Advanced Praise for
COMING HOME TO MYSELF

"You will be grateful to Jill Mellick for this book.
In it she takes us slowly through the rich layers of
Marion Woodman's imagery and offers us a choice of
those treasures which we have cherished for years.
She calls them "the shining bones" of Marion's writing.
Marion Woodman's keen observations and intuitions,
her touch and humorous stories and her healing
voice are all here in their naked essence."

—MEINRAD CRAIGHEAD, Artist and author of
The Mother's Song: Images of God the Mother

"A profoundly beautiful distillation.
Long-time students of Woodman will savor the
new light Mellick casts on these golden strands and new
readers will hold the key to understanding the essential
work of one of our greatest teachers."

—ROBERT JOHNSON, author of *He* and *She*

COMING HOME
to MYSELF

COMING HOME *to* MYSELF

*Reflections for Nurturing a
Woman's Body and Soul*

MARION WOODMAN and JILL MELLICK

WATERCOLOR PAINTINGS by JILL MELLICK

Conari Press

First published in 2000 by
Conari Press
An imprint of Red Wheel/Weiser, LLC
With offices at:
500 Third Street, Suite 230
San Francisco, CA 94107
www.redwheelweiser.com

Cover Illustration: Copyright © The Bridgeman Art Library /
Lincoln Seligman, Girl on the Beach, 1992
Cover and Book Design: Suzanne Albertson

ISBN-10: 1-57324-566-6
ISBN-13: 978-1-57324-566-1

LIBRARY OF CONGRESS CATALOGING-IN-PUBLICATION DATA
Woodman, Marion.
Coming home to myself : daily reflections for a woman's
body and soul / Marion Woodman and Jill Mellick.
p.   cm.
ISBN: 1-57324-566-6 (paperback)
ISBN: 1-57324-100-8 (hardcover)
1. Women—Conduct of life. 2. Meditation.
I. Mellick, Jill. II. Title.

BJ1610.W66   1998   98-10067
158.1'28'082—dc21   CIP

Printed in the United States of America on recycled paper
RRD   10 9 8 7 6 5 4

To: SOPHIA

To our ShaSha sisters

To the vast community of women
who are loving their femininity,
themselves and each other

To the vast community of men
who are coming to grips with the lost
feminine in themselves.

—M.W.

and

And for Tara, Paloma, Ariana, Amiya, Povi,
and those who stand on the threshold.

—J.M.

Coming Home to Myself

Linearity does not come naturally
to me. It kills my imagination.
Nothing happens.

No bell rings.
No moment of here and now.
No moment that says yes.
Without these, I am not alive.

I prefer the pleasure
of the journey through the spiral.

Relax.
Enjoy the spiral.
If you miss something
on the first round,
don't worry.
You might pick it up
on the second—or third—or ninth.
It doesn't matter.

Relax.
Timing is everything.
If the bell does ring,
it will resonate
through all the rungs of your spiral.
If it doesn't ring,
it is the wrong spiral—
or the wrong time—
or there is no bell.

1

New Resonances

Marion Woodman

Coming Home to Myself is a surprise child. Born of the insight of my friend and colleague, Jill Mellick, and my growing curiosity as we revisioned my earlier work, this little book has happened. Our editor, Mary Jane Ryan, dared the intuitive leap that is re-birthing my work in a distilled form.

I began writing my journal when I was twelve. I am still writing because I am compelled to find meaning in my experience. In my late teens, I chose to sacrifice my beloved microscope for another kind of poetry, the poetry of word. Still, the scientist in me is always observing with a thinking heart, noting, comparing, articulating.

Twenty years ago, much to my surprise, people were interested in my thesis on eating disorders. Being an addict myself and profoundly introverted, I was fearful of publication. With the encouragement of Inner City Books, the thesis was revised and published as *The Owl Was a Baker's Daughter.*

Addiction to Perfection was my first attempt at writing a book. It came out of an inner drive to understand the repetitive themes in the dreams of my addicted clients. I put rows of dreams on the floor of my studio, organized and reorganized them by theme. I marveled at the overwhelming power of the unconscious and, at the same time, the intensity of its drive toward healing.

One theme became clear as I began work on *The Pregnant Virgin.* The way to healing an addiction lies in finding a connection between body and soul. Soul needs body as much as body needs soul. Each is out of context without the other, an abandoned fragment of what it is. A great cherishing mother is often the link that manifests in dreams. Sometimes she appears as a striding Presence in the sky, sometimes as a bigger-than-life cleaning lady or a down-to-earth crone. She has many names: Buffalo Woman, Black Madonna, Isis, Anna, Tara. In the Bible she is called Wisdom, translated from the Greek word, *Sophia.* Whatever her temporal form, she is divine; she understands our humanity and her love is fierce enough to permeate flesh and bone. Her humor rips away veils of illusion. She is the central figure in *Dancing in the Flames,*

(Shambhala, 1996) which I co-authored with my friend, Elinor Dickson.

As I watched the pregnant virgin coming to consciousness in dreams, I became increasingly alarmed by images of ravaged masculinity, masculinity and femininity both being ravaged by patriarchy. Men and women who have worked hard to find a strong feminine standpoint in Being are now working hard to release a masculinity strong enough to partner the evolving virgin consciousness. This theme began by exploring the tragedy of perfection as Keats' "unravished bride" in "Ode on a Grecian Urn." So the process went on through *The Ravaged Bridegroom, Conscious Femininity,* and *Leaving My Father's House.*

One thing has been distilled in my consciousness. By whatever name we call the two magnets that create this balance of energies in our bodies and in our planet—Masculine/Feminine, Shiva/Shakti, Yang/Yin, Spirit/Soul, Transcendence/Immanence, Doing/Being, we are now responsible for making space for the healing of body, soul, and spirit. We are being directed in the evolutionary process by divine guides through our dreams, our symptoms, our planet. New values are emerging—feminine values and masculine values that are free of patriarchal abuse. A totally new harmonic lies ahead in the new millennium.

I write this down not because I am trying to sell my books, but because, as an intuitive, I tend to take too much for granted—I fail to fill in the facts that would make my thinking clear. As my husband says as he walks past my studio door, "You're not a born writer, Marion. Every time I walk by, you're gazing at the trees. You think everything through and then you write down your conclusion. A born writer would keep writing the process down."

He is right. People who are not intuitive become frustrated trying to follow my unstated logic and sensation types throw up their hands or the book in alarm when they feel their body responding but not their mind. I try to put down the facts, but I think in images, so when I try to explain, I end up in another image, which only compounds the difficulty. Moreover, my mind is a tapestry of the many great writers whom I have studied all my life. Their imagery is the warp and woof of my own thinking.

As a professor and practitioner of psychotherapy and the creative arts, Jill has worked from my books for many years. As she says in her introduction, she has taken my books and "has allowed the armature, the bones of the writing to show through the transparent skin of the prose and emphasized the closely interwoven relationships between images or thoughts by reflecting their relationship in their syntax." Her own book, *The Natural Artistry of Dreams* (Conari Press, 1996), with its wealth of creative ideas for releasing the energy of dream imagery, is a splendid companion text for this book.

Jill in Palo Alto, and I in London, Canada have put

my writing under a microscope to look at the fine tuning that has sometimes made meaning difficult. In reshaping it, allowing words more space, more time, more repetitions, we have heard new resonances. We hope you, our readers, will also.

Jill calls our creations "adaptations." I call them "moments." We do not call them poems. We both love poetry and we do not presume. We offer them with Sophia's proverbial grain of salt. Too much of her salt makes her wisdom bitter; just enough brings out the flavor.

A rose is a rose is a rose. By whatever name, we hope the images come home to your hearts in *Coming Home to Myself.*

2

Women's Lives, Women's Stories

JILL MELLICK

A MUTUAL JOURNEY

This *book was conceived* one dawn as I was checking a quote from Marion I was including in a book. There it was: an inner voice declaring, "*Some*one—*some*time—should gather Marion's essential comments into one publication." Women who see me for psychotherapy tell me they often pick up Marion's books and open them anywhere, finding, "by chance," just what they need. I went on looking for the quote. Then I heard another, amused voice: "Well?" I couldn't believe my psyche was planting the seed for a new book before my current one was even published.

I leafed through *Addiction to Perfection*. Sentences and paragraphs containing strong images leaped out. I typed them out, each image to a page. When I looked at them, they demanded line breaks for better contemplation. The line breaks led to some restructuring of word flow. Quickly, the melody lines I had always heard in Marion's more orchestral prose began to sing a capella.

After I had played with these creations for days, I landed in reality with a spine-bruising thump. What was I *doing*? And who invited me? Yet the idea wouldn't leave. I found myself quoting lines when I was in session. People remembered them, often whispering them to themselves for days. I decided that, even if I were not the person for this project, it had merit. The next time Marion and I were together, I would show her these adaptations and suggest that *someone* might do something similar—preferably she, herself, or her husband, Ross, a poet and literary critic.

It seemed inevitable that Marion and I should have explored this idea as we walked through Whole Foods, an excellent food market in my home town of Palo Alto. As we wandered through its rich landscape—pyramids of bell peppers, towers of grains, hills of aromatic breads—we could barely remember what we had come to buy; our excitement about this wild idea was growing. The meeting of body and soul, which lies at the heart of Marion's life and work (and my own), was playing itself out in our simultaneously putting milk in the cart and imagining this book.

Surely this is what women do, how women walk through life, separately and together—never doing one task at a time, never moving in one realm at a time. Rarely is one activity segregated from another; rather each is woven into the complex fabric of daily responsibilities and relationship. The sacred and the heartfelt suffuse the ordinary.

Despite the comfort of putting bread and tea and irises into the cart, I found myself diffident about my possible role. Yet Marion responded with her usual blend of nonjudgment, openness, and discerning curiosity.

After lunch, I showed her the adaptations. What most pleased me was that she recognized her voice and essence in each. I invited her to read them aloud. They sounded like her to each of us. When they didn't, we both heard it and agreed quickly where and how to change it.

Marion refused to do the project herself and dubbed me "it." Her one reservation was my using the word "poetic" about her writing. She thought it sounded grandiose. She had never thought of her writing as "poetic." I disagreed but respected her reservation. I told her I would do the project only if she and Ross were to review each piece.

Over the next year, whenever we could carve out a few hours together, we would rework the latest pieces. Both having had previous lives as high school and college English teachers in Canada and Australia respectively, we found ourselves in happily familiar places—bandying word usage, punctuation, line breaks, puns, consonance, assonance, sustained metaphors, tense changes, alliteration. We trusted and respected each other's views and opinions in this realm, and our forthrightness had only mutuality in its tone. We became servants to the word and were united in that higher purpose. Later, Ross would run his ruthlessly honest, critical eye over each.

I am grateful to Marion for her generosity and for this opportunity to do so many things I love at one time. I am also grateful to Mary Jane Ryan of Conari Press who once again respected my ideas and idiosyncratic ways of realizing them. I am also thankful to Daryl Sharp of Inner City Books and Tami Simon of Sounds True Recordings, who each gave us free and unlimited rights to adapt material. Shambhala Press and Texas A and M University also allowed us free use of a generous amount of material. Dr. Jan Fisher worked with us on impeccable research, manuscript preparation, and cross referencing. My thanks to Stanton Mellick, Ph.D., Karen O'Connor, Ph.D., Paula Reeves, Ph.D., Jeanne Shutes, Ph.D., and Ross Woodman, Ph.D., who each supported aspects of my work in unique ways.

Working with Marion's prose in this way has been a delightful conjunction of passions and disciplines for me. Many of these we share: love of the English language and its literature, particularly poetry, both spoken and read; long histories as writers; long involvement with Jungian theory and practice; passion for essence; and profound and abiding respect for the healing power of metaphor.

Each of these pieces has been created from Marion's writing and talks. Criteria for selection are intuitive: the call of an image, the strength of a metaphor, the power of a tale or observation.

In the process, I felt more like an ocean swimmer than a writer. I delighted in being sustained by the larger oceanic flow of Marion's writing and then in feeling an image, a metaphor, swell like a wave, which I rode to shore until it reabsorbed itself into greater tidal directions.

If I caught the wave too late, I lost elevation and thrust from the metaphor; if I caught it too early, I wasted energy splashing around and was unprepared to cleanly ride the wave. If I abandoned the wave too early, I lost the benefit of being carried to clear shallows of consciousness; if I hung on too long, I beached my awareness where it could no longer move easily and all I could see was the metaphor being sucked back to sea.

Once the image came into focus, the form shaped itself, claiming its authority over me. I have added no ideas—to which the quickest scan of the original will attest. Rather, mine has been a quiet exercise in distilling essence. With Marion's encouragement, I have let explicatory material fall quietly away; then, with literary devices such as meter, repetition, and parallel construction, and by emphasizing through syntax relationships between images or thoughts, I have tried to reveal the armature, the shining bones of the writing.

When I reread narratives from Marion's personal life, quietly woven into the larger flow of her prose, I was startled. I was further startled when I reread sections that Marion flagged for me—stories and dreams she was now ready to identify as her own (Katherine's story in *The Owl Was a Baker's Daughter*, for example). As I lifted them from their explanatory and discursive contexts, their starkness stunned me. How did I miss their unflinching honesty before?

At first, I felt intrusive highlighting these stories as independent entities. My reaction seemed odd, given that they had been read or heard by thousands. I even felt odd showing them to Marion. I felt as though I had been reading her personal journals without permission. When we did sit down together to read these narratives—each with its umbilical cord to the book cut and tied—my experience was confirmed indirectly; Marion was silent and still, as though once more absorbing into heart and body her original experience.

Reviewing them quietly together, making small changes here and there, we spoke sporadically. I did mention how strongly working with these stories affected me, how I needed to work slowly with each until my heart could accommodate its impact. I said little else; the narratives were their own commentary.

Marion did ask one question, half to herself: "I wonder why people sentimentalize my writing. These stories aren't sweet, Jill."

I ventured a recent understanding. "You provide a gentler, larger context in which to hold more shocking material. You soften the impact. You make it easier for us to digest. Even when you talk, you balance a terrible story with humor. I'm not being as protective here. These stories: when they're removed from their context, they are stark, they are from the bone, they are shocking." I paused briefly. "Is this acceptable to you?"

Marion also waited a little. I could almost see her listening to her bones to hear whether they resonated with the bones of the narratives. Then she answered, "This is the way they are for me. This is what happened, Jill. No, I don't want to soften them. The Crone tells life as it is."

Many of the other stories belong to Marion's friends and to some who have been in Jungian analysis with her. There is no sentimentality here, just silent receptivity, nonjudgmental observation, and fierce, tender honesty. Marion also makes clear that while we might hold another's pain with a loving heart, we cannot remove it. Our souls must heal and grow in their own time. These stories remind us to receive nonjudgmentally both our own and others' unveiled moments of light and darkness. They remind us of the ways in which we each struggle with demons and dance with angels.

Marion is happiest when she knows that her writing has proven to be a helpful departure point for our own journeys, considerations, and insights, independent of hers. We encourage you to use this book in just that way.

I hope I have done my dear and respected friend's imagery justice by catching more waves than I have lost and by lightly riding their graceful, spiraling forms home, only to begin the journey again.

GROWING THINGS IN DARKNESS AND IN LIGHT

Rare is the woman or man who arrives in adulthood unscathed by the vicissitudes of Western contemporary culture. Most of us have developed creative adaptations to make up for the fact that our movement, both inner and outer, is frequently impeded by old injuries that flare up.

These pages gently, fiercely bring us into the presence of some possible truths about the adaptations we have made as women. They invite us to be courageous enough to see—without collapsing—what we have fled from seeing in ourselves and others. As women seeking to grow into psychological and spiritual maturity, we need to acknowledge the subtle and not so subtle spiritual, cultural, emotional and physical damage we have experienced and to consciously choose new adaptations.

Healing does not mean wallowing in or identifying with injury. Nor does it mean defensive inaction. It means having the courage to see, acknowledge, grieve, and repair the holes ourselves (with, if we are fortunate, loving help from others). It means moving on, patches and all.

Marion alerts us to places of injury, to what we might have sacrificed in order to fit into a patriarchal culture. In capitulating to this unconscious patriarchal energy, we have been giving up even more than our souls. We have been handing over other birthrights: the right to our own feelings, and the right to take up conscious residence in our body—with love.

Often this self-betrayal, which happened silently and effortlessly in childhood, reemerges through the appearance of an addiction in later life. Marion makes many references to food addictions. These were the starting point of her work with the abandoned feminine and the need for its redemption. It quickly became clear to her that the suffering of addicts is not relevant to them alone. They are the canaries in the mine. Their cries are first. Their suffering alerts us to what is suffocating us in our dark and indentured daily descents into the perilous shafts of patriarchal society. Addictions are spiritual rituals that have been played out in a material world—accommodation to principles and rules, perfectionism, power, sexual longing and insecurity, pursuit of the perfect body, alcoholism, drugs, success in business, being the perfect mother (or all of these). Only through seeing these as metaphoric expressions of longing for soul and its rituals can we transcend limited lives and visions.

Ursula LeGuin, in a commencement speech given years ago to the women of Mills College in Oakland, California, emphasized that women grow things in darkness, not in light. It is darkness—with its secrets, earthiness, and joys, with its pains, losses, and despair—that we celebrate.

The woman who takes the time to grow herself in the darkness becomes familiar—perhaps for the first time—with the real source and containment of her psychic strength. No longer is her strength dissipated in obeying an idealized father figure, in pleasing a lover, in trying to satisfy a perpetually unsatisfied mother figure, in accommodating to a patriarchal organization or culture, in appeasing the inner witch who tells her she is worthless. No longer is her strength lost to obeying compulsions, drives, and obsessions that can slip in during the dark night of the soul and substitute for the real thing.

And what is the real thing, the thing for which she longs? The love affair with her own spirit, the inner marriage that commits her to her destiny, the rituals of soul that feed her deepest hunger, and the sense of being pregnant with her Self, her creative essence.

The journey to India that Marion describes in this book contains experiences that characterize all of our mythic journeys into the farthest regions of ourselves in search of the real thing: awakening; the call; the journey; the descent; the darkness; a healing crisis; an epiphany; the ascent; accepting unlikely companions on the journey; new visions of self and the world.

Later, Marion tells the story of an initiation on Krishna's birthday. Once again, we find the pattern characteristic of all initiations: the planning of the expected journey; the invitation to the unknown; the placing of trust in the situation and in one who initiates; the loss of the known and the entry into the unknown; the loss of personal identity; the fear of the initiation; facing the fear; active surrender; the epiphany; the restoration of personal identity; the return to the known world, this time with more spiritual understanding and lived knowledge; the long integration of the experience into daily life. These are developmental steps we all face if we actively surrender to the call of our soul.

To become whole, body and soul, we need to depart from the safety of the childhood house of beliefs into the wilderness, into the cave, with only the psychic necessities. We rarely have the safety of leaving one house of beliefs when we can clearly see the new house ahead lighted and warm. More often, we need to leave the old without any promise of the new, need to spend time as forest dwellers, just surviving. If we do survive, we find that we are no longer handmaidens to an outer authority that rules by principle rather than loving mutuality; we have reached a new cycle of maturity where we are consciously connected to our hearts, our bodies, our deepest values, and the people we love.

Our meandering paths into this new home are various, as these stories show. For each of us, there is a unique journey—it can come through the mind, through the body, through creativity, through the heart, through dealing with addictions, through age and cronehood, or through a unique mix of these.

We know that our journey to our old, new home is cyclical, that we shall never move in once and for all, and that we are well accompanied by other women and by ourselves. This book is also a companion on the journey, an encouragement, and, we hope, a source of quiet contemplation in which you might find your own rich images and creativity.

THE MEANDER PATTERN OF OUR LIVES AND STORIES

The feminine principle described in this book is neither linear nor unidirectional in its development. Catherine Bateson, in *Composing a Life*, remarks that women's outer lives are rarely led along trajectories toward unchanging goals. They are complex patterns of tasks, passions, and responsibilities that *intentionally live in response to* changing demands. To evaluate the achievements of such lives by objective linear measures is to miss the truth of how we really experience our lives and what we really value.

As women, we teach and pass on our wisdom through story—and we have done so through the ages. Story is one of the strongest containers for pain, joy, wisdom, fear. These stories in this book are no more linear than our lives. They don't begin, climax, and end where we might expect; they cycle back and forth through the maze, meander into the light, and disappear again into the dark.

This meander pattern—this map of the feminine spirit moving through women's inner and outer lives—informs the movement of Marion's original prose and these adapted contemplations. Through taking images important to you into body, heart, and soul, you can deepen the experience of your inner and outer journeys. Each journey has its gifts. Not all of the gifts are welcome but each does, indeed, carry the potential for quiet transformation.

WAYS TO DEEPEN YOUR WORK WITH THIS BOOK

Read with Your Body. Trinh Minh Ha, author of *Woman Native Other* reminds us that many women write not with the head but with the whole body. This kind of writing requires a different receptivity.

When you read this book daily, dip and surface, wander, alight. Do not bind yourself to reading word by word, line by line, page after page. As Marion says, if you miss the meaning the first time round, don't worry; it will pass by again in a new form. Read each piece more than once. The first time, read with your intuitive eye. The second, feel the body's resonance with phrases; these are the words that are plucking the strings of your heart and soul. When you reverberate, lay the book on your lap and go within. Actively open up to the image; experience the image taking up residence in your bones.

These are designed to be read daily, one at a time. But, if you are reading for longer periods, make time at least once an hour to get up and move. The body needs to allow the reading it is absorbing to move through it. Stretch, walk around the block, do deep breathing, move to music for five minutes—but do not sit for hours immersed in reading this book while your patient body waits in discomfort for you to return to it. That would contradict what you are reading!

This book does not ask to be read; it asks to be lived. To read with our whole body, we need more than a minute and a seat. No longer is it truly satisfying to snatch a moment between waking and sleeping, between throwing out the garbage and throwing on the pasta. Of course, if these moments are all we have, they are worthwhile. If they are all that we *ever* have, we miss experiencing the deep, abiding, embodied shift in consciousness. Open to a reflection at random. Become the quiet student of the intersection of randomness and meaning: trust the synchronicity of where the page opens for you each day. Work with one piece daily. Let your intuition and body be the authorities on how it is most fruitful for you to explore these. Quietly dance, paint, contemplate or otherwise embody these reflections.

Many of us say, when we reread journals from years

earlier, that we are shocked at how much we knew and have since forgotten, only to learn again in the next cycle of living and experience. "Why don't I remember the first time?" we ask, shocked, wondering why we spend so much energy on inner work that seems to vanish into the netherlands of our unconscious. We all know why, really: we continue to learn the same things again and again at each spiral in the path, each time taking the understanding deeper, each time embodying it more, each time able to recall it more quickly in demanding times. In a similar way, these pages might be able to remind you of what you already know deep down.

A Place of One's Own. When Virginia Woolf delivered her lecture on the importance of having a place of one's own, she spoke to Everywoman. If we are committed to tending our inner lives, we need a physical place in which to do this without interruption or intrusion. If you are reading this half-seated on a chair in the kitchen, munching, partly distracted by your need to prepare dinner, or your children's needs for a snack, you are probably missing any deep shifts in awareness you might experience.

Many women enter my consulting room feeling squeezed out of their lives—only to realize that, on a literal as well as metaphoric level, they have no place to call their own. However, even in a crowded home, simple changes can create a minimally private place. If you have not already done so, clear a space, no matter how small, that is yours alone. By your making this space physically, emotionally, and spiritually yours, it can become your temple.

In Japan, temple paths closed to the public often have a small, round stone tied four ways with string at the entry. A subtle, silent, effective gesture. If you live in a crowded space with house members who might not respect such a simple sign, you might even use a locked closet. Size doesn't matter (although it helps, undoubtedly!). What matters is your attending to your need for solitude. If even closet space is unavailable, make a temporary place for yourself. Lay out a special cloth or shawl on the floor. Place on it the things you want to use—paints, music. Keep a journal beside you for notes, drawings, mandalas, dreams—a large, cheap, blank book. This place and its tools will become treasured symbols of your time alone.

Create an Altar. When you have established your private place, you might consider adding a personal altar for certain kinds of inner work including the creative work this book is based on. A box can function as a movable (and closable) altar. Cover it with material whose color, history, or feel is quieting. Select symbols that will keep you mindful—of what you value, of who you are at your best, of how small you are in relation to larger forces at work in the universe. Choose pieces according to your spiritual or religious tradition. Preferably do not include any (or many) strongly connected with important people in your life. This time at your altar is for you alone. For example, your children might be central in your life and you might love parenting; however, this time and place are set aside to explore who you are *beyond* your daily roles.

Tend your place daily in a simple way consonant with your beliefs—a prayer, a meditation, a hymn, a chant, a quiet walk around the circumference, a vase of fragrant flowers, a sprig from a tree, a stick of incense, a candle. Do this with quiet attention. When you finish using your space, you might like to reverse whatever ritual you began with, covering private materials until the following day.

Choose Clothing Consciously. Be both practical and symbolic in your choice. Choose carefully what you wear for inner work. Choose it for comfort so that you can dance, paint, and read in it. Choose it, too, for personal significance. Do the color and fabric put you in touch more with your inner life? How have you used it in the past? Can you see yourself using it in this way now?

Play Music. Music creates an invisible yet palpable environment, and evokes a rich response from the body. Select favorite music to play during your reading or creative exploration: quiet music for meditation; flowing and smooth for movement; rhythmically varied for quick and slow gestures; and rousing for caged emotion. It may be wise to choose music you do not associate with a particular person or moment. Unless you intend to evoke new understanding of old memories carried in your body, choose music you will associate purely with your time alone.

Consider Using a Mirror. Our healing and growth comes from accepting ourselves for who we are, free of labels. At both real and symbolic levels, looking at ourselves in the mirror, being able to not only tolerate but celebrate looking at ourselves, can be helpful. If it feels timely and appropriate, use a large mirror for creative contemplation.

Explore Through the Arts and Dreams. Our soul speaks to us through metaphor and symbol and we best experience and express these through the creative arts. To explore your whole-body responses to these contemplations, you need little money and absolutely no talent. Newsprint and oil crayons or chalks are enough—plus a willingness to let your body make marks on a page. If you wish, keep malleable modeling clay on hand. For simple mask making, paper plates, poster paint, and cheap brushes suffice. Finger paints and finger paint paper also encourage full body expression.

Show others only creative pieces that you are really ready to have seen by other eyes. As Marion's image of the chrysalis reminds us, we need to protect what is gestating until is has been born and grown. This is delicate business, which gathers energy in the cooking pot of inner work. Lift the lid too soon or too often, and the food will never cook.

Metaphors, similes, symbols, and images abound on these pages. Find creative ways to express the effect certain images have on you—through collage, dance, claywork, haiku, poetry, personal story, or painting. Do not try to represent the image realistically; rather, focus on expressing the feeling you get from the image. Explore these images through movement. If you are working with a particular kind of body therapy, integrate your experience of these images into those times.

Record your dreams as you read this book and review recent dreams. Can you find threads of the themes that weave through these pages? How do these dream images play out in your life?

Exploring the inner world through creative expression is an important part of psychological healing and development. If you are unfamiliar with or want more ways to use simple media to enhance your inner life and dream work, *The Natural Artistry of Dreams* provides many easy ways for "nonartistic" (and artistic) people to explore the creative unconscious—through fairy tale and myth, poetry making, mask making, dialogue, movement, energy paintings, claywork, and ritual.

We read with more than our minds. So do not be too respectful of these printed pages. Mark them up! Mark lines to which your body responds with pleasure, tears, restlessness, stupor, anxiety. Note briefly on the page your body's response. Photocopy or transcribe pieces that carry intensity for you. Speak them out loud. Does a common theme weave through them? What is the smallest thing you can do this week to bring this new insight into your daily world?

List questions that come to you about yourself. Your questions are more valuable than the answers (which change from day to day). Don't bother to write in full-sentence, linear format. Jot down images, memory flashes, phrases. Intuitive insights are like fish in the water; they flash in the sunlight and then dive deep again, only enticed to the surface again by morsels of conscious attention.

Let the metaphors on these pages dance through your imagination. Allow the images to take up residence in consciousness, heart, and body. Once embraced, they will continue to grow in the chrysalis. One day, they will emerge, mature, as butterflies in your psychic life.

About the Paintings

The landscape paintings that divide each section carry a story. For years, several other women and I assisted at Marion's summer retreat for a small group of women. The five-day retreat was held on ShaSha, Marion and Ross's jewel of an island in Georgian Bay in Ontario. To reach the island was a pilgrimage just in itself; we left our lives behind and, as the boat made its way through the tricky channels between the islands—the journey prepared heart, soul, and body for the intensity of the days to come. In the same way, the voyage back allowed a gentle transition into our daily worlds.

To stay on the island brought healing and a beauty that haunts our dreams still. We listened to each others' stories, wept, laughed, sang, woke with the dawn, listened to loons, fought mosquitos, visited natural stone altars, lit candles, took turns cooking, braced the house against thunderstorms, and anointed our own and each others' bodies in the breathtakingly chill, clear waters of Georgian Bay. Over the years, I recorded that landscape in different media. I hope that these watercolors invite you into your own inner ShaSha, where you will spin, in spirit, one more thread of that invisible web that connects our community of women.

3

Learning to Trust & Receive

Infants *have central lessons* to learn after birth. As developmental theorists have described them, they need to learn to trust and receive from their caretaker, their environment, and ultimately themselves.

Because we are human, some of these lessons are incomplete. We might have learned—not inaccurately from the difficult situation into which we were born— that at least one of these three is not fully trustworthy. Such early learning dies hard. As adults, we have had years to confirm our findings. It takes leaps of faith for us to learn to trust and receive again.

As you reflect on trust and receptivity, consider the people you trust, in what areas you trust yourself, and what aspects of the environment you trust.

—J.M.

The fear of receiving resonates
in the deepest levels of the psyche.
To receive is
to let life happen,
to open to grief and loss,
to open to love and delight.

———————

Only when we experience trust
in the mother's love—
through dreams or waking life—
can our body surrender its defenses.
Only then can it move
to a new sexuality
with woman or with man.

If I surrender
to what you're saying,
if I take a listening role
while you're talking,
I take in what you are saying.
I receive.
There is such energy in receiving.

———

No amount of therapy
can heal a heart that cannot trust.
To learn to trust
is often
the heart of the therapy.

I use the word *mystery*,
rather than *magic*.

I loved magic.
Something magic was always going to happen.
When it did, it never did anything
but land me in trouble.

Mystery is the depth of the sacred.

The second daughter:
she was second, always second.
Her father rarely noticed her;
her mother, she always feared.

Only one thing she knew for sure:
what her mother was,
she was not.

She swung into life in red heels
and fell in love
with a handsome priest
who loved her
and who, of course,
had to give her up.

She came to know herself
through the gentle love
of a woman.

She was crying.
I don't know what to do
You tell me I have to recognize my feelings.
Most of the time I don't do anything
I want to do because I don't feel it would be right.
I was driving here,
and I had a desire—
to bring you a muffin.
I know you would love a muffin,
but no I won't buy it.
You don't take your analyst a muffin.
But then I got into such a state,
I was just sweating,
because I wanted to get the muffin so much.
I stopped the car, went back,
got the muffin,
and I have the muffin in the bag,
but I don't know whether to give it to you or not.
I feel like such a stupid child,
but I don't know what to do.
Well, I said, *I want to receive the muffin.*
I broke it in two.
And because she was received,
it was a communion.

So long as we're doing
one two three around the floor,
dancing is a bloody bore.
Only when we surrender
to the spirit of the music
can we truly dance.

———

Never interpret a work
until the work has had a chance
to interpret itself.

We receive life through our orifices:
eyes, ears, noses, pores, vagina.
When we truly receive,
we grow continually.

We are terrified of trust,
terrified of making ourselves vulnerable.
The leap into forgiveness is immense.
And after the leap, again the waiting.
And again another opening into love,
And again the terror.
It's the body that's terrified.

4

My Body

O *ur bodies,* with all their blessings and blemishes, give us pleasure and pain. They are also a vast, often untapped source of wisdom. Because most of us are in a culture that devalues the information our body gives us, we can fail to see, hear, taste, touch, and smell the subtle signals it sends us—in waking and sleeping—about our emotional states, spiritual well-being, physical health, and mental functioning.

You can begin to listen to those signals and to send constructive signals back to your body in many ways, using imagery, meditation, biofeedback, touch, and simple, loving attention.

Research and experience indicate that mind and body are not separate but part of a seamless, intricate network of intelligence. From a more intuitive perspective, your body can be considered a reservoir of cellular memory, wisdom, and guidance. If you attend, it can richly reward your journey into the unconscious with understanding about your deepest being and about the ways in which you might find healing and wholeness.

—J.M.

A body whose wisdom
has never been honored
does not easily trust.
An animal with a crazy trainer
   learns crazy habits,
runs wild.

———————

When we take ourselves seriously,
we accept the responsibility
of knowing and loving our body.

Body work is soul work.
Imagination is the bridge
between body and soul.
To have healing power,
an image needs to be taken
into our body on our breath.
Only then can the image connect
with the life force.
Only then can things change.

The ego that refuses to submit
to the demands of the body
will eventually have to submit
to the powers of nature.

———

If the dream says something is wrong
with your body, check.
Long before you do, your body knows
when something is wrong.

If you can listen to the wisdom of your body,
love this flesh and bone,
dedicate yourself to its mystery,
you may one day
find yourself
smiling from your mirror.

How many people do you know
who are willing to trust
their deepest understanding?
Test body wisdom in your office:
just try asking your boss
to breathe a decision
into his belly to check its resonance. . . .

Body work, like dream work, is soul work.
Body and dream illuminate
the point where spirit and matter
touch and do not touch.

Energy enters you
from the one sleeping beside you.
If that energy is depressed, angry,
doesn't like you tonight,
it might appear in your dreams.

—————

If we breathe deeply,
feeling erupts,
grows too intense for us.
So we keep our breath shallow.
To breathe deeply
is to receive
and that is the feminine incarnate.

To be in my body
also means to suffer.

————

Often we listen to a cat
with more precision
than we listen to our body.

We cherish the cat.
It purrs.
Our body may have to release
a scream, a symptom,
to be heard by us at all.
Too often, our soul can find
no other way to be heard.

To sit in a chair and analyze
is heady stuff,
but it does not help you
live the power of the image.

Put your image into your body.
Does it waken a response?

Of course:
your rage, your grief,
your great Buddha laugh.

Just put the image into your body
and wait.

This is your body,
your greatest gift,
pregnant with wisdom you do not hear,
grief you thought was forgotten,
and joy you have never known.

Give your body an hour a day.
If it's not worth an hour a day,
there's nothing
your body can tell you
and not much
anyone else can do.

5

Beyond Addiction & Possession

U*sually, we associate* "addiction" with food, drugs, and sex. Yet anything that begins to dominate and control our lives, *regardless of cost to our well-being*, can become an addiction—perfectionism, work, order, analytic thinking, approval, money, the Internet, intensity, worry....

When addicted to an emotion, thought pattern, or action, we are powerless to resist or exercise choice; we engage in unconscious repetitions that seem to have meaning at the time, but later appear empty, without purpose. We are possessed again and again by a familiar yet alien drive that overrides all else. We become obsessed with obtaining, usually through an inner or outer ritual, something not tangibly obtainable such as peace, love, or wholeness.

If we can recognize the addiction or state of possession and understand what it is really trying to give us, we can patiently begin to provide for ourselves what we truly desire in less costly, longer-lasting, and more effective ways.

As you turn these pages, reflect on ways in which you might recognize and break free from obvious and subtler patterns of addiction and possession.

—J.M.

Illness or addiction can be the pathway
to the feminine side of God.

———————

What is my addiction trying to tell me?

A compulsive relationship
may be just the one we need
to work our way
into a conscious relationship.

———————

If you find yourself
falling in love again
with the wrong man
and you can't help it,
take one minute
to shout in your own ear,
What am I doing?

The last curtain was the best.
The sets had been struck before we left.

We had a party—a memorable party.
The discipline over,
we clung to a world
that no longer existed.
We danced, ate, and drank
in no-man's land—
hadn't quite left,
hadn't quite returned.

About two in the morning
he crossed the room to thank me—
deliberate, serious.
But the party's not over, I said.
There's no performance tomorrow.

I have to go now, he said.
Quiet, decisive.
I have some serious drinking to do—
a rendezvous
with the one he had loved all his life
but could never marry.

I remember standing
in the midst of the dancers
looking into his proud eyes.

It was on my tongue to tell him
there was plenty of booze on the table.
But I sensed that was irrelevant.

Possession that drives us
can be our yearning
for conscious femininity.

———————

Sexuality without love is matter without spirit.

She had been
an outstanding student,
a good athlete,
a good leader.

At twenty-three, she was eating
nothing but popcorn,
unable to make decisions,
unable to speak to others
for fear they would load her
with more work.

When she could work no longer,
she entered the hospital.

Weeks later,
she showed me her lists—
yearly, monthly, weekly,
daily, special—
each organized perfectly.
I can't help it, she said.
*If one thing is missing,
what else might be?*

Can you make room, I asked.
for spontaneity?

She dutifully agreed
and one week later showed me her daily list:
"2:15-2:30 P.M.: Spontaneity."

She is riding home on the subway.
She decides she won't alight
at her usual stop.
There's a muffin stand one stop earlier.
A walk would do her good.

She stays on.
She is nervous.
Two more stops,
she's out,
forgets the panic in the dark,
races back to buy them—
holy, hated, taboo muffins.

She is alone, of course.
She is already being walked.
She hurries home,
locks the door,
unplugs the phone,
puts on her always dress,
takes her always position,
and begins.

Loved, secure,
protected, enthroned,
at first she is calm.
The calm becomes ecstasy
and she becomes wolf.

If she is obese,
she falls into bed in a stupor.
If she is thin,
she puts her finger down her throat.

Possessed but not possessing,
she feels betrayed.
The goddess did not appear.

We view ourselves as works of art.
Somewhere in us there is
a perfect image,
a perfect work,
a well-wrought mask
that cuts us off
from flesh and blood.

Our real terror is that the work,
being precious,
may, in an instant, be destroyed.

Medusa wants everything
permanent, perfect,
engraved in stone.

———

We are all addicts.
We experience ourselves
as emptiness
swinging in empty space
between spirit and matter,
located nowhere.
Metaphor can heal.
Metaphor can link
spirit and matter.

6

Beyond Perfection & Duty

Having high standards and a sense of duty that transcends personal self-interest is laudable. However, when our standards are so high that we deem ourselves unacceptable unless we meet them, we are in trouble.

We know yet forget that to be human *is* to be flawed. Even the finest endeavor contains minor imperfections. In some Eastern cultures, certain works of art are deliberately flawed so that the gods will not be angry because an artist is competing with their perfection.

Perfectionism and blind duty can ravage a woman's body, spirit, emotions, relationships, self-respect, self-care, and equanimity. As a goal, perfection is usually lethal because it is never met and our failure leaves us with the pain of comparison. And doing one's duty is empty and soul-withering unless it is fed by love.

—J.M.

As long as we try to transcend ourselves,
reach for the sky,
pull away from ground and into spirit,
we are heroes carved in stone.
We stand atop the pillar alone
blind to the pigeon's droppings.

Do not try to transform yourself.
Move *into* yourself.
Move into your human unsuccess.
Perfection rapes the soul.

I was committed to becoming conscious
as quickly as possible.
Then suddenly, a black hole.
Chaos.
I knew the only solution
was to understand exactly
what was going on.
I read day and night for a week.

Bursting with knowledge,
I leapt into his office.
I knew what was wrong with me
and I knew how to cure it.
I spent the hour elaborating,
weaving profundities.
He wilted in his chair.
The more he wilted,
the faster I talked.
At the end of the hour,
he silently helped me on with my coat
and took me to the elevator.
With a twinkle in his eighty-year-old eyes
he pushed the button.
If I were you, Mrs. Woodman,
I would take my animus for a good drink.

I was so angry I didn't even take him a muffin.

If we are trying to live by ideals,
we are constantly plagued
by a sense of unreality.

————

It is easier to try
to be better
than you are
than to be
who you are.

Perfection does not allow for feeling.

————

Perfection is not interested
in staying in the body.
It wants to fly,
wants ideals,
wants beauty,
wants truth,
wants light,
and you sure don't get these here.

Perfection massacres the feminine.
Our culture pulses to the pressure of perfection.

———

To move toward perfection
is to move out of life
or never to enter.

She has foolproof recipes
for everything.
If strictly followed
(and to follow is to follow strictly),
they guarantee success.

Her real world is the world of things,
things that work efficiently.

She is impatient of error,
having no room for it;
there is no need for it.
Anyone learning under her jurisdiction
will be oriented from the start
to objects and goals,
clearly defined.

Her daughter knows herself as a thing,
thinks of herself as an object
designed for high efficiency.
She does not know
her mother's knowledge
is not wisdom,
is without human meaning,
is without personal love.

Her daughter has no standpoint
of her own.
There is no danger
of her opening
to her own weeping.
There is no danger
of her singing
her own song.

Eventually we have to face the fact that we are not God.

7

Reclaiming My Own Energies

We often look elsewhere for what we have already; we project. We turn to others to give us a level of acceptance we can only give ourselves. We invest people, institutions, situations, and things with certain attributes that they might indeed have, yet which do not belong solely to them but to us as well. We attribute to others flaws we need to come to terms with in our own character; we credit others with fine qualities that we are unable to acknowledge in ourselves; we turn to institutions and leaders to give us answers, to rescue us from confusion and helplessness, to bring a level of meaning and order that can come only from within. Every time we reclaim some of our own energies, stop projecting onto others attributes of ourselves, we become more whole, more present.

—J.M.

The ghostly lover
does not remain in the shadows.

She:
    The day I married,
    I married not the man I loved
    but the man my father chose.
    As I walked down the aisle, I said to myself,
    I'm not enough for him,
    not good enough,
    not beautiful enough,
    not smart enough.

    He said *Jump*!
    I asked, *How high*?
    Finally, I did not ask again.

    Now everything's gone wrong.
    It's my fault.
    I should have been different.

    My inner home is a prison.
    I do get out, only to return.
    I cannot forgive myself for a crime
    I must have committed,
    though I don't know what it is.
    My heart is in white knots.
    The voice I hear within

is disdainful, says I am worthless,
won't let me live.
When I hear it,
I have no sexuality
and fear it will never come back.

He:
I always feel her fear,
but she rarely puts it out.
Except in other forms.

If I say anything against her,
she pulls a power trip.
She argues like a phony lawyer.
When she gets angry,
I draw back, become a nice guy.
She sees that and grows more violent.
I listen, I give sympathy.
The calmer I get,
the wilder she becomes.
The more I try to meet her demands,
the stronger, more insistent they become.

I go up the mountain of niceness,
but by heaven I come down fast
into the valley of rage.
Once I'm there, there's no road out

that's not divorce or the knife.

I am son, father,
no longer lover,
probably never husband.

———

A mother who is identified with being mother
has to have children who will eat
what she gives them to eat
and do what she wants them to do.
They must remain children.

A mother who is only "Mother"
makes her children eat
what she gives them to eat.
When there's a full breast,
somebody has to drink.

8

Unmasking Myself

W*e all have roles* we need to play and masks (the "faces") we need to wear. Many are vital and constructive: parent, partner, employee. However, roles and masks can be harmful if they conflict with our values, ethics, well-being, health, or real nature. They are also harmful when they become the only way we know how to feel confident or acceptable. And they are harmful if we identify completely with them.

Some masks fit us better than others; some no longer fit well; others never really fit at all. Sometimes, as children, we learned to play roles that became so necessary to our survival that they took the place of the person we really are. Now, as adult women, we only know that something is wrong because we have a pervasive weariness, depression, emptiness, or sense of unreality about us, despite success in our outer lives.

Are you familiar with the roles and masks you wear? Which are helpful? Which compromise you? Who lies beneath the masks? When and where does she reveal herself?

—J.M.

Hypocrisy, sentimentality, distraction,
are veils that hide reality.

———————

I look in the mirror.
I see the lines.
I put on makeup.

A tired, painted face.
I've aged ten years in two.
I've never felt my age before.

I want me.
Just me.
I won't pretend.
I want to live before I die.

One day perhaps you shall look
beyond the mask
into your own mirror
at your own reality.

Are you appalled?
Are the terrified eyes
that look back at you
the eyes of your own child?

Sentimentality robs us of our feeling.
Sentimentality makes us pity
those who really feel.
Sentimentality looks down on life
being fully lived
and betrays relationship.
It is terrified of real feeling;
real feeling blasts away sentimentality.

———

There is no growth without real feeling.
Children not loved for who they are
do not learn how to love themselves.
Their growth is an exercise in pleasing others,
not in expanding through experience.
As adults, they must learn to nurture
their own lost child.

There's personal anger,
but underneath
there's often universal rage;
And when we are possessed,
God help the man
who's on the end of that.

Deep rage is not about the man;
Deep rage is this:

Nobody ever saw me.
Nobody ever heard me.
As long as I can remember,
I've had to perform.
When I tried to be myself,
I was told, *That's not what you think,
that's not what you ought to do.*
So, just like my mother and her mother,
I put on a false face.
My life became a lie.

That's deep rage.

We have lived our lives
behind a mask.
Sooner or later
—if we are lucky—
the mask will be smashed.

What a relief to be human
instead of the god or goddess
my parents imagined me to be
or I imagined them.

9

Finding My Own Voice

To *find my own voice* is to give truthful expression to how I experience myself and the world I live in. I might or might not be "right" by others' standards and measurements. But I can be truthful to my experience and to my way of expressing my experience. Such expression is unique to me and to this moment.

Sometimes, we silence our beliefs in the face of self-doubt, self-criticism, fear of judgment, or lack of confidence in our capacity to express ourselves in the way that we believe others will respect and understand. While forces in the environment certainly push against our finding our own voice, all too often the force that silences comes from within.

There are many ways of finding your voice, both alone and with others: keeping a journal; working with symbols and metaphors in dreams and in literature; exploring verbal and nonverbal ways of expression through the arts. Talent is of no help or consequence in this kind of self-expression. The "voice" you find will be yours, with all its beauty and flaws.

—J.M.

She dreamed a voice told her,
Go to the attic and find a black box.
Still dreaming, she found it
and slipped her hand in.
She gently lifted out a bird,
tiny, skeletal, starving.
Stricken, she wept
for this bird she had loved as a child
and then forgotten.
Her tears changed its body
into a radiant small boy who said,
I only wanted to sing my song.

Such a dream will change your life
—if you remember you once had a song to sing.

The more I talk
the more my inner voice is saying,
No, that's not it at all.

———

Who am I?
What are my values?
What are my needs?
Am I true to myself?
Do I betray myself?
What are my feelings?
Am I capable of love?
Am I true to my love?

Femininity is taking responsibility
for who I am,
not only what I do,
not how I seem to be,
not what I accomplish.
When all the doing is done,
I have to face myself
in my naked reality.

———

However veiled,
the feminine
is always naked.

The feminine finds its own voice
in the virgin:
the initiated feminine
who is who she is
because her values and emotions
are grounded in her musculature.

———

Only by discovering and loving the goddess
lost within our rejected body
can we hear our own authentic voice.

———

Without our body we cannot speak truthfully.
We may think we are speaking the truth,
but if we lie down
and somebody puts a hand
on our heart and belly,
we will cry.
There's truth in those tears.

A life truly lived
constantly burns away
veils of illusion,
opening our eyes
to our uniqueness.

A life truly lived
burns away
what is no longer relevant,
gradually reveals
our essence
until, at last,
we are strong enough
to stand in our naked truth.

A man may be shocked
when he sees you've really changed.
He thought you'd been
scribbling in your journal
—a sentimental, little Victorian girl
writing in your little book,
naive and uninitiated.
Suddenly, when you say,
Look, this is what I think,
he can't believe
what's coming out of your mouth.
Mother puts up with anything.
Mother is unconditional love.
When you say,
See me as I am,
you are no longer mother,
no longer his ideal woman.
You've changed.
He thought you'd been
scribbling in your journal.

If we are full of rage
we have to get it out of our body.
We have to express it—
to ourselves—
or it will take another form,
perhaps illness.

———————

Anger is personal; rage, transpersonal.
We fear becoming angry
because we are terrified
of being possessed by rage.
So we skate.
In our dreams we skate or ski,
It takes ice and snow to skate and ski.
Feeling is frozen.
Rather than live in summer and spring,
we freeze.
No gentleness, no flow!
We feel nothing:
no anger, no rage.
No love.
The heart is closed.

Medusa appears, dark and devouring,
there to do battle.
When we wake to her
we cannot move.
She turns our creativity to stone.
Do not give up.
Keep telling her,
Your voice is not mine.
Do not give up.
Use all your courage.
Use all your strength.

————

Don't talk about *being true to myself*
until you are sure
to what voice you are being true.

It takes hard work to differentiate *our* inner voices,
and in crises,
there is no time to waste.
So spend an hour a day writing.
Separate real from unreal,
what stays from what goes.
Then leap beyond anything you ever imagined.

If you travel far enough,
one day you will recognize yourself
coming down the road to meet you.
And you will say
YES.

10

Leaving My Father's House

Blind *patriarchal authority* as it shows itself in men and women, adheres to prevailing opinion and expectation, to standing rules and regulations. It values goals and achievement; linear thinking, rationality, observable phenomena, measurable outcomes, and right and wrong.

To leave our father's house is not to wage war against our personal fathers. It is an invitation to trust inner wisdom, an invitation that may ask us to stand up to unthinking, rule-bound authorities. It also invites us to confront those same forces *within*.

Finding our inner wisdom can be difficult. How do we find something if we neither recognize nor trust it easily, if we do not know we ever possessed or lost it?

We should not follow every urging, impulse, and intuition regardless of sound outer wisdom and information. We need discernment. But we can give our deepest values and perceptions at least an equal hearing. As you turn these pages, reflect on ways you can listen to inner wisdom and values in the face of forceful inner and outer rulemakers.

—J.M.

We discuss the feminine principle,
read our notes, talk fast,
our bodies wound in knots.
We contradict what comes out of our mouths,
use feminine language
to mask our patriarchal thoughts.

———

How does it feel
in your empty apartment,
hearing voices inside
you thought were outside?
Do you wonder if finding yourself
is all it's cracked up to be?
Can you be the person
you have always denied?

How does it feel
to leave your father's house?
Your father-husband's house?

How does it feel
to look in his eyes
and see yourself as betrayer
of the one man
who has always trusted you?

How does it feel
to leave the security of his love
even though he never knew
who you were?

In psychic incest, lines between parent and child
are unclear, weak, or nonexistent.
The daughter merges with the father,
both human and divine.

———

Matriarchs are often more authoritarian
than patriarchal men.

The message is the same:
In our dreams, we are trapped—
in our home,
in a tomb,
in frozen water,
in a sinking ship,
in the stillness,
in the darkness,
in a prison,
in a concentration camp,
in a cave with a rock for a door.

Old Mother God, Old Father God—
they keep us trapped.
And we do give up.
We pull the covers over our head,
and go back to sleep.

Only to dream of old dragons,
old alligators, old crocodiles
drinking our blood.
To dream of cold-eyed lawmakers saying,
This is the way it's always been done.
It works.
It will stay this way.
And you will obey.

Only to dream we are riding
in our father's old car,
and he is driving.
To dream
we are in our mother's kitchen,
eating food she is cooking,
not cooking our own.

Only to dream we are looking
through father's or mother's,
or somebody's, anyone's glasses,
but not our own.

Only to dream
a banquet is spread
and we cannot eat.

She lived to please him,
lover, jailer, father,
lived to share his pursuits,
to meet his standards of perfection.
She was his beloved
(her mother, absent or rival).

Now, in the night,
she dreams of her demon lover.
In the day, she enacts her dream,
fearing its power:
she loves a man who cannot marry
—too young, too old,
blond priest,
blue-eyed homosexual.
All through her life,
she arrives too late.
She lives without her body.

She dreams she is in a glass coffin.
From her prison, details have beauty.
In her aloneness, she imagines emotions.

Her husband is the perfect bridegroom,
the trickster, the small boy looking for mother.
She is goddess and mirror,
siren and friend,
femme fatale and sacrificing wife.

He is attracted to her girlhood purity,
her desire to sacrifice, to serve.
At first he may be flattered:
she sees him as a god.

Ultimately, he will reject her
knowing he cannot live
up to her demands.

If he matures, he will grow bored with her
whom he can never reach,
as she walks her tightrope above the abyss
and wonders why men call her cruel.

When he calls your feminine approach
rambling, lacking in clarity,
coherence, emphasis,
do you wonder if you are stupid?

How does it feel
to say *no* to the one man
to whom you have always said *yes?*

How does it feel
when you stand up to him
and reject all he has never questioned?

11

Active Surrender

In defeat, we are forced to lay down our sword; in active surrender, we consciously choose to lay it down. We consciously accept that certain things are beyond our control. We consciously accept that certain things should be beyond our control. We learn to separate out what needs action from what requires our acceptance and embrace. We choose the unknown.

Practicing active surrender is important because it is as much a source of energy and freedom as taking action is. And it is often needed when we approach situations with love rather than power.

—J.M.

Do you think I have a father complex?
I asked my analyst,
with just enough bravado
to cover my shame.
That is your destiny, he said.
Celebrate it.
You're going to walk that path
whether you like it or not.
You can go like a squealing pig
to slaughter,
or you can walk
with as much dignity as you can muster.

We are so sure
that to be receptive
is to surrender control;
that to open to fate is
to plummet through the dark.
We know no loving arms will open
to receive us as we fall.
We know we dare not;
the consequences would be fatal.

The door of our cage stands open.
We dare not walk through.
If we act out of instinct,
voice our feelings,
we open ourselves to fate.
Better, silence.
Better, the roles—
daughter, wife, mother—
as we have always—even half-heartedly—
understood them.

Indeed, we may be making
the only choice we can.

I dream I am
walking in darkness.
I come upon
a volcano, round and black.
I am not sure it is dead
or what I might stir up
if I jump in.
The mud is heavy, foul.

Then comes a voice,
more plea than command,
Throw yourself into the abyss.
I walk to the brink.
All around, the voices echo,
Trust.

I jump.
As I fall I see,
at the bottom of the abyss,
two golden S's,
Spiritus Sanctus,
float and unite to make infinity.
I land in its center
and infinity stands on end.
Its crown bursts into flame and carries me
to the top of darkness.

Just when the sun came to noon,
total eclipse.
Words must be spoken
but there is nobody to speak.
No body.

Where to go?
Down what street that does not
smell of dead lilacs?

He is gone.
Three words.
I open my mouth:
an animal howl.

———————

Fear keeps us chattering,
fear that wells up from the past,
fear of repercussions,
fear of blurting out
what we really fear.

Healing needs listening
with the inner ear,
stopping the incessant blather,
listening.

I was traveling alone;
this city, my last stop.
Fasting was part of my plan
to overcome the pain.
Six weeks of near starvation
had made me bodiless,
more ready to free myself into death
at twenty-five
than into life again.

I was crossing
from one railway station to another
when he forced me into the alley.
He said he would rape and kill me.

I tried to run. He was stronger.
I saw the man, I saw myself,
and accepted death.
He could not kill what had already died.
I relaxed and looked into his eyes.

His fingers loosened their grip on my throat.
You don't even fight,
you're no fun to kill.

If I'm going to die, I'm going to die,
I said quietly, never taking my eye from his.

He was confused.
I put my hands over his
and gently took them from my throat.
He began to cry, grabbed my wrist,
yanked me into a nearby pub,
and told me he had watched me in the train.
I had been unaware of him.
He believed
I was pretending to read,
was casting a spell,
was luring him into my web.
I listened and waited
and when he went into the urinal,
I escaped.

I returned home unraped,
ravaged, for the first time seeing
in his desperate eyes my stillness.

The house of cards collapses.
Somewhere, we think,
there must be joy.
It can't be all
must and ought and have to.
When the crunch comes,
we have to realize the truth:
we weren't there.

———

To surrender is to accept
life as it is:
winter today, spring tomorrow;
cruelty with beauty;
aloneness after love.

In fateful crises, we may really have no choice.

———

We know what we feel,
know what we desire,
then slowly surrender
to accept what is, and forgive.
What might have been
the salt of bitterness
becomes the salt of wisdom.
Sophia understands well
the salt that gives life savor.

When the path is blocked,
we can accept or fight.
When we fight, doors slam.
When we surrender to the mystery
and say,
Well, what do you need?
doors open.

———

Life becomes hectic.
We try to exert control,
create secure little pigeonholes,
believe we are in control.
And all the time we know
chaos leaps eternally
at our edges.

Whether we understand it or not,
sometimes we know
that Someone is moving us.
To know this
is to be known.

12

The Black Madonna: Embodied Feminine

*I*n many cultures, important transcendent qualities are personified as divine beings. Some qualities are perceived as specifically feminine, and are widely represented by female deities. Certain central feminine qualities are personified in the figure of the Black Madonna.

She manifests in sexuality, in childbirth, in nature—in the earthiest sides of our womanhood. She is the mother of a divine son who embodies a new consciousness in the darkness that holds the light.

—J.M.

The Black Madonna is sacredness in matter,
the intersection of sexuality and spirituality.

———

The Black Madonna's energy has smoldered.
Rejected by the patriarchy,
now she is erupting
in the world and in us,
demanding conscious recognition.

The Black Madonna walked into the kitchen,
munched carrots, and said,
So where are your pearls?
The dreamer replied, *They're upstairs.*

Get them, she said.
The dreamer climbed the stairs.
The pearls were not there.
Shame-faced, the dreamer went downstairs.

Of course you couldn't find them, she said.
I found them—in a ditch.
You weren't taking care of them.
It's the third time I've found them.
I won't bring them back again.
Next time it's up to you.

The Black Madonna weeps at times.
At times she is austere.
At times her fierce humor
cuts through our daily madness.

———————

The Black Madonna is larger than life itself.
Nature impregnated by spirit,
she presides over fertility, sexuality, childbirth.
She accepts her body as chalice for spirit,
presides over the sacredness of matter,
the meeting of sex and spirit.
Rejected by the patriarchy,
her energy has smoldered for generations.
Now she erupts in us and in the world,
demands conscious recognition,
demands redemption of matter.

When she comes in a dream,
She may take us on her lap,
put our head beside her heart,
and rock.

And we know
we have never heard that heartbeat,
never felt so loved.

Sometimes she is strict.
Her discipline is part of her love.
She knows what she is fighting.

13

Sophia: Feminine Wisdom

I f the sum total of our spirituality is larger than our minds can encompass, then we can better appreciate particular qualities through their personification as certain spiritual figures. The figure of Sophia carries, within certain Christian traditions, that aspect of our spirituality thought of as feminine wisdom. Her wisdom is rooted in experience, in compassion. She thinks with her heart and is more concerned with the processes than with the products of a life lived fully. She does not value the presence of power but the power of presence. We all carry Sophia in our hearts and when we connect to our feminine wisdom, we embody her in all her magnificence.

—J.M.

On Friday I sent the clothes
I would wear for my Sunday speech
to the hotel cleaners.
On Saturday night, at five, I called.
They said they'd been delivered
—*to a room.*
(They had no idea which.)
I would receive them—*sometime.*

They did turn up.
And I rose early Sunday to meditate
and work on my speech, then thought,
I'll put on those clothes
and see if they still fit.
The hem of the skirt was ripped out.
I'm not adept with a needle and thread
and have no idea how to hem
so you can't see the hem on the other side.
And I couldn't thread the needle,
(The thread was too thick for the eye of the needle.
If you've tried a hotel needle, you'll understand.)
My husband was still sleeping
so there I was, on the toilet, mending
and digging the needle into my finger,
and bleeding instead of meditating.

And I could hear Sophia laughing.

So if you dream of Isis—fine.
If you dream of your grandmother
—great mother—
and she becomes Her—
fine.
Call her Sophie,
Call her Anna.
Call her Buffalo Woman.
It doesn't matter.
Call her whatever
you like.

But call her.

If it bothers you, change it.
Try not to get stuck on little things.
God, Goddess;
Shiva, Shakti;
Yin with Yang
embracing Yang with Yin;
we get caught in old words.
Call it what you want.

But call it.

Sophia dances in the flames.
Horror and beauty blaze in her love.

———

To surrender to Sophia
takes strength and long travail.
She is opposition
transformed into paradox.

Sophia is
the receptive Being in whom
divine and human meet.

———

Sophia is the bridge.
She is the mystery.

———

Sophia is the stillness
at the center of the whirlpool,
the eye of the hurricane.
Without her,
there is no dance.

Sophia is the wisdom
that grows within each cell.
Beauty and horror
both blaze in her love,
and She is dancing in the flames.

———

Sophia wants things
moving,
breathing,
touching,
creating.

Sophia is
body opening to spirit,
illumination rising
from icy waters.

14

The Crone

If the *Black Madonna* may be said to carry our embodied spirituality and Sophia, to carry a timeless wisdom of the heart, then the Crone may be said to personify the wise older woman who has lived long, suffered loss and pain, survived to tell the truth to herself (and others if they are ready to hear), laughed with kindness at herself, learned to let go of expectations, and forgiven herself and others for their shortcomings. As you turn these pages, you might like to remember those women who have given you a glimpse of their hard-earned, lightly-held wisdom. Perhaps you will even want to find ways to express your appreciation to them inwardly or outwardly. In doing this, you might remember the wisdom of the Crone that is already taking up silent residence in your bones.

—J.M.

Age does not make a crone.
The fortunes and misfortunes of her life
do have something to do
with her maturing.

———

The Crone acts as a tuning fork
in an environment.
Because she is true
to her own feeling,
she rings a true tone
that resonates with others.

The Crone can afford to be honest.
She's not playing games anymore.
She brings you into that place
where outer conflicts dissolve
and you can experience your essence.

———

The Crone cuts.
She cuts with love.
Her sword has
a well-honed golden blade
and a silver handle.

The Crone has gone
through one crossroads after another.
She has reached a place of surrender
where her personal demands are no longer relevant.
She is a surrendered instrument
and therefore detached.

———

The Crone has nothing to lose.
She can be who she is,
can live with the naked truth.

The Crone has nothing to lose.
There is no power operating.
She has no reason to persuade you
to do anything
or to be anything
other than what you are.
She's a perfect mirror.

———

The Crone has seen enough
to be able to separate
irrelevance from essence.
She has neither time nor energy
to waste on superficialities.

The Crone is strong enough
to hold the container
in which men can experience
their hidden rage
without destroying themselves or others.
The Crone takes life
with Sophia's proverbial grain of salt.
She can smile at the divine comedy.

———————

If the Crone hasn't lived
through her own crossroads,
don't trust her.
She'll want power.

To the Crone, detachment is not indifference.
It means she has lived,
and suffered,
and, having suffered,
can draw back
and see with her heart.

15

Conscious Femininity

Conscious femininity is not about being self-consciously female. It is an inner experience for both women and men. Yet, at a recent meeting of women—all committed to conscious femininity—when one woman asked, "What *is* it?" there was silence! We could not define it! Hours later it still defied definition, although the room resounded with stories and rich descriptions.

In these pages, we glimpse it in experiences of presence, process, paradox, embodied soul, thinking with the heart, receptivity, and resonance.

—J.M.

Feminine consciousness
is the transformative energy
that can contain the energies of matter
and, through the fire of love,
connect them to the energies of soul.

———

In man or in woman,
the virgin
has the courage to BE
and the flexibility
to be always becoming.

Lunar consciousness unites,
thinks with the heart,
incorporates past, present, and future
in time out of time.

———

The feminine
is an ocean of eternal being;
she contains the primordial animals,
contains the seeds for life.

The feminine is grounded
in the instincts;
she knows the laws of nature
and exacts them with ruthless justice.

————

The feminine
has slower rhythms,
meanders,
moves in spirals,
turns back on herself,
finds what is meaningful to her,
and plays.

The feminine
is always on the side of life.
loves life.
Loves.
If penetrated by the creative,
she flows into life
with a constant flow:
new hope,
new faith,
new dimensions of love.

––––––––

The feminine is often lost to us
yet never forgotten in our dreams:
purses are lost;
a wild wolf bites our hand;
little cats die.

We must not only hear
the feminine,
but act.
If we abandon her,
she turns her dark face,
revengeful, depressed, suicidal.
We need to accept
that our lives
are turning inside out.

16

Integrating Masculine Energy

Qualities of active receptivity, resonance, loving presence, process, paradox, and intuition have been traditionally associated by many theorists with the feminine aspects of spirituality. Their complements have been traditionally associated by many with masculine aspects of spirituality including initiative, directedness, discernment, analysis, decisiveness, strength of purpose, and clarity of mind. Some women—particularly younger—might not find that these distinctions parallel their experience. However, most of us might agree that, for every characteristic that has been nurtured in us by culture and family, there is a complementary quality that has probably been nurtured less.

To be well rounded individuals, we need to find graceful ways to move back and forth between "feminine" and "masculine" qualities, ways that allow those opposites to act synergistically.

—J.M.

At the moment of awakening,
we have to ask real questions
and be prepared to take real action.
It doesn't matter any more
what mother did to me,
what father did to me.
Shall I stay in this job?
Shall I stay in this relationship?
Am I going to live,
even if I don't know what that means?

Solar consciousness
cuts and clarifies,
makes well-defined boundaries.

———

We must first awaken
to our needs, feelings and values.
Then the masculine can grow up
and say:
I shall stand up
for these needs, these feelings, these values.
I shall put them out there in the world,
I shall work with you in all your creativity.

Positive masculine energy
is goal oriented,
has the strength of purpose
to move toward that goal.
It disciplines itself
to make the most of its gifts,
physical, intellectual, spiritual.
It attempts to bring them into harmony.
It learns to hold the tension
between a firm standpoint and a surrender
to the creative feminine within.

————

Solar consciousness
analyzes and discriminates.

I am no sailor
but I love to crew:
he and I, barefoot and flying,
skim, toss, veer
with treacherous current and vagaries of wind
through the waters of Georgian Bay.

Poised, excited, he takes easy command,
straining to keep the craft upright—
strong body, keen mind in harmony,
tuned to the fierce energies
through which we sail.

One slip, one moment of indecision
would hurl us headlong.
We strain back over the water,
hang on with our toes.

We moor,
I step out, feet bloody,
thighs burning.
He takes down the sails,
ties the ropes, smiles,
and walks up the cliff,
confident, relaxed, erect.
He trusts his animal body.
The eternal has blown through.

17

The Inner Marriage

*I*t's easy to feel that we are only whole when we are in relationship with another person whose qualities complete our picture of ourselves, both inner and outer. We rely on or long for that person who, we believe, can give us a completeness, purpose, and meaning we think we cannot have otherwise. When we fall prey to this belief, we underestimate ourselves and overburden our loved ones with unrealistic expectations.

When we stop expecting another to give us wholeness, we can take the risk of finding our own sense of wholeness; we can discover and encourage our own complementary energies, the inner masculine and feminine aspects of ourselves.

—J.M.

Masculinity is in men and women.
Femininity is in women and men.
Develop each to its fullest.

In relationship, each needs
full masculine and full feminine
to make things flow.
We are still so far from that.

————

The first time we fall helplessly in love,
we are in love with our own projected image.
Slowly, after many projections,
we recognize they are all alike at their core,
these ones to whom we are fatally drawn.
Slowly we recognize ourselves.
We have been falling in love with ourselves.

The graveyard was just behind
the family homestead;
The movement from life to immortality,
merely an adjustment of focus;
immortality, a presence.

Her father presided
with puritan severity,
broken, at times,
by tenderness and warmth.
She lived to please him,
share his pursuits,
meet his standards of perfection.

Another entered her life
when she was thirty-one.
He was married.
How well she knew him, we do not know.
Three years later, he moved away.

Left her
with willpower and a mask
to cover the blistering wound.

She was the perfect seedbed
for the demon lover.
Every encounter with friend and flower
released bolts of energy.

Determined to save her life,
she wore only white,
tended her garden
and a few close friends,
baked daily bread.

And, in one year alone,
wrote 366 poems.

He isn't a god after all.
The real god is inside.
Slowly, you recognize
the illusions, the delusions,
the pain of human limitation.
Then gradually it dawns
what a huge mistake you've made.

Hold your divinity within.
Then ask yourself,

Do I love this human being?
You may find that you do;
that there's something noble in his suffering,
something noble in your own;
that you're walking parallel paths,
not holding each other up.

It's a marvelous thing,
to love another human being this way.

If we are depending on our partner
to make us whole,
we're in trouble.
Sooner or later, we shall feel betrayed.
Sooner or later, we shall hate the dependence,
Sooner or later, we may be the one
who does the betraying.
Wholeness is within.

Something, someone, more intense,
is luring her out of life.
Her ghostly lover was merely the altar boy
for this, her Demon Lover.

Fiery, suave, seductive with royal charm,
he lives at her core,
a lover-killer within.
His magnetism lures her
toward death.

Her God is sadistic:
does not say Yes to her prayers.
God is her demon assailant
and she, enraged.

Her heart could stop,
not from death
but from fury
at the inevitability of loss.

Her awareness of immanence
may yet turn her round
with will
to live her own life.

She can make a choice.
She can choose surrender;

demon can become daimon,
her spirit guide within.

His wounding may become his blessing
and he, her inner king,
her creative genius;
this union, the true creative act.

She need not succumb,
need not retreat,
nor need she harden into bitterness.
She can begin a love affair
with her own life.

Spiritual birth, like biological birth,
requires a union of opposites,
from which the sacred child is born.

18

Creativity

Some people think of creativity as something that artists possess. It might be more helpful to think of it as Jung did, as an instinct. We can bring creativity to almost every life activity. Moreover, we can use certain imaginative forms of creative expression through the arts to explore personal, spiritual, and psychological development. These forms do not need artistic talent but simply artistic expression for the soul's sake. Metaphor, imagination, symbol can be said to be the soul's native language.

As you turn these pages, you might invite yourself to remember the ways in which you already express your creativity and quietly vow to yourself that you will also find other ways to free the creativity you ignore.

—J.M.

Creativity is divine:
the virgin soul opens to spirit
and conceives the divine child.
We cannot live without it.
It is the meaning of life,
this creative fire.

———

When *doing* is all we know,
being is just another word
for ceasing to exist.
When *being* begins to flow
through dance and paint and song,
joy is no longer luxury
but absolute need.

If you paint,
I say *yes, yes* to that.

If you use clay,
I say *yes, yes* to that.

If you set your dreams to music,
I say *yes, yes* to that.

I say *yes* to anything
that says *yes* to the soul.

.

In her dream
a pen, a paintbrush.

Do you ever paint?
    Nope. No, I can't paint.
    My sister's a good painter.
    I could never paint.

Her dreams are full
of brushes, colors,
a woman painting.

        Something happened.
        I stopped.

Her dreams are full
of brushes, colors,
a woman painting.

        I really do love painting.

Sooner or later
we have to take responsibility
for who we were born to be.

In our creating, we are created.

———

Just give him the paints.
Let him go to it
and discover his own soul.

If we give ourselves half an hour a day
with our creativity,
our dreams, our music,
the soul becomes quiet.
We are in our body
and we feel nourished.

———

Let your body become the music.
Let her sing.
Let your pen walk in the twilight
between consciousness and unconscious.
There, it will find
such images, such ideas
as you could never find.

Once you dance for a year,
it's part of your day.
I mean, it's prayer.
Dance your dreams each morning,
Let your images move in your body.

19

Dream Wisdom

Messengers *between* the creative unconscious and consciousness, dreams speak their own language, a language of image, symbol, and metaphor. When we bring our imagination, openness, and discernment to them, they are possible sources of inner guidance, wisdom, revelation, healing, and development.

Dreams live in a universe free of time and space restrictions. Only the fluidity of the arts—movement, poetry, myth, and art—truly carry their messages well to waking awareness. If we limit the dream to verbal analysis and reductive definitions, the dream dries up. However, if we feed our dreams with our creativity and curiosity, they will nourish our understanding for days, even years.

Let your memory bring you gifts from your dream world.

—J.M.

The dream keeps us
in touch with that soul
in which we all live.
The dream keeps us
in touch with our place
in that one creation.
The dream puts us
into a time and space
in which we are restored.

———

Our dreams give us the images
for our personal lives and for the earth.
Integrating these images
takes hours in meditation
and we may make fools of ourselves
when we first put them into life.
But when we've seen with new eyes,
when we've heard with new ears,
we can't go back.
However painful the fire,
we're in our own fire now.
We're learning what love is.

Our dreams disturb in order to illumine.

———

To make prose sense of a dream
subjects the dream
to a grammatical logic
that may be alien
to the symbolic logic
of the dreaming state.
The dream is closer
to poetry than prose.

We never know exactly
what a symbol means.
The symbol carries
meaning for the mind,
meaning for the heart,
meaning for the imagination.
We can never say,
That is what the dream means.
Years later we say,
Ah! That's what the dream was about!
A symbol opens and opens and opens.

————

If the dream uses a symbol
and you say, *That's bizarre!* Chuck it,
you're chucking gold.

Our banquet of dreams is spread each night.
We can choose to eat.
We can choose not to eat.

———

Write dreams down.
Work with them.
Talk with trusted others.
It will amaze you
how much comes through.
Be subjective and objective
at the same time.
Listen to your dream
with your third ear.

A dream can often tell us
what and where a problem is
long before a doctor can diagnose.

———

The dream arises from the instinctual world.

It usually comes after working on the body.
The dream will bring it to you:
a shift in sexuality,
a wave of creativity,
a welcoming of shadow.

———

God is the dream maker
revealed through the dream.

Dreams are the quickest way
into our inner world.
They astonish us with their wisdom
about past, present, future.

———————

Once we know what the dream world is,
to be without it is to be rudderless.
The dream continually corrects
our waking course.

Sleep brings body into balance;
dream brings psyche into balance.

———

The dream's language is not two-dimensional.
It carries its meaning
through imagination, emotion, and intellect.

We say, *That's it! That's it. I've got it!*
We know who we are.
Then, feeling whole, we walk out the door
and run into a reality we barely understand.
Yet, still reverberating with that moment of
wholeness, we can say,
This, this is my inner truth.
I shall try to stand in that today.

Tonight may bring a new image.

We cannot take in the dream
when we have it.

We glimpse ourselves and think,
That's crazy! Can't be!
Will never happen!

One day we shall find ourselves
walking into an image from a dream
we had years ago.

———

If you don't believe
something is trying to bring you
to full potential,
the dream world is impossible.
It takes you through dark water,
demonic territory.
You'll say, *No more of this!*

Balance of wind and water.
A small sail boat
accommodating the wind:
that is the dream process.
It must follow the currents,
yet we must hold firm
on the rudder and the sail.

———

The dream comes
from the world of the eternal,
the great *I am.*

20

Holding Conflict Creatively

Holding *an inner* or outer conflict quietly instead of attempting to resolve it quickly is a difficult idea to entertain. It is even more challenging to experience! However, as Carl Jung believed, if we held the tension between the two opposing forces, there would emerge a third way, which would unite and transcend the two. Indeed, he believed that this transcendent force was crucial to individuation. A woman might be torn between leaving her husband for a lover and staying with him out of loyalty and guilt. If she can be quiet enough and step back from her conflict, she may find, to her surprise, that she now *wants* to stay with her husband because she feels a new kind of love for him, or she might find, again to her surprise, that what she really wants is to live *alone*. Or she may find new life in her lover.

Whatever the third way is, it usually comes as a surprise, because it has not penetrated our defenses until now. A hasty move to resolve tension can abort growth of the new. If we can hold conflict in psychic utero long enough, we can give birth to something new in ourselves.

—J.M.

Both arms on the cross,
we dare not drop the tension.

If we reject one part,
we give up our past;
if we reject the other,
we give up our future.

Whether we like it or not,
we need to hold to our roots
and build from there.

If we can hold the conflict of opposites—
what we want and
what destiny has ordained—
if we can hold
while mind thinks and heart feels
we can learn to think with the heart.

———

In our dreams, we dance
along a fence,
up stairs, down stairs,
on sands beside the sea,
on dance floors we have known
and on others we have yearned to know.
In dreams and in life, we dance,
holding our balance between the opposites.

I'm brave.
Brave also means
being nervous.

————

We are not animals only.
We are not gods only.

Sentimentality refuses to suffer,
fears the heat
of passion, anger, grief.
Real feeling is tempered in fire,
moves into conflict
and holds the opposites
until the new is born.

———

A free woman has a strong neck,
an open connection between heart and head,
a balance between reality and ideals.

So long as we divide ourselves
with ancient dualities—
spirit or matter,
white or black,
we cannot know
the sacredness of matter.
We are blind to the unity
that nurtures diversity.

———

Life is a continual attempt
to balance yin and yang.
The further we move toward radiance,
the blacker the energy that gathers
behind our back.
The more we force ourselves
to perfect our ideal image of ourselves,
the more overflowing toilet bowls
we shall have in our dreams.

What do we do
when everything rational says,
Let go!
and everything emotional says,
I cannot!

———

We can swing back and forth
between opposites indefinitely.
Better to stand
on the stillpoint
at the center.

21

Finding Meaning in Darkness

Certain *things grow* in darkness—babies, dreams, roots. . . .
We often associate darkness with negativity, but darkness
has both positive and negative sides. Dark times in our
life might or might not contain inherent meaning; our
view of this depends on our religious and spiritual per-
spectives.

Yet there seems little doubt that dark times can provide opportunities for the student of the heart to learn.
Even times that seem ravaged by loss and pain can be
used as occasions for us to grow and mature. By
approaching situations from the point of view of the student, we might learn from the dark.

—J.M.

There's another way
to look at darkness.

———————

Creative work comes from that level
where we share our suffering,
just the sheer suffering
of being human.
That's where real love is.

No matter how awful it is,
the truth sets us free.

———————

Suffering and conflict
are one way to grow.
As life moves from phase to phase,
we suffer the death of one,
the birth of the other.

There is great danger
in trying to make everything sacred.

———————

I almost envy them, sometimes,
the happy ones.
I'm sure they don't envy me.
They say,
You're always grief-stricken,
always worrying,
always trying to understand,
always trying to 'bring to consciousness'...
(as if that were a dirty word).
Some just keep asking, *Why?*

Without the divine, the imagination,
the grief, the struggle,
life is two-dimensional.
One foot drags after the other,
without meaning.

I lived like that once.
I couldn't go on.

What if the symptoms of my illness
are trying to heal me?

There's nothing worse
than meaningless pain
and meaningless suffering.

———————

Once we find the right question
we soon realize
the answer lies in the
unconscious.
Question and answer are two sides of one
thought once we find the right questions.

Stand in the middle.
Let suffering pass through.
Let joy pass through.

Do not identify,
as though there is
nothing but suffering,
nothing but joy.

Yes, there is joy.
Yes, there is suffering.
Say, *I suffer.*
I can *go through this*
and learn what is to be learned.

Stand in the middle,
knowing the suffering will pass,
knowing the joy will pass.

22

Living with Paradox

Most of us have grown up in a culture that divides things into two piles, into dualities: spirit or matter, feminine or masculine, alive or dead, male or female, adult or child, good or bad, light or dark, joyful or painful. We believe things cannot belong in both piles.

In other cultures, this assumption is not experienced as true. What if we were to suspend our belief in it for a while? What if we were to consider the possibility that things are light *and* dark, good *and* bad, joyful *and* painful, spirit *and* matter? We might learn to entertain the notion of paradox, the holding as true of two apparently contradictory ideas, facts, beliefs, or observations at the same time. In so doing, we shall be more able to experience the richness of life, the truth of its beautiful complexity.

—J.M.

We learn to live
in paradox,
in a world where
two apparently exclusive views
are held at the same time.

In this world,
rhythms of paradox are circuitous,
slow, born of feeling
rising from the thinking heart.

Many sense such a place exists.
Few talk or walk from it.

In feminine consciousness,
spiritual and physical
are two aspects of one whole.
This paradox defies
the logic of prose,
demands metaphor, the poet's leap.
Frogs among lilypads
leap from leaf to leaf.

Intimacy reveals our deepest anguish.

————

The paradox of life and death
returns in a new form
at each new spiral of growth.
If we accept this,
we are not torn apart
by opposites.

So what is the rose in the fire?
It is soul
suffering
in the fire
of physical pain and passion.
It is spirit
languishing
as it descends
into physical limitation.
It is matter
ascending towards spirit.
It is the creation
of subtle body.
It is time
in timelessness.
It is light
in matter.

Soulmaking is
allowing eternal essence
to live and experience the outer world
through all the senses
—seeing, smelling, hearing, tasting, touching—
so that soul grows during its time on earth.

Soulmaking is
constantly confronting the paradox
that an eternal being is dwelling
in a temporal body.
That's why it suffers.
That's why it learns by heart.

———

Soul hears with eternal ears,
sees with eternal eyes,
smells with eternal nose.
Yet, having no tongue
other than the transitory language
of the body,
it learns to speak in metaphor.

Birth is the death of the life
we have known;
death, the birth of the life
we have yet to live.

23

Delighting in Play & Imagination

I f play is the work of the soul, imagination is its language. In order to be playful, we need to be in a trustworthy environment where we and those around us respect our vulnerabilities.

Loving parents create places in which their children can play safely. We, too, can provide these so that our playful energies can emerge. Play and imagination are the raw material of adult self-expression in the arts. Children don't need to be talented to enjoy painting or dancing; they do it because they enjoy it. Adults do not need talent either, just a willingness to let go of set ideas about what it means to express themselves in the arts.

The world of play and imagination invites us to let go of expectations and to open up spontaneous creativity in which unexpected wisdom and delight can emerge.

—J.M.

Most of us have forgotten how to play,
forgotten the joy of creativity.
Without joy, we run from pain.
Without creativity, we run from emptiness.
The faster we run, the more severe our
addictions.
We cannot face our nothingness,
the ultimate anguish of living a life knowing
who we are not,
not who we are.

———

Allow the body to play.
Give it space.
Let it make whatever movements
it wants to make.
Just as a dream is an invitation
to the unconscious,
so releasing your body
into spontaneous movement or play
is an invitation to the unconscious.

Seeing is looking with the eyes.
Perceiving is looking
with the eyes of the imagination.

———

The images we take in
are the nutrients of our subtle body.

A gift of the feminine,
metaphor transforms,
crosses from one state to another,
connects psyche and soma.

———————

Without metaphor,
culture, dreams, illness, and religion
have no meaning.
Drugs, sports, sex may revive metaphor
for a few hours before flatness
settles in again.
Life without metaphor is intolerable.

To be childlike is
to be spontaneous,
to live in the moment—
concentrated, imaginative, creative.

Your images are a picture
of your spiritual condition.

To turn the tomb into a womb,
move with the imagination.

———

We all want to play.
Play lives close to the imagination.
Every minute is new
because something new is constantly happening.
In a relationship, we each need to say,
Let's see how we can play.
Without this, we die.
It doesn't take money.
Just a long leap of faith.

Food and metaphor:
both feed our bodysoul;
both deserve discernment.

How long shall we go on
feeding ourselves
poisoned food and poisoned images?

———

To live a rich life,
we have to be in contact
with our inner world.

24

Beyond Power & Patriarchy

Both *men and women* suffer when power is exercised for its own sake by rule- and authority-bound women and men. Powermongers usually win their own games; they are operating on home territory. To go beyond power and the structures that support it usually involves quietly stepping aside. We do not step aside to disengage but to evolve creative alternatives to power struggles.

We may not be able to do as much as we would like about the way things turn out on sociopolitical battlegrounds, that often require well-coordinated strategies involving many people. However, we can certainly begin with ourselves. We do not have to react in kind. We can learn to choose how we want to respond.

Who are your inner powermongers? What do they say? How do they keep the rules?

—J.M.

Don't blame anyone out there.
You have been treated with power,
and you treat others
as you have been treated.
Have courage:
face the power in yourself.

———————

If we have been tyrannized,
we can be fairly sure
we're tyrannizing
someone else—
at least ourselves,
perhaps our bodies.
As we were treated,
so we treat ourselves and others.

In a patriarchy
everything is split.
It's *either or.*
In the feminine realm,
it's *both and.*

————

Living by principles
is not
living your own life.

Men have not escaped
the bludgeoning of the patriarchy.

———————

Patriarchy isn't "men"
and isn't only found in men.

The move from power to love
involves immense suffering.

———

Recognizing the difference
between power and love is difficult
if we were raised in a home
where power was disguised as love.

She inherited their beauty and intelligence.
Her mother groomed her to queenhood,
acquainted her
with Yves St. Laurent, Chanel, Harvard,
with the best princes Oxford could offer.
She carried her crown on her regal head—
performed meticulously,
smiled at the right times, wept at the right,
knew when to raise lashes and when to lower.

She did not prosper with the princes;
she became queen of Wall Street,
regal in pinstriped suit and heels.
Always, she carried her insignia,
her black briefcase full of papers, pills, and salve
for headaches, constipation, psoriasis.

And in her chrome and glass apartment,
before she went to bed,
she turned off her computer and stereo,
turned off her rheostat lights,
turned on her electric blanket.

She heard her mother crooning
Old Mother Hubbard,
She went to the cupboard
To give her poor doggie a bone...

She dreamed a computer
was printing out musical scores,
printing each note as a hole
through which she heard
the music for which she yearned.

An unconscious father's daughter
colludes with the lies of patriarchy.

We often repeat
the pattern of our own birth
each time life requires us to move
into new awareness.

25

Practicing Presence

Being *present invites us* to set aside comparison of our situation with another's, to set aside anticipation and rehearsal of future statements or actions, to set aside memories that interfere with or misinterpret the present moment. Being present invites us to be fully committed to the moment while not being attached to controlling what is not fully under our control: the outcome of whatever is happening right now.

Being present invites us to set aside judgment yet still retain discernment, to set aside sympathy yet hold to empathy, to set aside power yet be responsible for influence. It invites us to bring head, heart, and body into this moment.

—J.M.

The feminine
was, is, and shall be.
It lives in the eternal now.

————

If we could allow the pace of our meetings
to slow down to the pace of our hearts,
we might find genuine understanding.

The feminine mystery lives now.
Its energies are concentrated
on what is happening in this moment:
the scent of wet pine,
a hesitant hand.
The feminine does not save itself
for some glorious moment
in the future,
does not grieve over a lost moment
in the past.
It holds nothing back.
Now is all there is.

Oh sometimes, of course, the soul
enjoys homemade bread and jam,
and sex.

And when you dwell on a candle
in waking or dreaming,
dwell with all of you:
with gut,
with feeling,
with spirit,
with breath,
with mind!
And yes, all the senses
if you're really into it.

You go out
and the moment breaks.
But take it anyway,
knowing that it will break.

When one person in a room is more conscious,
the consciousness of all in the room changes.
If one person in a family is becoming conscious,
everyone in the family changes—
for better or for worse.

———

We go to great lengths
not to hear our inner voices.
If there's nobody home
we have to hang on for dear life.
Only when there is presence
can we let go.

We suffer but we also know
the joy of seeing that tree, that tree!
There! Look!
We know we're here,
present in the moment!
We give; we receive—
continual flow.

When we face death,
if we've lived life,
we'll be ready.
If we haven't lived it,
never been here,
never been present,
we'll be terrified;
our whole life will have been
an absence.

We shall have missed it.
Well, by heaven,
I don't intend to miss mine.

Femininity is Being
that knows its bone truth.

26

Trusting Deeper Processes

To believe *we understand* all the inner and outer forces in our lives is rather like believing we can understand ocean currents by observing the surface of the water. We all know that there are forces that we do not understand at work in our lives. Some people trust them; some distrust them; some believe them to be divine intervention; others simply live with not understanding them.

What are your own beliefs? Are there other views you might consider?

—J.M.

Conscious femininity gives us
the courage to trust in the moment
without knowing what the goal is.

———————

Distilling the truth of the image
is
the work,
a work
that is never finished.

I get up in the morning
to write in my journal.
While I wait for coffee, I wash a sweater.
Good suds! I might as well wash another.
While I'm trying to find it,
I find some soiled scarves
and, by heaven, there's the letter
I couldn't find six months ago.
I put the scarves to soak,
and water my plants.
And trying to find my good stationery
to reply to the old letter,
I find bills I have forgotten to pay
and then I decide to dance.
And I see the mess I'm creating.
So much to do.

Look at their beauty—
women for the first time
finding their sexuality,
men beginning
to know what sexuality is—
they are seeing the beauty
of their shadow,
at sixty-five or seventy.

Now that's grief—
but it's better to find it late
than not at all.
And, I tell you,
grief can open your heart
to incredible love.

———

Outer events are
not important.
Our response to them
is what matters.
It matters to them.

We spend years
building our lives on rotten foundations.

It takes years
to build new foundations
for a new life.

Where can I find an hour a day?
To turn away from duty,
to release that energy
into something creative for myself
is like being tossed into a washing machine.
Can I really believe
I am worth an hour a day?
Am I, who have given my life to others,
selfish enough to take one hour a day
to find myself?

27

Body-Soul Resonance

W*hen two things vibrate* at the same frequency, they resonate with each other. We, too, have experienced resonance within us: moments when everything in us said *yes* to someone or to something—an embrace, a piece of music, a new opportunity, an exquisite scene. Or moments when everything in us said *no*! These are occasions of body-soul resonance.

You might ask yourself: Do I have to wait for these occasional moments to experience this? Or might I begin to feel and trust this body-soul resonance in my daily life?

—J.M.

Whether we know or not,
our cells know
the love or lack of love
that comes toward us.

———

The earth is screaming.
Our bodies are in trouble.
Matter wants to be redeemed.

A mother who is out of touch
with her own body
cannot give her baby
the sense of harmony with self and universe
fundamental to a later sense of totality.

————

If we are robbed
of our feminine birthright
we are not here.
Our body is not here.

If we are whole,
we resonate
physically, psychically.
Our soul is incarnate.

Abandoned souls
bring themselves forth
whether we work
with ourselves or not.
They seem insatiable because we fail
to understand their language.

When we connect with our souls,
we connect with the soul
of every human being.
We resonate with all living things.
That's where healing is.

Conscious femininity is aware
of the energy in rock, bird, tree, sunset,
aware of living in the world soul.
The body is attuned, concentrated, alive,
open, receptive, alert,
aware in the marrow
of the harmony of the universe.

28

Rites of Passage

I f *we had lived in another time,* we would have passed through life passages with rituals different from those we have (or do not have) now. Puberty, a first sexual experience, becoming an adult, childbirth, the loss of a loved one, illness, the taking on of authority vested in us by age: these transitions from one phase of our lives into another are intense but sadly and too often noted only in passing and half-consciously in our time.

Perhaps it is only in retrospect that we recognize some of our rites of passage. However, we can still remember and celebrate them. And we can be more aware of how we approach them in the future—for ourselves, for others, and for new generations who might once again benefit from having these rites of passage overtly acknowledged.

—J.M.

Transitions are hell.
Our beloved dies or leaves
and we are alone.
That is hell.
It is also time to grow.

Converse alone with body, with soul.
Their wisdom is what we need for wholeness.
Their wisdom makes clear
what is real, what is illusion.
Their wisdom strips false pride.
Their wisdom makes us human.

Each hell burns off more illusions.
We go into the fire, die,
and are reborn.

Rites of passage
are inner and outer,
body and psyche at limit.
We journey through
the labyrinth of our souls.
The mystery
lures us into death,
which leads us into life.

———

Rites of passage are accompanied
by image.
The image partakes of spirit and matter,
belongs to neither,
is possessed by neither.
The image is the map
for the new country.
We hold the tension
until the new image comes;
if we do not, the gold is lost,
the initiation fails.

Rites of passage are accompanied
by surrender.
We let ourselves drop
into our charged body.
Soul surrenders to spirit.
Our relationship to ourselves
and to the world is recreated.

————

Rites of passage are accompanied
by tenacity.
The tunnel of death and rebirth
demands supreme effort,
demands holding on
without orientation
until the light.

Rites of passage are accompanied
by concentration.
Concentration directs energy
toward consciousness,
learns to take direction
from within,
discovers a world with its own order.
Every minute is new.
Every minute is now.

———

Rites of passage are accompanied
by preparation and purification:
a bath,
a garment,
a dance,
a sacrifice....

Rites of passage are accompanied
by strength.
Possession blinds.
We grow strong enough
to surrender
free of possession
by instinct or spirit.

———

Rites of passage are accompanied
by intensity.
Intensity brings us
to the moment
when the mystery bursts through.

Change and flux:
in the decay of the old
and the birth of the new,
the rhythm of the feminine.

29

The Shadow

When we stand in the light, we cast a shadow. Light and shade are to each other as breathing in is to breathing out. Some aspects of ourselves are in the light, visible to us and others. Other aspects, positive and negative, are in shadow, unseen by us, even when seen by others. These are parts of ourselves that have been neglected, disowned, forgotten, judged, unrecognized, or undeveloped.

Some of the ways we can glimpse what is in the psychological shade include noting what we idealize or denigrate in others; recognizing our uneasiness about others' perceptions of us (good and bad); and paying attention to our bodies, where shadow can sometimes reside as a physical symptom (an aching back, a pain in the stomach).

Our shadow is an infinite reservoir of energy. Learning to recognize and to take responsibility for our shadow qualities gives us more choice in responding consciously and creatively to the possibilities life offers us.

—J.M.

The shadow is anything
we are sure we are not;
it is part of us we do not know,
sometimes do not want to know,
most times do not want to know.
We can hardly bear to look.

Look.
It may carry the best of the life
we have not lived.

If we're ever to get along with our mates,
we have to deal with our shadow.
How can we have intimacy with another
when we lie to ourselves?

———

If we allow ourselves to receive,
to be ravished by the irrational,
we are compelled to face our own evil.
Trust takes on new dimension:
In knowing our own darkness,
we know what another's darkness can release.
We learn to forgive and to love.
There we don't know
from moment to moment
what will happen next.
That is God's country.

Once we've recognized our shadow,
once we've accepted it
as part of who we are,
and begun to civilize it,
we are no longer judgmental of others.

———————

Intuitive people are blessed and cursed.
They are confounded by possibilities,
driven this way and that by what might be.
They are rarely in the present,
never quite filling their bodies.

Their bodies become vulnerable
to all the pain in their environment.
Through osmosis they pick up
others' unconscious garbage.
Intuitive people are blessed and cursed.

Repressed energy returns
to haunt us
in symbols and symptoms.

———————

God preserve me
from being reduced to my shadow.

Trying to be a god or a goddess
all week
can flip us into being an animal
all weekend.

———

Our shadow may contain
the best of ourselves.

How the energy in the body
has been caged!
Released (which happens quickly),
there is danger in accepting it
without reserve
as a saving grace.

It is shadow.
Do not embrace it
as a long-lost sister.

Recognize.
Don't act impulsively.
Maintain healthy suspicion.
To live out is not to integrate.
Chew and digest.

Don't use
a whip that will kill its spirit.
Put a rider on the wild horse.

To claim our unlived parts
is to stand in our own shoes.
crumpled as they may be.

———————

We cannot kill energy.
It goes underground.
It always rises again
in another, strange way.

The Self
pushes the neglected forward
for recognition.
Do not disregard it.
It holds energy
of highest value.
It is the gold in the dung.
Do not disregard the dung.

30

Coming to Love

The kind of loving into which we are invited in the following pages may be familiar or unfamiliar. It certainly goes beyond personal attachment and physical attraction. This love walks in with an open heart, open hands, open eyes, and open mind. This love is not blind to human flaws in itself or in others. Rather it invites us to embrace others with full awareness of both the light and the dark.

Can we experience this kind of love for ourselves, for others, from others?

—J.M.

Whatever their outcome,
the profound relationships in our lives
give us the riches of loving.
That wealth is the only wealth
that means anything in the end.

———————

The mystery of God touches us—
or does not—
in the smallest details:
giving a strawberry,
with love;
receiving a touch,
with love;
sharing the snapdragon red
of an autumn sunset,
with love.

Only by opening ourselves to inner reality
do we open
to the possibility of love.
Action and choice are needed:
we can accept;
we can reject;
we can withdraw.

We cannot make it happen.
Love chooses us.

———

He is.
I am.
Tough stuff!

Imagine BEING love.

————

Real love happens
when soul in the body
meets soul in the body.
Not in that disembodied world of spirit
where we want to be perfect,
but in life,
where we're changing the diapers
of one we love who is dying,
swabbing the lips,
doing things we never thought we could do.
Stripped of all pride, of everything unreal,
we have no false modesty.
Where soul meets soul, that is love.

One day you shall be able to say,
I am.
I am loved.
I can receive love.
I do love myself.
I do love.
Perhaps today.

31

Trusting the Mystery

T*he mystery* this section contemplates is not the kind found in a detective novel. Rather, it is the gatekeeper of the sacred. To dispel this kind of mystery with too harsh a light—to explain away everything about our dream, about love, about commitments—is to tear down the gate and allow sacred ground to be trampled. Mystery keeps us humble, keeps our rationality aware of its ignorance.

Sustaining awareness of the mystery of what it is to be human, of what our dreams are, of what certain piercing moments "mean," reminds us what a wonderfully small part of a larger life flow we are.

As you reflect on these pages, you might ask yourself where you experience a sense of mystery in your life.

—J.M.

Why should we have more faith
in an amaryllis bulb
than in ourselves?
We know, perhaps,
that the amaryllis lives
by an inner law
with which we have lost touch
in ourselves.

The blossom dies;
with rest and darkness,
another bloom will come
we know, next year.
In this place of the goddess,
we accept birth and death.

When we listen to the amaryllis,
resonate with its silence,
its eternal stillness, we find ourselves
at the heart of the mystery.

Consciousness changes the perceived.
Science knows this.
Psychology is slower to believe.

———

I trust there is a healing process
going on in my unconscious.
If I can keep in touch with it,
my life flows forward;
I constantly open to what
I could never have imagined.

If you watch a caterpillar
you might catch the moment
when the crawling stops.
Delicate membranes attach to a twig,
old skin is shed, pupal skin hardens.

The caterpillar chooses the food
the butterfly will need,
chooses the exact space
to later spread its wings.
Without the space,
the wings would never fly.

The chrysalis is essential.
It is the twilight zone,
a precarious world
between past and future.

The grub will not emerge
as a high class caterpillar.
Does it know
what will go on inside?
Does it prepare
for the winged beauty
that slowly and painfully emerges,
that will live by a new set of laws?

If you're a happy carrot,
why wouldn't you remain a happy carrot?
If you're happy, and your life is mostly joy,
why would you want to be conscious?

Few of us come to consciousness
without great pain;
something unbearable
has happened.

Don't try to take others
out of carrothood.
You'll be responsible
for trying to make them conscious,
and that is misuse of power.
Some people are happy carrots.
God bless them!

———

Unconscious means
not conscious!

Our stillpoint at center:
the psychic pendulum swings
through to the left.
We say,
I despair,
but I am not despair.
This shall pass.
It swings through to the right.
We say,
I am in love,
hopelessly in love.
This too shall pass.

———

As we once entered the world,
so we still enter
each new spiral of growth.

Until consciousness intercedes.

Once we are in the flow
of our life's river,
we experience synchronicity.
Outer and inner
become
much the same.

32

Listening to My Soul

However we define "soul," we know when we encounter it. We don't have to ask. We are suffused with it.

Unless we invite our soul into our lived experience, we can miss its gifts to us in daily life—whether in an intimate encounter with another, in nature, in the arts, in spiritual setting or through our bodies, in illness and in healing and in health.

Here we are reminded to listen closely, for the soul often speaks in a whisper, easily drowned out in the busyness of daily life.

—J.M.

As long as we are determined
to move at our swift, logical pace,
our child remains hidden.
The soul-bird put away
in a dark box in childhood
needs time, needs silence
to learn to trust again.

If you see yourself
as no one worth looking at;
if you believe you are
not worth listening to;
if your parents didn't find
you worth looking at,
worth listening to;
if they told you,
That's not what you saw,
not what you heard,
not what you think,
you cannot trust yourself,
you are lost.

Don't look to others to find you,
to love and take care of you now.
You'll suck them dry.

No one out there is responsible.
Go back and find your soul.
Be mother and father to yourself,
Until the divine parents arrive.

In his eighties, he was my analyst.
I had been in England
seeing him for six months,
and was still trying to be efficient.
On Christmas Eve I learned my dog,
who was in Canada, had been killed.
I decided not to waste my evening session
talking about my dog.
I arrived as organized as usual.
At the end, he sat quietly,
then asked me what was wrong.
Nothing, I said, as I put on my coat.
You have not been here, he said.
I told him my dog was dead.
He wept. Wept over my dog.
Asked me how I could waste Christmas Eve
chattering when my soul animal had just died.
Suddenly his weeping made me feel
what I was doing to my soul.
We wept together.
That's when my analysis began.

Loss of soul connection,
loss of connection to our femininity,
may be the real cause of our anguish.
If we have no bridge
to the depths that drive us,
our rational attempts
to correct our situation
are merely Band-aids.

———

Shame was put upon you.
It is not yours.
Your soul need not
be limited by shame.

Our souls cry out
from underneath the rubble of our lives,
like children who have not known love,
children begging us to say,
You are not alone.
I love you.

————

In living the abandoned child
within herself
the woman becomes pregnant
with herself.

When we identify with our childish side
we say,
I was always a victim.
I will always be a victim
and it's all my parents' fault,
then walk around with a hangdog face
the rest of our lives.

When we gather our child into our arms,
we say,
My parents were victims of a culture,
as were their parents and their parents.
I shall not be a victim.
I shall take responsibility for my own life.
I shall live creatively.
I shall live now.

The soul may go into hiding,
but it does not die.

———

The soul
is,
present tense,
now.
Dancing in the flames.

Sooner or later we find her.
In dreams, she appears, that child,
(never at the beginning,
never at the beginning—
we would go crazy with grief).
She is starving in a pile of garbage,
in a basement under the basement.
Somebody tried to kill her.
Frightened, she ran downstairs.
She may even accuse you.

She is the age she was
when she fled.
And she must be fed.

One hour a day, let her play,
let her sing, let her dance,
let her be with her dreams.
Feed her.
She will grow strong and beautiful.

33

Timely Sacrifices

If *we are connected* to others through caring, friendship, or love, we know what it is to make sacrifices on a daily basis. We regularly set aside immediate personal wishes for the common good or to accommodate other legitimate needs.

At certain times, we also hear inner calls—to sacrifice old ways, old beliefs, old attachments, old attitudes. These sacrifices are more challenging because usually they carry with them no promise, no guarantee, no contract.

We need courage to open up heart, mind, and body to something as yet unformed. All we know is that the old way is no longer working and that we have no choice but to embrace the unknown.

—J.M.

Most of us are dragged
toward wholeness.
We do not understand
the breakdown of what has gone before.
We do not understand.
We cling to the familiar,
refuse to make necessary sacrifices,
refuse to give up habitual lives,
resist our growth.
We do not understand rebirth,
do not accept the initiation rites.
Most of us are dragged
toward wholeness.

————

If we must surrender a close bond,
we need to learn
to sacrifice the relationship
without sacrificing the love.

Once you have explored the depths,
don't wallow in them.
It's not only boring,
it's destructive.
Let grace enter.
It brings with it
a new understanding of love.

———————

Out of the chrysalis,
in its first moment,
perhaps in first flight,
the butterfly voids
a drop, frequently red.

We, too, may sacrifice
a drop of the past,
turn to the future,
unfold our wings,
and say,
I am.

Periods of renunciation
are the initiations in life
when we realize
God is not running a day care center.

————

Sometimes only with distance
may the depth of the root
of a relationship become apparent.
The plant may be cut off
almost to the ground
and still, with care,
rejuvenate.

Through failures, symptoms, problems,
we are prodded
to renounce attachments,
redundant now.
With the breakdown of what has gone before,
the possibility of rebirth comes.

We fall into old habits:
afraid to lose old friends,
afraid to lose our relationship,
afraid to lose our job,
afraid to make a fool of ourselves.

Friends say,
You never were like this.
I don't like you like this.

Your mate says,
You're not the person I married.
I don't like this one.
Why don't you stop?

You say,
This is who I am!
Your mate says,
If this is who you are, good luck.
I didn't promise to live with this person.

Most of us can only let so much go at a time.

Simplifying is the most elegant of tasks in our cluttered culture.

34

Initiation into the
Deep Feminine

In these pages, we find the story of one woman's unexpected initiation into a deeper, embodied understanding of feminine energies. Fear, courage, pain, joy, and openness accompany such initiations.

As you follow this journey, you might reflect on the phases of initiation: departure, loss of an old identity and psychic death accompanied often by physical suffering, insight into new possibilities, rebirth, and reintegration of the new understandings and new identity into the familiar world.

Where do your experiences intersect, parallel, or contrast with these? How have you been initiated into your deeper knowing? How might you be more courageous and more open to the initiatory experiences in your life?

—J.M.

One winter night
I was alone.
I needed a taxi.
I raised my arm
but the taxis didn't stop.
I was not forthright enough.

I walked through the snow
in the dark to where I was going.
Something had to change.
I knew I would buy
a ticket to India
and hoped I might
encounter God
in an ashram in Pondicherry.

I stay first in Delhi.
Terror becomes my gasoline.

Hands grasp at me—
crippled beggars,
black market hustlers
demanding American dollars,
professional lovers
assuring me they are second
only to Africans.

And two tiny waifs, older, here, than I.
Each morning they wait at the entrance.
All day they cling to my dress.
Each evening I sew up the seams.

I brush kisses with a cow,
step in her pancake.
People shout,
Good evening
in the morning.
I know something is wrong
when I shout back,
Good evening.

She picked up a bag of bones.
I've often thought of that woman.
She asked me if I was alone.
I said *Yes* and fainted dead away.
She picked up the bones from the street,
put them in a taxi, and took them with her.
She had no idea what she had.
She took me to her hotel,
determined I was going home.
I knew I had to stay.

I teem with elusive images.
In this monsoon season, the hotel balcony teems
with drenched crows
croaking *Nevermore*
and the bathtub is alive
with cockroaches.
I fall on the tile floor.
How long I am there,
I do not know.

I awake on the ceiling,
soul looking down at body
caked in dry vomit and excrement.
Helpless, still,
it takes a breath.
Poor dummy, I think,
Don't you know you're dead?
And give it a kick.

I watch it take another breath.
Will they burn it?
Will they send it home?
Then I remember my dog, trusting, faithful,
waiting for me to return.
I look at my body, trusting, faithful,
waiting for me to return.

It takes another breath.
I come down, move in.
We drag ourselves to the little bed.

I do my best to take care of her.

There is no one to phone,
no one to visit,
nothing to do.
All escapes cut.

In this descent into hell
for days, perhaps nine,
I lie in this narrow hotel bed reading
Shakespeare's sonnets,
the New Testament
and my passport
aloud.

On the tenth day,
the worst illness passes,
I venture to the lobby.
I sit on the couch writing a letter.
A woman in gold-trimmed sari,
fat arm warm and black,
squeezes between me
and the end of the couch.

I pull away
to make room to write.
She cuddles against me.
I move again. She moves.
I smile. She smiles.
She speaks no English.

By the time I finish my letter,
we are both at the other end,
her body pressed to mine.

The next day, still fearful of outside,
I return. And she returns.
The dignified game goes on.
And does for days.

One morning, as I am returning
to my room, he steps up.
You're all right now, he says.
You were dying.
I sent my wife to sit with you.
I knew the warmth of her body
would bring you back to life.
She won't need to come again.

I am ravished:
stench of urine
and perfume of jasmine;
flies in a baby's eyes
and a blaze of red silk;
screams of a beaten dog
and sweetness of a sitar
on this summer night.

The taxi driver's enigmatic smile,
the narrow roadway,
the featureless fields:
I hope we are on our way to the caves.
I see a dog with a canary yellow eye.
I see a cow with turquoise horns.
I see an elephant, translucent pink.

The driver is not disturbed.
He is conjuring ways to get me
into the front seat.
It is Krishna's birthday. Do you want to go?
Yes.
Singing, he swings the taxi into the ditch
and through the fields.

Four pairs of hands take
sandals, camera, purse, belt.
The faces of twenty men regard me.
I never thought I would die this way.
They bow in low salaam and straighten
until green eyes meet fiery black.
I will not faint.

They raise me above their heads.
Chanting, they carry me,
lay me gently on the ground.

The priest places grass in my mouth,
prays over me.
He divides my grass among the men.
They eat it as if it is holy.
They raise me, place me on an altar,
chant and dance slow around.

They salaam and carry me
away from holy ground,
give me sandals, camera, purse, and belt.
The driver reappears,
smiling his nonchalant smile.
We bounce across the fields.

In dark arms and dusty field,
I hear Her.
I know the grass between my lips is holy.
I know my milkmaid's body,
Krishna's bride.

She returned
triumphant and transformed:
it was not that way at all.

When I passed through Amsterdam,
I was shattered by noise.
I saw a woman in boots
with yellow hair, pink lipstick,
and turquoise eye shadow.
She must be going
to Krishna's birthday.

Why did you go to India?
Each time I went for analysis,
he asked me again.

You must be going senile.
You ask every time I come.

And every time you give me a different answer.
When I was a brigadier in India,
we had a hard time with some of the soldiers.
They didn't want to fight.

They put seeds in their eyes,
to make them blind,
and then they were sent home.
You think about that.

I've been taking seeds out of my eyes
for sixteen years.

————

In ancient rites
we would have met the mystery
in an underground passage,
an inner surrender
to our deepest eroticism.

Giving up desire,
in aloneness and despair
we would have surrendered
to what we believed was death.
We would have known the coming together
of matter and spirit,
of human and divine:
a love marriage with the god.

We cannot go back.
We cannot go back to the ancient mysteries.
Yet we can make the journey
below and back again.
We can know the light in our darkness,
can find again, within our body,
the sacred mystery.

Every night I dreamt
I was falling.

One night I landed.
Landed in strange terrain.
Frightened, paralyzed,
I felt around with my fingers,
and thought what I felt was sand.

It wasn't sand.
It was feathers,
and I was seated
on the wings of the Holy Spirit.

That dream changed my life.

In my dream,
I was a priestess
and had prepared
the altar for great celebration.
The flowers were almost in place,
the roses almost in the center
of the sunlit altar.
(I could not make the roses fit
within the light.)
A shadow the shape of a cross
came through a window.

An old man came to me and said,
Your hymns will never rise to heaven
until you clean up your mess in the basement.

But there's no basement in this temple, I said.
That's the problem: there is, he replied.

Down the rotting old steps we went
and found a slimy lagoon.
A water wheel,
joining basement to temple, lay still.

A huge serpent writhed,
trying and failing and trying again
to center its head on the wheel.
It knew its task was to turn the wheel—

quiet, rhythmic—with its head.

I tried to move the wheel towards the serpent
and it struck.
The old man pulled me out of danger,
You can't move so fast
She doesn't trust you.
Hasten slowly;
you will make her your friend.

For twenty years,
the wheel has creaked but turned;
The lagoon, fresh;
the serpent, Sophia;
the roses, not yet in place.

References

Woodman, Marion. *Addiction to Perfection: The Still Unravished Bride*. Toronto: Inner City Books, 1982.

_____. *Conscious Femininity: Interviews with Marion Woodman*. Toronto: Inner City Books, 1993.

_____. *Dreams: Language of the Soul* (cassette recording no. A131). Boulder, CO: Sounds True Recordings, 1991.

_____. *Emily Dickinson and the Demon Lover* (cassette recording no. A225). Boulder, CO: Sounds True Recordings, 1993.

_____. *Holding the Tension of the Opposites* (cassette recording no. A138). Boulder, CO: Sounds True Recordings, 1991.

_____. *Leaving My Father's House: A Journey to Conscious Femininity* (with Kate Danson, Mary Hamilton, and Rita Greer Allen). Boston: Shambhala, 1992.

_____. *The Owl Was a Baker's Daughter: Obesity, Anorexia Nervosa and the Repressed Feminine*. Toronto: Inner City Books, 1980.

_____. *The Pregnant Virgin: A Process of Psychological Transformation*. Toronto: Inner City Books, 1985.

_____. *The Ravaged Bridegroom: Masculinity in Women*. Toronto: Inner City Books, 1990.

_____. *Rolling Away the Stone* (cassette recording no. A095). Boulder, CO: Sounds True Recordings, 1989.

_____. *The Stillness Shall Be the Dancing: Feminine and Masculine in Emerging Balance* (cassette recording). College Station, TX: Texas A&M University Press, 1994.

Woodman, Marion and Dickson, Elinor. *Dancing in the Flames: The Dark Goddess in the Transformation of Consciousness*. Boston: Shambhala, 1996.

Alphabetical Index

The following works have been cited and are abbreviated as follows in the text:

The references from which the selection has been taken are listed after the abbreviation so that those familiar with Marion Woodman's work may revisit material of value to them and so that those less familiar may quickly find entry through a particular perspective that touches them.

Without our body we cannot speak truthfully	HTO
Write dreams down	DLS
Your images are a picture	RAS

Index by Reference

Conscious Femininity

If the dream uses a symbol
If we are full of rage
If we have been tyrannized
If you don't believe
If you paint
If you see yourself
If you're a happy carrot
In her dream
Masculinity is in men and women
Once you are in the flow
Once you dance for a year
Once we know what the dream world is
Patriarchy isn't "men"
The shadow is anything
Sleep brings the body into balance
Sooner or later we find her
Stand in the middle
There's nothing worse
To live a rich life
To sit in a chair and analyze
We cannot take in the dream
We fall into old habits
We spend years
What on earth is that person
When the path is blocked

Oh sometimes, of course, the soul
On Friday I sent the clothes
Our banquet of dreams is spread each night
So if you dream of Isis—fine
To turn the tomb into a womb
We cannot kill the energy
We project god and goddess out
When she comes in a dream
Your images are a picture

The Stillness Shall Be the Dancing
Any woman who takes herself seriously
A compulsive relationship
Consciousness changes the perceived
Do you think I have a father complex?
Femininity is Being
Food and metaphor
God preserve me
How many people do you know
Hypocrisy, sentimentality, distraction
If we are depending on our partner
If we could allow the pace of our meetings
If you find yourself
Intimacy reveals our deepest anguish
Once we find the right question
Our shadow may contain

Marion Woodman, Ph.D.

Marion Woodman, Ph.D. (Hon.) is a widely read and acclaimed author, leader in feminine development research and teaching, and a Jungian analyst. She is the author of many widely respected books that bridge the fields of analytical psychology and feminine psychology, including *Addiction to Perfection* (Inner City Books, Toronto, 1982), *The Pregnant Virgin* (Inner City Books, 1985), and *Leaving My Father's House* (co-authored) (Shambhala, 1992). Her other well-known works include *The Owl Was a Baker's Daughter* (Inner City Books, 1980), *The Ravaged Bridegroom* (1990), *Conscious Femininity* (Inner City Books, 1992) *Dancing in the Flames* (Shambhala, 1996) and *Bone* (Viking Press, 2000). Her works have been published in over fifteen editions and translated into nine languages. She is also the author of many articles and audio tapes, including a set of tapes on dreams, *Dreams: Language of the Soul,* which are available from Sounds True Recordings.

Marion Woodman has presented at or led over two hundred workshops and conferences and well over three hundred lectures in Canada, the United States, and Europe. Most recently, she has been leading workshops on fairytales with her friend, poet and leader in the men's movement, Robert Bly, and a series of excellent videotapes of their work *"Bly and Woodman on Men and Women"* is available from Applewood, Belleville, Canada.

She has a graduate degree in English from the University of Western Ontario, London, Ontario and several honorary doctorates including one from her alma mater and one from ITP. Until she became a Jungian analyst, she was a highly popular English and drama teacher at a high school in London, Ontario. She brings her lifelong love of literature and drama to her Jungian workshops, writing, and lectures. She has traveled widely and, until recently, spent most summers with family on her island retreat in Georgian Bay in Northern Ontario.

JILL MELLICK, PH.D.

An Australian by birth and upbringing, Dr. Jill Mellick has been in private practice for many years as a Jungian-oriented clinical psychologist and registered expressive arts therapist in Palo Alto, California. Her earlier graduate work was in English Language and Literature.

She is a multidisciplinary artist: A published poet, she also has held one-woman art shows of her landscapes and her work is held in private collections in Canada, Australia, France, Scandinavia, and the U.S; her photography is exhibited on the Soarts virtual gallery.

The author of *The Worlds of P'otsunu* (with Jeanne Shutes) (University of New Mexico Press, 1996) and *The Art of Dreaming* (Conari, 2001) she is also a Full Professor and Director of Creative Expression Studies at the masters and doctoral level at the Institute of Transpersonal Psychology.

She travels and teaches internationally, focusing on the use of the arts for psychospiritual dimensions. She has also spent twenty-five years visiting and living part-time in Santa Fe, New Mexico, where she has worked with the Pueblo peoples of the state as a clinician, writer, colleague, and friend.

THE

UNIVERSAL ENCYCLOPEDIA

OF

MATHEMATICS

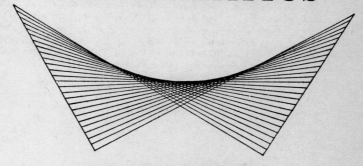

WITH A FOREWORD BY

JAMES R. NEWMAN

SIMON AND SCHUSTER
NEW YORK

Published by Simon and Schuster, A Gulf + Western Company
Rockefeller Center, 630 Fifth Avenue, New York, New York 10020

ISBN 0-671-77406-9
ISBN 0-671-20348-7 Pbk.
Library of Congress Catalog Card Number: 63-21086

Manufactured in the United States of America

5   6   7   8   9   10

4   5   6   7   8   9   10   Pbk.

CONTENTS

FOREWORD

I AM GLAD of the opportunity to say a few words about this clearly written, sensibly arranged and reliable reference work.

It is a translation of a widely used German compendium, designed to serve the needs of high school and college students, which encompasses many branches of mathematics from arithmetic through the calculus and includes a collection of essential formulae and tables. While the higher branches such as group theory or algebraic topology are not treated, the coverage within the limits indicated is succinct and to the point, and it is safe to predict that the book will be a much consulted companion, a comfort for the student, engineer or teacher to have within arm's reach.

The thought may readily cross one's mind that there must be several, if not indeed many, references of similar scope already available. Curiously enough, despite the immense growth in popularity of mathematical studies since the last world war, and the expanding mathematical curricula in the schools, this is not the case. Popularizations of mathematics abound, and the textbook field has been almost literally swamped with new approaches and innumerable revisions of standard works; also, there has been an outpouring of self-help and self-teaching guides. But if you are looking for an explicit, simply written, alphabetically arranged lexicon of mathematics, geared to average requirements, which explains such matters as angles, the design and operation of calculating machines, conic sections, continued fractions, mathematical induction, regular polygons, the Pythagorean theorem, the real number system, infinite series, nomography, logarithms, linear transformations, the solution of equations, the binomial distribution, complex numbers, Archimedes' spiral, the computation of interest, the indefinite integral, Pascal's triangle, the Roman number system, rigid motions, Platonic solids, the use of determinants, the nature of vectors, trigonometric relations, and many other concepts, methods and applications of mathematics, you will find this book unique.

The treatment of most topics seems to me just right. A straightforward, unencumbered definition is usually followed by a more detailed discussion, which often includes a number of carefully selected and worked out examples. Where diagrams are used they are helpful and utilitarian, not introduced for decoration. It is not assumed that you already know about a subject before looking it up, but it is assumed, and quite properly, that you are equipped to make your own way at that level. For instance, if you look up affine transformations, you are assumed to be reasonably conversant with the fundamentals of analytical geometry, and if logarithms are your quarry you must at least have some notion of the behavior of exponents. It would, of course, be a mistake to suppose that you can teach yourself all about a topic by reading the relevant article in the encyclopedia. That is not its purpose. What it sets out to do and what I believe it is successful in doing in a remarkably high proportion of its entries is to explain the elements of a concept or method, to indicate its connections and relations with other parts of mathematics and to give the reader the proper bearings and a good start in following up, if he is so inclined, by consulting appropriate texts and monographs.

Teachers will, I believe, be grateful for this book, for themselves and for their students. Parents will like it, as will the adult reader who still retains a flickering interest in mathematics which his earlier schooling has not extinguished. The book is a prize I wish I had had when I was a student, and even now I look forward to having it on my shelf.

JAMES R. NEWMAN
CHEVY CHASE, MD.
SEPTEMBER 1963

PUBLISHER'S NOTE

WE believe this to be the first popular encyclopedia or reference book of mathematics of its kind, arranged in alphabetical order of subjects. It is based on the *Rechenduden* of the Bibliographisches Institut in Mannheim. Well over 200,000 copies of this were sold within two years. The present version has been thoroughly adapted to Anglo-American needs and has been considerably altered in the process. We are grateful to the mathematicians on both sides of the Atlantic who have undertaken this task or helped us with their advice.

The ground covered is the mathematics from beginning High School, through College, but stopping short of a degree in mathematics. The book is therefore not addressed to the professional mathematician, but it will help the student to become one. It is intended for the Man in the Street, the harassed parent and the technical student; or for the scientist, engineer and accountant for whom mathematics has not lost its fascination.

The encyclopedia is reliable and the explanations clear. It contains a large collection of formulae (arithmetical, algebraic, geometric, trigonometric, special functions, series, differential and integral calculus). There are also tables of mathematical functions (powers, square and cube roots, logarithms, trigonometrical functions, exponential functions, length of arcs and angles in degrees and radians, tables of differences)—every value electronically calculated separately, with no interpolated values.

ALPHABETICAL ENCYCLOPEDIA
UNDER SUBJECTS

Absolute value

The absolute value of a real number a, written $|a|$ (read: mod a), equals a if a is positive, and $-a$ if a is negative, e.g. $|-2| = 2$, $|+2| = 2$. The absolute value of a complex number $z = a + ib$ is reckoned as $z = \sqrt{a^2 + b^2}$. In the *Argand diagram* (see below), the absolute value (modulus) of a complex number is the distance from the origin of the point representing the number.

Acute triangle

A triangle is said to be acute if each of the three interior angles is less than 90° (*i.e.* if all interior angles are acute).

Addition

Addition is one of the four fundamental operations of arithmetic. The addition sign is '+' (read: plus). The numbers which are added are called summands.

$$4 \quad + \quad 3 \quad = \quad 7$$

Summand plus Summand equals Sum

Addition of fractions

Fractions can be added directly only if they have equal denominators, e.g. $\dfrac{3}{17} + \dfrac{4}{17} = \dfrac{7}{17}$.

If fractions with unequal denominators are to be added they must first be brought to their *least common denominator* (see below).

Addition of literal numbers

Identically-named numbers can be added (and subtracted) by adding the coefficients:

$$2a + 3b + a + 4b = 3a + 7b.$$

Summands may be interchanged (*commutative law*):

$$a + b = b + a.$$

With more than two summands, brackets may be inserted (*associative law*):

$$a + b + c = (a + b) + c = a + (b + c).$$

Addition of directed numbers

No further rule is needed for the addition of positive numbers:

$$a + (+b) = a + b, \quad 5 + (+3) = 5 + 3 = 8.$$

To add one negative number to another, its absolute value is subtracted:

$$a + (-b) = a - b, \qquad (-a) + (-b) = -(a + b);$$
$$5 + (-3) = 5 - 3 = 2, \quad (-5) + (-3) = -(5 + 3) = -8.$$

Addition of powers and surds

Powers and surds must be treated like literal numbers for the purposes of addition, *e.g.*

$$a^2 + 4 \cdot b^3 + 4 \cdot c^3 + 4 \cdot a^2 = 5 \cdot a^2 + 4(b^3 + c^3);$$
$$3\sqrt{2} + 5\sqrt{3} + \sqrt{2} = 4\sqrt{2} + 5\sqrt{3}.$$

Addition of complex numbers

In adding complex numbers the real and imaginary parts must be added separately, *e.g.*

$$(5 + 3i) + (17 - i) = 22 + 2i.$$

Addition theorems for trigonometric functions

The addition theorems enable us to calculate the functions $\sin (\alpha + \beta)$, $\cos (\alpha + \beta)$, $\sin (\alpha - \beta)$ and $\cos (\alpha - \beta)$, given $\sin \alpha$, $\sin \beta$, $\cos \alpha$ and $\cos \beta$, and to calculate $\tan (\alpha + \beta)$, $\tan (\alpha - \beta)$, $\cot (\alpha + \beta)$, $\cot (\alpha - \beta)$, given $\tan \alpha$, $\tan \beta$, $\cot \alpha$, $\cot \beta$.

The addition theorems are as follows:

$$\text{I.} \quad \sin (\alpha + \beta) = \sin \alpha \cos \beta + \cos \alpha \sin \beta$$
$$\text{II.} \quad \sin (\alpha - \beta) = \sin \alpha \cos \beta - \cos \alpha \sin \beta$$

III. $\cos(\alpha + \beta) = \cos\alpha\cos\beta - \sin\alpha\sin\beta$

IV. $\cos(\alpha - \beta) = \cos\alpha\cos\beta + \sin\alpha\sin\beta$

V. $\tan(\alpha + \beta) = \dfrac{\tan\alpha + \tan\beta}{1 - \tan\alpha\tan\beta}$

VI. $\tan(\alpha - \beta) = \dfrac{\tan\alpha - \tan\beta}{1 + \tan\alpha\tan\beta}$

VII. $\cot(\alpha + \beta) = \dfrac{\cot\alpha\cot\beta - 1}{\cot\beta + \cot\alpha}$

VIII. $\cot(\alpha - \beta) = \dfrac{\cot\alpha\cot\beta + 1}{\cot\beta - \cot\alpha}$

The proof of formulae I–IV can be derived with the help of the following figures.

In Fig. 1, clearly,

$$\overline{OD} = \cos\beta,\ \overline{DE} = \overline{OD}\sin\alpha = \sin\alpha\cos\beta,$$
$$\overline{OE} = \overline{OD}\cos\alpha,\ \overline{AD} = \sin\beta,\ \overline{CD} = \overline{AD}\sin\alpha.$$

Further, $\quad \overline{AC} = \overline{AD}\cos\alpha = \sin\beta\cos\alpha.$

Then $\quad \sin(\alpha + \beta) = \dfrac{\overline{AB}}{\overline{AO}} = \overline{AB} = \overline{AC} + \overline{CB} = \overline{AC} + \overline{DE},$

that is, $\quad \sin(\alpha + \beta) = \sin\alpha\cos\beta + \sin\beta\cos\alpha.$

Similarly,

$$\cos(\alpha + \beta) = \dfrac{\overline{OB}}{1} = \overline{OB} = \overline{OE} - \overline{BE} = \overline{OE} - \overline{CD},$$

that is, $\quad \cos(\alpha + \beta) = \cos\alpha\cos\beta - \sin\alpha\sin\beta.$

In Fig. 2, similarly,

$$\overline{AD} = \sin\beta,\ \overline{DE} = \overline{AD}\cos\alpha = \cos\alpha\sin\beta,$$
$$\overline{OD} = \cos\beta,\ \overline{DC} = \overline{OD}\sin\alpha = \cos\beta\sin\alpha,$$
$$\overline{OC} = \overline{OD}\cos\alpha = \cos\beta\cos\alpha,$$
$$\overline{AE} = \overline{AD}\sin\alpha = \sin\beta\sin\alpha.$$

13

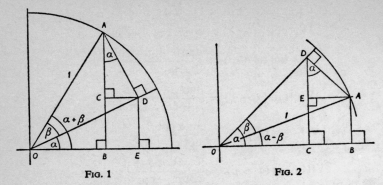

FIG. 1   FIG. 2

Then $\sin(\alpha - \beta) = \overline{AB} = \overline{EC} = \overline{DC} - \overline{DE} = \sin\alpha\cos\beta - \cos\alpha\sin\beta,$

and $\cos(\alpha - \beta) = \overline{OB} = \overline{OC} + \overline{CB} = \overline{OC} + \overline{EA} = \cos\alpha\cos\beta + \sin\alpha\sin\beta.$

Formulae V–VIII are obtained immediately from the relations

$$\tan\phi = \frac{\sin\phi}{\cos\phi} \quad\text{and}\quad \cot\phi = \frac{\cos\phi}{\sin\phi}.$$

Trigonometric functions of double angles

If the values of $\sin\alpha$, $\cos\alpha$, $\tan\alpha$ and $\cot\alpha$ are known, $\sin 2\alpha$, $\cos 2\alpha$, $\tan 2\alpha$ and $\cot 2\alpha$ can be calculated by putting $\beta = \alpha$ in the addition theorems:

$$\sin 2\alpha = 2\sin\alpha\cos\alpha;$$
$$\cos 2\alpha = \cos^2\alpha - \sin^2\alpha = 2\cos^2\alpha - 1 = 1 - 2\sin^2\alpha;$$
$$\tan 2\alpha = \frac{2\tan\alpha}{1 - \tan^2\alpha}; \quad \cot 2\alpha = \frac{\cot^2\alpha - 1}{2\cot\alpha}.$$

More generally, $\sin(n\alpha)$ and $\cos(n\alpha)$ can be calculated, given $\sin\alpha$ and $\cos\alpha$ (n a positive integer):

$$\sin(n\alpha) = \binom{n}{1}\cos^{n-1}\alpha\sin\alpha - \binom{n}{3}\cos^{n-3}\alpha\sin^3\alpha +$$

$$+ \binom{n}{5}\cos^{n-5}\alpha\sin^5\alpha - \ldots,$$

14

$$\cos(n\alpha) = \cos^n \alpha - \binom{n}{2} \cos^{n-2} \alpha \sin^2 \alpha + \binom{n}{4} \cos^{n-4} \alpha \sin^4 \alpha$$
$$- \ldots .$$

Trigonometric functions of half angles

Given $\sin\alpha$, $\cos\alpha$, $\tan\alpha$, and $\cot\alpha$, then $\sin\dfrac{\alpha}{2}$, $\cos\dfrac{\alpha}{2}$, $\tan\dfrac{\alpha}{2}$ and $\cot\dfrac{\alpha}{2}$ can be calculated as follows.

Since we know $\cos 2\alpha = 2\cos^2\alpha - 1 = 1 - 2\sin^2\alpha$,

we have
$$\cos\alpha = 2\cos^2\frac{\alpha}{2} - 1 = 1 - 2\sin^2\frac{\alpha}{2},$$

that is, $\sin\dfrac{\alpha}{2} = \sqrt{\dfrac{1-\cos\alpha}{2}}$; $\cos\dfrac{\alpha}{2} = \sqrt{\dfrac{1+\cos\alpha}{2}}$.

Dividing, we have
$$\tan\frac{\alpha}{2} = \sqrt{\frac{1-\cos\alpha}{1+\cos\alpha}} = \frac{\sin\alpha}{1+\cos\alpha} = \frac{1-\cos\alpha}{\sin\alpha};$$

and similarly
$$\cot\frac{\alpha}{2} = \sqrt{\frac{1+\cos\alpha}{1-\cos\alpha}}.$$

Affine

Two figures (solid or plane) which are derivable one from the other by an *affine transformation* (see below) are called affine with respect to one another. *E.g.* an ellipse can be regarded as the affine image of the circle on its major axis. Ellipse and circle are affine with respect to one another.

Affine-symmetrical

A plane figure is called affine-symmetric if a straight line exists such that the part of the figure lying on one side of the line is transformed into the part lying on the other side by an *affine*

15

reflection (see *Reflection, affine*). *E.g.* the oblique kite-like figure of Fig. 3 is affine-symmetrical with respect to the diagonal $\overline{AC}$. The other diagonal $\overline{BD}$ gives the direction of reflection.

An ellipse is affine-symmetrical with respect to a diameter d_1. The conjugate diameter d_2 gives the direction of reflection (see *Ellipse*).

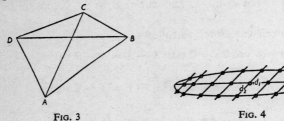

FIG. 3   FIG. 4

Affine transformation

An affine transformation of the points of space is a reversible *single-valued* (one-to-one) transformation in space, in which the ratios of distances separating three points P, Q, R which lie on a straight line remain unchanged. *I.e.* if P', Q', R' are the image points of P, Q, R, and if $\dfrac{\overline{PQ}}{\overline{QR}} = c$, then $\dfrac{\overline{P'Q'}}{\overline{Q'R'}} = c$.

If a general point P has coordinates x, y, z in a given rectangular coordinate system and the image point P' has coordinates x', y', z' in the same coordinate system, then the sets of coordinates are connected by equations of the following form:

$$x' = a_1 x + a_2 y + a_3 z + a_4,$$
$$y' = b_1 x + b_2 y + b_3 z + b_4,$$
$$z' = c_1 x + c_2 y + c_3 z + c_4.$$

Here the coefficients a_i, b_i, c_i are real numbers which satisfy the condition that the determinant

$$D = \begin{vmatrix} a_1 & a_2 & a_3 \\ b_1 & b_2 & b_3 \\ c_1 & c_2 & c_3 \end{vmatrix} \neq 0.$$

(If $D = 0$, all the image points P' lie on a single line.)

Under affine transformation straight lines transform into straight lines. If two straight lines are parallel the image lines are parallel also.

Types of plane affine transformation

(In what follows, $P(x, y)$ is to have the image point $P'(x', y')$ in the same rectangular coordinate system.)

1. *Parallel displacement.* Equations:

$$x' = x + a_4$$
$$y' = y + b_4$$

Displacement distance: $d = \sqrt{a_4^2 + b_4^2}$. The direction of the parallel displacement is that of the line joining the origin to the point $Q(a_4, b_4)$.

2. *Reflection in a straight line in the plane*

Reflection in the x-axis: in the y-axis:

$$x' = x, \qquad\qquad x' = -x,$$
$$y' = -y; \qquad\qquad y' = y.$$

3. *Rotation about a point in the plane*

(a) Rotation about the origin through angle δ,

$$x' = x \cdot \cos \delta + y \cdot \sin \delta,$$
$$y' = (-x) \cdot \sin \delta + y \cdot \cos \delta.$$

(b) Rotation about the point $P(x_z, y_z)$ through angle δ,

$$x' - x_z = (x - x_z) \cdot \cos \delta + (y - y_z) \cdot \sin \delta,$$
$$y' - y_z = -(x - x_z) \cdot \sin \delta + (y - y_z) \cdot \cos \delta.$$

The transformation 1, 3(a) and (b) are so-called *Rigid motions* (see below) or congruent transformations in the plane. In a rigid motion the originating figure and the image figure are always congruent. All rigid motions in the plane can be obtained by compounding transformations 1 and 3(a).

4. *Magnification*

(a) Parallel to the x-axis,   (b) Parallel to the y-axis,

$$x' = a_1 x, \qquad\qquad x' = x,$$
$$y' = y; \qquad\qquad y' = b_1 y.$$

17

(c) In the direction of the line joining the origin to the point $Q(a_1, b_1)$,

$$x' = a_1 x,$$
$$y' = b_1 y.$$

(d) If the magnifications (a) and (b) are effected simultaneously we obtain

$$x' = a_1 x,$$
$$y' = b_1 y.$$

If $a_1 = b_1 = a$, we obtain the similarity transformation $x' = ax$, $y' = ay$, in which all lines proceeding from the origin are magnified in the ratio $a:1$.

All affine transformations of the plane can be obtained by combining transformations 1, 2, 3(a), 4(a) and 4(b).

Important examples of affine transformations in space

(In what follows, $P(x, y, z)$ is to have image point $P'(x', y', z')$ in the same rectangular coordinate system.)

1. *Parallel displacement*

$$x' = x + a_4,$$
$$y' = y + b_4,$$
$$z' = z + c_4.$$

The direction of the parallel displacement is that of the line joining the origin to the point $Q(a_4, b_4, c_4)$. The displacement distance is $d = \sqrt{a_4^2 + b_4^2 + c_4^2}$.

2. *Reflection in a plane*

(a) in the (x, y)-plane,

$$x' = x,$$
$$y' = y,$$
$$z' = -z;$$

(b) in the (y, z)-plane,

$$x' = -x,$$
$$y' = y,$$
$$z' = z;$$

(c) in the (x, z)-plane,

$$x' = x,$$
$$y' = -y,$$
$$z' = z.$$

3. *Rotation about a straight line*

(a) about the x-axis,

$$x' = x,$$
$$y' = y \cdot \cos \delta + z \cdot \sin \delta,$$
$$z' = -y \cdot \sin \delta + z \cdot \cos \delta;$$

(b) about the y-axis,

$$x' = x \cdot \cos \varepsilon + z \cdot \sin \varepsilon,$$
$$y' = y,$$
$$z' = -x \cdot \sin \varepsilon + z \cdot \cos \varepsilon;$$

(c) about the z-axis,

$$x' = x \cdot \cos \zeta + y \cdot \sin \zeta,$$
$$y' = x \cdot \sin \zeta + y \cdot \cos \zeta,$$
$$z' = z.$$

4. *Reflection in a point*

(a) in the origin:

$$x' = -x,$$
$$y' = -y,$$
$$z' = -z;$$

(b) in the point P, (x_p, y_p, z_p):

$$x' - x_p = -(x - x_p),$$
$$y' - y_p = -(y - y_p),$$
$$z' - z_p = -(z - z_p).$$

Transformations 1 and 3 belong to the rigid motions in space (see *Rigid motions*).

5. *Magnification parallel* to the

(a) x-axis:

$$x' = ax,$$
$$y' = y,$$
$$z' = z;$$

(b) y-axis:

$$x' = x,$$
$$y' = by,$$
$$z' = z;$$

(c) z-axis:

$$x' = x,$$
$$y' = y,$$
$$z' = cz.$$

The magnifications (a), (b), (c) can be effected simultaneously,

$$x' = ax, \qquad y' = by, \qquad z' = cz.$$

If $a = b = c$ we obtain a

6. *Similarity transformation.* In the similarity transformation, all lines proceeding from the origin are magnified in the ratio $a:1$.

Algebra

For historical reasons elementary algebra embraces a wide variety of topics, but its central problem is the study of algebraic equations (see *Equations*).

Modern (abstract) algebra generalises the study of ordinary addition and multiplication, and is the theory of systems of elements on which operations with specified properties are defined.

Algebraic curves

A curve is called algebraic if an algebraic function can be found which represents it.

Examples:

Straight lines, Conic sections
Neil's parabola
Folium of Descartes
Lemniscate
Conchoid
Cissoid

Algebraic numbers

Every algebraic number is the solution of an *algebraic equation* (see *Equations*):

$$a_0 x^n + a_1 x^{n-1} + \ldots + a_n = 0,$$

where $a_0, a_1, \ldots, a_n$ are rational coefficients.

The following are examples of algebraic numbers:

$$x = 2, \ x = \tfrac{3}{4}, \ x = \sqrt{2 + \sqrt{3}}, \ x = \sqrt[4]{2 + \sqrt{2}}.$$

$x = 2$	satisfies $x - 2 = 0,$
$x = \tfrac{3}{4}$	satisfies $4x - 3 = 0,$
$x = \sqrt{2 + \sqrt{3}}$	satisfies $x^4 - 4x^2 + 1 = 0,$
$x = \sqrt[4]{2 + \sqrt{2}}$	satisfies $x^8 - 4x^4 + 2 = 0.$

Classification of the algebraic numbers

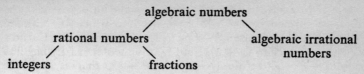

Many algebraic numbers are expressible as surds, *e.g.*

$$x = \sqrt{2 + \sqrt{3}}.$$

But there are also algebraic numbers which cannot be expressed by means of roots, for algebraic equations of order higher than 4 cannot in general be solved in terms of roots. Those algebraic numbers which can be expressed by means of roots are of special interest, particularly those expressible in terms of square roots, *e.g.*

$$x = \sqrt{2 + \sqrt{3}}.$$

These can be represented by line-segments, since they can be constructed in the plane by the use of ruler and compass only. Conversely, every line-segment which can be constructed by means of ruler and compass may be represented by a surd in which only square roots enter (see *Duplication of the cube, Trisection of the angle*).

Algebraic sum

An algebraic sum is a sum of directed numbers, *e.g.*

$$(+5) + (-3a) + (-4b^2) + (-0{\cdot}6) + (+5ab).$$

Instead of, as here, adding the negative numbers, one can also subtract the absolute values of these negative numbers. The example above then becomes:

$$5 - 3a - 4b^2 - 0{\cdot}6 + 5ab.$$

This type of expression also is called an algebraic sum.

Alternate angles

Alternate angles occur where two parallel lines are intersected by a third line. Alternate angles lie on opposite sides of the transversal and opposite sides of the parallel lines, and are equal (see *Angle*).

Altitude theorem (Euclid)

In a right-angled triangle the square on the altitude equals the rectangle formed by the two segments into which the altitude divides the hypotenuse: $h^2 = pq$ (Fig. 6). Proof: By Euclid's theorem, $b^2 = cq = (p + q)q$; but by the theorem of Pythagoras $b^2 = h^2 + q^2$. Therefore $(p + q)q = h^2 + q^2$, that is, $pq = h^2$ (Fig. 6).

By means of this theorem a rectangle can be transformed into a square of equal area. We lay the sides p and q of the rectangle alongside one another, construct the Thales circle on the combined segment $p + q$, and erect at F the perpendicular whose intersection with the circle C, gives the length of side $h = \overline{FC}$ of the required square (Fig. 5). Similarly, of course, a square can be transformed by means of the altitude theorem into a rectangle of equal area, with one side given.

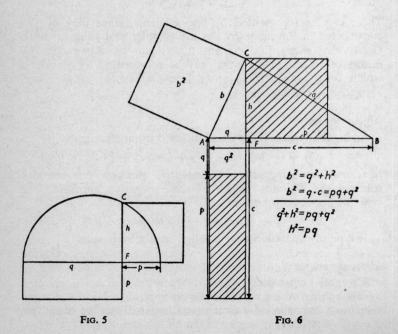

$$b^2 = q^2 + h^2$$
$$b^2 = q \cdot c = pq + q^2$$
$$\overline{q^2 + h^2 = pq + q^2}$$
$$h^2 = pq$$

FIG. 5   FIG. 6

Altitudes of a triangle

The perpendicular from a vertex of a triangle onto the opposite side is called an altitude of the triangle. Every triangle has three altitudes (h_a, h_b, h_c) which may lie either inside or outside the triangle or may coincide (for right angled triangles) with a side (leg of the right-angled triangle).

An acute-angled triangle has three internal altitudes.

An obtuse-angled triangle has one internal and two exterior altitudes.

A right-angled triangle has one internal altitude, the others coinciding with the legs of the triangle.

The three altitudes of a triangle intersect in the *orthocentre*. The three *feet* of the altitudes form a new triangle (see *Triangle*).

Analysis

Analysis is that part of mathematics concerned with the investigation of functions. Nowadays one usually understands by Analysis (the term *higher analysis* is also used) the differential and integral calculuses and the branches of mathematics which have developed from them.

Analytical geometry

Analytical geometry is the study of geometrical relations by means of the techniques of analysis. In this way one field of mathematics is used to assist the development of another. As it was Descartes who first unified geometry and algebra in this way, the use of coordinates or sets of numbers to represent points and other geometrical structures is spoken of as Cartesian geometry, although Descartes did not himself use 'Cartesian coordinates'. We have an everyday use of coordinates in map-references, and coordinates in analytical geometry are developed and refined from such examples as this. In the translation from geometry to algebra, those points which have a given property (which lie for example on a circle or sphere) translate into sets of coordinates satisfying an algebraic equation; points with two properties (such as lying on two different circles) translate into sets of coordinates satisfying two algebraic equations; and so on.

Although by taking n coordinates ($n = 1, 2, 3, \ldots$) it is easy to define a geometry of n dimensions, we shall confine ourselves to $n = 2$ (analytical geometry of the plane) and $n = 3$ (analytical geometry of space) in what follows below. By means of quadratic equations we can develop elegantly the theory of conic sections (see *Conic sections, Curves of the second order, Ellipse, Hyperbola*) and of quadric surfaces (see *Surfaces of the second order*).

Analytical geometry of the plane

1. *Points in rectangular coordinate systems.* If an aircraft is to be directed to a given position, we may give the instructions geometrically, in terms of a map with positions marked and distances drawn, or algebraically, in terms of an agreed set of coordinates, those of latitude and longitude. This is possible because each position has coordinates of latitude and longitude and (within agreed ranges of values) conversely.

In analytical geometry we operate with coordinates in much the same way. In place of the equator and the meridian of Greenwich we take two lines or *axes* at right-angles to each other, a 'vertical' line or y-axis and a 'horizontal' line or x-axis. The first or x-coordinate of a point P is the distance of P from the y-axis, measured positively to the right or negatively to the left. The second or y-coordinate of P is the distance of P from the x-axis, measured positively upwards and negatively downwards. In analytical geometry we translate problems involving points such as P into problems involving coordinates such as (x, y).

We note that if P is on the y-axis then $x = 0$, while if P is on the x-axis then $y = 0$. In fact these equations are necessary and sufficient conditions for P to lie on one or other axis.

We note also that if P lies in the upper-right-hand quadrant of the plane, conventionally known as the 'first' quadrant, then both x and y are positive. Similar rules apply to the other quadrants, numbered in anti-clockwise direction by convention.

	x	y
I	+	+
II	−	+
III	−	−
IV	+	−

A point lying on the x-axis has ordinate $y = 0$.
A point lying on the y-axis has abscissa $x = 0$.

2. *Distance between two points.* The distance between two points $P_1(x_1, y_1)$ and $P_2(x_2, y_2)$ by Pythagoras's theorem (Fig. 7) is $d = \sqrt{(x_2 - x_1)^2 + (y_2 - y_1)^2}$.

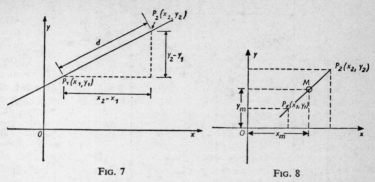

FIG. 7   FIG. 8

3. *Mid-point of a line-segment.* The mid-point M of a line-segment with end-points $P_1(x_1, y_1)$ and $P_2(x_2, y_2)$ has coordinates which are the average of the coordinates of P_1 and P_2, *i.e.*

$$x_m = \frac{x_1 + x_2}{2}, \quad y_m = \frac{y_1 + y_2}{2} \quad \text{(Fig. 8)}.$$

4. *Division of a line-segment in the ratio* $\lambda = \dfrac{m}{n}$ (Fig. 9).

(a) Inner division: $\lambda = \dfrac{m}{n}$ (positive). If $P_1(x_1, y_1)$ and $P_2(x_2, y_2)$ are the end-points of the line-segment, then the point of division $P_3(x_3, y_3)$ has coordinates:

$$x_3 = \frac{nx_1 + mx_2}{n + m} = \frac{x_1 + \lambda x_2}{1 + \lambda}; \quad y_3 = \frac{ny_1 + my_2}{n + m} = \frac{y_1 + \lambda y_2}{1 + \lambda}.$$

(b) Outer division: $\lambda = \dfrac{m}{n}$ (still positive). The point of division has coordinates

$$x_4 = \frac{-nx_1 + mx_2}{m - n} = \frac{x_1 - \lambda x_2}{1 - \lambda},$$

$$y_4 = \frac{-ny_1 + my_2}{m - n} = \frac{y_1 - \lambda y_2}{1 - \lambda}.$$

25

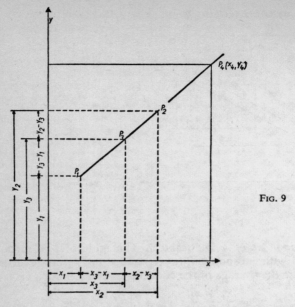

Fig. 9

5. *Area of a triangle*. Suppose the triangle has vertices $P_1(x_1, y_1)$, $P_2(x_2, y_2)$ and $P_3(x_3, y_3)$, the three points being laid out in the anticlockwise sense. The area of the triangle is

$$A = \tfrac{1}{2}[x_1(y_2 - y_3) + x_2(y_3 - y_1) + x_3(y_1 - y_2)].$$

(This expression is obtained by subtracting the trapezia $\bar{P}_1P_1P_2\bar{P}_2$ and $\bar{P}_2P_2P_3\bar{P}_3$ from the trapezium $\bar{P}_1P_1P_3\bar{P}_3$; Fig. 10.)

Fig. 10

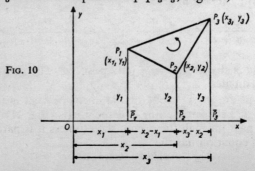

This formula can be written as a *determinant* (see below):

$$A = \tfrac{1}{2} \begin{vmatrix} 1 & x_1 & y_1 \\ 1 & x_2 & y_2 \\ 1 & x_3 & y_3 \end{vmatrix}$$

6. *Equation of a straight line.* The straight line through the points P_1 and P_2 consists of all the points $P(x, y)$ such that the area of the triangle PP_1P_2 is zero, that is,

$$\begin{vmatrix} 1 & x & y \\ 1 & x_1 & y_1 \\ 1 & x_2 & y_2 \end{vmatrix} = 0,$$

or $(x_1y_2 - x_2y_1) + x(y_1 - y_2) + y(x_2 - x_1) = 0$, which we may rewrite as

$$Ax + By + C = 0, \tag{a}$$

where A, B and C are constants (independent of x and y). It follows that every straight line has the form (a). Conversely, every equation of the form (a) represents a line, in fact the line joining the points $\left(0, \dfrac{-C}{B}\right)$ and $\left(\dfrac{-C}{A}, 0\right)$, unless $A = 0$ or $B = 0$ in which cases we have a line parallel to one of the axes.

It is convenient to be able to recognize the equation (a) of lines which are specially situated, and in general to be able to adapt the equation into equivalent forms which reflect more readily the properties with which we happen to be concerned.

(i) *Lines specially situated.* A line parallel to the x axis (equation $y = 0$) has equation of the form $y = b$, where b is the distance between the line and the axis. Similarly, a line parallel to the y-axis has equation of the form $x = a$. A line through the origin, that is, the point $(0, 0)$ at which the two axes intersect, has equation of the form $Ax + By = 0$, which it is convenient to write as $y = mx$.

(ii) *Convenient forms of the equation of a line.* As we have just seen, a line through the origin has equation of the form $y = mx$. m is a measure of the slope of the line, in fact it is the tangent of the angle between the line and the x-axis (Fig. 11). If the line does not pass through the origin, then (unless it is parallel to the y-axis) its equation has the form

$$y = mx + n,$$

27

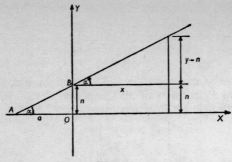

FIG. 11

and this time the line passes through the point $B(0, n)$ on the y-axis and again makes an angle with the x-axis with tangent m.

More generally, the line through the point $P_1(x_1, y_1)$ and making a similar angle with the x-axis has equation of the form

$$y - y_1 = m(x - x_1).$$

The straight line meeting the x-axis in $P(a, 0)$ and the y-axis in $Q(0, b)$ has the equation (Fig. 12)

$$\frac{x}{a} + \frac{y}{b} = 1, \quad (a \neq 0, b \neq 0).$$

If the equation of a straight line in the general form $Ax + By + C = 0$ is divided through by the constant

$$\pm\sqrt{A^2 + B^2}$$

the result is the Hessian normal form. This equation

$$\frac{Ax + By + C}{\pm\sqrt{A^2 + B^2}} = 0$$

has the following properties (Fig. 12):

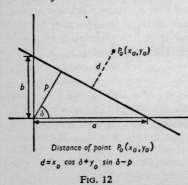

Distance of point $P_0(x_0, y_0)$

$d = x_0 \cos \delta + y_0 \sin \delta - p$

FIG. 12

$$-p = \frac{+C}{\pm\sqrt{A^2 + B^2}}$$

represents the absolute distance of the straight line from the origin if the sign of the root is taken so that p is positive. If δ is the angle which the perpendicular from the origin to the straight line makes with the positive x-axis then:

$$\cos \delta = \frac{A}{\pm \sqrt{A^2 + B^2}} \quad \text{and} \quad \sin \delta = \frac{B}{\pm \sqrt{A^2 + B^2}}.$$

The equation may then be written

$$x \cos \delta + y \sin \delta - p = 0.$$

The distance d of a point $P_0(x_0, y_0)$ from the straight line can be calculated with the help of the Hessian normal form:

$$d = x_0 \cos \delta + y_0 \sin \delta - p \quad \text{or} \quad d = \frac{Ax_0 + By_0 + C}{\pm \sqrt{A^2 + B^2}}$$

(Fig. 12).

The distance of the origin from the line is a special case of this formula.

Example: The straight line $y = -\frac{4}{3}x + 4$ has the Hessian normal form

$$\frac{4x + 3y - 12}{\sqrt{16 + 9}} = 0, \; i.e. \; \frac{4x + 3y - 12}{5} = 0.$$

By substituting the coordinates of a chosen point in the equation $d = \dfrac{4x + 3y - 12}{5}$, we can obtain the distance of the point from the straight line. The distance of the origin is $d = -\frac{12}{5}$. The distance of the point $P_0(8, 0)$ from the line is

$$d = \frac{4 \times 8 + 3 \times 0 - 12}{5} = 4.$$

Note that in reckoning the distance of points from a straight line by means of the Hessian normal form, we assign to all points which lie on one side of the line positive distances and to points on the other side negative distances.

7. The intersection of two lines

(i) *Point of intersection of two straight lines (two curves).* The coordinates of the intersection of two straight lines (curves) must satisfy the equations of both lines (curves). The coordinates of the point of intersection are thus the solutions of a system of two equations with two unknowns.

Example: Intersection of the straight lines $y = x + 2$ and $y = 5x - 2$. Let the coordinates of the point of intersection be (x_s, y_s). Then: I. $y_s = 5x_s - 2$,

$$\text{II. } y_s = x_s + 2.$$

This system of equations has the solution

$$x_s = 1, \, y_s = 3 \text{ (Fig. 13)}.$$

(ii) *Angle of intersection of two straight lines*. The angle of intersection of two straight lines with equations $y = m_1x + n_1$ and $y = m_2x + n_2$ can be determined from the formula

$$\tan \phi = \frac{m_2 - m_1}{1 + m_1m_2} \text{ (Fig. 14)}.$$

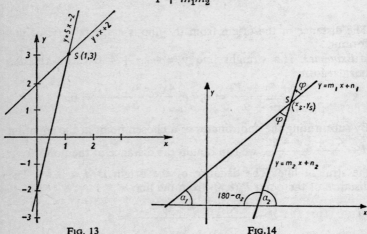

FIG. 13   FIG. 14

The angle obtained is that specified by moving anticlockwise from the first line to the second. In the above example (under (i)) $m_1 = 1$ and $m_2 = 5$, so that $\tan \phi = \dfrac{5 - 1}{1 + 5} = \dfrac{2}{3}$, that is $\phi = 33°\ 42'$.

If the denominator $(1 + m_1m_2)$ is zero $m_2 = -\dfrac{1}{m_1}$ and the lines are perpendicular to one another.

8. *Analytical geometry of the circle.*

Equation of the circle. For every point of the circumference of a circle with the origin of the coordinate-system as centre we have from Pythagoras's theorem the equation

$$x^2 + y^2 = r^2 \text{ (Fig. 15)}.$$

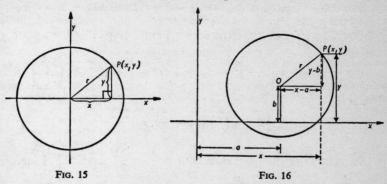

FIG. 15   FIG. 16

If the centre is not the origin, but some other point $O(a, b)$, the equation of the circle is

$$(x - a)^2 + (y - b)^2 = r^2 \text{ (Fig. 16)}.$$

The significant features of this equation are that the coefficients of x^2 and y^2 are equal and there is no term in xy. These are necessary conditions for the general equation of the second degree, which then has the form

$$Ax^2 + Ay^2 + 2Bx + 2Cy + D = 0,$$

to represent a circle, and if we exclude from consideration pairs of lines they are sufficient. We can obtain the coordinates of the centre from this equation. Dividing through by A we obtain

$$x^2 + y^2 + 2\frac{B}{A}x + 2\frac{C}{A}y + \frac{D}{A} = 0.$$

If we then complete the square we have

$$x^2 + 2\frac{B}{A}x + \frac{B^2}{A^2} + y^2 + 2\frac{C}{A}y + \frac{C^2}{A^2} = \frac{-D}{A} + \frac{B^2}{A^2} + \frac{C^2}{A^2},$$

that is,

$$\left(x + \frac{B}{A}\right)^2 + \left(y + \frac{C}{A}\right)^2 = -\frac{D}{A} + \frac{B^2}{A^2} + \frac{C^2}{A^2},$$

31

which is the equation of the circle centre $O\left(-\dfrac{B}{A}, -\dfrac{C}{A}\right)$ and radius

$$r = \sqrt{-\frac{D}{A} + \frac{B^2}{A^2} + \frac{C^2}{A^2}}.$$

Example: The equation $4x^2 + 4y^2 + 12x + 20y - 3 = 0$ represents a circle since the coefficients of x^2 and y^2 are equal and there is no term in xy. Division by 4 and completing the square gives

$$x^2 + 3x + \left(\frac{3}{2}\right)^2 + y^2 + 5y + \left(\frac{5}{2}\right)^2 = \frac{3}{4} + \left(\frac{3}{2}\right)^2 + \left(\frac{5}{2}\right)^2.$$

That is

$$\left(x + \frac{3}{2}\right)^2 + \left(y + \frac{5}{2}\right)^2 = \frac{37}{4}.$$

The centre of the circle is $O\left(-\dfrac{3}{2}, -\dfrac{5}{2}\right)$ and the radius $r = \dfrac{1}{2}\sqrt{37}$.

(i) *Equations of circles specially related to the coordinate system.* Centre lying on the x-axis: $O(a, O)$

$$(x - a)^2 + y^2 = r^2.$$

Centre lying on the y-axis: $O(O, b)$

$$x^2 + (y - b)^2 = r^2.$$

A circle whose centre $O(a, O)$ lies on the x-axis and which touches the y-axis has the equation:

$$(x - a)^2 + y^2 = a^2 \quad \text{or} \quad x^2 - 2ax + y^2 = 0 \text{ (Fig. 17)}.$$

Similarly, the equation of a circle which touches the x-axis and has its centre $O(O, b)$ on the y-axis has the equation:

$$x^2 + (y - b)^2 = b^2 \quad \text{or} \quad x^2 - 2by + y^2 = 0.$$

(ii) *Equation of a circle through three given points.* If a circle passes through three points $P_1(x_1, y_1)$, $P_2(x_2, y_2)$ and $P_3(x_3, y_3)$, the coordinates of these points must satisfy the equation of the circle. In this way we obtain the three conditions necessary to define uniquely the quantities c, d and r, where (c, d) are the coordinates of the centre and r is the (positive) length of the radius:

$$(x_1 - c)^2 + (y_1 - d)^2 = r^2,$$
$$(x_2 - c)^2 + (y_2 - d)^2 = r^2,$$
$$(x_3 - c)^2 + (y_3 - d)^2 = r^2.$$

(iii) *Intersection of a circle and a straight line* (Fig. 18). Given the circle $x^2 + y^2 = r^2$ and the straight line $y = mx + n$. Required, the points of intersection of these two curves.

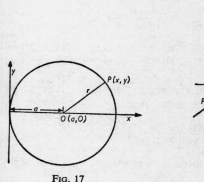
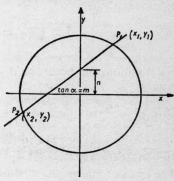

FIG. 17   FIG. 18

We have the system of equations

$$\begin{cases} \text{I.} \quad x^2 + y^2 = r^2 \\ \text{II.} \qquad\quad y = mx + n \end{cases}$$

to solve. The second equation gives $y^2 = m^2x^2 + 2mnx + n^2$. Put this in the first equation and we get $x^2 + m^2x^2 + 2mnx + n^2 = r^2$. This is a quadratic equation for the x-coordinate of the point of intersection and has solutions

$$x_{1,2} = \frac{-mn}{1 + m^2} \pm \frac{1}{1 + m^2} \sqrt{r^2(1 + m^2) - n^2}.$$

We now use the second equation, $y = mx + n$, to calculate the y-coordinate of the points of intersection, namely,

$$y_{1,2} = \frac{n}{1 + m^2} \pm \frac{m}{1 + m^2} \sqrt{r^2(1 + m^2) - n^2}.$$

33

The expression under the root-sign, $D = r^2(1 + m^2) - n^2$, is called the *Discriminant* of the circle. The discriminant allows one to decide whether a straight line has no points in common with a given circle, whether it touches it or whether it intersects it in two points.

1. $D = r^2(1 + m^2) - n^2$ negative. The solutions given above, x_1 and x_2 as well as y_1 and y_2, are pairs of conjugate complex numbers, *i.e.* there are no (real) points of intersection.

2. $D = r^2(1 + m^2) - n^2 = 0$. x_1 and x_2 are equal, as are y_1 and y_2, and so the line touches the circle in the point which has coordinates

$$x = \frac{-mn}{1 + m^2}, \quad y = \frac{n}{1 + m^2}.$$

3. $D = r^2(1 + m^2) - n^2$ positive. In this case there are two real solutions for both x and y. The line cuts the circle in two points.

(iv) *Mid-points of parallel chords.* A chord of the circle $x^2 + y^2 = r^2$ with gradient m has mid-point

$$M\left(\frac{-mn}{1 + m^2}, \frac{n}{1 + m^2}\right).$$

The locus of mid-points of chords with gradient m is the straight line $y = -\dfrac{1}{m} x$, *i.e.* the diameter of the circle which cuts the chords at right-angles.

(v) *Tangent to the circle $x^2 + y^2 = r^2$.*

1. A straight line with gradient m is a tangent to the circle $x^2 + y^2 = r^2$ if the equation $r^2(1 + m^2) - n^2 = 0$ is satisfied, *i.e.* if the intercept of the line with the y-axis is $n = r\sqrt{1 + m^2}$. It follows that for a given direction the equation of a tangent is $y = mx + r\sqrt{1 + m^2}$. The point of contact has coordinates

$$x = \frac{-mr}{\sqrt{1 + m^2}}, \quad y = \frac{r}{\sqrt{1 + m^2}}.$$

2. If the point $P_1(x_1, y_1)$ lies on the circle $x^2 + y^2 = r^2$, the tangent through this point has gradient $m = -\dfrac{x_1}{y_1}$ (perpendicular

to the radius through P_1), and the equation of the tangent is $y - y_1 = \dfrac{-x_1}{y_1}(x - x_1)$. This reduces to $xx_1 + yy_1 = r^2$.

(vi) *Tangent to the circle* $(x - a)^2 + (y - b)^2 = r^2$. The general equation of a tangent for this circle is $(x - a)(x_1 - a) + (y - b)(y_1 - b) = r^2$, where a and b are the coordinates of the centre $O(a, b)$, and x_1 and y_1 respectively the coordinates of the point at which the tangent touches the circle.

(vii) *Polar line of a point with respect to the circle* $x^2 + y^2 = r^2$. Suppose the two tangents are drawn to a circle from a point $P_0(x_0, y_0)$ outside the circle. Let the points of contact of these tangents be $P_1(x_1, y_1)$ and $P_2(x_2, y_2)$. The line joining these points is called the polar line or polar of the point P_0, and P_0 is called the pole of the line P_1P_2. The polar line of a point P_0 with respect to the circle $x^2 + y^2 = r^2$ has equation $x_0x + y_0y = r^2$. The polar line of a point with respect to the circle $(x - a)^2 + (y - b)^2 = r^2$ has equation $(x - a)(x_0 - a) + (y - b)(y_0 - b) = r^2$.

(viii) *The Radical Axis of two circles.* If the equations of two circles are given with the coefficient of x^2 the same in both, the equation of the radical axis is obtained by subtracting one equation from the other.

Example: To determine the radical axis of the circles $x^2 + y^2 - 36 = 0$ and $(x - 3)^2 + (y - 2)^2 - 25 = 0$. Subtraction gives $6x - 9 + 4y - 4 - 36 + 25 = 0$, that is,

$$6x + 4y = 24, \text{ or } y = -\tfrac{3}{2}x + 6.$$

9. *Analytical Geometry of the ellipse, parabola and hyperbola.* (See *Conic sections, Curves of the second order, Ellipse, Hyperbola* and *Parabola*.)

Analytical geometry of space

1. *Position of a point relative to the coordinate axes and the coordinate planes.* A three-dimensional space is divided by a rectangular coordinate-system into eight octants by a straightforward extension of the method used in two-dimensional space. The positive direction of the z-axis is chosen in the manner of a right handed screw when associated with increasing angles in the xy-plane. The octant in which the point $P(x, y, z)$ lies can be then determined from the signs of the coordinate-values (see *Co-ordinate-systems*).

The possibilities are:

	x	y	z
I	$+$	$+$	$+$
II	$-$	$+$	$+$
II	$-$	$-$	$+$
IV	$+$	$-$	$+$
V	$+$	$+$	$-$
VI	$-$	$+$	$-$
VII	$-$	$-$	$-$
VIII	$+$	$-$	$-$

A point $P(x, y, z)$ lies in one of the coordinate planes if one of its coordinates is zero:

for points in the xy-plane, $z = 0$;
for points in the yz-plane, $x = 0$;
for points in the zx-plane, $y = 0$.

A point lies on a coordinate axis if two of its coordinates are zero:

points on the x-axis have $y = 0$ and $z = 0$;
points on the y-axis have $x = 0$ and $z = 0$;
points on the z-axis have $x = 0$ and $y = 0$.

2. *Distance between two points.* By Pythagoras's theorem, two points $P_1(x_1, y_1, z_1)$ and $P_2(x_2, y_2, z_2)$ have distance apart

$$d = \sqrt{(x_2 - x_1)^2 + (y_2 - y_1)^2 + (z_2 - z_1)^2}.$$

3. *Direction of a line-segment.* The direction of a line-segment with end-points $P_1(x_1, y_1, z_1)$ and $P_2(x_2, y_2, z_2)$ is specified by the three numbers

$$\cos \alpha = \frac{x_2 - x_1}{\sqrt{(x_2 - x_1)^2 + (y_2 - y_1)^2 + (z_2 - z_1)^2}},$$

$$\cos \beta = \frac{y_2 - y_1}{\sqrt{(x_2 - x_1)^2 + (y_2 - y_1)^2 + (z_2 - z_1)^2}},$$

$$\cos \gamma = \frac{z_2 - z_1}{\sqrt{(x_2 - x_1)^2 + (y_2 - y_1)^2 + (z_2 - z_1)^2}}.$$

α, β and γ are the angles which a line through the origin and parallel to the line-segment makes with the coordinate axes. $\cos \alpha$, $\cos \beta$, and $\cos \gamma$ are called the *direction-cosines* of the line-segment. They satisfy the relation

$$\cos^2 \alpha + \cos^2 \beta + \cos^2 \gamma = 1.$$

4. *Straight line*. In discussing plane coordinate geometry (above, p. 27), we saw that the general equation of a line l can be put in the form

$$y = mx + n,$$

where m and n are constants. If we now put $x = a_1 + a_2 t$, where t is variable and a_1 and a_2 are (arbitrary) constants, we have

$$y = m(a_1 + a_2 t) + n = (ma_1 + n) + ma_2 t$$
$$= b_1 + b_2 t \text{ (say)},$$

where b_1 and b_2 are constants. In other words, points on the line l have coordinates of the form

$$(a_1 + a_2 t, \; b_1 + b_2 t).$$

We confirm that the locus of such points is identical with our original line by noticing that substituting these coordinates into the equation of any line l' defines exactly one value t' of t, giving the point of intersection of l and l' if t' is finite or showing the lines to be parallel if t' is infinite.

In the same way, a straight line in space can be represented by three linear functions of a parameter t:

$$x = a_1 + a_2 t, \; y = b_1 + b_2 t, \; z = c_1 + c_2 t.$$

Substituting all possible real values of t we obtain the coordinates of all points $P(x, y, z)$ which lie on the straight line.

One of a_2, b_2 and c_2 is certainly non-zero, since otherwise we have only a single point. If $c_2 \neq 0$, then $t = \dfrac{z - c_1}{c_2}$. This value can be substituted in the two other equations, giving

$$\text{I.} \quad x = a_1 + \frac{a_2}{c_2}(z - c_1),$$

$$\text{II.} \quad y = b_1 + \frac{b_2}{c_2}(z - c_1).$$

37

This is one example of the general property of a straight line, namely that it can also be represented by a system of two linear equations in the three variables x, y and z. If a definite value k is substituted for one variable (say z) we can calculate the x and y coordinates of the point on the straight line whose z-coordinate is k.

5. *The plane.* A plane can be represented by a linear equation $Ax + By + Cz + D = 0$. We confirm this by noting that (in general) three planes, or one plane and one line, intersect in a unique point. If the equation is divided through by $-D$ we get the equation in a form from which the intercepts of the plane on the coordinate axes can be obtained:

$$\frac{x}{\dfrac{-D}{A}} + \frac{y}{\dfrac{-D}{B}} + \frac{z}{\dfrac{-D}{C}} = 1.$$

The plane cuts the x-axis in the point $P_x\left(-\dfrac{D}{A}, 0, 0\right)$, the y-axis in the point $P_y\left(0, -\dfrac{D}{B}, 0\right)$ and the z-axis in the point $P_z\left(0, 0, -\dfrac{D}{C}\right)$. The usual way of indicating the *intercept-form* is

$$\frac{x}{a} + \frac{y}{b} + \frac{z}{c} = 1.$$

If the equation of a plane $Ax + By + Cz + D = 0$ is divided through by $\pm\sqrt{A^2 + B^2 + C^2}$, we obtain the Hessian normal form. The sign of $\pm\sqrt{A^2 + B^2 + C^2}$ is chosen as opposite to that of D. The Hessian normal form is therefore

$$\frac{Ax + By + Cz + D}{\sqrt{A^2 + B^2 + C^2}} = 0.$$

The perpendicular from the origin on to the plane has length

$$p = -\frac{D}{\pm\sqrt{A^2 + B^2 + C^2}},$$

and the direction-cosines of the plane (defined as those of a line perpendicular to the plane) are

$$\cos \alpha = \frac{A}{\pm \sqrt{A^2 + B^2 + C^2}}, \quad \cos \beta = \frac{B}{\pm \sqrt{A^2 + B^2 + C^2}},$$

$$\cos \gamma = \frac{C}{\pm \sqrt{A^2 + B^2 + C^2}}.$$

If we substitute the coordinates of an arbitrary point $P(x_1, y_1, z_1)$ in the equation, we obtain the distance d

$$d = \frac{Ax_1 + By_1 + Cz_1 + D}{\sqrt{A^2 + B^2 + C^2}},$$

of the point from the plane.

6. *Surfaces of the second order*. A functional equation of degree two in three variables x, y and z has the general form:

$$F(x, y, z) = a_{11}x^2 + a_{22}y^2 + a_{33}z^2 + 2a_{12}xy + 2a_{13}xz$$
$$+ 2a_{23}yz + 2a_{14}x + 2a_{24}y + 2a_{34}z + a_{44} = 0$$

Such an equation represents a locus of points in space which has two points in common with a general line and so is a surface of the second order (see *Surfaces of the second order*).

Angle

An angle is formed by two rays l and m proceeding from a point A. l and m are termed the arms or sides of the angle and A the vertex (Fig. 19). Angles are usually denoted by small Greek letters, by $\angle A$ where A is the vertex (if this is unambiguous), or, if B and C are points on l and m, by $\angle BAC$ (where we note that the vertex is the middle letter).

An angle divides the plane in which it lies into two parts, the interior and the exterior of the angle, where vertex and arms are taken to belong to neither part.

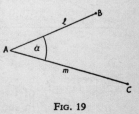

Fig. 19

Construction of an angle (with ruler and compass). Given an angle α with arms *a*, *b* and vertex *O*; to mark off this angle on a straight line *m* in the clockwise sense, with the given vertex *V* (see Fig. 20), describe about *O* and *V* equal circles with arbitrary radius *r*.

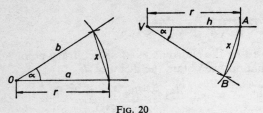

Fig. 20

The angle α cuts off an arc *x* on the circumference of the circle with centre *O*. This arc is marked off (with the compass) on the circle about *V*, measured from the point of intersection of the circle with *m*. The end point *B* gives one point of the required arm, which is obtained by joining *VB*.

Sum of two angles (construction). To construct the sum of two angles we lay out the angle α on one arm of β (alternatively β on α) in such a way that no point of the interior of α lies in the interior of β (Fig. 21).

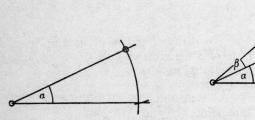

Fig. 21

Difference of two angles (construction). To construct the difference α − β of two angles α and β we lay out the angle α on one arm of β in such a way that the interior of β lies wholly within the interior of α. The part of the interior of α which does not lie within β is then the interior of the angle α − β (Fig. 22).

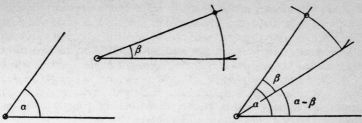

FIG. 22

Comparison of angles (Fig. 23). Given any two angles α and β, α with arms *m* and *n* and vertex *O*, β with arms *a* and *b* and vertex *V*. If we lay out the angle β on *m* with vertex *O* so that the arm *a* lies on *m*, and *b* lies on the same side of *m* as *n*, then *b* lies

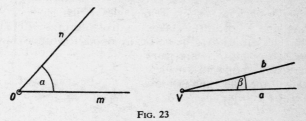

FIG. 23

either in the interior of α, or on *n*, or outside the angle α. In the first case β < α, in the second case the angles are equal, and in the third case β > α (Fig. 24).

Adjacent supplementary angles. If two angles α and β have vertex and one arm in common, and if the other two arms lie in a straight line, they are said to be adjacent supplementary (Fig. 25).

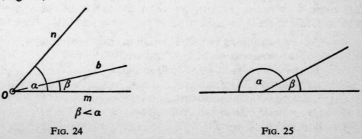

FIG. 24   FIG. 25

41

Right angles. An angle which is equal to its adjacent supplementary angle is called a 'right angle'. The right angle is assigned the size 90° (90 degrees, see below *angular measure*), and so adjacent supplementary angles add up to 180°, *i.e.* to two right angles, in other words, they form a *straight angle* (see below).

Acute angle, obtuse angle, straight angle, convex angle, round angle. An angle which is less than one right angle is said to be *acute*. An angle which is greater than one right angle and less than two right angles is said to be *obtuse*.

Acute angles are less than 90°.
Obtuse angles are between 90° and 180°.
The straight angle equals 180°.
Convex angles are between 180° and 360°.
The round angle (perigon) equals 360°.

Vertically opposite angles. Two angles which have vertex in common and whose arms taken in pairs form two complete straight lines are said to be vertically opposite to one another. In Fig. 26 α, γ and β, δ are pairs of vertically opposite angles. Vertically opposite angles are equal. Thus $\alpha = \gamma$ and $\beta = \delta$.

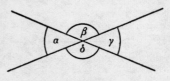

FIG. 26

Angular measure

  (i) *Sexagesimal measure:*

    1° (= 1 degree) is $\frac{1}{90}$th of a right angle.
    1′ (= 1 minute) is $\frac{1}{60}$th of a degree.
    1″ (= 1 second) is $\frac{1}{60}$th of a minute.

  (ii) *Radian measure:* the measure of an angle in radian (circular) measure is the length of arc cut off by the angle on the unit circle (*i.e.* circle with radius 1) with centre at the vertex of the angle. Radius and arc must be measured to the same scale. We have:

    360° = 2π radians = 6·28319 radians (approximately),
    180° = π radians = 3·14159 radians,
     90° = $\pi/2$ radians = 1·57080 radians,
     1° = 0·017,453,3 radians,
     1′ = 0·000,290,9 radians,
     1″ = 0·000,004,8 radians,
  1 radian = 57° 17′ 44·8″.

In scientific work the angular unit is often omitted in representing an angle, it being understood that the measure is in radians.

Measurement of angles is carried out by means of a protractor, that is, a half-circle of metal or plastic graduated into 180°.

Angles formed by transversal to parallel lines. The angles formed by a transversal to a set of parallel lines (Fig. 27) are called step

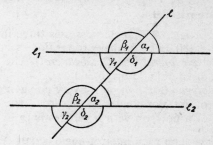

FIG. 27

or corresponding angles, alternate angles and opposite angles. They arise when two parallel lines l_1 and l_2 are intersected by a third line l which is not parallel to the first two, but lies in the same plane as they do (Fig. 27).

Step angles: step or corresponding angles lie on the same side of the transversal l, and on corresponding sides of the parallels l_1, l_2.

Opposed angles: opposed angles lie on the same side of the transversal l, and on different sides of the parallels l_1, l_2.

Alternate angles: alternate angles lie on different sides of the transversal l and on different sides of the parallels l_1, l_2.

In Fig. 27:

α_1 and α_2, β_1 and β_2, γ_1 and γ_2, δ_1 and δ_2 are step angles;

α_1 and δ_2, β_1 and γ_2, γ_1 and β_2, δ_1 and α_2 are opposed angles;

α_1 and γ_2, β_1 and δ_2, γ_1 and α_2, δ_1 and β_2 are alternate angles.

Properties of angles formed by a transversal

(1)   Pairs of step-angles are equal.
(2)   Pairs of alternate angles are equal.
(3)   Pairs of opposed angles are supplementary (add up to 180°).

Conversely: If two lines l_1 and l_2 are cut by a third line l and if:

(a) the angles of a pair on the same side of l and of l_1, l_2 are equal; or

(b) the angles of a pair on opposite sides of l and of l_1, l_2 are equal; or

(c) the angles of a pair on the same side of l and on different sides of l_1, l_2 add up to 180°;

then l_1 and l_2 are parallel.

Angles of a triangle. A triangle possesses three interior angles which add up to 180°. For further propositions see *Triangle*.

Angles of a quadrilateral (see *Quadrilateral*). The four interior angles of a quadrilateral add up to 360°.

Angles of a polygon (see *Polygon*). Every polygon possesses the same number of interior angles as vertices. The sum of the interior angles of a polygon with n vertices is $(n - 2)\,180°$, and so for a regular n-agon each interior angle equals $\dfrac{n-2}{n}\,180°$.

Angles in a circle

Circumference angle (Fig. 28): A circumference angle α is formed by two chords of a circle proceeding from a single point on the circumference. The circumference angle cuts off an arc on the circle.

Central angle (Fig. 28): A central angle is formed at the centre of a circle by two radii. It too determines an arc of the circle. The central angle is double the circumference angle corresponding to the same arc.

Circumference angles on equal arcs of a circle are equal. Two circumference angles whose arcs together comprise the full circle, add up to 360°.

Circumference angles on a semi-circle are right angles (see the Theorem of Thales, p. 428).

Angle between chord and tangent (Fig. 28): The angle between a chord

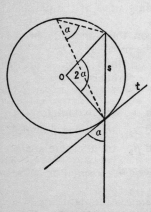

Fig. 28

44

s of a circle and the tangent *t* at an end-point of the chord is equal to the circumference angle α on the arc which lies between *t* and *s*.

Angle of sight. The lines of sight which proceed from the eye to the end-points of a line-segment form together the angle of sight, the angle suspended by the segment at the eye of the observer (Fig. 29).

Two points can be distinguished by the eye if the angle of sight determined by the points is not too small. The angle of sight

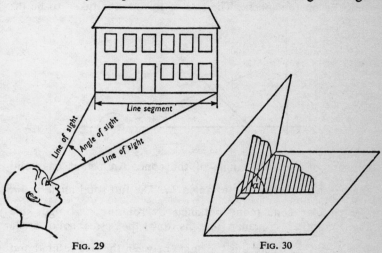

Line segment

Line of sight

Angle of sight

Line of sight

Fig. 29   Fig. 30

must be at least 60″–90″ for a normal eye to distinguish the points concerned. Optical instruments (magnifying glass, telescope, microscope) serve to enlarge the angle of sight.

An angle of sight in a vertical plane is called an angle of elevation.

Angle between two planes. Non-parallel planes intersect in a straight line. At a point on this line, perpendiculars to the line can be constructed in each plane (Fig. 30). These two perpendiculars determine a new plane and form an angle α with one another in it which is called the *angle of intersection* or *angle of inclination* of the two planes.

Angle between a straight line and a plane. A straight line, which is not parallel to a given plane, intersects the plane in a point (its

45

trace). The projection of the line onto the plane forms with the line an angle, which is called the angle between the line and the plane, or the angle of inclination of the line to the plane.

Solid angle. A cone comprises the system of all rays proceeding from a fixed point and passing through the points of a given curve. Cones may be measured in solid angular measure, by taking the sphere of unit radius with the vertex of the cone as centre and evaluating the area of the surface segment cut out by the cone on the sphere. The size of this area is taken to be the

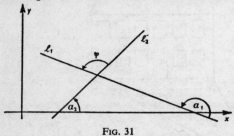

FIG. 31

measure of the solid angle of the cone. An octant has solid angle $\frac{\pi}{2}$, a hemisphere solid angle 2π. The full solid angle is 4π. The circular cone (cone obtained by rotating a straight line about another coplanar line as axis) possesses solid angle $\Phi = 4\pi \sin^2 \frac{\alpha}{2}$, where $\frac{\alpha}{2}$ is the angle between the line rotated and the axis of rotation.

Complementary angles. Two angles which add up to 90° are said to be complementary, *e.g.* the angles adjacent to the hypotenuse of a right-angled triangle are complementary.

Supplementary angles. Two angles which add up to 180° are said to be supplementary, *e.g.* neighbouring interior angles of a parallelogram are supplementary.

Angle between two curves

The angle which two curves C_1 and C_2 form with one another at their point of intersection is defined to be the angle formed by the tangents t_1 and t_2 to the two curves at the point of intersection (see Fig. 32).

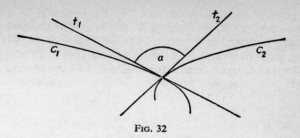

FIG. 32

Angle-bisector

The bisector of a given angle is the straight line which passes through the vertex of the angle and divides the angle into two equal angles. The bisector of an angle is its axis of symmetry.

Construction of the bisector of an angle (see *Fundamental constructions*). In a triangle three angle-bisectors (w_α, w_β, w_γ), corresponding to the internal angles, can be constructed. The term *angle-bisectors of a triangle* is usually applied to the line-segments extending from the vertices of the bisected angles to the opposite sides of the triangle. They intersect in a common point, the centre of the inscribed circle, and divide the sides of the triangle in the ratio of the sides adjacent to the angle bisected (see *Triangle*).

Angle of intersection of two lines

The angles of intersection of two straight lines is the angle formed by the lines at their point of intersection. The angle of intersection ψ of two straight lines l_1 and l_2 can be calculated from the gradients of the lines as follows:

Gradient of 1st line l_1: $m_1 = \tan \alpha_1$

Gradient of 2nd line l_2: $m_2 = \tan \alpha_2$

Since $\psi = \alpha_1 - \alpha_2$ and $\tan \psi = \dfrac{\tan \alpha_1 - \tan \alpha_2}{1 + \tan \alpha_1 \tan \alpha_2}$, we have

$$\tan \psi = \frac{m_1 - m_2}{1 + m_1 m_2}.$$

(see Fig. 31).

47

Angle of sight

The lines of sight, proceeding from the eye to the end points of a segment, together form the angle of sight (see *Angle*). If the angle of sight occurs in a vertical plane we speak of the *angle of elevation*. In surveying, etc., a theodolite is used to measure angles of sight.

Angle (solid)

For the measurement of a solid angle, see *Solid angle* and *Spherical trigonometry*.

Angles, measurement of

The measurement of an angle in drawing is carried out by means of a protractor; for surveying, and similar applications, a theodolite is used.

Annulus

The area bounded by two concentric circles in a plane is called an annulus (or circular ring). If the circles have radii R and r, where $R > r$, then the area of such a figure is

$$A = \pi R^2 - \pi r^2 = \pi(R + r)(R - r).$$

Apollonius (Apollonius of Perga, *c.* 200 B.C.)

The circle of Apollonius can be used to construct a triangle for which the ratio of two sides, the third side and a further independent element are given. The circle of Apollonius passes through the point of intersection of the sides of the triangle whose ratio is known. Its centre O lies on the third side. Further, it cuts the third side in two points which together with the endpoints of the side form a harmonic range (Fig. 33).

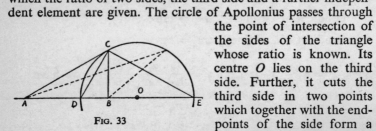

FIG. 33

Apollonius's problem

The problem of Apollonius is to construct a circle which touches each of three given circles (see *Circle*).

Arc

A segment of a circular line bounded by two end-points is called an arc. The straight line obtained by joining the two end-points of the arc is called the chord of the arc. The angle which has the centre of the circle as vertex and which is obtained by drawing the radii through the end-points of the arc is called the central angle of the arc. If an arc of length b lies on a circle of radius r and has central angle of α degrees then:

$$b = 2\pi r \, \frac{\alpha}{360}.$$

Archimedes's spiral

The archimedean spiral is a transcendental curve which can be represented in polar coordinates by the equation $r = a\theta$, a constant (Fig. 34).

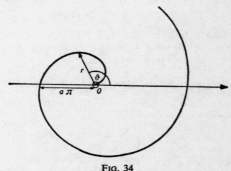

FIG. 34

Area, calculation of

For some purposes the area of a figure is determined by the number of unit squares contained in it (see *Square measure*). Congruent figures have equal area, but of course figures with equal areas need not be congruent.

49

Areas of rectangle and square. A rectangle with sides a and b has area

$$A = a \cdot b.$$

A square with side a has area

$$A = a^2.$$

Area of a parallelogram (Fig. 35)

From Fig. 35 we see that the parallelogram $ABCD$ must have the same area as the rectangle $ABEF$, since the rectangle $ABEF$ arises out of the parallelogram by cutting off the triangle BEC, at the same time adding to it the congruent triangle AFD. This shows that the area of a parallelogram is $A = gh$, that is, the product of a side and the associated altitude is.

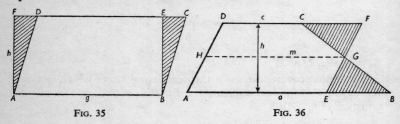

FIG. 35   FIG. 36

Area of a trapezium. A trapezium $ABCD$ can by Fig. 36 be transformed into a parallelogram of equal area. We have:

$$A = m \cdot h = \frac{a + c}{2} \cdot h,$$

that is, the mean parallel multiplied by the altitude.

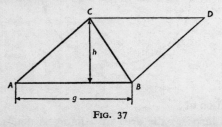

FIG. 37

Area of a triangle (Fig. 37). On any side of a triangle a congruent triangle can be placed diagonally opposite to the original triangle. The resulting figure is a parallelogram whose area is double that of the triangle. The area of a triangle is therefore equal to half the product of one side of the associated altitude. If we denote the altitude associated with a side by the appropriate suffix we have:

$$A = \frac{g \cdot h}{2} = \frac{a \cdot h_a}{2} = \frac{b \cdot h_b}{2} = \frac{c \cdot h_c}{2}.$$

Heron's Formula: If we denote by $s = \dfrac{a + b + c}{2}$ half the perimeter of a triangle, the area of the triangle is

$$A = \sqrt{s(s - a)(s - b)(s - c)}.$$

Trigonometrical Formulae for the calculation of the area of a triangle (in these formulae a, b, c are the sides of the triangle, α, β, γ the angles of the triangle, r the radius of the circumscribed circle, ρ the radius of the inscribed circle, $s = \dfrac{a + b + c}{2}$):

I. $A = \rho s,$

II. $A = \frac{1}{2}bc \sin \alpha = \frac{1}{2}ca \sin \beta = \frac{1}{2}ab \sin \gamma,$

III. $A = \dfrac{1}{2} a^2 \dfrac{\sin \beta \sin \gamma}{\sin \alpha} = \dfrac{1}{2} b^2 \dfrac{\sin \gamma \sin \alpha}{\sin \beta} = \dfrac{1}{2} c^2 \dfrac{\sin \alpha \sin \beta}{\sin \gamma},$

IV. $A = \dfrac{a \cdot b \cdot c}{4r}.$

Area of a right angled triangle. The area of a right angled triangle is equal to half the product of the shorter sides,

$$A = \frac{a \cdot b}{2}.$$

Area of an isosceles triangle (Fig. 38)

$$A = \frac{c}{2} \cdot h_c = \frac{c}{2} \sqrt{a^2 - \frac{c^2}{4}}.$$

51

Area of an equilateral triangle (Fig. 39).

$$A = \frac{a^2}{4}\sqrt{3}.$$

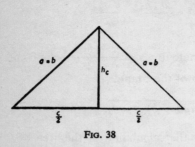

Fig. 38

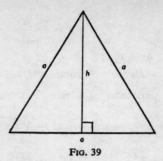

Fig. 39

The area of a figure with a curved boundary can, in particular cases, be determined by integration (see *Integration*). An elementary and rough method for determining the area of a figure with a curved boundary is the following graphical one (Fig. 40): We

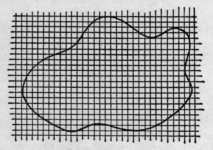

Fig. 40

cover the figure with a grid of squares of equal size, and count the number of squares which lie wholly within the figure; we then estimate the area of squares part of which lie within the figure. Naturally an approximate value only is obtained. Millimetre paper serves well for this purpose.

Area of a circle

$$A = \pi r^2 \; (r = \text{radius}),$$

or, equivalently,

$$A = \pi \cdot \frac{d^2}{4} \quad (d = \text{diameter}), \qquad \pi = 3 \cdot 1415 \ldots.$$

Area of an ellipse. With semi-axes a and b, the area is

$$A = \pi a b.$$

Area, measurement of

In the metric system the unit of area is the *are* $= 100 \, \text{m}^2$ (square metres).

$$
\begin{aligned}
1 \, \text{km}^2 &= 1 \text{ square kilometre} &&= 10^6 \, \text{m}^2, \\
& 1 \text{ hectare} &&= 10^4 \, \text{m}^2, \\
& 1 \text{ are} &&= 10^2 \, \text{m}^2, \\
1 \, \text{dm}^2 &= 1 \text{ square decimetre} &&= 10^{-2} \, \text{m}^2, \\
1 \, \text{cm}^2 &= 1 \text{ square centimetre} &&= 10^{-4} \, \text{m}^2, \\
1 \, \text{mm}^2 &= 1 \text{ square millimetre} &&= 10^{-6} \, \text{m}^2.
\end{aligned}
$$

In English measure:

$$
\begin{aligned}
144 \text{ square inches} &= 1 \text{ square foot}, \\
9 \text{ square feet} &= 1 \text{ square yard}, \\
4840 \text{ square yards} &= 1 \text{ acre}, \\
640 \text{ acres} &= 1 \text{ square mile}.
\end{aligned}
$$

Area-preserving transformation

In such a transformation corresponding segments of surfaces contain equal areas.

The congruent transformations (rigid motions) are area-preserving.

Arithmetic

Subdomain of *Mathematics* (see below). We distinguish: (i) common arithmetic, that is, calculation with definite numbers, (ii) literal arithmetic, calculation with numbers represented by alphabetical letters (algebraic calculation). In both the same laws hold for calculation.

There are four fundamental operations: (i) *Addition* = counting together. The result of an addition of summands is called the sum. (ii) *Subtraction* = taking away, the inverse of addition. The result of taking subtrahend from minuend is called a difference. (iii) *Multiplication* = making manifold. The result of multiplying factors together is called a product. (iv) *Division* = splitting into parts, the inverse of multiplication. The result of dividing a dividend by a divisor is called a quotient. The following laws hold for addition and multiplication: (i) Commutative Law: $a + b = b + a$; $p \cdot q = q \cdot p$. (ii) *Associative Law:* $(a + b) + c = a + (b + c)$ and $(a \cdot b) \cdot c = a \cdot (b \cdot c)$. (iii) *Distributive Law:* $(a + b)c = ac + bc$. When the minuend is less than the subtrahend, subtraction can only be carried out if negative numbers are introduced. If the dividend is not an exact multiple of the divisor, the division of integers leads to fractions.

A *fraction* represents an implied division; the dividend is the numerator, the divisor the denominator. Numerator and denominator are divided by a horizontal or sloping fraction bar, or by a double point, *e.g.* $\frac{3}{4} = 3/4 = 3 \div 4$. Fractions with numerator 1 are called unit fractions $\left(\frac{1}{2}, \frac{1}{3}, \frac{1}{4}, \ldots\right)$. According as the numerator is smaller or larger than the denominator the fraction is called proper or improper. An improper fraction (mixed numbers) is an integer plus a proper fraction, *e.g.* $\frac{17}{5} = 3\frac{2}{5}$. The value of a fraction is unaltered if numerator and denominator are both multiplied or divided by the same number. The rules for calculating with common fractions are illustrated by the following examples:

$$\frac{3}{7} + \frac{2}{7} - \frac{4}{7} = \frac{1}{7};$$

$$5\frac{4}{9} \cdot 1\frac{13}{14} = \frac{49}{9} \cdot \frac{27}{14} = \frac{7}{1} \cdot \frac{3}{2} = \frac{21}{2} = 10\frac{1}{2};$$

$$3\frac{1}{2} \div 5\frac{5}{6} = \frac{7}{2} \div \frac{35}{6} = \frac{7}{2} \cdot \frac{6}{35} = \frac{1}{1} \cdot \frac{3}{5} = \frac{3}{5}.$$

To add or subtract fractions with different denominators we reduce each to a common denominator, *e.g.*

$$\frac{4}{5} + \frac{2}{7} = \frac{4 \cdot 7}{5 \cdot 7} + \frac{2 \cdot 5}{7 \cdot 5} = \frac{28 + 10}{35} = \frac{38}{35} = 1\frac{3}{35}.$$

The least common denominator is the least common multiple of individual denominators, and is the most economical common denominator to use. A double fraction is a fraction in which numerator and denominator are themselves fractions, *e.g.* $\frac{7}{8}\Big/\frac{3}{5}$. Two fractions whose product is unity are called reciprocal, each being called the reciprocal of the other, *e.g.* $\frac{35}{6}$ and $\frac{6}{35}$, 3 and $\frac{1}{3}$. Continued fractions (see art.) may be used to yield approximations to fractions with large numbers.

Fractions whose denominators are powers of 10 are called decimal fractions. Proper fractions have zero unit, *e.g.* 0·34. The unity-entry is divided from the decimal-entry by a point, *e.g.* 6·205. Every common fraction can be transformed into a (finite or infinite) decimal fraction, if a sufficient number of zeros is appended, with a decimal point, to the numerator which is then divided by the denominator. If a denominator contains only 2 and 5 as prime factors the division is terminated in a finite number of terms, *e.g.* $\frac{5}{16} = 5 \cdot 0000 \div 16 = 0 \cdot 3125$; the decimal fraction has a finite number of places. If the denominator contains other prime factors the division results in an infinite decimal fraction in which a sequence of figures constantly repeats itself, *e.g.* $\frac{3}{7} = 0 \cdot \dot{4}2857\dot{1}$. The rules for calculating with decimal fractions correspond to those for integers.

Other calculating operations are *raising to a power, extraction of a root*, and *taking of the logarithm*. Explanation: Power = product of equal factors, *e.g.* $a^4 = a \times a \times a \times a$ (read, *a* to the fourth); *a* = base, 4 = power (exponent). In raising *a* to the power *n*, *a* and *n* are known and we wish to find $a^n = b$. The first inversion of this procedure comprises the extraction of a root: $a = \sqrt[n]{b}$ (read: *n*th root of *b*), where *n*, the degree of the root and *b*, the radicand are known, and we wish to find *a*. The second inversion comprises the taking of the logarithm, when a and b are known and we wish to find n: $n = \log_a b$ (read: log b to base a); b is an antilogarithm: $3 = \log_{10} 1000$, since $10^3 = 1{,}000$; $10 = \log_2 1024$, since $2^{10} = 1{,}024$. The notion of a power is extended to fractional exponents by means of the definition $\sqrt[n]{b} = b^{\frac{1}{n}}$, e.g. $\sqrt[4]{a^3} = a^{\frac{3}{4}}$; to negative exponents by means of the definition $\dfrac{1}{a^n} = a^{-n}$; and can be extended further to irrational exponents. The rules for calculating with logarithms follow from the rules for calculating with powers. $a^p \cdot a^q = a^{p+q}$ implies $\log_a a^{p+q} = p + q$, whence (putting $a^p = b$ and $a^q = c$): $\log_a bc = \log_a b + \log_a c$. Similarly we get $\log_a \dfrac{b}{c} = \log_a b - \log_a c$ and $\log_a b^t = t \cdot \log_a b$. In taking a logarithm the base and the number taken must both be positive.

Natural logarithms, in which the base is

$$e = 2 \cdot 718,281,828,495 \ldots$$

are of particular importance in theoretical mathematics; $\log_e$ is written ln. Common Briggsian logarithms are used for practical calculations (base 10; written as log). *E.g.* (rounded off to four decimal places).

$$\log 27 \cdot 38 = 1 \cdot 4374, \quad \log 27{,}380 = 4 \cdot 4374,$$
$$\log 0 \cdot 02738 = 0 \cdot 4374 - 2;$$

the whole number of the logarithm (1, 4, −2 in the examples) is called the *characteristic* and the decimal-part the *mantissa*. The characteristic is equal to one less than the number of digits behind the decimal point; the mantissa depends only on the sequence of digits in the number.

Literal calculation introduces, in place of definite numbers, letters of the alphabet, in order that rules and laws of calculation can be represented as general 'formulae'. An algebraic sum is a sum of terms comprising arbitrary signs which is called binomial, trinomial, etc., according as it contains 2, 3, etc., terms. The trinomial $5a^3 + 17a^2b + 9abc$ is said to be homogeneous and of the third degree since every term contains three literal factors (aaa, aab, abc). The fixed numbers 5, 17, 9 are called *coefficients*;

they do not enter into the degree of the expression. Thus $ax^4 + 4bx^3y - 6cx^2y^2 + 13dxy^3 - 2ey^4$ is a polynomial with five terms, homogeneous in x and y of degree 4. On the other hand if the various terms have different numbers of literal factors the expression is non-homogeneous (e.g. $5a^3 - 2ab$).

Manipulation of polynomial expressions

(i) $(a + b)(a - b) = a^2 - b^2$.

(ii) $x^n - y^n = (x - y)(x^{n-1} + x^{n-2}y + x^{n-3}y^2 + \ldots$
$$+ xy^{n-2} + y^{n-1});$$

here the second bracket contains a sum of n terms each with $(n - 1)$ factors ordered according to diminishing powers of x and increasing powers of y.

(iii) The *binomial theorem*: the powers of a binomial expression $(a + b)$ are:

$$(a + b)^2 = a^2 + 2ab + b^2; \quad (a + b)^3 = a^3 + 3a^2b + 3ab^2 + b^3;$$

$$(a + b)^n = a^n + na^{n-1}b + \frac{n(n - 1)}{1 \cdot 2} a^{n-2}b^2$$

$$+ \frac{n(n - 1)(n - 2)}{1 \cdot 2 \cdot 3} a^{n-3}b^3 + \ldots + nab^{n-1} + b^n.$$

If the exponent is n, then the expression on the right is a sum of $(n + 1)$ terms of the nth degree. The coefficients of the individual summands are given, for different values of n, by *Pascal's Triangle* in which each number is obtained as the sum of the two numbers to the right and left above it. For the nth power the kth binomial coefficient (see below) is

$$\frac{n(n - 1)(n - 2) \ldots (n - k + 1)}{1 \cdot 2 \cdot 3 \ldots k} = \binom{n}{k}.$$

Arithmetic mean

The mean (average = average value = arithmetic mean) x_0 of a set of n numbers is obtained by dividing the sum of the numbers by n.

The general expression is

$$x_0 = \frac{1}{n}(x_1 + x_2 + \ldots + x_n) = \frac{1}{n}\sum_{k=1}^{n} x_k;$$

Example: The A.M. of the six numbers 8, 9, 13, 8, 12, 10 is:

$$x_0 = \frac{8 + 9 + 13 + 8 + 12 + 10}{6} = \frac{60}{6} = 10.$$

In our example:

$$x_1 = 8 \quad x_3 = 13 \quad x_5 = 12 \quad n = 6$$
$$x_2 = 9 \quad x_4 = 8 \quad x_6 = 10 \quad k = 1, 2, \ldots, 6.$$

The APPARENT ERROR of a measurement is the difference between this measurement and an *estimate* of its true value, calculated as the A.M. of a number of measurements.

If x_1, x_2, x_3, . . ., x_n are n measurements of an unknown quantity X made under the same conditions, the most likely value of X is conventionally taken to be the A.M. of the measurements.

$$\bar{x} = \frac{x_1 + x_2 + \ldots + x_n}{n}.$$

The apparent errors v_i of the individual measurements are then:

$$v_1 = \bar{x} - x_1, v_2 = \bar{x} - x_2, \ldots, v_n = \bar{x} - x_n.$$

The apparent errors have the following properties:

(1) *The sum of the apparent error is zero*

$$v_1 + v_2 + \ldots + v_n = (\bar{x} - x_1) + (\bar{x} - x_2) + \ldots + (\bar{x} - x_n)$$
$$= n \cdot \bar{x} - (x_1 + x_2 + \ldots + x_n)$$
$$= n \cdot \frac{x_1 + x_2 + x_3 + \ldots + x_n}{n}$$
$$- (x_1 + x_2 + \ldots + x_n) = 0.$$

(2) *Minimal property of arithmetic mean.* The sum of squares of apparent errors associated with the arithmetic mean $\bar{x}$ as estimated value,

$$\sum_{i=1}^{n} v_i^2 = (\bar{x} - x_1)^2 + (\bar{x} - x_2)^2 + \ldots + (\bar{x} - x_n)^2,$$

is less than the corresponding expression with any other mean value x' taken as estimate.

We prove this as follows. If $v_1' = x' - x_1$, $v_2' = x' - x_2$, ..., $v_n' = x' - x_n$ are the apparent errors formed using the mean value $x' \neq \bar{x}$, then

$$\sum_{i=1}^{n} v_i'^2 = v_1'^2 + v_2'^2 + \ldots + v_n'^2$$

$$= (x' - x_1)^2 + (x' - x_2)^2 + \ldots + (x' - x_n)^2$$

$$= nx'^2 - 2x'(x_1 + x_2 + \ldots + x_n) + x_1^2 + x_2^2 + \ldots + x_n^2$$

$$= nx'^2 - 2x' \cdot n \cdot \bar{x} + x_1^2 + x_2^2 + \ldots + x_n^2,$$

while with the arithmetic mean $\bar{x} = \dfrac{x_1 + x_2 + \ldots + x_n}{n}$

$$\sum_{i=1}^{n} v_i^2 = v_1^2 + v_2^2 + \ldots + v_n^2 = (\bar{x} - x_1)^2 + \ldots + (\bar{x} + x_n)^2$$

$$= n\bar{x}^2 - 2\bar{x}(x_1 + x_2 + \ldots + x_n) + x_1^2 + x_2^2 + \ldots + x_n^2$$

$$= n\bar{x}^2 - 2n\bar{x}^2 + x_1^2 + x_2^2 + \ldots + x_n^2.$$

If we subtract the first expression from the second we have

$$n(x'^2 - 2x'\bar{x} + \bar{x}^2) = n(x' - \bar{x})^2 \geqslant 0,$$

that is, the first expression is positive if $x' \neq \bar{x}$ and zero if $x' = \bar{x}$, as required.

For a continuous distribution with distribution function $F(x)$ (see *Statistics*) the mean value $E(x)$ is calculated from the integral

$$E(x) = \int_{-\infty}^{+\infty} x \, dF(x).$$

Arithmetic sequence

An arithmetic sequence is a sequence of numbers in which two consecutive terms always have the same difference. If the difference is d, the terms of the sequence are:

$$a_1 = a, \quad a_2 = a + d, \quad a_3 = a + 2d, \quad a_4 = a + 3d, \ldots,$$
$$a_n = a + (n - 1)d.$$

Example: $a_1 = 2$, $a_2 = 4$, $a_3 = 6, \ldots$; $d = 2$.

$a_1 = a$ is called the initial term and a_n the general term of the sequence. In an arithmetic sequence each term is the *arithmetic mean* of its neighbours:

$$a_n = \tfrac{1}{2}(a_{n-1} + a_{n+1}).$$

If we form the differences of consecutive terms of the sequence we obtain a new sequence, the first *difference-sequence*, which comprises equal terms. We therefore call the original sequence an arithmetic sequence of the first order.

Example: Arithmetic sequence of first order: 3, 9, 15, 21, . . .

1st difference-sequence: 6, 6, 6, . . .

Arithmetic series

The (unevaluated) sum of terms of an arithmetic sequence is called an arithmetic series. If the series has only a finite number n of terms its sum S_n can be calculated:

$$S_n = a_1 + (a_1 + d) + \ldots + (a_1 + (n - 1)d)$$

and, reversing the order of the terms,

$$S_n = (a_1 + (n - 1)d) + (a_1 + (n - 2)d) + \ldots + a_1.$$

Adding pairs of corresponding terms, we have

$$2S_n = (a_1 + (a_1 + (n - 1)d)) + ((a_1 + d) + (a_1 + (n - 2)d))$$
$$+ \ldots + ((a_1 + (n - 1)d) + a_1)$$
$$= n(2a_1 + (n - 1)d),$$

that is,

$$S_n = \frac{n}{2}(2a_1 + (n - 1)d) = \frac{n}{2}(a_1 + a_n).$$

Example: To calculate the sum of the numbers from 1 to 100. We have $n = 100$, $a_1 = 1$, $d = 1$ and $a_n = 100$. Thus:

$$s_{100} = 50(1 + 100) = 5050.$$

Interpolation

If new terms are inserted between the terms of an arithmetic sequence in such a way that the extended sequence is also arithmetic, an interpolation is said to have been effected.

Example: 4 new terms are to be inserted between each pair of terms of the sequence 1, 4, 7, ... Let the new terms be b_1, b_2, b_3, b_4; b_5, b_6, b_7, b_8; b_9, ...

The new sequence is:

$$1, b_1, b_2, b_3, b_4, 4, b_5, b_6, b_7, b_8, 7, b_9, \ldots .$$

We must have:

$$4 = 1 + 5d, \text{ that is, } d = \tfrac{3}{5}.$$

Accordingly, the new sequence runs:

$$1, 1 \cdot 6, 2 \cdot 2, 2 \cdot 8, 3 \cdot 4, 4, 4 \cdot 6, 5 \cdot 2, 5 \cdot 8, 6 \cdot 4, 7, \ldots .$$

Arithmetic sequences and linear functions

The values of the linear function $y = a + dx$ form, for equidistant values of x, an arithmetic sequence of the first order. Conversely: the terms of an arithmetic sequence with initial term a and difference d are values of the linear function $y = a + dx$, the numbers 0, 1, 2, 3 . . . being substituted for x.

Example: $y = 2 + 3x$

$x =$	0	1	2	3	4	. . .
$y =$	2	5	8	11	14	. . .

Arithmetic sequences of higher order

A sequence of numbers whose kth difference is constant is called an arithmetic sequence of the kth order.

Example:

(i) *The sequence of square-numbers* is an arithmetic sequence of the second order.

Primary sequence: 1   4   9   16   25   36   49 . . .

1st difference-sequence: 3   5   7   9   11   13 . . .

2nd difference-sequence: 2   2   2   2   2 . . .

61

(ii) *A sequence of the fourth order:*

$$-1 \quad -3 \quad 9 \quad 71 \quad 243 \quad 609 \quad 1277 \ldots$$

1st difference-sequence:	$-2 \quad 12 \quad 62 \quad 172 \quad 366 \quad 668 \ldots$
2nd difference-sequence:	$14 \quad 50 \quad 110 \quad 194 \quad 302 \ldots$
3rd difference-sequence:	$36 \quad 60 \quad 84 \quad 108 \ldots$
4th difference-sequence:	$24 \quad 24 \quad 24 \ldots$

Arithmetic sequences and rational integral functions

The rational integral function

$$y = b_0 x^k + b_1 x^{k-1} + \ldots + b_{k-1} x + b_k$$

yields an arithmetic sequence of the kth order if equidistant numbers (*e.g.* the natural numbers $n = 1, 2, 3, 4, 5, \ldots$) are substituted for x. Conversely, the general term of an arithmetic sequence of the kth order can be represented by a rational integral function of the kth degree.

Example: The sequence

$$-1, -3, 9, 71, 243, 609, 1277, \ldots$$

is an arithmetic sequence of the 4th order. To determine the general term. This must be of the form:

$$a_n = b_0 n^4 + b_1 n^3 + b_2 n^2 + b_3 n + b_4$$

For $n = 1$, $a_1 = -1$, whence:

$$b_0 + \quad b_1 + \quad b_2 + \quad b_3 + b_4 = -1,$$

for $n = 2$, $a_2 = -3$, whence:

$$16b_0 + \quad 8b_1 + \quad 4b_2 + 2b_3 + b_4 = -3,$$

for $n = 3$, $a_3 = 9$, whence:

$$81b_0 + \quad 27b_1 + \quad 9b_2 + 3b_3 + b_4 = 9,$$

for $n = 4$, $a_4 = 71$, whence:

$$256b_0 + \quad 64b_1 + 16b_2 + 4b_3 + b_4 = 71,$$

for $n = 5$, $a_5 = 243$, whence:

$$625b_0 + 125b_1 + 25b_2 + 5b_3 + b_4 = 243.$$

We have 5 equations in 5 unknowns (viz. b_0, b_1, b_2, b_3 and b_4). This system of equations has solution

$$b_0 = 1, \ b_1 = -4, \ b_2 = 6, \ b_3 = -7 \text{ and } b_4 = 3.$$

The general term is therefore

$$a_n = n^4 - 4n^3 + 6n^2 - 7n + 3$$

and the sequence is obtained by substituting the numbers 1, 2, 3, 4, . . . for n in this expression.

If an arithmetic sequence of the kth order has a finite number of terms, these terms can be added to give their sum, which is an expression of the form:

$$s_n = b_0 n^{k+1} + b_1 n^k + b_2 n^{k-1} + \ldots + b_{k-1} n^2 + b_k n + b_{k+1}.$$

Example: What is the sum of the first n square numbers?

Sequence of squares:	1	4	9	16	25	36
Sum-sequence:	1	5	14	30	55	91

From this we calculate

1st difference-sequence:	4	9	16	25	36
2nd difference-sequence:	5	7	9	11	
3rd difference-sequence:	2	2	2		

To obtain the sum we put

$$s_n = b_0 n^3 + b_1 n^2 + b_2 n + b_3$$

For $n = 1$ we have: $s_1 = 1$, so that:

$$b_0 + \quad b_1 + \quad b_2 + b_3 = 1,$$

for $n = 2$ we have: $s_2 = 5$, so that:

$$8b_0 + \quad 4b_1 + 2b_2 + b_3 = 5,$$

for $n = 3$ we have: $s_3 = 14$, so that:

$$27b_0 + \quad 9b_1 + 3b_2 + b_3 = 14,$$

for $n = 4$ we have: $s_4 = 30$, so that:

$$64b_0 + 16b_1 + 4b_2 + b_3 = 30.$$

Solving these equations we obtain

$$b_0 = \frac{1}{3}, \ b_1 = \frac{1}{2}, \ b_2 = \frac{1}{6}, \ b_3 = 0.$$

The sum of the first n square numbers is therefore:

$$s_n = \frac{1}{3} n^3 + \frac{1}{2} n^2 + \frac{1}{6} n = \frac{n}{6} (n + 1)(2n + 1).$$

Arithmetic series

An arithmetic series is the (uncalculated) sum of the terms of an *arithmetic sequence* (see above).

Associative law

An associative law asserts the irrelevance of the order in which operations are performed:

$$a + (b + c) = (a + b) + c \qquad \text{for addition;}$$
$$a \cdot (b \cdot c) = (a \cdot b) \cdot c = a \cdot b \cdot c \quad \text{for multiplication.}$$

Asymptote

A straight line is called an asymptote of a curve, if the curve and the line approach indefinitely close together but never meet.

Examples: The function $y = \frac{1}{x}$ has the straight lines $x = 0$ (the y-axis) and $y = 0$ (the x-axis) as asymptotes.

The hyperbola $\frac{x^2}{a^2} - \frac{y^2}{b^2} = 1$ has asymptotes $y = + \frac{b}{a} x$ and $y = - \frac{b}{a} x.$

Axial symmetry

A plane figure is called *axially symmetric* if a straight line exists, the *axis of symmetry*, such that the figure can be superposed on itself by *rotation* about or *reflection* in the line. *E.g.* an equilateral triangle is axially symmetric with respect to each of its altitudes (Fig. 41).

Axioms

Propositions which are laid down without proof, in order to prove further propositions (theorems) from them. Euclid's geometry is the classic example of the number and variety of theorems that can be proved from a few simple axioms.

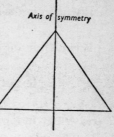

Axis of symmetry

Fig. 41

Binary system

The binary system is a number system using only two symbols, for example 0 and 1. The base of the binary system is 2. Every number can be uniquely represented as the sum of powers of 2, and so can be uniquely represented in the binary system, *e.g.*

$$58 = 32 + 16 + 8 + 2$$
$$= 1 \cdot 2^5 + 1 \cdot 2^4 + 1 \cdot 2^3 + 0 \cdot 2^2 + 1 \cdot 2^1 + 0 \cdot 2^0$$
$$= 111010 \text{ when written in binary notation.}$$

Conversely the binary number,

$$10011 = 1 \cdot 2^4 + 0 \cdot 2^3 + 0 \cdot 2^2 + 1 \cdot 2^1 + 1 \cdot 2^0$$
$$= 16 + 0 + 0 + 2 + 1 = 19 \text{ when written in decimal notation.}$$

Decimal Number	Binary Number
0	0
1	1
2	10
3	11
4	100
5	101
6	110
7	111
8	1000
9	1001
10	1010

Similarly we can transform decimal fractions into binary fractions, *e.g.*

$\frac{1}{2}$ is written in the binary system $1 \div 10 = 0{\cdot}1$;

$\frac{1}{3}$ is written in the binary system $1 \div 11 = 0{\cdot}0101\ldots$;

$\frac{1}{4}$ is written in the binary system $1 \div 100 = 0{\cdot}01$;

$\frac{1}{5}$ is written in the binary system $1 \div 101 = 0{\cdot}001,100,11\ldots$.

Every fraction which is a negative power of 2 is represented by a finite fraction in the binary system; all other fractions are represented by infinite periodic binary fractions. Calculation with binary numbers is widely used in electronic calculating machines (see *Calculating instruments and machines*).

Binomial coefficients (see *Binomial Theorem*)

Binomial coefficients are the coefficients appearing in the expansion of powers of binomials, and are written

$\binom{n}{k}$, read '*n* over *k*' (*n* and *k* positive integers).

For $n \geq k \geq 1$,

$$\binom{n}{k} = \frac{n(n-1)(n-2)\ldots(n-k+1)}{1 \cdot 2 \cdot 3 \ldots k}$$

(see also *Theory of combinations*), and in particular

$$\binom{n}{n} = 1.$$

For consistency we put

$$\binom{n}{0} = 1, \quad \binom{0}{0} = 1, \quad \text{and} \quad \binom{n}{k} = 0 \text{ if } k \text{ is a positive}$$

integer greater than *n*.

66

If for conciseness we put $1 . 2 . 3 \ldots n = n!$ for positive integers n (read n-factorial or factorial n), see *Factorial*, and $0! = 1$, then

1. $\binom{n}{k} = \binom{n}{n-k} = \left(\dfrac{n!}{(n-k)!k!}\right)$ for $n \geq k \geq 0$.

Further,

2. $\binom{n+1}{k+1} = \binom{n}{k} + \binom{n-1}{k} + \binom{n-2}{k} + \ldots + \binom{k}{k}$.

3. $\binom{n+1}{k} = \binom{n}{k} + \binom{n}{k-1}$.

4. If m is also a positive integer we have

$$\binom{m+n}{k} = \binom{m}{k}\binom{n}{0} + \binom{m}{k-1}\binom{n}{1} + \binom{m}{k-2}\binom{n}{2} + \ldots$$

$$+ \binom{m}{1}\binom{n}{k-1} + \binom{m}{0}\binom{n}{k}.$$

Binomial coefficients can also be formally calculated for negative integers and for fractional numbers (see *Binomial series*).

Binomial distribution

If the probability of a given event is p, and the probability of the event not occurring is $1 - p = q$, then the probability of the event occurring m times out of n trials is $\phi(m) = \binom{n}{m} p^m q^{n-m}$. The function $\phi(m)$ represents the binomial distribution for the given number n. In particular, if $p = q$ (as in tossing a coin to obtain 'heads'), the values occurring in the binomial distribution are proportional to the binomial coefficients (see art.).

Example: The probability of drawing a black ball from an urn containing b black and w white balls is $p = \dfrac{b}{b+w}$ and the probability of drawing a white ball is $q = \dfrac{w}{b+w}$. If this experiment is repeated m times, each time the ball being put back in the urn and the balls shuffled afresh, the probability of drawing a black ball x times in the m trials is $\phi(x) = \binom{m}{x} p^x q^{m-x}$.

The mean value of the binomial distribution is $mp = m(1 - q)$. The variance is $mpq = mp(1 - p)$.

When m is large, the binomial distribution approximates to the Gaussian normal distribution (see *Frequency curve*).

Binomial equations have the form $x^n - a = 0$ (see *Equations*).

Binomial expression (see *Polynomial*)

An expression with two terms and having the form $a + b$ or $a - b$ is called a binomial expression. For the powers $(a + b)^n$ and $(a - b)^n$, see *Binomial Theorem*.

Binomial formulae

The powers of the binomial expressions $(a + b)$ and $(a - b)$. These are

$$(a + b)^0 = 1,$$
$$(a + b)^1 = a + b,$$
$$(a + b)^2 = a^2 + 2ab + b^2$$
$$(a + b)^3 = a^3 + 3a^2b + 3ab^2 + b^3, \text{ etc.}$$
$$(a - b)^0 = 1,$$
$$(a - b)^1 = a - b,$$
$$(a - b)^2 = a^2 - 2ab + b^2,$$
$$(a - b)^3 = a^3 - 3a^2b + 3ab^2 - b^3, \text{ etc.}$$

In general

$$(a + b)^n = a^n + \binom{n}{1} a^{n-1}b + \binom{n}{2} a^{n-2}b^2 + \ldots$$
$$+ \binom{n}{n-1} ab^{n-1} + b^n,$$

$$(a - b)^n = a^n - \binom{n}{1} a^{n-1}b + \binom{n}{2} a^{n-2}b^2 - \ldots + (-1)^n b^n$$

(the last term, $(-1)^n b^n$ is positive if n is even and negative if n is odd; see *Binomial Theorem*).

Binomial series

The binomial series is as follows:

$$(1 + x)^\alpha = 1 + \binom{\alpha}{1} x + \binom{\alpha}{2} x^2 + \binom{\alpha}{3} x^3 + \ldots = \sum_{k=0}^{\infty} \binom{\alpha}{k} x^k.$$

The expansion holds for all fixed real α and for all x in the interval $-1 < x < +1$. The coefficients $\binom{\alpha}{k}$ are the *Binomial coefficients* (see above). They are calculated according to the formula:

$$\binom{\alpha}{k} = \frac{\alpha(\alpha - 1)(\alpha - 2) \ldots (\alpha - k + 1)}{k!}.$$

1. If α is a positive integer the series is identical with the *Binomial theorem* (see above) and holds for all x.

2. If α is a positive number the series also converges for $x = -1$ and we have

$$1 - \alpha + \binom{\alpha}{2} - \binom{\alpha}{3} + \binom{\alpha}{4} - \binom{\alpha}{5} + \ldots = 0.$$

3. If α is a number greater than -1 the series also converges for $x = +1$ and we have $1 + \alpha + \binom{\alpha}{2} + \binom{\alpha}{3} + \ldots = 2^\alpha$.

In all other cases the binomial series is divergent.

Binomial Theorem

The binomial theorem is as follows:

$$(a + b)^n = a^n + \binom{n}{1} a^{n-1}b + \binom{n}{2} a^{n-2}b^2 + \ldots$$

$$+ \binom{n}{n-1} ab^{n-1} + b^n.$$

Here the coefficients $\binom{n}{1}$, $\binom{n}{2}$, . . ., $\binom{n}{n-1}$ are the *Binomial*

69

coefficients (see above). These are calculated according to the formula:

$$\binom{n}{k} = \frac{n(n-1)(n-2)\ldots(n-k+1)}{1.2.3\ldots k} \quad \text{for } n \geqslant k \geqslant 1.$$

e.g. $\quad \binom{6}{5} = \frac{6.5.4.3.2}{1.2.3.4.5} = 6, \quad \binom{6}{3} = \frac{6.5.4}{1.2.3} = 20,$

$$\binom{6}{4} = \frac{6.5.4.3}{1.2.3.4} = 15, \quad \binom{6}{2} = \frac{6.5}{1.2} = 15,$$

$$\binom{6}{1} = \frac{6}{1} = 6,$$

so that

$$(a+b)^6 = a^6 + 6a^5b + 15a^4b^2 + 20a^3b^3 + 15a^2b^4 + 6ab^5 + b^6.$$

The binomial theorem is proved by induction. That is, it is shown to hold for $n = 1$, and further shown that *if* it holds for any given value of n *then* it also holds for the next higher value of n.

The binomial coefficients can be arranged in the form of *Pascal's triangle* (see below), in which each interior number is the sum of the nearest two numbers in the previous row. In the first row of the triangle are the coefficients of $(a+b)^0$, in the second those of $(a+b)^1$, in the third those of $(a+b)^2$, in the fourth of $(a+b)^3$ and so on.

Expansion:
(for further terms, see *Pascal's triangle*)

$$\binom{0}{0} \qquad\qquad 1$$

$$\binom{1}{0} \quad \binom{1}{1} \qquad\qquad 1 \quad 1$$

$$\binom{2}{0} \quad \binom{2}{1} \quad \binom{2}{2} \qquad 1 \quad 2 \quad 1$$

$$\binom{3}{0} \quad \binom{3}{1} \quad \binom{3}{2} \quad \binom{3}{3} \qquad 1 \quad 3 \quad 3 \quad 1$$

In the binomial theorem the exponent n is a positive integer. To calculate the powers $(a + b)^n$ when n is a negative integer or a fraction see *Binomial series*.

Biquadratic equation

Equation of the fourth degree, containing the unknown raised at most to the fourth power. Its normal form is:

$$x^4 + ax^3 + bx^2 + cx + d = 0$$

(see *Equations*).

Bisection of an angle

Describe a circle of arbitrary radius r about the vertex O, intersecting the arms in A and B, and then describe about A and B two equal circles intersecting in C; the line w joining C to O bisects the angle. The angle bisector w is the line of symmetry of the angle (see *Axial symmetry*, Fig. 42).

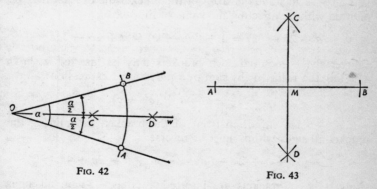

FIG. 42

FIG. 43

Bisection of a segment

Describe about the end points A and B of the segment circles of equal radii $r \left(r > \dfrac{\overline{AB}}{2} \right)$. The circles intersect in the points C and D. The straight line through C and D intersects the segment in its mid-point M (Fig. 43). It is the *perpendicular bisector* (see below) of the segment $\overline{AB}$. It is also the axis of symmetry of the points A and B. The points A and B lie symmetrically, as mirror images, about the line through C and D (see *Axial symmetry*).

Brackets

The bracket is a mathematical symbol which expresses a calculating instruction and means that the calculation symbolised within the brackets must be carried out before the others. Thus $a \cdot (b + c)$ signifies that b and c should be added and then multiplied by a whereas $a \cdot b + c$ means by convention that a and b should be multiplied, and the product added to c. The first expression given is therefore essentially a product, the second a sum.

Example: $3 \cdot (5 + 2) = 3 \cdot 7 = 21,$

$$3 \cdot 5 + 2 = 15 + 2 = 17.$$

The following rules are used in calculation with brackets:
If a '$+$'-sign stands in front of the bracket the bracket may be omitted without affecting the value of the sum:

$$(a + 2b - 3c) = a + (2b - 3c) = a + 2b - 3c.$$

Conversely, if required such brackets may be inserted without affecting the value of the sum of a polynomial expression:

$$a + 3b - c = a + (3b - c).$$

If a '$-$'-sign stands in front of the bracket, in omitting the bracket all signs within must be reversed:

$$-(3a - b + 2c - 4d) = -3a + b - 2c + 4d.$$

Conversely, if brackets are inserted after a '$-$'-sign, all signs enclosed must be reversed:

$$a + 2b - c - d + 3e = (a + 2b) - (c + d - 3e).$$

Association of terms of a sum in groups by means of brackets does not alter the value of the expression (*associative law*):

$$a + (b + c) = (a + b) + c; \quad 3 + 4 + 2 = 3 + 6 = 7 + 2.$$

Multiple brackets

If an expression contains a bracketed expression within which a further part stands in brackets, and we wish to eliminate the brackets, then the innermost pair of brackets must be dealt with first. In such circumstances different types of brackets are commonly used to avoid confusion; round brackets, (), are sometimes referred to as *parentheses* and curled brackets, {}, as *braces*, the term *bracket* itself then being reserved for the square type, [].

$$a - \{b + [2c - (d + 4e)]\} = a - \{b + [2c - d - 4e]\}$$
$$= a - \{b + 2c - d - 4e\}$$
$$= a - b - 2c + d + 4e.$$

Brianchon (1785–1871, Paris)

Brianchon's Theorem. In every hexagon circumscribing a circle or conic, the straight lines g, h and k joining opposite vertices meet in a single point Q, the 'Brianchon Point'. Here one vertex is said to be opposite to another if the two are separated by two vertices. Thus in Fig. 44 A and D, B and E, C and F, are pairs of opposite vertices.

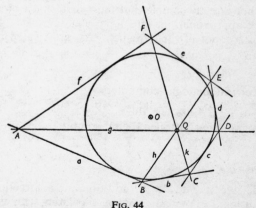

FIG. 44

Calculating instruments and machines

There exists a great variety of machines and instruments for carrying out numerical calculations. According to the principle on which their operation is based, we distinguish between *analogue* and *digital* devices. In an *analogical procedure* a particular physical process is taken to represent either another physical process or an abstract mathematical model. Numbers are represented by continuously varying quantities (*e.g.* lengths, angles of rotation, electrical tensions). A calculation is carried out by operating with these physical quantities, using known physical laws.

To the class of analogue devices belong the *slide-rule* (addition of segments) and the *planimeter* (pointer moving round a geometrical figure to register the figure's area). Analogue methods are particularly suited to the type of problem in which a rapid survey is required of the influence of a parameter or parameters in a given physical set-up.

Digital computers operate with discrete entities, counted, for example, by the movement of cog-wheels or by electrical current impulses. To this class belong hand-calculating machines, business machines, punched-card devices and programme-controlled digital computers. Using digital machines one can work with numbers to an arbitrary number of places, and consequently reach any desired degree of accuracy. Equations with infinitesimal terms are not directly soluble, but must first be transformed, by methods of approximation, into finite equations. The following devices, on account of their frequent use, are treated in greater detail below:

1. The slide-rule
2. Electrical analogue computers
3. Desk calculating-machines
4. Programme-controlled digital computers.

1. *The slide-rule*

The slide-rule operates by the addition and subtraction of line-segments, using the laws employed in calculating with logarithms.

The numbers from 1 to 10 are laid out on a logarithmic scale of length l, i.e. 1 is taken as the origin of the scale (since $\log 1 = 0$), 2 as $0.3010l$ ($\log_{10} 2 = 0.3010$), 3 as $0.4771l$ ($\log_{10} 3 = 0.4771$) and 10 as $1l$ ($\log_{10} 10 = 1$). Two identical logarithmic scales are constructed, so that they can slide along one another, one on the frame and the other on the lower edge of the *slide*.

Multiplication and division. Application of the rules that multiplication corresponds to the addition of logarithms and division to subtraction yields the appropriate procedures. Calculation is carried out with mantissae only, *i.e.* without regard to the characteristic. The position of the decimal point has to be determined mentally. Since 1 and 10 have equal mantissae, identical scales can be thought of as cyclically laid out to the right or to the left. Whether the slide is drawn out to the right or left depends on which side the result can be read off.

Example 1: 2·5 × 1·5

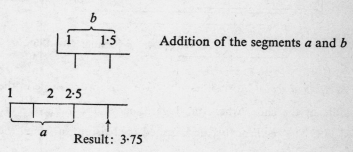

Addition of the segments *a* and *b*

Result: 3·75

Example 2: 3·5 × 5·6

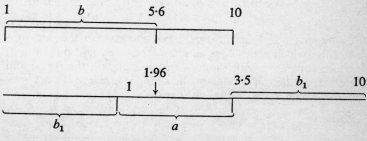

Result: 1·96 → 19·6

Addition of segments *a* and *b* using scale-cycle.

Example 3: 8 ÷ 2·4   Subtraction of the segments *a* and *b*.

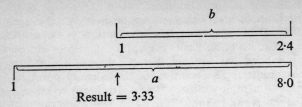

Result = 3·33

Example 4: 3 ÷ 5   Subtraction of the segments *a* and *b* using scale-cycle

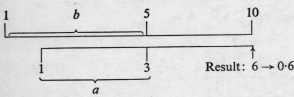

Result: 6 → 0·6

Reciprocal scale. Most slide-rules have a reciprocal scale in the middle of the slide, where the logarithms of the values $\frac{10}{x}$ are laid out. The reciprocal scale is suited to division, in which the form $a \times \frac{10}{b}$ is used instead of $a \div b$, the adjustments being chosen as for *examples 1* and *2*, and to multiplication in which $a \cdot \frac{10}{b}$ is used instead of $a \div b$, adjustments being chosen as for *examples 3* and *4*.

Upper scales. A slide rule usually possesses two further logarithmic scales which slide along one another, each laid out in half-measure compared with the lower scales, one on the frame and the other on the upper edge of the slide. The *square* is the corresponding magnitude on the lower scales.

Example 5: $4^2 = 4 \times 4$ 1   Result = 16

76

The *square-root* is obtained in a similar way. The given number is expressed in the form $x \times 10^n$ where x lies between 1 and 10 and n is an integer. The given number is taken on the left or right of the upper scale according as n is even or odd, the result being read off on the lower scale.

Example 6: $\sqrt{400}$ ($400 = 4 \times 10^2$, n is even)

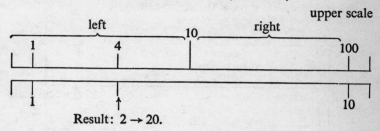

Result: 2 → 20.

Example 7: $\sqrt{0\cdot 6}$ ($0\cdot 6 = 6 \times 10^{-1}$; n is odd)

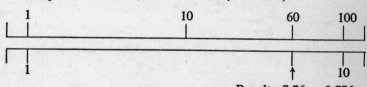

Result: 7·76 → 0·776

Multiplication and division can be carried out as in *examples 1–4* using the upper pair of scales; however, the lower scales are preferable for accuracy, there being twice as much room for interpolation and reading off.

Further scales. Various types of slide-rule have other scales, for example e^x, trigonometrical functions, log, $1 - x^2$, x^3, etc. These in general relate to the lower normal scale, results being obtained directly using the cursor (reading window).

Notes on procedure. We aim at the smallest possible loss of accuracy in carrying out a calculation.

(a) In order to place the decimal point correctly, each calculation must be roughly carried out mentally.

(b) For multiplication and division, employ the lower scales and the reciprocal scale only.

(c) For expressions of the form

$$\frac{a_1 \times a_2 \times \ldots \times a_m}{b_1 \times b_2 \times \ldots \times b_m},$$

alternately divide and multiply, so that the number of settings is kept as small as possible.

(d) For multiple products, use the reciprocal scale.

Example 8: $3 \cdot 5 \times 68 \times 0 \cdot 26$ (one setting)

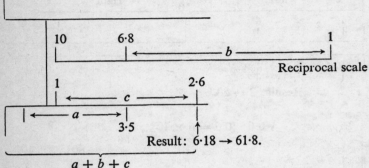

Special applications. To solve the quadratic equation

$$x^2 + Ax + B = 0,$$

the form $x + A + \dfrac{B}{x} = 0$ is used.

Example 9: $x - 5 \cdot 58 + \dfrac{7}{x} = 0$

The rule is set to give values a and $b = \dfrac{7}{a}$. We require $a + b = 5 \cdot 58$.

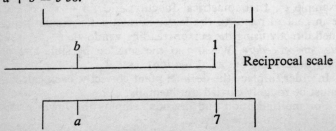

The solution is obtained by systematic testing with this setting.

a	$b = \dfrac{7}{a}$	$a + b$
1·75	4	5·75
2·0	3·5	5·5
1·9	3·68	5·58
x_1	x_2	

Some other types of equations with three terms can be solved by the same procedure, using square- or cube-scales.

Example 10: $x^4 - 6\cdot11x - 4 = 0$

(The equation $x^4 + ax^3 + c = 0$ can be put in this form by taking $x = \dfrac{1}{z}$.)

Divide by x to get $x^3 - 6\cdot11 - \dfrac{4}{x} = 0$, and set the scale as shown.

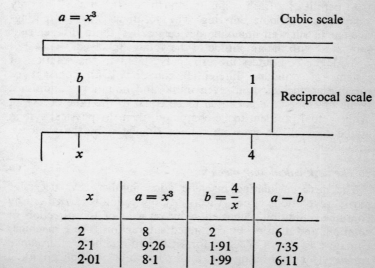

x	$a = x^3$	$b = \dfrac{4}{x}$	$a - b$
2	8	2	6
2·1	9·26	1·91	7·35
2·01	8·1	1·99	6·11

2. *Electrical analogue computers*

These computers contain a series of calculating elements. For each element the terminal voltage bears a specified relation to the input-voltages, the magnitudes used in a calculation being represented by electrical tensions. Present-day analogue computers have calculating-elements for:

- (a) Summation
- (b) Integration
- (c) Multiplication by a constant factor
- (d) Multiplication
- (e) Reversal of sign.

There are further devices available yielding approximations to special functions, as well as devices presenting the results of computations in graphical form (as curves).

The programming of a mathematical problem is effected by standardising the variables of the problem to bring them into correspondence with the machine-variables and by suitable juxtaposition of the machine-elements (either directly or by way of a switch-board). Initial conditions can be inserted or altered in accordance with the outcome of a particular computation, so as to permit of a fresh computation. In general, time is the only independent variable entering. The accuracy of a computing-element in such an analogue device reaches about 0·1 per cent compared with the amplitude of the voltage involved.

Analogue computers are especially suited to the solution of systems of ordinary differential equations with constant or variable coefficients and given initial and boundary conditions. If the machine-time is chosen to be equal to the time occurring in the actual problem to be computed, then the physical system at the root of the problem can be simulated by the analogue computer.

3. *The desk calculating machine*

The desk calculating machine adds numbers by successive partial revolutions of cog-wheels. Multiplication is carried out by continued addition, subtraction by reversal of the direction of rotation, and division by continued subtraction. These machines contain a *keyboard* or levers for setting up numbers, a *revolution register* (for registering the multiplier in a multiplication), a *product register* (recording the results of addition, multiplication and subtraction) and, in some cases, a storage register for the later use of intermediary results. The revolution and product registers can be moved sideways on a carriage to facilitate calculation with multi-digit multipliers. Further, most machines have a transfer-device which, for example in the case of the product $a . b . c$, does away with the need to set up by hand the intermediary result $a . b$ on the keyboard. The machine is operated either electrically or by hand. There are also in use machines provided with a tabulator for printing results, *e.g.* certain business-machines.

Procedures
for carrying out practical calculations

1st Step. Prior mathematical work.

(a) Determination of method of solution of the problem (the formulae involved are either evaluated directly or an appropriate method of approximation is employed, *e.g.* the Runge-Kutta procedure for integration).

(b) Determination of the degree of accuracy required (number of decimal places to be employed).

(c) Systematic control of errors.

On account of possible mistakes it is necessary to check the calculation, *e.g.* by sample testing. To avoid unnecessary waste of time in long calculations it is advisable to build in as many tests as possible (*e.g.* column-sums tests).

2nd Step. Design of computing-blank.

During the actual carrying out of a computation, the whole attention of the operator must be concentrated on the machine. Accordingly the calculating procedure is first divided into unit operations, and a computing-blank is prepared, giving, for each step, the requisite computing-instructions and the parameters involved. Actual intermediary and final results are later entered in this blank.

Example: Evaluation of $y = ax^2 + bx + c$

say, $$y = 2x^2 + 1 \cdot 5x + 3$$

Computing-blank with actual entries:

(1) x	(2) $x^2 = (1)^2$	(3) $2x^2 = 2(2)$	(4) $1{\cdot}5x = 1{\cdot}5(1)$	(5) $y = (3) + (4) + 3$
0·1	0·01	0·02	0·15	3·17
2	4	8	3	14·0

3rd Step. Actual computation.

In electrically-operated machines, keys are provided for individual operations.

In hand-operated machines, all operations are effected by turning a crank. Division is carried out by repeated subtraction, continued until a negative number appears in the product register. The operator proceeds to the next step only after a single addition has restored a positive value in the product-register. A calculation should be carried out independently by two persons, particularly if no built-in checks are possible.

Special calculations

1. *Square root, $a = \sqrt{A}$.* We commence with an approximate value for the root, a_0; a better approximation is given by the value $\dfrac{A/a_0 + a_0}{2}$ and further improved approximations are given by the iterative formula

$$a_{n+1} = \frac{\dfrac{A}{a_n} + a_n}{2}$$

(the number of valid places is roughly doubled at each step).

Example:
$$a = \sqrt{3}$$
$$a_0 = 2$$
$$a_1 = \frac{\dfrac{3}{2} + 2}{2} = 1{\cdot}75$$
$$a_2 = 1{\cdot}732143$$
$$a_3 = 1{\cdot}732051$$
$$a_4 = 1{\cdot}732054 \text{ etc.}$$

2. *Cube root,* $a = \sqrt[3]{A}$. Corresponding iterative procedure: first approximation, a_0;

$$a_{n+1} = \frac{\dfrac{A}{a_n^2} + 2a_n}{3}, \qquad n = 0, 1, 2, \ldots .$$

3. *Calculation with double accuracy.* The usual desk machine has a keyboard allowing for 10-digit numbers, a revolution-register with 10 places, and a product-register with 20 places, thus permitting calculation with 10-figure numbers. However, a higher degree of accuracy than this may well be required (*e.g.* for Fourier-analysis in radio-technology). To carry out a computation with 20-place accuracy, we proceed as follows.

We split up the numbers involved into their first and second ten places

$$A = (10^{10}A_1 + A_2)$$

$$B = (10^{10}B_1 + B_2)$$

We form $A \pm B$ by separate calculation of $A_1 \pm B_1$ and $A_2 \pm B_2$ with appropriate carrying-over; for the product we have

$$A \cdot B = (10^{10}A_1 + A_2)(10^{10}B_1 + B_2)$$

$$= (A_1 \times B_1)10^{20} + (A_1 \times B_2 + A_2 \times B_1)10^{10}.$$

(The term $A_2 \times B_2$ yields, after rounding-off, a quantity giving at most 1 in the last decimal place of the 20-place result, and thus can usually be neglected.)

$$\frac{A}{B} = \frac{A}{10^{10}B_1}\left(\frac{1}{1 + \dfrac{B_2}{10^{10}B_1}}\right)$$

$$= \frac{A}{10^{10}B_1}\left(1 - \frac{B_2}{10^{10}B_1}\right) \text{ approximately.}$$

Care must be taken that the first place of $B_1 \neq 0$, so that quadratic and higher terms can be neglected in the development of

$$\frac{1}{1 + B_2/10^{10}B_1} = \sum_{\nu=0}^{\infty}\left(-\frac{B_2}{10^{10}B_1}\right)^{\nu}.$$

4. *Programme-controlled digital computers*

Construction. In the modern electronic computer, the step-by-step control of the calculating procedure is taken over by the machine's control unit. The individual instructions of a programme, the data to be manipulated and intermediary results are held ready in a storage unit. An arithmetic unit carries out the fundamental arithmetic operations as for desk machines, and tests for sign or zero-value. Input and output devices regulate the reading-in of the programme and the initial data, and the presentation of results. Schematically the interrelationship of components is as follows (Fig. 45):

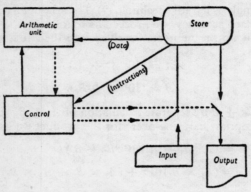

FIG. 45

The arithmetic unit. The arithmetic unit is essentially a device for addition. Subtraction can be carried out with complements, multiplication by continued addition, and division by continued subtraction. These four basic operations are usually wired into the computer, and can be called upon as occasion demands by single instructions. In addition, some computers have an instruction for extracting the square root. For problems in which the range of values occurring in intermediary and final results cannot be anticipated, most machines use the 'floating decimal-point' principle. With base 10, a number is expressed as the product of a power of ten and a number lying between 1 and 10. The so-called characteristic of the number is obtained by augmenting the exponent of the power of 10 by a fixed integer, *e.g.* 50. The number itself is represented by sign, characteristic and mantissa, *e.g.* the 8 leading places. Thus we have a kind of semi-logarithmic representation.

Examples:

1. $1 \cdot 234 = 1 \cdot 234 \times 10^0$ 50   1234000;

2. $-0 \cdot 001234 = -1 \cdot 234 \times 10^{-3}$ -47 1234000;

3. $12340 = 1 \cdot 234 \times 10^4$ 54   1234000.

The addition of this number 50 (the base of the characteristic) ensures that the characteristic is positive over a very wide range. In using a floating-decimal-point in place, *e.g.* of 10 fixed decimal places, a range of values covering 100 decimal places

$$(10^{-50} \leqslant x < 10^{50})$$

is obtained.

We speak of the *standard form* of a number if the first figure of the mantissa is non-zero, of unstandardised form otherwise. *E.g.* given 50 1234000 = 51 01234000, the left side is in standard form, the right unstandardised. The need for unstandardised calculations can arise in considering the accuracy of a result. It may well happen that in the subtraction of nearly equal numbers, the first places of the mantissa vanish, and subsequent standardisation may then suggest a spurious accuracy in the result.

The arithmetic unit can test whether a number in one of its registers has a particular sign (sign-testing), or is zero (zero-testing), or that a given number is in a given position. The result of the test is reported back to the control so that further progress of the calculation can be made dependent on this (logical) decision. The arithmetic unit provides for the carrying out of its operations in the following (or similar) registers:

(a) *Accumulator-register*, in which the result of an addition or subtraction appears.

(b) *Multiplicand-divisor register*—for registering multiplicands or divisors.

(c) *Multiplier-quotient register*—registering multipliers or quotients.

The basic individual element from which an arithmetic unit is constructed is a switch, *e.g.* a mechanical switch, electromagnetic relay, valve or transistor. Modern valve or transistor computers achieve 200,000 or more additions of 10-place decimal numbers in a second. Since the switches involved are in general capable of only two states, the internal use of the binary number-system is required (the digits 0 and 1 alone being effectively used).

The binary system uses the number 2 as base. Any number can be represented by the sum of powers of 2. For example:

$$13 = 8 + 4 + 1 = 1 \times 2^3 + 1 \times 2^2 + 1 \times 2^0 = 1101$$
$$156 = 128 + 16 + 8 + 4 = 1 \times 2^7 + 1 \times 2^4 + 1 \times 2^3$$
$$+ 1 \times 2^2 = 100\ 111\ 00$$

The use of other number codes can offer the advantage of automatic checks on accuracy, as against the drawback of smaller calculating speeds.

Storage unit. When called on, the store takes up information (data; intermediary results; in stored-programme computers, the programme as well). It contains a number of storage-locations each of which can be 'called on' by reference to a unique 'address'.

The following devices are used for storage: Small ferromagnetic rings (magnetic cores); drums, tapes or discs with magnetic coating (magnetic drum, magnetic tape, or magnetic-disc stores); paper tapes, or cards with fixed storage by means of punched holes (punched tape, punched cards); pins with changeable positions (mechanical storage); relays (electromagnetic storage). There exist two types of store, internal and external. An internal store is in loose connection only with the computer, *i.e.* it can be separated without affecting the functioning of the computer. An external store sometimes serves for the temporary storage of blocks of numbers from the internal store, parts of which can thus be released for information more urgently needed in the computation.

The different methods of storage are distinguished by the *access-times* they allow, *i.e.* the time taken from a call on the store to the transfer of the information required from the store to the arithmetic unit. Modern computers with magnetic-core storage have access-times as small as $(4 - 6) \times 10^{-6}$ secs. and storage-capacities of up to 32,000 10-place numbers. In assessing the efficiency of a computer, storage-capacity and access-time must be taken into account as well as actual calculating-speed.

Input and output. Input and output comprise the procedures of giving in and taking out data and instructions, and controlling exchanges with an internal store. Keyboards, punched tape, punched cards and magnetic tape are used as input media. The most rapid means of input is afforded by magnetic tape, and, using this, at the present time up to 40,000 alphabetical or numerical characters can be fed per second into a magnetic-core store; punched cards reach input speeds of about 500–600 characters per second; punched tape for normal rates of operation with photoelectric sensing, between 200 and 1,000 characters per sec. Output likewise can be effected by punched tape, punched cards and magnetic tape; and frequently also by means of tele-printer, tabulating machine, or automatic typewriter. Oscillo-graphs are also used for graphical representation of output functions (photography being used for permanent records). Output speeds are smaller than input speeds, except in the case of magnetic tape. In order that calculation should not be inter-rupted during input- and output-times, so-called buffer-stores are frequently introduced.

In large modern computers input and output are undertaken almost exclusively with magnetic tape. Separate devices are used for transferring information to and from the tapes, *e.g.* from or to punched cards. Choice of input and output units depends pre-dominantly on the nature of the problems being dealt with. Such problems fall into two broad groups.

(a) Commercial data-processing problems (characteristically involving the handling of large quantities of data, frequent input and output, little calculation).

(b) Scientific and technological problems (emphasis on actual computation; smaller quantities of data involved).

Thus for commercial problems, computers with rapid input and output units are preferable; on the other hand scientific problems usually call for rapid computation.

The control unit. The control unit controls the actual computa-tion. According to the way in which the control unit is given its individual instructions, we distinguish between plug-board, punched-tape, punched-card and stored-programme computers. Special computers with built-in programmes are also in use. In plug-board computers the sequence of calculating-steps is deter-mined by connecting wires on a plug-board. The small flexibility of such apparatus restricts its use to situations in which small numbers of standard calculations are continually repeated (for instance, in pay-roll calculation). The more conventional punched-card machines (tabulators, calculating punches) belong in this category.

For punched-tape and punched-card-controlled machines (not to be confused with machines in which programmes are inserted in an internal store by means of punched-cards or punched-tape) successive instructions are delivered directly from punched tape or from a sequence of punched-cards. This type of control is required if storage-capacity is small. On account of the large access-time, these machines are very slow. The control unit itself is similar in construction to those of stored-programme machines.

In stored-programme machines, the control unit contains an order-register which takes up orders and interprets them. An order contains an operation part, in which the type of operation to be performed (arithmetic operation, position-shift, sign-test or input or output operation) occurs, numerically coded. It also contains at least the store-address of the operand (for example, the address of the number to be added to the content of the accumulator, the address of the location in which a result from the accumulator will be stored, or the address of the storage location whose contents are to be abstracted). An instruction-counter contains the address of the next order. If the access-time to all storage-locations are equal, as with magnetic core stores, the computer operates in such a way that instructions are stored at successive locations and successively called upon. In this case an instruction does not need to contain the address of the subsequent instruction. On the other hand, in the case of machines with magnetic drum storage it may be possible for the programme to be so arranged that after carrying out an order, the storage-location of the next instruction is immediately accessible.

We distinguish according to the number of operands which are taken up in an order, between *single and multiple address systems*. For example, the Bell-System of the IBM 650 is a 3-address programme system; the instruction 3 A B C means: multiply (operation code = 3) the contents of the storage-location A by the contents of storage location B and bring the result into the storage location C. According to whether a subsequent address is or is not given, we further speak of (multiple- or single-, + 1) address-systems or (multiple- or single-, + 0) address systems. (The Bell-System is thus a (3 + 0) address-system; provision of an operand and a subsequent address comprises a (1 + 1) address-system.)

In the case of stored-programme machines, calculation with orders can be carried on exactly as with numbers. This makes possible the use of a section of a programme for different storage domains, provided the addresses are suitably transformed. This *address-calculus* is an essential part of the programming.

In practice problems frequently arise where similar operations are performed on data placed in consecutive storage-locations, *e.g.* matrix-operations. In such cases, so-called *index-registers* are useful. For 'indexed operations', the contents of an index register under consideration are taken from or added to the address part of the order. The control unit works with this *'effective address'*, the order itself being unchanged in its storage-location. Special testing and addition orders on the index register make it possible to establish how often the particular section of the programme is to be run through.

Example: Suppose we wish to evaluate the sum

$$y = \sum_{i=1}^{N} x_i = x_1 + x_2 + \ldots + x_N,$$

where $N = 30$, x_1 being entered in the storage-location 1000, x_2 in 1001, . . ., x_{30} in 1029.

The written programme for this runs as follows:

Order 1: Insert 30 in index register A.

Order 2: Clear the accumulator.

Order 3: Add the contents of the storage-location (1030—content of A) to the accumulator.

Order 4: Subtract 1 from the number in the index register and test whether result is zero or not. If $[A] \neq 0$ proceed to order 3, otherwise to 5. By this means order 3 is gone through exactly 30 times, corresponding to locations 1000 to 1029.

Order 5: Store accumulator (giving the required value y).

The functions of the control unit and storage unit ('memory') have suggested the often-used expression 'Electronic brain'.

Actually, of course, each step the computer takes will have been programmed by a human controller.

Programming. Before actual encoding, a problem must be thought through with a view to all possible contingencies. In order to formalise the method of solution clearly a *flow-diagram* is constructed (Fig. 46).

Example: Calculation of

$$y = f(x) = \begin{cases} x^2 + 2x + 1 & \text{for } x \leqslant 1 \\ x^2 + 3x & \text{for } x > 1 \end{cases}$$

(input by means of punched cards, printed output).

The following signs and symbols are sometimes used in writing out flow-diagrams (Fig. 47).

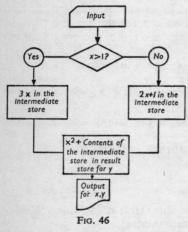

(a) Decision, switches, branchings;

(b) Direction of data flow, next step of procedure;

(c) Arithmetic operations, etc.;

(d) Programme-modifications;

(e) Error-stop;

(f) Punched-card (input or output);

(g) Magnetic tape (input or output);

(h) Printed output;

(i) Drum (external store), input or output.

Fɪɢ. 46

In order to translate a flow diagram into the machine code, it is first of all necessary to be familiar with the type of machine to be employed (type of calculating register, type of orders allowable, whether a one- or many-address machine). It is further necessary to provide a system of *storage-allocation, i.e.* it is necessary to know which quantity is lodged in which storage location.

In manual programming there exist great possibilities of error in both these procedures, but it is possible to let part of the

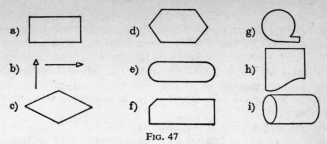

FIG. 47

programming work be done by the machine itself. Thus a series of aids to programming have come into existence.

1. *Sub-programmes*. Every calculating centre possesses a library of programmes comprising frequently occurring calculating routines. Subject to certain modifications (in the specification of parameters, type of entry, store-locations used) such sub-programmes can be incorporated into a programme as required. For routine problems (*e.g.* solution of systems of linear equations) the sub-programme becomes the working-programme, the actual programming required being confined to preparation of the input quantities.

2. *Auxiliary programmes*. For input or output, etc., there are different procedures dependent on the type of machine used. In order not to burden every programmer with these procedures, input and output programmes are available in programme-libraries for as many special cases as possible.

3. *Superprogrammes* (symbolic input programmes, etc.). For complete encoding in the machine code, and the allocation of storage there exist programmes which translate a *pseudo-code* (order-code not directly suited to the machine) into the machine code. There are two types of such superprogrammes, interpretative programmes and translation programmes.

(i) *Interpretative programmes*. The initial coding uses a pseudo-code. An additional input super-programme then translates the pseudo-programme order by order into machine steps which the machine then carries out.

Example: Bell-system for the IBM 650. The pseudo-order 3 A B C is first interpreted as a multiplication order for data occurring in the locations A and B, on the basis of which the sub-programme for this multiplication is run off and the result stored in the location C, whereupon the next pseudo-instruction is interpreted. In the above case the interpretative programme occupies 1,000 of the 2,000 storage locations. The number of orders needed is always essentially less for programmes using the 3-address code than for those using the one-address machine code. The possibility of calling on elementary mathematical functions by means of a single order is a further advantage of this system.

Disadvantages of interpretative systems are the reduction of calculating speeds occasioned by the necessary interpretation of each order, and the reduction in storage-locations occasioned by the storage of the super-programme.

Interpretative systems exist for many useful types of calculations which cannot be directly programmed (*e.g.* matrix operations, floating point operations for machines without built-in floating point).

(ii) *Translation programmes*. In translation programmes the machine programme is produced from a pseudo-programme by the machine itself. In an *entirely separate* operation, the super-programme translates the pseudo-instructions and provides the machine programme, ready for use, on punched cards or magnetic tape. Compared with the interpretative programme, this has the advantage that the translation time occurs once only. But of course this time, since the output time for the machine programme must be allowed for, is greater than the unit interpretation time, and so an interpretive system is preferable for a programme which is employed only a small number of times.

Different degrees of this *automatic programme-preparation* are possible with translation programmes.

(a) Symbolic Programming.

Instead of the usual numerical operation code, standard abbreviations (*e.g.* ADD for the addition operation) are introduced. For data- and instruction-stores no numerical addresses are given, symbols being substituted (*e.g.* X for the store containing a variable x). The direction of symbols to fixed storage-addresses is undertaken by the machine itself, as is the choice of subsequent addresses. For the rest, programming takes place analogously to the procedure using a machine code with exact references to special machine components. The advantage of symbolic programming lies primarily in the avoidance of errors in coding and of the duplication of entries in the store, and also in the full utilisation of the capacity of the computer, programmes being run through in the shortest possible time.

(b) Formula Programming.

(1) The programme language should depart as little as possible from the customary symbolic language of mathematics, and be independent of the machine, *i.e.* the programme-rules should be kept to a minimum. (ALGOL (algorithmic language) groups have been set up by several scientific societies for the development of such a general pseudo-programme language.)

(2) It should be possible to feed in a programme in a simple way (perhaps by direct input of a formula, or even by the spoken word). Such a method of programming requires for each type of computer a separately worked-out programme which in a preliminary run-through translates these formula-instructions into a proper machine-programme. The best-known development today in this field is the FORTRAN (formula-translator) system for the computers IBM 704, 709 and 7090. The programme for summing $x_1, \ldots, x_{30}$ appears in the following way in Fortran:

$$Y = 0$$
$$\text{DO } 1 \text{ I} = 1 \cdot 30$$
$$1 \ Y = Y + X(\text{I})$$

Each row corresponds to an alphanumerically punched punched-card. The value Y, which later is going to contain the sum, is first put equal to 0. In this example, the abbreviation DO corresponds to the mathematical symbol for summation; it means that this section of the programme is run through up to the order with numerical label 1 (this 1 can only occur once in the programme) from $I = 1$ to $I = 30$. The symbols all occur in the above form, and in such a way as to be intelligible to the machine. In the Fortran system floating-point arithmetic is used. The super-programme consists of about 25,000 orders, and the individual types of operation are translated by built-in sub-programmes. Every programmer is in a position to write such a programme after a very short time spent in getting acquainted with the procedures used (usually 2–3 days). The time spent in programming is as short as could be wished (about one-tenth or one-fifth of that required for a symbolic programme). A disadvantage is that the programmer has no direct insight into the machine programme. Improvements in the machine-programme are barely possible, and must therefore usually be carried out in the original pseudo-programme, involving a further translation-procedure.

Special procedures for automatic computers

1. *Commercial data-processing problems.* Here, collection and transfer of data, not calculation, are the primary problems. This requires simultaneous access to 2 or more files (a basic card-index and one or more moving files). Special large-volume stores (*e.g.* the RAMAC (random-access) store of IBM with storage for 6 million alphanumerical characters and more) make possible the storage of a basic file.

The simultaneous use of several files is possible if individual files are stored according to some common characteristic (*e.g.* personnel number). For punched cards, the sorting is carried out by special *sorting-machines*. In sorting, a batch of cards is divided according to one column into 10 compartments (one for each of the figures 0–9) and subsequently reunited so that cards in the 0-category come at the beginning and those in the 9-category at the end. If the key to the sorting extends to more than one column we repeat for the tens-column the procedure gone through already with the units-column using the sorted batch. This yields the sequence:

00, 01, 02, . . ., 09. 10, 11, . . ., 90, 91, . . ., 98, 99.

Continuing the process for further columns, any required sequence can be obtained.

In using magnetic tape, at least two input and two output tapes are required for sorting. Instead of being on punched cards, records appear on successive sections of magnetic tape. First of all the store is filled from an input tape. The record with the smallest reference-number is then sent out on an output tape and the empty location in the store filled from the input tape. The record with reference number next lowest (compared with that of the one just sent out) is transferred to the output tape and the procedure continued until no suitable record is available in the store. (This results in a so-called *string* on the first output tape.)

By the same means a further string is produced on the second output tape. In proceeding from one string to another it is important that a different output tape should be chosen: the third string, for example, must either be put on a third output tape or added to the contents of the first tape. In the second sorting-stage (or 'pass') the output tapes become input tapes. Before being fed into the store the two tapes must be compared to find out which contains the record with the lowest reference-number.

Example: (two locations in store used). Given input tape with reference numbers to be sorted: 123, 101, 088, 211, 100.

> *First pass*
> Store 1   :   123, 101
> Output tape 1:   101
> Input   :   088
> Output tape 1:   123
> Input   :   211
> Output tape 1:   211
> Input   :   100
> No number available in the store is now larger than 211.
> Output tape 2:   088, 100
>
> *Second pass*
> Input tape 1 :   101
> Input tape 2 :   088
> Output   :   088
> Input tape 2 :   100 ($<$ 123, which would be the next record on tape 1);
> Output   :   100
> Input tape 1 :   100 (contents of tape 2 have been exhausted);
> Output   .:   101
> Input tape 1 :   211
> Output   :   123, 211. Sorting complete.

On the average strings contain, after each pass with n store and locations used, at least n times as many records as before. The first input tape can be regarded as comprising strings of one record each, so that for A records the maximum number of passes required, r, is such that $n^{r-1} < A \leqslant n^r$.

For commercial applications are usually needed: straightforward storage organisation; capacity for massive output; and choice of input and output media so that output data can readily be used again, punched cards or magnetic tape being almost always most favourable on account of their suitability for sorting. The computer should be rapid, reliable and simple to programme and if possible should operate directly with decimal numbers.

2. *Technical and mathematical problems.* The algorithmic method of writing is especially suited for the programming.

Example: $\quad e^x = \sum_{i=0}^{\infty} \dfrac{x^i}{i!} = \sum_{i=0}^{\infty} t_i$

with $\quad\quad\quad t_0 = 1, t_n = \dfrac{x}{n} t_{n-1}.$

The formation of a new t_n and subsequent summing can take place over and over again using the same section of the programme up to the point where the next term (t_i) does not contribute to the prescribed accuracy.

In choosing between several procedures, preference will not always be given to the shortest; the expense of the programming must be taken into account. Iterative procedures are especially suitable. To conserve storage-space, functions should be calculated wherever possible and not abstracted from tables. (In place of series, approximations in which maximum departures from actual values are known should be used where available.) Fixed decimal point calculation should only be used if the range of all intermediary values can be anticipated before the calculation is carried out. Desirable qualities in the computer used are: rapid calculation-time (parallel-working machines are very suitable), large storage-capacity, and if at all possible, built-in floating-point, and index register.

The extent to which the calculation is proof against machine errors (failure of valves, etc.) must be determined for all problems. Independent calculation checks are in use; such methods use so-called *twin-control*, in which the same calculation is performed twice independently, any discrepancy in the result causing the computer to stop, so indicating that an error has occurred. In all other cases checks must be built into the programme.

Programme testing

After preparation of a computer programme (directly, or by translation of a pseudo-programme), it is necessary to test its accuracy. This is done by calculations of simple test-examples for all sections of the programme. The possibility of errors gives rise to a sequence of diagnostic or post-mortem programmes, which help in localising programming errors. Tests for errors must be effected with as small as possible expenditure of machine-time. Three types of diagnostic programme are in use:

1. Inspection of the whole or part of the contents of store and register (to check to what extent the intermediary results are correct; this is the least used method).

2. For a branching programme (in which the machine selects one of two or more possible subprogrammes): intercalation of an intermediary programme which prints out the conditions which lead to branching and the intermediary results.

3. Recording of each step of the computation with the associated register- and store-contents.

Procedure in working with programme-controlled automatic computers

1st step: Establishment of numerical procedure (degree of accuracy required, fixed or floating point, input and output arrangements, built-in checks for non-automatically checked computers).

2nd step: Construction of the flow-diagram.

3rd step: Choice of operations-code (pseudo-code or machine-code) and coding.

4th step: Computing of simple test-example (programme testing).

5th step: Carrying out of computation (automatic).

Calculus of observations

In the calculus of observations the aim is to obtain the most probable value for quantities of which varying observations have been taken. In general the adjustment of errors of observation follows the Method of Least Squares, introduced by Legendre and Gauss (see *Error*).

Catenary

The catenary is a transcendental curve which can be represented by the equation

$$y = \frac{a}{2}\left(e^{\frac{x}{a}} + e^{-\frac{x}{a}}\right),$$

where a is a constant and $e = 2 \cdot 718, \ldots$ is 'Euler's number' (see e), (Fig. 48).

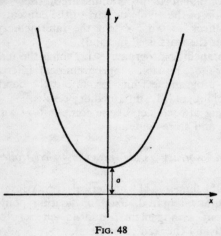

FIG. 48

In a suitably chosen coordinate system, an (ideal) chain suspended from two points, not immediately above one another, has the above equation..

Cavalier perspective

This is a method of mapping used in descriptive geometry. In cavalier perspective a three-dimensional rectangular coordinate system, together with the object to be mapped, is projected by general (oblique) parallel projection onto an image plane; the image plane is taken to be vertical and to lie parallel to the y, z-plane of the coordinate system which is to be transformed. The y-axis lies horizontally, the z-axis vertically. All figures which lie in a plane parallel to the image-plane are transformed congruently. The image of the positive x-axis is in general inclined at an angle of $45°$ to the negative y-axis. In the direction of the x-axis segments are in general shortened in the ratio $1:2$.

Cavalieri (1598–1647)

Cavalieri's theorem. If two solid bodies are of equal height and have bases of equal area, and if all plane sections parallel to the

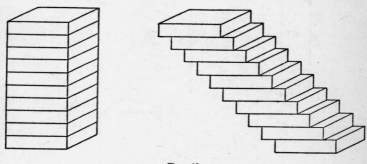

FIG. 49

bases and at the same distances from the corresponding bases are equal in area, then the two solids are equal in volume. Cavalieri's theorem cannot be proved by the methods of elementary mathematics, but the above figures make the proposition plausible (Fig. 49).

Central angle

An angle between two radii of a circle (see *Angle, Circle*).

Central perspective

Central perspective is used to provide a clear two-dimensional representation of a three-dimensional object. In central perspective the object to be depicted is projected from a fixed point P, the centre of projection (or point of sight), by rays of projection onto a projection, image or picture plane. The image is then seen as viewed from the point of sight P. In Fig. 50 a square prism is represented in central perspective. The prism stands perpendicular on a horizontal plane; it is viewed from the point of sight, P, and projected onto the image-plane. The point of sight is distant h above the horizontal plane, and d from the image-plane. If the perpendicular is dropped from the point of sight P onto the image

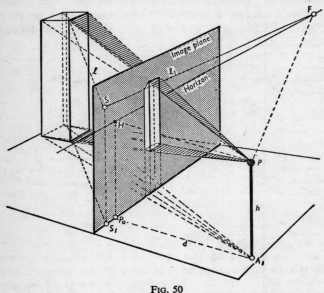

FIG. 50

plane we obtain the *principal point* H. $\overline{P_0 H} = h$ and $PH = d$. The line in the image plane through H parallel to the horizontal plane is called the *horizon*.

The fundamental laws of central perspective are suggested by the figure.

(1) The images of straight lines perpendicular to the horizontal plane are straight lines perpendicular to the horizon.

(2) The images of straight lines parallel to the horizon are straight lines parallel to the horizon.

(3) The image of a straight line l is also a straight line and passes through the point S in which l intersects the image plane. The projection ray through P parallel to l intersects the image

plane in the vanishing point F of l. The image line l_1 of l is determined by F and S. The vanishing points of horizontal straight lines lie on the horizon. Parallel lines have the same vanishing point. The vanishing point is the image of the 'infinitely distant point' of a line.

Central projection

From a point (the centre of the central projection) are constructed rays joining the point to some solid or plane figure (the projection rays); these intersect an image plane in the image points, or the image figure. The image figure is said to arise from central projection onto the image plane.

Central symmetry

Central symmetry in a plane is a special case of *axial symmetry* (see *Symmetry*). A figure is said to be centrally symmetric with respect to a point, the *centre of symmetry*, if when rotated through 180° about the centre of symmetry, the figure comes into coincidence with itself.

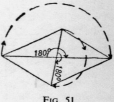

FIG. 51

Example: A parallelogram is centrally symmetric with respect to the point of intersection of its diagonals (Fig. 51).

Central symmetry in space

A solid figure is said to be centrally symmetric with respect to a point, the centre of symmetry, if on reflection in the point the figure coincides with itself (see *Reflexion in a point*).

Example: A cube is centrally symmetric with respect to the point of intersection of its space-diagonals.

Centre of similarity of two circles

The intersection of the common outer tangents of two circles is called the outer centre of similarity of the two circles; the intersection of the common inner tangents of two circles is called the inner centre of similarity of the two circles. The centres of similarity of two circles lie on the line of centres of the two circles and divide the line of centres harmonically (see *Circle*).

101

Centroid of a triangle

The centroid of a triangle is the point of intersection of the lines joining vertices to the mid-points of opposite sides. Each of these lines is divided by the centroid in the ratio 1:2 (see *Triangle*).

Ceva (1648–1734)

Ceva's theorem. Three concurrent lines passing through the three vertices of a triangle intersect the sides of the triangle in such a way that the product of three non-adjacent intercepts on the sides is equal to the product of the other three intercepts (Fig. 52): $\overline{AY}.\overline{BZ}.\overline{CX} = \overline{AZ}.\overline{BX}.\overline{CY}$.

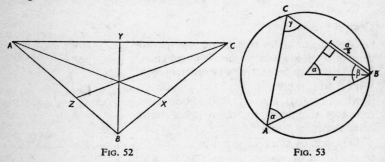

FIG. 52   FIG. 53

Chord

A chord of a circle is a straight line joining two points of the circle (see *Circle*).

Chord formula of plane trigonometry

If a, b and c are the sides of a triangle, α, β, γ its angles and r the radius of its circumcircle, then

$$a = 2r \sin \alpha, \ b = 2r \sin \beta \ \text{and} \ c = 2r \sin \gamma,$$

that is,
$$\frac{a}{\sin \alpha} = \frac{b}{\sin \beta} = \frac{c}{\sin \gamma}.$$

This formula rests on the fact that a peripheral angle is half as big as a central angle on the same chord (Fig. 53).

102

Chord theorem

If two straight lines intersect in the point *P* in the interior of a circle and cut the circle respectively in points *A* and *B*, and *C* and *D*, then

$$\overline{PA}:\overline{PC} = \overline{PD}:\overline{PB} \quad \text{(Fig. 54)}.$$

Circle

Definition and terminology (Fig. 55). The circle is the locus of points having the same distance from a fixed point *O*, called the *centre* of the circle. A line joining two points on the circle and passing through the centre of the circle, is called a *diameter* (*d*).

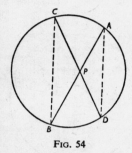

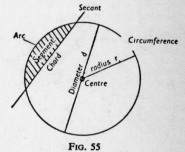

FIG. 54   FIG. 55

A line joining the centre to a point on the circle is called a *radius* (*r*) of the circle. We have *d* = 2*r*. The totality of points on the circle is called the *circumference* of the circle. The circumference bounds the area of the circle, which lies to the left if the circumference is described in the anti-clockwise sense. A point belongs to the interior of a circle if its distance from the centre of the circle is less than the radius *r*. A point lies outside the circle if its distance from the centre of the circle is greater than the radius *r*.

Circle and straight line

A circle and a straight line can have either two, one, or no points in common.

If the line has two points in common with the circle, it is called a *secant* of the circle. The segment of the line lying between the two points is called a *chord* of the circle (Fig. 55).

A secant divides the area of the circle and its circumference, each into two parts. The parts of the circumference are called *arcs*. The parts of the area are called *segments*.

A diameter of a circle is a line of symmetry of the circle. A diameter of a circle divides the circumference into two semi-circular arcs, and the area of the circle into two semicircles.

A straight line which has only one point in common with a circle, is called a *tangent* of the circle. The common point of circle and tangent is called the *point of contact* of the tangent (Fig. 56).

A tangent to a circle is perpendicular to the radius at the point of contact. There is a tangent through every point of the circumference of a circle.

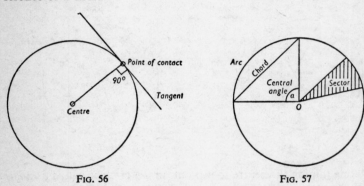

FIG. 56   FIG. 57

Angles in a circle

If we draw a chord of a circle, the end-points of the chord cut off an arc on the circle. If we construct the radii which pass through the end-points, we obtain an angle α which has the centre of the circle as vertex; we call this the *central angle* belonging to the chord and to the arc (Fig. 57). The part of the area of the circle lying within a central angle is called a *sector* of the circle. Equal chords in circles with equal radii have equal arcs corresponding to them, and subtend equal angles at the centre. If we draw through each end-point of a chord a line, such that the two lines intersect on the circumference of the circle, an angle is formed whose vertex lies on the circumference. This is called a *peripheral angle*.

Different peripheral angles can be constructed corresponding to the same chord. These may lie on different sides of the chord, with their vertices lying on opposite arcs. A peripheral angle is half the size of the central angle associated with the same chord. Peripheral angles whose vertices lie on opposite arcs, add up to 180° (Fig. 58; $\alpha + \beta = 180°$). All peripheral angles belonging to equal chords, and with vertex on one and the same side of the

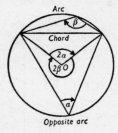

FIG. 58

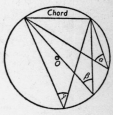

FIG. 59

chord, are equal (Fig. 59; $\alpha = \beta = \gamma = \ldots$). If we draw a tangent to the circle at one end-point of a chord, an angle is formed which does not contain the centre of the circle. This angle is equal to the peripheral angle associated with the chord.

Constructions

1. *Circle through three given points*. The perpendicular from the centre of a circle onto one of its chords bisects the chord, the arcs associated with the chord, and the central angle of the chord (Fig. 60).

Conversely the perpendicular bisector of a chord passes through the centre of the circle. It follows that, given three points A, B and C which are to lie on the circle, the centre of the circle must lie on the perpendicular bisectors of the segments $\overline{AB}$, $\overline{BC}$ and $\overline{CA}$. The centre of the circle is thus the point of intersection of any two of the three perpendicular bisectors. The circle is the circumcircle of the triangle (Fig. 61). The segments $\overline{AO}$, $\overline{BO}$ and $\overline{CO}$ are all radii of the circle.

2. *Circle of Thales*. The locus of right-angle vertices of right-angled triangles with the segment $\overline{AB}$ as hypotenuse is a circle,

called the Thales circle on $\overline{AB}$. To construct it we take the midpoint O of the segment as centre and half the length $\overline{AB}$ as radius (Fig. 62).

3. *To construct the locus of points at which the segment* $\overline{AB}$ *subtends a given angle* ε (Fig. 63). Draw at A the angle ε adjacent

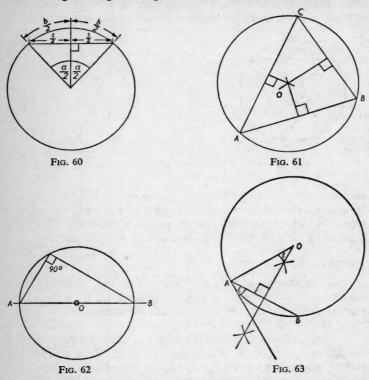

FIG. 60

FIG. 61

FIG. 62

FIG. 63

to the segment; next, erect at this point the perpendicular to the free arm of the angle ε and draw the perpendicular bisector of the given segment. The two lines intersect in a point O. Describe about O the circle with radius $\overline{OA}$. This circle is the required locus, for peripheral angles on it corresponding to the chord $\overline{AB}$ are equal to the angle ε between the tangent at A and the chord itself.

4. *Tangent to a point of a circle.* Draw the radius $\overline{OB}$ at the point B of the circle. Then the perpendicular to $\overline{OB}$ at B is the required tangent t (Fig. 64).

5. *Tangents from a point to a circle* (Fig. 65). Join the point P to the centre of the circle O, and construct the Thales circle on the segment $\overline{OP}$ (with mid-point H of $\overline{OP}$ centre of Thales circle, and $\overline{HP} = \overline{HO}$ = radius of Thales circle). The Thales circle cuts the given circle in two points B_1 and B_2. The straight lines through

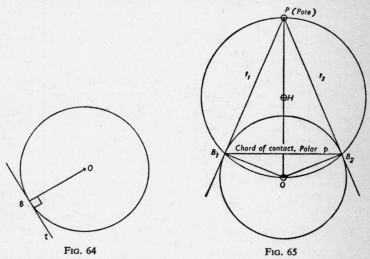

FIG. 64   FIG. 65

P and B_1 and through P and B_2 are the required tangents from P to the circle. B_1 and B_2 are the points of contact of the tangents. The segment joining B_1 and B_2 is called the chord of contact, and the straight line through B_1 and B_2 is the *polar* (or polar line) of the point P. The point P itself is called the *pole* of the line through B_1 and B_2. Pole and polar uniquely and reversibly determine one another (see *Polarity*). The correspondence 'pole–polar' is called a polarity. Finally, the tangent segments $\overline{PB_1}$ and $\overline{PB_2}$ are equal in length.

6. *Circle touching three given straight lines.* The centre of a circle which touches two given straight lines a and b lies on the bisector of the angle which the lines make with one another. If

a third line *c* is given, the centre of the circle also lies on the bisector of the angle between *a* and *c* (and on the bisector of the angle between *b* and *c*). By Fig. 66 we see that there are four centres O, O_a, O_b and O_c. These are the centres of the incircle of the triangle *ABC* and of the three excircles (escribed circles) of this triangle. The radii are obtained by dropping perpendiculars from the centres onto a side of the triangle *ABC*.

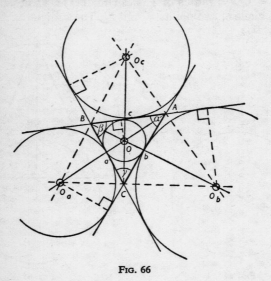

Fig. 66

Congruence and similarity of circles

All circles of equal radius are congruent. All circles are similar to one another.

Circle and triangle

For every triangle, a circle can be constructed which passes through the three vertices of the triangle; we call it the circumscribed circle of the triangle. For its construction, see the construction of a circle through three points. The circle which touches the three sides of a triangle and lies wholly within the triangle is called the *incircle* (inscribed circle) of the triangle.

108

The circles which lie wholly outside the triangle and which touch the three sides of the triangle or their extensions are called *excircles* (escribed circles) of the triangle. For the construction of these circles see the construction of circles which touch three straight lines (Fig. 66). The segments on the sides of the triangle measured up to the points of contact of the incircle and excircles can be calculated. They are (Fig. 67):

$$\overline{CE} = \overline{CF} = \frac{a+b+c}{2} = s,$$

$$\overline{CG} = \overline{CH} = \frac{a+b-c}{2} = s - c,$$

$$\overline{AG} = \overline{AK} = \frac{b+c-a}{2} = s - a,$$

$$\overline{BH} = \overline{BK} = \frac{a+c-b}{2} = s - b,$$

$$\overline{AD} = \overline{AE} = \frac{a+c-b}{2} = s - b,$$

$$\overline{BD} = \overline{BF} = \frac{b+c-a}{2} = s - a.$$

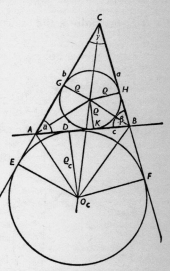

$$\overline{AD} + \overline{DB} = c$$

$$\overline{CE} = \overline{CF} = \frac{a+b+c}{2}$$

Fig. 67

The radius of the incircle can also be calculated (see *Half-angle theorems*). We have:

$$\tan \frac{\alpha}{2} = \frac{\rho}{s-a} = \sqrt{\frac{(s-b)(s-c)}{s(s-a)}},$$

and so

$$\rho = (s-a)\tan \frac{\alpha}{2} = \sqrt{\frac{(s-a)(s-b)(s-c)}{s}}.$$

Similarly,

$$\tan\frac{\beta}{2} = \frac{\rho}{s-b} = \sqrt{\frac{(s-a)(s-c)}{s(s-b)}}, \text{ and so } \rho = (s-b)\tan\frac{\beta}{2};$$

$$\tan\frac{\gamma}{2} = \frac{\rho}{s-c} = \sqrt{\frac{(s-a)(s-b)}{s(s-c)}}, \text{ and so } \rho = (s-c)\tan\frac{\gamma}{2}.$$

For the radii of the excircles we have:

$$\rho_a = s \cdot \tan\frac{\alpha}{2}, \ \rho_b = s \cdot \tan\frac{\beta}{2}, \ \rho_c = s \cdot \tan\frac{\gamma}{2};$$

or, equivalently,

$$\rho_a = \sqrt{\frac{s(s-b)(s-c)}{s-a}}, \quad \rho_b = \sqrt{\frac{s(s-a)(s-c)}{s-b}},$$

$$\rho_c = \sqrt{\frac{s(s-a)(s-b)}{s-c}}.$$

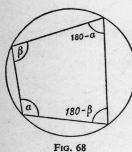

FIG. 68

The following relations hold between the radius ρ of the incircle, the three radii ρ_a, ρ_b, ρ_c, and the radius r of the circumscribed circle:

$$\frac{1}{\rho} = \frac{1}{\rho_a} + \frac{1}{\rho_b} + \frac{1}{\rho_c}; \ \rho_a + \rho_b + \rho_c - \rho = 4r;$$

$$s(s-a)(s-b)(s-c) = \rho \cdot \rho_a \cdot \rho_b \cdot \rho_c$$

(see also *Triangle*).

Circle and quadrilateral

In general the vertices of a quadrilateral do not lie on a circle. If they do, opposite angles add up to 180° (Fig. 68). The area of such a quadrilateral with sides a, b, c, d and semi-perimeter $s = \dfrac{a+b+c+d}{2}$ is

$$A = \sqrt{(s-a)(s-b)(s-c)(s-d)}.$$

110

The radius r of the circumscribed circle of this quadrilateral is

$$r = \frac{1}{4A} \cdot \sqrt{(ab + cd)(ac + bd)(ad + bc)}.$$

We have for the diagonals e and f: $ef = ac + bd$ (Ptolemy's Theorem, Fig. 69).

$$e = \sqrt{\frac{(ad + bc)(ac + bd)}{ab + cd}}, \quad f = \sqrt{\frac{(ab + cd)(ac + bd)}{ad + bc}}.$$

In general the sides of a quadrilateral are not tangent to a single circle. They are if, and only if, the sums of opposite sides are equal (Fig. 70).

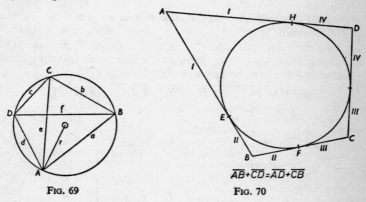

$$\overline{AB} + \overline{CD} = \overline{AD} + \overline{CB}$$

FIG. 69   FIG. 70

Circle and polygon

In general a polygon will possess neither an inscribed nor a circumscribed circle. However, the regular polygons (those whose sides and angles are equal) possess both (see *Regular polygons*).

Relations of proportionality in the circle

Secant theorem and chord theorem. Suppose two straight lines pass through a point P and intersect a circle in A, B and C, D respectively. Then the four segments $\overline{PA}$, $\overline{PB}$, $\overline{PC}$ and $\overline{PD}$ satisfy the proportionality relation $\overline{PA} : \overline{PC} = \overline{PB} : \overline{PD}$. This theorem is called the secant theorem (Fig. 71) if the point P lies outside the

111

circle and the chord theorem (Fig. 72) if P lies inside the circle. There is no corresponding theorem for when P lies on the circumference of the circle.

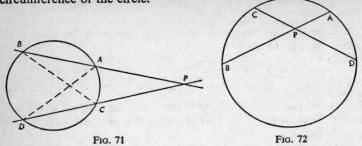

FIG. 71   FIG. 72

Tangent theorem. The tangent theorem is a special case of the secant theorem. If a secant and a tangent intersect in a point P the segment between P and the point of contact of the tangent is the geometric mean of the segments formed by P and the points of intersection of the secant with the circle.

$$(PB)^2 = \overline{PC}.\overline{PD}; \quad \overline{PC}:\overline{PB} = \overline{PB}:\overline{PD} \text{ (Fig. 73).}$$

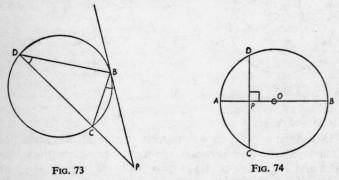

FIG. 73   FIG. 74

Special case of chord theorem. If we have two perpendicular chords one of which passes through the centre of the circle (*i.e.* is a diameter) then (Fig. 74) $\overline{PA}:\overline{PC} = \overline{PD}:\overline{PB}$. Since the segments on the chord which do not pass through the centre are equal ($\overline{PC} = \overline{PD}$), we have $\overline{PC}^2 = \overline{PA}.\overline{PB}$. That is, half the length of a chord is the geometric mean of the intercepts on the diameter perpendicular to it.

112

Construction of arithmetic, geometric, and harmonic means

Draw a diameter $\overline{AB}$ of the circle and perpendicular to it any chord $\overline{CD}$ cutting the diameter in the point P. Draw through P another chord $\overline{EF}$ such that $\overline{PE}$ is equal to the radius of the circle. Then we have for the segments $\overline{PA} = a$ and $\overline{PB} = b$:

PE is the arithmetic mean between a and b, $\overline{PE} = \dfrac{a+b}{2}$;

$\overline{PC} = \overline{PD}$ is the geometric mean between a and b, $\overline{PC} = ab$; since $\overline{PF}:\overline{PC} = \overline{PD}:\overline{PE}$ (Fig. 75),

$\overline{PF}$ is the harmonic mean between a and b, $\overline{PF} = \dfrac{2ab}{a+b}$.

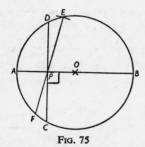

FIG. 75

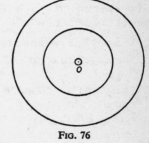

FIG. 76

Two circles, position relative to one another

If two circles have the same centre, they are called *concentric* (Fig. 76); if they have different centres they are called *eccentric*. The radii and the distance between the two centres together determine the position of the circles relative to one another.

Distance between centres	Relative position of circles	
$c = 0$	concentric position	
$c < r_1 - r_2$	no intersection, smaller within larger circle $\Big\}$	no common tangents
$c = r_1 - r_2$	contact from within	one common tangent
$r_1 + r_2 > c > r_1 - r_2$	two points of intersection	two common tangents
$c = r_1 + r_2$	contact from without	three common tangents
$c > r_1 + r_2$	no intersection	four common tangents

113

The common chord of two intersecting circles is perpendicular to the line of centres and is bisected by it (Fig. 77).

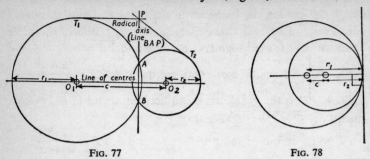

FIG. 77   FIG. 78

Common tangents of two circles. From the table on the previous page we can determine when two circles have common tangents:

I. There is one common tangent when $c = r_1 - r_2$ (Fig. 78).

II. There are two common tangents when $r_1 + r_2 > c > r_1 - r_2$ (Fig. 79).

III. There are three common tangents when $c = r_1 + r_2$ (Fig. 80).

IV. There are four common tangents when $c > r_1 + r_2$ (Fig. 81).

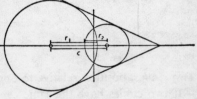

FIG. 79

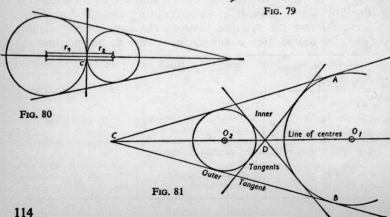

FIG. 80

FIG. 81

Construction of the common tangents.

(a) Outer tangents: Describe about the mid-point O_1 of the one circle an auxiliary circle with radius $r_1 - r_2$ ($= \overline{O_1C_1}$), and on the segment $\overline{O_1O_2}$ construct the Thales circle. These two circles intersect in the points C_1 and D_1. Draw those radii of the circle with centre O_1 and radius r_1 which pass through C_1 and D_1; let the end-points of these radii be A_1 and B_1 respectively. Then the lines through A_1 and B_1 parallel to $\overline{C_1O_2}$ and $\overline{D_1O_2}$ respectively are the required common outer tangents (Fig. 82).

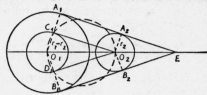

FIG. 82

(b) Inner tangents: Describe about O_1 an auxiliary circle with radius $r_1 + r_2$ ($= \overline{O_1C_1}$). By means of the Thales circle on the line of centres construct the tangents from O_2 to the auxiliary circle, $\overline{O_2C_1}$ and $\overline{O_2D_1}$. The required inner tangents pass through A_1 and B_1 parallel to $\overline{O_2C_1}$ and $\overline{O_2D_1}$ respectively (Fig. 83).

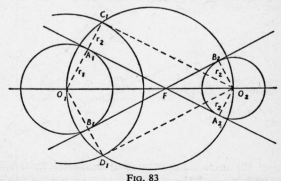

FIG. 83

Centre of similarity of two circles. The intersection of the two common inner tangents is called the inner centre of similarity of the two circles, and the intersection of the two common outer

115

tangents the outer centre of similarity. In Fig. 81 C is the outer and D the inner centre of similarity of the two circles. The centres of similarity of two circles lie on the line of centres of the circles, and they divide the line of centres harmonically in the ratio of the radii. In Fig. 82 E is the outer centre of similarity and we have $\overline{EO_2}:\overline{EO_1} = r_2:r_1$. In Fig. 83 we have for the inner centre of similarity (F) $\overline{FO_2}:\overline{FO_1} = r_2:r_1$.

Three circles

Centre of similarity of three circles. The three outer centres of similarity A_1, A_2 and A_3 of three circles lie on a straight line.

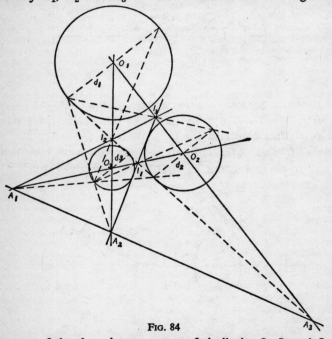

FIG. 84

Any two of the three inner centres of similarity I_1, I_2 and I_3 are collinear with one of the outer centres of similarity (Fig. 84; Theorem of *Monge*, 1746–1818, Paris). These straight lines are called the axes of similarity. The line through A_1, A_2, A_3 is called the outer axis of similarity, the others inner axes of similarity.

Construction: Draw the three lines of centres $\overline{O_1 O_2}$, $\overline{O_2 O_3}$ and $\overline{O_3 O_1}$. In the three circles construct parallel diameters d_1, d_2 and d_3. Join the end-points of the diameter d_1 and d_2, and let the joins intersect the line of centres through O_1 and O_2 in A_3 and I_3. Carry out the same construction with the diameters d_2 and d_3 and with the diameters d_3 and d_1, so obtaining in turn the centres of similarity A_1 and I_1, and A_2 and I_2.

Problem of Apollonius. The problem of constructing a circle to touch each of three given circles is called the problem of Apollonius.

1. If two circles with centres O_1 and O_2 and radii r_1 and r_2 are given together with a third circle, with centre O_3 and radius r_3, which touches the first two circles externally at the points B_1 and B_2 respectively, then the products of the segments from the external centre of similarity A to the points B_1 and B_2 is constant.

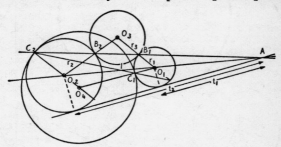

FIG. 85

That is, $\overline{AB_1} \cdot \overline{AB_2} = t_1 \cdot t_2$, where t_1 and t_2 are the distances from A to the points of contact of the common tangent of the first two circles (Fig. 85). In the same way, given a circle with centre O_4 touching the given circles at the points C_1 and C_2 (one externally, and enclosing the other), then if I is the inner centre of similarity of the given circles the product $\overline{IC_1} \cdot \overline{IC_2}$ is constant independent of the size of the third circle.

2. Construction of the tangent circle of three given circles. We construct first the radical centre P of the three circles (radical centre = intersection of the three radical axes of the three circles, see above), mark off their outer centres of similarity A_1, A_2, A_3 and the straight line through $A_1 A_2 A_3$ (outer axis of similarity), and determine the pole of this line with respect to each of the three

117

given circles; in this way we obtain the points Q_1, Q_2, Q_3. [Construction of the pole of a line with respect to a circle, see above: we join any point of the line to the centre of the circle, and draw the two tangents from the point of the circle. The chord joining the points of contact of the tangents intersects the line through the centre of the circle perpendicular to the straight line in the pole of the line.] If we join the points Q_1, Q_2, Q_3 to the radical centre P, the points of intersection of these lines with the given

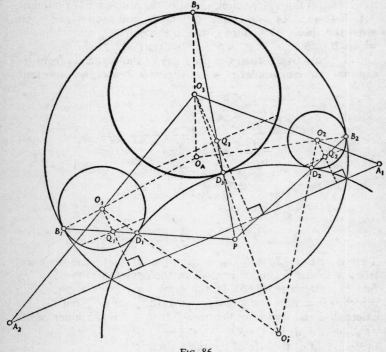

FIG. 86

circles are the six points of contact B_1, B_2, B_3 and D_1, D_2, D_3 (Fig. 86).

To construct the remaining tangent circles, we determine the pole of each of the three inner centres of similarity with respect to the three given circles, and join the poles to the radical axis;

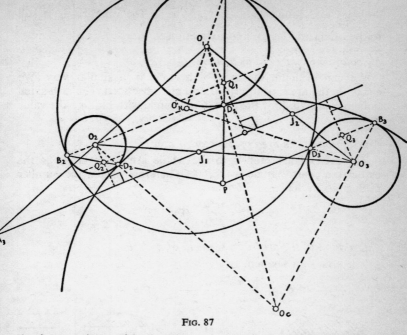

FIG. 87

the intersections with the given circles are the required points of contact (Fig. 87).

Calculation of the circumference of a circle

Archimedes of Syracuse (287–212 B.C.) calculated the circle's circumference by comparing the length of the circumference with the lengths of the perimeters of inscribed and circumscribed regular polygons each of *n* sides. As *n* increases, the sequence of perimeter lengths of inscribed polygons progressively increases while that of circumscribed polygons progressively decreases. The two sequences have a common limit, the circumference *C*. This is

$$C = 2r \times 3 \cdot 141 \ldots$$

The number $3 \cdot 141 \ldots$ which appears here is denoted by the Greek letter π.

Archimedes extended his calculation as far as polygons with 96 sides and found that $\frac{22}{7} < \pi < \frac{223}{71}$. The number $\frac{22}{7}$ is still today often used as an approximation to π.

Calculation of the area of a circle

We can evaluate the area of a circle in a similar way. We calculate the areas of inscribed and circumscribed regular *n*-sided polygons and find for the area A of a circle with radius r the value $A = \pi r^2$.

Calculation of the area of a sector of a circle

The area of a sector is to the whole area of a circle as the associated central angle is to 360°. Therefore, if α is the number of degrees in the central angle,

$$A_s = \frac{\pi r^2 \alpha}{360} \quad \text{(Fig. 88)}.$$

Calculation of the area of a segment of a circle

The area of a segment is:

$$S_g = \frac{\pi r^2 \alpha}{360} - \frac{s(r - h)}{2}. \quad \text{(Fig. 89)}.$$

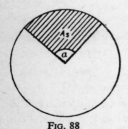

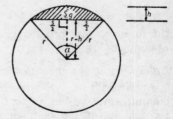

FIG. 88   FIG. 89

Circle, sector of

The area of a circle cut out by a central angle is called a sector of the circle. Let the circle have radius r and let the central angle be α degrees. Then the area A of the sector is

$$A = \frac{\pi r^2 \alpha}{360}.$$

Now the circumference of the circle has length $2\pi r$, and so the arc associated with the central angle α has length $l = \dfrac{2\pi r \alpha}{360}$. We therefore have

$$A = \frac{lr}{2}. \quad \text{(Fig. 90)}$$

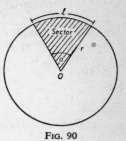

Circle, segment of

If a circle is divided into two parts by a *secant* the parts are called segments (see *Circle*).

FIG. 90

Circular cone

A cone whose base is a circle is called a circular cone (see *Cone*).

Circular measure

The size of an angle in circular measure is the arc-length which the angle cuts off on a unit circle ($R = 1$) having the vertex of the angle as centre. The size of a right angle in circular measure is $\dfrac{\pi}{2}$, or $\dfrac{\pi}{2}$ *radians*. The circular measure of an angle is related to the measure of the angle in degrees by the equation:

$$\alpha \text{ degrees} = 2\pi \frac{\alpha}{360} \text{ radians.}$$

Tables relating degrees to radians are useful in calculation (see *Table III*; also *Angle, Angular measurement*).

Circumcircle

A circle which passes through all the vertices of a polygon is called the circumcircle, or circumscribed circle, of the polygon. Not all polygons possess a circumcircle. The following are examples of those which do: all triangles, squares, rectangles, isosceles trapezia and *regular polygons* (see art.).

121

Circumference

The circumference of a circle, *i.e.* the complete circular arc, is of length $2\pi r$, where r is the radius of the circle (see *Circle*).

Circumference angle

The angle between two chords of a circle, whose point of intersection lies on the circumference of the circle (see *Angle, Circle*).

Cissoid

The Cissoid is the algebraic curve with the equation

$$y^2(a - x) = x^3,$$

or in polar coordinates

$$r = a \sin \phi \tan \phi.$$

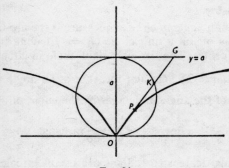

FIG. 91

Coefficient

The determinate (constant) numbers which occur as factors of literal terms in an algebraic sum are called coefficients, *e.g.* in $7a + \frac{3}{2} x = 4$, 7 and $\frac{3}{2}$ are coefficients.

The multiplication sign between coefficient and literal expression is commonly omitted.

Combinatory analysis

Combinatory analysis is the branch of mathematics concerned with the ways in which a given number of objects (elements) can be grouped together, or arranged together in groups. Every grouping of an arbitrary number n of objects is called an arrangement; it is called an arrangement without repetition if each element occurs once only.

(1) *Simple permutations.* The simple permutations of n elements comprise the possible orderings of the n elements taken all together. If the objects are all different, there are n candidates for the first position, $n - 1$ remaining candidates for the second, $n - 2$ for the third, and so on. The number of such permutations is therefore $n(n - 1)(n - 2) \ldots 2 . 1 = n!$

Example: three objects a, b, c can be ordered in $3! = 6$ ways.

$$abc, \; acb, \; bca, \; bac, \; cab, \; cba.$$

If of the n objects, p_1 are alike of one kind, p_2 alike of a second kind, etc., the number of different orderings possible is reduced to

$$\frac{n!}{p_1! p_2! \ldots p_k!}.$$

Example: three objects, a, a, $b (n = 3, p_1 = 2, p_2 = 1)$; number of distinguishable orderings $= \dfrac{3!}{2!1!} = 3$, viz.

$$aab, \; aba, \; baa.$$

(2) *General permutations.* Here we consider the number of arrangements (permutations) of n (different) objects taken r at a time with or without repetition.

(i) *Without repetition:* There are n candidates for the first position, $n - 1$ remaining candidates for the second, . . ., $n - r + 1$ for the rth. The number of permutations is therefore

$$n(n - 1)(n - 2) \ldots (n - r + 1) = \frac{n!}{(n - r)!}.$$

Example: three objects a, b, c; $r = 2$; $\dfrac{3!}{(3 - 2)!} = 6$; the permutations are:

$$ab, \; ac, \; bc, \; ba, \; ca, \; cb.$$

(ii) *With repetition:* There are n candidates for each of the r positions, and so the number of permutations is n^r.

Example: three objects a, b, c; $r = 2$; $3^2 = 9$; the permutations are:

$$aa, \ ab, \ ac, \ bb, \ bc, \ ba, \ cc, \ cb, \ ca.$$

(3) *Combinations.* The combinations of n elements taken r at a time are the ways in which r elements can be chosen from the total number, no regard being paid to the order of elements within the new group.

(i) *Without repetition:* Each element can occur only once. Each combination corresponds to $r!$ permutations, so that the number of possible combinations is $\dfrac{n!}{(n-r)!} \cdot \dfrac{1}{r!}$, that is, $\dbinom{n}{r}$.

Example: four elements, a, b, c, d. The combinations of pairs, elements being taken without repetition, are: ab, ac, ad, bc, bd, cd. The number is $\dbinom{n}{r} = \dbinom{4}{2} = \dfrac{4 \cdot 3 \cdot 2 \cdot 1}{1 \cdot 2 \cdot 1 \cdot 2} = 6$.

(ii) *With repetition:* Each element can be chosen more than once for a particular combination. The number of possible combinations is then $\dbinom{n+r-1}{r}$.

Example: $n = 4$, $r = 2$ a, b, c, d: aa ab ac ad

$$bb \ bc \ bd$$
$$cc \ cd$$
$$dd$$

$$\binom{4+2-1}{2} = \binom{5}{2} = \frac{5 \cdot 4}{1 \cdot 2} = 10.$$

Commensurables

Two or more quantities are called commensurable if they are both measurable or divisible by a third quantity.

Examples: 20 and 25 are commensurable, since they have the same divisor, 5.

The distances 20 yards and 12 yards are commensurable, since they can both be exactly measured by the distance 4 yards.

Quantities which cannot be measured or divided by a third quantity without remainder are called incommensurable, *e.g.* lines of length 1 and $\sqrt{2}$ are incommensurable.

Commutative Law

For addition: $a + b = b + a,$

that is, summands are interchangeable.

For multiplication: $a \cdot b = b \cdot a,$

that is, factors are interchangeable.

In both cases a and b may be either real or complex numbers.

Compasses

A pair of compasses serves primarily for the construction of circles. It comprises two arms, held together at one end by a joint, so that they can be separated and held apart at a constant angle. One arm has a pointed end, which can be stuck in the surface, the other ends in a pencil or drawing-pen and serves to describe the circle.

Complementary angles

Two angles which add up to 90° (one right angle) are said to be complementary. *E.g.* the angles adjacent to the hypotenuse of a right-angled triangle are complementary angles (Fig. 92), $\alpha + \beta = 90°$.

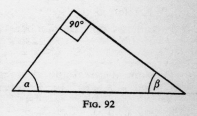

FIG. 92

Completion of a parallelogram (see also treatment of *Surfaces*)

Given a parallelogram *ABCD*, an arbitrary point *P* on a diagonal and lines $\overline{EG}$, $\overline{FH}$ through this point parallel to the sides of the parallelogram, then the two parallelograms *EBFP* and

125

HPGD (which are not cut by the diagonal) are equal in area (Fig. 93).

Proof: The triangles denoted by Roman numbers are pairwise congruent (I to II and III to IV), and so if they are taken away from the triangles *ABC* and *ACD*, which are likewise congruent, then the residual figures are equal in area.

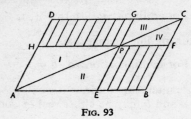

FIG. 93

Complex numbers

A complex number is the sum of a *real number* (see below) and the square root of a negative number.

Example: $5 + \sqrt{-3}$.

Since the square of a real number is always positive, the square roots of the negative real numbers form a new type of number, misleadingly referred to as *imaginary numbers*. Since every negative number is the product of (-1) and the corresponding positive number it suffices to introduce a new number for $\sqrt{-1}$, which is referred to as the imaginary unit, and is denoted by i; if b signifies a positive number, then $\sqrt{-b} = i \cdot \sqrt{+b}$, e.g.

$$\sqrt{-5} = i \cdot \sqrt{+5}.$$

The sum of a real and an imaginary number is referred to as a complex number.

Examples: $1 + i$, $5 + 3i$, $\frac{3}{5} + 7.83i$, $\sqrt{2} + i \cdot \sqrt{3}$.

The real summands are called the *real parts* of the complex numbers.

Example: In $1 + i$ the real part is 1; 1 is called the real unit.

The imaginary summands are called the *imaginary parts* of the complex parts. *E.g.* $1 + i$ has imaginary part i; i is called the imaginary unit. A complex number whose imaginary part is equal to zero is a real number. If the real part of a complex number is equal to zero, we have a (pure) imaginary number. A one-to-one correspondence can be established between the complex numbers and the points of a plane, the *Gaussian number plane*. The complex number $z = a + ib$ with real part a and imaginary part ib is associated with the point P with abscissa a and ordinate b in the Gaussian plane (see *number plane* and further below).

The *absolute value* $|z|$ of a complex number $z = a + ib$ is defined as

$$|z| = +\sqrt{a^2 + b^2} = r.$$

In the number plane, $|z|$ is equal to the distance r of the point $P(a, b)$ corresponding to z, from the origin of the number plane.

Example: $z = 1 + i$ has the absolute value

$$|z| = +\sqrt{1 + 1} = +\sqrt{2}$$

The angle ϕ, which the line joining the point $P(a, b)$ to the origin makes with the positive real axis, is called the *argument* of the complex number $z = a + ib$ (r and ϕ are the polar coordinates of the point $P(a, b)$ in the plane). As we see from Fig. 94, r and ϕ are related to the numbers a and b by the following equations:

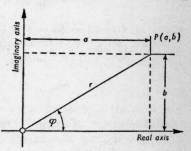

Fig. 94

$$a = r \cos \phi \qquad\qquad r = \sqrt{a^2 + b^2}$$

$$b = r \sin \phi \qquad\qquad \cos \phi = \frac{a}{r} = \frac{a}{\sqrt{a^2 + b^2}}$$

$$\sin \phi = \frac{b}{r} = \frac{b}{\sqrt{a^2 + b^2}}.$$

From this we get: $z = a + ib = r(\cos \phi + i \sin \phi)$. This is Euler's form of the complex number z. $(\cos \phi + i \sin \phi)$ is a complex number with absolute value 1. Complex numbers with absolute value 1 lie on the unit circle in the number plane, with centre at the origin.

Two complex numbers $z_1 = a + ib$ and $z_2 = a - ib$ which differ only in the sign of their imaginary parts are called *conjugate* with respect to one another. This is often written $z_2 = \overline{z_1}$ or $z_1 = \overline{z_2}$ (read: 'z-one equals z-two bar'), *e.g.*

$$z_1 = 1 + i, \; \overline{z_1} = 1 - i.$$

Two complex numbers are equal, if they coincide in respect of both their real and imaginary parts.

Addition of complex numbers. Two complex numbers $z_1 = a_1 + ib_1$ and $z_2 = a_2 + ib_2$ are added by adding the real and imaginary parts of each number; the result is the new complex number

$$z = z_1 + z_2 = (a_1 + ib_1) + (a_2 + ib_2) = a_1 + a_2 + i(b_1 + b_2);$$

e.g. $(5 + i) + (3 - 2i) = 8 - i$.

Subtraction of complex numbers. The subtraction of two complex numbers is carried through as in addition:

$$z_1 - z_2 = a_1 + ib_1 - (a_2 + ib_2) = a_1 - a_2 + i(b_1 - b_2);$$

e.g. $(7 - 3i) - (2 + 3i) = 5 - 6i$.

Multiplication of complex numbers. Two complex numbers $z_1 = a_1 + ib_1$ and $z_2 = a_2 + ib_2$ are multiplied by carrying out formal multiplication of the binomial expressions and putting $i^2 = -1$:

$$z_1 \cdot z_2 = (a_1 + ib_1)(a_2 + ib_2) = a_1a_2 - b_1b_2 + i(a_1b_2 + a_2b_1);$$

e.g. $(1 + i)(2 - i) = 2 + 1 + i(2 - 1) = 3 + i$.

Division of complex numbers. In the division of complex numbers, we write the quotient of the complex numbers to be divided as a fraction, and multiply numerator and denominator by a number (the conjugate of the denominator) which makes the denominator real. Thus, if $z_1 = a_1 + ib_1$, and $z_2 = a_2 + ib_2 \neq 0$:

$$z_1 \div z_2 = \frac{z_1}{z_2} = \frac{a_1 + ib_1}{a_2 + ib_2} = \frac{(a_1 + ib_1)(a_2 - ib_2)}{(a_2 + ib_2)(a_2 - ib_2)}$$

$$= \frac{a_1 a_2 + b_1 b_2 + i(a_2 b_1 - a_1 b_2)}{a_2^2 + b_2^2}$$

$$= \frac{a_1 a_2 + b_1 b_2}{a_2^2 + b_2^2} + i\,\frac{a_2 b_1 - a_1 b_2}{a_2^2 + b_2^2}.$$

E.g. $(5 - i) \div (1 + i) = \dfrac{5 - i}{1 + i} = \dfrac{(5 - i)(1 - i)}{(1 + i)(1 - i)}$

$$= \frac{5 - 1 - 5i - i}{1 + 1} = \frac{4}{2} - i\frac{6}{2} = 2 - 3i.$$

Multiplication of complex numbers in the Eulerian representation

If the numbers $z_1 = r_1(\cos \phi_1 + i \sin \phi_1)$ and $z_2 = r_2(\cos \phi_2 + i \sin \phi_2)$ are multiplied together we have:

$$z_1 . z_2 = r_1 (\cos \phi_1 + i \sin \phi_1) . r_2 (\cos \phi_2 + i \sin \phi_2)$$
$$= r_1 r_2 (\cos \phi_1 \cos \phi_2 - \sin \phi_1 \sin \phi_2 + i \cos \phi_1 \sin \phi_2$$
$$+ i \cos \phi_2 \sin \phi_1).$$

By the addition theorems for the cosine and sine functions, we have:

$$\cos \phi_1 \cos \phi_2 - \sin \phi_1 \sin \phi_2 = \cos (\phi_1 + \phi_2)$$
$$\sin \phi_1 \cos \phi_2 + \sin \phi_2 \cos \phi_1 = \sin (\phi_1 + \phi_2),$$

and so

$$z_1 . z_2 = r_1 r_2 [\cos (\phi_1 + \phi_2) + i \sin (\phi_1 + \phi_2)].$$

In words: in multiplying complex numbers together absolute values are multiplied and arguments added. *E.g.*

$$2 (\cos 60° + i \sin 60°) . 3 (\cos 45° + i \sin 45°)$$
$$= 6 [\cos (60° + 45°) + i \sin (60° + 45°)]$$
$$= 6 [\cos 105° + i \sin 105°] = 6 . [-\cos 75° + i \sin 75°].$$

In particular,

$$z^n = [r (\cos \phi + i \sin \phi)]^n = r^n (\cos \phi + i \sin \phi)^n$$
$$= r^n [\cos (n\phi) + i \sin (n\phi)].$$

In words: in raising a complex number z to the power n, the absolute value, r, of the number is raised to the power n, and the argument ϕ of z is multiplied by n.

Example:
$$z = 1 + i = \sqrt{2} \, . \, (\cos 45° + i \sin 45°)$$
$$z^2 = 2 \, (\cos 90° + i \sin 90°) = 2i$$
$$z^3 = 2\sqrt{2} \, (\cos 135° + i \, . \sin 135°)$$
$$= 2\sqrt{2} \, . \, (-\tfrac{1}{2}\sqrt{2} + i \, . \, \tfrac{1}{2}\sqrt{2})$$
$$= -2 + 2i.$$

Division of complex numbers in the Eulerian representation

Similarly, in dividing a complex number z_1 by a complex number z_2, the absolute value r_1 of z_1 is divided by the absolute value r_2 of z_2, and the argument ϕ_2 of z_2 is subtracted from the argument ϕ_1 of z_1.

$$z_1 \div z_2 = r_1 \, (\cos \phi_1 + i \sin \phi_1) \div r_2 \, (\cos \phi_2 + i \sin \phi_2)$$

$$= \frac{r_1}{r_2} \, [\cos (\phi_1 - \phi_2) + i \sin (\phi_1 - \phi_2)];$$

e.g. $2 \, (\cos 60° + i \sin 60°) \div 3 \, (\cos 45° + i \sin 45°)$

$$= \frac{2}{3} \, [\cos (60° - 45°) + i \sin (60° - 45°)]$$

$$= \frac{2}{3} \, (\cos 15° + i \sin 15°).$$

Roots of complex numbers

De Moivre's formula

$$(\cos \phi + i \sin \phi)^n = \cos (n\phi) + i \sin (n\phi)$$
$$(\cos \phi - i \sin \phi)^n = \cos (n\phi) - i \sin (n\phi)$$

may also be used for the extraction of roots of complex numbers.

The nth root of a complex number z is obtained by taking the nth root of the absolute value r and dividing the argument ϕ by n.

$$\sqrt[n]{z} = \sqrt[n]{r \, (\cos \phi + i \sin \phi)} = \sqrt[n]{r} \left(\cos \frac{\phi}{n} + i \sin \frac{\phi}{n} \right).$$

This is the so-called *principal value* of $\sqrt[n]{z}$. There are $(n-1)$ further values for $\sqrt[n]{z}$, for given any integer k we have

$$\cos(\phi + k \cdot 360°) = \cos\phi \text{ and } \sin(\phi + k \cdot 360°) = \sin\phi.$$

We therefore have

$$\sqrt[n]{z} = \sqrt[n]{r}\,[\cos(\phi + 2k\pi) + i\sin(\phi + 2k\pi)]$$

$$= \sqrt[n]{r}\left(\frac{\cos\phi + 2k\pi}{n} + i\sin\frac{\phi + 2k\pi}{n}\right).$$

For $k = 0$ this yields the principal value.
For $k = 1, 2, 3, \ldots, n-1$ we obtain different secondary values.

Example: the nth root of unity $z = \sqrt[n]{1}$. We have

$$1 = \cos 0 + i \sin 0,$$

and so: $z_0 = \cos 0 + i \sin 0,$

$$z_1 = \cos\frac{360°}{n} + i\sin\frac{360°}{n},$$

$$z_2 = \cos\frac{720°}{n} + i\sin\frac{720°}{n},$$

$$\ldots$$

$$z_{n-1} = \cos\frac{2(n-1)180°}{n} + i\sin\frac{2(n-1)180°}{n}.$$

For $n = 3$, $z_0 = \cos 0 + i\sin 0 = 1,$

$$z_1 = \cos\frac{360°}{3} + i\sin\frac{360°}{3} = \cos 120° + i\sin 120°$$

$$= -\frac{1}{2} + \frac{i}{2}\sqrt{3},$$

$$z_2 = \cos\frac{720°}{3} + i\sin\frac{720°}{3} = \cos 240° + i\sin 240°$$

$$= -\frac{1}{2} - \frac{i}{2}\sqrt{3}.$$

Geometrical interpretation of calculation with complex numbers

(1) *Conjugate complex numbers* (see above; Fig. 95). The numbers $z_1 = a + ib$ and $z_2 = a - ib$ are conjugate complex. In the number plane, these correspond to mirror-image points in the real axis. In the Eulerian representation

$$z_1 = r (\cos \phi + i \sin \phi)$$
$$z_2 = r (\cos \phi - i \sin \phi).$$

The mirror-image relationship is reflected in the difference between the arguments of the two conjugates. If the argument of z_1 is ϕ, that of z_2 is $-\phi$. (We have $\cos (-\phi) = \cos (+\phi)$ and $\sin (-\phi) = - \sin (+\phi)$, see *Trigonometry*.)

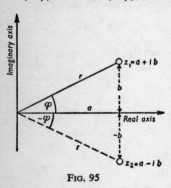

Fig. 95

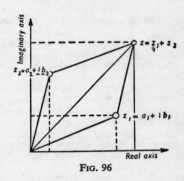

Fig. 96

(2) *Addition.* The sum is $z = z_1 + z_2 = a_1 + a_2 + i(b_1 + b_2)$ (see p. 128). The addition of complex numbers corresponds to the addition of *Vectors* (see below). We construct a parallelogram corresponding to the two numbers (Fig. 96), and the diagonal passing through the origin terminates in the point $z_1 + z_2$.

(3) *Multiplication.* The point of the number plane corresponding to the product $z_1 z_2$ has argument $\phi_1 + \phi_2$ and absolute value $r_1 . r_2$ (Fig. 97).

(4) *Division.* Similarly, the Eulerian representation provides the easiest geometric representation of division. The point in the number plane corresponding to the quotient $\frac{z_1}{z_2}$ has argument $\phi_1 - \phi_2$ and absolute value $\frac{r_1}{r_2}$ (Fig. 98).

132

(5) *Raising to a power* (Fig. 99). In the Eulerian representation the nth power of a complex number $z = r (\cos \phi + i \sin \phi)$ is $z^n = r^n [\cos (n\phi) + i \sin (n\phi)]$, which at once gives the geometric representation.

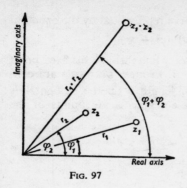

FIG. 97

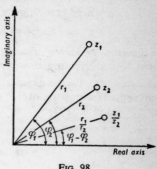

FIG. 98

(6) *Extraction of roots.* The principal value $\sqrt[n]{z}$ of the nth root of a complex number z has as argument the nth part, $\dfrac{\phi}{n}$, of the argument ϕ of z (Fig. 100) and as absolute value $\sqrt[n]{r}$ where r is the absolute value of z (see above).

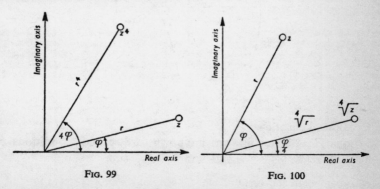

FIG. 99   FIG. 100

Concave

Concave = curved from the inside (see also *Convex*).

Concentric

Two circles with the same centre are said to be concentric with respect to one another.

Conchoid

The conchoid is an algebraic curve represented by the equation

$$x^2y^2 = (x - a)^2 (c^2 - x^2).$$

Construction: We draw an arbitrary line through the fixed point $A(a, 0)$, intersecting the y-axis in B. From B outwards are constructed the two segments $\overline{BP}$ of length c on the straight line chosen. The end-points P of these segments are points of the conchoid (Fig. 101).

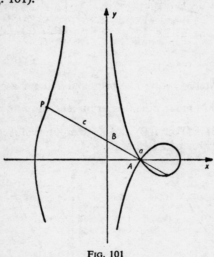

Fig. 101

Conditional equations

Equations involving an unknown are called conditional equations (see *Equations* (2)).

Cone

Given a closed curve c lying in a plane, and a point S not in the plane, then a cone is formed by joining S by a straight line to each point of the curve. These lines (elements or generators s) may be regarded as infinitely extended in both or one direction; or they may be thought of as line-segments lying between S and c. In the latter case, the surface of the cone is formed of the generators together with the plane area enclosed by c. S is the vertex of the cone.

The length of the perpendicular from the vertex onto the base is called the altitude H of the cone. The volume of a cone is $V = \dfrac{G \cdot H}{3}$, where G is the area of the base. In particular, for a circular cone in which c is a circle radius r, $V = \dfrac{\pi r^2 H}{3}$.

A *right* circular cone is a circular cone whose vertex lies directly above the centre of the circle which forms the cone's base. Other circular cones are called *oblique*. The axis of a cone is the line joining the vertex to the centre of the base (Fig. 102). A plane

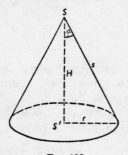

FIG. 102

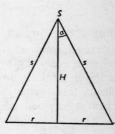

FIG. 103

through the axis of a right circular cone intersects the cone in an isosceles triangle whose principal altitude is the axis of the cone and whose base is a diameter of the circle forming the base of the cone.

A plane through the axis of an oblique circular cone is a non-isosceles triangle.

The angle between the axis and any generator of a right circular cone is called the angle, α, of the cone (Figs. 102, 103).

The lateral area of a right circular cone is (r = radius of base) $A = \pi r s$ (Fig. 104) and the total area of the surface is $\pi r(r + s)$.

By the theorem of Pythagoras, in a right circular cone with

altitude H, length of a generator s and radius of the base-circle r, we have: $s^2 = r^2 + H^2$.

If the lateral surface of a right circular cone is slit along a generator it can be developed (i.e. 'rolled out') onto a plane. There results a sector of a circle with radius s and central angle $\phi = \dfrac{360 \cdot r}{s}$ degrees (Fig. 105).

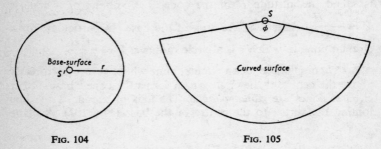

Base-surface

Curved surface

FIG. 104   FIG. 105

Conformal transformation

A transformation is called conformal (angle-preserving, isogonal) if every angle is transformed into another angle of equal size. Rigid motions are conformal transformations, as are the similarity transformations and the transformations of (complex) function theory defined by differentiable functions.

Congruent

Congruent figures are identical in shape and size. Two segments are called congruent (symbol: $\cong$) if one segment is obtained by marking off the other.

Two *angles* are called congruent, if one can be obtained from the other by marking off on an arbitrary line.

The following axiom links the congruence of segments with the congruence of angles. If, for two triangles $\triangle ABC$ and $\triangle A_1B_1C_1$, the congruences $\overline{AB} \cong \overline{A_1B_1}$, $\overline{AC} \cong \overline{A_1C_1}$ and $\angle BAC \cong \angle B_1A_1C_1$ hold, then the congruence $\angle ABC \cong \angle A_1B_1C_1$ is also satisfied. For other plane figures congruence can always be referred back to the congruence of segments and angles.

136

The notion of congruence is closely related to that of *rigid motion* (see below). The rigid motions are *transformations* (see below) in which the image of a figure is always a congruent figure. Translation, rotation and mirror-reflection are examples of rigid motions.

Conic sections

A plane figure which can be obtained as the intersection of a plane with a right circular cone is called a conic section. The following cases arise:

1. The plane passes through the vertex of the cone and cuts the axis at an angle greater than the angle, α, of the cone. This yields a single point of intersection.

2. The plane passes through the vertex of the cone and intersects the cone in two straight lines which themselves pass through the vertex of the cone (*i.e.* are generators).

3. The plane does not pass through the vertex of the cone but intersects the axis in some other point and at an angle of 90°. The plane figure formed by the intersection is a circle (Fig. 106).

4. The plane intersects the axis of the cone in such a way that the angle between the axis and the plane is less than 90° but greater than the angle, α, of the cone. The resulting figure is an ellipse (Fig. 107).

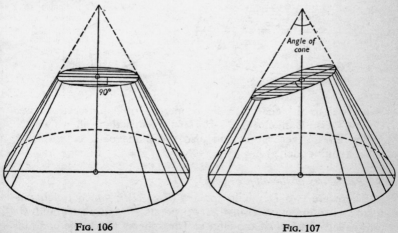

FIG. 106   FIG. 107

5. If the intersecting plane is parallel to a generator, the section is a parabola (Fig. 108). But if it touches the cone along a generator the generator itself is the figure resulting from the intersection.

6. If the intersecting plane cuts the axis of the cone at an angle which is less than the angle of the cone, the section is a hyperbola. In this case the plane also intersects the cone formed by extending the generators of the given cone beyond its vertex, and so the complete hyperbola has two branches (Fig. 109).

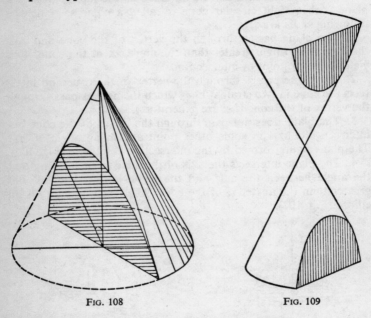

FIG. 108   FIG. 109

To derive the characteristic properties of conic sections we follow Pierre Dandelin (1794–1847) in constructing spheres which touch all the generators and also the plane of intersection E (Dandelin's spheres).

1. *Properties of the ellipse*

There are two Dandelin spheres (Fig. 110), which touch the plane of intersection E in the two points F_1 and F_2. F_1 and F_2 are called the foci of the ellipse. The spheres touch the cone in circles with diameters $\overline{B_1C_1}$ and $\overline{B_2C_2}$. If we construct the generator of the cone which passes through an arbitrary point P of the ellipse and join P to F_1 and F_2, then $\overline{PF_1} = \overline{PD_1}$ and $\overline{PF_2} = \overline{PD_2}$ (being tangents to the sphere); therefore:

$$\overline{PF_1} + \overline{PF_2} = \overline{PD_1} + \overline{PD_2} = \overline{D_1D_2} = \overline{C_1C_2} = \overline{B_1B_2}.$$

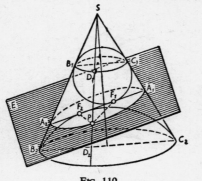

FIG. 110

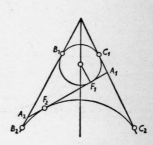

FIG. 111

The distance between the circles of contact of the two Dandelin spheres is, for a given plane of intersection, a constant quantity $\overline{C_1C_2}$, so the points F_1 and F_2 are fixed. Thus we have:

The ellipse is the locus of points for which the sum of the distances from two fixed points F_1 and F_2 is constant ($= \overline{C_1C_2}$).

From Fig. 111 we see that

$$\overline{A_2F_2} + \overline{F_2A_1} + \overline{A_2F_1} + \overline{F_1A_1} = \overline{B_2A_2} + \overline{A_1C_2} + \overline{A_2B_1} + \overline{A_1C_1}$$
$$= \overline{B_1B_2} + \overline{C_1C_2} = 2\overline{C_1C_2}$$
$$= 2\overline{B_1B_2} = 2\overline{A_1A_2}.$$

$\overline{A_1A_2}$ is called the major axis of the ellipse. The length of the major axis is denoted by $2a$.

The mid-point O of the major axis is called the centre of the ellipse. The distance $\overline{OF_1} = \overline{OF_2} = e$ is called the linear eccentricity of the ellipse. If the perpendicular $\overline{B_1B_2}$ to the major axis at O is constructed then $\overline{F_1B_1} + \overline{B_1F_2} = 2a$. Since $\overline{B_1F_2} = \overline{B_1F_1}$ then we must have $\overline{B_1F_1} = \overline{B_1F_2} = a$ (Fig. 112). From the right-angled triangle OB_1F_1 we obtain the relation $\overline{OB_1^2} = a^2 - e^2$. $\overline{B_1B_2}$ is called the minor axis and its length n is denoted by $2b$. We have: $a^2 = b^2 + e^2$. The segments $\overline{F_1P}$ and $\overline{F_2P}$ are called focal distances of the point P on the ellipse.

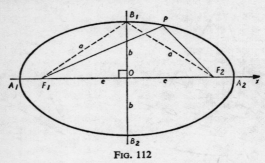

FIG. 112

Construction of the ellipse. For the point by point construction of an ellipse, the two foci F_1 and F_2 and the length of the major axis, $2a$, must be given.

(1) *Construction according to the definition of the ellipse.* The segment $2a$ is divided into two arbitrary parts, *e.g.* $\overline{A_1D}$ and $\overline{DA_2}$. We describe about the foci F_1 and F_2 circles with radii $\overline{A_1D}$ and $\overline{DA_2}$ respectively (Fig. 113). The points of intersection of the circles are points P_1, P_2, P_3, P_4 of the ellipse.

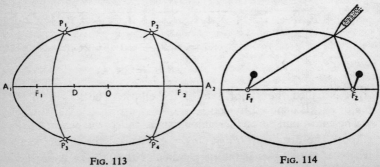

FIG. 113   FIG. 114

140

(2) *The string construction.* A loop of string of length $2a + 2e$ is laid round two fixed points whose distance apart is $2e$. The loop is stretched by a pencil. The pencil is moved in the stretched position and then describes an ellipse (Fig. 114). For further properties of the ellipse see *Curves of the second order.*

2. *Properties of the parabola*

The intersecting plane parallel to a generator will be perpendicular to the plane containing the generator and the axis of the cone. It yields only one Dandelin sphere; this touches the intersecting plane in the focus of the parabola, and the cone in a circle (diameter $\overline{BC}$) (Fig. 115).

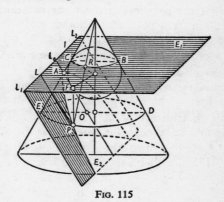

Fig. 115

Let the generator $\overline{SP}$ through the point P of the parabola touch the Dandelin sphere in R and let the plane of the circle of contact of the Dandelin sphere cut the intersecting plane E_2 in a straight line 1. Consider the plane through P perpendicular to the axis of the cone. This intersects the cone in a circle with the diameter $\overline{ED}$. Join P and F. Then we have:

$$\overline{PR} = \overline{PF} \qquad \text{(tangents to the sphere),}$$

$$\overline{PR} = \overline{CE} \qquad \text{(generators between two parallel circles)}$$

$$\overline{CE} = \overline{AE} + \overline{AC}.$$

The triangles AEO and L_0AC are isosceles, since their sides run

141

parallel to the generators of the cone which lie in the plane determined by D, S and E. It follows that

$$\overline{AE} = \overline{AO} \quad \text{and} \quad \overline{AC} = \overline{AL_0}.$$

Thus
$$\overline{CE} = \overline{AO} + \overline{AL_0} = \overline{OL_0}.$$

$\overline{OL_0}$ is perpendicular to the line 1. Draw through P in the plane E_2 $\overline{LP}$ parallel to $\overline{OL_0}$, so that $\overline{LP} = \overline{L_0O}$. Thus

$$\overline{PF} = \overline{PR} = \overline{CE} = \overline{L_0O} = \overline{LP}, \quad \overline{PF} = \overline{PL}.$$

It follows that the parabola is the locus of points which are equidistant from a fixed point P, the focus, and a fixed line, the directrix. The line through F perpendicular to the directrix is called the *axis* of the parabola. The line segment $\overline{FL_0}$ is referred to as the *parameter* of the parabola ($\overline{FL_0} = p$).

Construction of the parabola. For point by point construction, the focus and directrix must be given.

(a) Through an arbitrary point D of the axis of the parabola (Fig. 116) the line parallel to the directrix is drawn. The circle with radius $\overline{DL_0}$ is described about the focus F. The points of intersection of the circle with the parallel line are then points of the parabola, P_1 and P_2.

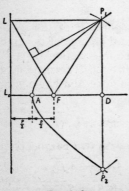

(b) If a point P_1 of the parabola is joined to F and the perpendicular $\overline{P_1L}$ from P_1 onto the directrix drawn, then the triangle $\overline{FLP_1}$ is isosceles. A point of the parabola is therefore obtained if we take the line parallel to the axis of the parabola through an arbitrary point L of the directrix and let this line intersect the perpendicular bisector of the segment $\overline{LF}$. For further properties of the parabola see *Curves of the second order*.

FIG. 116

3. *Properties of the hyperbola* (Fig. 117)

The plane of intersection cuts both the cone itself and its extension on the other side of the vertex. A Dandelin sphere can be inscribed in each part of cone. The spheres touch the plane of intersection in the points F_1 and F_2 and the cone in the circles with the radii $\overline{B_1C_1}$ and $\overline{B_2C_2}$.

A point P of the hyperbola is joined to F_1 and F_2 and the generators, $\overline{D_1S}$ and $\overline{D_2P}$, passing through it are drawn. We have

$$\overline{PF_1} = \overline{PD_1}. \; \overline{PF_2} = \overline{PD_2} \quad \text{(tangents to the sphere).}$$

Thus: $\quad \overline{PF_1} - \overline{PF_2} = \overline{PD_1} - \overline{PD_2} = \overline{D_1D_2} = \overline{C_1C_2}.$

For a fixed plane of intersection $\overline{C_1C_2}$ is a constant quantity which we denote by $2a$.

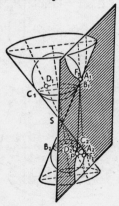

FIG. 117

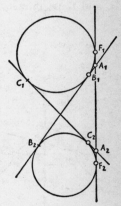

FIG. 118

The hyperbola is thus the locus of points the difference of whose distances from two fixed points, the foci, is constant and equal to $2a$. By Fig. 118 we have

$$2\overline{A_1A_2} = \overline{A_1F_2} - \overline{F_2A_2} + \overline{A_2F_1} - \overline{F_1A_1}$$
$$= \overline{A_1B_2} - \overline{A_2C_2} + \overline{A_2C_1} - \overline{B_1A_1}$$
$$= \overline{A_1B_2} - \overline{A_1B_1} + \overline{A_2C_1} - \overline{A_2C_2}$$
$$= \overline{B_1B_2} + \overline{C_1C_2} = 2\overline{B_1B_2} = 2\overline{C_1C_2}.$$

143

$\overline{A_1A_2}$ is called the major axis of the hyperbola and is of length $2a$. If the perpendicular at the mid-point O of the major axis is erected and its points of intersection with the circle, radii $\overline{F_1O} = e$, centres F_1 and F_2, denoted by B_1 and B_2, then $\overline{B_1B_2}$ is called the minor axis of the hyperbola, and its length is denoted by $2b$. e is called the linear eccentricity of the hyperbola. In the right-angled triangle $\overline{OB_1A_2}$ we have $e^2 = a^2 + b^2$.

The segments $\overline{P_1F_1}$ and $\overline{P_1F_2}$ are called focal distances of the point P_1 of the hyperbola (Fig. 119).

Construction of the hyperbola. For point by point construction of hyperbola the fixed points F_1 and F_2 and the segment $2a$ must be given. A point D is chosen on the major axis $\overline{A_1A_2}$ (Fig. 119). Circles are then described about F_1 and F_2 with radii $\overline{A_2D}$ and $\overline{A_1D}$, and these intersect in four points of the hyperbola P_1, P_2, P_3, P_4.

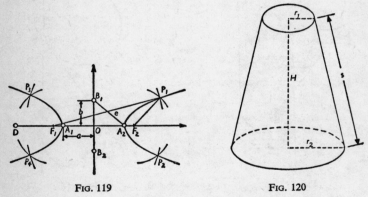

FIG. 119   FIG. 120

Conical frustrum

If a circular cone is cut off by a plane parallel to the base of the cone and at a height H above it the result is a conical frustrum (Fig. 120). Putting $H =$ height, $r_2 =$ radius of base-circle, $r_1 =$ radius of upper-circle, the volume of a frustrum is

$$V = \pi \frac{H}{3} (r_1^2 + r_1r_2 + r_2^2).$$

This holds for both right and oblique conical frustrums.

The lateral area of the surface of a right conical frustrum is:

$$S = \pi s(r_1 + r_2)$$

where s is the length of a generator.

Constant

A constant is an invariable quantity, as opposed to *variable* (see below).

Example: In the functional equation $y = ax + b$, a and b are constant numbers, x and y are variables.

Construction, geometrical

In a geometrical construction the required geometrical figure is constructed from known elements (points, segments, angles, straight lines, rays, planes, etc.), using only ruler and compass.

The following types of constructions are of special importance.

(1) *Fundamental geometrical constructions.* These are:

Measuring-off of a segment;
Construction of an angle on a line;
Bisection of a segment;
Erection of a perpendicular on a straight line;
Dropping of a perpendicular from a point onto a straight line;
Drawing of a parallel to a straight line through a given point;
Drawing of a parallel to a straight line at distance a;
Bisection of an angle.

These constructions are described under *Fundamental constructions.*

(2) *Triangle constructions* (see *Triangle*).
(3) *Quadrangle constructions* (see *Quadrangle*).
(4) *Conic section constructions* (see *Conic sections*).

CONTINUED FRACTIONS

Continued fractions

Every rational number $\frac{a}{b}$ (a, b positive integers) can be developed as a continued fraction. This development is obtained by means of the *Euclidean algorithm* (see below). If $a > b$ we put

$$a = q_0 \cdot b + r_1 \qquad 0 < r_1 < b$$

$$b = q_1 \cdot r_1 + r_2 \qquad 0 < r_2 < r_1$$

$$r_1 = q_2 \cdot r_2 + r_3 \qquad 0 < r_3 < r_2$$

$$r_2 = q_3 \cdot r_3 + r_4 \qquad 0 < r_4 < r_3$$

$$\cdots\cdots\cdots \qquad \cdots\cdots\cdots$$

$$r_{n-2} = q_{n-1} \cdot r_{n-1} + r_n \qquad 0 < r_n < r_{n-1}$$

$$r_{n-1} = \quad q_n \cdot r_n + 0.$$

These equations can be transformed as follows,

$$\frac{a}{b} = q_0 + \frac{r_1}{b} = q_0 + \frac{1}{\frac{b}{r_1}}; \qquad \frac{r_1}{r_2} = q_2 + \frac{r_3}{r_2} = q_2 + \frac{1}{\frac{r_2}{r_3}};$$

$$\frac{b}{r_1} = q_1 + \frac{r_2}{r_1} = q_1 + \frac{1}{\frac{r_1}{r_2}}; \qquad \frac{r_2}{r_3} = q_3 + \frac{r_4}{r_3} = q_3 + \frac{1}{\frac{r_3}{r_4}};$$

$$\cdots\cdots\cdots\cdots\cdots$$

$$\frac{r_{n-2}}{r_{n-2}} = q_{n-1} + \frac{r_n}{r_{n-1}} = q_{n-1} + \frac{1}{\frac{r_{n-1}}{r_n}};$$

$$\frac{r_{n-1}}{r_n} = q_n + 0 = q_n.$$

Substituting these fractions step-wise back into the first formula, we obtain the continued fraction for the rational number $\frac{a}{b}$,

$$\frac{a}{b} = q_0 + \cfrac{1}{q_1 + \cfrac{1}{q_2 + \cfrac{1}{q_3 + \cdots \cfrac{}{q_{n-1} + \cfrac{1}{q_n}}}}}.$$

Example: To develop $\frac{693}{147}$ as a continued fraction.

We have
$$693 = 4 \cdot 147 + 105$$
$$147 = 1 \cdot 105 + 42$$
$$105 = 2 \cdot 42 + 21$$
$$42 = 2 \cdot 21 + 0$$
so
$$\frac{693}{147} = 4 + \cfrac{1}{1 + \cfrac{1}{2 + \cfrac{1}{2}}}.$$

Irrational numbers can be developed as infinite continued fractions. Conversely every infinite continued fraction is an irrational number; *e.g.*

$$a = \cfrac{1}{1 + \cfrac{1}{1 + \cfrac{1}{1 + \cdots}}}$$

is the development of $a = \dfrac{\sqrt{5} - 1}{2}$ which is a solution of the equation $x = \dfrac{1}{1 + x}$.

Continuous transformation

All transformations which can be represented by continuous functions are called continuous transformations.

Convex (= curved from the outside)

A plane figure or solid is called convex if, given two points in its interior, the segment joining these points lies wholly within it.

147

Coordinate systems

Coordinate systems in a plane

Two straight lines in a plane, which intersect in a point O, the origin, can be used to establish the relative positions of points of the plane. These lines are then called coordinate axes. The first coordinate axis is called the abscissa-axis (x-axis) and the second the ordinate-axis (y-axis). The origin divides each coordinate axis into two parts. On each coordinate axis a unit-point is fixed, denoted by E and E'. The direction OE fixes the positive direction of the x-axis and that of OE' the positive direction of the y-axis; by convention OE' is to the left as one moves from O to E. If the coordinate axes intersect at right angles, the coordinate system is called rectangular. If the coordinate axes do not intersect at right angles the coordinate system is described as *oblique* (Fig. 121).

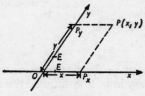

FIG. 121

To establish the position of a point P we draw the lines through P parallel to the axes, intersecting the axes in the points P_x and P_y (Fig. 121). The ratio $\dfrac{\overline{OP_x}}{\overline{OE}}$ is called the abscissa x of the point P, the ratio $\dfrac{\overline{OP_y}}{\overline{OE'}}$ the ordinate y of P. The numbers x and y are called the coordinates of P and we write $P(x, y)$ or $P(x; y)$. The abscissa of P is always written first.

If $\overline{OE}$ and $\overline{OE'}$ are each of unit distance the coordinates are simply the distances of the points P_x and P_y from the origin.

$\overline{OE}$ and $\overline{OE'}$ can however be different.

If the coordinate system is rectangular and $\overline{OE} = \overline{OE'} = 1$, we can also say that the distance of P from the y-axis is the abscissa x of P and the distance of P from the x-axis is the ordinate y of P.

148

Polar coordinates in a plane (Fig. 122). If in a plane we fix a point O (the origin, or pole), a line-segment $\overline{OE}$ with unit point E proceeding from O, and a positive direction of rotation, then the position of any point P in the plane can be identified by two numbers. The first number is the distance ρ of P from O, measured by means of the unit length $\overline{OE}$. The second number is the angle ϕ between the directions $\overline{OE}$ and $\overline{OP}$. This establishes a so-called system of polar coordinates. The segment $\overline{OE}$ is called the axis of the system, ρ the radius vector and ϕ the amplitude (or polar angle) of the point P.

Relationship between rectangular and polar coordinates of a point (Fig. 123). From the figure we obtain for the coordinates of a point P:

$$x = \rho \cos \phi \qquad \rho = \sqrt{x^2 + y^2}, \quad \frac{x}{y} = \tan \phi.$$
$$y = \rho \sin \phi$$

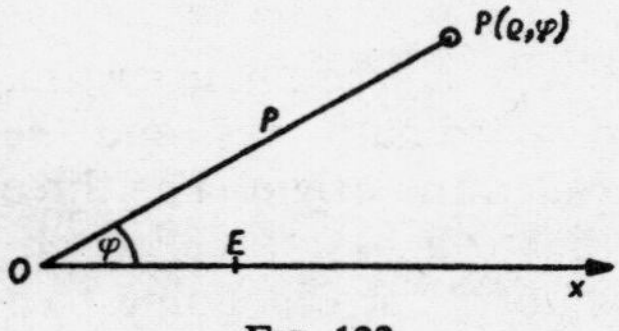

FIG. 122

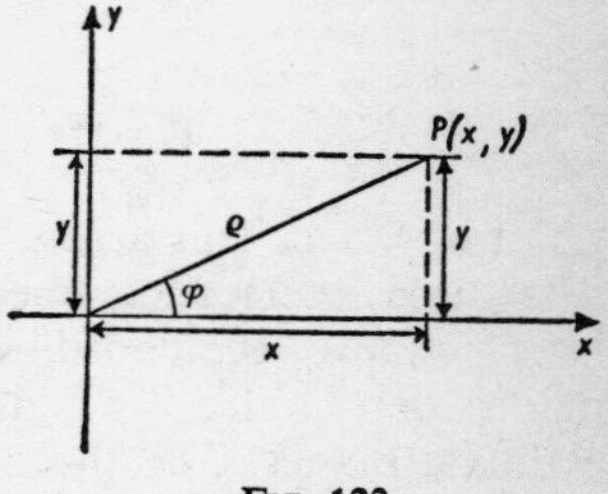

FIG. 123

Coordinate systems in space (Fig. 124)

Rectangular coordinate system in space. We can use three straight lines in space which intersect in a point O and are mutually perpendicular to establish the relative positions of points in space. If the perpendiculars are dropped from P onto the three coordinate axes, we obtain the points P_x, P_y and P_z. The distances of these three points from the origin, measured according to the unit lengths taken, are called the coordinates of the point P and are denoted by x, y and z. We write $P = P(x, y, z)$. The order of the three numbers is to be taken as fixed. To each point of space there corresponds a set of three numbers in a definite order, and with every set of three points in a fixed order is associated a

149

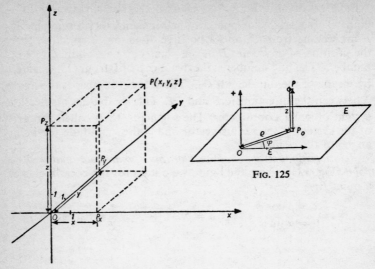

FIG. 124

FIG. 125

point of space. This arrangement establishes a coordinate system. The three intersecting lines are called coordinate axes, and the intersection of the coordinate axes is called the origin. The three planes determined by pairs of coordinate axes are called coordinate planes. The three ordered numbers corresponding to a point are called coordinates of the point.

Cylindrical coordinates (Fig. 125). Suppose we have in space a plane E, and in the plane a system of polar coordinates; and suppose further that we assign which part of space is to be regarded as positive with respect to the plane. A point of space can then be fixed by the polar coordinates ρ and ϕ of the point P_0 (the perpendicular projection of P onto the plane E) and the distance z of P from the plane E, taken to be positive if P lies on the positive side of E and negative if P lies on the negative side of E.

Spherical polar coordinates (Fig. 126). It is often useful to assign the position of a point in space in polar coordinates. For this purpose we use the radius vector, *i.e.* the distance r of the point from the origin, the 'longitude' λ, *i.e.* the angle which the projection of the radius vector onto the xy-plane makes with the x-axis and the 'latitude' ϕ, *i.e.* the angle which the radius vector makes with the xy-plane. We have then:

$$x = r \cos \phi \cos \lambda,$$
$$y = r \cos \phi \sin \lambda,$$
$$z = r \sin \phi.$$

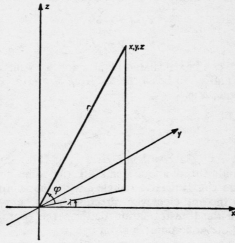

FIG. 126

Coordinate transformations

If two coordinate systems are given in a plane or in space, then a fixed point P has coordinates in respect of both systems. The transition from the coordinates of the point in the first system to the coordinates of the same point in the second system is called a coordinate transformation. A coordinate transformation can be represented by a system of equations between the co-ordinates of the point in the first and second systems.

Coordinate transformations representing the transition from one rectangular coordinate system to another rectangular system are of especial importance. These are referred to as orthogonal transformations (orthogonal = rectangular).

151

1. *Orthogonal transformations in a plane*

(1) *Translation of the coordinate axes.* Let the point P have coordinates x and y in the first coordinate system and x' and y' after the translation, and denote the origin of the first system by O and that of the second by O'. Let O' have coordinates c and d in the first coordinate system (Fig. 127). Then the transformation equations between the coordinates x and y of the point P and the coordinates x' and y' of the same point are:

$$x' = x - c,$$
$$y' = y - d,$$

and x' and y' can be calculated from x and y by means of these equations. x and y can be calculated from x' and y' by means of the inverse equations:

$$x = x' + c,$$
$$y = y' + d.$$

(2) *Rotation of the coordinate axes* (Fig. 128). Suppose the origins of both coordinate systems are the same and that the x-axis and the x'-axis make an angle δ with one another, δ being measured in the anti-clockwise direction from the x-axis to the x'-axis. Then the transformation between the coordinates x, y and x', y' of the same point is given by:

$$x' = x \cos \delta + y \sin \delta \qquad x = x' \cos \delta - y' \sin \delta$$
$$y' = -x \sin \delta + y \cos \delta \qquad \text{and} \qquad y = x' \sin \delta + y' \cos \delta.$$

(3) *The transformation*

$$x' = x$$
$$y' = -y$$

changes the direction of the y-axis (in three dimensions this transformation would signify a rotation of $180°$ about the x-axis); it also is an orthogonal transformation.

2. *Orthogonal transformations in space*

(1) *Translation of the coordinate axes.* Suppose the origin O' of the new system has coordinates (a, b, c) in the old system and

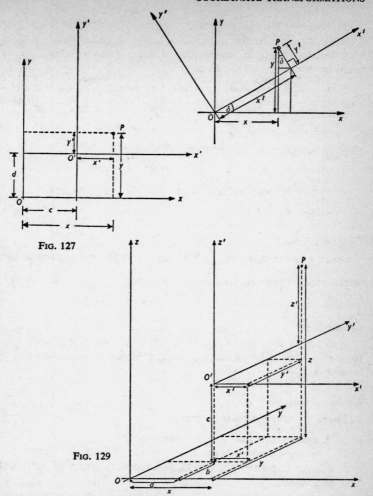

FIG. 127

FIG. 129

let the point P have coordinates (x, y, z) in the old system and (x', y', z') in the new. Then:

$$x' = x - a \quad \text{and} \quad x = x' + a$$
$$y' = y - b \qquad\qquad y = y' + b$$
$$z' = z - c \qquad\qquad z = z' + c \quad \text{(Fig. 129)}.$$

(2) *Rotation of the coordinate axes*. A transition from one rectangular coordinate system to another rectangular system with the same origin, but different orientation of the axes, is given by equations of the form:

$$x = a_1 x' + b_1 y' + c_1 z' \quad \text{and} \quad x' = a_1' x + b_1' y + c_1' z$$
$$y = a_2 x' + b_2 y' + c_2 z' \qquad\qquad y' = a_2' x + b_2' y + c_2' z$$
$$z = a_3 x' + b_3 y' + c_3 z' \qquad\qquad z' = a_3' x + b_3' y + c_3' z.$$

Here the coefficients satisfy the conditions:

$$\begin{vmatrix} a_1 & b_1 & c_1 \\ a_2 & b_2 & c_2 \\ a_3 & b_3 & c_3 \end{vmatrix} = \pm 1 \quad \text{and} \quad \begin{vmatrix} a_1' & b_1' & c_1' \\ a_2' & b_2' & c_2' \\ a_3' & b_3' & c_3' \end{vmatrix} = \pm 1.$$

Cosecant (cosec)

Cosec α is the ratio of the hypotenuse to the side opposite the angle α in a right-angled triangle, and equals $\dfrac{1}{\sin \alpha}$ (see *Trigonometry*).

Cosine (cos)

The cosine function $\cos \alpha$ is the ratio of the side adjacent to the angle α to the hypotenuse in a right-angled triangle (see *Trigonometry*).

Cosine theorem

There are three such theorems:

1. A theorem of plane trigonometry;
2. The angle cosine theorem of spherical trigonometry;
3. The cosine theorem for sides, also a theorem of spherical trigonometry.

1. The cosine theorem of plane trigonometry states that if a, b and c are the sides and α, β and γ the angles of a triangle then:

$$\text{I} \quad a^2 = b^2 + c^2 - 2bc \,.\, \cos \alpha$$
$$\text{II} \quad b^2 = c^2 + a^2 - 2ca \,.\, \cos \beta$$
$$\text{III} \quad c^2 = a^2 + b^2 - 2ab \,.\, \cos \gamma.$$

The cosine theorem of plane trigonometry can be used to solve a triangle if the three sides of the triangle are given or if two sides and the included angle are given.

2. The angle cosine theorem of spherical trigonometry states that if a, b and c are the sides and α, β and γ the angles of a spherical triangle then:

I $\cos \alpha = -\cos \beta \cos \gamma + \sin \beta \sin \gamma \cos a$

II $\cos \beta = -\cos \gamma \cos \alpha + \sin \gamma \sin \alpha \cos b$

III $\cos \gamma = -\cos \alpha \cos \beta + \sin \alpha \sin \beta \cos c.$

3. The cosine theorem for the sides of the same triangle runs:

I $\cos a = \cos b \cos c + \sin b \sin c \cos \alpha$

II $\cos b = \cos c \cos a + \sin c \sin a \cos \beta$

III $\cos c = \cos a \cos b + \sin a \sin b \cos \gamma.$

The angle cosine theorem can be used if three angles of a spherical triangle are given, or if one side and the two adjacent angles are given. The cosine theorem for the sides of a spherical triangle can be used if three sides or two sides and the included angle are given (see *Spherical trigonometry*).

Cotangent (cot)

Cot α is the ratio of the side adjacent to the angle α of a right-angled triangle to the side opposite (see *Trigonometry*).

Cube

The cube is a solid bounded by six congruent squares (Fig. 130). The six squares meet one another in twelve edges of equal length. Each face is perpendicular to its neighbouring faces. The twelve edges meet in eight vertices (corners), each vertex comprising the intersection of three mutually perpendicular edges. A cube with edges of

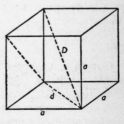

FIG. 130

length a has volume $V = a^3$, surface area $S = 6a^2$; the length of the diagonal of a face is $d = a\sqrt{2}$ and the space-diagonal $D = a\sqrt{3}.$

Cubic equation

Equations which contain the unknown raised to the third power. Normal form: $x^3 + ax^2 + bx + c = 0$ (see *Equations*).

Cubic numbers

The third powers of the natural numbers, *i.e.* 1, 8, 27, 64 . . . (see *Number, types of*).

Curvature

Deviation of a curve (surface) from a straight line (plane). The curvature of a curve at a point is more marked the more rapidly it departs from its tangent in the neighbourhood of the point. In a plane only a circle has equal curvature at all points of its length; the curvature of a circle increases as the radius decreases, and the magnitude $\frac{1}{r}$ is taken as the curvature of the circle. To determine the curvature of a general curve at one of its points, we take the curvature of the circle which fits most closely to the curve at this point. This circle is called the circle of curvature (or *osculating circle*) at the point concerned; the radius of this circle is called the *radius of curvature* and its centre the *centre of curvature*; the latter lies on the normal to the curve at the point concerned. The *Differential calculus* (see *Infinitesimal calculus*) is used to determine the curvature of a mathematically defined curve.

Curves

Curves are geometrical structures in space which for many purposes can be regarded as derivable from a straight line by a reversible transformation.

A curve segment arises from a reversible transformation of a straight line segment.

A curve, or curve segment, is called continuous, if the transformation through which it arises is continuous.

A curve is called closed, if a reversible transformation of the curve into a straight line segment can be found such that a single point on the curve corresponds to both end points of the line.

Plane curves

A curve which lies wholly in a plane is called a plane curve, *e.g.* straight line, parabola, circle, ellipse, hyperbola.

Skew curves

Curves which do not wholly lie in a plane are called skew curves, *e.g.* helix.

Parametric representation of a curve

If the variable *t* ranges over all numbers corresponding to points in a closed interval on a straight line, and if three functions $u(t)$, $v(t)$, $w(t)$ are given, then the point P with coordinates

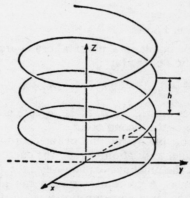

Fig. 131

$x = u(t)$, $y = v(t)$, $z = w(t)$ can be put into correspondence with the point *t* of the straight line. The equations $x = u(t)$, $y = v(t)$, $z = w(t)$ are called the parametric equations of the curve, *t* being the parameter. Since the numbered straight line is an orientated line (see *Orientation*) the curve with parametric equations $x = u(t)$, $y = v(t)$, $z = w(t)$ is also an orientated curve. Of two points on the curve one is behind, or earlier than the other, if it corresponds to the smaller value of the parameter. The other point is the later of the two. If the curve is described continuously from earlier to later points, the curve is said to be described in the positive sense.

157

Examples: 1. The circle. If t ranges over the interval $-\pi < t \leqslant +\pi$, a circle in the xy-plane is represented by the equations

$$x = x_m + r \cos t, \; y = y_m + r \sin t.$$

The centre O of the circle has coordinates $O(x_m, y_m)$; the radius is r.

2. The helix. If t ranges over all numbers in the interval $-\infty < t < +\infty$, the functions $x = r \cos t$, $y = r \sin t$, $z = \dfrac{ht}{2\pi}$ represent the helix of Fig. 131. The radius of the helix is r, the *pitch* is h.

Curves of the second order

The totality of points in a plane whose coordinates satisfy a functional equation of the form

$$F(x, y) = a_{11}x^2 + a_{22}y^2 + 2a_{12}xy + 2a_{13}x + 2a_{23}y + a_{33} = 0,$$

where the coefficients a_{11}, a_{22}, a_{12}, . . ., a_{33} are any real numbers, is called a curve of the second order.

It is always possible by rotation of the coordinate system and subsequent parallel translation to refer the curve to a coordinate system in which the functional equation has the simplest possible form. In particular, a coordinate system can always be found such that the functional equation possesses no term in xy. The curve is then referred to its principal axes, and in this form the following cases arise:

1. *The parabola*

$y^2 - 2px = 0$, where p is a positive number.

2. *The ellipse*

$\dfrac{x^2}{a^2} + \dfrac{y^2}{b^2} = 1$, where a and b are two positive numbers.

In particular if $a = b = r$ we have the circle $x^2 + y^2 = r^2$.

158

3. *The hyperbola*

$\dfrac{x^2}{a^2} - \dfrac{y^2}{b^2} = 1$, where a and b are two positive real numbers.

4. *Degenerate curves of the second order*

(a) $x^2 + y^2 = 0$. The curve comprises one point only, the origin.

(b) $x^2 + y^2 = -1$. No point with real coordinates is associated with this equation.

(c) $(ax + by + c)^2 = 0$. The curve comprises the straight line $ax + by + c = 0$.

(d) $(ax + by + c)(dx + ey + f) = 0$. The curve comprises straight lines $ax + by + c = 0$ and $dx + ey + f = 0$.

In other words, the curves of the second order are identical with the conic sections.

For special properties of the conic sections see *Circle, Ellipse, Parabola, Hyperbola*.

5. *General properties of curves of the second order (conic sections)*

1. *Vertex equations.* The equation of any non-degenerate conic section can be brought to the form $y^2 = 2px - (1 - \varepsilon^2)x^2$ (where p is positive). This is called the vertex equation of the conic section. The x-axis is then the major axis of the conic section and the y-axis a tangent. We have:

a circle, if $\quad p = r$ and $\varepsilon^2 = 0$ (r is the radius of the circle),

an ellipse, if $\quad \varepsilon < 1$,

a parabola, if $\quad \varepsilon = 1$,

a hyperbola, if $\varepsilon > 1$.

p is termed the parameter of the conic section, ε the numerical eccentricity. The origin is a (or in the case of the parabola, the) vertex of the curve (Fig. 132). In the figure:

$$y^2 = 2x - x^2: \qquad \text{Circle} \qquad \varepsilon^2 = 0,$$

$$y^2 = 2x - \frac{1}{2}x^2: \qquad \text{Ellipse} \qquad \varepsilon^2 = \frac{1}{2},$$

$$y^2 = 2x: \qquad\qquad \text{Parabola} \qquad \varepsilon^2 = 1,$$

$$y^2 = 2x + \frac{1}{2}x^2: \qquad \text{Hyperbola} \qquad \varepsilon^2 = \frac{3}{2}.$$

159

2. *The directrix of a conic section* (curve of second order). A curve of the second order (ellipse, hyperbola, parabola) is determined by a straight line (directrix l), a fixed point (focus, F) and the constant ratio ε of the distances of its points from the focus to their distances from the directrix. If $\varepsilon < 1$ we have an ellipse, if $\varepsilon = 1$ we have a parabola and if $\varepsilon > 1$, a hyperbola. The ratio ε is equal to the numerical eccentricity (Fig. 133).

3. *Equation of a conic section in polar coordinates* (ρ, ϕ). The general equation of a conic section in polar coordinates is:

$$\rho = \frac{p}{1 - \varepsilon \cos \phi}.$$

Here p is the parameter and ε is the numerical eccentricity. The focus F_1 is the origin of the coordinate system. The direction from F_1 to the more distant vertex is the zero-direction for ϕ, and ϕ is measured in the anti-clockwise sense.

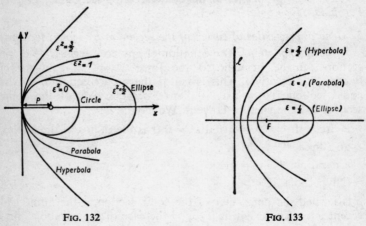

Fig. 132   Fig. 133

Cycloid (Fig. 134)

If a circle is rolled along a straight line, the curve traced out by a point on its circumference is called a cycloid. With the angle t as parameter it is represented by

$$x = \rho(t - \sin t)$$
$$y = \rho(1 - \cos t), \quad t \text{ in angular measure.}$$

If y is expressed in terms of x, y is a periodic function whose period is equal to the radius $2\pi\rho$ of the rolling circle.

An *epicycloid* is the curve obtained by rolling one circle on the exterior of another circle instead of on a straight line. A *hypocycloid* is obtained by rolling the first circle on the inner side of the circumference of the other circle. All these curves are transcendental.

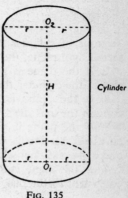

Cylinder

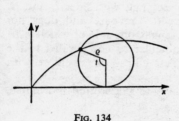

FIG. 134

FIG. 135

Cylinder

If the end-points of parallel radii of two circles of equal radius lying in parallel planes are joined we obtain a *circular cylinder* (Fig. 135). The line-segments joining the two circles are called *generators* of the cylinder. If they are perpendicular to the parallel planes we speak of a right cylinder, otherwise of an oblique cylinder. The distance apart of the two parallel planes is called the altitude H of the cylinder.

Cylinders are obtained by joining the points of any two congruent figures in parallel planes by parallel segments, *e.g.* elliptical cylinder; two congruent ellipses lying in parallel planes form the base and upper surface.

The volume of the cylinder is

$$V = A \cdot H \quad (A = \text{area of base}).$$

For the circular cylinder

$$V = \pi r^2 H \quad (r = \text{radius of circle}).$$

161

For the elliptical cylinder

$$V = \pi abH \quad (a, b = \text{semi-axes of the ellipse}).$$

Area of lateral surface of circular cylinder

$$L = 2\pi rH.$$

Area of complete surface

$$S = 2\pi r(r + H).$$

Sections of cylinder (right cylinder only). If a cylinder is intersected by a plane, the following figures can arise:

1. If the plane is perpendicular to the base and contains the axis of the cylinder the section is a rectangle with sides $2r$ and H.

2. If the plane is perpendicular to the base and does not contain the axis the section is a rectangle, one side of which is H.

3. If the plane is neither perpendicular to nor parallel to the bases the section is either a complete ellipse or an ellipse with one or two segments cut off.

4. If the plane is parallel to the base the section is a circle, congruent to the base circle.

Decimal fractions

Fractions with denominator 10, 100, 1000, . . . are called decimal fractions, *e.g.*

$$\frac{573}{1000}, \quad \frac{3578}{1000}.$$

These fractions can be briefly written as *decimal numbers*: we divide the decimal fraction into a whole number and a 'proper' decimal fraction; we write the whole number first, put a 'decimal point' after it and set down to the right the tenths, hundredths, thousandths, etc.; *e.g.*

$$\frac{573}{1,000} = 0.573; \quad \frac{3,578}{1,000} = 3.578.$$

When we have a proper decimal fraction for clarity we set a 0 to the left of the point. 0·573 is read: 'nought (or zero)-point-five-seven-three'.

Decimal system

The decimal system originated in India and reached Europe through the Arabs. In the decimal system the numbers are written using 10 signs:

$$0, 1, 2, 3, 4, 5, 6, 7, 8, \text{ and } 9.$$

These numbers have different values according to the position they occupy in the written number. On the furthest right they have unit value, immediately to the left tenfold value, to the left of that one hundredfold, and so on, *e.g.*

20,349 = 9 units + 4 tens + 3 hundreds + 0 thousands
+ 2 tenthousands.

The decimal method of writing numbers is possible because every number can be written as a sum of the form

$$x = a_0 \times 10^n + a_1 \times 10^{n-1} + a_2 \times 10^{n-2} + \ldots + a_n \times 10^0,$$

$$\text{where } 0 \leq a_i < 10, \text{ all } i.$$

E.g. $\quad 3059 = 3 \times 10^3 + 0 \times 10^2 + 5 \times 10^1 + 9 \times 10^0$

$$= 3,000 + 50 + 9.$$

The exponent n, and the coefficients which appear, are uniquely determined.

The decimal method of writing numbers can be extended to all the real numbers, *e.g.*

$$3 \cdot 01 = 3 \text{ units} + 0 \text{ tenths} + 1 \text{ hundredth}.$$

Degenerate transformation

A projective transformation of the points of a plane or of space is called degenerate, if different points give rise to the same image point.

Example: Suppose in a rectangular coordinate system in a plane a point P with coordinates (x, y) has image point $P'(x, 0)$. In this transformation a single image point corresponds to all points with the same x-coordinate (the transformation being in fact perpendicular projection of the plane onto the x-axis). An equivalent definition is as follows: A projective transformation is degenerate if it is not one-to-one (= reversibly single-valued) (see *Single-valued transformation*).

163

In the representation of the transformation by a system of equations the determinant of a degenerate transformation has value zero.

Degree (see also *Angle, Angular measurement*)

$1° = 1$ degree = ninetieth part of a right angle;

$1°$ is divided into $60'$ (60 minutes);

$1'$ is divided into $60''$ (60 seconds).

Deltoid

A deltoid (kite-shaped figure) is a quadrilateral in which two pairs of neighbouring sides are equal (see *Quadrilateral*).

De Moivre's formula

The powers and roots of complex numbers are obtained by means of de Moivre's formula:

if $$z = r\,(\cos\phi + i\sin\phi),$$

then $$z^n = r^n\,(\cos n\phi + i\sin n\phi)$$

and $$\sqrt[n]{z} = \sqrt[n]{r}\left(\cos\frac{\phi}{n} + i\sin\frac{\phi}{n}\right)$$

(see *Complex numbers*).

Descriptive geometry

Descriptive geometry is the branch of mathematics concerned with the representation of three-dimensional objects as plane figures. For this purpose central projections, general parallel projections and orthogonal parallel projections are used. Central projection can be regarded as corresponding to the act of seeing. The three-dimensional object is projected onto a projection plane from a centre of projection lying at a finite distance. This sort of projection gives a very good qualitative picture, but is less suitable for the assessment of quantitative relations, so that if an actual measurement has to be derived from measurement of the projected image a roundabout procedure must be employed.

A general parallel projection is a projection in which all lines of projection are parallel and intersect the projection plane at the same angle. It is the general parallel projection which is used for representation of objects in so-called oblique perspective (see below). (The illustrations in this book are mostly done in this fashion.)

Orthogonal parallel projection is usually used for the representation of technical objects. This projection yields very unrealistic-looking images, but the true measurements of the objects represented can easily be taken from the mapping.

The representation of three-dimensional objects can be effected by means of one, two or more projection planes.

In oblique and horizontal projections a single plane is used, and in such cases we speak of one-plane projection.

In mapping by means of orthogonal parallel projection or by means of central projection, two or more planes of projection are often used; the planes are called the plan (top view) and the elevation (vertical projection), and we talk of two-plane projection.

Determinants

An n-rowed determinant is a quantity depending upon n^2 numbers arranged in the form of a square. The numbers themselves are called the elements of the determinant.

Two-rowed determinants

A two-rowed determinant is defined by:

$$\begin{vmatrix} a_{11} & a_{12} \\ a_{21} & a_{22} \end{vmatrix} = a_{11}\, a_{22} - a_{12}\, a_{21}.$$

a_{ik} is used to indicate the element in the ith row and the kth column.

(a_{11}, read: a one one.)

Example:

$$\begin{vmatrix} 2 & 3 \\ 0 & 1 \end{vmatrix} = 2 \cdot 1 - 3 \cdot 0 = 2, \qquad \begin{vmatrix} 5 & 6 \\ 2 & 1 \end{vmatrix} = 5 \cdot 1 - 6 \cdot 2 = -7.$$

Two-row determinants can be used for the solution of a system of equations with two unknowns. The system of equations

I. $a_{11}\, x + a_{12}\, y = b_1$

II. $a_{21}\, x + a_{22}\, y = b_2$

165

has the solution

$$x = \frac{\begin{vmatrix} b_1 & a_{12} \\ b_2 & a_{22} \end{vmatrix}}{\begin{vmatrix} a_{11} & a_{12} \\ a_{21} & a_{22} \end{vmatrix}}; \quad y = \frac{\begin{vmatrix} a_{11} & b_1 \\ a_{21} & b_2 \end{vmatrix}}{\begin{vmatrix} a_{11} & a_{12} \\ a_{21} & a_{22} \end{vmatrix}}.$$

Example:

I. $x + 7y = 21$

II. $4x - 3y = 22$

$$x = \frac{\begin{vmatrix} 21 & 7 \\ 22 & -3 \end{vmatrix}}{\begin{vmatrix} 1 & 7 \\ 4 & -3 \end{vmatrix}} = \frac{-217}{-31} = 7; \quad y = \frac{\begin{vmatrix} 1 & 21 \\ 4 & 22 \end{vmatrix}}{\begin{vmatrix} 1 & 7 \\ 4 & -3 \end{vmatrix}} = \frac{-62}{-31} = 2.$$

Two-rowed determinants are also used for the calculation of the 'outer-product' (vector product) of two vectors (see *Vector product*).

Three-rowed determinants

A three-rowed determinant is defined by:

$$\begin{vmatrix} a_{11} & a_{12} & a_{13} \\ a_{21} & a_{22} & a_{23} \\ a_{31} & a_{32} & a_{33} \end{vmatrix} = a_{11}\ a_{22}\ a_{33} + a_{12}\ a_{23}\ a_{31} \\ + a_{13}\ a_{21}\ a_{32} - a_{13}\ a_{22}\ a_{31} \\ - a_{12}\ a_{21}\ a_{33} - a_{11}\ a_{23}\ a_{32}.$$

A simple method of evaluating three-rowed determinants is as follows: Extend the determinant, by repeating the first two columns, and form the products of terms in the direction of the principal diagonals and the secondary diagonals. Then subtract the sum of the products in the direction of the secondary diagonals from the sum of the products in the direction of the principal diagonals.

$$\begin{array}{ccc|cc} a_{11} & a_{12} & a_{13} & a_{11} & a_{12} \\ a_{21} & a_{22} & a_{23} & a_{21} & a_{22} \\ a_{31} & a_{32} & a_{33} & a_{31} & a_{32}. \end{array}$$

Principal diagonal: Secondary diagonal:

$$
\begin{array}{ccc}
a_{11} & \cdot & \cdot \\
\cdot & a_{22} & \cdot \\
\cdot & \cdot & a_{33}
\end{array}
\qquad
\begin{array}{ccc}
\cdot & \cdot & a_{13} \\
\cdot & a_{22} & \cdot \\
a_{31} & \cdot & \cdot
\end{array}
$$

Minors (subdeterminants)

If one row and one column of a three-rowed determinant are struck out, there remain four elements only, in the form of a square. These remaining numbers, in the arrangement in which they occur, form a minor. Since there are nine possibilities corresponding to the number of ways in which one row and one column can be eliminated, we obtain nine minors from a three-rowed determinant. To every element there corresponds in a natural way one minor: to the element in the ith row and the kth column there corresponds the minor A_{ik} arising from the elimination of the ith row and the kth column.

Example: $\begin{vmatrix} a_{11} & a_{12} & a_{13} \\ a_{21} & a_{22} & a_{23} \\ a_{31} & a_{32} & a_{33} \end{vmatrix}$.   Strike out the first row and the second column, giving

$$A_{12} = \begin{vmatrix} a_{21} & a_{23} \\ a_{31} & a_{33} \end{vmatrix}.$$

Expansion of a determinant about one row or column.

A determinant can be expanded as follows about one row: (example, 1st row)

$$\begin{vmatrix} a_{11} & a_{12} & a_{13} \\ a_{21} & a_{22} & a_{23} \\ a_{31} & a_{32} & a_{33} \end{vmatrix} = a_{11} \begin{vmatrix} a_{22} & a_{23} \\ a_{32} & a_{33} \end{vmatrix} - a_{12} \begin{vmatrix} a_{21} & a_{23} \\ a_{31} & a_{33} \end{vmatrix} + a_{13} \begin{vmatrix} a_{21} & a_{22} \\ a_{31} & a_{32} \end{vmatrix},$$

$$\begin{vmatrix} a_{11} & a_{12} & a_{13} \\ a_{21} & a_{22} & a_{23} \\ a_{31} & a_{32} & a_{33} \end{vmatrix} = a_{11}A_{11} - a_{12}A_{12} + a_{13}A_{13}.$$

n-rowed determinants

The value of an n-rowed determinant is likewise defined so that it can be calculated by developing about one row or column and then evaluating the $(n-1)$-rowed minors. We have (developing about the first row):

$$\begin{vmatrix} a_{11} & a_{12} & a_{13} \ldots a_{1n} \\ a_{21} & a_{22} & a_{23} \ldots a_{2n} \\ \cdot & \cdot & \cdot \; \cdots \\ \cdot & \cdot & \cdot \; \cdots \\ a_{n1} & a_{n2} & a_{n3} \ldots a_{nn} \end{vmatrix} = \begin{aligned} & a_{11}A_{11} - a_{12}A_{12} + a_{13}A_{13} - \ldots \\ & + (-1)^{n+1}a_{1n}A_{1n}. \end{aligned}$$

Here a_{ik} is the element in the ith row and the kth column, and A_{ik} is the $(n-1)$-rowed minor obtained by eliminating the ith row and the kth column.

Development about the ith row:

$$\begin{vmatrix} a_{11} & a_{12} & a_{13} \ldots a_{1n} \\ a_{21} & a_{22} & a_{23} \ldots a_{2n} \\ \cdot & \cdot & \cdot \; \cdots \\ a_{n1} & a_{n2} & a_{n3} \ldots a_{nn} \end{vmatrix} = \begin{aligned} & (-1)^{i+1}a_{i1}A_{i1} + (-1)^{i+2}a_{i2}A_{i2} \\ & + \ldots + (-1)^{i+n}a_{in}A_{in}. \end{aligned}$$

Example: Calculation of a five-rowed determinant (developing about the second row):

$$\begin{vmatrix} 5 & 4 & 3 & 2 & 1 \\ 0 & 0 & 0 & 1 & 2 \\ 1 & 1 & 1 & 1 & 0 \\ 1 & -2 & -3 & -4 & -2 \\ 1 & 0 & 1 & 1 & 1 \end{vmatrix} = (-1)^{2+4} \cdot 1 \begin{vmatrix} 5 & 4 & 3 & 1 \\ 1 & 1 & 1 & 0 \\ 1 & -2 & -3 & -2 \\ 1 & 0 & 1 & 1 \end{vmatrix}$$

$$+ (-1)^{2+5} \cdot 2 \begin{vmatrix} 5 & 4 & 3 & 2 \\ 1 & 1 & 1 & 1 \\ 1 & -2 & -3 & -4 \\ 1 & 0 & 1 & 1 \end{vmatrix}$$

$$= 10 - 2 \cdot (-2) = 14.$$

In this the minors have been calculated as follows:

$$\begin{vmatrix} 5 & 4 & 3 & 1 \\ 1 & 1 & 1 & 0 \\ 1 & -2 & -3 & -2 \\ 1 & 0 & 1 & 1 \end{vmatrix} = (-1)^{2+1} \begin{vmatrix} 4 & 3 & 1 \\ -2 & -3 & -2 \\ 0 & 1 & 1 \end{vmatrix}$$

$$+ (-1)^{2+2} \begin{vmatrix} 5 & 3 & 1 \\ 1 & -3 & -2 \\ 1 & 1 & 1 \end{vmatrix} + (-1)^{2+3} \begin{vmatrix} 5 & 4 & 1 \\ 1 & -2 & -2 \\ 1 & 0 & 1 \end{vmatrix}$$

(develop about the second row)

$$= 0 - 10 + 20 = +10;$$

$$\begin{vmatrix} 5 & 4 & 3 & 2 \\ 1 & 1 & 1 & 1 \\ 1 & -2 & -3 & -4 \\ 1 & 0 & 1 & 1 \end{vmatrix} = (-1)^{4+1} \begin{vmatrix} 4 & 3 & 2 \\ 1 & 1 & 1 \\ -2 & -3 & -4 \end{vmatrix}$$

$$+ (-1)^{4+3} \begin{vmatrix} 5 & 4 & 2 \\ 1 & 1 & 1 \\ 1 & -2 & -4 \end{vmatrix} + (-1)^{4+4} \begin{vmatrix} 5 & 4 & 3 \\ 1 & 1 & 1 \\ 1 & -2 & -3 \end{vmatrix}$$

(develop about the last row)

$$= 0 - 4 + 2 = -2.$$

(Short cut: use for development a row or column with as many zeros as possible.)

Theorems on n-rowed determinants

1. The value of a determinant is unaltered if the rows are written as columns and the columns as rows (reflection in the principal diagonal); for the expansion of the original determinant by its first row is identical with expansion of the reflected determinant by its first column.

2. If two rows of a determinant are interchanged, the sign of the determinant is altered; for expansions of the determinants by one of the rows in its original and transposed position gives corresponding terms equal but of opposite sign.

3. Similarly, if two columns of a determinant are interchanged, the sign of the determinant is altered.

4. If corresponding elements of two rows (columns) of a determinant are equal or proportional, the determinant is equal to zero; for by (2) (or by (3)) the determinant is equal or proportional to its negative.

5. The value of a determinant is unaltered if to the elements of one row (or column) are added a fixed multiple of the corresponding elements of another row (or column); for the modified determinant is equal to the original determinant plus a determinant which (by (4)) is zero.

Applications of determinants

Cramer's Rule. The system of equations

$$a_{11}x_1 + a_{12}x_2 + \ldots + a_{1n}x_n = b_1$$
$$a_{21}x_1 + a_{22}x_2 + \ldots + a_{2n}x_n = b_2$$
$$\cdots\cdots\cdots\cdots\cdots\cdots\cdots$$
$$a_{n1}x_1 + a_{n2}x_2 + \ldots + a_{nn}x_n = b_n$$

with unknowns $x_1, x_2, \ldots, x_n$, possesses exactly one set of solutions $x_1, x_2, \ldots, x_n$ provided

$$D = \begin{vmatrix} a_{11} & a_{12} & a_{13} \ldots a_{1n} \\ a_{21} & a_{22} & a_{23} \ldots a_{2n} \\ \cdots\cdots\cdots\cdots\cdots \\ a_{n1} & a_{n2} & a_{n3} \ldots a_{nn} \end{vmatrix} \neq 0.$$

If $D = 0$, then the left-hand members of the equations are not independent of each other.

The values of $x_1, x_2, x_3, \ldots, x_n$, are quotients of n-rowed determinants $D_1, D_2, \ldots, D_n$ and the coefficient-determinant D, where

$$D_1 = \begin{vmatrix} b_1 & a_{12} & a_{13} \ldots a_{1n} \\ b_2 & a_{22} & a_{23} \ldots a_{2n} \\ \cdots\cdots\cdots\cdots\cdots \\ b_n & a_{n1} & a_{n2} \ldots a_{nn} \end{vmatrix}, \quad D_2 = \begin{vmatrix} a_{11} & b_1 & a_{13} \ldots a_{1n} \\ a_{21} & b_2 & a_{23} \ldots a_{2n} \\ \cdots\cdots\cdots\cdots\cdots \\ a_{n1} & b_n & a_{n3} \ldots a_{nn} \end{vmatrix}, \ldots,$$

$$D_n = \begin{vmatrix} a_{11} & a_{12} & a_{13} \ldots b_1 \\ a_{21} & a_{22} & a_{23} \ldots b_2 \\ \cdots\cdots\cdots\cdots\cdots \\ a_{n1} & a_{n2} & a_{n3} \ldots b_n \end{vmatrix}.$$

In these determinants the coefficients of the unknown in question are replaced in the coefficient-determinant by the constant terms of the equations. The solution of the system of equations is then:

$$x_1 = \frac{D_1}{D}, \quad x_2 = \frac{D_2}{D}, \quad x_3 = \frac{D_3}{D}, \quad \ldots, \quad x_n = \frac{D_n}{D}.$$

Example:

$$x_1 + x_2 + x_3 + x_4 = 4$$
$$2x_1 + x_2 \qquad\qquad = 3$$
$$2x_2 + x_3 \qquad = 4$$
$$x_3 + x_4 = 2$$

The determinant D is:

$$D = \begin{vmatrix} 1 & 1 & 1 & 1 \\ 2 & 1 & 0 & 0 \\ 0 & 2 & 1 & 0 \\ 0 & 0 & 1 & 1 \end{vmatrix} = (-2) \begin{vmatrix} 1 & 1 & 1 \\ 2 & 1 & 0 \\ 0 & 1 & 1 \end{vmatrix} + 1 \begin{vmatrix} 1 & 1 & 1 \\ 0 & 1 & 0 \\ 0 & 1 & 1 \end{vmatrix} = -1.$$

The determinants D_1, D_2, D_3 and D_4 are:

$$D_1 = \begin{vmatrix} 4 & 1 & 1 & 1 \\ 3 & 1 & 0 & 0 \\ 4 & 2 & 1 & 0 \\ 2 & 0 & 1 & 1 \end{vmatrix} = (-3) \begin{vmatrix} 1 & 1 & 1 \\ 2 & 1 & 0 \\ 0 & 1 & 1 \end{vmatrix} + 1 \begin{vmatrix} 4 & 1 & 1 \\ 4 & 1 & 0 \\ 2 & 1 & 1 \end{vmatrix} = (-3) + 2 = -1,$$

$$D_2 = \begin{vmatrix} 1 & 4 & 1 & 1 \\ 2 & 3 & 0 & 0 \\ 0 & 4 & 1 & 0 \\ 0 & 2 & 1 & 1 \end{vmatrix} = (-1) \begin{vmatrix} 2 & 3 & 0 \\ 0 & 4 & 1 \\ 0 & 2 & 1 \end{vmatrix} + 1 \begin{vmatrix} 1 & 4 & 1 \\ 2 & 3 & 0 \\ 0 & 4 & 1 \end{vmatrix} = (-4) + 3 = -1,$$

$$D_3 = \begin{vmatrix} 1 & 1 & 4 & 1 \\ 2 & 1 & 3 & 0 \\ 0 & 2 & 4 & 0 \\ 0 & 0 & 2 & 1 \end{vmatrix} = (-1) \begin{vmatrix} 2 & 1 & 3 \\ 0 & 2 & 4 \\ 0 & 0 & 2 \end{vmatrix} + 1 \begin{vmatrix} 1 & 1 & 4 \\ 2 & 1 & 3 \\ 0 & 2 & 4 \end{vmatrix} = -8 + 6 = -2,$$

$$D_4 = \begin{vmatrix} 1 & 1 & 1 & 4 \\ 2 & 1 & 0 & 3 \\ 0 & 2 & 1 & 4 \\ 0 & 0 & 1 & 2 \end{vmatrix} = +1 \begin{vmatrix} 1 & 0 & 3 \\ 2 & 1 & 4 \\ 0 & 1 & 2 \end{vmatrix} - 2 \begin{vmatrix} 1 & 1 & 4 \\ 2 & 1 & 4 \\ 0 & 1 & 2 \end{vmatrix} = 4 - 4 = 0.$$

The solution is therefore

$$x_1 = \frac{D_1}{D} = \frac{-1}{-1} = 1, \qquad x_2 = \frac{D_2}{D} = \frac{-1}{-1} = 1,$$

$$x_3 = \frac{D_3}{D} = \frac{-2}{-1} = 2, \qquad x_4 = \frac{D_4}{D} = \frac{0}{-1} = 0.$$

Diameter

A diameter of a circle is a *chord* which passes through the centre of the circle. In length the diameter of a circle is double the radius (see *Circle*).

Dilatation

If a segment undergoes a change of length the ratio of the increase of length to the original length is called the dilatation.

Dimension

Dimension is a property of the basic *geometrical elements* (see below) and the derived geometrical structures. Points have dimension zero. The straight line has dimension 1. The plane has dimension 2. Space has dimension 3. Derived geometrical structures have their dimension defined so as to conform to these values. Thus a curve lying in a plane and defined by a single algebraic equation has the same dimension as a straight line; a surface in space defined by a single equation has the same dimension as a plane; a curve in space defined as the intersection of two surfaces has the same dimension as a straight line. In physics dimension often has a quite different meaning, being used to denote physical measures. *E.g.* cm/sec is the dimension of a velocity.

Diophantine equations

Equations of the form $ax + by = c$ are called diophantine. Here a, b and c are given integers, and integral number-pairs x and y are required which satisfy the equation. We find solutions by first solving the equation $ax + by = 1$. Thus if U, V is a pair of values which satisfies the equation $ax + by = 1$, *i.e.* $aU + bV = 1$, then $x = cU + bp$ and $y = cV - ap$ with p an arbitrary integer is the general solution of the equation $ax + by = c$ (verify by substitution). In the same way we obtain from a pair of values U, V satisfying $aU - bV = 1$ the general solution of the equation $ax - by = C$ by putting $x = cU + bp$, $y = cV + ap$, where p is an arbitrary integer. The solutions of the equation $ax + by = 1$ are obtained by developing $\dfrac{a}{b}$ as a continued fraction. The penultimate convergent gives (apart from sign) U as denominator and V as numerator.

Example: $\qquad\qquad 31x - 164y = 7.$

The development of $\dfrac{31}{164}$ as a continued fraction is, by the Euclidean algorithm (see *Continued fractions*):

$$164 \div 31 = 5 \text{ Remainder } 9$$
$$31 \div 9 = 3 \quad\text{,,}\quad 4$$
$$9 \div 4 = 2 \quad\text{,,}\quad 1$$
$$4 \div 1 = 4 \quad\text{,,}\quad 0.$$

This gives the continued fraction development

$$\frac{31}{164} = \cfrac{1}{5 + \cfrac{1}{3 + \cfrac{1}{2 + \cfrac{1}{4}}}} ,$$

and the convergents are

$$\frac{1}{5}, \quad \cfrac{1}{5 + \cfrac{1}{3}} = \frac{3}{16}, \quad \cfrac{1}{5 + \cfrac{1}{3 + \cfrac{1}{2}}} = \frac{7}{37}$$

and $\dfrac{31}{164}$. The penultimate convergent has numerator $7 = \pm V$ and denominator $37 = \pm U$. If we choose $U = -37$ and $V = -7$ then we have

$$31x - 164y = 31(-37) - 164(-7) = -1147 + 1148 = +1.$$

From this we get the general solution:

$$x = cU + bp = 7(-37) + 164 \cdot p$$

and $\qquad y = cV + ap = 7(-7) + 31 \cdot p,$

that is

$$x = -259 + 164p \text{ and } y = -49 + 31p.$$

Distributive law

In its usual form, this establishes a relation between addition and multiplication: $a(b + c) = ab + ac$.

Division

Division is the fourth fundamental operation of calculation.

Dividend divided by Divisor gives Quotient

$$\underbrace{12 \quad \div \quad 4}_{\text{Quotient}} = 3$$

It is the inverse of multiplication (as the inverse of the multiplication $3 \times 4 = 12$ we have the division $12 \div 4 = 3$). The division of integers does not always lead to integral results, *i.e.* in the domain of integers, division (without remainder) cannot always be carried out. On the other hand, in the domain of rational numbers all four basic operations are unrestrictedly possible (with the exception of division by zero, see below); *i.e.* if one of the basic operations is performed on any two rational numbers, the result is another rational number. A domain of numbers with this property is called a (number) field, *e.g.* the field of rational numbers, the field of complex numbers. A quotient can also be written as a fraction, *e.g.*

$$a \div b = \frac{a}{b}, \qquad 12 \div 4 = \frac{12}{4}.$$

If we interchange the dividend and the divisor, we obtain the reciprocal of the quotient, *e.g.*

$$4 \div 12 = \frac{4}{12} \text{ is the reciprocal of } \frac{12}{4}.$$

Division of directed numbers

Directed numbers are divided according to the following rules of signs:

1. If dividend and divisor have the same sign, the quotient is positive:

$$\frac{-6}{-2} = +3, \qquad \frac{8a}{2a} = 4.$$

2. If dividend and divisor have different signs, the quotient is negative:

$$\frac{-6}{+2} = -3, \qquad \frac{6a}{-2a} = -3.$$

Rules for fractional calculations with literal numbers

The rules for fractional calculations with literal numbers are the same as for fractions composed of ordinary numbers:

1. Fractions can be reduced (see *Reduction of fractions*), e.g. $\frac{3abc}{3b} = ac$ (reduced by $3b$). And, conversely, if $d \neq 0$, $\frac{a}{b} = \frac{ad}{bd}$.

2. Fractions can only be added directly if they have the same numerator:

$$\frac{a}{c} + \frac{b}{c} = \frac{a+b}{c}.$$

Other fractions must first be reduced to a common denominator:

$$\frac{a}{b} + \frac{c}{d} = \frac{ad}{bd} + \frac{cb}{bd} = \frac{ad+cb}{bd}.$$

3. In multiplying fractions, numerators and denominators are multiplied together:

$$\frac{a}{b} \cdot \frac{c}{d} = \frac{ac}{bd}.$$

4. To divide two fractions the first fraction is multiplied by the reciprocal of the second:

$$\frac{a}{b} \div \frac{c}{d} = \frac{a}{b} \cdot \frac{d}{c} = \frac{ad}{bc}.$$

Division of an algebraic sum by a number

An algebraic sum (polynomial) is divided by a number when each of the terms are divided by the number and the resulting quotients added.

Example: $(54xz - 72yz - 25) \div 9z = 6x - 8y - \dfrac{25}{9z}.$

Division of algebraic sum by algebraic sums

We use the following procedure: First we order the terms of the dividend and of the divisor in the same way, the literal numbers in alphabetical order and arranged according to decreasing or increasing powers.

Example: $(12ac - 7b^2 - 23ab + 3bc + 20a^2) \div (4a + b)$

will be ordered as

$$(20a^2 - 23ab + 12ac - 7b^2 + 3bc) \div (4a + b).$$

Then, as in the division of one multi-digit number by another, we divide the first term of the dividend by the first term of the divisor, multiply the complete divisor by the partial quotient we have obtained, and subtract the resulting product from the dividend. If necessary we reorder the remainder of the dividend and divide its first term by the first term of the divisor, multiply the complete divisor by the second partial quotient, subtract the product from the remainder, and continue until either no remainder is left or until the remainder is no longer divisible by the first term of the divisor; in the first case the division is exact, in the second case, not.

Example 1:

$$(20a^2 - 23ab + 12ac - 7b^2 + 3bc) \div (4a + b) = 5a - 7b + 3c$$
$$\underline{-(20a^2 + 5ab)}$$
$$\qquad -28ab + 12ac - 7b^2 + 3bc$$
$$\qquad \underline{-(-28ab \qquad\quad - 7b^2)}$$
$$\qquad\qquad\qquad +12ac \qquad\quad + 3bc$$
$$\qquad\qquad\quad \underline{-(+12ac \qquad\quad + 3bc)}$$
$$\qquad\qquad\qquad\qquad\qquad\qquad 0$$

Example 2:

$$(2x^2 + 7xy + 4y^2) \div (x + 3y) = 2x + y + \frac{y^2}{x + 3y}$$
$$\underline{-(2x^2 + 6xy)}$$
$$\qquad\qquad xy + 4y^2$$
$$\qquad \underline{-(+\ xy + 3y^2)}$$
$$\qquad\qquad\qquad y^2$$

Division of powers

(a) Equal bases. Here we subtract the exponent of the divisor from the exponent of the dividend: $\dfrac{a^p}{a^q} = a^{p-q}$

e.g. $\qquad \dfrac{a^5}{a^3} = a^2, \qquad \dfrac{a^5}{a^7} = a^{5-7} = a^{-2}.$

(b) Equal exponents. Here we retain the common exponent and divide the bases: $\dfrac{a^n}{b^n} = \left(\dfrac{a}{b}\right)^n$

e.g. $\qquad \dfrac{10^3}{5^3} = \left(\dfrac{10}{5}\right)^3 = 2^3 = 8.$

Division of roots

(a) Equal indexes. Here we retain the index and divide the radicand; *e.g.*

$$\frac{\sqrt[n]{a^p}}{\sqrt[n]{b}} = \sqrt[n]{\frac{a^p}{b}}, \qquad \frac{\sqrt[3]{64}}{\sqrt[3]{8}} = \sqrt[3]{\frac{64}{8}} = \sqrt[3]{8} = 2.$$

(b) Equal radicands. We must first make the orders of the roots equal and then use rule (a) above: $\dfrac{\sqrt[n]{a}}{\sqrt[m]{a}} = \dfrac{\sqrt[nm]{a^m}}{\sqrt[nm]{a^n}} = \sqrt[nm]{a^{m-n}};$

e.g. $\qquad \dfrac{\sqrt[4]{8}}{\sqrt[3]{8}} = \dfrac{\sqrt[12]{8^3}}{\sqrt[12]{8^4}} = \sqrt[12]{8^{-1}} = \sqrt[12]{\dfrac{1}{8}}.$

(c) Roots can be written as powers with fractional exponents, and so can be divided by using the corresponding rules for powers; *e.g.*

(a) $\dfrac{\sqrt[n]{a}}{\sqrt[n]{b}} = \dfrac{a^{\frac{1}{n}}}{b^{\frac{1}{n}}} = \left(\dfrac{a}{b}\right)^{\frac{1}{n}}, \qquad \dfrac{\sqrt[4]{8}}{\sqrt[4]{9}} = \dfrac{8^{\frac{1}{4}}}{9^{\frac{1}{4}}} = \left(\dfrac{8}{9}\right)^{\frac{1}{4}}.$

(b) $\dfrac{\sqrt[n]{a}}{\sqrt[m]{a}} = \dfrac{a^{\frac{1}{n}}}{a^{\frac{1}{m}}} = a^{\frac{1}{n}-\frac{1}{m}}, \qquad \dfrac{\sqrt[4]{8}}{\sqrt[3]{8}} = \dfrac{8^{\frac{1}{4}}}{8^{\frac{1}{3}}} = 8^{\frac{1}{4}-\frac{1}{3}} = 8^{-\frac{1}{12}} = \dfrac{1}{\sqrt[12]{8}}.$

Division of complex numbers

To divide two complex numbers $a + ib$ and $c + id$ we write the division as a fraction and by multiplication rearrange this fraction so that the denominator becomes real. Then we gather together real parts and imaginary parts in the numerator:

$$(a + ib) \div (c + id) = \frac{a + ib}{c + id} = \frac{(a + ib)(c - id)}{(c + id)(c - id)}$$

$$= \frac{ac + bd + i(bc - ad)}{c^2 + d^2}.$$

E.g. $(1 + i) \div (5 + 6i) = \dfrac{1 + i}{5 + 6i} = \dfrac{(1 + i)(5 - 6i)}{(5 + 6i)(5 - 6i)}$

$$= \frac{5 + 6 - i}{25 + 36} = \frac{11 - i}{61} = \frac{11}{61} - \frac{1}{61} i.$$

Division ratio

If A, B and C are three points on a straight line, the quotient $\dfrac{\overline{CA}}{\overline{CB}}$ is referred to as a division ratio.

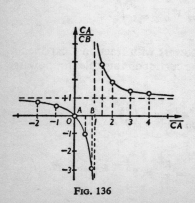

If C lies between A and B, C is said to divide the segment $\overline{AB}$ internally. If C lies outside the segment $\overline{AB}$, C is said to divide AB externally. For interior points C the segments $\overline{CA}$ and $\overline{CB}$ have opposite directions and the division ratio is given a negative value (see *Vector calculus*). For exterior points C the segments $\overline{CA}$ and $\overline{CB}$ have the same direction and the division ratio is positive.

Fig. 136

If C coincides with A the division ratio is 0. As C approaches B, the division ratio tends to $+\infty$ or $-\infty$ according as C approaches from the exterior or the interior of the segment $\overline{AB}$. In Fig. 136 the division ratio of a segment is taken as ordinate and the distance of C from A as abscissa. The division ratio remains unaltered under affine transformations (see *Transformation, affine*).

Dodecahedron

Dodecahedra are solids bounded by twelve surfaces. In the case of rhombic dodecahedra, these are twelve rhombuses, and in the case of pentagon dodecahedra (pentadodecahedra) twelve regular pentagons. The pentadodecahedron is one of the so-called *Platonic solids* (see below).

Duplication of the cube

The duplication of the cube, or Delic problem, is the problem of constructing with ruler and compass alone the edge of a cube having twice the volume of a cube with given edge. It has been studied since the fifth century B.C. In spite of its apparent simplicity it cannot be solved by these elementary methods, but attempts to solve it have led to important advances in mathematics.

$e = 2{\cdot}718,281,828\ldots.$

The number e is the limit of the sequence with general term

$$b_n = \left(1 + \frac{1}{n}\right)^n.$$

The term e for this limiting value derives from Leonhard Euler (1731).

Properties of the number e

1. The number e is also the limiting value of the sequence

$$a_n = \left(1 + \frac{1}{n}\right)^{n+1}.$$

179

2. For all natural numbers n we have:

$$\left(1 + \frac{1}{n}\right)^n < e < \left(1 + \frac{1}{n}\right)^{n+1}.$$

3. $\quad e = \lim_{n \to \infty} \left(1 + \frac{1}{1!} + \frac{1}{2!} + \frac{1}{3!} + \frac{1}{4!} + \ldots + \frac{1}{n!}\right).$

e can be quickly calculated to any desired degree of accuracy by using this last series, the terms of which diminish rapidly; e.g. for $n = 12$ we already have an approximation accurate to 9 places of decimals:

$$e = 2 \cdot 718,281,828.$$

4. e is a *transcendental number* (proved by *Charles Hermite*, 1873).

5. e is the base of the *exponential function* $y = e^x$ (see below).

Ellipse

An ellipse may be defined as the locus of points, the sum of whose distances from two fixed points F_1 and F_2 (the foci) is constant and equal to $2a$. The mid-point of the line segment $\overline{F_1 F_2}$ is the centre O of the ellipse (see *Conic sections*). If we construct on the straight line through F_1 and F_2 segments of length a on either side of O, we obtain the end points A_1 and A_2 of the major axis of the ellipse. The perpendicular to the major axis through O cuts the ellipse in points B_1 and B_2, the end points of the minor axis of the ellipse. The points B_1 and B_2 are distant b from the centre of the ellipse and each is distant a from each of the foci. If $e^2 = a^2 - b^2$, e is called the eccentricity of the ellipse (also, focal distance), and is equal to the distance from a focus to the centre of the ellipse. The ellipse is symmetric with respect to both its axes. It is a closed curve. For the construction of the ellipse see below and *Conic sections*.

Particular equations of the ellipse

1. *Central equation.* If the coordinate system is chosen so that the origin of the system is the centre of the ellipse and the coordinate axes coincide with the axes of the ellipse (the abscissa axis being the major axis), we can derive the central equation

from the definition of the ellipse (see above; expressed as a formula, it is $\rho_1 + \rho_2 = 2a$):

$$\frac{x^2}{a^2} + \frac{y^2}{b^2} = 1.$$

2. *Equation of the ellipse with arbitrary centre.* If the centre of the ellipse does not lie at the origin of the coordinate system but has coordinates $O(x_m, y_m)$, and if the axes are parallel to the coordinate axes, the equation is:

$$\frac{(x - x_m)^2}{a^2} + \frac{(y - y_m)^2}{b^2} = 1.$$

3. *Vertex equation of the ellipse.* If a vertex of the ellipse lies at the origin of the coordinate system and the centre of the ellipse lies on the abscissa axis then the ellipse has the equation:

$$\frac{(x - a)^2}{a^2} + \frac{y^2}{b^2} = 1.$$

This equation can be expanded to read:

$$y^2 = \frac{2b^2}{a} x - \frac{b^2}{a^2} x^2.$$

If we put $\frac{b^2}{a} = p$, $\frac{e}{a} = \varepsilon$, p being termed the parameter and ε the numerical eccentricity of the ellipse, the vertex equation reads:

$$y^2 = 2px - (1 - \varepsilon^2)x^2.$$

(*Cf.* the general apse equation of a conic section in the article *Curves of second order*.) p and ε are positive numbers, and since we are dealing with an ellipse ε is less than 1.

Length of the focal distances (Fig. 137): If the point $P(x_1, y_1)$ lies on the ellipse with equation $\frac{x^2}{a^2} + \frac{y^2}{b^2} = 1$, the focal distances $\overline{PF_1}$ and $\overline{PF_2}$ are $\overline{PF_1} = \rho_1 = a - \frac{e}{a} x_1 = a - \varepsilon x_1$ and $\overline{PF_2} = \rho_2 = a + \frac{e}{a} x_1 = a + \varepsilon . x_1.$

181

Affine relation between circle and ellipse: The ellipse $\dfrac{x^2}{a^2} + \dfrac{y^2}{b^2} = 1$ can be obtained as an affine transformation of the circle $x^2 + y^2 = a^2$ (or as an affine transformation of the circle $x^2 + y^2 = b^2$).

The circle $x^2 + y^2 = a^2$ is the circle on the major axis of the ellipse; it passes through the two vertices of the ellipse. The circle $x^2 + y^2 = b^2$ is the circle on the minor axis. Let a radius $\overline{OP_K}$ of the circle on the major axis cut the circle on the minor axis

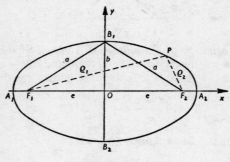

FIG. 137

in the point R. Draw through R the line parallel to the x-axis and through P_K the line parallel to the y-axis. Let the two lines intersect in the point P_E, and let the foot of the perpendicular from P_K on the x-axis be Q.

By the first theorem on rays $\overline{P_K O}:\overline{RO} = \overline{P_K Q}:\overline{P_E Q}$. Let the coordinates of P_K be (x, y_K) and of P_E be (x, y_E). Then Q has coordinates $(x, 0)$. We have $y_K:y_E = \overline{P_K O}:\overline{RO} = a:b$, that is, $y_E = \dfrac{b}{a} \cdot y_K$. Since P_K lies on the circle $x^2 + y^2 = a^2$, we have

$$y_K^2 = a^2 - x^2 \quad \text{and so} \quad y_E^2 = \frac{b^2}{a^2} y_K^2 = \frac{b^2}{a^2}(a^2 - x^2), \quad \text{that is,}$$

$$\frac{x^2}{a^2} + \frac{y_E^2}{b^2} = 1.$$

We have therefore proved: If $P_K(x, y_K)$ is a point on the circle $x^2 + y^2 = a^2$ and if we shorten the ordinate of this point in the ratio $b:a$ $(b < a)$, the resulting point P_E with coordinates $\left(x, \dfrac{b}{a} y_K\right)$ lies on the ellipse with axes a and b (Fig. 138).

We say that the ellipse is the affine image of the circle on its major axis. Constructions for tangents to an ellipse and for conjugate diameters of an ellipse can be derived from the properties of the affine transformation.

1. **Point by point construction of the ellipse.** We draw the circles on the major and minor axes and construct points on the ellipse (Fig. 138) as already described above.

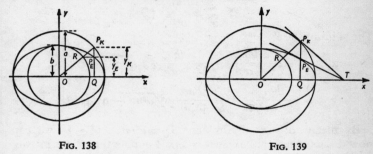

Fig. 138   Fig. 139

2. **To construct the tangent at a point P_E of an ellipse** (Fig. 139). Draw through P_E the line parallel to the y-axis. This cuts the circle on the major axis in the point P_K. Draw the tangent to the circle at P_K and let it intersect the x-axis in the point T. Then the line TP_E is the required tangent.

3. **Conjugate diameters.** A chord of an ellipse is called a diameter if it passes through the centre of the ellipse.

Given the circles on the two axes of an ellipse and two diameters $\overline{P_K Q_K}$ and $\overline{S_K R_K}$ of the circle on the major axis perpendicular to one another. Construct the points on the ellipse P_E and S_E corresponding to the points P_K and S_K (Fig. 140), and draw the straight lines through these points and the centre of the ellipse. These are *conjugate diameters* of the

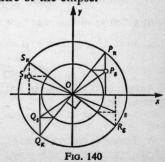

Fig. 140

183

ellipse, and they arise, by affine transformation, from two perpendicular diameters of the circle on the major axis.

Ellipse and straight line

1. *Discriminant of the ellipse*. The coordinates of the points of intersection of a straight line $y = mx + n$ and the ellipse $\frac{x^2}{a^2} + \frac{y^2}{b^2} = 1$ are obtained as solutions of the system of equations:

$$\text{I. } y = mx + n,$$

$$\text{II. } \frac{x^2}{a^2} + \frac{y^2}{b^2} = 1.$$

The solutions are:

$$x_{1,2} = -\frac{a^2mn}{b^2 + a^2m^2} \pm \frac{ab}{b^2 + a^2m^2}\sqrt{a^2m^2 - n^2 + b^2},$$

$$y_{1,2} = \frac{b^2n}{b^2 + a^2m^2} \pm \frac{abm}{b^2 + a^2m^2}\sqrt{a^2m^2 - n^2 + b^2}.$$

By means of the discriminant $D = a^2m^2 + b^2 - n^2$ we can now decide whether the line $y = mx + n$ cuts the ellipse in two, one, or no points. We have:

for $D = a^2m^2 + b^2 - n^2 > 0$ two points of intersection;

for $D = a^2m^2 + b^2 - n^2 = 0$ one point of intersection, that is, the line is a tangent;

for $D = a^2m^2 + b^2 - n^2 < 0$ no point of intersection.

2. *Tangents to an ellipse with given gradients*. A line $y = mx + n$ with given gradient m is tangent to the ellipse $\frac{x^2}{a^2} + \frac{y^2}{b^2} = 1$ if the discriminant is zero, *i.e.* if $n^2 = a^2m^2 + b^2$, that is, if

$$n = \pm\sqrt{a^2m^2 + b^2}.$$

A tangent to the ellipse with given gradient m must therefore have equation

$$y = mx \pm \sqrt{a^2m^2 + b^2}.$$

3. *Tangents to an ellipse at a given point $P_1(x_1, y_1)$*. The gradient of the tangent at the point P_1 is given, by differentiation, as

184

$-\dfrac{b^2 x_1}{a^2 y_1}$. From this gradient together with the coordinates of P_1 we obtain the equation of the tangent as:

$$\frac{xx_1}{a^2} + \frac{yy_1}{b^2} = 1.$$

Where the centre is not at the origin but at the point (x_m, y_m), the equation is:

$$\frac{(x_1 - x_m)(x - x_m)}{a^2} + \frac{(y_1 - y_m)(y - y_m)}{b^2} = 1.$$

4. *Polar of a point $P_0(x_0, y_0)$ with respect to an ellipse*. The polar of P_0 with respect to an ellipse is the straight line which passes through both points of contact of the tangents from P_0 to the ellipse. The equation of the polar has the same form as the tangent equation given under 3, that is:

$$\frac{xx_0}{a^2} + \frac{yy_0}{b^2} = 1,$$

or more generally,

$$\frac{(x_0 - x_m)(x - x_m)}{a^2} + \frac{(y_0 - y_m)(y - y_m)}{b^2} = 1.$$

5. *Conjugate diameters of the ellipse*. A straight line through the centre of an ellipse is called a diameter of the ellipse. The mid-points of all chords of the ellipse with given slope m lie on the straight line $y = \dfrac{-b^2}{a^2 m}\, x$, which passes through the centre and so is a diameter of the ellipse. The lines $y = mx$ and $y = \dfrac{-b^2}{a^2 m}\, x$ are conjugate diameters. The tangents at the end-points of a diameter of an ellipse are parallel to the conjugate diameter.

General theorems on the ellipse

1. The tangent and normal at a point P of the ellipse bisect the angle which the focal lines through P make with one another.
2. The feet of the perpendiculars from a focus onto the tangents of the ellipse lie on the circle on the major axis. The mirror image

of a focus with respect to a tangent lies on the circle with radius $2a$ described about the other focus.

3. The product of the distances of the foci from a tangent is constant, and equal to b^2.

4. The ellipse is the locus of points whose distance from a fixed point (a focus) bears a constant ratio ε to its distance from a fixed line (the directrix). The directrix has equation $x = \dfrac{a^2}{e} = \dfrac{a}{\varepsilon}$.

5. An ellipse and the hyperbola confocal with it intersect at right angles (an ellipse and a hyperbola are confocal if they have the same foci).

Construction of tangents to an ellipse

(a) *At a point of the ellipse.* We draw the two focal lines of the point and bisect the angle between one of them and the extension of the other.

(b) *From a point outside the ellipse.* Draw from the given point P the straight line through one of the foci F_2 of the ellipse, and describe the Thales circle on the segment $\overline{PF_2}$. This cuts the circle on the major axis of the ellipse in the points H which lie on the

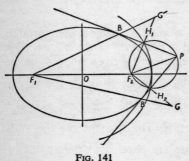

FIG. 141

required tangents (by theorem 3 above). The straight lines through P and H_1, and P and H_2 are the required tangents.

If we construct the perpendicular to a tangent through H_1 and extend it to meet the circle with radius $2a$ and centre F_1 in G, then the straight line through G and F_1 cuts the tangent in its point of contact B (Fig. 141).

Equality sign

If the equality sign '=' occurs between two mathematical expressions it means that the expressions on the right and left hand sides of the equality sign are equal. The following laws hold for the relation of equality:

1. Every quantity is equal to itself:

$a = a$ (Reflexivity).

2. Right and left hand sides in an equality may be interchanged:

$a = b$ implies $b = a$ (Symmetry).

3. If two quantities are equal to a third, they are equal to one another:

$a = b$ and $b = c$ implies $a = c$ (Transistivity).

Two quantities which are not equal to one another are called unequal (sign: $\neq$).

The equality sign does not signify that two quantities which are equal are necessarily identical in form, *e.g.* $\frac{2}{4} = \frac{4}{8}$.

Equations

An equation implies the judgement, or the establishing of the fact that, two mathematical quantities are equal to one another. We distinguish between *identical equations* (see below), *conditional equations* (see below) and *functional equations* (see *functions*).

1. *Identical equations*

An identical equation (identity) asserts that two given constant mathematical expressions are equal, *e.g.*

$$2 + 2 = 4, \quad a + b = b + a.$$

2. *Conditional equations*

If any number in an equation is unknown we call such an equation a conditional equation. The unknown is usually denoted by one of the last letters of the alphabet, x, y or z. If such an equation is given, the problem arises of determining the unknown x so that the meaning of the equation is fulfilled, *e.g.*

$$x - 5 = 4.$$

x is to be determined so that 4 is the difference $x - 5$. We must take for x the number 9 in order that the equation be satisfied. $x = 9$ is called a solution or root of the equation. More than one unknown can arise in an equation. We speak then of equations with several unknowns (see *Equations, linear systems of; Diophantine equations*).

Types of conditional equation. We distinguish between *algebraic equations* (see below) and equations which are not algebraic (see *Transcendental equations*). In an algebraic equation the known and unknown quantities are associated together by means of algebraic operations (addition, subtraction, multiplication, division and raising to a power, the last being merely a shortened way of writing a multiplication) alone.

Example: $$x^5 + 4x^3 + 4x + 1 = 0.$$

For the classification of *algebraic equations*, see below.

Transcendental (non-algebraic) equations contain transcendental functions of the unknowns, thus, *e.g.*

1. Exponential equations, *e.g.* $10^x + x = 2^x$

2. Logarithmic equations, *e.g.* $\log x + 5 = \log x + x^2$

3. Trigonometric equations, *e.g.* $\sin x = \cos x - 0 \cdot 5$

See *Transcendental equations, Exponential equations, Logarithmic equations* and *Trigonometric equations.*

Differential equations (see above) (ordinary and partial) are conditional equations for unknown functions.

Algebraic equations

A. *With one unknown.* The standard form of these equations is

$$a_0 x^n + a_1 x^{n-1} + a_2 x^{n-2} + \ldots + a_{n-1} x + a_n = 0.$$

Here x is the unknown, n a given fixed positive integer and

$$a_1, a_2, \ldots, a_{n-1}, a_n$$

are given fixed numbers. n is called the degree of the equation and we speak of equations of the

1st degree (*linear equations*) $3x - 5 = 0$

2nd degree (*quadratic equations*) $2x^2 - 3x + 5 = 0$

3rd degree (*cubic equations*) $3x^3 - 2x^2 + 2x - 1 = 0$

4th degree (*biquadratic equations*) $5x^4 - x^3 + 2x^2 - x + 1 = 0$

and in general of equations of the nth degree.

B. With several unknowns. In the general case such an equation contains terms of the form

$$a_k x^n y^m \ldots z^p.$$

Here a_k is a fixed number, x, y, z, $\ldots$ are unknowns. The sum of the exponents of a term, $n + m + \ldots + p$ is called the degree of the term, *e.g.*

$$x^2 y^2 z^2 + x^3 + yx^4 + z^6 + 5 = 0.$$

The first term is of degree 6, the second of degree 3, etc. The equation itself is of degree 6.

Equations in which all terms are of the same degree are said to be homogeneous, *e.g.*

$$x^4 + x^3 y + y^4 = 0$$

is homogeneous, of degree 4.

Of particular importance are equations of the first degree in several variables, *e.g.*

$$5x + 6y - 7z + 3u = 0.$$

There are called linear equations. They arise in number theory as *diophantine equations* (see above) and above all in *analytical geometry* (see above).

C. Systems of algebraic equations. If more than one equation is given for the determination of the unknowns, we speak of a system of equations.

The unknowns can be uniquely determined only if the number of unknowns is equal to the number of equations. With more equations than unknowns, we become involved in problems of the *Calculus of Observations* (see above).

General theorems on algebraical equations of the nth *degree*

1. The general equation of the nth degree

$$A_0 x^n + A_1 x^{n-1} + A_2 x^{n-2} + \ldots + A_n = 0$$

is reduced by division throughout by A_0 to the normal form

$$f(x) = x^n + a_1 x^{n-1} + a_2 x^{n-2} + \ldots + a_n = 0,$$

where a_i is written for $\dfrac{A_i}{A_0}$.

2. If the given equation $f(x) = 0$ has the root x_1, $f(x)$ can be divided through by the linear factor $(x - x_1)$,

$$f(x) = (x - x_1)g(x),$$

say, where the degree of $g(x)$ is 1 less than that of $f(x)$.

3. Every algebraic equation with rational coefficients

$$x^n + a_1 x^{n-1} + \ldots + a_n = 0$$

has at least one (real or complex) root x_1 (Fundamental theorem of algebra).

4. If $f(x)$ is divisible by $(x - x_1)^r$ but not by $(x - x_1)^{r+1}$, x is called an *r*-fold root.

5. As a consequence of 2, 3 and 4 we have: Every equation of the *n*th degree has exactly n roots, each root being counted according to its multiplicity.

6. If $x_1, x_2, x_3, \ldots, x_n$ are the roots of the equation $f(x) = 0$ then

$$f(x) = (x - x_1)(x - x_2)(x - x_3) \ldots (x - x_n)$$

(decomposition into linear factors).

7. The following relations hold between the coefficients and the roots of the equation $f(x) = 0$:

$$\left.\begin{aligned}
a_1 &= -(x_1 + x_2 + x_3 + \ldots + x_n) \\
a_2 &= +(x_1 x_2 + x_1 x_3 + \ldots + x_2 x_3 \ldots + x_{n-1} x_n) \\
a_3 &= -(x_1 x_2 x_3 + x_1 x_2 x_4 + \ldots + x_2 x_3 x_4 + \ldots \\
&\qquad\qquad\qquad\qquad\qquad\qquad + x_{n-2} x_{n-1} x_n) \\
&\;\;\cdot\;\;\cdot\;\;\cdot\;\;\cdot\;\;\cdot\;\;\cdot\;\;\cdot\;\;\cdot\;\;\cdot \\
a_n &= (-1)^n x_1 x_2 x_3 \ldots x_n
\end{aligned}\right\} \begin{array}{l} \text{Viète's} \\ \text{relations.} \end{array}$$

In words: The coefficient of

x^{n-1} is equal to the negative sum of the roots.

x^{n-2} is equal to the positive sum of products of roots taken two at a time.

x^{n-3} is equal to the negative sum of products of roots taken three at a time.

x^{n-4} is equal to the positive sum of products of roots taken four at a time.

In general, x^{n-k} is equal to $(-1)^k$ times the sum of products of roots taken k at a time.

The constant term is the product of all the roots, with sign $(-1)^n$.

8. If an equation $f(x) = 0$ with real coefficients has the complex root $x_1 = a + ib$, it also has the conjugate complex number $x_2 = a - ib$ as a solution.

9. The general equation of the nth degree, $n > 4$, is not soluble by means of radicals, *i.e.* for such equations there is no solution-formula by which the solutions can be calculated from the coefficients by rational operations and the extraction of roots. For equations of the 1st, 2nd, 3rd and 4th degrees, such general methods of solution do exist.

However, special forms of the equation of the nth degree can be solved by radicals, *e.g. binomial equations* (see below) and *symmetrical equations* of the 5th and 7th degrees.

Solution of equations with one unknown

An equation is said to be solved when all numbers have been determined which, when substituted for x in the equation, satisfy it. These numbers are called solutions, or roots, of the equation. For special equations (algebraic equations of the 1st, 2nd, 3rd and 4th degrees, symmetrical equations, binomial equations) there are procedures for solution. All such methods of solution start from the normal form of the equations, and so in such cases the equation must first be brought into suitable normal form. For this purpose the following rules are useful. Note that all equations remain true if their left- and right-hand sides are subjected to the same procedures of calculation. These general rules also illustrate the rules for solution of particularly simple conditional equations.

Addition of the same number to left and right:

$$\begin{array}{r} x - 2 = 4 \\ +2 +2 \\ \hline x = 6. \end{array}$$

Subtraction of the same number:

$$x + 5 = 10$$
$$\underline{-5 \quad -5}$$
$$x = 5.$$

Multiplication by the same number:

$\dfrac{x}{4} = 3$, so, multiplying by 4, we have

$x = 12.$

Division by the same number (other than 0):

$7x = 63$, so, dividing by 7, we have

$x = 9.$

Raising to equal powers or taking roots of equal orders:

$$4x^2 = 36, \qquad\qquad \sqrt[3]{x} = 2,$$
$$\text{so } 2x = 6. \qquad \text{so} \quad x = 8.$$

Taking the logarithm of both sides:

$$2^x = 37.$$
$$\text{so } x \log 2 = \log 37.$$

Interchange of the two sides:

$$a + x = 2b - c \quad \text{and}$$
$$2b - c = a + x \quad \text{are equivalent.}$$

The following examples illustrate the application of these rules in bringing an equation to normal form:

1. Equations in which the unknown occurs in the denominator of a fraction:

$\dfrac{9x + 1}{8x - 24} + 2 + \dfrac{x + 5}{x - 3} = \dfrac{9x - 7}{2x - 6}$. Least common denominator:

$$8(x - 3).$$

We multiply numerator and denominator of all fractions so that each possesses the denominator $8(x - 3)$:

$$\frac{9x + 1}{8x - 24} + \frac{2 \cdot 8(x - 3)}{8x - 24} + \frac{8(x + 5)}{8x - 24} = \frac{4(9x - 7)}{8x - 24}.$$

Now we multiply the whole equation by the common denominator, obtaining an equation of the first degree:

$$9x + 1 + 16(x - 3) + 8(x + 5) = 4(9x - 7).$$

We multiply out and add corresponding numbers:

$$9x + 1 + 16x - 48 + 8x + 40 = 36x - 28,$$

that is, $$33x - 7 = 36x - 28.$$

We add 7 to both sides of the equation and subtract from both sides $36x$:

$$-3x = -21.$$

Finally, we divide through by -3:

$$x = 7.$$

2. Equations in which the unknown enters under a root sign: Only in special cases do these equations lead to equations of the first degree. Here is an example in which we arrive at a quadratic equation:

$$\sqrt{5 + x} - \sqrt{5 - x} = 2.$$

We square the equation:

$$5 + x + 5 - x - 2\sqrt{(5 + x)(5 - x)} = 4.$$

We then rearrange the equation so that the root is isolated on one side of it:

$$2\sqrt{(5 + x)(5 - x)} = 6$$

and square once more:

$$4(5 + x)(5 - x) = 36.$$

We calculate the product and divide through by 4:

$$25 - x^2 = 9.$$

In this way we reach a quadratic equation

$$x^2 - 16 = 0$$

with solutions

$$x_1 = +4$$

and $$x_2 = -4.$$

In such 'root-equations' it is essential to test possible solutions in the original equation. We substitute the calculated value $x_1 = 4$ for x in the original equation; if an identical equation arises, x_1 is a solution of the root-equation.

$$\sqrt{5+4} - \sqrt{5-4} = 2$$

is evidently true, so $x_1 = 4$ is a solution.

But if we substitute $x_1 = -4$ for x we have,

$$\sqrt{5-4} - \sqrt{5+4} = 1 - 3 = -2,$$

so $x_2 = -4$ is not a solution.

Methods of solution for algebraic equations

(1) *Equations with one unknown*

(a) *Equations of the first degree* (linear equations with one unknown): Equations of the first degree contain the quantity to be determined raised at most to the first power. The normal form of these equations is:

$$ax + b = 0.$$

We refer to ax as the linear term and to b as the constant term.

Example: $\qquad\qquad 4x - 8 = 0.$

To solve this type of equation we subtract b from both sides, obtaining $ax = -b$. Finally we divide each side by a, which gives $x = \dfrac{-b}{a}.$

Example: If $\qquad\qquad 4x - 8 = 0,$

then $\qquad\qquad\qquad\quad 4x = 8,$

that is, $\qquad\qquad\qquad\quad x = 2.$

(b) *Equations of the second degree* (quadratic equations with one unknown): Equations of the second degree contain the unknown raised at most to the second power. The normal form of these equations is

$$x^2 + px + q = 0$$

Here x^2 is the square term, px the linear term and q the constant term. If $p = 0$, no linear term is present, and we have a pure quadratic equation; if $p \neq 0$, we have a mixed quadratic equation.

Example: $x^2 - 9 = 0$ is a pure quadratic equation;

$x^2 + 5x - 10 = 0$ is a mixed quadratic equation.

Solution of the pure quadratic equation.

In the equation $x^2 + q = 0$ we can subtract q from both sides to obtain: $x^2 = -q$. On extracting the root we have:

$$x_1 = +\sqrt{-q} \quad \text{or} \quad x_2 = -\sqrt{-q}.$$

Examples:

$$x^2 - 9 = 0, \qquad\qquad x^2 + 4 = 0,$$
$$\text{or } x^2 = 9, \qquad\qquad \text{or } x^2 = -4,$$
$$\text{that is, } x_1 = 3 \qquad \text{that is, } x_1 = +2i$$
$$\text{and } x_2 = -3. \qquad\qquad \text{and } x_2 = -2i.$$

A pure quadratic equation has two solutions, x_1 and x_2. These differ only in sign. If the constant term of the pure quadratic equation is positive the equation has two so-called imaginary solutions which also differ only in sign.

Solution of the mixed quadratic equation

$$x^2 + px + q = 0.$$

In this equation we first subtract q from both sides, giving

$$x^2 + px = -q.$$

Now we 'complete the square', *i.e.* we add the number $\left(\dfrac{p}{p}\right)^2$ to each side of the equation

$$x^2 + px + \left(\frac{p}{2}\right)^2 = -q + \left(\frac{p}{2}\right)^2.$$

The left hand side of this equation is identical with

$$\left(x + \frac{p}{2}\right)^2,$$

and so the equation now reads

$$\left(x + \frac{p}{2}\right)^2 = \left(\frac{p}{2}\right)^2 - q.$$

By taking the square root of both sides of the equation we get

$$x + \frac{p}{2} = \pm\sqrt{\left(\frac{p}{2}\right)^2 - q}.$$

Finally we now subtract $\frac{p}{2}$ from both sides of the equation. The solutions of the mixed quadratic equation are therefore:

$$x_1 = -\frac{p}{2} + \sqrt{\left(\frac{p}{2}\right)^2 - q}, \quad x_2 = -\frac{p}{2} - \sqrt{\left(\frac{p}{2}\right)^2 - q}.$$

The following solution formula is widely used: The quadratic equation

$$ax^2 + bx + c = 0$$

has solutions:

$$x_1 = \frac{-b + \sqrt{b^2 - 4ac}}{2a}, \qquad x_2 = \frac{-b - \sqrt{b^2 - 4ac}}{2a}.$$

Example 1: $x^2 - x - 30 = 0$. Here $p = -1$, $q = -30$,

so
$$x_1 = \frac{1}{2} + \sqrt{\frac{1}{4} + 30}, \qquad x_2 = \frac{1}{2} - \sqrt{\frac{1}{4} + 30},$$

that is, $\quad x_1 = \frac{1}{2} + \sqrt{\frac{121}{4}} = 6, \qquad x_2 = \frac{1}{2} - \sqrt{\frac{121}{4}} = -5.$

Example 2: $5x^2 - 10x - 120 = 0$. Here $a = 5$, $b = -10$, $c = -120$, so

$$x_1 = \frac{10 + \sqrt{100 - 4 \cdot 5\,(-120)}}{10} = \frac{10 + \sqrt{100 + 2400}}{10}$$

$$= \frac{10 + 50}{10} = 6,$$

and $x_2 = \dfrac{10 - \sqrt{100 - 4 \cdot 5(-120)}}{10} = \dfrac{10 - \sqrt{100 + 2400}}{10}$

$$= \frac{10 - 50}{10} = -4.$$

Every quadratic equation has two solutions which can be either different real numbers, the same real number, or conjugate complex numbers, depending on the value of the discriminant

$$D = b^2 - 4ac.$$

If $b^2 - 4ac$ is positive we have two different real solutions; if $b^2 - 4ac = 0$ we have a real double-solution; if $b^2 - 4ac$ is negative the equation has two conjugate complex solutions.

Example 1: $4x^2 - 12x + 5 = 0$. In this case

$$b^2 - 4ac = 12^2 - 4 \cdot 4 \cdot 5 = 144 - 80 = 64,$$

that is, $b^2 - 4ac$ is positive, so there are 2 different real solutions, *viz.*

$$x_1 = \frac{5}{2}, \quad x_2 = \frac{1}{2}.$$

Example 2:

$$4x^2 - 12x + 9 = 0; \; b^2 - 4ac = 12^2 - 4 \cdot 4 \cdot 9 = 0,$$

thus we have a real double-root, *viz.*

$$x_1 = x_2 = \frac{3}{2}.$$

Example 3:

$$4x^2 - 12x + 13 = 0; \; b^2 - 4ac = 12^2 - 4 \cdot 4 \cdot 13 = 144 - 208$$

is negative, so we have 2 conjugate complex roots, *viz.*

$$x_1 = \frac{3}{2} + i; \quad x_2 = \frac{3}{2} - i.$$

Note that if x_1 and x_2 are solutions of the quadratic equation

$$x^2 + px + q = 0,$$

we have $\quad x_1 + x_2 = -p; \; x_1 x_2 = q.$

(c) *Equations of the third degree* (cubic equations with one unknown): Equations of the third degree contain the unknown raised at most to the third power. The normal form of these equations is

$$x^3 + ax^2 + bx + c = 0.$$

By the substitution $x = y - \dfrac{a}{3}$ we obtain from the normal form the reduced form

$$y^3 + 3py + 2q = 0,$$

where

$$3p = -\frac{a^2}{3} + b, \quad \text{and} \quad 2q = \frac{2a^3}{27} - \frac{ab}{3} + c.$$

Solution of the reduced cubic equation

1. *Cardan's formula* (published 1545). If $q^2 + p^3 \geq 0$, we first calculate the (real) quantities:

$$u = \sqrt[3]{-q + \sqrt{q^2 + p^3}}, \qquad v = \sqrt[3]{-q - \sqrt{q^2 + p^3}}.$$

The solutions of the reduced equation are then:

$$y_1 = u + v$$

$$y_2 = -\frac{u + v}{2} + \frac{i}{2} \cdot \sqrt{3} \cdot (u - v)$$

$$y_3 = -\frac{u + v}{2} - \frac{i}{2} \cdot \sqrt{3} \cdot (u - v).$$

2. *Trigonometrical solutions* $(p \neq 0,\, q \neq 0)$:

(1) $q^2 + p^3 \geq 0$.

(a) $p > 0$. From the equations

$$\tan \phi = \frac{+\sqrt{p^3}}{q} \quad \text{and} \quad \tan \psi = \sqrt[3]{\tan \frac{\phi}{2}}$$

we evaluate the angles ϕ and ψ which lie in the intervals

$$-\frac{\pi}{2} < \phi < \frac{\pi}{2} \quad \text{and} \quad -\frac{\pi}{4} < \psi < \frac{\pi}{4}.$$

The solutions of the reduced equation can then be expressed as:

$$y_1 = -2 \underset{+}{\sqrt{p}} \cot 2\psi$$

$$y_2 = \underset{+}{\sqrt{p}} \left(\cot 2\psi + \frac{i\sqrt{3}}{\sin 2\psi} \right)$$

$$y_3 = \underset{+}{\sqrt{p}} \left(\cot 2\psi - \frac{i\sqrt{3}}{\sin 2\psi} \right).$$

(b) $p < 0$. From the equations

$$\sin \phi = \frac{\pm\sqrt{-p^3}}{q}, \qquad \tan \psi = \sqrt[3]{\tan \frac{\phi}{2}},$$

we evaluate ϕ and ψ, where

$$-\frac{\pi}{2} < \phi < \frac{\pi}{2}; \qquad -\frac{\pi}{4} < \psi < \frac{\pi}{4}.$$

The solutions of the reduced equation are then

$$y_1 = -2 \sqrt[+]{-p} \, \frac{1}{\sin 2\psi}$$

$$y_2 = \sqrt[+]{-p} \left(\frac{1}{\sin 2\psi} + i\sqrt{3} \cot 2\psi \right)$$

$$y_3 = \sqrt[+]{-p} \left(\frac{1}{\sin 2\psi} - i\sqrt{3} \cot 2\psi \right).$$

(2) $q^3 + p^3 \leq 0$ (irreducible case).
We evaluate the angle ϕ from the equation

$$\cos \phi = \frac{-q}{+\sqrt{-p^3}}, \qquad \begin{array}{l} \text{taking } \phi \text{ in the II quadrant, if } q \text{ is positive,} \\ \text{and } \phi \text{ in the I quadrant, if } q \text{ is negative.} \end{array}$$

The solutions of the equation can then be expressed as:

$$y_1 = 2 \sqrt[+]{-p} \, \cos \frac{\phi}{3}$$

$$y_2 = -2\sqrt[+]{-p} \cos \left(\frac{\phi}{3} + 60° \right)$$

$$y_3 = -2\sqrt[+]{-p} \cos \left(\frac{\phi}{3} - 60° \right).$$

The cubic equation therefore possesses

1. Three real and different solutions if $q^2 + p^3 < 0$,
2. Three real solutions, of which at least two are equal, if $q^2 + p^3 = 0$,
3. One real and two conjugate complex solutions if $q^2 + p^3 > 0$.

Example 1: $x^3 + 6x^2 - 60x - 416 = 0$. We have $a = 6$ and to obtain the reduced equation we put $x = y - 2$.

Then

$$(y - 2)^3 = y^3 - 6y^2 + 12y - \quad 8$$
$$6(y - 2)^2 = \quad + 6y^2 - 24y + \quad 24$$
$$-60(y - 2) = \quad \quad - 60y + 120$$
$$-416 = \quad \quad \quad \quad - 416$$

The reduced equation therefore reads

$$y^3 - 72y - 280 = 0$$

with $p = -24$, $p^3 = -13,824$, Therefore: $3p = -72$,
and $q = -140$, $q^2 = -19,600$. $2q = -280$,
and $q^2 + p^3 = 5776$.

We take

$$u = \sqrt[3]{140 + \sqrt{5776}} = \sqrt[3]{140 + 76} = \sqrt[3]{216} = 6$$

and $v = \sqrt[3]{140 - \sqrt{5776}} = \sqrt[3]{140 - 76} = \sqrt[3]{64} = 4$,

and the solutions of the reduced equations are therefore:

$$y_1 = u + v = 6 + 4 = 10,$$

$$y_2 = -\frac{u + v}{2} + \frac{i}{2}\sqrt{3}(u - v) = -5 + i\sqrt{3},$$

$$y_3 = -\frac{u + v}{2} - \frac{i}{2}\sqrt{3}(u - v) = -5 - i\sqrt{3}.$$

Putting $x = y - 2$ we have as solutions of the original equation:

$$x_1 = 8; \quad x_2 = -7 + i\sqrt{3}; \quad x_3 + -7 - i\sqrt{3}.$$

Example 2: $x^3 + 3x^2 - 36x + 36 = 0$. We have $a = 3$ and so we put $x = y - 1$. Then

$$(y - 1)^3 = y^3 - 3y^2 + \quad 3y - \quad 1$$
$$3(y - 1)^2 = \quad + 3y^2 - \quad 6y + \quad 3$$
$$-36(y - 1) = \quad \quad - 36y + 36$$
$$+36 \quad = \quad \quad \quad \quad + 36$$

and the reduced equation therefore reads

$$y^3 - 39y + 74 = 0 \qquad \text{Therefore: } 3p = -39,$$

with $p = -13$, $p^3 = -2197$, $\qquad\qquad\qquad 2q = \quad 74,$

and $q = 37$, $\quad q^2 = \quad 1369.$ $\qquad$ and $q^2 + p^3 = -828.$

(This is the irreducible case.)

We therefore put $\cos \phi = -\dfrac{37}{\sqrt{2197}}$.

$$\log \quad 37 = 1 \cdot 5682$$
$$\log 2197 = 3 \cdot 3418$$
$$0 \cdot 5 \log 2197 = 1 \cdot 6709$$

so that $\qquad \log(-\cos \phi) = 9 \cdot 8973 - 10$

and therefore $\qquad\qquad\qquad \phi = 142° \, 8'$

(in the II quadrant, since q is positive).

The solutions of the

| reduced equation are therefore: | original equation are therefore: |

$$y_1 = \quad 2\sqrt{13} \cos 47° \, 23' = 4 \cdot 881 \qquad x_1 = 3 \cdot 881$$

$$y_2 = -2\sqrt{13} \cos 107° \, 23' = 2 \cdot 154 \qquad x_2 = 1 \cdot 154$$

$$y_3 = -2\sqrt{13} \cos(-12° \, 37') = -7 \cdot 035 \quad x_3 = -8 \cdot 035$$

(d) *Equations of the fourth degree* (biquadratic equations): Equations of the fourth degree contain the unknown raised at most to the fourth power. The normal form of these equations is

$$x^4 + ax^3 + bx^2 + cx + d = 0.$$

By the substitution $y = x - \dfrac{a}{4}$ we obtain from the normal form the *reduced equation* of the fourth degree, containing no cubic term:

$$y^4 + py^2 + qy + r = 0.$$

We isolate y^4:

$$y^4 = -py^2 - qy - r.$$

201

We add now to both sides of the equation the expression $2y^2z + z^2$, where z is an unknown. We get

$$y^4 + 2y^2z + z^2 = -py^2 - qy - r + 2y^2z + z^2,$$

and so $$(y^2 + z)^2 = y^2(2z - p) - qy + z^2 - r.$$

We now choose z so that the expression on the right hand side of this equation becomes a perfect square. For this we must have $\dfrac{qy}{2z - p}$ equal to twice the product of y and $\dfrac{z^2 - r^2}{2z - p}$, and so the equation for z is

$$q^2 = 4(z^2 - r)(2z - p), \quad \text{the } \textit{cubic resolvent.}$$

This cubic resolvent is an equation of the third degree in z, and can therefore be solved. If z_1, z_2 and z_3 are the solutions, then the solutions of the reduced equation of the fourth degree are

$$y = \pm\sqrt{z_1} \pm \sqrt{z_2} \pm \sqrt{z_3},$$

where the signs are so chosen that

$$\sqrt{z_1} \cdot \sqrt{z_2} \cdot \sqrt{z_3} = -\frac{q}{8}.$$

Binomial equations. An equation of the form $x^n - a = 0$ is called a binomial equation. The equation

$$x^n = 1 = \cos 2k\pi + i \sin 2k\pi \quad (k \text{ any integer})$$

has n roots

$$x_1 = \cos \frac{2.0.\pi}{n} + i \sin \frac{2.0.\pi}{n},$$

$$x_2 = \cos \frac{2\pi}{n} + i \sin \frac{2\pi}{n},$$

$$x_3 = \cos \frac{2.2.\pi}{n} + i \sin \frac{2.2.\pi}{n}, \ldots,$$

$$x_{n-1} = \cos \frac{2(n-2)\pi}{n} + i \sin \frac{2(n-2)\pi}{n},$$

$$x_n = \cos \frac{2(n-1)\pi}{n} + i \sin \frac{2(n-1)\pi}{n}.$$

The equation

$$x^n = -1 = \cos(2k+1)\pi + i\sin(2k+1)\pi \quad (k \text{ any integer})$$

has n roots:

$$x_1 = \cos\frac{\pi}{n} + i\sin\frac{\pi}{n}, \; x_2 = \cos\frac{3\pi}{n} + i\sin\frac{3\pi}{n},$$

$$x_3 = \cos\frac{5\pi}{n} + i\sin\frac{5\pi}{n}, \ldots,$$

$$x_n = \cos\frac{(2n-1)\pi}{n} + i\sin\frac{(2n-1)\pi}{n}.$$

Example 1: $x^2 = +1$; the roots are

$$x_1 = \cos 0 + i\sin 0 = +1, \quad x_2 = \cos\pi + i\sin\pi = -1.$$

Example 2: $x^2 = -1$; the roots are

$$x_1 = \cos\frac{\pi}{2} + i\sin\frac{\pi}{2} = +i, \; x_2 = \cos\frac{3\pi}{2} + i\sin\frac{3\pi}{2} = -i.$$

Example 3: $x^3 = +1$; the roots are $x_1 = 1$,

$$x_2 = \cos\frac{2\pi}{3} + i\sin\frac{2\pi}{3} = \cos 120° + i\sin 120° = -\frac{1}{2} + \frac{i}{2}\sqrt{3},$$

$$x_3 = \cos\frac{4\pi}{3} + i\sin\frac{4\pi}{3} = \cos 240° + i\sin 240° = -\frac{1}{2} - \frac{i}{2}\sqrt{3}.$$

Example 4: $x^3 = -1$; the roots are

$$x_1 = \cos\frac{\pi}{3} + i\sin\frac{\pi}{3} = \cos 60° + i\sin 60° = \frac{1}{2} + \frac{i}{2}\sqrt{3},$$

$$x_2 = -1,$$

$$x_3 = \cos\frac{5\pi}{3} + i\sin\frac{5\pi}{3} = \cos 300° + i\sin 300° = +\frac{1}{2} - \frac{i}{2}\sqrt{3}.$$

Example 5: The equation $x^n - a = 0$, a positive, can now be solved in the following way. We put

$$x^n = a = a \cdot (\cos 2k\pi + i\sin 2k\pi).$$

By $\sqrt[n]{a}$ we denote the real positive nth root of a. It follows by de Moivre's theorem that

$$x_1 = \sqrt[n]{a}\,(\cos 0 + i\sin 0)$$

$$x_2 = \sqrt[n]{a}\left(\cos\frac{2\pi}{n} + i\sin\frac{2\pi}{n}\right)$$

$$x_3 = \sqrt[n]{a}\left(\cos\frac{4\pi}{n} + i\sin\frac{4\pi}{n}\right)$$

. . . .

$$x_n = \sqrt[n]{a}\left(\cos\frac{2(n-1)\pi}{n} + i\sin\frac{2(n-1)\pi}{n}\right).$$

The solutions of the equation $x^n + a = 0$, a positive, correspondingly read

$$x_1 = \sqrt[n]{a}\left(\cos\frac{\pi}{n} + i\sin\frac{\pi}{n}\right)$$

$$x_2 = \sqrt[n]{a}\left(\cos\frac{3\pi}{n} + i\sin\frac{3\pi}{n}\right)$$

. . . .

$$x_n = \sqrt[n]{a}\left(\cos\frac{(2n-1)\pi}{n} + i\sin\frac{(2n-1)\pi}{n}\right).$$

Integral solutions of algebraic equations of the nth degree with integral coefficients

We note first that the solutions of an algebraic equation of the nth degree with integral coefficients, the coefficient of x^n being unity, *e.g.*

$$x^3 - 6x^2 + 11x - 6 = 0,$$

are either integral numbers, irrational numbers or complex numbers, but never rational non-integral numbers. Now the constant term in such an equation is, by Viète's relations, the product of all the roots, and so if an integral equation possesses an integral root, this root must be a factor of the constant term in the equation. In such an equation, therefore, we can take all the factors of the constant term and determine one by one whether they are solutions of the equation. If in doing this we find no solutions of the equation, then there are no rational solutions of the equation. We must then use methods of approximation to find the real irrational solutions of the equation.

Example: $\qquad x^4 - x^3 - 21x^2 + x + 20 = 0.$

The factors of the constant term are:

$+1, -1, +2, -2, +4, -4, +5, -5, +10, -10, +20, -20.$

We insert these values in turn in the equation:
$x = +1; 1 - 1 - 21 + 1 + 20 = 0.$

> For $x = +1$ an identity arises. $x_1 = 1$ is a root of the equation.

$x = -1; 1 + 1 - 21 - 1 + 20 = 0.$

> For $x = -1$ the equation is satisfied. $x_2 = -1$ is the second root.

$x = +2; 16 - 8 - 84 + 2 + 20 = -54.$

> $x = +2$ is not a root of the equation.

$x = -2; 16 + 8 - 84 - 2 + 20 = -42.$

> $x = -2$ is not a root of the equation.

$x = +4; 256 - 64 - 336 + 4 + 20 = -120.$

> $x = 4$ is not a root of the equation.

$x = -4; 256 + 64 - 336 - 4 + 20 = 0.$

> For $x = -4$ the equation is satisfied. $x_3 = -4$ is the third root of the equation.

$x = +5; 625 - 125 - 525 + 5 + 20 = 0.$

> $x = 5$ is the fourth root of the equation.

Hence the four roots of the equation have been found.

If the equation is not given in normal form, then we must first express it in this form. If

$$a_0x^n + a_1x^{n-1} + a_2x^{n-2} + \ldots + a_n = 0$$

is the given equation, we must first multiply through by a_0^{n-1} and then write z in place of $a_0 x$. We then have the following equation:

$$z^n + a_1 z^{n-1} + a_2 a_0 z^{n-2} + a_3 a_0^2 z^{n-3} + \ldots + a_n a_0^{n-1} = 0.$$

If we know a solution, z_1, of this equation, we can obtain a solution of the original equation by putting $x_1 = \dfrac{z_1}{a_0}$.

Example: $\qquad 10x^3 + 7x^2 - 4x - 1 = 0.$

Multiply through by 100:

$$(10x)^3 + 7 \cdot (10x)^2 - 40 \cdot 10x - 100 = 0.$$

We write $10x = z$ and obtain:

$$z^3 + 7z^2 - 40z - 100 = 0.$$

The factors of 100 are:

$+1, -1, +2, -2, +4, -4, +5, -5, +10, -10, +20, -20,$
$+25, -25, +50, -50, +100, -100.$

We insert these values in the equation:

$z = +1; \quad 1 + 7 - 40 - 100 \neq 0$ (no solution),

$z = -1; \; -1 + 7 + 40 - 100 \neq 0$ (no solution),

$z = +2; \quad 8 + 28 - 80 - 100 \neq 0$ (no solution),

$z = -2; \; -8 + 28 + 80 - 100 = 0;$

$z_1 = -2$ is a root of the equation.

Instead of continuing this procedure, we can divide the left hand side of the equation by the linear factor $z + 2$:

$$(z^3 + 7z^2 - 40z - 100) \div (z + 2) = z^2 + 5z - 50,$$

$$\begin{array}{l} \underline{-(z^3 + 2z^2)} \\ \quad 5z^2 - 40z \\ \quad \underline{-(5z^2 + 10z)} \\ \qquad -50z - 100 \\ \qquad \underline{-(-50z - 100)} \\ \qquad\qquad 0 \end{array}$$

and find the remaining two solutions from the equation:

$$z^2 + 5z - 50 = 0.$$

This has solutions

$$z_2 = +5, \quad z_3 = -10.$$

Lastly, we obtain from z_1, z_2 and z_3:

$$x_1 = \frac{-2}{10} = -\frac{1}{5}, \; x_2 = \frac{5}{10} = \frac{1}{2}, \; x_3 = \frac{-10}{10} = -1.$$

Symmetrical equations

An equation is called *reciprocal* or *symmetrical* if the reciprocal value of every root is also a root.

Example: $x^2 - \dfrac{5}{2} x + 1 = 0$ is a reciprocal equation since it has solutions $x_1 = 2$ and $x_2 = \frac{1}{2}$.

Every reciprocal equation of odd degree has as one root either $x_1 = +1$ or $x_1 = -1$.

If we write $\dfrac{1}{x}$ in place of x everywhere in a reciprocal equation, the equation transforms into itself, and every reciprocal equation is therefore symmetrical in its coefficients. Every reciprocal equation of odd degree is divisible by $x - 1$ or $x + 1$; it then becomes a reciprocal equation of even degree. If we divide a reciprocal equation of degree $2n$ ($2n$ is always even if n is a natural number) through by x^n then the equation

$$A_{2n}x^{2n} + A_{2n-1}x^{2n-1} + \ldots + A_n x^n + A_{n-1}x^{n-1} + \ldots$$
$$+ A_1 x + A_0 = 0$$

becomes:

$$A_{2n}x^n + A_{2n-1}x^{n-1} + \ldots + A_n + A_{n-1} \cdot \frac{1}{x} \ldots$$
$$+ A_1 \cdot \left(\frac{1}{x}\right)^{n-1} + A_0 \cdot \left(\frac{1}{x}\right)^n = 0.$$

On account of the symmetry of the coefficients, we can associate

207

the first with the last term, the second with the next to the last, and so on, and write

$$x + \frac{1}{x} = u,\ x^2 + \frac{1}{x^2} = u^2 - 2,\ x^3 + \frac{1}{x^3} = u^3 - 3u,\ \ldots,$$

or

$$x - \frac{1}{x} = u,\ x^2 + \frac{1}{x^2} = u^2 + 2,\ x^3 - \frac{1}{x^3} = u^3 + 3u,\ \ldots..$$

We obtain then an equation of degree n with unknown u. If we can find the solutions $u_1, u_2, \ldots, u_n$ of this equation, we can calculate the roots of the original equation.

Example: $6x^5 + 11x^4 - 33x^3 - 33x^2 + 11x + 6 = 0.$

By substitution we establish that $x_1 = -1$ is a solution. We divide through by $x + 1$ to obtain:

$$6x^4 + 5x^3 - 38x^2 + 5x + 6 = 0.$$

Dividing through by x^2 we get:

$$6x^2 + 5x - 38 + \frac{5}{x} + \frac{6}{x^2} = 0.$$

We next collect together symmetrical terms:

$$6 \left(x^2 + \frac{1}{x^2} \right) + 5 \left(x + \frac{1}{x} \right) - 38 = 0.$$

Putting $x + \frac{1}{x} = u$, we have

$$x^2 + \frac{1}{x^2} = u^2 - 2,$$

so that

$$6(u^2 - 2) + 5u - 38 = 0.$$

The solutions of this equation are:

$$u_1 = \frac{5}{2},\ \ u_2 = -\frac{10}{3}.$$

Then

$$x + \frac{1}{x} = \frac{5}{2}, \quad \text{giving} \quad x_2 = 2,\ x_3 = \frac{1}{2},$$

and

$$x + \frac{1}{x} = -\frac{10}{3}, \quad \text{giving} \quad x_4 = -3, \; x_5 = -\frac{1}{3}.$$

Equations, linear systems of

If we have to determine the values of unknowns occurring in a number of equations which are simultaneously true, we speak of a system of equations, *e.g.* a system comprising two equations with two unknowns:

$$\text{I.} \quad x + y = 5,$$
$$\text{II.} \quad x - y = 3.$$

Where more than two or three unknowns occur, it is usual to denote the unknowns by x_1, x_2, x_3, . . . (read: 'x-one, x-two, x-three'); *e.g.*

$$\text{I.} \quad 5x_1 - 2x_2 + x_3 = 1,$$
$$\text{II.} \quad x_1 \qquad - x_3 = 0,$$
$$\text{III.} \qquad\qquad x_2 + x_3 = -1.$$

Two linear equations with two unknowns

The following methods of solution are available:

A. Substitution method
B. Equating method
C. Addition method
D. Determinant method (see *Determinants*).

A. *The Substitution method.* Here we use one of the equations to obtain the value of one of the unknowns in terms of the other, and then substitute this value in the other equation. This provides an equation in one unknown; *e.g.*

$$\text{I.} \quad x + 7y = 21,$$
$$\text{II.} \quad 4x - 3y = 22.$$

From the first equation we obtain $x = 21 - 7y$. We substitute this value of y in the second equation, getting

$$4(21 - 7y) - 3y = 22,$$
$$\text{that is,} \quad -31y = -62,$$
$$\text{or} \quad y = 2.$$

If we substitute back in the equation $x = 21 - 7y$, we have

$$x = 21 - 14 = 7,$$

and so the system of equations has the solution $x = 7$, $y = 2$.

B. *The Equating method.* Here we calculate the same unknown from each equation, *e.g.* x, and equate the results. In this way we obtain an equation in one unknown, which we solve and then obtain the value of the other unknown by substitution.

Example: I. $x - y = 3$ giving: $x = 3 + y$

              II. $2x + 2y = 14$ giving: $x = 7 - y$

Equating the results we have:

$$3 + y = 7 - y \text{ with the solution } y = 2.$$

Substitute $y = 2$ in equation I: $x - 2 = 3$, or $x = 5$. Solution of the system is then: $x = 5$, $y = 2$.

C. *Addition or Subtraction method.* Here we obtain an equation in only one of the unknowns by adding suitable multiples of the original equations. The remaining unknown is calculated from this equation and the result substituted in one of the original equations so that the other unknown may be calculated.

Example: I. $x - y = 3$ (-2) (numbers in brackets

          II. $2x + 2y = 14$ $(+1)$ are the multiples taken)

$$-2x + 2y = -6$$
$$2x + 2y = 14$$

Adding, we have $4y = 8$,

or $y = 2$.

We put $y = 2$ in equation I, and obtain $x - 2 = 3$, that is, $x = 5$.

Three (or more) equations with three (or more) unknowns

The procedures used in systems of equations with two unknowns can also be used for systems with more than two unknowns.

Example 1:   I. $2x + 3y = 12$,

                II. $3x + 2z = 11$,

                III. $3y + 4z = 10$.

Using the substitution method we proceed as follows:

From equation I we obtain $3y = 12 - 2x$. This is substituted in equations II and III:

$$\text{II.} \quad 3x \qquad + 2z = 11,$$
$$\text{III.} \quad 12 - 2x + 4z = 10.$$

These are two equations in two unknowns.

From equation II we obtain $2z = 11 - 3x$. If we substitute this in equation III:

$$12 - 2x + 22 - 6x = 10,$$

we get $24 = 8x$, or $\underline{x = 3}$.

From this we can calculate z and y.

$$2z = 11 - 9 \qquad 3y = 12 - 6$$
$$\underline{z = 1} \qquad\qquad \underline{y = 2}$$

Example 2:
$$\text{I.} \quad x + y + z = 7,$$
$$\text{II.} \quad 2x + y - z = 14,$$
$$\text{III.} \quad x - y \qquad = 2.$$

Using the equating method we proceed as follows:

$$\text{I.} \quad y = 7 - x - z,$$
$$\text{II.} \quad y = 14 - 2x + z,$$
$$\text{III.} \quad y = x - 2.$$

Equating the expressions on the right in pairs we obtain two equations in two unknowns:

(A) $\quad 7 - x - z = x - 2;$ that is, $2x + z = 9$

(B) $\quad 14 - 2x + z = x - 2;$ that is, $3x - z = 16.$

Equation (A) gives $\qquad z = 9 - 2x,$

equation (B) gives $\qquad z = 3x - 16;$

equating, we have $3x - 16 = 9 - 2x$, giving

$$5x = 25 \qquad y = x - 2 \qquad z = 9 - 10$$
$$\underline{x = 5} \qquad y = 5 - 2 \qquad \underline{z = -1}$$
$$\qquad\qquad \underline{y = 3}$$

211

Example 3:

I. $3x + 2y + z = 8$ | (-2) | 1
II. $2x + 3y + 2z = 11$ | 3 |
III. $x - y + 2z = 6$ | | (-3)

Using the addition method we add (-2) times equation I to 3 times equation II, to give equation (A) below. We add equation I to (-3) times equation III to give equation (B).

$$(A) \ 5y + 4z = 17,$$
$$(B) \ 5y - 5z = -10.$$

Subtracting equation (B) from equation (A) we have

$$9z = 27,$$

that is,

$$z = 3.$$

Substituting $z = 3$ in equation (A) we get

$$5y + 12 = 17,$$

that is,

$$5y = 5,$$
$$\underline{y = 1.}$$

Lastly, substituting $z = 3$ and $y = 1$ in equation III we get

$$x - 1 + 6 = 6,$$
$$\underline{x = 1.}$$

Equilateral triangle

If all three sides of a triangle are equal it is called equilateral. The three internal angles of an equilateral triangle are equal to 60°. For further theorems, see *Triangle*.

Error

If a measurement is taken twice and the results differ, as is likely if the measurements are read to many significant figures, this difference is called the observation-difference d.

The so-called mean error (m^*) of the observation-difference is

$$m^* = \frac{d}{\sqrt{2}} = 0 \cdot 707 \ d.$$

The error of one of a sequence of measurements can be defined as the deviation of the single reading a_n from the actual unique true value a of the entity concerned. In the theory of error the apparent error is the deviation from an estimate (usually the *arithmetic mean*; see above) based on the totality of different readings. An error is called *systematic* if it is constant and arises from a cause which is usually recognisable (*e.g.* temperature changes in the surroundings). Such an error is not considered in the theory of error.

An accidental error is an error ε, whose cause is frequently unknown, such as to be legitimately regarded as outside our control and unavoidable. This type of error alone is a subject for the *theory of error*. Where many readings are available, its character can be established by means of the frequency-diagram, or histogram (see *Error, theory of*).

A true error is the deviation ε_n of a measurement a_n from the (usually unknown) true value, a, of the object measured: $\varepsilon_n = a - a_n$.

v_n (the apparent error) is the deviation of a_n from the mean value, μ_1, of the differing readings: $v_n = \mu_1 - a_n$.

Suppose in the measurement of a quantity a the values $a_1, a_2, \ldots, a_n$ are observed. If a_0 is the true value of the quantity to be measured $a_0 - a_1 = \varepsilon_1, a_0 - a_2 = \varepsilon_2, \ldots, a_0 - a_n = \varepsilon_n$ are called the true errors of the individual observations. But usually the true value and the true error are unknown. However, the occurrence of a large sequence of values for one and the same measurement can serve to yield, not indeed the true value, but the most probable estimate of it. If the frequency curve has been demonstrated to be symmetric *Gauss's* method of least squares can be used (see *Method of least squares*).

The *probable error* w is 0·674 times the standard error of the mean (see below)

$$w = 0{\cdot}674 \cdot m = 0{\cdot}674 \sqrt{\frac{\Sigma v^2}{N(N-1)}} = 0{\cdot}674 \sqrt{\frac{[v\,v]}{N(N-1)}}.$$

There is the same probability that the true value lies inside or outside the range $a_m \pm w$.

The *mean error* δ is the arithmetic mean of the individual

213

errors in a sequence of measurements taken without regard to sign.

$$\delta = \frac{\Sigma v}{N} = 0.7979m.$$

The *standard error of the single observation a_n* of a sequence of measurements is for N observations

$$\mu = \sqrt{\frac{\Sigma v^2}{N-1}} = \sqrt{\frac{[v\,v]}{N-1}}.$$

The *standard error m of the arithmetic mean* is, for N observations,

$$m = \sqrt{\frac{\Sigma v^2}{N(N-1)}} = \sqrt{\frac{[v\,v]}{N(N-1)}}.$$

Error, theory of

The theory of error enables one, given a large number of observations (a_n) on one and the same quantity, to calculate that value which probably lies closest to the true and unknown value (a). In addition it enables us to provide a measure of the accuracy of a sequence of measurements. If the end result is given in the form $a \pm \Delta a$, or in numbers, *e.g.* as 345 ± 3, it is important to make clear whether (taking ± 3 as an example) we mean

(a) an absolute bound (tolerance); *i.e.* the true value certainly lies in the range 345 ± 3;

(b) a mean error (u) of the individual measurement;
a mean error (m) of the arithmetic mean;
a probable error (w) of the arithmetic mean,

where in the last case (w) the probabilities that the true value lies within and outside the range 345 ± 3, are both equal to $\frac{1}{2}$, while the probability of the true value lying in double the range, (345 ± 6), is 95 per cent. The difference between the true value and the observation is called the error. Since the true value is usually unknown, the difference v between observation and arithmetic mean is also called the error.

The theory of error deals only with accidental errors (see above). Their nature can be investigated by means of the frequency curve.

An example of a method in the theory of error is the *Method of least squares*. For further information, see *Error, Frequency curves, Mean value, Distribution, Method of least squares*.

Escribed circle

A circle which touches one side of a triangle externally and touches the extensions of the other two sides is called an escribed circle of the triangle. A triangle has three escribed circles (see *Triangle*).

Euclidean algorithm

The euclidean algorithm is a procedure for determining the highest common factor of two numbers. If a and b are two positive integers and $a > b$, then in carrying out the euclidean algorithm we perform the following divisions:

$$a = q_0 \cdot b + r_2 \qquad (0 < r_2 < b)$$
$$b = q_1 \cdot r_2 + r_3 \qquad (0 < r_3 < r_2)$$
$$r_2 = q_2 \cdot r_3 + r_4 \qquad (0 < r_4 < r_3)$$
$$\cdots \cdots \cdots \qquad \cdots \cdots$$
$$r_{n-2} = q_{n-2} \cdot r_{n-1} + r_n \qquad (0 < r_n < r_{n-1})$$
$$r_{n-1} = q_{n-1} \cdot r_n + 0$$

This procedure must eventually end since the remainders progressively decrease and are positive integers. The last remainder r_n is the highest common factor of the two numbers a and b.

Example: To determine the highest common factor of 693 and 147. Dividing, we have

$$693 = 4 \cdot 147 + 105$$
$$147 = 1 \cdot 105 + 42$$
$$105 = 2 \cdot 42 + 21$$
$$42 = 2 \cdot 21 + 0$$

The highest common factor of 693 and 147 is therefore 21.

Euclid's theorem

In every right-angled triangle the square on one of the shorter sides (legs) is equal in area to the rectangle formed by the hypotenuse and the projection of this leg on the hypotenuse; $b^2 = cq$ or $a^2 = cp$ (Fig. 142).

By means of this theorem a rectangle can be transformed into a square of equal area. If c and q are the sides of the given rectangle we mark off the shorter side from one end point of the longer (in Fig. 143 $q < c$). From the point thus obtained we erect the perpendicular to the longer side $\overline{AB}$ and determine the point of intersection, C, of this perpendicular with the Thales circle on $\overline{AB}$. The segment $\overline{AC}$ is the side of the required square.

In the same way Euclid's theorem can be used to transform a square into a rectangle of equal area with one side given.

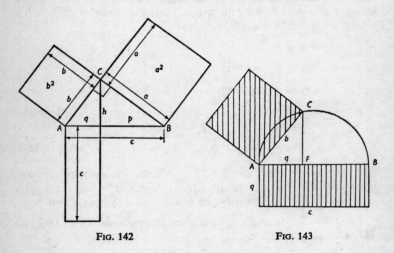

FIG. 142   FIG. 143

Euler's line

In a triangle the centre of the circumscribed circle, the ortho-centre and the centroid (intersection of side-bisectors) all lie on a straight line, known as *Euler's line*. The centroid divides the segment between the other two points in the ratio $1:2$.

Euler's theorem on polyhedra

Euler's theorem on polyhedra is as follows: If a convex polyhedron has s surfaces, e edges and v vertices, then $v + s = e + 2$ (see *Polyhedron*).

Exponential equations

Exponential equations are equations in which the unknown appears in the exponent of a power, *e.g.*

$$3^x = 6561; \quad 7^{x+1} = 3^{2x-1} + 3^{2x+1}.$$

Simple exponential equations can be solved by taking the logarithm of both sides (possibly reforming the equation before doing so, see example (ii)); *e.g.*

(i) $3^x = 6561$; take logarithms:

$$x \cdot \log 3 = \log 6561$$

$$0 \cdot 47712 \cdot x = 3 \cdot 81697$$

$$x = \frac{3 \cdot 81697}{0 \cdot 47712}$$

$$x = 8 \cdot 00002; \text{ that is, } x \approx 8.$$

(ii) $7^{x+1} = 3^{2x+1} + 3^{2x-1}$; take out the factor 3^{2x} on the right hand side.

Then $7^{x+1} = 3^{2x} \left(\dfrac{1}{3} + 3 \right)$; taking logarithms of both sides we have

$$(x + 1) \log 7 = 2x \log 3 + \log \left(\frac{1}{3} + 3 \right);$$

that is

$$x \left(\log 7 - 2 \log 3 \right) = \log \left(3 + \frac{1}{3} \right) - \log 7,$$

or

$$x \log \frac{7}{3^2} = \log \frac{10}{3} - \log 7,$$

that is,

$$x \log \frac{7}{9} = \log \frac{10}{21}, \text{ or } x = \frac{\log \frac{10}{21}}{\log \frac{7}{9}} = \frac{-0 \cdot 32222}{-0 \cdot 10914} = 0 \cdot 29524.$$

There is no general method for the solution of exponential equations. In difficult cases numerical or graphical methods must be used (see *False position, rule of, Newton's method of approximation*).

Exponential function

A function of the form $y = a^x$, where a is an arbitrary constant greater than zero and x is variable between $-\infty$ and $+\infty$, is termed exponential.

An exponential function has the property:

$$a^{x_1} \cdot a^{x_2} = a^{x_1 + x_2}.$$

If $a = e$ we have the important exponential function $y = e^x$. The inverse of this function $y = e^x$ is $y = \ln x$ (see Fig. 144). It was proved by Leibniz that exponential functions are transcendental (see also *Infinitesimal calculus* and *Inverse functions*).

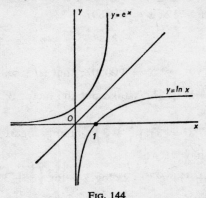

FIG. 144

Exponential series

The exponential series

$$e^x = 1 + \frac{x}{1!} + \frac{x^2}{2!} + \frac{x^3}{3!} + \cdots$$

converges for all x. In particular we have

$$2 \cdot 7182818 \ldots = e^1 = 1 + \frac{1}{1!} + \frac{1}{2!} + \frac{1}{3!} + \cdots + \frac{1}{n!} + \cdots.$$

With base a the exponential series reads (a a fixed positive number)

$$a^x = e^{x \ln a} = 1 + \frac{(\ln a)}{1!} x + \frac{(\ln a)^2}{2!} x^2 + \frac{(\ln a)^3}{3!} x^3 + \ldots$$

$$+ \frac{(\ln a)^n}{n!} x^n + \ldots .$$

This series also converges for all values of x.

Exterior angles

The exterior angles of a polygon lie outside the polygon and between its sides or the extensions of its sides; they are adjacent to (and supplementary to) interior angles. Since the extension can be of either side there corresponds to every interior angle two equal exterior angles. The sum of either set of exterior angles of a polygon ($\alpha_1 + \beta_1 + \gamma_1 + \delta_1 + \varepsilon_1$ in Fig. 145) is always $360°$.

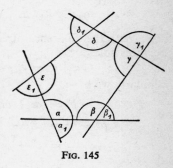

Fig. 145

Factorial, $n!$ (read: 'n-factorial')

For positive integers n the product of the first n natural numbers is called 'n-factorial' and is written $n! = 1 . 2 . 3 \ldots (n-1) . n$. For $n = 0$, $0!$ is defined as 1.

Examples: $1! = 1$ $\qquad 3! = 1 \times 2 \times 3 = 6$

$2! = 1 \times 2 = 2$ $\qquad \ldots \ldots$

For large numbers the approximation $n! = n^n . e^{-n} \sqrt{2\pi n}$ can be used (*Stirling's Formula*).

Factorisation

The formation of a product from a sum is called factorisation; *e.g.*

$$a^2 + 2ab + b^2 = (a + b)(a + b).$$

219

The following simple procedures can be used for finding factors:

1. Factors common to several terms of a sum can be taken out.

$$35a^2x + 15bx^2 - 28a^3 - 12abx$$
$$= 5x(7a^2 + 3bx) - 4a(7a^2 + 3bx)$$
$$= (7a^2 + 3bx)(5x - 4a).$$

2. Given the square of a binomial expression, the formula

$$a^2 + 2ab + b^2 = (a + b)^2$$

can be compared with the given expression:

$$9x^4 + 6x^2 + 1 = (3x^2 + 1)(3x^2 + 1).$$

3. With the difference of two squares the following important relation holds:

$$a^2 - b^2 = (a + b)(a - b).$$

Similarly we have

$$a^3 - b^3 = (a^2 + ab + b^2)(a - b)$$
$$a^4 - b^4 = (a^2)^2 - (b^2)^2 = (a^2 + b^2)(a^2 - b^2)$$
$$= (a^2 + b^2)(a + b)(a - b)$$
$$= (a + ib)(a - ib)(a + b)(a - b).$$

If the difference of two squares is multiplied by a factor this must first be taken out:

$$108x^2y^2c - 75a^2c = 3c(36x^2y^2 - 25a^2)$$
$$= 3c(6xy + 5a)(6xy - 5a).$$

4. If we suspect we have the product of two *linear factors*, the following formula can be tried:

$$x^2 + (a + b)x + ab = (x + a)(x + b),$$

e.g. $$x^2 + 3x - 10 = (x + 5)(x - 2).$$

5. In expressions of the form

$$x^n + a_1x^{n-1} + a_2x^{n-2} + \ldots + a_n = f(x)$$

a linear factor of the type $x - b$ can often be found by taking as b the factors of a_n, and so testing each factor of a_n in turn. This should only be done when all the coefficients $a_1, a_2, \ldots, a_n$

are integers, *e.g.*

$$f(x) = x^4 - 6x^3 + 3x^2 + 11x - 5$$
$$= (x - 5)(x^3 - x^2 - 2x + 1).$$

False position, rule of

The rule of false position is an iterative method for the solution of equations.

If the solutions of the conditional equation $f(x) = 0$ are required, we consider the functional equation $y = f(x)$. The zeros of this functional equation (that is, those values of the abscissa x in which the curve represented by the functional equation intersects the x-axis) are then the solutions of the conditional equation. If $f(x)$ is continuous in the interval $x_1 \leq x \leq x_2$ and $y_1 = f(x_1)$ and $y_2 = f(x_2)$ have opposite signs, then $f(x)$ has at least one zero, x_0 in the interval $x_1 \leq x \leq x_2$. The rule of false positions yields an approximate value for this zero. But the function $y = f(x)$ should not have a point of inflexion in the neighbourhood of the point under investigation.

According to the rule, the curve associated with the function is replaced between the points $P_1(x_1, y_1)$ and $P_2(x_2, y_2)$ by the straight line segment joining these points. Instead of the point of intersection of the function with the x-axis, the point of intersection x_3 of the straight line with the x-axis is taken as approximate value (see Fig. 146).

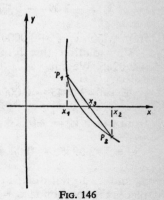

Fig. 146

The equation of the chord through the points $P_1(x_1, y_1)$ and $P_2(x_2, y_2)$ is

$$y = \frac{y_2 - y_1}{x_2 - x_1} x - \frac{x_1 y_2 - x_2 y_1}{x_2 - x_1}.$$

The point of intersection with the x-axis ($y = 0$) therefore has the abscissa

$$x_3 = \frac{x_1 y_2 - x_2 y_1}{y_2 - y_1} = \begin{cases} x_1 - y_1 \dfrac{x_2 - x_1}{y_2 - y_1} \text{ or} \\[2ex] x_2 - y_2 \dfrac{x_2 - x_1}{y_2 - y_1}. \end{cases}$$

221

The representation of x_3 is used for which the number subtracted (the correction) is smaller.

Example: (Calculation of the y-value can be carried out according to the Horner array method.) To solve the equation $x^3 - 2x + 5 = 0$. We put $y = x^3 - 2x + 5$, and note that for $x_1 = -2$, $y = 1$; for $x_2 = -2\cdot1$, $y_2 = -0\cdot061$. A solution of the equation must therefore lie between $x_1 = -2$ and $x_2 = -2\cdot1$. Using the formula

$$x_3 = x_1 - y_1 \cdot \frac{x_2 - x_1}{y_2 - y_1},$$

we have

$$x_3 = -2 - 1 \cdot \frac{-2\cdot1 + 2}{-0\cdot061 - 1} = -2\cdot094,$$

to which the corresponding value of y_3 is $0\cdot0061$. The solution must therefore lie between $x_3 = -2\cdot094$ and $x_2 = 2\cdot1$. We put again

$$x_4 = -2\cdot094 - 0\cdot0061 \cdot \frac{-2\cdot094 + 2\cdot1}{0\cdot0061 + 0\cdot061} = -2\cdot0945,$$

from which $y_4 = +0\cdot0006$.

The solution therefore lies between $x_2 = -2\cdot1$ and $x_4 = -2\cdot0945$. We put

$$x_5 = -2\cdot0945 - 0\cdot0006 \cdot \frac{-2\cdot0945 + 2\cdot094}{-0\cdot0006 - 0\cdot0061} = -2\cdot09455,$$

from which $y_5 = +0\cdot00002$. We put

$$x_6 = -2\cdot09455 - 0\cdot00002 \frac{-2\cdot09455 + 2\cdot0945}{-0\cdot00002 + 0\cdot0006} = -2\cdot094552.$$

x_5 and x_6 do not differ in the fifth decimal place, and so to five places the solution is $x_0 = -2\cdot09455$.

Extension of the rule of false position

The method of the rule of false position can be improved so that with the same number of steps a better approximation is obtained. Instead of as above setting up a straight line segment with two points $P_1(x_1, y_1)$ and $P_2(x_2, y_2)$ we now use three points. The third point $P_3(x_3, y_3)$, is so chosen that $x_3 - x_2 = x_2 - x_1$

$= h$ (where it is assumed that $x_1 \leq x_2 \leq x_3$). Corresponding to x_3 we must of course calculate $y_3 = f(x_3)$ (as above). With a new variable t we then form the function $x(t) = x_2 + ht$. This function takes

for $t = 0$ the value $x = x_2$

for $t = 1$ the value $x = x_2 + h = x_2 + (x_3 - x_2) = x_3$, and

for $t = -1$ the value $x = x_2 + h(-1) = x_2 - (x_2 - x_1) = x_1$.

We further form the function

$$y(t) = y_2 + \frac{1}{2}(y_3 - y_2 + y_2 - y_1)t + \frac{1}{2}[y_3 - y_2 - (y_2 - y_1)]t^2.$$

The functions $x(t)$ and $y(t)$ represent a parabola which passes through the three points $P_1(x_1, y_1)$, $P_2(x_2, y_2)$ and $P_3(x_3, y_3)$. The zero of the quadratic equation $y(t) = 0$ which belongs to the above parabola yields an approximation $x(t)$ to the zero of the function $y = f(x)$.

Example: To solve the equation $x^3 - 2x + 5 = 0$. We choose the values $x_1 = -2$, $x_2 = -2 \cdot 05$ and $x_3 = -2 \cdot 1$ giving

$$x(t) = x_2 + ht = -2 \cdot 05 - 0 \cdot 05t.$$

For $x_1 = -2$ we have $y_1 = x_1^3 - 2x_1 + 5$, *i.e.* $y_1 = +1$,

$x_2 = -2 \cdot 05$ we have $y_2 = +0 \cdot 4849$,

$x_3 = -2 \cdot 1$ we have $y_3 = -0 \cdot 061$.

The following lay-out is convenient to use:

$$\left.\begin{array}{l} y_1 = \quad 1 \\ y_2 = \quad 0 \cdot 4849 \\ y_3 = -0 \cdot 061 \end{array}\right\} \begin{array}{l} y_2 - y_1 = -0 \cdot 5151; \\ \qquad y_3 - y_2 - (y_2 - y_1) = -0 \cdot 0308, \\ y_3 - y_2 = -0 \cdot 5459; \\ \qquad y_3 - y_2 + (y_2 - y_1) = -1 \cdot 0610. \end{array}$$

Therefore

$$y(t) = 0 \cdot 4849 + \frac{1}{2}(-1 \cdot 0610)t + \frac{1}{2}(-0 \cdot 0308)t^2,$$

that is,

$$y(t) = 0 \cdot 4849 - 0 \cdot 5305t - 0 \cdot 0154t^2.$$

We now require those values of t for which $y(t) = 0$. It is sufficient to determine an approximate value, *e.g.* the value of t for which $0.4849 = 0.5305t$. This equation gives $t = 0.9140$. With this value of t we get:

$$x = -2.05 - 0.05t = -2.0957,$$

the required approximation. Corresponding to this we have

$$y = -0.0154t^2 = -0.013.$$

Feuerbach's Circle (1800–1834, Erlangen)

The circle of Feuerbach (the nine-point circle of a triangle) is determined by the three mid-points of the sides of a triangle. In addition, it passes through the feet of the three altitudes, and through the three points midway between the orthocentre (the intersection of altitudes) and the vertices. The Feuerbach circle touches the three escribed circles and the incircle of the triangle. The radius of the Feuerbach circle is equal to half the radius of the circumscribed circle, its centre lies on Euler's line and forms, together with the centre of the circumscribed circle, the orthocentre and the centroid, a harmonic range of points.

Folium of Descartes

The folium of Descartes belongs to the class of algebraic curves. It can be represented by the equation

$$x^3 + y^3 = 3axy.$$

In polar coordinates the equation of this curve is

$$r = \frac{3a \sin \phi \cos \phi}{\sin^3 \phi + \cos^3 \phi}$$

(see Fig. 147).

Formula

A formula is a frequently-used calculating rule expressed succinctly by means of literal numbers and mathematical signs, *e.g.*

$$(a + b)^2 = a^2 + 2ab + b^2.$$

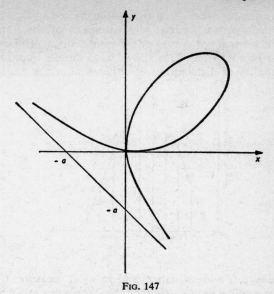

Fig. 147

Frequency curve (Fig. 148)

This is a graphical presentation of the distribution of accidental errors about an estimate (usually the *arithmetic mean*, see above) of the unknown true value. The number of measurements within a range $(a_n + \Delta a)$ is taken as ordinate, and the range of measurements itself as abscissa. Clearly this sort of presentation is only meaningful if a large number of measurements (at least 100) is being dealt with.

Gauss discussed the frequently-occurring and so-called *normal distribution* for accidental errors, and developed an analytical expression for this bell-shaped curve. If the intervals taken for ranges of measurements is made smaller and smaller (which is possible only when there is an infinite number of observations) we finally obtain a continuous function $F(x)$ whose integral

$$\int_{a_n}^{a_m} F(x)\, dx$$

represents the number of outcomes for which the observed value lies between n and m.

225

If the ordinates are divided by a value chosen so that the area beneath the frequency curve $= 1$ we speak of the normalised curve. The normalised curves of different sequences of measurements can be compared. This allows us to discuss questions such as the equality of distribution of either side of the mean value,

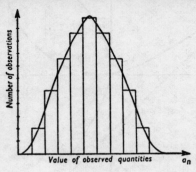

FIG. 148

and thereby to decide whether, and in what measure, the error calculus is applicable, *i.e.* whether the distribution which occurs actually is a chance distribution. Gauss's distribution is represented by

$$J = \frac{h}{\sqrt{\pi}}\, e^{-h^2 x^2},$$

where h is a parameter which gives the form (peaked or flat) of the curve.

The proportion of errors, according to a Gaussian distribution, which lie between $-v_1$ and $+v_1$ is

$$\frac{2h}{\sqrt{\pi}} \int_0^{v_1} e^{-h^2 v^2}\, dv.$$

Other expressions, given other assumptions, have been given for frequency curves, notably by Poisson.

Frequency, relative

If an experiment is performed N times and a particular outcome occurs g times the quotient $\frac{g}{N}$ is called the relative frequency of this outcome.

If a sufficient number of trials is made, the relative frequency of an outcome approaches the probability of occurrence of the event.

Examples: 1. If a die is thrown N times and a six occurs g times, the relative frequency of occurrence of 6 is $\frac{g}{N}$.

2. If in an experiment which is repeated N times, one of several outcomes can occur at each repetition, then a relative frequency can be determined for each possible outcome. The sum of the relative frequencies must then equal 1.

Of 30 children 5 have fair hair, 5 red, 10 brown and 10 black. The relative frequencies are then:

fair-haired: $\frac{5}{30}$; red-haired: $\frac{5}{30}$; brown-haired: $\frac{10}{30}$; and black-haired: $\frac{10}{30}$.

Function

Numerical dependence of a quantity on one or more other variable quantities. The area of a square is, *e.g.*, a function of the length of side, the frequency of a piano string a function of its length, cross-section and tension, the weight of a litre of dry air a function of pressure and of temperature. In the strict mathematical interpretation y is called a function of x if, corresponding to each permissible value of x, a value of y can be calculated or observed. We write: $y = f(x)$ and say: y is equal to f of x (or simply fx); other letters and symbols can be used in place of f (e.g. F, ϕ, f_1, f', etc.). x is called the argument; it is the *independent* variable. y is the dependent variable, since its value depends on x. If x can take all values in an interval, *e.g.* every value between -1 and $+1$, x is said to vary continuously. Further the function $y = f(x)$ is said to be continuous at a point x_0 in the given interval if as $x \to x_0$ y tends to a finite value which is equal to $f(x_0)$. It is often helpful to represent a continuous function of a single independent variable by the coordinates of a curve (graphical representation, graph of a function); for at each point P of the curve (Fig. 149) a value x on the horizontal axis is related to a definite value y on the perpendicular axis.

227

An *equation* involving x and y can give y as an 'implicit' function of x: *e.g.* $4x^2 + 9y^2 = 36$. Solution of this particular equation gives two 'explicit' functions

$$y = \pm 2\sqrt{1 - \left(\frac{x}{3}\right)^2},$$

i.e. in this example y is many-valued. If y is a function of x, x is usually also a function of y, called the *inverse function*. If we

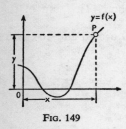

FIG. 149

have an equation linking three variables x, y and z then z (say) is determined as a function of x and y: $z = f(x, y)$. Such a function is represented graphically by a *surface*.

Graphical representation becomes impossible when we allow x to take complex values. The theory of functions, which was founded by *Riemann, Cauchy* and *Weierstrass*, deals with the general properties of functions.

A function $f(x)$ can also be determined by a *series*, a differential or integral equation, or by functional equations. Some common functions have special labels: examples are the *exponential function e^x*, the *trigonometrical* functions $\sin x$, $\cos x$, $\tan x$, $\cot x$, the *hyperbolic* functions $\sinh x$, $\cosh x$, $\tanh x$, $\coth x$, and the *inverse* trigonometric functions $\sin^{-1}$, etc. ($=$ arc $\sin x$; *i.e.* the angle, in radian measure, whose sine has the value x). The inverse of the function $y = a^x$ yields the function $x = \log_a y$ (*logarithm*). The *gamma-function*, $\Gamma(x)$, first discussed by Euler, is an extension of the *factorial* function $x!$, for factorials are defined only for positive integral x ($y = x! = 1 . 2 . 3 \ldots x$) (see p. 219).

For much-used functions there are available function-tables in which function-values y are calculated for sufficient numbers of values of x for practical purposes: *Tables of Logarithms, Tables of Exponential Functions*, etc. (see *Mathematical Tables: Table* 4).

Fundamental constructions

The following geometrical constructions are in frequent use and are referred to as fundamental constructions (see *Construction, geometrical*).

1. Measuring off a segment.
2. Construction of an angle on a line.
3. Bisection of a segment.
4. Erection of a perpendicular on a straight line.
5. Dropping of a perpendicular from a point onto a straight line.
6. Construction of a parallel to a straight line, through a given point.
7. Construction of a parallel to a straight line at distance *a*.
8. Bisection of an angle.

1. *Measuring off a segment.* If a given segment *a* is to be measured off from a point *P* on a straight line *l* we describe a circle about *P* with radius *a*. The circle intersects *l* in two points *A* and *B*, giving $\overline{PA}$ or $\overline{PB}$ as the required segment. In other words, we can measure off a segment from *P* on two different sides, and so the side required must be specified.

2. *Construction of an angle on a line* (Fig. 150). If the angle α has vertex *S* and arms *h* and *k* we describe about *S* a circle with arbitrary radius *r*. This circle cuts the arms of α in the points *H*

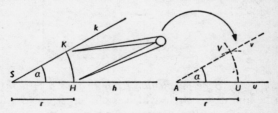

Fig. 150

and *K*. Suppose now the angle α is to be constructed at the point *A* on the straight line *u*. About the point *A* describe a circle of radius *r*, and about the point *U* describe another circle with radius $\overline{HK}$. This intersects the former circle in two points *V* and *V′*. Either the line $\overline{AV}$ or the line $\overline{AV'}$ is the required second arm of the angle; as in the marking off of a segment, the side of the line on which the angle is to lie must be specified.

3. *Bisection of a segment.* We describe about the end-points *A* and *B* two circles of equal size whose points of intersection *C*

and D we join. The join bisects the segment in M and is perpendicular to it, and so is called the perpendicular bisector of $\overline{AB}$ (Fig. 151).

4. *Erection of a perpendicular on the point P.* We describe about P a circle which intersects l in A and B, and about these points we describe two circles of equal size whose intersections are C and D, say. The line $\overline{CD}$ is the required perpendicular (Fig. 152).

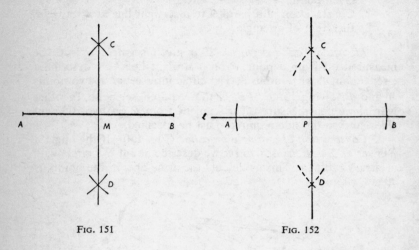

FIG. 151   FIG. 152

5. *Dropping of a perpendicular from P onto a straight line l.* We describe about P a circle which is chosen so as to intersect l in A and B, and about these points we describe two circles of equal size whose intersections C and D we join. The join passes through P and is the perpendicular from P onto the straight line (Fig. 153).

6. *To draw through P a parallel to a straight line l.* Draw through P a straight line l_1 which intersects l in A, and construct at P on l_1 the angle α which l makes with l_1; the free arm m of this angle is the required parallel (Fig. 154).

7. *To draw a parallel to a straight line at distance a.* Erect at any point A of the straight line l the perpendicular h, mark off on this the segment of length a and through the end point B draw the perpendicular l_1 to h (Fig. 155).

230

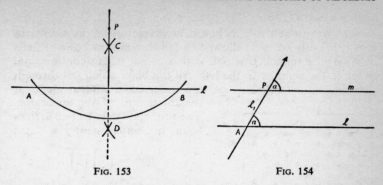

FIG. 153   FIG. 154

8. *Bisection of an angle.* Describe a circle of arbitrary radius r about the vertex S, intersecting the arms in A and B, and then describe about A and B two equal circles intersecting in C; the line joining C to S bisects the angle (Fig. 156).

Fundamental theorem of algebra

The fundamental theorem of algebra is as follows: Every algebraic equation of the nth degree

$$a_0 x^n + a_1 x^{n-1} + \ldots + a_{n-1} x + a_n = 0$$

whose coefficients are real numbers possesses at least one (real or complex) root. An algebraic equation of the nth degree with one unknown, and real coefficients, possesses exactly n roots, provided every solution (real and complex) is counted according to its multiplicity.

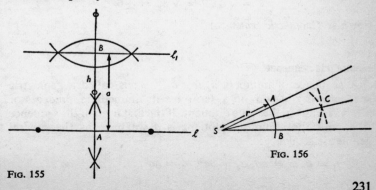

FIG. 156

FIG. 155

Galton's board (1822–1911)

Nails are driven into a board in several rows, as shown in Fig. 157. Balls are now allowed to fall through the rows of nails by way of a funnel. If a ball strikes a nail it can continue on, either to the right or to the left. All the balls which fall through are collected in compartments at the lower end of the apparatus. The probability that a ball arrives below in compartment x is then:

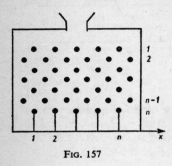

FIG. 157

$$f(x) = \binom{n}{x}\left(\frac{1}{2}\right)^n.$$

As there are n rows of nails, $(n+1)$ compartments are required. Given five rows of nails we would expect to find the following proportions of balls in the six compartments, reading from left to right:

$$\frac{1}{32}, \frac{5}{32}, \frac{10}{32}, \frac{10}{32}, \frac{5}{32}, \frac{1}{32}.$$

Geometric mean

The geometric mean of two numbers, a, b is $x = \sqrt{ab}$.

Example: The geometric mean of the numbers 4 and 9 is:

$$x = \sqrt{4 \cdot 9} = \sqrt{36} = \pm 6$$

(see also *Geometric sequence*).

Geometric sequence

A sequence of numbers a_1, a_2, a_3, . . . is called a geometric sequence if division of a term by its immediate predecessor always results in the same quotient. If the first term of the sequence is a_1 and the common quotient is q we have as the general geometric sequence:

$$a_1 = a, \ a_2 = aq, \ a_3 = aq^2, \ a_4 = aq^3, \ . . ., a_n = aq^{n-1}.$$

232

Thus a geometric sequence is uniquely determined by its initial term and the quotient q. In a geometric sequence every term is the *geometric mean* of its neighbouring terms:

$$a_n = \sqrt{a_{n-1} \cdot a_{n+1}}.$$

The following cases of geometric sequences can be distinguished:

1. $q > 1$

   The sequence increases, *e.g.* 1, 2, 4, 8, 16, ...

2. $q = 1$

   All terms of the sequence are equal, *e.g.* 2, 2, 2, ...

3. $0 < q < 1$

   The sequence is decreasing, *e.g.* $a_1 = 2$, $q = \frac{1}{2}$: 2, 1, $\frac{1}{2}$, $\frac{1}{4}$, $\frac{1}{8}$, $\frac{1}{16}$, $\frac{1}{32}$, ...

4. $0 > q > -1$

   The terms of the sequence are alternately positive and negative, *e.g.* $a = 1$, $q = -\dfrac{1}{10}$: 1, $-\dfrac{1}{10}$, $\dfrac{1}{100}$, $-\dfrac{1}{1000}$, ...

5. $-1 > q$

   The terms of the sequence have alternately positive and negative signs and their absolute values increase, *e.g.*

   $$a = 1, \dot{q} = -2:$$

   $$1, -2, +4, -8, +16, \ldots .$$

Sequences with $q > 1$ and with $-1 > q$ are *divergent sequences* (see below). Sequences with $q = -1$ are oscillatory. Sequences with $-1 < q \leq +1$ are convergent.

Geometric series

The sum of an (unevaluated) geometric sequence is called a geometric series:

$$s_n = a + aq + aq^2 + \ldots + aq^{n-1} + \ldots .$$

Sum of a finite geometric series. The sum of a geometric series with a finite number of terms can be evaluated. It is

$$s_n = a + aq + aq^2 + aq^3 + aq^4 + \ldots + aq^{n-1} = a\,\frac{(1-q^n)}{1-q}.$$

Example: $a = 3, q = 2, n = 10$.

$$s_{10} = 3 + 6 + 12 + 24 + \ldots + 3 \cdot 2^9 = 3 \cdot \frac{(1 - 1024)}{1 - 2}.$$
$$= 3 \cdot 1023 = 3{,}069.$$

Infinite geometric series. An infinite geometric series is one formed from an infinite geometric sequence.

The sum of an infinite geometric series

The sum

$$s_n = a + aq + aq^2 + aq^3 + \ldots + aq^{n-1}$$

is a partial sum of an infinite geometric sequence. The partial sums for $n = 1, 2, 3, 4, \ldots$ can be determined, and so we have a sequence of partial sums. This sequence has the terms

$$s_1 = a = \frac{a(1-q)}{1-q},$$

$$s_2 = a + aq = \frac{a(1-q^2)}{1-q},$$

$$s_3 = a + aq + aq^2 = \frac{a(1-q^3)}{1-q},$$

$$s_4 = a + aq + aq^2 + aq^3 = \frac{a(1-q^4)}{1-q},$$

. . . .

$$s_n = a + aq + aq^2 + aq^3 + \ldots + aq^{n-1} = \frac{a(1-q^n)}{1-q},$$

. . . .

If we consider the general term of the sequence of partial sums

$$s_n = \frac{a(1-q^n)}{1-q} = \frac{a}{1-q} - \frac{aq^n}{1-q},$$

we find as its *limit* the value $s = \dfrac{a}{1-q}$, provided $|q| < 1$.

$s = \dfrac{a}{1-q}$ is defined to be the sum of the infinite geometric series.

Example: $a = 2, q = \dfrac{1}{4}$.

$$s = 2 + \frac{1}{2} + \frac{1}{8} + \frac{1}{32} + \ldots = \frac{2}{1 - \frac{1}{4}} = \frac{8}{3}.$$

Geometric series

The unevaluated sums of the terms of a *geometric sequence* (see above) is referred to as a geometric series.

Geometrical elements

The fundamental element of linear geometry is the point.

The fundamental elements of plane geometry are the point and the straight line.

The fundamental elements of solid geometry are the point, the straight line and the plane.

These geometrical elements are regarded as directly given. Their properties are determined by the axioms of the geometry.

Golden section

A segment is said to be divided in golden section if the larger segment is the mean proportional between the complete segment and the smaller segment. This is equivalent to saying that the ratio of the complete segment to the larger segment is equal to the ratio of the larger segment to the smaller.

Construction: Draw a circle, with centre O, whose radius is half the length of the complete segment $a = \overline{AB}$ which is to be divided in golden section (Fig. 158). Let $\overline{AC}$ be a diameter of the circle. Draw the tangent to the circle at A and mark off on it from A a segment of length a, with end-point B. Draw the secant

235

of the circle from B through O, cutting the circle in points D and E. BD is the larger of the two segments required. This follows from the *Tangent theorem* (see below) which tells us that

$$\overline{BD} . \overline{BE} = \overline{AB}^2$$

that is,

$$a^2 = x(a + x), \text{ or } a(a - x) = x^2,$$

that is,

$$a:x = x:(a - x).$$

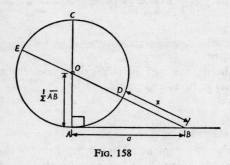

Fig. 158

The actual ratios of the section can be calculated from the relation $a:x = x:(a - x)$, i.e.

$$x = \frac{a}{2}(\sqrt{5} - 1), \ a - x = \frac{a}{2}(3 - \sqrt{5}).$$

If the original segment is of length 1 the lengths of the two sections are 0·618 and 0·382 approximately.

The ratio of the two sections is irrational, since $\sqrt{5}$ is, of course, irrational. This ratio can be approximated to by rational numbers. For example, we can take as approximations:

$$\frac{5}{8}, \frac{8}{13}, \frac{13}{21}, \frac{21}{34}, \ \cdot \ \cdot \ \cdot \ \cdot$$

Properties of the golden section: If the smaller segment is marked off on the corresponding larger segment then the larger segment is itself divided in golden section.

If the original segment is extended by the length of its larger

236

sub-segment then the original segment divides the extended segment in golden section. With the help of these two theorems, given a single golden section an arbitrary number of further golden sections can be constructed.

Gradient of a straight line

The gradient of a straight line is tan α, where α is the angle which the straight line makes in a rectangular coordinate system with the positive x-axis (see Fig. 159).

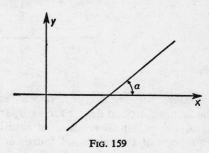

FIG. 159

Graphical solution of equations

If an equation is to be solved graphically it must be put in the form $f(x) = 0$. The conditional equation $f(x) = 0$ yields the functional equation $y = f(x)$. This equation can be represented in a *coordinate system* (see above) by a curve (see *Function*). The points of intersection of this curve with the x-axis give the required solutions.

Equations of the first degree. The functional equations associated with equations of the first degree yield straight lines.

Example: $3x - 4 = 0$.

The associated functional equation is: $y = 3x - 4$ (Fig. 160).

Equations of the second degree. Here the type of curve we get is a parabola.

Example: $7 - \dfrac{x^2}{2} = 0$. The functional equation is: $y = 7 - \dfrac{x^2}{2}$.

The solutions are: $x_1 = 3\cdot8$ and $x_2 = -3\cdot8$ (Fig. 161).

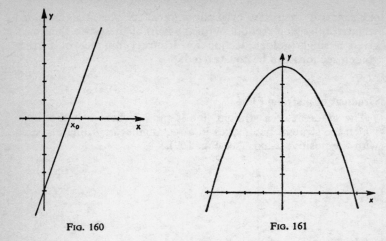

FIG. 160   FIG. 161

Algebraic equations of higher degree, transcendental equations.
Equations of the first and second degree are easily solved directly;
the application of the graphical method of solution is tedious
and inexact. Equations of the third and fourth degree with one
unknown can also be solved formally, but the calculations
required may be extensive. Algebraic equations of higher degree,
and transcendental equations, in general cannot be formally
solved, but their graphical representation provides the possibility
of discovering approximate solutions which can then be used,
following various known methods, to give solutions as accurately
as desired (see *False position, rule of*).

With transcendental equations a knowledge of the relations
between functions can facilitate graphical representation.

Equations of third and higher degrees. For ease of graphical
representation it is often convenient to split a function into two
functions and obtain the required solutions from their intersections, *e.g.*

$$f(x) = x^2 + \frac{1}{x} - 2 = 0, \; i.e. \; x^2 - 2 = -\frac{1}{x}$$

may be handled by means of $y = x^2 - 2$ and $y = -\frac{1}{x}$ (Fig.
162), *i.e.* two functions whose difference is $f(x)$. The abscissae of

238

their points of intersection are solutions of the equation $f(x) = 0$. We conclude that the equation of the third degree

$$x^3 - 2x + 1 = 0$$

has three roots whose approximate values are: $-1 \cdot 6$, $+0 \cdot 6$, and $+1 \cdot 0$.

Graphical solution of equations with first degree with two unknowns

Example: $x + 2y = 4 \qquad 2x - y = 1$ (Fig. 163)

1st equation: $y = 2 - \dfrac{x}{2}$;   2nd equation: $y = 2x - 1$

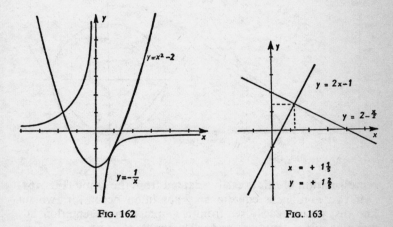

FIG. 162   FIG. 163

Each equation can be represented by a straight line. These lines intersect in a point, whose coordinates are the only values which satisfy both equations. They represent, therefore, the solution of the equations:

$$x = +1\tfrac{1}{5}; \quad y = +1\tfrac{2}{5}.$$

Graphical solution is particularly useful and instructive in the case of so-called equations of motion.

Example: A passenger train leaves a station at 7.38 at a speed of 40 m.p.h.; at 7.55 an express follows at 85 m.p.h. When will

239

this overtake the passenger train? According to the graphical representation derived from the following table this happens (after 21·2 miles) at 8.10 (Fig. 164).

Passenger train		Express	
7.38	0 miles	7.55	0 miles
7.53	10 miles	8.10	21·25 miles
8.08	20 miles	8.25	42·50 miles

Suppose, for example, after 19 miles the slow train must wait on a siding at a station to let the express go by and can only proceed when the express has passed through the station. A visual

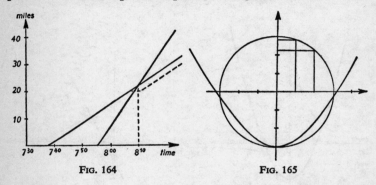

FIG. 164   FIG. 165

representation of this is easily adapted from the graph (Fig. 164).

If two non-linear equations of condition occur for two unknowns, we can easily see from a graphical representation how many solutions there are and whereabouts they lie.

Example (Fig. 165): The pair of equations

$$y = \frac{x^2}{4} - 3 \quad \text{and} \quad y = \sqrt{(3 + x)(3 - x)}$$

has three solutions:

$$x_1 = 2\sqrt{2} \qquad x_2 = -2\sqrt{2} \qquad x_3 = 0$$
$$y_1 = -1 \qquad y_2 = -1 \qquad y_3 = -3.$$

The detailed treatment of this type of question is a matter for *Analytical geometry* (see above).

Half angle theorems

The half angle theorems are theorems of plane trigonometry. If a, b and c are the sides, α, β, γ the angles, ρ the radius of the inscribed circle of a triangle and s half the length of the perimeter $\left(s = \dfrac{a + b + c}{2}\right)$, then

$$\rho = \sqrt{\frac{(s - a)(s - b)(s - c)}{s}},$$

$$\tan \frac{\alpha}{2} = \frac{\rho}{s - a} = \sqrt{\frac{(s - b)(s - c)}{s(s - a)}},$$

$$\tan \frac{\beta}{2} = \frac{\rho}{s - b} = \sqrt{\frac{(s - c)(s - a)}{s(s - b)}},$$

$$\tan \frac{\gamma}{2} = \frac{\rho}{s - c} = \sqrt{\frac{(s - a)(s - b)}{s(s - c)}}.$$

Harmonic division

A segment is said to be harmonically divided in a given ratio $m:n$ if it is divided both internally and externally in the same ratio $m:n$ (see *Straight line segments, ratios of*).

Harmonic mean

The expression $\dfrac{2ab}{a + b}$ is called the harmonic mean of the numbers a and b.

Example: The harmonic mean of the numbers 4 and 6 is:

$$x = \frac{2 \cdot 4 \cdot 6}{4 + 6} = \frac{48}{10} = 4 \cdot 8$$

(see also *Harmonic series*).

Harmonic series

The harmonic series $1 + \dfrac{1}{2} + \dfrac{1}{3} + \dfrac{1}{4} + \dfrac{1}{5} + \ldots$ is divergent.

The following series are also called harmonic:

$$\sum_{n=1}^{\infty} \frac{1}{n^\alpha} = 1 + \frac{1}{2^\alpha} + \frac{1}{3^\alpha} + \frac{1}{4^\alpha} + \frac{1}{5^\alpha} + \ldots$$

These series converge for all exponents α which are greater than 1 (in symbols, $\alpha > 1$).

In the harmonic series $1 + \frac{1}{2} + \frac{1}{3} + \frac{1}{4} + \frac{1}{5} + \ldots$ each term is the *Harmonic mean* (see above) of its 2 neighbouring terms.

Since $\displaystyle\sum_{n=1}^{2^N} \frac{1}{n} = 1 + \frac{1}{2} + \left(\frac{1}{3} + \frac{1}{4}\right) + \left(\frac{1}{5} + \frac{1}{6} + \frac{1}{7} + \frac{1}{8}\right) + \ldots$

$$+ \left(\frac{1}{2^{N-1}+1} + \ldots + \frac{1}{2^N}\right)$$

$$> 1 + \frac{1}{2} + \left(\frac{1}{4} + \frac{1}{4}\right) + \left(\frac{1}{8} + \frac{1}{8} + \frac{1}{8} + \frac{1}{8}\right) + \ldots$$

$$+ \left(\frac{1}{2^N} + \ldots + \frac{1}{2^N}\right)$$

$$= 1 + \frac{1}{2} + \frac{1}{2} + \frac{1}{2} + \ldots + \frac{1}{2}$$

$$= 1 + \frac{N}{2} \to \infty \quad \text{as} \quad N \to \infty, \text{ the series diverges.}$$

Heron's formula (Heron of Alexandria, first century A.D.)

If we denote by $s = \dfrac{a+b+c}{2}$ the semi-perimeter of a triangle, then the area of a triangle with sides a, b and c is

$$\triangle = \sqrt{s(s-a)(s-b)(s-c)}.$$

Highest common factor (greatest common divisor)

The highest common factor of two integers is the largest integer which is a factor of both numbers. *E.g.* the highest common factor of 20 and 25 is 5. The evaluation of the highest common factor of two numbers can be effected by splitting each number into its prime factors, or if these are not known by using the *Euclidean algorithm* (see above).

Example: To determine the highest common factor of 84 and 105.

Division into prime factors gives:

$$84 = 2^2 . 3 . 7,$$
$$105 = 3 . 5 . 7;$$

the highest common factor is therefore $3 . 7 = 21$.

Hippocrates (Hippocrates of Chios, 440 B.C.; one of the 'Pythagoreans')

The 'lunes (crescents) of Hippocrates' are named after Hippocrates. The sum of the lunes on the legs of a right-angled triangle is equal to the area of the triangle (Fig. 166; see also *Pythagoras, Theorem of*).

For a square we have similarly: the sum of the lunes on the side of a square is equal to the area of the square (Fig. 167).

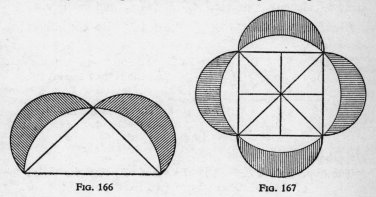

FIG. 166   FIG. 167

Horizontal

A plane or line is said to be horizontal if it is at right angles to the perpendicular (plumb line). In practical situations a spirit level can be used to determine whether a plane is horizontal or not. The opposite of horizontal is *vertical* or *perpendicular*.

243

Horner's array

Horner's array may be used for calculating the values of rational integral functions. By continued bracketing of x, the rational integral function

$$y = a_0 x^n + a_1 x^{n-1} + \ldots + a_n$$

can be written

$$y = a_n + x(a_{n-1} + x(a_{n-2} + x(\ldots + x(a_1 + xa_0))\ldots)).$$

We write

$$A_1 = a_0 x + a_1, \quad A_2 = x(a_0 x + a_1) + a_2 = x \cdot A_1 + a_2,$$

$$A_3 = x \cdot A_2 + a_3, \text{ and so on.}$$

With these quantities we then form the following array:

a_0	a_1	a_2	a_3	a_4	a_5	$\ldots a_{n-1}$	a_n
+	$a_0 x$	$A_1 x$	$A_2 x$	$A_3 x$	$A_4 x \ldots$	$A_{n-2} x$	$A_{n-1} x$
a_0	A_1	A_2	A_3	A_4	A_5	$\ldots A_{n-1}$	y

In place of x we can set any number we like, and then use the array to calculate in turn $A_1, A_2, \ldots, A_{n-1}$, and finally y.

Example: $y = 0 \cdot 9 x^4 + 0 \cdot 7 x^2 - x + 1 \cdot 2$. The coefficients $a_0, \ldots, a_4$ are

0·9	0	0·7	−1	1.2	and for $x = 2$ we calculate
					the rest of the array:
	1·8	3·6	8·6	15·2	
0·9	1·8	4·3	7·6	16·4.	This gives the result,

$$y = 16 \cdot 4.$$

Hyperbola

The hyperbola is defined as the locus of points for which the *difference* of their distances from two fixed points, the *foci*, is constant, $= 2a$ say.

If the foci are F_1 and F_2, then the mid-point of the segment $\overline{F_1 F_2}$ is called the *centre*, O, of the hyperbola. If segments of length a are drawn on either side of O on the straight line through F_1 and F_2 we obtain the *vertices* A_1 and A_2 of the hyperbola. $\overline{A_1 A_2}$ is the *transverse axis* of the hyperbola. If we erect the

244

perpendicular to the segment $\overline{F_1F_2}$ at O and describe about each vertex a circle of radius $\overline{OF_1} = e$ we obtain as intersections of these circles with the perpendicular to $\overline{F_1F_2}$ the *secondary vertices* B_1 and B_2 of the hyperbola. $\overline{B_1B_2}$ is called the *conjugate axis* of the hyperbola and the length of $\overline{B_1B_2}$ is denoted by $2b$. By the theorem of Pythagoras, $e^2 = a^2 + b^2$ (Fig. 168). e is called the *linear eccentricity* of the hyperbola. The hyperbola is not a closed curve but comprises two branches; it lies symmetrically about

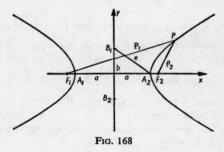

FIG. 168

both its transverse and its conjugate axes. The point by point construction of the hyperbola derives from the definition given above (see Fig. 168 and *Conic sections*).

Particular equations of the hyperbola

1. *Central equation.* If a coordinate system is used whose x-axis coincides with the transverse axis of the hyperbola and whose y-axis coincides with the conjugate axis (and whose origin is in consequence the centre of the hyperbola), the equation of the curve is:

$$\frac{x^2}{a^2} - \frac{y^2}{b^2} = 1.$$

2. *Equation of the hyperbola with arbitrary centre.* If the centre of the hyperbola has coordinates $O(x_0, y_0)$ and its transverse axis is parallel to the x-axis, its equation is:

$$\frac{(x - x_0)^2}{a^2} + \frac{(y - y_0)^2}{b^2} = 1.$$

245

3. *Vertex equation of the hyperbola.* If one vertex of the hyperbola lies at the origin of the coordinate system, and if the centre lies on the x-axis, then the hyperbola has the equation:

$$\frac{(x + a)^2}{a^2} - \frac{y^2}{b^2} = 1.$$

This equation can be rewritten as

$$y^2 = 2\frac{b^2}{a}x + \frac{b^2}{a^2}x^2 \text{ (vertex equation).}$$

If we put $\frac{b^2}{a} = p$, $\frac{e}{a} = \varepsilon$, p being termed the parameter and ε the numerical eccentricity (eccentricity) of the hyperbola, the vertex equation reads:

$$y^2 = 2px - (1 - \varepsilon^2)x^2 \qquad \varepsilon > 1.$$

(Cf. the general vertex equation of the conic section in art. *Curves of the second order.*)

p and ε are always positive, and since we are dealing with an hyperbola ε is greater than unity.

Rectangular hyperbola

If the axes of the hyperbola are equal in length, the hyperbola is called rectangular. Its standard equation is $x^2 - y^2 = a^2$.

The focal lengths of a point $P(x_1, y_1)$ of the hyperbola $\frac{x^2}{a^2} - \frac{y^2}{b^2} = 1$ are (Fig. 168):

$$\overline{PF_1} = \frac{e}{a}x_1 + a = \varepsilon x_1 + a; \ \overline{PF_2} = \frac{e}{a}x_1 - a = \varepsilon x_1 - a.$$

Hyperbola and straight line

1. *Discriminant of the hyperbola.* The coordinates of the points of intersection of a straight line $y = mx + n$ with the hyperbola $\frac{x^2}{a^2} - \frac{y^2}{b^2} = 1$ are obtained as solutions of the system of equations

$$\text{I. } y = mx + n$$

$$\text{II. } \frac{x^2}{a^2} - \frac{y^2}{b^2} = 1.$$

The solutions are

$$x_{1,2} = \frac{a^2mn}{b^2 - a^2m^2} \pm \frac{ab}{b^2 - a^2m^2} \sqrt{n^2 + b^2 - a^2m^2}$$

$$y_{1,2} = \frac{nb^2}{b^2 - a^2m^2} \pm \frac{abm}{b^2 - a^2m^2} \sqrt{n^2 + b^2 - a^2m^2}.$$

By means of the discriminant $D = n^2 + b^2 - a^2m^2$ we can now decide whether the line $y = mx + n$ intersects the hyperbola in two, one or no points.

We have:

> for $D > 0$ two points of intersection;
> for $D = 0$ one point of intersection (tangent);
> for $D < 0$ no intersections.

2. *Tangents to the hyperbola with given gradients*. A straight line $y = mx + n$, with given gradient m, is tangent to the hyperbola if the discriminant D is equal to 0, that is, if $n^2 = a^2m^2 - b^2$ or $n = \pm\sqrt{a^2m^2 - b^2}$. A tangent to the hyperbola which has the given gradient m must therefore have equation

$$y = mx \pm \sqrt{a^2m^2 - b^2}.$$

3. *Tangents to the hyperbola at a given point $P_1(x_1, y_1)$*. The gradient of the tangent at the point P_1 is given by differentiation as $\dfrac{b^2x_1}{a^2y_1}$. From this gradient together with the coordinates of P_1 we obtain the equation of the tangent as

$$\frac{xx_1}{a^2} - \frac{yy_1}{b^2} = 1.$$

Where the centre of the hyperbola is not at the origin but at the point (x_0, y_0) the equation of the tangent reads:

$$\frac{(x - x_0)(x_1 - x_0)}{a^2} - \frac{(y - y_0)(y_1 - y_0)}{b^2} = 1.$$

4. *Polar line of a point $P_1(x_1, y_1)$ with respect to a hyperbola.* The polar line of P_1 with respect to a hyperbola is the straight line which passes through both points of contact of the tangents

from P_1 to the ellipse. The equation of the polar has the same form as the tangent equation (see above 3), that is:

$$\frac{xx_1}{a^2} - \frac{xy_1}{b^2} = 1$$

or more generally

$$\frac{(x - x_0)(x_1 - x_0)}{a^2} - \frac{(y - y_0)(y_1 - y_0)}{b^2} = 1.$$

5. *Conjugate diameters of the hyperbola*. A straight line which passes through the centre of a hyperbola is called a diameter of the hyperbola. The mid-points of all chords of the hyperbola with given slope m lie on a straight line which passes through the

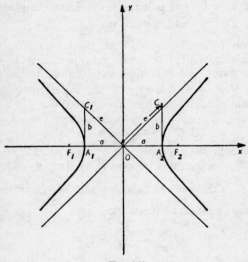

Fig. 169

centre of the hyperbola and which is called the conjugate diameter with respect to the original diameter. The equation of the diameter conjugate to the diameter $y = mx$ has equation

$$y = \frac{b^2}{a^2 m} x.$$

6. *Asymptotes of the hyperbola*. The ordinate of a point of a

hyperbola is given by the equation of the hyperbola as

$$y = \pm \frac{b}{a} \sqrt{x^2 - a^2} \quad \text{or} \quad y = \pm \frac{b}{a} x \sqrt{1 - \frac{a^2}{x^2}}.$$

Now $\frac{b}{a} x \sqrt{1 - \frac{a^2}{x^2}} - \frac{b}{a} x$ tends to zero as x tends to infinity,

and so the hyperbola and the lines $y = \pm \frac{b}{a} x$ approach indefinitely close together as x increases. Such a straight line, which approaches a curve indefinitely closely but never meets it, is called an asymptote. The equations of the asymptotes of the hyperbola are therefore $y = \pm \frac{b}{a} x$ (Fig. 169).

Construction of the asymptotes of the hyperbola $\frac{x^2}{a^2} - \frac{y^2}{b^2} = 1$.
Draw the perpendiculars to the transverse axis at the vertices of the hyperbola and mark off segments of length b on each and in the same direction. Join the end points C_1 and C_2 of the two segments to the centre of the hyperbola. The line through O and C_2 (as drawn) is the asymptote $y = \frac{b}{a} x$ and that through O and C_1 is the asymptote $y = -\frac{b}{a} x$ (Fig. 169). The asymptotes of a rectangular hyperbola are perpendicular to one another.

Construction of the tangent to a hyperbola at the point P. We draw the focal lines from P and bisect the angle between them. The angle bisector is the required tangent.

Construction of the tangents from a point P_0 to a hyperbola (Fig. 170). Describe about P_0 a circle with radius $\overline{P_0F_1}$, and about the other focus F_2 a circle with radius $2a$. Let these circles intersect

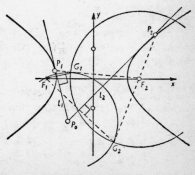

Fig. 170

249

in the points G_1 and G_2. Then drop the perpendiculars from P_0 onto $\overline{F_1 G_1}$ and $\overline{F_1 G_2}$. These are the required tangents t_1 and t_2. The points of contact P_1 and P_2 of these tangents are obtained by joining F_2 to G_1 and G_2 and extending these lines to meet t_1 and t_2.

General theorems on the hyperbola

1. Given a line segment perpendicular to the transverse axis of a hyperbola and with its end points on the two asymptotes; then if one point of intersection with the hyperbola divides the segment into two segments l and m, then $lm = b^2$.

2. The product of the two line segments drawn parallel to the asymptotes from a point D of an hyperbola to the asymptotes is a constant.

3. The two segments $\overline{CD}$ and $\overline{EF}$ lying between the curve and the asymptotes on a secant of a hyperbola, are equal.

4. The segment $\overline{PA}$ lying between the asymptotes on a tangent to a hyperbola is divided into equal parts by the point of contact of the tangent.

5. All triangles formed by a tangent and the asymptotes have the same area, namely ab, where a and b are the axes of the hyperbola.

6. The feet of perpendiculars from the foci on to tangents lie on the circle with the transverse axis of the hyperbola as diameter.

7. The mirror images of a focus with respect to a tangent lie on the circle with the other focus as centre and radius $2a$.

Hypotenuse

The side opposite the right angle in a right-angled triangle is called the *hypotenuse* of the triangle. The *legs* of the triangle are the sides adjacent to the right angle.

i is the (so-called) imaginary unit.

$i = +\sqrt{-1}$ (see *Complex numbers*). We have

$$i^2 = -1 \qquad\qquad i^5 = i \qquad\qquad i^8 = +1$$
$$i^3 = -i \qquad\qquad i^6 = -1 \qquad\qquad \text{etc.}$$
$$i^4 = +1 \qquad\qquad i^7 = -i$$

In electrical engineering $\sqrt{-1}$ is sometimes denoted by j.

Icosahedron

The regular icosahedron is one of the so-called platonic solids. It is bounded by twenty equilateral triangles (see *Platonic solids*).

Identical transformation

If, for a transformation in a plane or in space, all points coincide with their image points, the transformation is said to be *identical*.

Identically named numbers

For general numbers, as in

$$2a + 3a + 4b = 5a + 4b$$

$2a$ and $3a$ are referred to as identically named and can be added together—here as $5a$ (see *Addition*); $5a$ and $4b$ are not identically named and cannot be added together.

Imaginary numbers

The (so-called) imaginary numbers are among the *complex numbers* (see above): complex numbers whose real parts are zero are called imaginary, *e.g. i, $2i$, $-3i$*.

The imaginary numbers are multiples of the imaginary unit $i = \sqrt{-1}$. In the representation of complex numbers on the *Gaussian number plane* (Argand diagram), the imaginary numbers lie on the y-axis (see *Complex numbers, Number-plane*).

Indicatrix (*Dupin's conic section*)

A method, due to *Charles Dupin*, for recognising the nature of the curvature of a surface at a particular point. We imagine a plane E drawn a very small distance from and parallel to the tangent plane E at the point P, and cutting the surface. The curve in which E' cuts the surface is the *indicatrix*.

Indirect proof

If a proposition is proved true by demonstrating that its negation is false, the proof is said to be indirect.

251

Example of an indirect proof: To prove that $\sqrt{2}$ is an irrational number: We assume that the negation of the proposition is true, and show that this leads to a contradiction. We therefore suppose $\sqrt{2}$ to be a rational number, $\sqrt{2} = \dfrac{p}{q}$ (say), where p and q may be taken to be integers with no common factors. We now take the square of both sides of this equation and obtain $2 = \dfrac{p^2}{q^2}$. Multiplying both sides by q^2, we obtain $2q^2 = p^2$. From this we infer that p^2, and therefore p as well, must be even, say $p = 2r$. Substituting in the equation we have: $2q^2 = 4r^2$, so that q also must be an even number. That is, from the assumption that $\sqrt{2}$ is rational and so of the form $\dfrac{p}{q}$ where p and q have no common factors we can deduce that p and q are both even, and have the common factor 2. In other words we have a contradiction, and so the original assumption that $\sqrt{2}$ is rational must be false. Consequently $\sqrt{2}$ is irrational.

Inequality

If mathematical expressions are connected by one of the ordering-symbols $<$, $>$, $\leq$ or $\geq$, the resulting proposition is referred to as an inequality; *e.g.*

$$3 < 5 \text{ denotes } 3 \text{ less than } 5,$$

$$3x \leq 6 \text{ denotes } 3x \text{ less than or equal to } 6.$$

In calculating with inequalities (as for example in approximation problems) we have the following simple rules,

1. $|a + b| \leq |a| + |b|; \qquad |a - b| \leq |a| + |b|.$

2. $|a + b| \geq |a| - |b|; \qquad |a - b| \geq |a| - |b|.$

3. $a > b$ implies $a + c > b + c$ for all c.

4. $a > b$ implies $pa > pb$ if $p > 0$.

5. $a > b$ implies $\dfrac{1}{a} < \dfrac{1}{b}$ if $ab > 0$.

When expressing these symbols in words,

for $a < b$ read: a less than b,
for $c > d$ read: c greater than d,
for $e \leq f$ read: e less than or equal to f,
for $g = h$ read: g equals h,
for $k \geq m$ read: k greater than or equal to m.

Infinite series

The unevaluated sum of terms of an infinite sequence of numbers is called an infinite series. The abbreviation $\sum_{k=1}^{\infty} a_k$ is used for the infinite series $a_1 + a_2 + a_3 + \dots$. We say: 'Sigma ak from one to infinity' (see *Summation sign*), *e.g.*

$$\sum_{k=1}^{\infty} \frac{1}{k} = 1 + \frac{1}{2} + \frac{1}{3} + \frac{1}{4} + \frac{1}{5} + \dots$$

The sequence with a finite number of terms

$$s_n = \sum_{k=1}^{n} a_k = a_1 + a_2 + a_3 + \dots + a_n$$

is called a *partial sum* of the infinite series. A partial sum of an infinite series can be formed for every natural number n. If, for a given infinite series, the sequence of partial sums, s_n, is convergent (oscillatory, or divergent) the infinite series is also said to be convergent (oscillatory, or divergent).

If the sequence of partial sums s_n converges to the value s, then s is referred to as the value or the sum of the infinite series,

$$s = \sum_{k=1}^{\infty} a_k.$$

Given a divergent series, we similarly say that the series diverges to $+\infty$ or $-\infty$ according to the behaviour of the sequence of partial sums.

Examples:

1. $\sum_{k=1}^{\infty} \frac{1}{2^{k-1}} = 2$ (geometric series with ratio $\frac{1}{2}$ and initial term 1).

2. $\sum\limits_{k=1}^{\infty} k$ is divergent.

3. $\sum\limits_{k=0}^{\infty} (-1)^k = 1 - 1 + 1 - 1 + 1 - \ldots$ is oscillatory.

4. $\sum\limits_{k=1}^{\infty} \frac{1}{k} = \frac{1}{1} + \frac{1}{2} + \frac{1}{3} + \frac{1}{4} + \ldots$ is divergent.

Particular infinite series
1. Geometric series (see *Geometric sequence*).
2. Binomial series (see *art.*).
3. Exponential series (see *art.*).
4. Trigonometrical series (see *art.*).
5. Power-series (see *art.*).
6. Taylor's series (see *art.*).
7. Maclaurin's series (see *art.*).
8. Harmonic series (see *art.*).

Infinitesimal calculus

The infinitesimal calculus is concerned with the treatment of limits (originally with 'infinitely small' quantities). Elementary infinitesimal calculus is divided into two parts, the differential calculus, and the integral calculus; higher domains are differential and integral equations, differential geometry and the calculus of variations.

Differential calculus

An (unrigorous but) intuitive idea of the differential calculus is most easily grasped by reference to the graph (Fig. 171) of a function $y = f(x)$, represented in rectangular coordinates by a curve which has a tangent at every point. Join two points P_1 and P_2 of the curve by the chord $s = \overline{P_1P_2}$, so that the gradient of the curve is fixed by the difference quotient $(y_2 - y_1) \div (x_2 - x_1)$, or $\Delta y \div \Delta x$ (delta y divided by delta x), *i.e.* the ratio of the increment of y to the increment of x. Now let P_2 approach P_1 along the curve so that the chord s rotates until it coincides with the tangent t at P_1. To this geometrical limiting process there corresponds an algebraic process in which the difference quotient $\Delta y \div \Delta x$ tends to a limit:

$$\lim_{\Delta x \to 0} \frac{\Delta y}{\Delta x} = \frac{dy}{dx} = y' = f'(x)$$

(read: limit as x tends to 0; *differential coefficient*, or first derivative, of y with respect to x). y' is the measure of the gradient of the tangent to the curve (with angle c) at each point of the curve.

In Fig. 171 $y' = \dfrac{\overline{QT}}{P_1 Q} = \dfrac{dy}{dx}$. dy and dx are called *differentials*. If the scales on the x- and y-axes are equal, the differential coefficient is the tangent of the angle c $\left(\dfrac{dy}{dx} = \tan c\right)$.

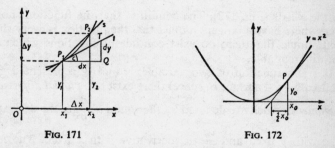

FIG. 171   FIG. 172

We may be able to differentiate $f'(x)$ as well, *i.e.* if the curve for $f'(x)$ has a tangent at every point in the range considered, we obtain the second derivative $y'' = f''(x) = \dfrac{d^2 y}{dx^2}$ (read: d two y by dx-squared). In this way we can form derivatives of higher orders of which the nth, if it exists, is written

$$y^{(n)} = f^{(n)}(x) = \frac{d^n y}{dx^n}.$$

In order to differentiate the elementary functions we usually derive the appropriate limits. For example if $y = x^2$ we proceed as follows: we have

$$y_1 = x_1^2, \text{ and } y_2 = y_1 + \Delta y = (x_1 + \Delta x)^2,$$

255

so that

$$y_2 - y_1 = \Delta y = (x_1 + \Delta x)^2 - x_1^2 = 2x_1\Delta x + (\Delta x)^2,$$

that is

$$\Delta y \div \Delta x = 2x_1 + \Delta x.$$

Taking the limit we obtain as gradient of the tangents:

$$\lim_{\Delta x \to 0} (2x + \Delta x) = 2x, \ \textit{i.e.,} \ \frac{d(x^2)}{dx} = 2x.$$

Now $2x = x^2 \div \frac{1}{2}x = y \div \frac{1}{2}x$ and this says, in geometrical terms, that the tangent to the parabola $y = x^2$ at an arbitrary point $P(x_0, y_0)$ can be obtained by joining P to the point $x = \frac{1}{2}x_0$ on the x-axis (Fig. 172). The condition that the function should everywhere have a tangent implies that the function is everywhere continuous. But there do exist continuous functions which are not differentiable.

If z is a function of two variables x and y (represented geometrically by a surface in space) there exist two *partial differential coefficients* which are denoted by the round ∂: $\frac{\partial z}{\partial x}$ is the derivative of z with y fixed and $\frac{\partial z}{\partial y}$ the derivative with x fixed. The *total differential* of z is $dz = \frac{\partial z}{\partial x}dx + \frac{\partial z}{\partial y}dy$.

Integral calculus

An intuitive idea of the integral calculus is likewise most easily grasped geometrically (see Fig. 173). The curve $y = f(x)$ between $P_0(x_0, y_0)$ to $P(x_n, y_n)$ forms with the ordinates y_0 and y_n and the part of the x-axis of length $x_n - x_0$ lying between them an area $F(x)$ which is therefore a function of $f(x)$. The finding of $F(x)$ is called the quadrature of the area, and this calculation of areas is the basic problem of the integral calculus; as in the case of the differential calculus, it is solved by a limiting process. We subdivide the area by means of a number of ordinates y_1, y_2, . . . which are spaced at equal intervals Δx, so that we can form two sums of rectangles one of which is greater and the other less than the required area F; in Fig. 173:

$$y_0\Delta x + y_1\Delta x + y_2\Delta x + y_3\Delta x + y_4\Delta x < F$$
$$< y_1\Delta x + y_2\Delta x + y_3\Delta x + y_4\Delta x + y_n\Delta x.$$

The difference of the two sums is the shaded rectangle in Fig. 173, whose area decreases as we make Δx smaller, *i.e.* as we increase the number of strips into which we divide the area we are investigating. Now let Δx tend to 0, so that the two sums

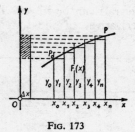

FIG. 173

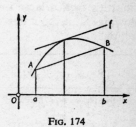

FIG. 174

become equal to one another and to the required area. In order to express this briefly, we need two symbols for summation: Σ (Greek *sigma*) for sum and the old long $s = \int$ which is now called *integral*. In this way we obtain, given the initial and final values of the abscissa as x_0 and x respectively, the equation

$$\lim_{\Delta x \to 0} \sum_{x_0}^{x} y\Delta x = \int_{x_0}^{x} f(x)dx = F(x).$$

If we displace the initial ordinate y_0 to the left or to the right, we alter the area F by a fixed amount, namely by the area introduced or cut off. There corresponds then to an 'integrand' $f(x)$ an infinite number of integrals, each of which can be derived from any given one by the addition or subtracting of a constant, the (arbitrary) constant of integration. Such an integral is therefore usually written without specification of the limits, and is then called an indefinite integral. If, on the other hand, the limits are given, *e.g.* $x_0 = a$ as the lower, $x = b$ as the upper, $\int_a^b f(x)dx$ is referred to as a *definite integral*.

The length of the arc of a curve is also found by integration. The volume V of a solid and the area of a curved surface are determined by multiple integrals, *e.g.*

$$V = \iiint f(x, y, z)dx\, dy\, dz.$$

Now the problem of quadrature, *i.e.* of integration, is the inverse of the tangent problem, *i.e.* of differentiation:

$$\text{if } \frac{dF(x)}{dx} = f(x) \text{ then } \int f(x)dx = F(x)$$

Using this fact, a large number of integrals can be solved. The following table contains the first derivatives of the simplest functions:

y	y'	y	y'
x^n	nx^{n-1}	e^x	e^x
$\sin x$	$\cos x$	a^x	$a^x \ln a$
$\cos x$	$-\sin x$	$\ln x$	$\dfrac{1}{x}$
$\tan x$	$\dfrac{1}{\cos^2 x}$	$\log_a x$	$\dfrac{1}{x \ln a}$
$\cot x$	$-\dfrac{1}{\sin^2 x}$		

Here $e = \lim\limits_{n \to \infty} \left(1 + \dfrac{1}{n}\right)^n$, an irrational number whose value is approximately $2\cdot71828$. The function e^x is called the *exponential function*; logarithms to base e are called *natural logarithms* (ln). The following five rules help in calculation of the derivatives—when they exist—of more complex functions:

1. $(u + v)' = u' + v'$.

2. $(uv)' = uv' + u'v$.

3. $\left(\dfrac{u}{v}\right)' = \dfrac{u'v - uv'}{v^2}$.

4. *Chain-rule:* If $y = f(u)$ then $y' = \dfrac{df(u)}{du} \cdot \dfrac{du}{dx}$.

5. *Derivative of the inverse function:* If $y = f(x)$ is differentiable and has the inverse function $x = \phi(y)$ then

$$\frac{d\phi(y)}{dy} = 1 \div \frac{df(x)}{dx} \quad \text{or} \quad \frac{dx}{dy} = 1 \div \frac{dy}{dx}.$$

The rationale of the integral calculus is based on the *mean value theorem*, which, in geometrical terms, asserts: if a curve $y = f(x)$ possesses a tangent for all values of x between a and b, then there exists at least one value $x = \xi$ between a and b for which the tangent to the curve is parallel to the chord joining A to B (Fig. 174). For proof we use the theorem of *Rolle* (1690) with $f(a) = f(b)$.

Applications of the differential calculus

1. *Indeterminate forms,* when a function $y = f(x)$ for $x = a$ gives rise to one of the indeterminate expressions $\dfrac{0}{0}$, $\dfrac{\infty}{\infty}$, $0 \times \infty$, $\infty - \infty$, 0^0, ∞^0. The function does not strictly speaking exist for this value; but the limiting value $\lim\limits_{x \to a} f(x)$ may well exist and be used to fill in the gap in the function values. Thus for the function $y = (e^x - e^{-x})/x$ denominator and numerator are both equal to zero for $x = 0$, so that y does not exist there. We can invoke here the rule given by *Joh. Bernoulli:* If $\phi(x)$ and $\psi(x)$ are zero for $x = a$ and are differentiable in its neighbourhood then

$$\lim_{x \to a} \frac{\phi(x)}{\psi(x)} = \lim_{x \to a} \frac{\phi'(x)}{\psi'(x)}$$

(provided this limit exists). In the above example the derivative of the numerator, $e^x + e^{-x}$ takes the value 2 for $x = 0$; the derivative of the denominator is 1; therefore $\lim\limits_{x \to 0} \dfrac{e^x - e^{-x}}{x} = 2$.

2. *Maxima and minima,* occurring when the slope of the tangent is horizontal, that is, when $f'(x) = 0$.

3. *Sequences.*

4. *Differential equations,* i.e. equations in which differential

coefficients of unknown functions occur; such equations are of great importance in theoretical physics and astronomy.

5. *Differential geometry* deals with applications of the differential calculus to the geometry of curves and surfaces.

Graphical and numerical procedures

If the graph of $y = f(x)$ is given, graphs of the derivative $y' = f'(x)$ and of an integral $\int f(x)dx$ can be found diagrammatically without recourse to calculation. Moreover there exist numerical and mechanical methods. Of numerical methods for obtaining a definite integral $\int_b^a f(x)dx$, *Simpson's Rule* is noteworthy: we divide the interval a,b into an even number $2m$ of equal parts of width $h = \dfrac{b-a}{2m}$; the ordinates $y_1, y_2, \ldots, y_{2m-1}$, correspond to the points of division and y_a and y_b to $x = a$ and $x = b$. Then:

$$\int_a^b f(x)dx \approx \frac{h}{3}(y_a + 4y_1 + 2y_2 + 4y_3 + 2y_4 + \ldots$$
$$+ 4y_{2m-1} + y_b).$$

Various instruments exist (planimeters, integrators) for use in this connection.

Inflexion, point of inflexion of a curve

A point of inflexion on a curve is a point in which the curve changes from being concave to being convex (or *vice versa*).

Inscribed circle

The circle which touches all sides of a polygon on the inside is called the inscribed circle of the polygon. Not all polygons possess inscribed circles.

Integers

The set of integers comprises the positive whole numbers, the negative whole numbers and zero. The positive integers are identical with the *natural numbers*. In the domain of integers we can add, subtract and multiply without restriction, *i.e.* every sum, every difference and every product of two integers is also an integer. On the other hand, the division of one integer by another can take us outside the domain of integers, *e.g.* $5 \div 7 = \dfrac{5}{7}$.

Interest

Simple interest

Interest is the increase accruing to capital put out on loan. The amount of interest is calculated from the *principal* (*i.e.* capital) P, the *rate of interest p* and *time of duration* of the loan t. In the calculation of simple interest it is usual to regard a year as containing 360 days. The rate of interest p specifies how much interest is to be paid to the lender of a principal of £100 for one year. Thus a year's interest on a principal P is $p\%$, that is, $\dfrac{P \times p}{100}$.

In t years the interest yielded is $I = \dfrac{P \times t \times p}{100}$.

E.g. A principal $P =$ £400 is loaned for 3 months at 4%.

We have: $P =$ £400, $p = 4\%$, $t = 3$ months $= 0.25$ years, and so

$$I = \frac{400 \times 4 \times 0.25}{100} = \text{£4}.$$

That is, the principal brings in £4 interest.

The rate of interest is usually given for a year. This can be emphasised by adding the phrase *per annum*.

If we are concerned with the calculation of interest on different principals at the same ratio of interest *interest-numbers* can be used. If a principal P is lent for t days at $p\%$ (per annum) the quantity $\dfrac{P \times t}{100}$ is referred to as the interest-number, and $\dfrac{360}{p}$ as the interest-divisor. Thus the interest due is calculated as

$$I = \frac{P \times t}{100} \div \frac{360}{p} = \frac{\text{Interest-number}}{\text{Interest-divisor}}.$$

If several principals are to yield interest, we first calculate all the interest-numbers, add them and divide the sum by the interest-divisor; *e.g.* How much interest is obtained at the end of a year if the following deposits are made into a savings account ($p = 3\%$, one year taken as containing 360 days)?

Date	Deposit	No. of days t	Interest-number
Jan. 15	£40	345	138
Feb. 10	£20	320	64
May 10	£17 10s.	230	40·25

$$242\cdot25$$

Interest-divisor: $\dfrac{360}{3} = 120$.

$$\text{Interest} = \frac{\text{Sum of interest-numbers}}{\text{interest divisor}} = \frac{242\cdot25}{120}.$$

Interest obtained = £2·019 = £2 0s. 5d.

Compound interest

Interest is said to be compound if the interest is added to the principal at the end of each *conversion-period* (such as a month

Capital at beginning of year	Interest	Capital at end of year	Time elapsed in years
P_0	$\dfrac{P_0 \cdot p}{100}$	$P_1 = P_0 + P_0 \cdot \dfrac{p}{100} = P_0\left(1 + \dfrac{p}{100}\right) = P_0 q$	1
P_1	$\dfrac{P_1 \cdot p}{100}$	$P_2 = P_1 + P_1 \cdot \dfrac{p}{100} = P_1\left(1 + \dfrac{p}{100}\right) = P_0 q^2$	2
P_2	$\dfrac{P_2 \cdot p}{100}$	$P_3 = P_2 + P_2 \cdot \dfrac{p}{100} = P_2\left(1 + \dfrac{p}{100}\right) = P_0 q^3$	3
...	...	....	...
P_{n-1}	$\dfrac{P_{n-1} \cdot p}{100}$	$P_n = P_{n-1} + P_{n-1} \cdot \dfrac{p}{100} = P_{n-1}\left(1 + \dfrac{p}{100}\right)$ $= P_0 q^{n-1} \cdot q = P_0 q^n$	n

or a year) and thereafter itself earns interest. The final capital P_n is calculated from the original capital P_0, the number of years and the rate of interest p; conversion period, 1 year. (We put $1 + \frac{p}{100} = q$ and refer to this quantity as the interest-factor.)

Interest-factors

p \\ n	3·5%	4%	4·5%	5%	5·5%	6%	7%
1	1·035	1·04	1·045	1·05	1·055	1·06	1·07
2	1·07123	1·0816	1·09203	1·1025	1·11303	1·1236	1·1449
3	1·10872	1·12486	1·14117	1·15763	1·17424	1·19102	1·22504
4	1·14752	1·16986	1·19252	1·21551	1·23882	1·26248	1·31080
5	1·18769	1·21665	1·24618	1·27628	1·30696	1·33823	1·40255
6	1·22926	1·26532	1·30226	1·34010	1·37884	1·41852	1·50073
7	1·27228	1·31593	1·36086	1·40710	1·45468	1·50363	1·60578
8	1·31681	1·36857	1·42210	1·47746	1·53469	1·59385	1·71819
9	1·36290	1·42331	1·48610	1·55133	1·61909	1·68948	1·83846
10	1·41060	1·48024	1·55297	1·62889	1·70814	1·79085	1·96715
11	1·45997	1·53945	1·62285	1·71034	1·80209	1·89830	2·10485
12	1·51107	1·60103	1·69588	1·79586	1·90121	2·01220	2·25219
13	1·56396	1·66507	1·77220	1·88565	2·00577	2·13293	2·40985
14	1·61869	1·73168	1·85194	1·97993	2·11609	2·26090	2·57853
15	1·67535	1·80094	1·93528	2·07893	2·23248	2·39656	2·75903
16	1·73399	1·87298	2·02237	2·18287	2·35526	2·54035	2·95216
17	1·79468	1·94790	2·11338	2·29202	2·48480	2·69277	3·15882
18	1·85749	2·02582	2·20848	2·40662	2·62147	2·85434	3·37993
19	1·92250	2·10685	2·30786	2·52695	2·76565	3·02560	3·61653
20	1·98979	2·19112	2·41171	2·65330	2·91776	3·20714	3·86968
21	2·05943	2·27877	2·52024	2·78596	3·07823	3·39956	4·14056
22	2·13151	2·36992	2·63365	2·92526	3·24754	3·60354	4·43040
23	2·20611	2·46472	2·75217	3·07152	3·42615	3·81975	4·74053
24	2·28333	2·56330	2·87601	3·22510	3·61459	4·04893	5·07237
25	2·36324	2·66584	3·00543	3·38635	3·81339	2·29187	5·42743
26	2·44596	2·77247	3·14068	3·55567	4·02313	4·54938	5·80735
27	2·53157	2·88337	3·28201	3·73346	4·24440	4·82235	6·21387
28	2·62017	2·99870	3·42970	3·92013	4·47784	5·11169	6·64884
29	2·71188	3·11865	3·58404	4·11614	4·72412	5·41839	7·11426
30	2·80079	3·24340	3·74532	4·32194	5·98395	5·74349	7·61226

Result: We have

$$P_n = P_0 \times q^n \text{ for the final capital,}$$

$$p = 100 \left(\sqrt[n]{\frac{P_n}{P_0}} - 1 \right) \text{ for the rate of interest,}$$

$$n = \frac{\log P_n - \log P_0}{\log q} \text{ for the number of years.}$$

Shorter conversion period

The formula $P_n = P_0 q^n$ enables the final capital P_n to be calculated provided interest is added to capital yearly. If on the other hand the interest is added more often, say m times a year, the capital after one year with interest-rate $p\%$ per annum is

$$P_1 = P_0 \left(1 + \frac{p}{100m} \right)^m,$$

after n years

$$P_n = P_0 \left(1 + \frac{p}{100m} \right)^{mn}.$$

Examples: To what sum does £20,000 increase after 4 years at 3·5% compound interest?

From the table, p. 263, we get: £1 increases in 4 years at 3·5% to £1·14752. Thus $P_4 = £20,000 \times 1·14752 \cong £22,950$.

Interior angles

An interior angle is one formed by neighbouring sides of a figure and lying within the interior of the figure.

Interpolation

The determination of an intermediary value of a function by means of a sequence of known values of the function is called interpolation. It often happens that the value of a function is required which corresponds to an argument-value for which the function-value is not tabulated, and the required function-value must then be obtained by interpolation. Interpolation can only be carried out between values contained in the available table: an extrapolation beyond the limits within which a function is defined in a table is seldom possible except in relatively trivial problems.

Linear interpolation

The simplest, and for most purposes sufficient, form of interpolation—especially if the function concerned is closely tabulated —is linear interpolation. Here it is assumed that increments of the functional value may be taken as proportional to corresponding increments of the argument: for values $x_0 + th$ in the interval h $(0 < t < 1)$,

$$y(t) = t \cdot \frac{y_1 - y_0}{x_1 - x_0}.$$

Quadratic interpolation

The first refinement of linear interpolation is quadratic interpolation, in which the function is replaced by the parabola passing through three neighbouring points. Thus, in this type of interpolation, we make use not only of the two values which lie on either side of the intermediary value but of a third value as well (see *False position, Newton's method of approximation, Interpolation formulae* p. 511).

Intersection, point of

Two non-parallel straight lines lying in a plane intersect in a unique point. If the straight lines are specified by their equations relative to a coordinate-system in the plane, the coordinates of the point of intersection P can be calculated by regarding the equations of the straight lines as a system of two equations in two unknowns and solving for these unknowns.

Example: line l_1 $y = 3x - 1$,

line l_2 $y = 3x + 5$.

System of equations: 1. $y - 3x = -1$,

$\qquad\qquad\qquad$ 2. $y + 3x = 5$.

Solution of the system of equations: $x = 1$, $y = 2$.
Point of intersection: $P(1, 2)$ (Fig. 175).

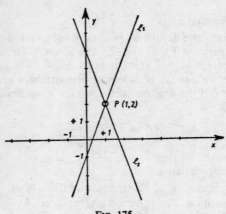

Fig. 175

Intersection of two curves

The points of intersection of two curves (in a plane or in three dimensions) are those points which the two curves have in common. If the curves are specified by their equations (in a rectangular coordinate system) the coordinates of the point of intersection can be calculated by regarding the two equations representing the curves as a system of equations in two unknowns.

Example: Points of intersection of a parabola and a circle.

$\qquad$ Equation of circle, $x^2 + y^2 = 144$.

$\qquad$ Equation of parabola, $y^2 = 10x$.

$\qquad$ System of equations, 1. $x^2 + y^2 = 144$,

$\qquad\qquad\qquad\qquad\qquad$ 2. $\qquad y^2 = 10x$.

266

Solutions:

$x_1 = 8$, $y_1 = +4\sqrt{5}$; point of intersection: $P_1(8, +4\sqrt{5})$.

$x_1 = 8$, $y_2 = -4\sqrt{5}$; point of intersection: $P_2(8, -4\sqrt{5})$.

$x_2 = -18$ gives no real solution for y (Fig. 176).

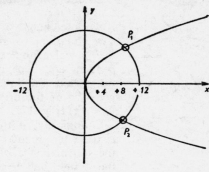

FIG. 176

Interval

The totality of all numbers which lie between two fixed numbers a and b is called an open interval. a and b are the limits of the interval [Symbolically: (a, b)].

If the limits themselves are included in the totality of numbers in the interval, this new set of numbers is called a closed interval (Symbolically: $[a, b]$). If only one limit is included, we speak of a one-sided closed (or half-open) interval. If the left limit belongs to the interval and the right not, we have an interval closed on the left and open on the right [Symbolically: $[a, b)$].

Intervals can be represented by *inequalities* (see above):

I.   Open interval: $a < x < b$; all numbers x which satisfy these inequalities lie in the interval (a, b).

II. Closed interval: $a \leq x \leq b$; all numbers x which satisfy these inequalities lie in the closed interval $[a, b]$.

III. Interval open to the left: $a < x \leq b$.

IV. Interval open to the right: $a \leq x < b$.

In the representation of numbers on a straight line, an interval forms a segment where, in the case of an open interval, it is agreed that neither end-point belongs to the interval, for a half-open interval that one end-point (right or left) belongs, and for a closed interval that both end-points belong.

Inverse function

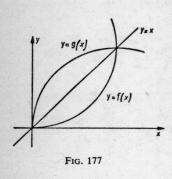

FIG. 177

Solution of a functional equation $y = f(x)$ for x gives $x = g(y)$. If we interchange x and y in this new equation, to give x and y their usual connotations of independent and dependent variable, we obtain the inverse function $y = g(x)$ of the original function $y = f(x)$ (Fig. 177).

Graphically, if the same scale is used for x and y, $y = g(x)$ is the mirror-image of $y = f(x)$ in the straight line $y = x$.

Original function		Inverse function	
Square,	$y = x^2$	Root,	$y = \sqrt{x} = x^{1/2}$
Power,	$y = x^n$		$y = \sqrt[n]{x} = x^{1/n}$
Exponential functions,	$y = a^x$	Logarithm,	$y = \log_a x$
	$y = e^x$		$y = \ln x$
	$y = 10^x$		$y = \log x$
Sine,	$y = \sin x$	Inverse sine,	$y = \sin^{-1} x$
Hyperbolic sine,	$y = \sinh x$	Inverse sinh,	$y = \sinh^{-1} x$

Inverse trigonometric series

Of these the $\tan^{-1}$ series and the $\sin^{-1}$ series are the most important. We have, for all x in the range $-1 < x \le +1$ (and for these values only),

$$\tan^{-1} x = x - \frac{x^3}{3} + \frac{x^5}{5} - \ldots + (-1)^k \frac{x^{2k+1}}{2k+1} + \ldots;$$

for all x in the range $-1 \leq x \leq +1$,

$$\sin^{-1} x = x + \frac{1 \cdot x^3}{2 \cdot 3} + \frac{1 \cdot 3 \cdot x^5}{2 \cdot 4 \cdot 5} + \cdots$$

$$+ \frac{1 \cdot 3 \cdot 5 \cdot \ldots \cdot (2k-1) \cdot x^{2k+1}}{2 \cdot 4 \cdot 6 \cdot \ldots \cdot (2k) \cdot (2k+1)} + \cdots.$$

In particular, $\frac{\pi}{4} = \tan^{-1} 1 = 1 - \frac{1}{3} + \frac{1}{5} + \frac{1}{7} + \cdots.$

Inversion

An inversion occurs in a *permutation* (see below) if two elements in the permutation are interchanged as compared with their original order.

Example: Let the elements a, b, c, d, e be given in the permutation a, c, e, d, b. This permutation is obtained by carrying out 4 inversions, namely by interchanging successively c and b; d and b; e and b; e and d.

Even and odd permutations

A permutation is called even if it contains an even number of inversions and odd if it contains an odd number of inversions.

If two different elements in a permutation are interchanged, a new permutation arises, and the number of inversions is altered by an odd number.

Irrational number

The real numbers are sub-divided into the *rational numbers* (see below) and the *irrational numbers*. The irrational numbers are thus the non-rational real numbers, *e.g.* $\sqrt{2}$, $e = 2 \cdot 718 \ldots$ (see below).

(For the proof that $\sqrt{2}$ is irrational see *Indirect Proof*.)

As with all irrational numbers, neither of these numbers can be represented by the ratio of two integers.

Amongst the irrational numbers we distinguish those, *e.g.*

irrational square roots, which are the roots of algebraic equations
—*algebraic-irrational numbers* (see *Algebraic numbers*)—from
transcendental numbers (see below), *e.g.* $\pi = 3\cdot141,592,6\ldots$, for
which this is not the case.

Isosceles triangle

A triangle with two sides equal is called isosceles. The equal
sides are called the lateral sides, and the third side the base. The
intersection of the lateral sides is called the apex (vertex) of the
triangle. The angles adjacent to the base are equal (see *Triangle*).

Jointed quadrilateral

If four rods are jointed together we get a jointed quadrilateral
ABCD (Fig. 178). A jointed quadrilateral does not have a definite
shape, as a jointed triangle would; if, for example, one rod, $\overline{AB}$,
is held fixed, the rods $\overline{BC}$ and $\overline{AD}$ can still rotate, within certain
limits, about A and B (see *Quadrilateral*).

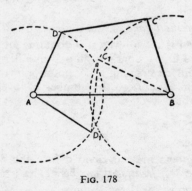

FIG. 178

Kepler's star polyhedra

If the edges of a pentadodecahedron or of an icosahedron are
extended there arises in either case a new solid called respectively
dodecahedron-star and the icosahedron-star (Figs. 179, 180).

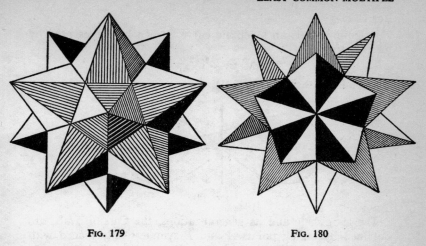

FIG. 179   FIG. 180

Least common denominator

The least common denominator of a number of fractions is the least common multiple (l.c.m.; see below) of their denominators, *e.g.* $\frac{1}{2}$ and $\frac{1}{3}$ have least common denominator 6.

Reduction to a common denominator makes possible the addition of fractions of different type, *e.g.*

$$\frac{1}{2} + \frac{1}{3} = \frac{3}{6} + \frac{2}{6} = \frac{5}{6}.$$

Least common multiple (L.C.M.)

The least common multiple of two numbers is the smallest number which contains both numbers as a factor. The least common multiple of two or more numbers can be determined by dividing each number into its prime factors, *e.g.* 8 and 12 have the least common multiple 24. For we have $8 = 2^3$ and $12 = 2^2 . 3$, and so the least common multiple must contain the factors 2^3 and 3.

271

Lemniscate

A lemniscate is an algebraic curve. It can be represented by the equation

$$(x^2 + y^2)^2 - 2a^2(x^2 - y^2) = 0,$$

where a is a constant (Fig. 181).

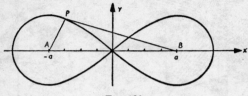

FIG. 181

The lemniscate and its generalizations, the Cassini ovals, are obtained by taking points A and B symmetrically placed with respect to the origin and distant $2a$ apart, and determining points P such that $PA \times PB = $ constant $(= b^2)$. If $a = b$, we have the lemniscate; if $b > a$ the Cassini oval lies outside and encloses the lemniscate; if $b < a$ the curve lies wholly within the two loops of the lemniscate.

The equation of the Cassini ovals is

$$(x^2 + y^2)^2 - 2a^2(x^2 - y^2) = b^4 - a^4.$$

Length, measurement of

The unit of linear measurement in the metric system is the metre. The length of the metre m was established (1889) as the distance between marks on a bar of platinum–iridium preserved in Paris. In the comparable system of measurement used in the United States and in countries of the British Commonwealth (mainly for commercial purposes) the yard is the unit of linear measurement. 1 yard is now uniformly defined as 0·9144 m. We have:

1 Kilometre (km)	$= 10^3$ m	$(= 0\cdot6214$ mile)
1 Hectometre (hm)	$= 10^2$ m	$(= 328$ feet 1 inch)
1 Decametre (Dm)	$= 10$ m	$(= 393\cdot7$ inches)
1 Metre (m)	$= 10^0$ m	$(= 39\cdot37$ inches)

1 Decimetre (dm) $= 10^{-1}$ m $(= 3\cdot937$ inches)
1 Centimetre (cm) $= 10^{-2}$ m $(= 0\cdot3937$ inches)
1 Millimetre (mm) $= 10^{-3}$ m $(= 0\cdot03937$ inches)
1 Micron (μ) $= 10^{-6}$ m
1 Millimicron (mμ) $= 10^{-9}$ m
1 Ångstrom (Å) $= 10^{-10}$ m
1 Micromicron $(\mu\mu)$ $= 10^{-12}$ m

	yard	feet	inches	lines	metres
1 mile	1,760	5,280	63,360	760,320	1,609
1 yard	—	3	36	432	0·914
1 foot		—	12	144	0·305
1 inch			—	12	0·025
1 line				—	0·0021

Other units of length

1 light year = distance travelled by light in 1 year = $9\cdot4608$ 10^{12} km $\approx 10^{13}$ km.

1 parsec = distance of a star at which the angle subtended by the radius of the earth's orbit is $1''$ (*i.e.* parallax of the star amounts to $1''$) = $3\cdot258$ light years = $3\cdot0826 \times 10^{13}$ km.

1 nautical mile = $1\cdot852$ km = $6,080\cdot3$ feet = $\dfrac{1}{60}$ meridian degree.

Length-preserving transformation

A transformation is called length-preserving if in the transformation every section of a curve corresponds to a section of a curve with equal length. The congruent transformations (= rigid motions) are length-preserving.

Limit

If the terms of an infinite sequence approach a definite value l in such a way that if we select some quantity, however small, we can always find a number N so that every term of the sequence after the Nth differs from l by less than the selected small quantity, then l is said to be the limit of the sequence.

If the terms of the sequence are denoted by $a_1, a_2, \ldots$, then we write:

$$\lim_{n \to \infty} a_n = l \text{ or } a_n \to l \text{ as } n \to \infty.$$

(See *Sequence*.)

Example: The sequence $0 \cdot 3$; $0 \cdot 33$; $0 \cdot 333$; $0 \cdot 3333$; $\ldots$ has the limit $\frac{1}{3}$.

Evaluation of limits

1. The limit of a sum (or difference, or product) is equal to the sum (or difference, or product) of the limit.

2. The limit of a quotient is equal to the quotient of the limits, provided the limit of the denominator differs from zero.

Formally:

$$\lim_{n \to \infty} (a_n + b_n) = \lim_{n \to \infty} a_n + \lim_{n \to \infty} b_n; \lim_{n \to \infty} a_n \cdot b_n = (\lim_{n \to \infty} a_n)(\lim_{n \to \infty} b_n)$$

$$\lim_{n \to \infty} (a_n - b_n) = \lim_{n \to \infty} a_n - \lim_{n \to \infty} b_n$$

$$\lim_{n \to \infty} \frac{a_n}{b_n} = \frac{\lim_{n \to \infty} a_n}{\lim_{n \to \infty} b_n}, \text{ where } \lim_{n \to \infty} b_n \neq 0.$$

Examples:

$$a_n = 2 + \frac{1}{n}; \; b_n = 3 + \frac{1}{2n}; \; \lim_{n \to \infty} a_n = 2; \; \lim_{n \to \infty} b_n = 3$$

$$\lim_{n \to \infty} (a_n + b_n) = \lim_{n \to \infty} \left(\left[2 + \frac{1}{n}\right] + \left[3 + \frac{1}{2n}\right] \right)$$

$$= \lim_{n \to \infty} \left(5 + \frac{3}{2n}\right) = 5$$

$$\text{and} \lim_{n \to \infty} a_n + \lim_{n \to \infty} b_n = 2 + 3 = 5.$$

$$\lim_{n \to \infty} (b_n - a_n) = \lim_{n \to \infty} b_n - \lim_{n \to \infty} a_n = 3 - 2 = 1$$

$$\text{and } \lim_{n \to \infty} \left(\left[3 + \frac{1}{2n} \right] - \left[2 + \frac{1}{n} \right] \right)$$

$$= \lim_{n \to \infty} \left(1 - \frac{1}{2n} \right) = 1.$$

$$\lim_{n \to \infty} a_n b_n = \lim_{n \to \infty} a_n \lim_{n \to \infty} b_n = 2 \cdot 3 = 6$$

$$\text{and } \lim_{n \to \infty} \left(2 + \frac{1}{n} \right) \left(3 + \frac{1}{2n} \right) = \lim_{n \to \infty} \left(6 + \frac{3}{n} + \frac{1}{n} + \frac{1}{2n^2} \right) = 6.$$

$$\lim_{n \to \infty} \frac{a_n}{b_n} = \frac{\lim_{n \to \infty} a_n}{\lim_{n \to \infty} b_n} = \frac{2}{3} \text{ and } \lim_{n \to \infty} \left(\frac{2 + \frac{1}{n}}{3 + \frac{1}{2n}} \right) = \frac{2}{3}.$$

These rules can be used for the evaluation of limits.

Example:

$$\lim_{n \to \infty} \frac{4n - 1}{n - 1} = \lim_{n \to \infty} \frac{\frac{4n - 1}{n}}{\frac{n - 1}{n}} = \lim_{n \to \infty} \frac{4 - \frac{1}{n}}{1 - \frac{1}{n}} = \frac{\lim_{n \to \infty} \left(4 - \frac{1}{n} \right)}{\lim_{n \to \infty} \left(1 - \frac{1}{n} \right)}$$

$$= \frac{\lim_{n \to \infty} 4 - \lim_{n \to \infty} \frac{1}{n}}{\lim_{n \to \infty} 1 - \lim_{n \to \infty} \frac{1}{n}} = \frac{4 - 0}{1 - 0} = 4.$$

Linear equation

Equations of the first degree, *i.e.* containing the unknown raised to at most the first power.

The normal form is $ax + b = 0$ (see *Equation*).

275

Linear transformation

Linear transformations are transformations of the complex z-plane onto the complex w-plane, carried out by means of complex linear functions. The theory of these linear transformations belongs to the foundations of the 'Theory of Functions'.

In what follows z denotes a complex variable: $z = x + iy$; similarly, w is a complex variable: $w = u + iv$. The constants a, b, c, d etc., denote complex numbers.

1. *Transformation by means of integral linear functions* $w = az + b$

(1) $a = 1$, $w = z + b$; this is a translation along the vector b. For $b = 0$ we have $w = z$, the identical transformation.

(2) $b = 0$, $w = az$, where $a \neq 0$. These are similarity transformations in which rotation occurs about the origin O through an angle $\alpha = \arg a$ and stretching occurs in the ratio $1 : |a|$ ($|a|$ is the absolute value of a). If in particular $|a| = 1$, *i.e.*

$$a = \cos \alpha + i \sin \alpha,$$

we have a pure rotation through the angle α. If a is a real number we have to deal with a pure stretching in all directions with similarity ratio $1 : |a|$ and origin O left unchanged.

The transformation $w = az + b$ $(a \neq 0)$ (the requirement $a \neq 0$ is essential since the transformation $w = b$ maps all points of the w-plane on to a single point of the z-plane and is thus degenerate) therefore means that to obtain the image w of the point z we first rotate and stretch the position vector z, and then translate the point along the vector b.

2. *Transformation by means of the function* $w = \dfrac{1}{z}$

If $z = r (\cos \alpha + i \sin \alpha)$ then $w = \dfrac{1}{r} \cos (-\alpha) + i \sin (-\alpha)$.

The image point of z thus has as absolute value the reciprocal of the absolute value of z and as argument (-1) times the argument of z. The transformation can best be carried out in two steps.

(1) Transition to the negative argument, *i.e.* we determine the point which has the same absolute value as z but negative argument, that is to say the point z' which is the conjugate complex with respect to z.

(2) We seek the point which has the same argument as z' but reciprocal absolute value. This involves taking the mirror reflection in the unit circle, *i.e.* inversion with respect to the unit circle or transformation by reciprocal radii (see Figs. 182 and 183).

Figs. 182 and 183 show how the mirror image of z with respect to a circle is found. z is joined to the centre O of the circle and, if z lies outside the circle (Fig. 182), the tangents from z to the circle are drawn. The line joining the points of contact of the tangents

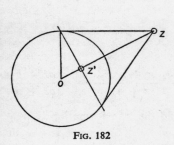

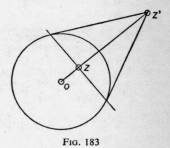

FIG. 182   FIG. 183

then intersects the line joining z to O in the required image-point z'. Alternatively, if z lies within the circle (Fig. 183), the perpendicular to the line joining z to O is constructed. This intersects the circle in two points. The tangent is constructed at each of these points, and these intersect in the required image-point z'.

3. *The general linear transformation* $w = \dfrac{az + b}{cz + d}$

A non-degenerate transformation of the z-plane on to the w-plane is defined by this function if the determinant

$$\begin{vmatrix} a & b \\ c & d \end{vmatrix} = ad - bc \neq 0.$$

A non-degenerate linear transformation of the above form can be carried out in three steps by splitting the given transformation into transformations of types 1 and 2.

(1) We first determine the point $z' = cx + d$ (as in 1).

(2) We then determine $z'' = \dfrac{1}{z'}$ (as in 2).

(3) Finally we carry out the transformation

$$w = \left(-\frac{ad - bc}{c}\right) z'' + \frac{a}{c} \text{ (as in 1).}$$

Then

$$w = \left(-\frac{ad - bc}{c}\right) z'' + \frac{a}{c} = \left(-\frac{ad - bc}{c}\right) \cdot \frac{1}{z'} + \frac{a}{c}$$

$$= \left(-\frac{ad - bc}{c}\right) \frac{1}{cz + d} + \frac{a}{c},$$

that is,

$$w = \frac{-ad + bc}{c(cz + d)} + \frac{a}{c} = \frac{-ad + bc + acz + da}{c(cz + d)} = \frac{az + b}{cz + d},$$

and so these three steps together yield the transformation

$$w = \frac{az + b}{cz + d}.$$

Note that if $ad - bc = 0$ we have $\dfrac{a}{c} = \dfrac{b}{d} = \dfrac{az + b}{cz + d}$ for all z, in other words all points z have the same image point $w = \dfrac{a}{c}$ and so the transformation is degenerate.

Literal numbers

Literal numbers are represented by letters of an alphabet (customarily the Latin and Greek alphabets). Any definite number can replace such a letter in a calculation, provided of course that the substitution is carried through consistently.

By convention the early letters of each alphabet are used as known fixed quantities, and the last letters to signify unknown fixed quantities, or variables. Frequently indices or other distinguishing marks are added to the letters of the alphabet, e.g.

$$a_1, \; b_7, \; A_4, \; \alpha_3, \; \beta', \; R_{\alpha\beta}.$$

The importance of literal numbers lies in their usefulness in presenting mathematical laws and rules clearly, compactly and comprehensively, by means of 'formulae'. *E.g.*

1. The commutative law of addition:
   In words: In addition, summands can be interchanged.
   As a formula: $a + b = b + a$.
2. In words: Powers of the same number are multiplied by retaining the base and adding the exponents.
   As a formula: $a^n \cdot a^m = a^{n+m}$.

Locus

The set of points satisfying certain conditions is called a 'locus'.

Examples:

(i) The locus of points distant r from a fixed point O is the circle with centre O and radius r.

(ii) The locus of points equidistant from two fixed points A and B is the perpendicular bisector of the segment $\overline{AB}$.

(iii) The locus of points distant d from a straight line l comprises the pair of lines parallel to l and distant d from it on either side.

(iv) The locus of points equidistant from two intersecting straight lines l and m is the pair of bisectors of the angle formed by l and m.

(v) The locus of the centres of circles which pass through two fixed points A and B is the perpendicular bisector of the segment $\overline{AB}$.

(vi) The locus of the centres of circles which touch a given straight line l in a given point A is the line through A perpendicular to l.

(vii) The locus of points the sum of whose distances from two fixed points F_1 and F_2 is constant and equal to $2a$ is the ellipse with foci F_1 and F_2 and major axis of length $2a$.

(viii) The locus of points the difference of whose distances from two fixed points F_1 and F_2 is constant is the hyperbola with foci F_1 and F_2.

(ix) The locus of points whose distances from a fixed point F and a fixed straight line l are equal is the parabola with focus F and directrix l.

If a point of the plane satisfies two conditions, it lies on the intersection of the two loci determined by these conditions.

Logarithm

A logarithmic function is the inverse of a power function.

The logarithm (of b to base a) is the exponent (n) to which the base (a) must be raised in order to obtain the antilogarithm (b).

$$
\begin{array}{ccc}
& \text{base} & \\
n & a & b \\
\text{logarithm} & & \text{antilogarithm}
\end{array}
$$

The logarithm of 1 is 0 for every base:

since $a^0 = 1$ for all a, $\log_a 1 = 0$.

If the base and antilogarithm are equal, the logarithm is 1:

since $a^1 = a$ for all a, $\log_a a = 1$.

Any positive number other than 0 and 1 can be used as base. In science and technology the base e ($e = 2 \cdot 718 \ldots$; see e) and the *natural logarithms* defined thereby (abbreviation: ln) are often used. The *common or Briggsian logarithms* widely employed in computation have base 10. This base is usually omitted when writing such logarithms: $\log_{10} a$ is abbreviated to $\log a$. We then have:

$$
\begin{array}{ll}
\log 10 = 1 & \log 0 \cdot 1 = -1 \\
\log 100 = 2 & \log 0 \cdot 01 = -2 \\
\log 1{,}000 = 3 & \log 0 \cdot 001 = -3 \text{ etc.}
\end{array}
$$

Since every positive number x can be written as the product of a number x' which lies between 1 and 10, and a power of 10, it is sufficient, for common logarithms, to calculate and tabulate the logarithms of numbers between 1 and 10 only. These logarithms lie between $\log 1 = 0$ and $\log 10 = 1$. Thus, in the table, figures will only occur to the right of the decimal place: if

$$x = 10^n x' \ (1 < x' < 10),$$

we have

$$\log x = n + \log x' \ (0 < \log x' < 1);$$

e.g. $20 = 10^1 \cdot 2, \ \log 20 = 1 + \log 2 = 1 + 0 \cdot 30103$

$0 \cdot 00002 = 10^{-5} \cdot 2, \ \log 0 \cdot 00002 = -5 + 0 \cdot 30103.$

n is called the *characteristic* of $\log x$. The characteristic is:

zero if x lies between 1 and 10;

positive if x is at least equal to 10;

negative if x is positive and less than 1.

$\log x'$ is called the *mantissa* of $\log x$. E.g.

$$\log 200{,}000 = \log (10^5 \times 2) = 5 + 0 \cdot 30103$$

has characteristic 5 and mantissa $0 \cdot 30103$.

Where the characteristic is positive, the characteristic and mantissa are to be added; *e.g.* $\log 200{,}000 = 5 \cdot 30103$. On the other hand, if the characteristic is negative we keep the characteristic and mantissa separate; *e.g.*

$$\log 0 \cdot 003 = \log 10^{-3} = -3 + \log 3 = 0 \cdot 47712 - 3.$$

Alternatively (and more commonly) we indicate a negative characteristic by a bar above it and append this characteristic to the mantissa, *e.g.*

$$\log 0 \cdot 003 = \bar{3} \cdot 47712.$$

Rules for calculating with logarithms

Example:

1. $\log_a (x \cdot y) = \log_a x + \log_a y$ \qquad $\log (7 \times 3) = \log 7 + \log 3$

2. $\log_a \left(\dfrac{x}{y} \right) = \log_a x - \log_a y$ \qquad $\log \dfrac{7}{3} = \log 7 - \log 3$

3. $\log_a (x^y) = y \log_a x$ \qquad $\log (7^3) = 3 \log 7$

4. $\log_a \sqrt[y]{x} = \dfrac{1}{y} \log_a x$ \qquad $\log \sqrt[3]{7} = \dfrac{1}{3} \log 7$

These formulae are simple consequences of the rules for calculating with powers.

There are as many systems of logarithms as there are possible base numbers $a > 0$. To obtain the relation between logarithms in one system with base a and those with base b, the following equation is used:

$$\log_b x = \log_b a \times \log_a x.$$

In particular for bases 10 and $e = 2\cdot71828\ldots$ we have

$$\log_{10} x = \log x = \log_{10} e \times \ln x.$$

Since $\log_{10} e = 0\cdot43429$ we have

$$\log x = 0\cdot43429 \ln x \text{ or } \ln x = \frac{1}{0\cdot43429} \log x.$$

Rules 1–4 explain why logarithms are of great practical use in numerical calculations. In calculating using logarithms each type of calculation is reduced to a simpler type: multiplication to addition, division to subtraction, etc. The accuracy of the calculation is of course limited by the number of places in the table of logarithms used.

Examples of numerical calculation using logarithms:

1. $\log (ab) = \log a + \log b$

    e.g. $x = 17 \cdot 0\cdot23$
    $\log 17 = 1\cdot23045$
    $\underline{\log 0\cdot23 = 0\cdot36173 - 1}$
    $\log x = 1\cdot59218 - 1$
    $\log x = 0\cdot59218$
    $\underline{x = 3\cdot910}$

2. $\log \left(\dfrac{a}{b}\right) = \log a - \log b$

    e.g. $x = 17 \div 0\cdot23$
    $\log 17 = 1\cdot23045$
    $\underline{\log 0\cdot23 = 0\cdot36173 - 1}$
    $\log x = 1\cdot86872$
    $\underline{x = 73\cdot913}$

    See also example 5.

3. $\log a^n = n \log a$

    e.g. $x = 37^3$
    $\log 37 = 1\cdot56820$

4. $\log \sqrt[n]{a} = \dfrac{1}{n} \cdot \log a$

    e.g. $x = \sqrt[3]{35}$
    $\log 35 = 1\cdot54407$

$3 \log 37 = 4 \cdot 70460$

$\log x = 4 \cdot 70460$

$x = 50652*$

$\frac{1}{3} \log 35 = 0 \cdot 51469$

$\log x = 0 \cdot 51469$

$x = 3 \cdot 2711$

See also example 6.

5.　　$\log \dfrac{a}{b} = \log a - \log b,$

e.g. $\log x = \dfrac{17}{1017}$

$\log 17 = 1 \cdot 23045$

$\underline{\log 1017 = 3 \cdot 00732}$

Here the subtraction cannot be carried out, since the subtrahend is greater than the minuend; we proceed as follows:

$\log 17 = 3 \cdot 23045 - 2$　　Thus for $\log 17 = 1 \cdot 23045$, 2 is

$\underline{\log 1017 = 3 \cdot 00732}$　　added and then taken away again.

$\log x = 0 \cdot 22313 - 2$

$x = 0 \cdot 016716$

6.　$\log \sqrt[n]{a} = \dfrac{1}{n} \log a$　　The characteristic -2 cannot be divided by 3, hence we add and subtract 1.

E.g.　　$x = \sqrt[3]{0 \cdot 017}$

$\log 0 \cdot 017 = 1 \cdot 23045 - 3$

$\underline{\frac{1}{3} \log 0 \cdot 017 = 0 \cdot 41015 - 1}$

$\log x = 0 \cdot 41015 - 1$

$x = 0 \cdot 25713$

Logarithmic tables. A table of logarithms (see *Table* 2) is a table containing the mantissae of the logarithms. According to the number of places given, we speak of 4-figure, 5-figure, etc., logarithm tables.

* Note that the result $x = 50652$ is short by 1. Errors like this occur in logarithmic calculations, since values in the table of logarithms used have been rounded off in the last decimal place.

Logarithmic functions (see *Functions*). The function $y = \log_a x$ is called a logarithmic function. For $a = 2$, the graph is shown in Fig. 184.

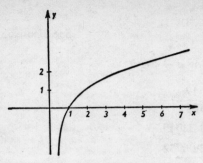

FIG. 184

Logarithmic series (see *Series*). The following development in series holds for the natural logarithms of numbers lying between (-1) and $(+1)$, *i.e.* for $-1 < x < 1$:

$$\ln(1 + x) = x - \frac{x^2}{2} + \frac{x^3}{3} - \ldots + (-1)^{n-1}\frac{x^n}{n} + \ldots$$

$$(-1 < x \le +1).$$

$$\ln\left(\frac{1}{1 - x}\right) = x + \frac{x^2}{2} + \frac{x^3}{3} + \ldots + \frac{x^n}{n} + \ldots$$

$$(-1 \le x < +1).$$

$$\ln\left(\frac{1 + x}{1 - x}\right) = 2\left(x + \frac{x^3}{3} + \frac{x^5}{5} + \ldots + \frac{x^{2k+1}}{2k + 1} + \ldots\right)$$

$$(-1 < x < +1).$$

Logarithms of the trigonometrical functions. Logarithms of the trigonometrical functions are sometimes given in tables of logarithms. Since the values of these functions are mostly less than 1, the tables are listed so that -10 must usually be appended to the given logarithm (exceptions are given in the tables).

Example: $\log \sin 37° \ 12' = 9{\cdot}7815 - 10.$

Interpolation in tables of logarithms. (For general remarks on interpolation, see *Interpolation.*) In logarithmic calculation it is sometimes necessary to achieve greater accuracy by interpolation. Suppose we wish to determine log 101·34, given

$$\log 101·3 = 2·0056,$$

and

$$\log 101·4 = 2·0060.$$

The difference of the arguments contained in the table is 0·1, and the difference of the associated logarithms is 0·0004. We assume now that the logarithm increases proportionately with the argument and accordingly take as approximating value

$$\log 101·34 = \log 101·3 + \frac{0·0004}{0·1} \times 0·04$$

$$= 2·0056 + 0·00016 = 2·0058.$$

Suppose we wish to solve the equation log x = 3·0419, and the latter value is not in the table. We seek the next smallest and the next largest logarithms in the table, *viz.*

$$\log 1101 = 3·0418$$

$$\log 1102 = 3·0422.$$

The difference of the logarithms is 0·0004. This corresponds to a difference in argument of 1. Thus a difference 0·0001 in the logarithm corresponds to a difference in the argument of $1 \times \frac{0·0001}{0·0004} = 0·25$; thus log 1101·25 = 3·0419 approximately.

In many tables of logarithms so-called *Proportional Parts* are given to aid in interpolation. These are either printed at the edges of individual pages or also at the beginning or end of the book on opposite pages. The use of these tables is illustrated by the following example.

To find

$$x = \log 246·57.$$

In the 5-figure table we find

$$\log 246 \cdot 5 = 2 \cdot 39182$$

and

$$\log 246 \cdot 6 = 2 \cdot 39199.$$

The difference of these logarithms is 0·00017. At the edge of the table we find the proportions table for the tabular difference 17; it reads:

	17
1	1·7
2	3·4
3	5·1
4	6·8
5	8·5
6	10·2
7	11·9
8	13·6
9	15·3

Since we have to determine log 246·57 we look for 7 in the left column of the table and find next to it the number 11·9. 11·9 is added to the last two figures of log 246·5 = 2·39182, *i.e.* to 82.*

Since we wish to calculate to 5 places, 11·9 is rounded off to 12, and we obtain: log 246·57 = 2·39194.

Logarithmic equation

Logarithmic equations are *conditional equations* in which the logarithm of the unknown appears, *e.g.*

$$5 \log x = x.$$

In general such equations must be solved by graphical or numerical methods, though sometimes a simple method can be found, *e.g.*

$$\log \sqrt{2x - 1} + \log \sqrt{x - 9} = 1.$$

We use the product rule for logarithms to get:

$$\log \sqrt{(2x - 1)(x - 9)} = \log 10.$$

---

* The addition of 11·9 to the last two figures 82 means in fact:
  $2 \cdot 39182 + 0 \cdot 000119 = 2 \cdot 391939 \approx 2 \cdot 39194$ (to 5 places).

If the logarithms of both sides of an equation coincide so must the antilogs. Thus:

$$\sqrt{(2x-1)(x-9)} = 10.$$

Whence it follows that:

$$2x^2 - 19x + 9 = 100 \qquad\qquad x = \frac{19}{4} \pm \frac{33}{4}$$

$$x^2 - \frac{19}{2}x - \frac{91}{2} = 0 \qquad\qquad x_1 = 13$$

$$x = \frac{19}{4} \pm \sqrt{\frac{361}{16} + \frac{728}{16}} \qquad\qquad x_2 = -\frac{7}{2}$$

Test 1. $\log \sqrt{2 \times 13 - 1} + \log \sqrt{13 - 9} = \log \sqrt{25} + \log \sqrt{4}$

$$= \log 5 + \log 2$$
$$= \log 5 \times 2$$
$$= \log 10 = 1.$$

2. $x_2 = \frac{7}{2}$ is not a root since $2x_2 - 1 = -7 - 1 = -8$ is negative and so $\sqrt{2x_2 - 1}$ is imaginary.

Logarithmic series

The series

$$\ln(1+x) = x - \frac{x^2}{2} + \frac{x^3}{3} - \frac{x^4}{4} + \ldots (-1)^{n-1} \frac{x^n}{n} + \ldots$$

converges for all x such that $-1 < x \leq 1$ (and only these values). $\ln$ = natural logarithm.

For $-1 \leq x < +1$,

$$\ln \frac{1}{1-x} = x + \frac{x^2}{2} + \frac{x^3}{3} + \frac{x^4}{4} + \ldots + \frac{x^n}{n} + \ldots.$$

For $-1 < x < 1$,

$$\ln \frac{1+x}{1-x} = 2\left(x + \frac{x^3}{3} + \frac{x^5}{5} + \ldots + \frac{x^{2k+1}}{2k+1} + \ldots\right).$$

These series are referred to as logarithmic series.

Logarithmic spiral

The logarithmic spiral has equation $r = me^{\varphi}$, where $m > 0$ is a constant number, $e = 2 \cdot 718\ldots$, and r and φ are polar co-ordinates (Fig. 185). The logarithmic spiral is a transcendental curve.

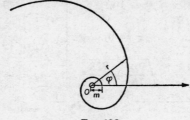

FIG. 185

Maclaurin's series

Maclaurin's series enables us to develop a given function $f(x)$ in powers of x, *i.e.* to provide a power series in x which represents the function $f(x)$. Maclaurin's series for the function $f(x)$ runs

$$f(x) = f(0) + \frac{f'(0)}{1!} x + \frac{f''(0)}{2!} x^2 + \frac{f'''(0)}{3!} x^3 + \ldots$$

Mathematical geography

To represent the position of a point on the earth's surface we refer it to the earth's axis (*i.e.* the diameter of the earth about which is executes in 24 hours its daily rotation). The two end-points of the axis are called the geographical poles (North and South). The great circle equidistant from both poles is called the equator; the half-circles running from North to South pole are called meridians and the circles running parallel to the equator, parallels of latitude. The position of a point on the earth's surface is denoted by its (geographical) latitude and longitude (Fig. 186). The latitude ϕ of a point is the angle between the normal to the earth's surface at the point and the normal at the equator. It ranges, to the North and to the South, from $0°$ to $90°$. The longitude of a point is the spherical angle at the pole between the meridian through Greenwich and the meridian of the point in question, or alternatively the arc between the two meridians at the equator. The longitude ranges from 0° to 180° to the east and to the west.

Mapping of the earth's surface

Cartography is concerned with the representation of the surface of the earth on a plane. This can only be done for limited areas without significant distortion. For larger areas the relative value of different mappings depends upon the purpose for which the map is being constructed. A mapping is essentially a transformation, and in this application angle-preserving (conformal), area-preserving, or length-preserving transformations are of especial interest (although length-preservation is only possible to a very restricted extent). We can recognise the relationship between mapped and map most simply by considering the image on the map of the latitude and longitude-circles.

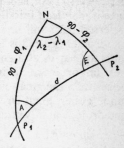

FIG. 186   FIG. 187

Position of two points relative to one another

The relative position of two points on the earth's surface is specified by the differences between their latitudes and longitudes. The angular length of the shortest line joining the two points (the section of the great circle which passes through them both) represents the distance apart of the two points, and is denoted in Fig. 187 by d. The angles between this line and the northerly

289

directions at P_1 and P_2 are denoted by A and E. We have

$$\cos d = \cos (90° - \phi_1) \cos (90° - \phi_2)$$
$$+ \sin (90° - \phi_1) \sin (90° - \phi_2) \cos (\lambda_2 - \lambda_1),$$

$$\cot A = \frac{-\sin \phi_1 \cos (\lambda_2 - \lambda_1) + \tan \phi_2 \cos \phi_1}{\sin (\lambda_2 - \lambda_1)},$$

$$\cot E = \frac{-\sin \phi_2 \cos (\lambda_1 - \lambda_2) + \tan \phi_1 \cos \phi_2}{\sin (\lambda_1 - \lambda_2)}.$$

The last two formulae are important for navigation. They need not be solved with great accuracy, since a course can only be steered to an accuracy of about 1°. Tables are available for the computation.

Loxodrome

The great-circle path is not the only one between two points on the earth's surface. In actual navigation it is often unsuitable, since it may lead into latitudes where ice is a danger. Usually the preferred path will be that with constant direction, the so-called loxodrome. Sea-maps are therefore usually maps in which such paths appear as straight lines (Mercator's map). In the latitudes most important in navigation the loxodrome is usually not much longer than the great-circle path. For air navigation, on the other hand, either great-circle routes are preferred, or routes with meteorological advantages.

Example: At 12 hrs., shore-time (the position of the ship at this time has to be registered in the ship's log), a ship is located at 38° 50′ N, 12° 17′ W, and steers in the direction 245° East of North at 14 knots. What will be its position at 19 hrs.?

The new position is calculated from the old by means of the changes in latitude and longitude during the period under consideration. The difference in latitude b follows from the direction and distance d; $b = d \cos \alpha$ (7 hours at 14 knots gives 98 nautical miles). $d \sin \alpha$, however, does not give the required difference in longitude l but the deviation a, related to the difference in longitude by the formula $l = a \cos \phi_m$, where ϕ_m is the mean of the initial and final latitudes (Fig. 188).

Distance $d = 98$ miles.

$\log d = 1\cdot9912 \qquad \log d = 1\cdot9912$

Direction $\alpha = 65°$

$\log \cos \alpha = \overline{1}\cdot6259 \quad \log \sin \alpha = \overline{1}\cdot9573$

$\log b = 1\cdot6171_n \qquad \log a = 1\cdot9485_n \qquad \log a = 1\cdot9485_n$

$b = -41\cdot4' \qquad\quad a = -88\cdot8\,\text{m} \quad \log \cos \phi_m = \overline{1}\cdot8936$

$\log l = 2\cdot0549$

Initial latitude:

38° 50′ N $\hspace{5cm}$ $l = 113\cdot5'\,\text{W}$

Final latitude:

38° 08·6′ N $\hspace{3cm}$ Initial longitude: 12° 17′ W

Mean latitude ϕ_m:

38° 29′ N $\hspace{3.5cm}$ Final longitude: 14° 10·5′ W

Vertex of the great circle

The point nearest the pole on a great circle path is calculated from the formulae;

$$\sin (90° - \phi_s) = \sin (90° - \phi_1) \sin A$$

$$\tan (\lambda_s - \lambda_1) = \frac{\cot A}{\sin \phi_1} \ \text{(Fig. 189)}$$

The navigator possesses special tables for this type of calculation.

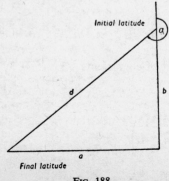

Fig. 188

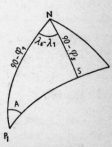

Fig. 189

Mathematical induction

Mathematical induction is a method of proving a general proposition involving an integer n which may be *any* positive integer (or any integer greater than some fixed N). Such a proof proceeds in the following way:

1. It is first proved that the proposition is true when n is equal to 1 (or whatever is the least integer $N + 1$ to which the proposition applies).

2. It is next proved that *if* the proposition is true for some arbitrary value of n, say k, greater than or equal to 1 (or $N + 1$), then it is also true for $n = k + 1$.

Now since by 1. the proposition is true for $n = 1$ (or $N + 1$), by 2. it is also true for $n = 2$ (or $N + 2$). Then by 2. it is also true for $n = 3$ (or $N + 3$), and so on for all the relevant values of n.

Example: $S_n = 1 + 2 + 3 + \ldots + n = \frac{1}{2} n(n + 1)$.

1. $S_1 = 1 = \frac{1}{2} \cdot 1 \cdot 2$, so the theorem is true for $n = 1$.

2. If $S_k = \frac{1}{2} k(k + 1)$, then $S_{k+1} = \frac{1}{2} k(k + 1) + k + 1 = \frac{1}{2}(k + 1)(k + 2)$; that is, if the theorem is true for $n = k$ it is true for $n = k + 1$.

The theorem is therefore true for all positive integral n.

Matrix

A matrix may be regarded as the array of coefficients of a system of linear equations; *e.g.*

$3x + 5y - 3z = 11$ has the matrix of coefficients $\begin{pmatrix} 3 & 5 & -3 \\ 2 & -1 & 4 \\ 2 & -3 & 1 \end{pmatrix}$.
$2x - y + 4z = 0$
$2x - 3y + z = 1$

The matrix $\begin{pmatrix} 3 & 5 & -3 & 11 \\ 2 & -1 & 4 & 0 \\ 2 & -3 & 1 & 1 \end{pmatrix}$

is called the augmented matrix of the system of equations.

A matrix can be either square or rectangular (*see* above examples). If certain rows and columns of a matrix are eliminated to leave a square matrix with (say) k rows and columns, the determinant of this matrix can be formed. This determinant is called a k-rowed *subdeterminant* of the matrix. The *rank* of a matrix is the highest order of non-zero subdeterminants.

Example: The matrix

$$\begin{pmatrix} 3 & 5 & -3 & 11 \\ 2 & -1 & 4 & 0 \\ 2 & -3 & 1 & 1 \end{pmatrix}$$

has at most rank 3. But the sub-determinant of the third order

$$\begin{vmatrix} 5 & -3 & 11 \\ -1 & 4 & 0 \\ -3 & 1 & 1 \end{vmatrix} = 5 \cdot 4 - 11 + 132 - 3 = 138$$

is non-zero. The rank of the matrix is thus 3.

Application: A system of linear equations is consistent if the matrix of coefficients and the augmented matrixes of the system have equal rank.

Mean proportional

The mean proportional x with respect to two quantities a and b (segments or numbers) is the number which satisfies the proportional relationship $a:x = x:b$. That is, $x^2 = ab$ and thus $x = \sqrt{ab}$. The mean proportional of two quantities a and b is identical with the *geometric mean*.

Measuring off an angle

To construct a given angle, α, at a point A on a straight line f (Figs. 190, 191).

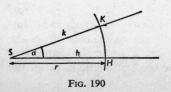
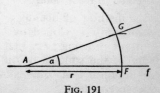

FIG. 190   FIG. 191

293

Suppose the given angle has vertex S and legs h and k. Describe about S and A equal circles with arbitrary radius r. Let the one circle cut h and k in H and K respectively and the other cut f in F. Now describe about F a circle with radius HK. This cuts the first circle in G, and the straight line through A and G is the second leg of the required angle. Note that the angle α can be measured off on different sides of f.

Median

The median of a number of observations is that value which has an equal number of observations greater and less than it. In the case of the Gaussian normal distribution the median coincides with the arithmetic mean.

Menelaos (1st century A.D., Alexandria)

Theorem of Menelaos. Every transversal cuts the sides of a triangle in such a way that the product of the ratios of the resulting segments, taken in the same sense round the triangle, is $+1$;

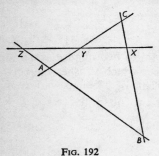

$$\frac{\overline{AZ}}{\overline{BZ}} \cdot \frac{\overline{BX}}{\overline{CX}} \cdot \frac{\overline{CY}}{\overline{AY}} = 1.$$

See Fig. 192.

FIG. 192

Method of least squares

A method of dealing with errors of observation (see *Error, theory of*), developed by Gauss, and named after its most important principle; *i.e.* that for a sequence of measurements the sum of the squares of differences from a particular value is a minimum if that value is taken to be the arithmetic mean of the measurements.

Consider a simple error-calculation made according to the method of least squares.

Suppose we have a sequence of measurements:

Obsv.	$\triangle$	$\triangle^2$
7	1·2	1·44
8	0·2	0·04
9	0·8	0·64
10	1·8	3·24
6	2·2	4·84
7	1·2	1·44
8	0·2	0·04
9	0·8	0·64
10	1·8	3·24
8	0·2	0·04
Σ 82	10·4	15·60

The arithmetic mean of the observations is 8·2, whence we get for the error:

$$\mu = \sqrt{\frac{15\cdot6}{9}} = \sqrt{1\cdot733}$$

$$m = \sqrt{\frac{15\cdot6}{90}} = \sqrt{0\cdot1733}$$

$$w = 0\cdot674\sqrt{0\cdot1733}$$

$$\delta = \frac{10\cdot4}{10} = 1\cdot04 = 0\cdot7979 \cdot \sqrt{0\cdot1733}.$$

Consequently, for the result, we have:

$$\beta = 8\cdot2 \pm 0\cdot674\sqrt{0\cdot1733},$$

the true value lying inside this range with probability 50%.

Mixed number

Sum of an integer and a fractional number, *e.g.*

$$1\frac{2}{3} = 1 + \frac{2}{3}$$

(see *Numbers, types of*).

Mollweide equations

Mollweide's equations belong to plane trigonometry and can be used for the solution of a triangle (sides *a*, *b*, *c*; angles α, β, γ).

The formulae are

$$\text{I. } \frac{a+b}{c} = \frac{\cos\dfrac{\alpha-\beta}{2}}{\cos\dfrac{\alpha+\beta}{2}} \qquad \text{II. } \frac{a-b}{c} = \frac{\sin\dfrac{\alpha-\beta}{2}}{\sin\dfrac{\alpha+\beta}{2}}$$

$$\frac{b+c}{a} = \frac{\cos\dfrac{\beta-\gamma}{2}}{\cos\dfrac{\beta+\gamma}{2}} \qquad \frac{b-c}{a} = \frac{\sin\dfrac{\beta-\gamma}{2}}{\sin\dfrac{\beta+\gamma}{2}}$$

$$\frac{c+a}{b} = \frac{\cos\dfrac{\gamma-\alpha}{2}}{\cos\dfrac{\gamma+\alpha}{2}} \qquad \frac{c-a}{b} = \frac{\sin\dfrac{\gamma-\alpha}{2}}{\sin\dfrac{\gamma+\alpha}{2}}$$

Monotonic

1. *Monotonic sequence*

A sequence x_n is said to be monotonic increasing if $x_n \leq x_{n+1}$ for all n, and monotonic decreasing if $x_n \geq x_{n+1}$ for all n. If $x_n < x_{n+1}$ or $x_n > x_{n+1}$ for all n we speak of strictly monotonic (increasing or decreasing) sequences.

2. *Monotonic functions*

If, for all $x_n < x_{n+1}$, $f(x_n) \leq f(x_{n+1})$, the function $f(x)$ is said to be monotonic increasing. Monotonic decreasing and strictly monotonic functions are defined similarly.

3. *Monotonic laws*

(a) for addition. If $a < b$ then $a + c < b + c$.
(b) for multiplication. If $a < b$ then, if c is positive, $ac < bc$.

Most probable value

The most probable value of a quantity with frequency distribution function $F(x)$ is the value of x for which the distribution function attains its maximum (see *Frequency curve*).

The binomial distribution $P_n(x) = \binom{n}{x} p^x q^{n-x}$ has mean value $E = np$. If the mean value is an integer, then it is also the most probable value of the distribution. If it is not an integer, it lies between two integers x_w and x_{w+1}. In this case, one other of these numbers is the most probable value, or both are regarded as most probable value if they are equally probable.

Example: 1. $p = q = \frac{1}{2}$, $n = 3$; $P_3(x) = \binom{3}{x} \left(\frac{1}{2}\right)^3$; mean value $E = \frac{3}{2}$, $P_3(0) = \frac{1}{8}$, $P_3(1) = \frac{3}{8}$, $P_3(2) = \frac{3}{8}$, $P_3(3) = \frac{1}{8}$.

$P_3(1)$ and $P_3(2)$ are equal and are the most probable values.

2. For $n = 4$, $p = q = \frac{1}{2}$, $P_4(x) = \binom{4}{x} \left(\frac{1}{2}\right)^4$ and $E = \frac{4}{2} = 2$; $x = 2$ is the most probable value. We verify that $P_4(0) = \frac{1}{16}$, $P_4(1) = \frac{1}{4}$, $P_4(2) = \frac{3}{8}$, $P_4(3) = \frac{1}{4}$, $P_4(4) = \frac{1}{16}$.

Multiplication

Multiplication is the third of the four fundamental calculating operations. It results from abbreviating the process of addition of equal summands:

$$a + a + a + a + a = a \times 5; \quad 3 + 3 + 3 = 3 \times 3.$$

The numbers multiplied together are called factors; the result of the multiplication is called the product. The first factor is sometimes called the multiplicand, the second factor the multiplier:

$$5 \quad \times \quad 3 \quad = \quad 15$$
$$\text{multiplicand} \times \text{multiplier} = \text{product}.$$

The commutative law holds for multiplication:

$$a \times b = b \times a; \text{ e.g. } 5 \times 3 = 3 \times 5.$$

No distinction need therefore be made in calculation between multiplicand and multiplier.

1. *Multiplication of general (literal) numbers*

By the product $a \times b$ of two general numbers we understand a sum of b summands each equal to a.

$$a \times b = a + a + a + \ldots (b \text{ times}), b \text{ integral}.$$

In particular b can be a definite number. We have then, for example,

$$a \times 5 = a + a + a + a + a.$$

In such a product 5 is called a coefficient. It is customary to omit the multiplication sign between coefficient and letter; the coefficient is placed in front of the letters and the latter placed in alphabetical order.

In multiplying general numbers together, the coefficients are first multiplied together, and then the letters.

$$(3a) \times (6b) = 18ab.$$

If a product contains equal factors, these can be grouped together as a power:

$$a \times a \times a \times a \times b \times b \times c = a^4 b^2 c \text{ (see } Power\text{)}.$$

If one factor of a product is zero the value of the product is zero. To multiply a product by a number, a factor may be multiplied by the number:

$$(3\sqrt{a}) \times 5 = 15 \times \sqrt{a}.$$

2. *Multiplication of relative numbers*

Relative numbers are multiplied by reference to the following sign rules: The product of two numbers with the same sign is positive; the product of two numbers with different signs is negative. (In what follows, '$\times$' is shortened to '.'.)

$$(+2) . (+3) = +6, \quad (-2) . (-3) = +6.$$
$$(+2) . (-3) = -6, \quad (-2) . (+3) = -6.$$
$$(+a) . (+b) = +ab, \quad (-a) . (-b) = +ab.$$
$$(-a) . (+b) = -ab, \quad (+a) . (-b) = -ab.$$

3. *Multiplication of algebraic sums*

To multiply an algebraic sum by a number, each term of the sum is multiplied by the number (distributive law):

$$x . (a + b - c) = ax + bx - cx.$$

To multiply algebraic sums together, every term of one sum is multiplied by every term of the other:

$$(a + 3) \cdot (2b - c) = 2ab + 6b - ac - 3c.$$

4. *Multiplication of powers*

(a) With the same base; multiply by adding the exponents and leaving the base unaltered:

$$a^3 \cdot a^7 = a^{10}; \quad a^m \cdot a^n = a^{m+n}.$$

(b) With the same exponent; multiply by leaving the exponent unaltered and taking the product of the bases:

$$a^m \cdot b^m = (a \cdot b)^m; \quad 5^3 \cdot 2^3 = (5 \cdot 2)^3 = 10^3.$$

5. *Multiplication of roots*

(a) With the same index; multiply by leaving the index unaltered and taking the product of the radicands:

$$\sqrt[n]{a} \cdot \sqrt[n]{b} = \sqrt[n]{a \cdot b}, \quad \sqrt[3]{5} \cdot \sqrt[3]{2} = \sqrt[3]{5 \cdot 2} = \sqrt[3]{10},$$

$$\sqrt{2} \cdot \sqrt{8} = \sqrt{16} = 4.$$

(b) With the same radicand; we make the roots similar and proceed according to the rule for roots with the same index, *e.g.*

$$\sqrt[n]{a} \cdot \sqrt[m]{a} = \sqrt[nm]{a^m} \, \sqrt[nm]{a^n} = \sqrt[nm]{a^{n+m}};$$

$$\sqrt[5]{3} \cdot \sqrt[7]{3} = {}^{5.7}\sqrt{3^7} \cdot {}^{7.5}\sqrt{3^5} = \sqrt[35]{3^7 \cdot 3^5} = \sqrt[35]{3^{12}}.$$

(c) Roots can be expressed as powers with fractional exponents and multiplication can then be carried out using the corresponding rules for powers, *e.g.*

$$\sqrt[n]{a} \cdot \sqrt[n]{b} = a^{\frac{1}{n}} \cdot b^{\frac{1}{n}} = (ab)^{\frac{1}{n}} = \sqrt[n]{ab};$$

$$\sqrt[3]{5} \cdot \sqrt[3]{2} = 5^{\frac{1}{3}} \cdot 2^{\frac{1}{3}} = (5 \cdot 2)^{\frac{1}{3}} = \sqrt[3]{5 \cdot 2} = \sqrt[3]{10};$$

$$\sqrt[n]{a} \cdot \sqrt[m]{a} = a^{\frac{1}{n}} \cdot a^{\frac{1}{m}} = a^{\frac{1}{n}+\frac{1}{m}} = a^{\frac{m+n}{mn}} = \sqrt[mn]{a^{m+n}};$$

$$\sqrt[5]{3} \cdot \sqrt[7]{3} = 3^{\frac{1}{5}} \cdot 3^{\frac{1}{7}} = 3^{\frac{1}{5}+\frac{1}{7}} = 3^{\frac{7+5}{35}} = 3^{\frac{12}{35}} = \sqrt[35]{3^{12}}.$$

6. *Multiplication of complex numbers*

Complex numbers are multiplied in the same way as algebraic sums, with i^2 put equal to -1, e.g.

$$(a + ib) \cdot (c + id) = ac - bd + i(bc + ad);$$
$$(7 + 5i) \cdot (1 + 3i) = 7 + 7 \cdot 3i + 1 \cdot 5i + 5i \cdot 3i$$
$$= 7 + 21i + 5i + 15i^2 = 7 + 26i - 15$$
$$= -8 + 26i.$$

Negative numbers

The introduction of the negative numbers is due to the need for subtraction to be performable without restriction. In the domain of positive numbers the subtraction $a - b = c$ can only be carried out if $a > b$ (a greater than b). If, on the other hand, $a < b$ (a smaller than b) we define $c = -(b - a)$, e.g. $5 - 7 = (-2)$. Here the '$-$ sign' on the left hand side of the equation represents an operation; on the right hand side it forms part of the number itself. In the case of positive numbers the associated sign ($+$) may be omitted, but not in the case of negative numbers. Representation of the numbers on a straight line clarifies the notion of a negative number.

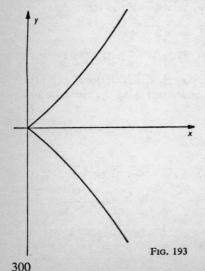

Neil's Parabola

This is an algebraic curve represented by the equation $ax^3 - y^2 = 0$, or in explicit form, $y = \pm\sqrt{ax^3}$ (a a fixed positive number, Fig. 193).

Newton's method of approximation

The improvement of an approximate solution $x = x_1$ of the equation $f(x) = 0$ by means of the differential

Fig. 193   calculus makes use of the

fact that the equation of the tangent at the point (x_1, y_1) on the curve given by $y = f(x)$, is

$$y - y_1 = f'(x_1)(x - x_1).$$

If x_1 is an approximate solution then $f(x_1)$ is not exactly zero. Suppose it equals y_1. A better approximation can be obtained by calculating the point x_t in which the tangent intersects the x-axis (*i.e.* $y = 0$). This is (Fig. 194)

$$x_t = x_1 - \frac{y_1}{f'(x_1)}.$$

Several applications of Newton's procedure rapidly lead to a sufficiently accurate approximation.

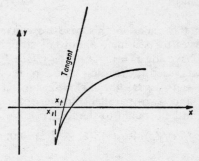

FIG. 194

Nomography

Representation of a functional relationship by a so-called nomogram is used when frequent graphical solution of the same equation with different parameters is required. After choice of scale (ratio of diagram lengths in cm. to actual quantities) a relation $y = f(x)$ can be represented as a nomogram scale in which the y values are plotted on a straight line, the x values being printed beside the relevant points (Fig. 195). Double-scales are also used, *i.e.* scales with two quantities having a simple relationship (*e.g.* frequency and wave-length, where the product is constant). Particular scales in frequent use are the logarithmic

301

scale ($y = c \log x$), the quadratic scale ($y = cx^2$) and the projective scale $\left(y = \dfrac{ax + b}{cx + d} \right)$. For three variables we speak of *function-nets*.

Example: graphs for $z = xy$ (Fig. 196).

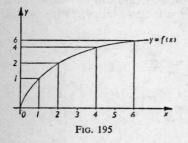

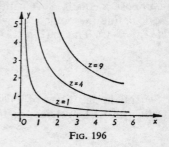

FIG. 195   FIG. 196

By adjusting the scales in this case we can arrange for the z-family of curves to become a family of straight lines: taking logarithms we have $\log z = \log x + \log y$ (see Fig. 197). These two function nets, used for reading off the relation $f(x, y, z) = 0$, are also called *net charts*. $f(x, y, z) = 0$ can be represented by one arbitrary and two parallel families of straight lines if $f(x, y, z) = 0$ can be brought to the form

$$f_1(x)f_3(z) + f_2(y)f_4(z) + f_5(z) = 0.$$

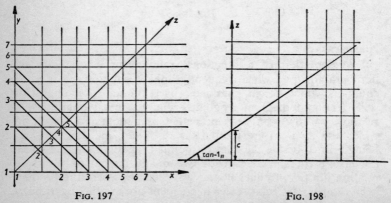

FIG. 197   FIG. 198

Examples of net charts

1. $z = cx^n$. Given scale-ratio l, we obtain:

$$l \log z = l \log c + ln \log x$$

(the use of *double logarithmic graph paper* is advantageous here, Fig. 198).

2. $z = cA^x + z_0$. If we take logarithms, the equation becomes

$$\log (z - z_0) = \log c + x \log A$$

(*simple logarithmic paper* is used here, Fig. 199).

Nomograms

The straight line joining two parameter values on two straight or curved lines laid out with appropriate scales gives a point of intersection on a third scale such that the required result is read off directly.

Example: $z = xy$ (particular case: $z = 12 = 3 \cdot 4$, Fig. 200).

The *code-equation* of a nomogram (*i.e.* of the functional relationship which the nomogram represents) and the scale of

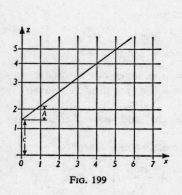

FIG. 199

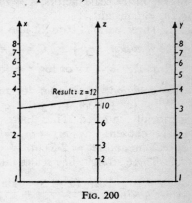

FIG. 200

the z-axis are given by representing the nomogram in a ξ- η-coordinate system and applying the straight-line conditions (Fig. 201).

303

For an arbitrary pair of values (x, y) the condition is that the determinant

$$\begin{vmatrix} \xi_1(x) & \eta_1(y) & 1 \\ \xi_2(x) & \eta_2(y) & 1 \\ \xi_3(x) & \eta_3(y) & 1 \end{vmatrix} = 0.$$

Application of this equation gives us the following code-equations for some frequently occurring nomograms (in what follows

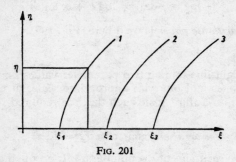

FIG. 201

m_f, m_g, m_h = scale factors, $A = m_f f(x)$; $B = m_g g(y)$; $C = m_h h(z)$; c_1, c_2 = constants):

1. Three parallel straight line scales.

Code-equation: $(c_1 + c_2) C = c_1 A + c_2 B$ (Fig. 202).

Example: $z = xy$ or $\log z = \log x + \log y$.

Code-equation: $(c_1 + c_2) m_h \log z = c_1 m_f \log x + c_2 m_g \log y$.

With $(c_1 + c_2) m_h = c_1 m_f = c_2 m_g$ the required equation is identically satisfied. Thus there are 3 quantities which can be freely chosen, say $m_f = m_g = 5$ cm and $c_1 = 2$ cm, giving $c_2 = 2$ cm and $m_h = 2 \cdot 5$ cm.

2. Three straight line scales intersecting in a point.

Code-equation: $\dfrac{\sin (\alpha + \beta)}{C} = \dfrac{\sin \alpha}{A} + \dfrac{\sin \beta}{B}$ (Fig. 203).

3. Triangular nomogram (equilateral triangle with measuring-lines parallel to edges).

Code-equation: $A + B + C = c_1$ (Fig. 204).

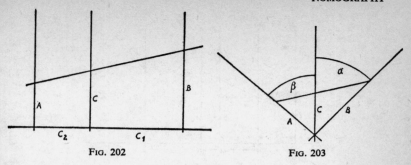

FIG. 202   FIG. 203

Nomograms for more than 3 variables

With more than 3 variables, unlabelled auxiliary lines are used (as scales for intermediate results for 2 adjacent variables, Fig. 205).

Example: $z = xyu$. Taking logarithms,

$$\log z = \log x + \log y + \log u$$

(Fig. 206).

With $c_1 = c_2$, and equating the scale factors m_x, m_y, we have for the scale factor m_h of the auxiliary line

$$(c_1 + c_2)m_h = c_2 m_x = c_1 m_y, \ i.e. \ m_h = \frac{m_x}{2},$$

and likewise with $m_u = m_h$ and $c_3 = c_4$,

$$(c_3 + c_4)m_z = c_4 m_h = c_3 m_u, \ i.e. \ m_z = \frac{m_h}{2} = \frac{m_x}{4}.$$

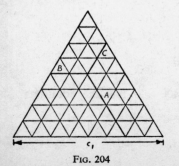

FIG. 204

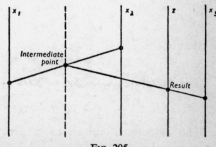

FIG. 205

305

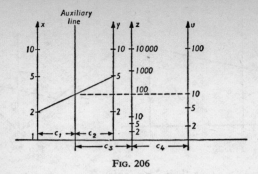

FIG. 206

Nonlinear systems of equations with two unknowns

If we have, for example, two nonlinear equations, then in order to eliminate one of the unknowns we make use of the *Resultant* (see art.) of the two equations, proceeding as follows. We order both equations according to the powers of one of the unknowns and then form their resultant by interpreting the preferred unknown as a known quantity. Since the two equations hold simultaneously the resultant must be 0. This gives us an equation with one unknown.

Example: I. $2x^2 - 3y^2 - 6 = 0$
II. $3x^2 - 2y^2 - 19 = 0$

The resultant is:

$$R = \begin{vmatrix} 2 & 0 & -3y^2 - 6 & 0 \\ 0 & 2 & 0 & -3y^2 - 6 \\ 3 & 0 & -2y^2 - 19 & 0 \\ 0 & 3 & 0 & -2y^2 - 19 \end{vmatrix}.$$

that is,

$$R = 25y^4 - 200y^2 + 400.$$

The equation $R = 25y^4 - 200y^2 + 400 = 0$ has the solutions

$$y_1 = 2, \quad y_2 = 2, \quad y_3 = -2, \quad y_4 = -2.$$

The associated values of x are: $x_1 = 3$, $x_2 = -3$, $x_3 = 3$, $x_4 = -3$.

Null sequence

A number-sequence whose limit is 0 is referred to as a null sequence.

Examples:

1. $1, \dfrac{1}{2}, \dfrac{1}{3}, \dfrac{1}{4}, \ldots, \dfrac{1}{n}, \ldots$

2. $1, \dfrac{1}{2}, \dfrac{1}{4}, \dfrac{1}{8}, \ldots, \left(\dfrac{1}{2}\right)^{n-1}, \ldots$

3. $1, -\dfrac{1}{2}, +\dfrac{1}{3}, -\dfrac{1}{4}, +\dfrac{1}{5}, \ldots, (-1)^{n-1} \cdot \left(\dfrac{1}{n}\right), \ldots$

Null vector

A vector whose length is zero is a null-vector (see *Vector*).

Number

Number is a fundamental concept of mathematics, and should be strictly distinguished from the concept of *numeral*. The numerals are merely the signs by means of which numbers are represented (see *Numerals, Number system*).

Number-plane

The number plane (also *Gaussian plane, Argand diagram*) provides a visual representation of the complex numbers (see above) in the same way as the real numbers are visualised as forming a straight line. A rectangular coordinate system is constructed, the horizontal axis usually being referred to as the real axis, and the perpendicular as the imaginary axis (Fig. 207).

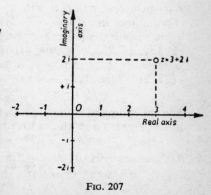

Fig. 207

The intersection of the two axes is denoted by O. On both axes unit lengths are laid out in both directions, the numbers . . . , -4, -3, -2, -1, 0, 1, 2, 3, 4, . . . being laid out on the real axis and . . . , $-3i$, $-2i$, $-i$, 0, i, $2i$, $3i$, . . . on the imaginary axis. In this way every point of the number plane is associated with a complex number and vice versa.

Number system

A number system is a method of representing numbers by means of symbols. Modern number systems are place-value systems. The Romans, Greeks, and Egyptians used number systems in which an individual number symbol had the same value essentially regardless of the position in which it occurred. (See *Numerals, Place-value system, Roman number system, Decimal system.*)

Number, types of

1. *Natural numbers*—cardinal numbers—1, 2, 3, 4, 5, . . .

   Even numbers: natural numbers divisible by two. 2, 4, 6, 8, 10, 12, 14, 16, ...

   Odd numbers: natural numbers not divisible by two. 1, 3, 5, 7, 9, 11, 13, 15, ...

   Prime numbers: numbers with no factor other than unity or the number itself. 2, 3, 5, 7, 11, 13, 17, 19, 23, 29, 31, ...

   Square numbers: squares (second powers) of natural numbers. 1, 4, 9, 16, 25, 36, 49, 64, 81, 100, 121, 144, ...

   Cubic numbers: third powers of natural numbers. 1, 8, 27, 64, 125, 216, 343, 512, 729, 1000, ...

2. *Integers* (integral numbers)—all positive integers (natural numbers), zero and all negative integers.

3. *Rational numbers* (fractions—fractional numbers).

   Proper fractions: the numerator of a proper fraction is less than its denominator, for example, $\frac{1}{2}, \frac{2}{5}, \frac{7}{9}$.

Unit fractions: unit fractions have numerator 1.

$$\frac{1}{2}, \frac{1}{3}, \frac{1}{4}, \frac{1}{5}, \frac{1}{6}, \frac{1}{7}, \frac{1}{8}, \cdots$$

Improper fractions: the numerator of an improper fraction is equal to or greater than its denominator, for example,

$$\frac{9}{2}, \frac{8}{3}, \frac{11}{7}, \frac{118}{20}.$$

Mixed numbers: sum of an integer and a proper fraction, for example, $3\frac{1}{2}$, $7\frac{2}{9}$.

Decimal fractions: fractions with denominator 10, 100, 1000, . . .; for example, 0·1987; 0·00876; 21·201.

4. *Decimal numbers*—numbers written according to the system using 10 as base (integral, rational or irrational numbers)

Finite decimal numbers: decimal numbers in which a finite number of digits come after the decimal point: for example, $\frac{1}{4} = 0·25$.

Infinite decimal numbers: decimal numbers in which an infinite number of places come after the decimal point.

Periodic decimal numbers: infinite decimal numbers in which a given sequence of figures constantly recurs: for example, 0·3333. . .; 0·173,173,173,. . .; 5·234,545,45. . . .

Pure periodic decimal numbers: periodic decimal numbers in which the period commences with the first place after the decimal point: for example, 0·333. . .; 1·212121.

Mixed periodic decimal numbers: periodic decimal numbers in which the period does not commence with the first place after the decimal point: for example, 0·00033333. . .; 0·4563333. . .; 0·465767676. . . .

5. *Irrational numbers* (non-rational numbers), for example $\sqrt{2}$, $\sqrt[3]{4}$, e, $\ln 2$, π.

Algebraic irrational numbers: those irrational numbers which satisfy an algebraic equation with rational coefficients; for example, $\sqrt[3]{2}$, $\sqrt{21}$, $\sqrt[3]{4}$.

Transcendental irrational numbers: those (irrational) numbers which do not satisfy any algebraic equation with rational coefficients; for example, e, e^5, ln 2.

6. *Real numbers.* (The real numbers comprise the rational and the irrational numbers.)

Relative numbers are real numbers furnished with a sign.

Absolute numbers. If real numbers are considered without their signs they are referred to as absolute numbers.

Denominate numbers. The real numbers may be provided with a labelling; for example, £3, $14, 5 miles, 6 lb.

7. *Complex numbers*

Imaginary numbers. The square root of a negative number is called an imaginary number; for example, $\sqrt{-1} = i$, $2i$, $3i$.

A complex number is a sum of a real number and an imaginary number: for example, $5 + 3i$, $7 - i\sqrt{3}$.

8. *Literal numbers.* (Letters used for representing mathematical formulae, such as a, b, c, . . ., α, β, γ, ...)

Numbers, representation on a straight line

The straight line serves to provide visual representation of the positive and negative numbers. It can be used to illustrate the addition and subtraction of relative numbers. A point, the origin, is fixed on a straight line. To the right and left a fixed segment, *e.g.* 1 cm, is laid out and the process repeated arbitrarily often. The points of division thus formed to the right of the origin are labelled from left to right 1, 2, 3, 4, . . ., and those formed to the left of the origin, from right to left -1, -2, -3, . . .,

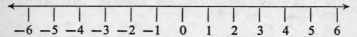

The positive numbers alone can be represented on a ray proceeding from an origin 0,

```
    0   1   2   3   4   5   6   7   8
    |   |   |   |   |   |   |   |   |
    |   |   |   |   |   |   |   |   |———————→  .
```

Numerals

The numerals are the symbols which are used to name the individual natural numbers (see *Number-system*, *Decimal system*, *Roman number system*).

Oblique triangle

A triangle is referred to as oblique if one of its interior angles is obtuse, *i.e.* greater than 90°.

Octahedron

The octahedron is one of the so-called Platonic solids. It is bounded by eight equilateral triangles (see *Platonic solids*).

Octant

If a three-dimensional rectangular coordinate system is set up then the space is divided by the coordinate planes into eight octants. Each octant is bounded by three mutually perpendicular coordinate planes (see *Coordinate systems*).

Opposite angles

Opposite angles or opposite-lying angles occur where parallel lines are cut by a transversal. Opposite angles lie on the same side of the transversal and on different sides of the parallel lines. Angles opposite to the intersecting parallels add up to 180° (see *Angle*).

Ordering

We can always establish for two real numbers which unique one of the three ordering-relations $<, =, >$ holds between them (see *Inequality*), *e.g.*

$$3 < 4, \quad -1 > -2, \quad \sqrt{2} < 2, \quad \frac{2}{3} = \frac{6}{9}$$

(read: 3 less than 4; −1 greater than −2; root 2 less than 2).

In the symbols $>$ and $<$ the vertex of the angle is always directed towards the smaller number.

Orientation (directional sense)

A line-segment, straight line or curve, is said to be oriented if some rule is given, according to which, of any two different points on the segment, one can be assigned as the earlier or preceding point, the other as the later or succeeding point. In these circumstances it is also said that the line segment, straight line or curve has been given an orientation or directional sense. The line is said to be described in the positive sense, if we proceed at every stage from earlier points towards later. If the curve is described in the opposite way, then it is said to be described in the negative sense.

Orthocentre

The point of intersection of the three altitudes of a *triangle* (see *Triangle*); it lies on the *Euler line of the Triangle*.

Pappus's theorem (3rd century A.D.)

On two sides of a triangle *ABC* construct arbitrary parallelograms *ACDE* and *BCFG*; extend the sides $\overline{ED}$ and $\overline{FG}$ to meet

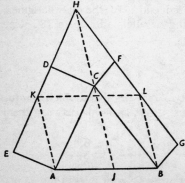

in the point H; draw lines through A and B parallel to $\overline{HC}$ meeting $\overline{HD}$ and $\overline{HF}$ in K and L respectively; join $\overline{KL}$. We now have a third parallelogram *ABLK* whose area is equal to the sum of the areas of the two original parallelograms (Fig. 208).

FIG. 208

312

Parabola

A parabola is the locus of points equidistant from a fixed point, the focus, and a fixed straight line, the directrix (see *Conic sections*).

The distance of the *focus F* from the *directrix l* is denoted by the *parameter p*. The standard equation of the parabola is $y^2 = 2px$. This is the *vertex equation* of the parabola, the vertex of the parabola (*i.e.* the point nearest the directrix) being taken in this representation to be the origin of the coordinate system (Fig. 209). The focus of the parabola then has coordinates $F\left(\dfrac{p}{2}, 0\right)$ and the directrix has equation $x = -\dfrac{p}{2}$.

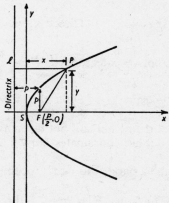

Fig. 209

The line perpendicular to the axis of the parabola and passing through the focus intersects the parabola in two points which are distant $2p$ apart. The parabola is symmetric about its axis and is an open curve. The further we proceed along the axis of the parabola from the vertex to and beyond the focus the greater is the distance of the points of the parabola from the axis. For construction of parabola, see *Conic sections*.

Particular equations of parabola

1. *Vertex equations.* According to the direction of the axis of the parabola, we have the following equations (the vertex of the parabola being taken each time as the origin):

(a) Axis of parabola = y-axis, focus $F\left(0, \frac{p}{2}\right)$ (opening above)

$$x^2 = 2py \qquad \text{Directrix: } y = -\frac{p}{2}$$

(b) Axis of parabola = y-axis, focus $F\left(0, -\frac{p}{2}\right)$ (opening below)

$$x^2 = -2py \qquad \text{Directrix: } y = +\frac{p}{2}$$

(c) Axis of parabola = x-axis, focus $F\left(\frac{p}{2}, 0\right)$ (opening to right)

$$y^2 = 2px \qquad \text{Directrix: } x = -\frac{p}{2}$$

(d) Axis of parabola = x-axis, focus $F\left(-\frac{p}{2}, 0\right)$ (opening to left)

$$y^2 = -2px \qquad \text{Directrix: } x = +\frac{p}{2}$$

2. If the vertex of the parabola is not taken as the origin of the coordinate system but has coordinates $S(a, b)$, then the following possibilities arise:

(a) Axis of parabola parallel to y-axis (opening above)

$(x - a)^2 = 2p(y - b)$, focus: $F\left(a, b + \frac{p}{2}\right)$, directrix: $y = b - \frac{p}{2}$.

(b) Axis of parabola parallel to y-axis (opening below)

$(x - a)^2 = -2p(y - b)$, focus: $F\left(a, b - \frac{p}{2}\right)$, directrix: $y = b + \frac{p}{2}$.

(c) Axis of parabola parallel to x-axis (opening to right)

$(y - b)^2 = 2p(x - a)$, focus: $F\left(a + \frac{p}{2}, b\right)$, directrix: $x = a - \frac{p}{2}$.

(d) Axis of parabola parallel to x-axis (opening to left)

$(y - b)^2 = -2p(x - a)$, focus: $F\left(a - \frac{p}{2}, b\right)$, directrix: $x = a + \frac{p}{2}$.

Equations of lines associated with the parabola

Tangents, normals, polars, diameters.

1. *Intersections* of the line $y = mx + n$ with the parabola $y^2 = 2px$.

Regarding the equations (i) $y = mx + n$ and

(ii) $y^2 = 2px$

as a system of equations specifying the points of intersection we have

$$x_{1,2} = -\frac{mn - p}{m^2} \pm \frac{1}{m^2} \sqrt{p(p - 2mn)};$$

$$y_{1,2} = +\frac{p}{m} \pm \frac{1}{m} \sqrt{p(p - 2mn)}.$$

Special case: $m = 0$, the straight line is parallel to the x-axis. The system of equations is then: $y^2 = 2px$, $y = n$. In this case there is only one point of intersection $P_1 \left(\frac{n^2}{2p}, n \right)$, and there is no tangent line having this direction.

In the general case we have ($D = p - 2mn$, the discriminant):

2 points of intersection if D is positive;

1 point of intersection if $D = 0$ (tangent);

no point of intersection if D is negative.

2. *Tangents to the parabola.* The line $y = mx + n$ is tangent to the parabola $y^2 = 2px$ if $D = p - 2mn = 0$, *i.e.* if $n = \frac{p}{2m}$. The equation of the tangent is then

$$y = mx + \frac{p}{2m}.$$

This line touches the parabola in the point $\left(\frac{p}{2m^2}, \frac{p}{m} \right)$.

The equation of the tangent to the parabola at the point (x_1, y_1) is

$$yy_1 = p(x + x_1).$$

The equation of the normal at the same point is

$$y - y_1 = -\frac{y_1}{p}(x - x_1).$$

3. *Polar equations.* If the tangents to the parabola from a point P_0 outside the parabola are to be constructed and their equations obtained, the points of contact of the required tangents are first calculated by means of the polar equation. This is $yy_0 = p(x + x_0)$.

4. *Diameters.* Straight lines with a fixed gradient m have equations of the form $y = mx + n$ and form a family of parallel chords of the parabola when n is varied. From the coordinates of the point of intersection we can derive the mid-points of the chords $\left(-\dfrac{mn - p}{m^2}, \dfrac{p}{m}\right)$ and their locus is defined to be a diameter of the parabola. The mid-points of chords of a family with common gradient m therefore lie on a line parallel to the x-axis and at distance $\dfrac{p}{m}$ from it. This line is called the diameter with reference to the direction m.

5. *Tangents to the parabolas* $y^2 = -2px$, $x^2 = 2py$, $x^2 = -2py$:

(a) The line $y = mx + n$ is tangent to the parabola $y^2 = -2px$ if $D = p + 2mn = 0$.

(b) The line $y = mx + n$ is tangent to the parabola $x^2 = 2py$ if $D = pm^2 + 2n = 0$.

(c) The line $y = mx + n$ is tangent to the parabola $x^2 = -2py$ if $D = pm^2 - 2n = 0$.

6. *Equations of tangent* at given point of contact $P_1(x_1, y_1)$ to the parabolas $(y - b)^2 = \pm 2p(x - a)$ or $(x - a)^2 = \pm 2p(y - b)$:
The equations of the tangents are

$$(y - b)(y_1 - b) = \quad p \cdot (x - a + x_1 - a)$$
$$\text{for the parabola } (y - b)^2 = \quad 2p(x - a),$$

$$(y - b)(y_1 - b) = -p \cdot (x - a + x_1 - a)$$
$$\text{for the parabola } (y - b)^2 = -2p(x - a),$$

$$(x - a)(x_1 - a) = \quad p \cdot (y - b + y_1 - b)$$
$$\text{for the parabola } (x - a)^2 = \quad 2p(y - b),$$

PARABOLA

$$(x - a)(x_1 - a) = -p \cdot (y - b + y_1 - b)$$

for the parabola $(x - a)^2 = -2p(y - b)$.

7. *Equations of polar* for given pole $P_0(x_0, y_0)$ in respect of the parabolas

$$(y - b)^2 = \pm 2p(x - a) \text{ and } (x - a)^2 = \pm 2p(y - b).$$

The equation of the polar line is identical with the equation of a tangent (see above under 6) and is obtained by substituting the coordinates (x_0, y_0) for (x_1, y_1) in the equation. The polar equation can be used to calculate the point of contact of tangents from P_0 to the parabola, and from these to set up the equations of the tangents.

General theorems on the parabola (Fig. 210).

1. Diameters of a parabola (with reference to families of parallel chords) are parallel to the axis of the parabola.

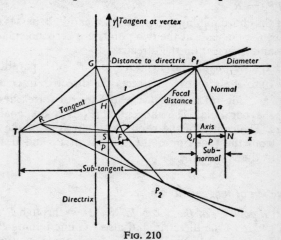

FIG. 210

2. The feet of perpendiculars from the focus to tangents to a parabola lie on the tangent at the vertex.

3. The point of intersection of two mutually perpendicular tangents lies on the directrix of the parabola.

4. The distance of the point of contact of a tangent from the focus is equal to the distance of the focus from the point of intersection of the tangent with the axis of the parabola. (In Fig. 210, $\overline{TF} = \overline{FP_1}$.)

5. The tangent at P_1 bisects the angle between P_1F and the perpendicular from P_1 onto the directrix.

6. The projection onto the axis of the parabola of the line-segment between the point of contact of a tangent and the point of intersection of the tangent with the axis, is bisected by the vertex. The segment bisected is referred to as the subtangent.

7. The projection onto the axis of the parabola of the segment lying on the normal, between its points of intersection with the parabola and with the axis, is called the subnormal. The subnormal has length p.

8. The mirror-image of the focus, with respect to a tangent, lies on the directrix of the parabola.

9. If the tangents at points P_1, P_2 of a parabola intersect in R, then $RFP_1 = RFP_2$.

10. If the chord joining two points of a parabola passes through the focus, the tangents at the two points are perpendicular to one another and intersect on the directrix.

11. If the perpendicular from a point P_1 of a parabola with focus F onto the directrix intersects the directrix in G then $\overline{P_1F}$ and $\overline{P_1G}$ are sides of a rhombus whose fourth vertex lies on the axis of the parabola. The tangent at P_1 is a diagonal of the rhombus. The centre of the rhombus is the foot of the perpendicular from the focus onto the tangent at P_1 and lies on the tangent at the vertex.

Construction of tangents to a parabola

(a) *At a point P_1 of the parabola.* We draw through P_1 the line perpendicular to the directrix and also the line joining P_1 to the focus. The tangent is the bisector of the angle between these two lines.

(b) *From a point P to the parabola* (Fig. 211). Join the point P to the focus F and describe on the segment $\overline{PF}$ the Thales circle. The point of intersection of this circle with the tangent at the vertex is the foot H of the perpendicular from the focus onto the required tangent. Join FH and let it intersect the directrix in G. G is the mirror-image of the focus with respect to the required tangent. Through G draw the line parallel to the axis of the parabola. This intersects the tangent in its point B of contact with the parabola.

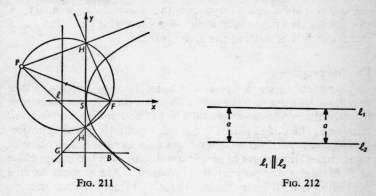

FIG. 211   FIG. 212

Parallel

Two straight lines which lie in one and the same plane and do not intersect are said to be parallel (Fig. 212).

Parallel axiom

If a is an arbitrary straight line and A a point which does not lie on a, then in the plane determined by a and A, there is just one straight line which passes through A and does not intersect a.

Consequences of the parallel axiom

1. If two parallel lines are intersected by a third, step angles and alternate angles are equal and conversely if step-angles and alternate angles are equal the two lines intersected by the transversal must be parallel.

2. The interior angles of a triangle add up to $180°$.

3. If l and m are two straight lines which are both parallel to a third line n, then l and m themselves are parallel.

4. If l and m are two parallel lines, P a point on l, and if $\overline{PF}$

is the perpendicular from P onto m, then PF is defined as the distance between the parallel lines. The distance defined in this way is the same wherever P is chosen to lie on l.

Parallel planes

Planes which do not intersect are said to be parallel.

Parallel planes are everywhere the same distance apart. A straight line is said to be parallel to a plane if it lies wholly in a plane which is parallel to the given plane.

Parallel projection

A *projection* (see art.) in which all rays of projection are parallel is called a parallel projection. The direction of these rays is called the *projection-direction*. The projection-direction is given relative to the image-plane. We speak of oblique parallel projection, if the rays of projection do not intersect the image plane at right angles. If the rays of projection do intersect the image-plane at right angles, the projection is *orthogonal*. The general parallel projection is used for representing solid objects by plane images, *e.g.* in *cavalier perspective* (see art.). Orthogonal parallel projection is used for *horizontal projection* and for *two-plane projection* (see art.).

Parallel translation (Fig. 213)

A parallel translation is a transformation in a plane or in space (see *Transformation*). A parallel translation in a plane can be specified by a translation-direction (measured by the angle α

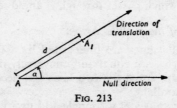

FIG. 213

formed with an agreed null-direction) and by a displacement-segment d. The image of a point A can be constructed by drawing from A the ray in the direction of translation, and marking off on it the displacement segment d. The end-point A_1 of the segment laid off is the image point of A. For representation by a system of equations, see *Rigid motions*.

Parallelogram

A quadrilateral in which pairs of opposite sides are parallel is called a parallelogram (see *Quadrilateral*).

Parallels to a straight line, construction of

1. To construct a straight line m through a given point, parallel to a straight line l. Draw through the given point P an arbitrary straight line l_1 intersecting l in the point A. l and l_1 form together the angle α (see Fig. 214). At P on l_1 lay out the angle α, on the same side of l_1, and in the same sense, from AP. Then the free arm of the new angle gives the direction of the required parallel m. l_1 may conveniently be chosen to be perpendicular to m ($\alpha = 90°$).

2. To construct a straight line m parallel to a given straight line l and at a distance a from it (Fig. 215). Take a point P on l

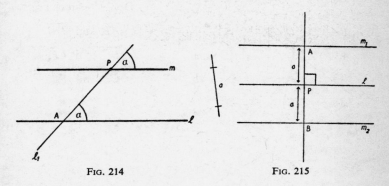

FIG. 214   FIG. 215

and erect the perpendicular to l at this point. Describe a circle with radius a about P. This intersects the perpendicular in two points A and B, such that P lies between A and B. Draw the lines parallel to l through A and B. There are two lines, m_1 and m_2 with the required property.

Parametric representation of a curve

The representation of the points $P(x, y, z)$ of a curve by three functions $x = u(t)$, $y = v(t)$, $z = w(t)$ dependent on a parameter t is described as a parametric representation of the curve (see *Curves*).

Parametric representation of a surface

The points $P(x, y, z)$ of a surface can be represented by three functions

$$x = u(s, t), \quad y = v(s, t), \quad z = w(s, t),$$

dependent upon two parameters, s and t. This is referred to as a parametric representation of the surface (see *Surface*).

Pascal's theorem (Blaise Pascal, 1623–1662)

The three points of intersection X, Y and Z of opposite sides of a hexagon inscribed in a circle (or conic) lie on a straight line (Pascal's line), opposite sides being sides separated from one another by two sides (Fig. 216).

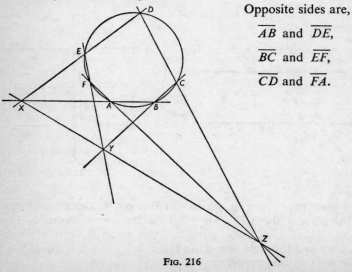

Opposite sides are,

$\overline{AB}$ and $\overline{DE}$,

$\overline{BC}$ and $\overline{EF}$,

$\overline{CD}$ and $\overline{FA}$.

FIG. 216

Pascal's triangle

Pascal's triangle is the following array of numbers, in which the individual numbers of the array are the binomial coefficients $\left(\dfrac{n}{k}\right)$, (see also *Binomial Theorem*).

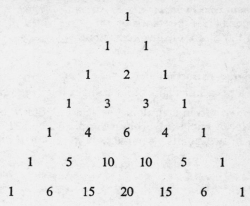

```
                    1
                 1     1
              1     2     1
           1     3     3     1
        1     4     6     4     1
     1     5    10    10     5     1
  1     6    15    20    15     6     1
```

The array has the following properties

1. Each number is the sum of the two numbers standing above it to the left and right; *e.g.* $10 = 4 + 6$.

2. Each number is equal to the sum of all numbers in the left or right diagonal, beginning with the number immediately above to the left or right, and proceeding upwards; *e.g.* $15 = 5 + 4 + 3 + 2 + 1$ and $15 = 10 + 4 + 1$.

3. Each diagonal is an *arithmetic sequence* (see art.); *e.g.*

1st diagonal: 1, 1, 1, 1, 1, . . .   Arithmetic sequence of zero order.

2nd diagonal: 1, 2, 3, 4, 5, . . .   Arithmetic sequence of 1st order.

3rd diagonal: 1, 3, 6, 10, 15, . . .   Arithmetic sequence of 2nd order.

4th diagonal: 1, 4, 10, 20, . . .   Arithmetic sequence of 3rd order.

And so on.

Perpendicular bisector

The perpendicular bisector of a given straight line segment $\overline{AB}$ is the straight line perpendicular to $\overline{AB}$, and passing through its mid-point.

The perpendicular bisector of a segment is the axis of symmetry of the segment (see *Fundamental constructions*, *Triangle*).

The perpendicular bisectors of the three sides of a triangle intersect in the centre of the circumcircle.

Perpendicular, construction of

To drop a perpendicular onto a straight line (Fig. 217).

Construction: Given a straight line l and a point P outside the line. Describe a circle (of arbitrary radius) about P so that it intersects l in two points A and B. About A and B draw circles

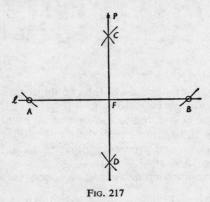

Fig. 217

large enough to intersect and join their points of intersection, C and D. The required perpendicular lies on the line through C and D, and is the join of P to the point F where l and CD intersect.

Perspective

Two figures or solid bodies which arise from one another by a *perspective transformation* (see art.) are said to be in perspective with respect to one another. The perspective image of a circle can, for example, be a parabola, and the parabola and the circle are then in perspective with respect to one another (see *Perspective transformation*).

Perspective transformation (= perspectivity)

Plane perspective transformation

In a perspective transformation in a plane, the points of two different straight lines are associated with one another in the following way:

If l and m are given straight lines and Z is a point of the plane which lies neither on l or m, then a point L of l is associated with the point of intersection, M, of $\overline{ZL}$ with m (M is the image-point of L). Z is called the centre of the perspectivity (Fig. 218). Thus in a perspectivity the image-points on m arise out of the points of l by central projection.

Such a perspectivity of the points of two straight lines possesses a fixed point (point whose image coincides with the point itself), namely the point of intersection P of the two lines.

Example of a perspective transformation in space

If E_1 and E_2 are two different planes in space, and Z is a point outside both E_1 and E_2, a perspectivity can be defined in the following way:

If P_1 is a point of E_1 the point of intersection P_2 of the line $\overline{ZP_1}$ with the plane E_2 is associated with P_1 as its image-point. The points of the line of intersection l of E_1 and E_2 are fixed points of this transformation (Fig. 219).

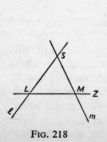

FIG. 218

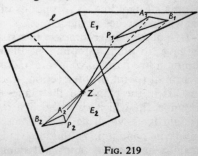

FIG. 219

325

'Central perspective' is an important mapping-procedure of *Descriptive geometry* (see art. under this title and also *Central perspective*).

The perspective transformations belong to the *projective transformations* (see art.).

Place-value system

A place-value system is a number system in which the value of a number-symbol depends not only on the symbol itself but also on the position in the number at which the symbol occurs. The *sexagesimal system* of the Babylonians, with base 60, our own *decimal system*, with base 10, and the *binary* system (base 2) used by many computing machines are examples. Each place-value system has a positive integral base and as many different number-symbols as this base allows.

A sexagesimal system must thus have 60 number-symbols; the decimal system uses the symbols 0, 1, 2, 3, 4, 5, 6, 7, 8 and 9; a binary system can use the symbols 0 and 1. See *Number system*, *Numerals*, *Decimal system*.

Plane

The plane is one of the basic geometric elements of space (the others are the *point* (see below) and the *straight line* (see below)).

Properties of the plane

A plane is uniquely determined by three points which do not lie on a straight line. If two points of a straight line lie in a plane, the whole line lies in the plane.

Two planes either intersect in a straight line (trace line or trace) or have no point in common. Planes which have no points in common are parallel. A plane and a straight line either intersect in a point (point of intersection, trace point, trace); or the whole line lies in the plane; or the plane and the line have no point in common, in which case the line is parallel to the plane. Two straight lines which lie in the same plane have either one or no points in common. A unique plane is determined either by a straight line and a point not lying on it, or by two different straight lines with a common point. A plane is unbounded on all sides and divides space into two parts. A plane is divided by every straight line within it into two parts. In dealing with different planes in space at the same time we sometimes denote the planes by capital Greek letters: A, B, Γ, Δ, E, Z, ...

Planetary orbits

The path of a planet in its motion about the sun is described as its orbit. The movement of the planets about the sun results from the force of attraction (gravitational force) between the planets and the sun. A planet moves in an orbit which obey the following three laws (Kepler's laws):

I. The planet describes an ellipse with the sun at one focus.

II. The radius vector from the sun to the planet sweeps out equal areas in equal times.

III. If the orbits of several planets are compared with one another, the squares of times of revolution are proportional to the cubes of the major axes of the orbital ellipses.

Planimetry

Planimetry, or 'plane geometry', comprises the study of figures lying in a plane. Parallel with plane geometry we speak of 'linear geometry', the study of geometrical structures lying in a straight line, and of stereometry or 'solid geometry' primarily concerned with geometrical structures in space which do not lie in a straight line or in a plane.

The term 'planimetry' is often confined to that part of plane geometry concerned with the measurement of plane figures.

Platonic solids

Platonic solids or regular polyhedra are convex polyhedra which are bounded by regular, mutually congruent, polygons. There are five Platonic solids, viz.

Tetrahedron, Hexahedron (cube), *Octahedron,*

Pentadodecahedron, and *Icosahedron.*

General properties

> *Notation:* v = number of vertices
> f = number of faces
> e = number of edges
> m = number of faces meeting at a vertex
> n = number of edges and vertices associated with a face
> a = number of angles.

We have $v + f = e + 2$ (*Euler's polyhedron theorem*).

Solid	m	n	f	v	e
Tetrahedron	3	3	4	4	6
Octahedron	4	3	8	6	12
Icosahedron	5	3	20	12	30
Hexahedron	3	4	6	8	12
Dodecahedron	3	5	12	20	30

Each of these solids possesses an inscribed and a circumscribed sphere, which has the same centre O. Further, the mid-points of all the edges of a platonic solid also lie on a sphere again with centre O. If we construct the inscribed sphere of a Platonic solid and join neighbouring points of contact of the sphere with the faces of the polyhedron, there results within the sphere another regular polyhedron, which has the same number of vertices as the original solid has faces, and the same number of edges as the original solid. The cube yields an octahedron, the icosahedron a dodecahedron, and the tetrahedron another tetrahedron.

Measurements of the Platonic solids

> *Notation:* lateral edge a, lateral surface G, total surface S, volume V, radius of circumscribed sphere r, radius of inscribed sphere ρ, angle between edges α and angle between faces ϕ.

	Tetra-hedron	Cube	Octa-hedron	Dodecahedron	Icosahedron
Lateral surface, G	$\frac{a^2}{4}\sqrt{3}$	a^2	$\frac{a^2}{4}\sqrt{3}$	$\frac{a^2}{4}\sqrt{25+10\sqrt{5}}$	$\frac{a^2}{4}\sqrt{3}$
Total surface, S	$a^2\sqrt{3}$	$6a^2$	$2a^2\sqrt{3}$	$3a^2\sqrt{25+10\sqrt{5}}$	$5a^2\sqrt{3}$
Volume, V	$\frac{a^3}{12}\sqrt{2}$	a^3	$\frac{a^3}{3}\sqrt{2}$	$\frac{a^3}{4}(15+7\sqrt{5})$	$\frac{5}{12}a^3(3+\sqrt{5})$
Radius, r	$\frac{a}{4}\sqrt{6}$	$\frac{a}{2}\sqrt{3}$	$\frac{a}{2}\sqrt{2}$	$\frac{a}{4}\sqrt{3}(1+\sqrt{5})$	$\frac{a}{4}\sqrt{10+2\sqrt{5}}$
Radius, ρ	$\frac{a}{12}\sqrt{6}$	$\frac{a}{2}$	$\frac{a}{6}\sqrt{6}$	$\frac{a}{4}\sqrt{\frac{50+22\sqrt{5}}{5}}$	$\frac{a}{12}\sqrt{3}(3+\sqrt{5})$
Angle between edges, α	60°	90°	60°	108°	60°
Angle between faces, ϕ	70° 33′	90°	109° 28′	116° 34′	138° 11′

Point

Points are basic elements of linear, plane and three-dimensional geometry. Properties of points: two distinct points determine a straight line (connecting line).

Two straight lines, which lie in a plane and are not parallel, intersect in a point (point of intersection).

If three distinct points lie on a straight line we can say of just one of these points that it lies between the other two. (Ordering of points on a straight line.)

Three points of space which do not lie on a straight line determine a single plane.

Point-sequence

If according to some prescribed rule a first point P_1 determines a second P_2, and P_2 determines a third P_3, and so on, these points are said to form a point-sequence:

$$P_1, P_2, P_3, P_4, \ldots\ldots$$

The points dealt with can be either in a plane or in three-dimensional space. Point-sequences are closely related to number-sequences. Thus, if the points are specified by their coordinates, three number sequences are formed from the coordinates $P_n(x_n, y_n, z_n)$ of the general point

$$x_1, x_2, x_3, \ldots, x_n, \ldots$$
$$y_1, y_2, y_3, \ldots, y_n, \ldots$$
$$z_1, z_2, z_3, \ldots, z_n, \ldots$$

Conversely, given an arbitrary number-sequence $a_1, a_2, a_3, \ldots$, a point-sequence can be derived in which the number a_n is associated with the point $A_n(a_n, 0)$ of the plane (x, y).

A point-sequence is said to *converge* to the point A ($P_n \to A$, or $\lim\limits_{n \to \infty} P_n = A$) if the distances $\overline{P_n A}$ form a null sequence. A point-sequence which is not convergent is said to be *divergent*. E.g. suppose the following points are given in a plane:

$$P_1\left(2 + \frac{1}{2}, 5\right), P_2\left(2 + \frac{1}{4}, 4 + \frac{1}{2}\right),$$
$$P_3\left(2 + \frac{1}{8}, 4 + \frac{1}{4}\right), P_4\left(2 + \frac{1}{16}, 4 + \frac{1}{8}\right), \ldots,$$
$$P_n\left(2 + \frac{1}{2^n}, 4 + \frac{1}{2^{n-1}}\right), \ldots$$

The sequence converges to the point $P(2, 4)$, since the sequence of distances

$$\overline{P_n P} = \sqrt{\left(2 + \frac{1}{2^n} - 2\right)^2 + \left(4 + \frac{1}{2^{n-1}} - 4\right)^2}$$
$$= \sqrt{\left(\frac{1}{2^n}\right)^2 + \left(\frac{1}{2^{n-1}}\right)^2} = \sqrt{\left(\frac{1}{2^n}\right)^2 (1 + 4)} = \frac{1}{2^n} \sqrt{5}$$

is a null sequence.

Pole

If, as $x \to x_0, f(x) \to \pm\infty$, $f(x)$ is said to have a pole at x_0. E.g.

$$f(x) = \frac{1}{x}, \text{ pole at } x = 0; \quad f(x) = \frac{1}{1-x}, \text{ pole at } x = 1.$$

Polygonal numbers

Polygonal numbers are numbers which form an *arithmetic sequence* (see art.) of the second order. The general term of these sequences is

$$z_n = \frac{n}{2}\,[2 + (n-1)d], \text{ where } d \text{ is one of the numbers } 1, 2, 3, \ldots$$

With $d = 1$ we obtain the *triangular numbers:* 1, 3, 6, 10, 15, . . .

With $d = 2$ we obtain the *square numbers:* 1, 4, 9, 16, 25, . . .

With $d = 3$ we obtain the *pentagonal numbers:* 1, 5, 12, 22, 35, . . .

The names of these numbers derive from a particular property, *i.e.* that the number of points ($\times$) indicated by the triangular (square) number can be arranged in the form of a triangle (square). Triangular numbers:

```
   1          3               6                    10
   ×          ×               ×                    ×
           ×   ×            ×   ×                 ×   ×
                         ×   ×   ×              ×   ×   ×
                                            ×   ×   ×   ×
```

Square numbers:

```
   1          4               9                    16
   ×        ×   ×           ×   ×   ×            ×   ×   ×   ×
           ×   ×           ×   ×   ×            ×   ×   ×   ×
                          ×   ×   ×            ×   ×   ×   ×
                                               ×   ×   ×   ×
```

Pentagonal, hexagonal and other such numbers are not so adequately represented in this way.

Polygons

The polygon defined by the points A_1, A_2, . . ., A_n lying in a plane is the figure bounded by the segments $\overline{A_1A_2}$, $\overline{A_2A_3}$, . . .,

331

$\overline{A_nA_1}$ (Fig. 220). When we define a polygon we usually assume that the points (or vertices) A_1, A_2, . . ., A_n, are all different, and that two segments have no point in common unless they are adjacent segments, in which case they have a vertex in common. Fig. 221 shows a polygon which does *not* satisfy these conditions.

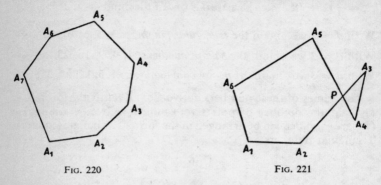

FIG. 220   FIG. 221

The sides of the polygon can also be denoted by a_1, a_2, a_3, . . ., a_n where $a_1 = \overline{A_1A_2}$, $a_2 = \overline{A_2A_3}$, $a_3 = \overline{A_3A_4}$, . . ., $a_{n-1} = \overline{A_{n-1}A_n}$, $a_n = \overline{A_nA_1}$. Every n-sided polygon possesses $n(n-3)/2$ diagonals. A diagonal is a segment joining two vertices which are not sides of the polygon, so that from each vertex proceed two sides and $(n-3)$ diagonals (Fig. 222, hexagon, 9 diagonals). Every n-sided polygon can be divided into $(n-2)$ triangles (Fig. 223, hexagon, 4 triangles); the sum of the interior angles of an n-sided polygon is therefore equal to $(n-2) \times 180°$.

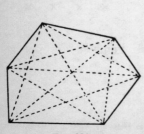

FIG. 222

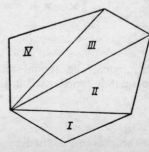

FIG. 223

The most important polygons are the regular polygons, *i.e.* polygons whose sides are of equal length and whose angles are of equal size (see *Regular polygons*).

Polyhedron

A polyhedron is a closed portion of space bounded on all sides by plane surfaces. The lines of intersection of these surfaces are called edges. The edges meet in the vertices of the polyhedron. In the case of convex polyhedra we have *Euler's theorem*: If a convex polyhedron has v vertices, e edges and f faces then $v + f = e + 2$.

If a denotes the number of angles, then we also have:

$$a = 2e, \, a \geq 3f, \, v \leq \frac{2}{3}e, f \leq \frac{2}{3}e, f \leq 2v - 4.$$

By means of Euler's theorem and the other relationships, it can be proved that only five regular solids, *i.e.* solids bounded by congruent regular polygons, can exist. These are referred to as the *Platonic solids* (see art.).

The so-called crystal-structures are of great interest in science (see textbooks of Mineralogy).

Polynomial

Expressions comprising one term, such as $2a$, $\frac{1}{2}bc$, can be added or subtracted from one another. Several literal numbers associated in this manner form a polynomial expression. $a + 2b - 4c - d$ for example is a polynomial of four terms. A polynomial of two terms is called *binomial*, *e.g.* $a + b$.

Position vector

A position vector is a vector whose point of origin is the origin of a coordinate system, and whose end-point is some other point. Position vectors cannot, like other vectors, be freely moved parallel to themselves; they are bound to the origin of the coordinate system (see *Vector*).

Powers

A power is a product of equal factors. *E.g.:*

$$4^3 = 4 \times 4 \times 4, \quad a^5 = a \times a \times a \times a \times a.$$

Evaluating the product, we obtain the value of the power; *e.g.*

$$4^3 = 64, \quad 3^2 = 9, \quad a^1 = a.$$

Nomenclature, $a^n = c$:

a = base; n = exponent (or power); c = value of power (also sometimes, power).

In particular we have: $1^n = 1$ and $0^n = 0$ for all values of n.
For integral values of the exponent n we have: A positive base raised to a positive power always has a positive value.

A negative base raised to an even power has a positive value and raised to an odd power has a negative value, *e.g.*

$$(-1)^2 = +1, \quad (-1)^5 = -1.$$

In general:

$$(-a)^{2n} = a^{2n}, \quad (-a)^{2n+1} = -a^{2n+1},$$

e.g. $\qquad (-1)^{2n} = +1, \quad (-1)^{2n+1} = -1.$

Any power can be multiplied by a number; *e.g.*

$$2 \times 3^2 = 2 \times 9 = 18; \text{ if } a^n = c \text{ then } b \times a^n = b \times c.$$

Addition and subtraction of powers. Powers can only be added or subtracted directly if they have the same base and exponent; *e.g.* $a^2 + a^2 = 2a^2$, but a^3 can only be added to a^2 if a determinate number is assigned to a.

Powers of a sum (see *Binomial Theorem*).

Powers of a product. In taking the power of a product we take the power of each factor and multiply these together.

$$(a \times b)^n = a^n \times b^n; \quad (3 \times 5)^2 = 3^2 \times 5^2.$$

Powers of a quotient (fraction). In taking the power of a quotient (fraction), we take the power of the dividend (numerator), and divide it by the power of divisor (denominator).

$$\left(\frac{a}{b}\right)^n = \frac{a^n}{b^n}; \quad (a \div b)^n = a^n \div b^n;$$

$$(12 \div 4)^2 = \left(\frac{12}{4}\right)^2 = 12^2 \div 4^2 = \frac{12^2}{4^2}.$$

Multiplication of powers.

(i) with the same base: the result of multiplying powers with the same base is an expression with the common base raised to exponent equal to the sum of the individual exponents.

$$a^p \times a^q = a^{p+q}, \quad 3^2 \times 3^3 = 3^{2+3} = 3^5$$

(ii) with the same exponent: in multiplying powers with the same exponent we take the product of the individual bases and raise to the common exponent.

$$a^n \times b^n = (a \times b)^n, \quad 3^3 \times 5^3 = (3 \times 5)^3 = 15^3$$

Powers of a power. To raise a power to a power, we raise the base to the product of the two given powers.

$$(a^p)^q = a^{pq}, \quad (3^3)^2 = 3^{3.2} = 3^6.$$

Division of powers.

(i) with the same base: to divide powers with the same base we raise the base to the difference between the exponent of the dividend and the exponent of the divisor:

$$\frac{a^p}{a^q} = a^{p-q},$$

E.g. $a^5 \div a^2 = a^{5-2} = a^3; \quad x^4 \div x^6 = x^{4-6} = x^{-2} = \dfrac{1}{x^2}$

(for $x^{-2} = \dfrac{1}{x^2}$, see below).

(ii) with the same exponent: to divide powers with the same exponent, we raise the quotient of the bases to the common power.

$$\frac{a^n}{b^n} = \left(\frac{a}{b}\right)^n,$$

e.g. $\quad \dfrac{12^2}{4^2} = \left(\dfrac{12}{4}\right)^2 = 3^2 = 9; \quad \dfrac{45^3}{9^3} = \left(\dfrac{45}{9}\right)^3 = 5^3.$

Powers with negative exponents. In dividing two powers with the same base and the same exponent, we get:

$$x^n \div x^n = x^{n-n} = x^0.$$

But since $\dfrac{x^n}{x^n}$ also equals 1, x^0 is defined as 1.

Similarly, so as to be able to extend the relation $\dfrac{a^p}{a^q} = a^{p-q}$ to all positive numbers p and q we define $x^{-n} = \dfrac{1}{x^n}$, e.g.

$$4^{-2} = \frac{1}{4^2} = \frac{1}{16}.$$

The rules given above hold unaltered for negative and zero exponents.

Powers with fractional exponents. In order to extend the relation $(a^p)^q = a^{p \cdot q}$ to fractional indices, we need to have $(a^{\frac{1}{q}})^q = 1$, and so we define $a^{\frac{1}{q}}$ to be the qth root of a. Then a power $a^{\frac{p}{q}}$ with fractional exponent $\dfrac{p}{q}$ represents the qth root of the power a^p.

$$a^{\frac{p}{q}} = \sqrt[q]{a^p},$$

e.g.
$$4^{\frac{3}{2}} = \sqrt[2]{4^3} = \sqrt[2]{64} = 8.$$

In particular,

$$a^{\frac{1}{n}} = \sqrt[n]{a}, \quad 2^{\frac{1}{2}} = \sqrt{2}, \quad 3^{\frac{1}{4}} = \sqrt[4]{3}.$$

The rules given above hold also for fractional exponents, e.g.

$$a^{\frac{1}{7}} a^{\frac{2}{9}} = a^{\frac{1}{7}+\frac{2}{9}} = a^{\frac{9+14}{63}} = a^{\frac{23}{63}} = \sqrt[63]{a^{23}}$$

$$b^{\frac{3}{2}} \cdot a^{-\frac{3}{2}} = b^{\frac{3}{2}} \cdot \frac{1}{a^{\frac{3}{2}}} = \frac{b^{\frac{3}{2}}}{a^{\frac{3}{2}}} = \left(\frac{b}{a}\right)^{\frac{3}{2}} = \sqrt{\left(\frac{b}{a}\right)^3}.$$

Powers of roots. To raise a root to a power we take the power of the radicand, and then extract the root (see *Roots, extraction of*). For powers of complex numbers, see *De Moivre's formula*.

Power-series

A series of the form

$$\sum_{k=0}^{\infty} a_k x^k = a_0 + a_1 x^1 + a_2 x^2 + a_3 x^3 + \ldots + a_n x^n + \ldots$$

is described as a power series in x. The numbers a_1, a_2, a_3, $\ldots$ are called the coefficients of the power-series. x is a variable. Polynomials of the form

$$a_0 + a_1 x^1 + a_2 x^2 + \ldots + a_p x^p$$

are also power-series with finite numbers of terms.

Examples: The binomial series, the exponential series, the logarithmic series, the trigonometrical series and the inverse trigonometrical series are power-series in the variable x (see individual articles).

Every power-series possesses an *interval of convergence* (see below) and a radius of convergence. If r is the radius of convergence of a power-series, the series converges for all values of x for which $|x| < r$, while the series diverges for all values of x with $|x| > r$. The interval $-r < x < +r$ is referred to as the *interval of convergence*. The radius of convergence can be 0, in which case the series only converges for the value $x = 0$. The radius of convergence may be ∞, in which case the series converges for all values of x.

Examples: 1. The exponential series

$$e^x = \sum_{k=0}^{\infty} \frac{x^k}{k!} = 1 + \frac{x}{1!} + \frac{x^2}{2!} + \frac{x^3}{3!} + \ldots$$

converges for all values of x.

2. The logarithmic series

$$\ln(1 + x) = x - \frac{x^2}{2} + \frac{x^3}{3} - \ldots + (-1)^{n-1} \frac{x^n}{n!} + \ldots$$

converges for $-1 < x \le +1$.

3. The power-series

$$\sum_{n=0}^{\infty} n! x^n = 1 + x + 2! x^2 + 3! x^3 + 4! x^4 + 5! x^5 + \ldots$$

converges only for $x = 0$.

Prism

A prism is a solid having polygons lying in parallel planes as base and upper surface, and bounded by parallelograms as lateral surfaces.

If the lateral surfaces of the solid are perpendicular to the base, it is said to be a right prism (Fig. 224), otherwise it is called an oblique prism (Fig. 225).

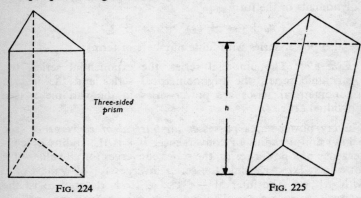

Three-sided prism

FIG. 224

h

FIG. 225

If the base of a prism is a regular n-agon, it is said to be a regular n-sided prism. The distance between the base and the upper surface is called the altitude. The volume of a prism with base-area B and altitude h is $V = B \cdot h$.

A four-sided right prism is also called a *right parallelepiped* or *rectangular solid* (see art.). A right parallelepiped whose altitude is equal to the edges of the base is a *cube*. A four-sided oblique prism is also called a *parallelepiped*. Prisms with bases of equal area and with equal altitudes have equal volumes.

Probability

If an event occurs n times, and if we may expect the event to turn out in a particular way (a favourable event, a success) m times out of the n trials, each of the events being equally probable, then the probability P of a success is

$$P = \frac{m}{n}.$$

Example 1: the probability of throwing a six with a cubical die is $\frac{1}{6}$, since the number of favourable cases is 1 and the number of possible cases is 6.

Example 2: according to a life-table, out of 100,000 20-year-old men 82,878 survive to the end of their 40th year. Thus the probability of a 20-year-old man completing his 40th year is

$$P = \frac{82,878}{100,000} = 0 \cdot 82878.$$

A probability is always a number between 0 an 1. If the probability of occurrence of an event is 1 the event will certainly take place. If, on the other hand, the probability of occurrence of an event is 0, then the event will certainly not take place.

Addition law of probability theory. If an event can come about in several *independent* ways, the overall probability that it will occur is equal to the sum of the individual probabilities.

Example: What is the probability P of throwing either a 6 or a 1 with a die? The probability of throwing a 6 is $\frac{1}{6}$ and of throwing a 1 is also $\frac{1}{6}$. Therefore the probability of throwing either a 6 or a 1 is $P = \frac{1}{6} + \frac{1}{6} = \frac{1}{3}$.

Multiplication law (compound probability). If an event is regarded as occurring if a number of sub-events independently occur, then the (compound) probability of the occurrence of the event is equal to the product of the probabilities of occurrence of the sub-events.

Example: What is the probability P of throwing first a 6 and then a 1 with a cubical die? Both individual probabilities are $\frac{1}{6}$, so the required probability $P = \frac{1}{6} \cdot \frac{1}{6} = \frac{1}{36}$.

Projection

A projection is a transformation in which the image-figure is obtained from the original figure (plane or three-dimensional) by drawing from the point of the original figure straight lines, which are either parallel (parallel projection), or concurrent (central projection), and which intersect the image-plane. The points of intersection of the straight lines (rays of projection) with the image-plane are the image-points, the totality of which yields the image-figure. The figure is said to be projected onto the image-plane.

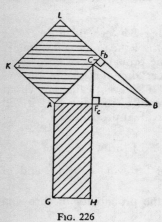

FIG. 226

Projection theorem for triangles

The rectangle formed from one side of a triangle and the projection of a second side onto it is equal to the rectangle formed by the second side and the projection of the first on the second. Area of the rectangle $AF_cHG =$ area of the rectangle AF_bLK.

$$\overline{AC} = \overline{AK}, \quad \overline{AB} = \overline{AG}. \quad \text{(Fig. 226)}$$

Projective

Two plane figures or two solids which arise from one another by a *projective transformation* (see art.) are said to be projective with respect to one another; *e.g.* the projective image of a circle is a conic section.

Projective transformation (Collineation, Projectivity)

Linear projective transformations are single-valued transformations of the points of space (or of a plane) for which the *cross-ratio* (see art.) of four points lying on a straight line remains fixed.

Properties of the projective transformations

Fundamental theorem of projective geometry: given 5 points of space, P_0, P_1, P_2, P_3, P_4, of which no four lie in a plane, and 5 further points Q_0, Q_1, Q_2, Q_3, Q_4, of which also no four lie in a plane, then there is exactly one projective transformation in which the point P_0 corresponds to the point Q_0, P_1 to Q_1, P_2 to Q_2, P_3 to Q_3 and P_4 to Q_4 as image points.

That is, a projective transformation of the points of space is uniquely determined by 5 points, no four of which lie in a plane, and by the images of these 5 points. For the projective transformation of points of a plane we have similarly:

A projective transformation of the points of a plane π is a one-valued transformation which is specified by four points P_0, P_1, P_2, P_3, of the plane π, no three of which lie on a straight line, and by the four image-points Q_0, Q_1, Q_2, Q_3, of which again no three are collinear. The points Q_0, Q_1, Q_2, Q_3, can lie in the same plane π or in another plane π_1.

Finally, for projective transformations of the points of a straight line: A projective transformation of the points of a straight line l is specified by three different points P_0, P_1, P_2, of l and the image-points Q_0, Q_1, Q_2 which must also be different and which can lie either on the same line l or on another straight line l_1.

Examples of projective transformations

1. The *perspective transformations* (see art.).
2. *Projective transformations* on a straight line.

Example: If A, B, C are three points of the straight line m which are to possess the image-points $A_1 = A$, B_1, C_1, the image-point D_1 corresponding to a further point D can be constructed as follows (Fig. 227).

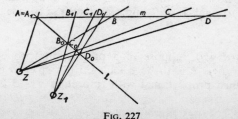

Fig. 227

We draw through the fixed point $A = A_1$ an arbitrary straight line l and choose a point Z which lies on neither l nor m. From Z we draw lines through the points A, B, C and D. These rays intersect the line l in the points A, B_0, C_0, D_0. We join the points B_0, C_0 to B_1 and C_1 respectively: let the lines $\overline{B_0 B_1}$ and $\overline{C_0 C_1}$ intersect in the point Z_1. Now we join Z_1 to D_0, and extend the segment beyond D_0. The point of intersection with m is the required image-point of D.

(The transformation $D \to D_1$ is a projective transformation in which $A \to A_1$, $B \to B_1$ and $C \to C_1$. By the fundamental theorem, it is the only such projective transformation.)

3. The three dimensional and plane *affine transformations* (see art.) are projective transformations. The affine transformations leave unchanged the division-ratio of three points on a straight line, and so, *a fortiori*, leave unchanged a cross-ratio formed from division-ratios. The affine transformations are those projective transformations which send infinitely distant elements (points, lines and planes at infinity) into other infinitely distant elements.

Proportion

If the ratio of the numbers a and b is equal to the ratio of the numbers c and d, *i.e.* if $a:b = c:d$ we speak of a ratio-equation or proportion. a and d are referred to as the outer terms, and b and c as the inner terms of the proportion. If the outer terms are interchanged and the inner terms are unchanged, the proportion remains valid. Inner terms can only be interchanged with outer terms if this is simultaneously done on both sides. The sides of a proportion may be interchanged. The product of the inner terms is equal to the product of the outer terms. $a:b = c:d$ implies $a \times d = b \times c$.

4th proportional. In the relation $a:b = c:d$, d is called the fourth proportional. If a, b, and c are given, d can be calculated:

$$d = \frac{b \times c}{a}.$$

3rd proportional. Suppose in a proportion with equal inner terms, $a:b = b:c$, c is to be calculated for given a and b. c is called the third proportional with respect to a and b. We have

$$c = \frac{b^2}{a}.$$

Mean proportional or geometric mean. In the proportion $a:m = m:d$, m is called the mean proportional or the geometric mean of a and d; $m = \sqrt{ad}$.

Derived proportions. If $a:b = c:d$, we have $\dfrac{a}{b} = \dfrac{c}{d}$. We can add ± 1 to each side of this equation. Thus

$$\frac{a}{b} \pm 1 = \frac{c}{d} \pm 1, \text{ so that } \frac{a \pm b}{b} = \frac{c \pm d}{d}.$$

That is, if $a:b = c:d$, then $a \pm b:b = c \pm d:d$.

Continued proportion. The pair of quantities

$$\frac{a}{b} = \frac{c}{d}, \quad \frac{c}{d} = \frac{m}{n}$$

can also be written as a continued proportion in the form

$$a:c:m = b:d:n.$$

Proportional

Two variable quantities are said to be proportional to one another if their quotient has a fixed value m. m is called the proportionality factor. For instance, the ratio of current intensity to voltage is constant for a direct current (Ohm's law).

Two numbers are said to be *directly proportional* if they stand in direct ratio to one another, *e.g.* time worked and money earned (the longer the time worked the more money earned).

Two numbers are said to be *inversely proportional* if they stand in reciprocal (indirect) ratio to one another, *e.g.* speed, and time taken to travel a certain distance at that speed (the greater the speed, the shorter the time taken).

Proportionality equation

We speak of a proportionality equation if the ratios of two pairs of numbers are equal;

$$a:b = c:d.$$

See *Proportion* for further treatment.

Protractor (see *Angle*)

A protractor is an instrument for measuring angles. It is made of metal, plastic, cardboard or paper and has the shape of a semicircle. The circumference of the semicircle is graduated into 180°.

Ptolemy's theorem (Ptolemy, 2nd century A.D., Alexandria)

If $ABCD$ is a quadrilateral inscribed in a circle with diagonals $\overline{AC} = e$ and $\overline{BD} = f$ and sides $\overline{AB} = a$, $\overline{BC} = b$, $\overline{CD} = c$ and $\overline{DA} = d$, then the area of the rectangle formed by the diagonals is equal to the sum of the areas of the rectangles formed by the two pairs of opposite sides: $ef = ac + bd$ (Fig. 228).

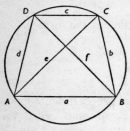

Ptolemy's theorem can be regarded as a generalisation of the theorem of Pythagoras. For, if the given quadrilateral is a rectangle, then $e = f$, $a = c$ and $b = d$, and the diagonal $e = \overline{AC}$ forms a right-angled triangle with the sides $\overline{AB}$ and $\overline{BC}$. That is, $e^2 = a^2 + b^2$.

FIG. 228

Pyramid

An n-sided pyramid is a solid bounded by an n-sided polygon as base and by n triangles as sides. The n triangles meet in a point, the apex, which does not lie in the plane of the base. The n sides have each one edge in common with the base.

If the base-surface of a pyramid possesses a circumcircle, and if the perpendicular from the apex passes through the centre of this circle, then the pyramid is said to be a right pyramid; otherwise it is said to be oblique. If the base-surface of a right pyramid is a regular n-agon the pyramid itself is said to be regular.

The sides of a pyramid meet in pairs in the lateral edges. The edges of the base surface are referred to as the *base edges*. Only in the case of 3-, 4- and 5-sided pyramids can the base- and lateral-edges of a regular n-sided pyramid be of equal length.

The regular three-sided pyramid whose base-edges and lateral-edges are equal is referred to as a *regular tetrahedron*. If a pyramid is intersected by a plane, parallel to, and distant H_1 from, the base, the figure formed by the intersection is similar to the base-surface; the area of the intersection-figure is to the area of the base-surface as the square of the distance $(H - H_1)$ of the intersecting plane from the vertex to the square of the altitude H of the pyramid; $G_1:G = (H - H_1)^2:H^2$ (Fig. 229). If we remove the part of the pyramid lying above the intersecting plane there remains a *truncated pyramid (frustrum)*. Pyramids with equal altitudes and bases of equal area, are intersected by planes at equal distances from the bases in figures of equal area. From this it follows, by the principle of *Cavalieri* (see art.) that pyramids with equal base-surfaces and altitudes have equal volumes. This gives an elementary method for calculating the volume of a pyramid.

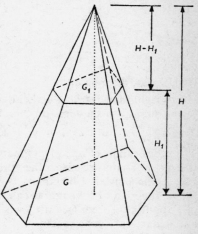

FIG. 229

We imagine a three-sided prism divided by two plane sections into three pyramids. Of these, I and II have equal bases (*ABC* and *DEF*) and the same altitude (as the prism), I and III have equal base-surfaces (*ABD* and *BDE*) and the same altitude (distance of the vertex *C* from *ABED*). In consequence they are equal in volume. Whence we have: a pyramid with base-area G and altitude h has volume $\frac{1}{3} Gh$ (Figs. 230 and 231). The volume of an *n*-sided pyramid is likewise $V = \frac{GH}{3}$. Thus the *n*-sided pyramid can be transformed into a three-sided pyramid of the same volume, if, leaving the altitude H unchanged, the *n*-sided base-surface is transformed into a triangle of equal area.

345

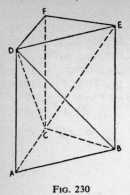

Fig. 230

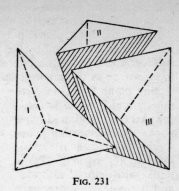

Fig. 231

Pythagoras, theorem of

In a right-angled triangle, the square on the hypotenuse is equal to the sum of the squares on the other two sides:

$$a^2 + b^2 = c^2 \text{ (Fig. 233).}$$

The proof can be effected by two applications of Euclid's theorem (see art.). There are also other proofs. The proof according to Fig. 234 is arrived at by comparison of areas.

The theorem of Pythagoras can be regarded as the special case of Pappus's theorem (see art.) where the triangle is right-angled and squares are constructed on its sides. Although this theorem is named after Pythagoras (sixth century B.C.), it was known to the Babylonians at least a thousand years earlier.

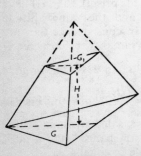

Fig. 232

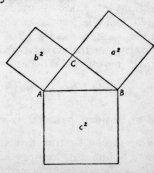

Fig. 233

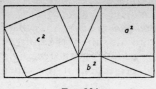

FIG. 234

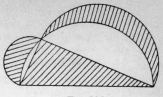

FIG. 235

Extension of the theorem of Pythagoras (Figs. 235 and 236). If semi-circles are constructed on the sides of a right-angled triangle, and if we multiply the equation $a^2 + b^2 = c^2$ through by $\frac{\pi}{8}$, we see that the area of the semi-circle on the hypotenuse is equal to the sum of the areas of the semi-circles on the other two sides.

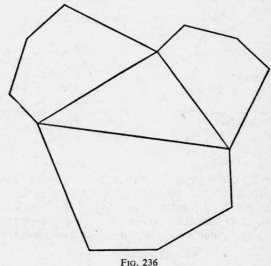

FIG. 236

For other figures the equation has to be multiplied through by other numbers, so that we have the general result: the area of any figure erected on the hypotenuse of a right-angled triangle is equal to the sum of the areas of similar figures erected on the other two sides.

Pythagoras's theorem holds for right-angled triangles only. Its generalisation allows its application to all triangles.

Generalisation of the theorem of Pythagoras (Fig. 237). The square on one side of a triangle is equal to the sum of the squares on the other sides, diminished or augmented by twice the rectangle formed by one of these sides and the projection of the other upon it.

$$c^2 = a^2 + b^2 \pm 2bq$$

The positive sign is taken if the two sides form an obtuse angle with one another, the negative sign if they form an acute angle.

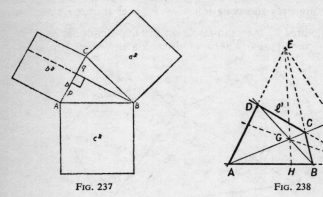

FIG. 237   FIG. 238

Quadrangle, complete

A 'complete quadrangle' is formed by four points lying in a plane, no three of which lie on a straight line, together with all the *six* straight lines joining them (Fig. 238). The four given points A, B, C, D are called vertices of the complete quadrangle. The vertices are joined by three pairs of opposite sides, *viz*.

$$AB \text{ and } CD$$
$$AC \text{ and } BD$$
$$AD \text{ and } BC.$$

Each pair of opposite sides intersects in a 'diagonal point'. Thus there are 3 diagonal points, E, F and G, which together form the 'diagonal triangle'.

At a diagonal point a harmonic pencil of lines is formed. At the point G in the figure the pencil is formed by AC and BD, which are opposite sides of the quadrangle, and GE and GF, sides of the diagonal triangle. The points A, B, H and F in which four points of the pencil intersect the side AB of the quadrangle form a harmonic range (see *Harmonic division*). The complete quadrangle can be used to construct the fourth harmonic of three given points. For example, in Fig. 238, we can construct the fourth harmonic point H of F with respect to A and B. To do this we choose any point E outside the line l on which A, B and F lie. We join EA, EB and EF, and through F draw an arbitrary line l'. Let l' intersect EA and EB in D and C respectively, and let G be the point of intersection of AC and BD. Then GE intersects AB in the required point H. (Note, the construction has been done without a compass.) The complete quadrangle and the complete quadrilateral are dual figures.

Quadrant

If a system of rectangular coordinates is set up in a plane, the plane is divided by the coordinate axes into four *quadrants*, each bounded by two mutually perpendicular coordinate axes.

Quadratic equation

Equations of the second degree, containing the unknown raised at most to the second power, are termed *quadratic*. The normal form of this equation is $x^2 + px + q = 0$ (see *Equation*).

Quadrature

The quadrature of a geometrical figure is the determination of its area. This may be done in geometric or arithmetic terms:

(1) *Geometric quadrature*. Here the task is to construct a square figure of area equal to the given one, and traditionally by ruler and compass only. The quadrature of the circle cannot be carried out by ruler and compass (see *Circle*).

(2) *Arithmetic quadrature*. Here the area is to be calculated in numerical terms.

Quadrilateral

Definition and nomenclature

If A, B, C, D are four distinct points in a plane, no three of which are collinear, and if the four segments $\overline{AB}$, $\overline{BC}$, $\overline{CD}$ and $\overline{DA}$ have no points in common other than A, B, C, D, these segments form a *quadrilateral*, or *quadrangle* (Fig. 239). The points A, B, C and D are called the *vertices* of the quadrilateral, and $\overline{AB} = a$, $\overline{BC} = b$, $\overline{CD} = c$ and $\overline{DA} = d$ the *sides* of the quadrilateral. The order of labelling does not matter, but by convention the vertices are labelled alphabetically in the anti-clockwise sense and the side a begins at the vertex A, the side b at the vertex B, and so on. If we think of the quadrilateral as being described, according to this labelling, in the anti-clockwise sense, then the *interior* of the quadrilateral lies to the left and the *exterior* to

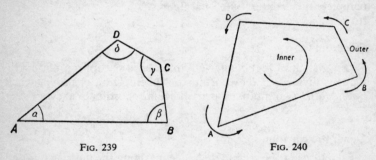

FIG. 239   FIG. 240

the right (Fig. 240). Each pair of neighbouring sides of the quadrilateral forms an *interior angle* of the quadrilateral. These are denoted by small Greek letters: α, β, γ, δ. The angle with vertex A is denoted by α, the angle with vertex B by β, and so on. If the sides of the quadrilateral are extended, each in the direction in which the quadrilateral has been described, four angles are produced in the exterior of the quadrilateral, which we denote by $\alpha_1, \beta_1, \gamma_1$ and δ_1. They are referred to as *exterior angles* (Fig. 241).

If the requirements that the segments $\overline{AB}$, $\overline{BC}$, $\overline{CD}$ and $\overline{DA}$ should have no points in common other than A, B, C, D is dropped, then we have a larger group of figures, in which sides may cut each other (Fig. 242). The theorems and properties which follow usually hold only for quadrilaterals as originally defined.

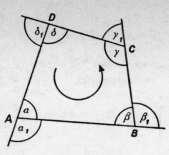

FIG. 241

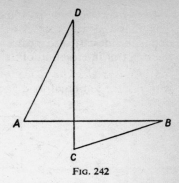

FIG. 242

Diagonals of a quadrilateral

The segments $\overline{AC}$ and $\overline{BD}$ are called the *diagonals* of the quadrilateral. Each of these diagonals divides the quadrilateral into two parts.

Relations between angles of quadrilateral

Since any quadrilateral is divided by a diagonal into two triangles, in each of which the sum of the angles is 180°, the sum of the interior angles of a quadrilateral must amount to 360°. The sum of the exterior angles is

$$4 \times 180° - 360° = 720° - 360° = 360°.$$

Classification of quadrilaterals

Quadrilaterals are classified by such properties of symmetry as they have.

Note to Fig. 243. The dotted lines are axes of affine symmetry; the full lines represent the usual (orthogonal) axes of symmetry; the centres of symmetry of central symmetries are denoted by small circles.

1. A *general quadrilateral* has no symmetrical properties.

2. An *oblique kite-shaped quadrilateral* (in which one diagonal is bisected by the other) is affine-symmetrical with respect to one of its diagonals.

3. A *trapezium with non-parallel sides unequal* is affine-symmetrical with respect to the line joining the mid-points of the parallel sides.

351

4. A *parallelogram* is affine-symmetrical with respect to its diagonals and with respect to the lines joining the mid-points of opposite sides. It also possesses central symmetry in respect of the point of intersection of its diagonals.

5. An *isosceles kite-shaped quadrilateral* (*deltoid*) is symmetrical with respect to one of its diagonals.

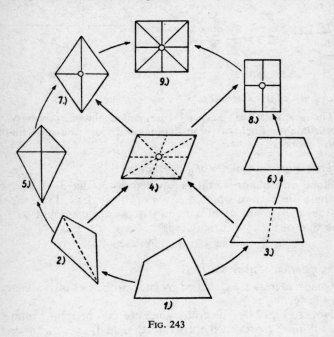

Fig. 243

6. A *trapezium with non-parallel sides equal* is symmetrical with respect to the line-joining the mid-points of the parallel sides.

7. A *rhombus* is symmetrical with respect to each of its diagonals and centrally symmetrical in respect of their point of intersection.

8. A *rectangle* is symmetrical with respect to each of the lines joining the mid-points of opposite sides, and centrally symmetrical with respect to their point of intersection.

9. A *square* is symmetrical with respect to each of its diagonals and to each of the lines joining the mid-points of opposite sides; it is centrally symmetrical in respect of the point of intersection of its diagonals.

Construction of a quadrilateral (Fig. 244)

Since a quadrilateral is divided by a diagonal into two triangles, and a triangle is determined by three independent elements, (*a*) three sides, (*b*) two sides and one angle *or* (*c*) one side and two angles (see *Triangle*), a quadrilateral can be constructed if 5 independent elements are known. Three elements are necessary to construct the first sub-triangle; and only two more for the second, since it has one side in common with the first. There can be given: 4 sides and one angle, 3 sides and two angles, or 2 sides and three angles; diagonals, altitudes and similar elements may also be given in the specification. Quadrangles which possess symmetrical properties can be constructed, if less than five elements are known. Four sides are sufficient to specify 2. and 3. in Fig. 243. Three sides are sufficient to specify 4., 5., and 6., two sides to specify 7. and 8., one side to specify 9.

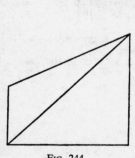

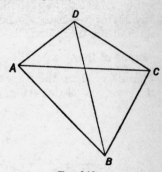

Fig. 244   Fig. 245

Properties of special quadrilaterals

The oblique kite-shaped quadrilateral. If the diagonals of a quadrilateral intersect in such a way that one diagonal $(\overline{AC})$ is bisected by the other $(\overline{DB})$ but not the second by the first, the quadrilateral is said to be an *oblique kite-shaped quadrilateral* (Fig. 245). It is affine-symmetrical with respect to the diagonal $\overline{BD}$.

The oblique trapezium. A quadrilateral with two parallel sides is called a *trapezium* ($\overline{AB}$ parallel to $\overline{CD}$, Fig. 246). If the non-parallel sides $\overline{AD}$ and $\overline{BC}$ are unequal the trapezium is said to be oblique, if equal, isosceles (see below). The trapezium is affine-symmetrical with respect to the line $\overline{M_1 M_2}$ joining the mid-points of the parallel sides.

The distance between the two parallel sides is called the altitude (Fig. 247). The two interior angles adjacent to a non-parallel side add up to 180°.

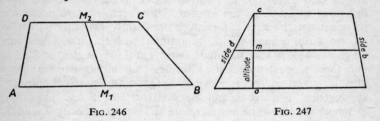

FIG. 246   FIG. 247

The line *m* mid-way between the two parallel sides bisects both non-parallel sides and both diagonals (Fig. 248). It also bisects any segment whose end-points lie each on one of the parallel sides of the trapezium. Its length is equal to half the sum of the lengths of the two parallel sides, $m = \dfrac{a + c}{2}$ (proof by Fig. 249).

The diagonals in the trapezium divide each other in the ratio of the two parallel sides (Fig. 248):

$$\frac{\overline{AG}}{\overline{GC}} = \frac{\overline{BG}}{\overline{GD}} = \frac{\overline{AB}}{\overline{CD}}.$$

$\overline{AE} = \overline{EC}$, $\overline{BF} = \overline{FD}$

FIG. 248   FIG. 249

The isosceles kite-shaped quadrilateral or deltoid. This is a quadrilateral in which sides are equal in adjacent pairs. It possesses an axis of symmetry, namely, one of its diagonals (Fig. 250). The diagonals intersect at right angles. The diagonal $\overline{AC}$ bisects the diagonal $\overline{BD}$ and the angles α and γ. The other angles of the quadrangle are equal ($\beta = \delta$). It possesses an inscribed circle (Fig. 250). The centre, O, of this circle is the point of intersection of the axis of symmetry and the bisector of the angle γ (or δ). The radius of the inscribed circle is the perpendicular from O onto a side of the quadrilateral.

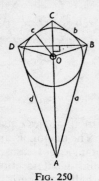

FIG. 250

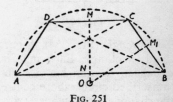

FIG. 251

The isosceles trapezium. If two sides of a quadrilateral are parallel, and the non-parallel sides are equal, we have an isosceles trapezium. An isosceles trapezium possesses an axis of symmetry, the common perpendicular bisector $\overline{MN}$ of the parallel sides (Fig. 251). Its diagonals are of equal length. The angles adjacent to its base are equal. Opposite angles add up to 180°. It possesses a circumscribed circle whose centre is obtained as the point of intersection, O, of the perpendicular bisectors of two sides. $\overline{OA}$ is the radius of the circumscribed circle (Fig. 251).

The parallelogram (Fig. 252). A quadrilateral in which both pairs of opposite sides are parallel is called a parallelogram. A parallelogram is centrally symmetrical about the point of intersection of its diagonals. The diagonals bisect each other. Opposite sides are of equal length, opposite angles are equal, and any two neighbouring angles add up to 180°.

The rhombus (Fig. 253). A rhombus (diamond, lozenge, rhomb) is a parallelogram in which all sides are of equal length. Its diagonals are the perpendicular bisectors of one another. It is axially symmetrical with respect to each diagonal. Opposite angles are equal. It possesses an inscribed circle, whose centre, O, is the point of intersection of the diagonals and whose radius is the length of the perpendicular from O on to a side.

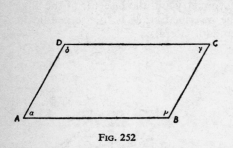

FIG. 252

FIG. 253

The rectangle (Fig. 254). A parallelogram with all angles equal is called a rectangle. Each angle is equal to 90°. The diagonals are of equal length, and bisect each other. A rectangle possesses a circumscribed circle whose centre, O, is the point of intersection of the diagonals and whose radius is equal to half the length of the diagonal. It possesses two axes of symmetry, namely, the common perpendicular bisectors $\overline{M_1M_3}$ and $\overline{M_2M_4}$ of the two pairs of opposite sides. It is centrally symmetrical about the point of intersection O of its diagonals.

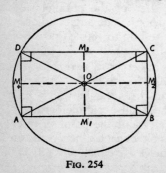

FIG. 254

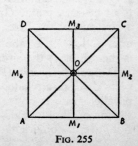

FIG. 255

The square (Fig. 255). The square is a rectangle with four equal sides (or equivalently, a rhombus with four equal angles). Its diagonals are equal, are the perpendicular bisectors of each other, and bisect its interior angles. It possesses four axes of symmetry, namely, the two diagonals and the lines joining the mid-points of opposite sides. It is centrally symmetric about the point O of intersection of the diagonals. It possesses a circumscribed and an inscribed circle whose centres coincide in O. The radius of the circumscribed circle is equal to half the length of the diagonal. The radius of the inscribed circle is equal to half the length of the side of the square.

Quadrilaterals with circumcircles

The sides of such a quadrilateral being chords of the circumcircle, a necessary and sufficient condition for a quadrilateral to be of this type is that the sum of opposite angles should be 180° (*e.g.* rectangle).

Quadrilaterals with incircles

The sides of such a quadrilateral being tangents of the incircle, a necessary and sufficient condition for a quadrilateral to be of this type is that the sum of two opposite sides should equal the sum of the other two sides (*e.g.* rhombus).

Linked quadrilateral

If four rods are jointed together we have a linked quadrilateral. Such a construction has no fixed shape, unlike a triangle formed in similar fashion. If one rod, *e.g.* $\overline{AB}$, is held stationary, the rods $\overline{AD}$ and $\overline{BC}$ can be rotated about the vertices A and B respectively. Such a linked quadrilateral is shown in Fig. 256. $ABCD$, ABC_1D_1, ABC_2D_2, ABC_3D_3 are four different positions of the rods. ABC_1D_1 and ABC_3D_3 are so-called limiting cases.

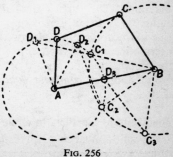

FIG. 256

357

Quadrilateral, complete

A 'complete quadrilateral' is formed by four straight lines lying in a plane, no three of which pass through a point, together with their six points of intersection (Fig. 257). The four given lines

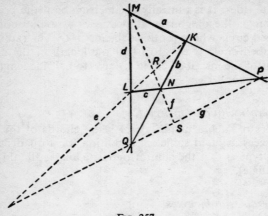

Fig. 257

a, b, c and d are called the sides of the complete quadrilateral. The sides intersect in three pairs of opposite vertices, namely

K and L,

P and Q,

M and N.

A line joining one of these pairs of opposite vertices is termed a 'diagonal'. The three diagonals, e, f and g, form the 'diagonal triangle' (or, strictly speaking, 'trilateral'). On each diagonal lie four harmonic points, *viz.* two opposite vertices and the point of intersection of the two other diagonals. In the figure, for the diagonal f, these points are M, N, R and S. The complete quadrilateral and the *complete quadrangle* (see *Quadrangle*) are dual figures.

Quadrilateral inscribed in circle

The sides of such a quadrilateral are chords of the circumscribed circle. A quadrilateral can be inscribed in a circle if, and only if, two opposite angles add up to 180°. The isosceles trapezium, the rectangle and the square satisfy this condition; the parallelogram and the rhombus in general do not (Fig. 258).

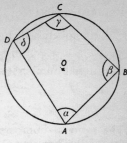

$$\alpha + \gamma = 180°,$$
$$\beta + \delta = 180°,$$

(circumference angles on opposite arcs add up to 180°).

FIG. 258

Radical axis

The radical axis of two circles is the locus of points from which tangents to the two circles have equal lengths. If the circles have one or two points in common the radical axis is the common tangent or the line including the common chord (see *Circle*).

Radius

The radius or semi-diameter of a circle is a line joining any point of the circle to the centre of the circle. The length of the radius is half the length of the diameter (see *Circle*).

Ratio

The ratio of two quantities a and b is their quotient $a:b = \dfrac{a}{b}$. We read 'a to b' or 'a over b'. If $a:b = m$, m is referred to as the value of the ratio. Two quantities, in order to possess a ratio, must be either pure numbers or measures of the same type, *e.g.*

$$20:5 = \frac{20}{5} = 4; \quad 15\,\mathrm{lb}:3\,\mathrm{lb} = 5.$$

The value of the ratio (proportionality factor) is always a pure number (see *Proportion*).

Rational integral

The rational integral numbers are the *integers* (see *Integers*), *e.g.* $+2$, -3. The rational integral functions are those rational functions (see *Function*) whose denominators do not contain the variable x; *e.g.* $y = a_0 x^n + a_1 x^{n-1} + \ldots + a_n$.

Rational numbers

All numbers which can be written in the form of a fraction $\frac{m}{n}$, where m and n are integral (positive or negative), are referred to as rational numbers; *e.g.*

$$\frac{3}{4}, \frac{-5}{6}, \frac{4}{-7} = \frac{-4}{7}.$$

The rational numbers can also be written as decimal numbers (see art.). The decimal expression of a rational number is obtained by dividing the numerator of the fraction by its denominator; *e.g.*

$$\frac{3}{4} = 3 \div 4 = 0.75; \quad \frac{-5}{6} = (-5) \div 6 = -0.833\ldots.$$

Any fraction whose denominator contains only the prime factors 2 or 5 yields a finite decimal fraction. Conversely common fractions can be derived again from finite and infinite-periodic decimal fractions; *e.g.*

1. $0.84 = \dfrac{84}{100} = \dfrac{21}{25}.$

2. $2.067,676,7\ldots = x$

$$1000x = 2067.67\ldots$$

$$\underline{10x = \quad 20.67\ldots}$$

$$990x = 2047$$

$$x = \frac{2047}{990}.$$

Infinite non-periodic decimal fractions cannot be written as fractions. These are referred to as *irrational numbers* (see art.).

Ray

The totality of points, lying on one and the same side of a point O on a straight line, is called the *ray* extending from O. O is called the *origin* of the ray.

Ray theorems

Two rays extending from a single point S comprise a double-ray; S is called the vertex of the double-ray.

1. *1st theorem on rays.* If a double-ray is cut by parallel lines the ratios of corresponding segments on the rays are equal. In Fig. 259 $\overline{SA}:\overline{SA'} = \overline{SB}:\overline{SB'}$.

Proof: We use the auxiliary lines $\overline{AB'}$ and $\overline{BA'}$. The triangles $AB'B$ and $AA'B$ are equal in area since they have the same base AB and equal altitudes ($\overline{AB}$ parallel to $\overline{A'B'}$). Further, triangles ABS and ABA' have the same altitudes, as also have triangles ABS and $AB'B$. But triangles with equal altitudes enclose areas proportional to their bases. (We denote by $\triangle(ABS)$ the area of the triangle ABS and by $\triangle(AA'B)$ the area of $AA'B$, etc.) Whence

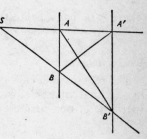

Fig. 259

$$\frac{\triangle(ABS)}{\triangle(AA'B)} = \frac{\overline{SA}}{\overline{AA'}}, \qquad \frac{\triangle(ABS)}{\triangle(AB'B)} = \frac{\overline{SB}}{\overline{BB'}}$$

and $\triangle(AA'B) = \triangle(AB'B)$.

From these three equations we get

$$\frac{\overline{SA}}{\overline{AA'}} = \frac{\overline{SB}}{\overline{BB'}}. \quad (1)$$

Similarly

$$\frac{\overline{SA'}}{\overline{AA'}} = \frac{\overline{SB'}}{\overline{BB'}}. \quad (2)$$

Dividing equation (1) by equation (2) we get

$$\frac{\overline{SA'}}{\overline{SA}} = \frac{\overline{SB'}}{\overline{SB}}.$$

361

2. *Converse of 1st ray-theorem*. If a double-ray is cut by two straight lines, and if the ratios of corresponding segments on the two rays are equal, then the transversals are parallel.

3. *2nd theorem on rays*. If a double-ray is cut by parallels, the ratio of the segments cut off on the transversals equals the ratio of the segments cut off on either ray. In the figure $\dfrac{\overline{AB}}{\overline{A'B'}} = \dfrac{\overline{SA}}{\overline{SA'}}$.

There is no converse to this theorem.

Real numbers

The real numbers are those numbers which can be represented by decimal numbers with finite or infinite number of places (periodic or non-periodic).

Real Numbers
(positive and negative real numbers)

Rational numbers (decimal numbers with finite no. of places and periodic decimals)		Irrational numbers (non-periodic decimal numbers with infinitely many places)	
Integers 3, −5	*Fractions* $\dfrac{3}{4}, \dfrac{-7}{3}$	*Algebraic* irrational nos. $\sqrt{2}, \sqrt[3]{9}$	*Transcendental* irrational nos. $e, \pi, \log 3, e^{\sqrt{2}}$

(see *Numbers, types of*).

Reciprocal equations

An equation is referred to as reciprocal if the reciprocals of its roots are also roots; *e.g.* $x^2 - \dfrac{5}{2}x + 1 = 0$ has the solutions $x_1 = 2$ and $x_2 = \frac{1}{2}$ (see *Equations*).

Rectangle

A rectangle is a parallelogram with four right-angles (see *Quadrilateral*).

Rectangular solid

A rectangular solid, or right parallelepiped, is a four-sided right prism. A rectangular solid is bounded by six rectangles, comprising three parallel and congruent pairs. The six surfaces meet in pairs in twelve edges which fall into three groups of four edges of equal length. A rectangular solid possesses eight vertices. At each vertex three edges meet forming right angles with one another in pairs. Let three such edges of a rectangular solid be denoted by a, b and c (Fig. 260). The diagonals of the faces are called plane-diagonals, and are denoted by d_1, d_2 and d_3. In addition to these there is a space diagonal, D. The volume of the rectangular solid is $V = abc$. The surface-area of the rectangular solid is

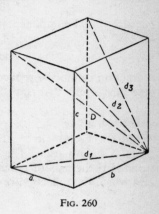

Fig. 260

$$S = 2(ab + bc + ca).$$

The plane-diagonals are calculated from the lengths of the edges as

$$d_1 = \sqrt{a^2 + b^2}$$

$$d_2 = \sqrt{b^2 + c^2}$$

and

$$d_3 = \sqrt{c^2 + a^2}.$$

The space-diagonal is $D = \sqrt{a^2 + b^2 + c^2}$ (by Pythagoras's theorem). A rectangular solid whose base is a square (*e.g.* $a = b$) is called a square prism. If all the edges of a rectangular solid are equal we have a cube (see *Prism*).

363

Reduction of fractions

A fraction is reduced, or cancelled, by dividing numerator and denominator by the same number, *e.g.*

$$\frac{5}{15} = \frac{1}{3} \text{ (5 cancelled)}.$$

The value of a fraction is unaltered by reduction. In the case of general numbers not only can coefficients be cancelled, *e.g.*

$$\frac{5a^2b}{15a^3} = \frac{a^2b}{3a^3},$$

but also literal components:

$$\frac{5a^2b}{15a^3} = \frac{1 \cdot b}{3 \cdot a}.$$

A fraction cannot be reduced if numerator and denominator are mutually prime, that is, if they have no common factors.

Reflection, affine

Affine reflection in a straight line is a particular case of an affine transformation. The image of a given point can be constructed if the axis of reflection is given together with the angle ψ in which the reflection-rays cut the axis.

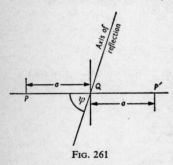

Construction of the affine reflection P' of a point P (Fig. 261): The straight line through P intersecting the axis of reflection in the given angle ψ is drawn. The segment $a = \overline{PQ}$ is marked out on the line from Q in the other direction to give QP' (Q lies between P and P'). P' is the affine reflection of P.

FIG. 261

Reflection in a plane

Reflection in a plane E is a three-dimensional affine transformation. The original point A and the image point A_1 arising out of it by the reflection are connected by a straight line which

364

is perpendicular to the plane E. The distances of A and A_1 from E are equal (Fig. 262).

For representation of the reflection by a system of equations, see *Transformation, affine.*

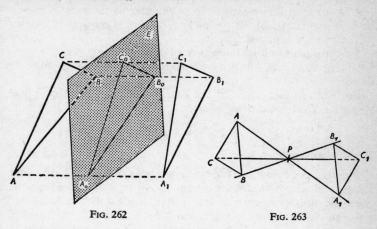

FIG. 262   FIG. 263

Reflection in a point

Reflection in a point P is a three-dimensional affine transformation. The image A_1 of a point A is obtained by constructing the line through A and the fixed point P, and from P marking off on the line the segment $\overline{A_1P}$, with end-point A_1 such that P lies between A and A_1. For the representation of reflection by a system of equations, see *Transformation, affine. Example—* reflection of a triangle ABC in a point P (Fig. 263).

Reflection in a straight line

Reflection in a straight line l is a plane affine transformation. The original point A and the point arising from it by reflection are connected by a straight line which is perpendicular to l. The distances A and A_1 from l are equal.

Properties of the reflection

1. Points on the axis of reflection remain unchanged under the reflection.

2. If two points A and B lie on a straight line c, then the straight line through the image points A_1 and B_1 is the image-line c_1 of c.

3. If two straight lines a and b intersect in a point C the image-lines a_1 and b_1 intersect in the image-point C_1 of C.

4. A straight line which is perpendicular to the axis of reflection, is identical with its image-line. The rays on opposite sides of the axis are interchanged.

5. A segment and its image are of equal length.

6. If an angle is transformed by reflection, its image-angle is of equal size.

For the representation of the reflection by a system of equations, see *Transformations, affine*.

Regular polygons

Regular polygons are polygons whose sides are all of equal length and whose angles are all equal. All regular polygons with the same number of vertices are similar to one another. A regular polygon possesses an inscribed and a circumscribed circle, which have common centre. If the centre of the circumscribed circle of a regular polygon is joined to the n vertices there arise n isosceles triangles whose lateral sides are equal to the radius of the circumcircle and whose bases are equal to the side of the regular polygon. The angle at the apex of such a triangle is $\frac{360°}{n}$ (Fig. 264). The two base angles together make up the interior angle of the polygon, namely,

$$180° - \frac{360°}{n} = 180° \times \frac{n-2}{n}.$$

The altitude is equal to the radius of the inscribed circle of the polygon.

Every regular polygon is *n-fold symmetric* about the centre of its circumcircle (*i.e.* it coincides with itself on rotation through $\frac{360°}{n}$).

Regular polygons with an even number of vertices are also centrally-symmetric with respect to the centre of the circumcircle.

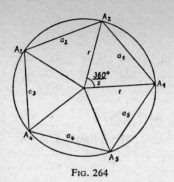

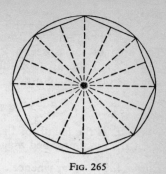

<table>
</table>

Fig. 264

Fig. 265

Regular polygons with an even number of vertices possess n axes of symmetry. $\frac{n}{2}$ of these axes are the joins of opposite vertices and $\frac{n}{2}$ the joins of the mid-points of opposite sides (Fig. 265).

Regular polygons with an odd number of vertices likewise possess n axes of symmetry. Each axis of symmetry passes through a vertex and the mid-point of the opposite side (Fig. 266).

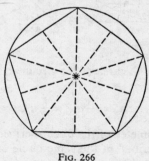

Fig. 266

Relations between radii of circumscribed and inscribed circles, sides, circumference and area

If a_n is the length of a side, r the radius of the circumcircle and ρ_n the radius of the incircle (Fig. 267) then

$$r^2 = \left(\frac{a_n}{2}\right)^2 + \rho_n^2,$$

367

that is,

$$a_n = 2\sqrt{r^2 - \rho_n^2} \quad \text{or} \quad \rho_n = \tfrac{1}{2}\sqrt{4r^2 - a_n^2}.$$

The area of the isosceles triangle discussed above is therefore $\triangle = \tfrac{1}{2}a_n\rho_n$; the area of the n-sided regular polygon, being n times as big, is therefore

$$A_n = \frac{n}{2}\, a_n\rho_n = \frac{1}{2}\,(na_n)\rho_n = \frac{1}{2}\, u_n\rho_n,$$

where u_n is the length of the perimeter of the n-agon. The sides a_n' of the circumscribed n-agon are calculated from the relationship $a_n : a_n' = \rho_n : r$, whence $a_n' = \dfrac{ra_n}{\rho_n}$.

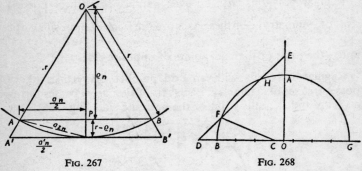

FIG. 267   FIG. 268

It follows that for the area of the circumscribed regular n-agon we have

$$A_n' = \frac{n}{2}\, a_n'r = \frac{r}{2}\, u_n',$$

where u_n' is the perimeter of the circumscribed n-agon. The sides of the $2n$-agon inscribed in the same circle can, by Fig. 267, be easily calculated. We have

$$a_{2n}^2 = \left(\frac{a_n}{2}\right)^2 + (r - \rho_n)^2,$$

so that

$$a_{2n}^2 = r^2 - \rho_n^2 + r^2 - 2r\rho_n + \rho_n^2 = 2r^2 - 2r\rho_n = 2r(r - \rho_n),$$

that is,

$$a_{2n} = \sqrt{2r(r - \rho_n)}.$$

Construction of the regular polygons

Gauss proved that a regular n-agon can be constructed using ruler and compass alone if, in the separation of n into prime factors, there appear only powers of two and prime numbers of the form $p = 2^{2^k} + 1$ raised to the first power, where k can be any integer. For $k = 0$ we obtain $p = 3$; for $k = 1$, $p = 5$; for $k = 2$, $p = 17$; for $k = 3$, $p = 257$, for $k = 4$, $p = 65{,}537$. For $k = 5$, however, $p = 2^{2^5} + 1$, but it is not a prime number since it possesses the factor 641. Thus the following regular polygons can be constructed, using ruler and compass:

triangle	square	pentagon	15-agon	17-agon
hexagon	octagon	decagon	30-agon	34-agon
dodecagon	16-agon	20-agon	60-agon	68-agon
etc.,	etc.,	etc.,	etc.,	etc.

The next sequences of n-agons which can be constructed using ruler and compass begin with the 51-agon, the 85-agon, the 255-agon, and the 257-agon.

Approximate constructions

Approximate constructions are obviously possible for every n-agon. For $n > 5$ we have:

Example: (Fig. 268). The diameter $\overline{BG}$ of a circle of radius r is divided into n equal parts (in the figure $n = 7$). The perpendicular $\overline{OA}$ to $\overline{BG}$ is drawn. $\overline{OA}$ and $\overline{OB}$ are each extended to E and D respectively. The straight line $\overline{ED}$ intersects the circle in two points F and H, F lying closest to D. F is now joined to C, the third point of division starting from B. Then $\overline{CF}$ is approximately equal to the side of the required n-agon.

Construction of particular regular polygons

Since all regular polygons with the same number of sides are similar, it is only necessary to construct one of a type to be able to construct all of that type. Further, a regular polygon can be drawn if the isosceles triangle associated with it can be constructed.

369

REGULAR POLYGONS

1. *Regular polygons with n = 4 × 2^k vertices.* The first polygon of this sequence is the square. If two mutually perpendicular diameters are drawn within a circle of radius *r* and their endpoints are joined, a square is obtained inscribed in the circle. Bisecting the angles which the diagonals make with one another and joining the points of intersection of the bisectors with the circle a regular octagon is obtained. The procedure can be continued to obtain successive members of the series.

2. *Regular polygons with n = 3 × 2^k vertices.* If chords of length *r* are successively laid out on the circumference of a circle of radius *r* the six vertices of a regular hexagon are obtained. Omit alternate vertices, and the three vertices of a regular triangle inscribed in the same circle are obtained. By bisection of the central angles of the associated isosceles triangles of the hexagon the regular dodecahedron is obtained, and this procedure can be repeated to give later members of the series.

3. *Regular polygons with n = 5 × 2^k vertices.* The second polygon of this series is the regular decagon. The associated isosceles triangle has angle 36° at the apex and angles of 72° at the base (Fig. 269). If one base angle is bisected, the angle *ABC* is obtained, which also has angles 36° (at *A*) and 72° (at *B* and *C*). The triangle *ABC* is thus similar to the triangle *AOB*. From

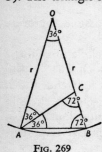

FIG. 269

this similarity is obtained the ratio of the sides $\overline{OA}:\overline{AB} = \overline{AB}:\overline{BC}$, since $\overline{AB} = \overline{AC} = \overline{OC}$, $\overline{OB}:\overline{OC} = \overline{OC}:\overline{CB}$. Thus the side of the regular decagon is equal to the larger segment of radius of the circumcircle when divided in continuous proportion. The regular pentagon is obtained from the regular decagon by omitting alternate vertices. The regular 20-agon, regular 40-agon, etc., are obtained by successive bisections of the central angles.

4. *Regular polygons with n = 15 × 2^k vertices.* The central angle of the 15-agon is 24°. This angle can be constructed as the difference of the angles 60° (equilateral triangle) and 36° (central angle of regular decagon). The construction of the regular 15-agon and of regular polygons with 15 × 2^k vertices follows immediately.

Regular n-agons inscribed in circle of radius r:

No. of vertices	3	4	5	6	8	10
Central angle α_n	$120°$	$90°$	$72°$	$60°$	$45°$	$36°$
Side s_n	$s_3 = r\sqrt{3}$	$s_4 = r\sqrt{2}$	$s_5 = \dfrac{r}{2}\sqrt{10-2\sqrt{5}}$	$s_6 = r$	$s_8 = r\sqrt{2-\sqrt{2}}$	$s_{10} = \dfrac{r}{2}(\sqrt{5}-1)$
Perimeter P_n	$P_3 = 3r\sqrt{3}$	$P_4 = 4r\sqrt{2}$	$P_5 = \dfrac{5r}{2}\sqrt{10-2\sqrt{5}}$	$P_6 = 6r$	$P_8 = 8r\sqrt{2-\sqrt{2}}$	$P_{10} = 5r(\sqrt{5}-1)$
Incircle radius ρ_n	$\rho_3 = \dfrac{1}{2}r$	$\rho_4 = \dfrac{r}{2}\sqrt{2}$	$\rho_5 = \dfrac{r}{4}(\sqrt{5}+1)$	$\rho_6 = \dfrac{r}{2}\sqrt{3}$	$\rho_8 = \dfrac{r}{2}\sqrt{2+\sqrt{2}}$	$\rho_{10} \times \dfrac{r}{4}\sqrt{10+2\sqrt{5}}$
Area A_n	$A_3 = \dfrac{3}{4}r^2\sqrt{3}$	$A_4 = 2r^2$	$A_5 = \dfrac{5}{8}r^2\sqrt{10+\sqrt{20}}$	$A_6 = \dfrac{3}{2}r^2\sqrt{3}$	$A_8 = 2r^2\sqrt{2}$	$A_{10} = \dfrac{5}{4}r^2\sqrt{10-2\sqrt{5}}$

Regular n-agons, length of side a:

No. of vertices	3	4	5	6	8	10
Circumcircle radius	$r_3 = \dfrac{a}{3}\sqrt{3}$	$r_4 = \dfrac{a}{2}\sqrt{2}$	$r_5 = \dfrac{a}{10}\sqrt{50+10\sqrt{5}}$	$r_6 = a$	$r_8 = \dfrac{a}{2}\sqrt{4+2\sqrt{2}}$	$r_{10} = \dfrac{a}{2}(\sqrt{5}+1)$
Incircle radius	$\rho_3 = \dfrac{a}{6}\sqrt{3}$	$\rho_4 = \dfrac{a}{2}$	$\rho_5 = \dfrac{a}{10}\sqrt{25+10\sqrt{5}}$	$\rho_6 = \dfrac{a}{2}\sqrt{3}$	$\rho_8 = \dfrac{a}{2}(\sqrt{2}+1)$	$\rho_{10} = \dfrac{a}{2}\sqrt{5+2\sqrt{5}}$
Area	$A_3 = \dfrac{a^2}{4}\sqrt{3}$	$A_4 = a^2$	$A_5 = \dfrac{a^2}{4}\sqrt{25+10\sqrt{5}}$	$A_6 = \dfrac{3}{2}a^2\sqrt{3}$	$A_8 = 2a^2(\sqrt{2}+1)$	$A_{10} = \dfrac{5a^2}{2}\sqrt{5+2\sqrt{5}}$

Relative numbers

Positive and negative numbers form together the relative numbers. Regarded apart from their signs, numbers are referred to as absolute numbers (see *Negative numbers, Numbers, representation on a straight line, Absolute value*).

Relative primes

Two numbers are said to be relative primes, or prime to one another, if they possess no common factor other than 1; *e.g.* 3 and 5 are relative primes.

To determine whether two numbers are prime to one another the *Euclidean algorithm* (see art.) can be used, or if their factors are known the numbers can be expressed as powers of primes and compared; *e.g.* 35 and 39 are prime to one another, for $35 = 5 \times 7$ and $39 = 3 \times 13$, and since no common prime factor occurs, the highest common factor must be 1.

Resultant

The resultant of two algebraic equations is a *determinant* (see art.) formed from the coefficients of the equations. The resultant can be used to ascertain whether the two equations possess a common root. Let the two equations be

$$f(x) = a_0 x^n + a_1 x^{n-1} + \ldots + a_n = 0.$$

$$g(x) = b_0 x^m + b_1 x^{m-1} + \ldots + b_m = 0.$$

Their resultant is

$$R = \left| \begin{array}{ccccccccc} a_0 & a_1 \ldots & & a_{n-1} & a_n & 0 & & \ldots 0 \\ 0 & a_0 \ldots & & a_{n-2} & a_{n-1} & a_n & 0 \ldots & 0 \\ \multicolumn{9}{c}{\dotfill} \\ 0 & 0 & \multicolumn{6}{c}{\dotfill a_n} \\ b_0 & b_1 \ldots & & b_{n-1} & b_n & 0 & & \ldots 0 \\ 0 & b_0 \ldots & & b_{n-2} & b_{n-1} & b_n & & \ldots 0 \\ \multicolumn{9}{c}{\dotfill} \\ 0 & 0 \ldots 0 & b_0 & b_1 & & \multicolumn{3}{c}{\ldots\ldots\ldots b_m} \end{array} \right| \begin{array}{c} \left. \rule{0pt}{30pt} \right\} m \text{ rows} \\ \left. \rule{0pt}{30pt} \right\} n \text{ rows} \end{array}$$

If the two equations have a common root the resultant R is equal to zero.

$$\textit{Example:} \qquad f(x) = x^2 - 3x + 2$$

and

$$g(x) = x^3 - x^2 - x + 1$$

have the resultant

$$R = \begin{vmatrix} 1 & -3 & 2 & 0 & 0 \\ 0 & 1 & -3 & 2 & 0 \\ 0 & 0 & 1 & -3 & 2 \\ 1 & -1 & -1 & 1 & 0 \\ 0 & 1 & -1 & -1 & 1 \end{vmatrix} = 0.$$

$f(x)$ and $g(x)$ have a common root which can be found by means of the *Euclidean algorithm* (see art.) as follows:

$$(x^3 - x^2 - x + 1) \div (x^2 - 3x + 2) = x + 2$$

$$\begin{array}{l} \underline{x^3 - 3x^2 + 2x} \\ \quad + 2x^2 - 3x + 1 \qquad (x^2 - 3x + 2) \div (3x - 3) = \left(\dfrac{x}{3} - \dfrac{2}{3}\right) \\ \quad\; \underline{2x^2 - 6x + 4} \qquad\quad \underline{x^2 - \;\; x} \\ \qquad + 3x - 3 \qquad\qquad\quad\; -2x + 2 \\ \qquad\qquad\qquad\qquad\qquad\quad\;\; \underline{-2x + 2} \\ \qquad\qquad\qquad\qquad\qquad\qquad\quad\; 0 \end{array}$$

that is,

$$x^2 - 3x + 2 = 3(x - 1)\left(\frac{x}{3} - \frac{2}{3}\right)$$

and

$$x^3 - x^2 - x + 1 = (x + 2)(x^2 - 3x + 2) + 3(x - 1),$$

or

$$x^3 - x^2 - x + 1 = (x - 1)\left[(x + 2)\left(\frac{x}{3} - \frac{2}{3}\right) \cdot 3 + 3\right].$$

The common factor is $(x - 1)$, and the common root, $x = 1$.

Rhombus

A rhombus is a parallelogram with four sides of equal length (see *Quadrilateral*).

Right angle

A right angle is an angle which is equal to its adjacent supplementary angle. Its measure in degrees is 90° and in circular measure is $\frac{\pi}{2}$ radians.

Construction of the right angle (Fig. 270)

To construct a straight line m cutting a given straight line l at right angles in a given point P.

Procedure. We describe about P a circle with arbitrary radius. This intersects l in the points A and B. We now describe about A and B circles of equal radius, which must be larger than the segment $\overline{AP}$. The two circles intersect in the points C and D. The required line m is determined by C and D (see *Perpendicular, construction of*). A set-square (see Figs. 271 and 272) serves to construct a right angle.

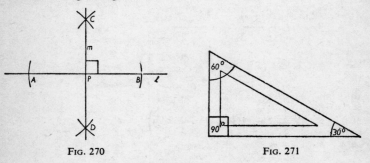

FIG. 270 FIG. 271

The *circle of Thales* (Fig. 273) can be used to construct a right angle whose arms pass through the end-points of a given segment $\overline{AB} = c$. It is the circle with radius $\frac{c}{2}$ and centre, O, the mid-point of the given segment $c = \overline{AB}$. The vertices of all right angles whose arms pass through A and B lie on this circle.

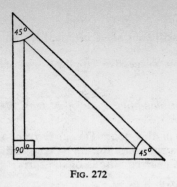

FIG. 272

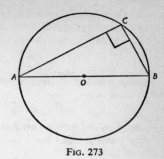

FIG. 273

Right-angled

A geometrical figure is said to be right-angled if a right angle occurs in it, *e.g. a right-angled triangle.*

Right-angled triangle

A triangle is said to be right-angled if one of its interior angles is a right angle. The side opposite the right angle is referred to as the *hypotenuse.* For theorems on the right-angled triangle see *Triangle.*

Rigid motions

The rigid motions (congruent transformations) are transformations (see *Transformation*) in space or in a plane, in which the original figure and its image are congruent. In particular: a line-segment and its image have equal length; an angle and its image are equal; a plane figure and its image are congruent and thus have equal area; a solid and its image are congruent and have equal volume. On account of these properties, the rigid motions are also called *congruent transformations.*

Rigid motions in a plane

1. Parallel displacement or translation.
2. Rotation about a point.
3. Transformations obtained by successive translations and rotations.

375

Rigid motions in space

1. Parallel displacement or translation.
2. Rotation about a straight line.
3. Transformations obtained by successive applications of transformations of types 1, 2.

Representation of rigid motions in a plane by means of systems of equations

If in the same coordinate system the point $P(x, y)$ is transformed into $Q(x', y')$ by means of a rigid motion, then (x, y) and (x', y') are related by a system of linear equations of the form:

$$x' = a_1x + a_2y + a_3,$$
$$y' = b_1x + b_2y + b_3.$$

This system of equations represents a rigid motion only if its *determinant* has absolute value 1:

$$D = \begin{vmatrix} a_1a_2 \\ b_1b_2 \end{vmatrix} = a_1b_2 - a_2b_1 = \pm 1.$$

Parallel displacement (Fig. 274)

$$x' = x + a_3,$$
$$y' = y + b_3.$$

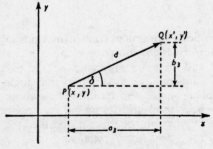

FIG. 274

The direction of the parallel displacement is given by the angle δ which the line-segment $\overline{PQ}$ makes with the positive x-axis, that is, by $\tan \delta = \dfrac{b_3}{a_3}$. The displacement distance d is: $d = \sqrt{a_3^2 + b_3^2}$.

Rotation about a point in the plane

(a) Rotation about the origin of the coordinate system (Fig. 275):

$$x' = x \cos \phi + y \sin \phi,$$
$$y' = -x \sin \phi + y \cos \phi.$$

(b) Rotation about the point $P_0(x_0, y_0)$ (Fig. 276):

$$x' - x_0 = (x - x_0) \cos \phi + (y - y_0) \sin \phi,$$
$$y' - y_0 = -(x - x_0) \sin \phi + (y - y_0) \cos \phi.$$

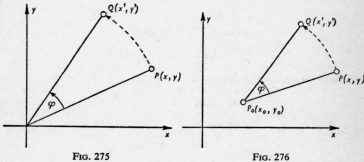

FIG. 275   FIG. 276

Representation of rigid motions in space by means of systems of equations

A system of equations,

$$x' = a_1 x + a_2 y + a_3 z + a_4,$$
$$y' = b_1 x + b_2 y + b_3 z + b_4,$$
$$z' = c_1 x + c_2 y + c_3 z + c_4,$$

in which x', y', z' and x, y, z are the coordinates of two points $P(x, y, z)$ and $Q(x', y', z')$ in the same coordinate system, represents a rigid motion in space if the *determinant D* of the system of equations has absolute value 1:

$$D = \begin{vmatrix} a_1 & a_2 & a_3 \\ b_1 & b_2 & b_3 \\ c_1 & c_2 & c_3 \end{vmatrix} = \pm 1.$$

377

Parallel displacement

$$x' = x + a_4,$$
$$y' = y + b_4,$$
$$z' = z + c_4.$$

The displacement distance is $d = \sqrt{a_4^2 + b_4^2 + c_4^2}$. The direction of the parallel displacement is in the direction of the point $P(a_4, b_4, c_4)$ from the origin.

Rotation about a straight line

Rotation about the x-axis:

$$x' = x,$$
$$y' = y \cos \phi + z \sin \phi,$$
$$z' = -y \sin \phi + z \cos \phi.$$

Rotation about the y-axis:

$$x' = x \cos \phi + z \sin \phi,$$
$$y' = y,$$
$$z' = -x \sin \phi + z \cos \phi.$$

Rotation about the z-axis:

$$x' = x \cos \phi + y \sin \phi,$$
$$y' = -x \sin \phi + y \cos \phi,$$
$$z' = z.$$

Rotation about a line parallel to the x-axis: The line cuts the yz-plane in the point $P_0(0, y_0, z_0)$, say, and has the parametric representation $x = at$, $y = y_0$, $z = z_0$: then

$$x' = x,$$
$$y' - y_0 = (y - y_0) \cos \phi + (z - z_0) \sin \phi,$$
$$z' - z_0 = -(y - y_0) \sin \phi + (z - z_0) \cos \phi.$$

Rotation about a line parallel to the y-axis: The line has the parametric representation $x = x_0$, $y = bt$, $z = z_0$, say, and cuts the xz-plane in the point $P_0(x_0, 0, z_0)$: then

$$x' - x_0 = (x - x_0) \cos \phi + (z - z_0) \sin \phi,$$
$$y' = y,$$
$$z' - z_0 = -(x - x_0) \sin \phi + (z - z_0) \cos \phi.$$

Rotation about a line parallel to the z-axis. The line has parametric representation $x = x_0$, $y = y_0$, $z = ct$, say, and cuts the xy-plane in the points $P_0(x_0, y_0, 0)$:

$$x' - x_0 = (x - x_0) \cos \phi + (y - y_0) \sin \phi,$$
$$y' - y_0 = -(x - x_0) \sin \phi + (y - y_0) \cos \phi,$$
$$z' = z.$$

Roman number-system

The Roman numerals were in general use in central Europe for upwards of 1,200 years. Today they are occasionally used for inscriptions and other special purposes. The Roman number-symbols have a fixed value, irrespective of its position in the number, in contrast with the place-value system of the Arabic numerals. The symbols are:

I = 1, V = 5, X = 10, L = 50, C = 100, D = 500, M = 1000.

The symbols I, C may be repeated, but in general not more than three times; a fourfold repetition is avoided by reversing the natural order of the symbols:

IV = 4, XL = 40, CD = 400; IX = 9, XC = 90, CM = 900.

In compound numbers, numerical values follow each other in order. This regular system involves addition of the corresponding values; *e.g.*

MMCMXLII = 2000 + 900 + 40 + 2 = 2942

I = 1	XI = 11	XXI = 21	XXXI = 31	XLI = 41
II = 2	XII = 12	XXII = 22	XXXII = 32	XLII = 42
III = 3	XIII = 13	XXIII = 23	XXXIII = 33	XLIII = 43
IV = 4	XIV = 14	XXIV = 24	XXXIV = 34	XLIV = 44

379

V = 5	XV = 15	XXV = 25	XXXV = 35	XLV = 45
VI = 6	XVI = 16	XXVI = 26	XXXVI = 36	XLVI = 46
VII = 7	XVII = 17	XXVII = 27	XXXVII = 37	XLVII = 47
VIII = 8	XVIII = 18	XXVIII = 28	XXXVIII = 38	XLVIII = 48
IX = 9	XIX = 19	XXIX = 29	XXXIX = 39	XLIX = 49
X = 10	XX = 20	XXX = 30	XL = 40	L = 50

Roots, extraction of

The calculation or *extraction* of a root is one of the operations inverse to that of raising to a power (the other being that of taking the *logarithm*, see art.). In raising a number to a power, the number is multiplied by itself a number of times, *e.g.* $5^3 = 5 \times 5 \times 5 = 125$. In extracting a root the problem is, *e.g.* given the number 125, to transform it into a product of a given number of equal factors. Since $125 = 5 \times 5 \times 5 = 5^3$, 5 is said to be the third, or cube, root of 125: $\sqrt[3]{125} = 5$. The root-sign can be regarded as a stylised *r*, the initial letter of the Latin word radix = root. The number 125 in our example is the number from which the root is obtained; it is called the radicand. The number 3, the number of equal factors into which the radicand is divided is called the index (or order) of the root.

General definitions

By the *n*th root of a number *a* is meant the number *b* whose *n*th power is equal to *b*. We write: $\sqrt[n]{a} = b$ and read: '*n*th root of *a* equals *b*'. Here *a* is called the radicand, *n* the index of the root, and *b* the value of the root.

In particular, the second root of a number is referred to as the square-root: the square root of a number *a* is the (positive) number, which multiplied by itself gives *a*. For square roots, it is customary to omit the index, 2, of the root, *e.g.*

$$\sqrt[2]{9} = \sqrt{9} = 3, \text{ since } 3 \times 3 = 9.$$

The third root of a number is referred to as the cube-root, *e.g.* $\sqrt[3]{27} = 3$.

The calculation of square- and cube-roots is facilitated by the use of tables (see explanation attached to tables of square and cubic numbers, p. 709).

380

Calculation of square-roots by means of the formula:

$$(a + b + c + d + \ldots)^2 = a^2 + (2a + b)b$$
$$+ [2(a + b) + c]c + [2(a + b + c) + d]d + \ldots.$$

To explain our method we first of all apply this formula to the development of a decimal number in powers of 10. *E.g.*

$$342 = 3 \times 100 + 4 \times 10 + 2 \times 1.$$

Denoting 300 by a, 40 by b, and 2 by c we have:

$$342^2 = (a + b + c)^3 = a^2 + (2a + b)b + (2a + 2b + c)c$$

where

$a^2 =$	90,000	
$2ab =$	24,000	
$b^2 =$	1,600	$342^2 = 116,964.$
$2ac =$	1,200	
$2bc =$	160	
$c^2 =$	4	

Suppose now that our task is to find the square root of 116,964. We first of all establish how many digits the root has. The square of a:

one-digit number has one or two digits
two-digit number has three or four digits
three-digit number has five or six digits
four-digit number has seven or eight digits, etc.

Conversely it follows that the square root of a:

one- or two-digit number has one digit
three- or four-digit number has two digits
five- or six-digit number has three digits, etc.

Thus, if we divide the radicand into groups of two digits, commencing with the units, we can count off how many digits there are in the square root; *e.g.*: 11'69'64, where we have placed a dash over the space between appropriate digits. (If a number has an odd number of digits, the group on the extreme left will contain only one digit.) In our example the root will have three digits. Thus it will lie between 100 and 1,000. We can also tell how many hundreds it contains, since we have

$$100^2 = \quad 10\ 000 \quad \text{and so} \quad \sqrt{10\ 000} = \quad 100$$
$$200^2 = \quad 40\ 000 \quad\quad\quad\quad \sqrt{40\ 000} = \quad 200$$
$$300^2 = \quad 90\ 000 \quad\quad\quad\quad \sqrt{90\ 000} = \quad 300$$
$$\cdots\cdots\cdots\cdots \quad\quad\quad\quad\quad \cdots\cdots\cdots\cdots$$
$$1000^2 = 1000\ 000 \quad\quad\quad \sqrt{1000\ 000} = 1000.$$

Now our number, 116,964, lies between 90,000 and 160,000 and so its square root lies between 300 and 400; the first digit is therefore a 3. That is, $a = 300$ and $a^2 = 90,000$. We now subtract 90,000 from 116,964. The remainder 26,964, must contain the terms $2ab$, b^2, $2ac$, $2bc$ and c^2. We write:

$$\sqrt{116,964} = \sqrt{11'69'64}.$$

We subtract a^2:
$$\sqrt{11'69'64}$$
$$9\ 00\ 00$$
$$\overline{2\ 69\ 64.}$$

In order to find b next we write $2a = 600$ after 26964:

$$\sqrt{11'69'64}$$
$$9\ 00\ 00$$
$$2\ 69\ 64 \quad \underbrace{600}_{2a}$$

Then we divide 26,964 by 600, taking note only of the tens $(26,964 \div 600 \approx 40)$ and obtain $b = 40$. We can now subtract $2ab + b^2 = 24,000 + 1,600 = 25,600$ from 26,964 to give 1,364. $2ac$, $2bc$ and c^2 must still be contained in this remainder. Thus $1,364 = (2a + 2b + c)c$.

To find c we divide 1364 (approximately) by $2a + 2b = 680$ and obtain $c = 2$. We write 680 and 2 beside 1364. After multiplication of $682 = 2a + 2b + c$ by c no remainder is left on subtraction, and so our number 116,964 was a square number. We can shorten the procedure by omitting the zeros occurring in the individual steps. $E.g.$

in full: abbreviated:

$$a \quad + \quad b + c$$

$$\sqrt{11'69'64} = 300 + 40 + 2 \qquad\qquad \sqrt{11\ 69\ 64} = 342$$

$$\begin{array}{ll} \underline{9\ 00\ 00}\ a^2 & \qquad\qquad \underline{9} \\ 2\ 69\ 64\ (2a+b)b = (600+40)\,.\,40 & \qquad\qquad 2\ 69 \div 64 \\ \underline{2\ 56\ 00} & \qquad\qquad \underline{2\ 56} \\ 13\ 64\ (2a+2b+c)\,.\,c = & \qquad\qquad 13\ 64 \div 682 \\ \underline{13\ 64}\ (600+80+2)\,.\,2 & \qquad\qquad \underline{13\ 64} \\ 0 & \qquad\qquad 0 \end{array}$$

If the radicand does not prove to be a square number the calculation can be continued by writing pairs of zeros after the decimal point. Radicands with terms to the right of the decimal place can be treated in a similar fashion. The decimal point is then inserted in the root when the two final digits of the radicand enter the calculation.

Example: $\sqrt{23\cdot167}$ $= 4\cdot8132$

$$\begin{array}{ll} \underline{16} & \\ 7\ 16 & 80\,.\,8 = 640 \\ & 8^2 = \ \ 64 \\ \underline{7\ 04} & \\ 1270 & 960\,.\,1 = 960 \\ & 1^2 = \ \ \ 1 \\ \underline{961} & \\ 30900 & 9620\,.\,3 = 28860 \\ & 3^2 \doteqdot \ \ \ \ 9 \\ \underline{28869} & \\ 203100 & 96260\,.\,2 = 192520 \\ & 2^2 = \ \ \ \ \ 4 \\ \underline{192524} & \\ 1057600 & 962640\,.\,1 \end{array}$$

As in division, the calculation is broken off when the required degree of accuracy has been achieved.

In evaluating square roots with a calculating machine, an 'iterative' procedure is adopted, *i.e.* step-by-step approximation by repeated application of the same procedure of calculation. For example, suppose that with a slide rule we have obtained the approximate value x_0 for $x = \sqrt{a}$. Now if x_0 differs from x by $\frac{1}{2}\varepsilon_0$ we have

$$(x_0 \pm \tfrac{1}{2}\varepsilon_0) = \sqrt{a},$$

and squaring both sides we get:

$$x_0^2 \pm \varepsilon_0 x_0 + \tfrac{1}{4}\varepsilon_0^2 = a.$$

ε_0 however is small compared with x_0 and we can neglect the term $\frac{1}{4}\varepsilon_0^2$, so that $\varepsilon_0 \approx \pm \left(\dfrac{a}{x_0} - x_0\right)$.

Accordingly we form the quotient $\dfrac{a}{x_0} = x_1$. If x_0 were equal to $\sqrt{a}$ then x_0 would equal x_1. However, with the approximate value x_0, we will have $x_1 = x_0 + \varepsilon_0$. ε_0 arises essentially out of the decimal places of x_1 lying beyond those of x_0, and these places can easily be read off in dividing on the machine. The arithmetic mean of x_0 and x_1 yields an improved value $x_2 = x_0 + \frac{1}{2}\varepsilon_0$. The procedure is repeated till the required accuracy is reached; in practice this occurs very quickly.

Example: $\sqrt{3} \approx 1 \cdot 73$.

$$y_0 = 1 \cdot 73$$

$3 \div 1 \cdot 73 = 1 \cdot 73410 \qquad \varepsilon_0 = 0 \cdot 00410 \qquad \dfrac{1}{2}\varepsilon_0 = 0 \cdot 00205$

$$x_2 = 1 \cdot 73205$$

$3 \div 1 \cdot 73205 = 1 \cdot 73205161 \quad \varepsilon_2 = 0 \cdot 00000161 \quad \dfrac{1}{2}\varepsilon_2 = 0 \cdot 00000080$

$$x_3 = 1 \cdot 73205080.$$

Calculation of nth roots. nth roots are calculated in practice by means of logarithms (see art.), or by iterative methods.

Multiplicity of roots. In taking the square root of a number b, two results are always obtained, namely $\sqrt{b} = +a$ and $\sqrt{b} = -a$. The results are distinguished only by their sign. We write $\sqrt{b} = \pm a$. For nth roots there are n (real or complex) values.

Roots of negative numbers. The nth root of a negative number can be another real number only if the index of the root is odd. If a is a positive number, $\sqrt[n]{-a} = \sqrt[n]{-1}\,\sqrt[n]{+a}$. Thus, if the index n is odd we have

$$\sqrt[n]{-a} = -\sqrt[n]{a}.$$

On the other hand, if the index is even, $\sqrt[n]{-a} = \sqrt[n]{-1}\,\sqrt[n]{+a}$ which is complex.

Example:

$$\sqrt{-1} = \pm i, \qquad \sqrt[3]{-1} = \begin{cases} -1 \\ +\dfrac{1}{2} + \dfrac{i}{2}\sqrt{3} \\ +\dfrac{1}{2} - \dfrac{i}{2}\sqrt{3}, \end{cases}$$

$$\sqrt[4]{-1} = \sqrt[2]{\sqrt[2]{-1}} = \begin{cases} \pm\sqrt[2]{+i} \\ \pm\sqrt[2]{-i}. \end{cases}$$

Addition and subtraction of roots. Roots with the same index and the same radicand can be collected into a single term:

$$\sqrt[n]{a} + 3\sqrt[n]{a} = 4\sqrt[n]{a}.$$

Roots of products. To extract the root of a product, take the root of each factor and multiply them together. To multiply roots with the same index, take the root of the product of the radicands; $\sqrt[3]{a}\,\sqrt[3]{b} = \sqrt[3]{ab}$. Factors in front of the root can be assimilated within the root-sign by raising them to the power equal to the index of the root; $a\sqrt[4]{b} = \sqrt[4]{a^4 b}$.

Roots of quotients (fractions). To extract the root of a fraction, take the roots of the numerator and denominator separately, and divide. Conversely, to divide roots with the same index, take the root of the quotient of the radicands:

$$\sqrt[n]{\frac{a}{b}} = \frac{\sqrt[n]{a}}{\sqrt[n]{b}}$$

Roots of powers. To extract the root of a power, take the root of the base and then raise to the given exponent:

$$\sqrt[n]{a^x} = (\sqrt[n]{a})^x$$

If the exponent of the power and the index of the root are each multiplied or divided by the same number, the value of the root is unaltered: $\sqrt[bn]{a^{bx}} = \sqrt[n]{a^x}$. If the exponent of the power and the index of the root are each divided by the latter, a fractional exponent is obtained: $\sqrt[n]{a^m} = a^{\frac{m}{n}}$.

Raising a number to a fractional power, $\frac{m}{n}$, implies that the number is to be raised to the mth power and then that the nth root is to be extracted; $\sqrt[n]{a^m} = a^{\frac{m}{n}}$. In particular, $\sqrt[n]{a} = a^{\frac{1}{n}}$.

Roots of roots. To take the root of a root-expression, multiply the indexes of the roots and retain the original radicand:

$$\sqrt[n]{\sqrt[x]{a}} = \sqrt[nx]{a}$$

Conversely, if the index of the root is a product, we can successively extract the roots whose indexes are the factors of the product:

$$\sqrt[4]{81} = \sqrt{\sqrt{81}} = \sqrt{9} = 3$$

In taking roots of roots the indexes of the roots can be interchanged, *i.e.* the sequence in which the roots are extracted is arbitrary:

$$\sqrt[6]{64} = \sqrt[3]{\sqrt{64}} = \sqrt[3]{8} = 2$$

$$\sqrt[6]{64} = \sqrt{\sqrt[3]{64}} = \sqrt{4} = 2$$

Roots of polynomials. The roots of polynomials can be extracted according to the same scheme used for numbers, employing the formula

$$(a + b + c + \ldots)^2 = a^2 + (2a + b)b + (2a + 2b + c)c + \ldots.$$

For roots of complex numbers, see *De Moivre's formula.*

Rotation

The rotations about a point in a plane and about a straight line in space belong to the *rigid motions* (see above).

Rotations in a plane

The rotations in a plane are determined by the point P in the plane which is unaltered by the rotation (centre of rotation), and by the angle of rotation ϕ.

The image point A_1 of a given point A can be constructed as follows. A circle with radius $\overline{PA}$ is described about P and the angle ϕ constructed on $\overline{PA}$ with vertex P. The intersection of the free arm of ϕ and the circle is the required image point A_1 (Fig. 277).

Example: Rotation of a triangle ABC about its vertex A through angle $\phi = 30°$. The image of the triangle is AB_1C_1 (Fig. 278).

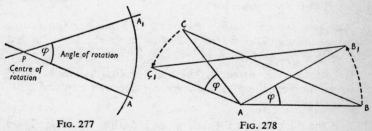

FIG. 277   FIG. 278

Rotations in space

A rotation in space is determined when an axis of rotation and an angle of rotation are given. For representation of rotations in a plane, see *Rigid motions.* Examples are also given there of rigid motions in space.

Rounding off

The correct rounding off of decimal fractions which do not terminate is often of importance. For example, the decimal fraction $\sqrt{2} = 1\cdot414213562\ldots$ does not terminate. It is therefore inevitable when evaluating such a number as a decimal fraction that the procedure be broken off after a definite number of places. Thus $\sqrt{2}$, calculated to three places, is $1\cdot414$. The most appropriate number of places can only be decided after examination of the problem in which the number occurs.

Naturally, if we calculate a number to n places only, when the exact expression of the number as a decimal fraction requires more than n places (whether finitely- or infinitely-many more), our calculation differs from the exact expression by what is (somewhat misleadingly) known as an 'error'. Our problem is to make this error as small as possible with the n decimal places at our disposal. To do this we require the number correct to $n + 1$ decimal places, or sometimes to a higher number of places if the digit in the $(n + 1)$th place is a 5. Knowing this we can decide whether we do better by leaving the digit in the nth place unaltered or by increasing it by 1. The rules we require are then as follows:

1. If the digit in the $(n + 1)$th place is less than 5, leave the digit in the nth place unaltered.

2. If the digit in the $(n + 1)$th place is more than 5, increase the digit in the nth place by 1.

Examples: To calculate $\sqrt{2}$ correct to 3 places: The fourth place has the digit 2, so we leave the 4 in the third place unaltered and write $\sqrt{2} = 1\cdot414$.

To calculate $\sqrt{2}$ correct to 7 places: The eighth place has digit 6, so we increase the 5 in the seventh place by unity and write $\sqrt{2} = 1\cdot4142136$.

3. If the digit in the $(n + 1)$th place is 5, then we normally do better by increasing the digit in the nth by unity. Two exceptions occur. (i) If the decimal fraction is finite and the 5 in the $(n + 1)$th place is the last non-zero figure in its exact expression, then it makes no difference whether we round 'up' or 'down'. By convention we round 'up' and increase the digit in the nth place by unity. (ii) If the expression we are given ends with the 5

in the $(n + 1)$th place, and if this is not exact but the result of a previous rounding-off process, then we must calculate more decimal places until we know whether the digit in the $(n + 1)$th place was originally a 4, in which case we leave the digit in the nth place unaltered, or a 5, in which case we increase the digit in the nth place by unity.

Examples:

(i) To three decimal places, $3·14156... = 3·142$.

(ii) By convention, to three decimal places $3·1415 = 3·142$.

(iii) If we are given $\sqrt{2·2} = 1·5$ to one decimal place, then before we can round off $\sqrt{2·2}$ to the nearest whole number we must calculate $\sqrt{2·2}$ to more decimal places, namely $\sqrt{2·2} = 1·48...$; and we then know we should round 'down' and put $\sqrt{2·2} = 1$ to the nearest whole number. If this further calculation is not possible, then as a matter of convention we normally round 'up'.

Scalar

By a scalar is meant a pure numerical quantity, the term being used in particular to distinguish such quantities from 'vectors' which have directions associated with them.

Scalar product

The scalar product of two vectors $\mathbf{a} = (a_x, a_y, a_z)$ and $\mathbf{b} = (b_x, b_y, b_z)$ is the scalar $\mathbf{a} . \mathbf{b} = a_x b_x + a_y b_y + a_z b_z$ (see *Vector*).

Secant

A secant is a straight line which intersects a circle in two points. Extension to other curves—a secant of a curve is a straight line which intersects the curve in at least two points (see *Circle*).

Secant (sec)

Sec α is the ratio of the hypotenuse to the adjacent side in a right-angled triangle. The function sec α is the reciprocal of cos α (see *Trigonometry*),

$$\sec \alpha = \frac{\text{hypotenuse}}{\text{adjacent side}} = \frac{1}{\cos \alpha}.$$

Secant theorem

If two lines passing through a point P (outside the circle) intersect a circle in the points A, B, and C, D we have

$$\overline{PA}:\overline{PC} = \overline{PD}:\overline{PB} \text{ (Fig. 279)}.$$

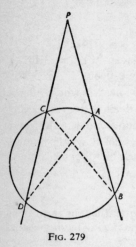

FIG. 279

Semicircle

A circle is divided by any diameter into two congruent parts, symmetrical with respect to the diameter. The parts are called semicircles.

Sequence of numbers

A sequence of numbers is of the form x_1, x_2, x_3, . . ., where the x's are numbers following one another in some defined manner. The numbers x_n are referred to as terms of the sequence. We can consider *finite* sequences or *infinite* sequences, according as the sequences do or do not possess a finite number of terms.

The rule according to which the members of the sequence are formed may be an explicit rule for calculation in which, apart from given constants, only the letter n—the number of the term to be calculated—occurs; *e.g.* the formula:

$x_n = \dfrac{1}{n}$ $(n = 1, 2, . . .)$ yields the sequence

$$1, \frac{1}{2}, \frac{1}{3}, \frac{1}{4}, \frac{1}{5}, . . ., \frac{1}{n}, . . .;$$

$x_n = \dfrac{1}{2^n}$ $(n = 1, 2, . . .)$ yields the sequence

$$\frac{1}{2}, \frac{1}{4}, \frac{1}{8}, \frac{1}{16}, \frac{1}{32}, . . ., \frac{1}{2^n}, . . .;$$

$x_n = 1 + 2n$ $(n = 1, 2, 3, . . .)$ yields the sequence

$$3, 5, 7, 9, 11, . . ., 1 + 2n, . . .$$

Properties of number sequences

1. A sequence is said to be bounded if a fixed positive number can be found greater than the absolute values of each of its terms, that is, if K can be found such that

$$|x_n| \leq K \text{ or } -K \leq x_n \leq +K \text{ for } n = 1, 2, 3, \ldots.$$

2. A sequence is said to be *bounded from below* (or *above*) if a number K_1 (or K_2) can be found such that

$$x_n \geq K_1 \text{ (or } x_n \leq K_2) \text{ for } n = 1, 2, 3, \ldots.$$

A bounded sequence is bounded from both above and below.

3. A sequence is said to be *monotonic increasing* if

$$x_n \leq x_{n+1} \text{ for } n = 1, 2, 3, \ldots.$$

The sequence is said to be *monotonic decreasing* if

$$x_n \geq x_{n+1} \text{ for } n = 1, 2, 3, \ldots.$$

Both types are referred to as monotonic sequences. *E.g.*

(i) The sequence $x_n = 2^n$ is monotonic increasing and bounded from below.

(ii) The sequence $x_n = \dfrac{1}{n}$ is monotonic decreasing and bounded.

4. A sequence a_n is said to be a convergent sequence, with limiting value a, if the terms of the sequence approach the value a in such a way that if we select any positive quantity ε, however small, then sooner or later *all* the terms of the sequence differ from a by less than ε. We say: 'The sequence tends (or converges) to a'. We write:

$$a_n \to a \text{ as } n \to \infty, \text{ or, } \lim_{n \to \infty} a_n = a.$$

a is also called the *limit* of the sequence.

For $a_n \to a$ we say: 'a_n tends to a'. For $\lim_{n \to \infty} a_n = a$ we say: 'The limit of a_n as n tends to infinity equals a'. *E.g.* the sequence $a_n = 1 + \dfrac{1}{2n}$ converges to 1.

5. A sequence with limit zero is called a *null sequence*; *e.g.* $a_n = \dfrac{1}{2n}$.

391

6. Sequences which do not converge to a finite limit are said to be *divergent*; e.g.

(i) The sequence of the natural numbers $a_n = n$ is divergent.

(ii) The *geometric sequence* (see art.) 2, 6, 18, 54, . . . with initial term 2 and quotient 3 and general term $a_n = 2 \times 3^{n-1}$ is divergent.

(iii) The alternating geometric sequence 1, -2, 4, -8, . . ., $a_n = (-1)^{n-1} 2^{n-1}$, . . . is divergent.

7. If for sufficiently large n, a_n and all later terms exceed any given number however large, the sequence is said to diverge to $+\infty$. We write:

$$a_n \rightarrow +\infty \text{ as } n \rightarrow \infty, \text{ or } \lim_{n \to \infty} a_n = \infty.$$

Similarly we speak of sequences which diverge or tend to $-\infty$; *e.g.* the *arithmetic sequence* (see art.) 2, -1, -4, -7, . . . diverges to $-\infty$.

Example: the sequence of natural numbers diverges to $+\infty$.

8. Sequences which neither converge nor diverge to $+\infty$ or $-\infty$ are said to be oscillatory. *E.g.*

the sequences   1, -2, $+4$, -8, $+16$, . . .,

$$+2, -2, +2, -2, +2, \ldots,$$

are oscillatory.

Series

A series is the unevaluated sum of terms of a (finite or infinite) sequence. *E.g.*

from the sequence a_1, a_2, a_3, a_4, . . . we form the series

$$a_1 + a_2 + a_3 + a_4 + \ldots.$$

The series can be abbreviated by means of the *summation sign* $\sum$ (see art.),

$$a_1 + a_2 + a_3 + \ldots + a_n + \ldots = \sum_{k=1}^{\infty} a_k;$$

or, if the series has only n terms,

$$a_1 + a_2 + a_3 + \ldots + a_n = \sum_{k=1}^{n} a_k.$$

Set-theory

A theory founded and widely developed by Georg Cantor (1845–1918) which forms the foundation of the theory of point-sets, of real functions and of topology. A set is a collection of definite and distinguishable objects, either concrete or conceptual, *e.g.* the whole numbers. Sets are finite or infinite. The infinite set of the natural numbers is said to be enumerable, and other sets are said to be enumerable if their elements can be put into one-to-one correspondence with elements of this set. There exist sets which are neither finite nor enumerable, *e.g.* the set of real numbers between 0 and 1.

Shear

Shearing consists in a transformation in a plane or in space in which the area of a plane figure or the volume of a solid is unaltered. Since angles are (in general) changed, the original and transformed figure are neither congruent nor similar.

Examples:

1. *ABCD* is a given parallelogram (Fig. 280). In a shearing motion parallel to the direction of $\overline{AB}$, the point *D* on the straight line *DC* passes to the final position *D′* which depends on the distance apart of the parallel straight lines $\overline{AB}$ and $\overline{DC}$.

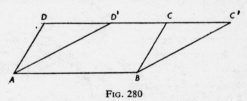

FIG. 280

2. In a plane rectangular coordinate system a shearing motion in the direction of the *x*-axis can be described by the following equations:

$$x' = x + ay,$$
$$y' = y,$$

where x, y denote the coordinates of the original point P and x', y' the coordinates of the image-point P', while a is a constant number $\neq 0$.

393

3. If *ABCDEFGH* is a given rectangular solid, a shearing motion in any direction in the plane *EFGH* parallel to *ABCD* produces a parallelepiped *ABCDE'F'G'H'* (Fig. 281).

4. In a three-dimensional rectangular coordinate system, a shearing-motion in any direction parallel to the x, y-plane can be represented by the following system of equations:

$$x' = x + az,$$
$$y' = y + bz,$$
$$z' = z,$$

where x, y, z denote the coordinates of an arbitrary point, x', y', z' the coordinates of the corresponding image-point and a, b two constants specifying the direction and magnitude of the shear.

Sickle of Archimedes (Archimedes, 287–212 B.C.)

If the diameter of a semi-circle $2r = 2r_1 + 2r_2$ is divided into any two parts of length $2r_1$ and $2r_2$ and if further semicircles are constructed on these segments as diameters, the resulting sickle of Archimedes has the same area as the circle with diameter $\overline{FC} = h$ (Fig. 282).

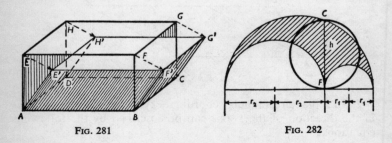

FIG. 281   FIG. 282

Sign

The two signs used before numbers are '+' (read: plus) and '−' (read: minus), positive numbers being indicated by the former, negative numbers by the latter. This use of + and −

must be carefully distinguished from their use as operations, when they serve to indicate which of two calculating-operations is to be carried out.

Similarity

Two geometrical figures are similar if they agree in respect of the main attributes of shape, *viz.* angles and the ratios of different linear measurements.

1. *Similarity of triangles*

Two triangles are called similar, if the angles and ratios of corresponding sides of one are equal to those of the other, symbol: $\sim$ (see *Triangle*).

2. *Similarity of polygons*

Polygons are called similar, if they agree in respect of all angles and ratios of pairs of sides. The areas of similar polygons vary as the squares of corresponding sides (see *Triangle, Polygon*).

3. *Similarity transformations*

A similarity transformation transforms any plane figure into a similar figure. Conversely, given two similar figures, a similarity transformation can always be found which will send one figure into the other (see *Similarity transformation*).

Similarity transformation

The similarity transformations belong to the *affine transformations* (see above). They comprise those affine transformations in which a figure (plane or solid) is transformed into a similar figure.

Sine (sin)

The sine function sin α is a trigonometric function, the ratio of the opposite side to the hypotenuse in a right-angled triangle (see *Trigonometry*),

$$\sin \alpha = \frac{\text{opposite side}}{\text{hypotenuse}}.$$

Sine theorem

1. *The sine theorem of plane trigonometry*

If a, b and c are the sides, and α, β and γ the angles of a triangle, then $a:b:c = \sin \alpha : \sin \beta : \sin \gamma$. The theorem can be used to solve a triangle if *one side, the opposite angle and a further side or a further angle are given* (see *Trigonometry*). For examples see *Solution of triangle*.

2. *The sine theorem of spherical trigonometry*

If a, b and c are the sides, and α, β and γ the angles of a spherical triangle, then $\sin a : \sin b : \sin c = \sin \alpha : \sin \beta : \sin \gamma$. The sine theorem of spherical trigonometry can be used to solve a spherical triangle if *one side, the opposite angle and a further side or a further angle are given* (see *Spherical trigonometry*).

Single-valued transformation

A transformation of points of one space into points of another is called *single-valued* if there corresponds to each point one image-point and one only. The transformation is called one-to-one, or reversibly single-valued, if there corresponds to each image-point one inverse-image point and one only.

Skew

Two lines in space are said to be skew (with respect to one another) if they neither intersect nor are parallel.

Solid

A solid is a bounded part of space. The boundaries are surfaces. The bounding surfaces can be either plane or curved. If all are plane the solid is a *polyhedron* (see above).

Solid angle

The measure of a solid angle is specified in a way analogous to the radian- (or arc-) measure of an angle in a plane. An auxiliary unit sphere is used and every cone has a measure, the solid angle Φ associated with it.

We consider the intersection of the given cone with the sphere of unit radius which has the vertex of the cone as centre. The area on the sphere cut out by the cone is taken as the measure of solid angle of the cone.

An octant of a sphere has solid angle $\frac{\pi}{2}$. The complete space-angle is 4π. A cone of revolution formed by rotating a straight line about an axis inclined to it at an angle α has solid angle

$$\Phi = 4\pi \sin^2 \frac{\alpha}{2}.$$

Solid of revolution

A solid of revolution can be regarded as a curve $y = f(x)$ rotated about the x-axis. The cross-section of such a solid for abscissa x is a circle with area $\pi y^2 = \pi(f(x))^2$. Thus the volume of the solid of revolution between x_0 and $x_0 + \Delta x$ is

$$\pi \int_{x_0}^{x_0 + \Delta x} y^2 \, dx.$$

Example: Ellipsoid of revolution; $y = \frac{b}{a} \sqrt{a^2 - x^2}$ is the equation of the ellipse referred to its principal axes. The volume of the solid of revolution is obtained by integrating from $-a$ to $+a$:

$$\pi \int_{-a}^{+a} \frac{b^2}{a^2} (a^2 - x^2) dx = \pi \frac{b^2}{a^2} \left(a^2 x - \frac{x^3}{3} \right) \Big|_{-a}^{+a} = \frac{4ab^2\pi}{3}.$$

(Fig. 283)

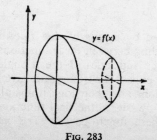

FIG. 283

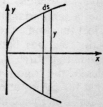

FIG. 284

The surface of a solid of revolution is obtained by the integration

$$2\pi \int_a^b y\sqrt{1 + y'^2}dx.$$

Example: Paraboloid of revolution; equation of parabola, $y^2 = 2px$,

$$\text{surface-area} = 2\pi \int_0^x \sqrt{2px}\sqrt{1 + \frac{p}{2x}}\,dx$$

$$= \frac{2\pi\sqrt{p}}{3}\left[(p + 2x)^{3/2} - p^{3/2}\right]$$

(Fig. 284).

Solution of the triangle
Elementary solution of the triangle

Sides of a triangle can be calculated by means of Euclid's theorem (theorem on altitudes), the theorem of Pythagoras, the projection theorems for triangles, the various extensions and generalisations of the Pythagorean theorem, and the proportionality relations obtained from the theory of similar triangles (*e.g.* theorem of Apollonius). But it is not possible by these means to calculate the angles of a triangle from a knowledge of its sides.

Trigonometrical solution of the triangle

A solution of the triangle with the help of the trigonometrical functions relies on the following theorems: sine theorem, cosine theorem, Mollweide equations, tangent theorem, half-angle theorem, and the relations between angles of a triangle. See references to individual words and *Trigonometry*, and below.

Solution of triangle, trigonometrical

The general triangle can be solved by means of the trigonometrical functions, the relations holding between these functions, and the relations between the angles and sides of the triangle, provided that three independent elements of the triangle are given. Tables of the trigonometrical functions and their logarithms are needed for the solution of triangles by trigonometrical functions and for other calculations with these functions (see *Trigonometrical Tables*).

Formulae for the general triangle (sides a, b, c, angles α, β, γ, radius of inscribed circle ρ, radius of circumscribed circle r, altitude h, area $\triangle$)

Relations between angles:

$$\alpha + \beta + \gamma = 180°, \text{ therefore:}$$

$$\sin(\beta + \gamma) = \sin(180 - \alpha) = \sin\alpha,$$

$$\cos(\beta + \gamma) = \cos(180 - \alpha) = -\cos\alpha,$$

$$\sin\frac{\beta + \gamma}{2} = \sin\left(90 - \frac{\alpha}{2}\right) = \cos\frac{\alpha}{2},$$

$$\cos\frac{\beta + \gamma}{2} = \cos\left(90 - \frac{\alpha}{2}\right) = \sin\frac{\alpha}{2}.$$

Altitude formulae:

$$h_a = b\sin\gamma = c\sin\beta,$$
$$h_b = a\sin\gamma = c\sin\alpha,$$
$$h_c = b\sin\alpha = a\sin\beta. \quad \text{(Fig. 285)}$$

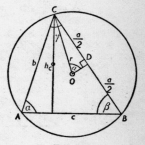

Sine theorem:

$$a:b:c = \sin\alpha:\sin\beta:\sin\gamma.$$

Chord formulae:

$$a:2r\sin\alpha; \quad b = 2r\sin\beta;$$
$$c:2r\sin\gamma \text{ (Fig. 285).}$$

Fig. 285

Tangent theorem:

$$\frac{b+c}{b-c} = \frac{\tan\dfrac{\beta+\gamma}{2}}{\tan\dfrac{\beta-\gamma}{2}}; \quad \frac{c+a}{c-a} = \frac{\tan\dfrac{\gamma+\alpha}{2}}{\tan\dfrac{\gamma-\alpha}{2}}; \quad \frac{a+b}{a-b} = \frac{\tan\dfrac{\alpha+\beta}{2}}{\tan\dfrac{\alpha-\beta}{2}}.$$

Mollweide equations:

$$\frac{b+c}{a} = \frac{\cos\dfrac{\beta-\gamma}{2}}{\sin\dfrac{\alpha}{2}}; \quad \frac{c+a}{b} = \frac{\cos\dfrac{\gamma-\alpha}{2}}{\sin\dfrac{\beta}{2}}; \quad \frac{a+b}{c} = \frac{\cos\dfrac{\alpha-\beta}{2}}{\sin\dfrac{\gamma}{2}}.$$

399

Cosine theorem:

$$a^2 = b^2 + c^2 - 2bc \cos \alpha,$$

$$b^2 = c^2 + a^2 - 2ca \cos \beta,$$

$$c^2 = a^2 + b^2 - 2ab \cos \gamma.$$

Radius of inscribed circle:

$$\rho = 4r \sin \frac{\alpha}{2} \sin \frac{\beta}{2} \sin \frac{\gamma}{2}.$$

Perimeter:

$$L = 8r \cos \frac{\alpha}{2} \cos \frac{\beta}{2} \cos \frac{\gamma}{2}.$$

Area:

$$\Delta = \frac{ab}{2} \sin \gamma = 2r^2 \sin \alpha \sin \beta \sin \gamma = \frac{abc}{4r}.$$

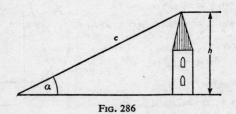

FIG. 286

Examples: (i) The angle of elevation of a tower of known height (60 metres) is measured as 5° 20′ (Fig. 286). How far is the point at which the measurement is taken from the top of the tower?

We have $\dfrac{h}{c} = \sin \alpha$, or $c = \dfrac{h}{\sin \alpha}$;

$$\log 60 = 11 \cdot 77815 - 10$$

$$\log 5° 20' = \underline{8 \cdot 96825 - 10}$$

$$\log c = 2 \cdot 80990.$$

That is, $\qquad\qquad c = 645 \cdot 5$ metres (Fig. 286).

(ii) Given $a = 15$, $\beta = 77°$ and $\gamma = 35°$.

Required: α, b and c.

First we have: $\alpha = 180° - \beta - \gamma$; that is,

$$\alpha = 180° - 77° - 35° = 68°.$$

By the sine theorem we have:

$$b = \frac{a \sin \beta}{\sin \alpha}, \text{ that is, } b = \frac{15 \sin 77°}{\sin 68°} = 15 \cdot 763,$$

$$c = \frac{a \sin \gamma}{\sin \alpha}, \text{ that is, } c = \frac{15 \sin 35°}{\sin 68°} = 9 \cdot 2792.$$

Computation:

$\log 15 =$	$1 \cdot 17609$	$\log 15 =$	$1 \cdot 17609$
$\log \sin 77° =$	$9 \cdot 98872 - 10$	$\log \sin 35° =$	$9 \cdot 75859 - 10$
	$11 \cdot 16481 - 10$		$10 \cdot 93468 - 10$
$\log \sin 68° =$	$9 \cdot 96717 - 10$	$\log \sin 68° =$	$9 \cdot 96717 - 10$
$\log b =$	$1 \cdot 19764$	$\log c =$	$0 \cdot 96751$
$b =$	$15 \cdot 763$	$c =$	$9 \cdot 2792$

(iii) The distance between two points A and B on the bank of a river is measured and the directions at A and B of a tower on the other side of the river with respect to the base-line $\overline{AB}$ are determined. How far is the tower from A? (Fig. 287).

We have

$$\gamma = 180° - \alpha - \beta$$

and

$$\frac{\overline{AT}}{\overline{AB}} = \frac{\sin \beta}{\sin \gamma},$$

so that

$$\overline{AT} = \overline{AB} \frac{\sin \beta}{\sin \gamma}.$$

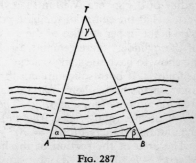

Fig. 287

401

Sphere

Definition: a sphere is the locus of points in space having a given fixed distance from a given point O. O is called the centre of the sphere, the fixed distance its radius (r). If a sphere is intersected by a plane they meet in a circle (Fig. 288).

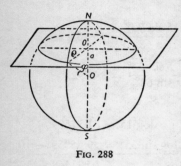

FIG. 288

The greater the distance a of the plane from the centre of the sphere the smaller is the radius ρ of the circle of intersection; we have $\rho = r \sin \phi$.

If the plane passes through the centre of the sphere ($a = 0$, $\phi = 90°$), it intersects the sphere in a *great* circle. If the distance a of the plane from the centre is r ($\phi = 0$) the plane touches the sphere, and is then called a tangent plane. If $a > r$ the plane does not intersect the sphere.

A segment is cut off by the sphere on a straight line which passes through the centre of the sphere. The segment is called a diameter of the sphere and its length is twice the radius.

Volume of the sphere

The volume of the sphere may be determined if we regard volumes of the cylinder and the cone as already known. We use a cylinder whose height and radius of base are each equal to the radius of the sphere. Within the cylinder is placed a cone, whose vertex is at the centre of the base-circle of the cylinder and whose base is the upper surface of the cylinder. If this cone is bored out of the cylinder, there remains a solid (of known volume) which we show to have the same volume as the upper half of the sphere, as follows. If both solids are cut through at height h the area laid open on the half-sphere is a circular area and on the other solid it is an annulus (circular ring). The inner radius of the annulus is h (isosceles right-angled triangle) and the outer, r. The area of the annulus is therefore $A_1 = \pi(r^2 - h^2)$.

The area of the section of the half-sphere is $A_2 = \pi\rho^2$, where $\rho^2 = r^2 - h^2$; that is, A_2 also equals $\pi(r^2 - h^2)$. Since the two surfaces are at equal height and are equal in area, it follows by Cavalieri's principle that the half-sphere and the bored-out cylinder have the same volume. That is, the volume of the half-sphere is

$$\pi r^2 \cdot r - \frac{1}{3} \pi r^2 \cdot r = \frac{2}{3} \pi r^3.$$

The volume of the whole sphere is therefore $V = \frac{4}{3} \pi r^3$.

Corollary: the volumes of a circular cylinder of height r and radius r, of a half-sphere of radius r, and of a circular cone with height r and radius r, are in the ratio $3:2:1$.

Calculation of the surface area of the sphere

Imagine the interior of the sphere to be filled by a large number of congruent pyramids, whose vertices lie at the centre of the sphere and whose base-curves lie on the inner surface of the sphere, the pyramids touching one another. Then the sum of the volumes of these pyramids is $W = \frac{h}{3} Bn$, where $B =$ area of base of a pyramid and $h =$ height. The larger n becomes, the nearer does nB come to the surface of the sphere ($nB \to S$), the nearer does h come to the radius r of the sphere ($h \to r$), and the nearer does W come to the volume of the sphere $\left(W \to V = \frac{4}{3} \pi r^3 \right)$.

Suppose the process is carried out to the limit; then

$$\frac{4}{3} \pi r^3 = \frac{r}{3} \times S.$$

That is, the area S of the surface of the sphere is $S = 4\pi r^2$.

Parts of the sphere

(1) *Spherical segment*. If a sphere is cut by a plane, we have on either of the plane *segments of the sphere*. The one segment has height $h = r - a$ (Fig. 289), the other has height $h_1 = r + a$. If ρ is the radius of the bounding circle, then:

$$\rho^2 = r^2 - a^2 = (r + a)(r - a),$$

or, if we put $r - a = h$, $\rho^2 = (2r - h)h$.

403

By adapting our method for determining the volume of the sphere we can easily show that the volume of the segment of the sphere with height h is $V = \pi \dfrac{h^2}{3}(3r - h)$, or, in terms of the radius ρ, $V = \pi \dfrac{h}{6}(3\rho^2 + h^2)$.

(2) *Spherical sector.* If a spherical segment is extended by including in the volume the cone whose vertex is the centre of the circle and whose base is the base of the segments, we obtain a spherical sector. The volume of the sector is $V = \dfrac{2\pi h}{3} r^2$, where h is the height of the segment.

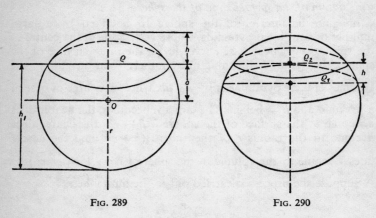

FIG. 289   FIG. 290

(3) *Spherical segment with two bases* (Fig. 290). If a sphere is cut by two parallel planes, distance h apart, between the planes there is a spherical segment of height h with two bases. Let the radii of the bounding circles be ρ_1 and ρ_2. The volume of the figure is the difference of the volumes of two spherical segments of the type discussed above:

$$V = \pi \frac{h}{6}(3\rho_1^2 + 3\rho_2^2 + h^2).$$

(4) *Spherical cap.* A spherical cap is that part of the surface of a sphere bounded by a circle lying on the sphere. The curved

404

part of the surface of a single spherical segment is a spherical cap. The area is:

$$S = 2\pi rh.$$

(5) *Spherical zone*. The curved part of the surface of a spherical segment with two bases (of height h) is called a spherical zone. Its area is:

$$S = 2\pi rh.$$

(6) If two planes intersect at an angle α in a diameter of a sphere of radius r they divide the sphere into 4 'spherical wedges', two of which have internal angle α. The volume of such a wedge (Fig. 291) is:

$$V = \frac{\pi r^3 \alpha}{270} \text{ (α measured in degrees).}$$

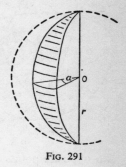

FIG. 291

Spherical trigonometry

The branch of mathematics concerned with geometry on the sphere is of special interest for problems of mathematical geography, of navigation and of astronomy. Mathematically speaking, the geometry of a curved surface is a non-euclidean geometry. Practical calculations are carried out with the trigonometrical functions, using logarithmic and numerical tables.

Great circles. If a plane contains the centre of a sphere, it intersects the sphere in a great circle; if not, it intersects the sphere in a small circle (or not at all). Great circles on a sphere afford the shortest distance between two points, and correspond to straight lines in plane geometry. Each point on a sphere may be associated with a great circle (*e.g.* the North or South pole on the earth may be associated with the equator). This makes possible 'polar formulae', *i.e.* formulae in which the 'sides' and 'angles' of a triangle on the surface of the sphere (spherical triangle) changes places. A great circle is the line of intersection of a plane through the centre of the sphere; the diameter of the sphere perpendicular to this plane cuts the sphere in two points, which are the poles of the great circle and lie at 'opposite positions' on the sphere.

Spherical triangle (Fig. 292). Consider a sphere of unit radius. Three planes each passing through the centre of the sphere cut the sphere in three great circles. Two great circles intersect in

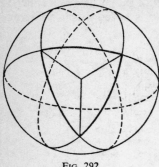

FIG. 292

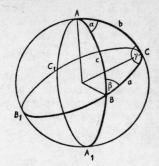

FIG. 293

two opposite points of the sphere; the planes determined by the great circles form the angle between the great circles, equal to the angle of inclination of the planes.

The figure bounded by the two great circles is referred to as a spherical lune. However, three further spherical lunes are determined by the two planes, namely two each of which when taken together with the first forms a hemisphere, and one which lies opposite to, and is congruent to, the first.

The third great circle divides each of these four spherical lunes into two spherical triangles, those belonging to opposite lunes being centrally symmetric in pairs. Notation for spherical triangles is as in the plane: vertices A, B, C; sides a, b, c; and angles α, β, γ. In what follows we shall only consider triangles which lie wholly on a hemisphere. The derivation of the formulae of spherical trigonometry follow from consideration of the trihedral angle concerned (Figs. 293 and 294).

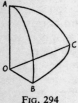

FIG. 294

Sine theorem of spherical trigonometry (Fig. 295)

We drop the perpendicular from the vertex A of the triangle onto the plane determined by the two other vertices, B and C.

406

This perpendicular, $\overline{AD}$, is the line of intersection of the planes through A perpendicular to OAC and OCB on the one side and to OAB and OCB on the other side. The first of these two planes cuts the plane OAC in the line $\overline{AF}$. The segment $\overline{AF}$ is the opposite side of the angle AOF in the right-angled triangle OAF with

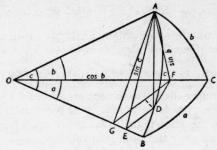

FIG. 295

hypotenuse 1, and thus is of length $\sin b$. Similarly, the line of intersection $\overline{AE}$ has length $\sin c$. The triangles ADF and ADE are right-angled and the angles at F and E in them are respectively the angles γ and β. AD can be calculated from both of these two triangles: $\overline{AD} = \sin \beta \sin c$ and $\overline{AD} = \sin \gamma \sin b$. Equating these two expressions we have the sine theorem:

$$\sin \beta \sin c = \sin \gamma \sin b,$$

which can be written alternatively as:

$$\frac{\sin \beta}{\sin b} = \frac{\sin \gamma}{\sin c} = \frac{\sin \alpha}{\sin a}.$$

The last term is obtained by cyclic permutation.

Cosine theorem of spherical trigonometry (Fig. 295)

To derive the cosine theorem of spherical trigonometry we drop the perpendicular from F onto the edge OB; the distance $\overline{OG}$ of the foot of this perpendicular from O is $\cos b \cos a$. We have $\overline{OE} = \cos c$, since $\overline{OE}$ is adjacent to the angle at O in the right-angled triangle OAE (hypotenuse 1). But the segment $\overline{GE}$ must

407

have length $\sin b \cos \gamma \sin a$, since $\angle OFD = 90°$ and $\angle OFG = 90° - a$; consequently $\angle GFD = a$, and $\overline{FD} = \sin b \cos \gamma$ as adjacent side in the right-angled triangle AFD whose hypotenuse $\overline{AF}$ is the length $\sin b$, as has already been shown in the proof of the sine theorem. $\overline{OE} = \overline{OG} + \overline{GE}$ gives then:

$$\cos c = \cos b \cos a + \sin b \sin a \cos \gamma.$$

By cyclic permutation we obtain analogous formulae for $\cos a$ and $\cos b$. The polar formulae

$$\cos \gamma = -\cos \beta \cos \alpha + \sin \beta \sin \alpha \cos c$$

and corresponding formulae for $\cos \alpha$ and $\cos \beta$ follow from the correspondence of pole and great circle mentioned above.

Combining the known theorems, we can obtain further formulae, of which only the cotangent theorem,

$$\cos c \cos \alpha = \cot b \sin c - \cot \beta \sin \alpha,$$

and the sine-cosine-theorem

$$\sin a \cos \beta = \cos b \sin c - \sin b \cos c \cos \alpha$$

are specially named. From these further formulae can be obtained by cyclic permutation (Fig. 296). For a complete collection of these formulae, see p. 532.

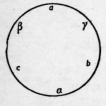

Fig. 296

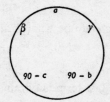

Fig. 297

Right-angled spherical triangles. The general formulae for spherical triangles take a simple form if one of the angles or one of the sides is 90°. If $\alpha = 90°$, formulae obtain which can be derived mechanically by Napier's rule. The cosine of any element in Fig. 297 is equal to the product of the sines of the elements separated from it, and to the product of the cotangents of the adjacent elements, as follows:

$$\cos a = \cos b \cos c$$

and $$\cos a = \cot \beta \cot \gamma;$$

$$\cos \beta = \cos b \sin \gamma, \text{etc.};$$

where of course we use the relations $\sin (90° - x) = \cos x$, $\cot (90° - x) = \tan x$.

Square

A square is a quadrilateral with four equal sides and four right angles (see *Quadrilateral*).

Square numbers

Square numbers are the squares of the natural numbers: 1, 4, 9, 16, . . . (see also *Polygonal numbers*).

Standard deviation

Expression for the average measure of a number of errors or deviations. We understand by the standard deviation, σ, the square root of the mean of the squares of deviations. If Σv^2 is the sum of the squares of deviation from the arithmetic mean, then

$$\sigma = \sqrt{\frac{\Sigma v^2}{n}}.$$

Example: Given observations $a_1 = 8$, $a_2 = 9$, $a_3 = 13$, $a_4 = 8$, $a_5 = 12$, $a_6 = 10$, then the arithmetic mean is:

$$\frac{8 + 9 + 13 + 8 + 12 + 10}{6} = \frac{60}{6} = 10,$$

whence:

$$\sigma^2 = \frac{2^2 + 1^2 + 3^2 + 2^2 + 2^2 + 0^2}{6} = \frac{22}{6},$$

and so $$\sigma = \sqrt{\frac{11}{3}} = 1 \cdot 91$$

(see also *Error*).

Statistics

In statistics we study a set or population of objects, persons, events, etc., and a basic problem is to determine a population's essential attributes (variates), and to describe its *Distribution* according to one or more of these attributes. The distribution relative to a single attribute can be specified by dividing the population into a sequence of classes according to the size and character of the attribute as it occurs in the individuals in the population. Where there exists only a limited sequence of possibilities (*e.g.* children in a marriage, pips on a die) the distribution is said to be discontinuous; if an unlimited number of possibilities exists, it is said to be continuous (*e.g.* physical measurements, height, weight). We may represent continuous distributions by means of a continuous curve; but in the case of discontinuous distributions such a curve is, strictly speaking, not permissible (see *Frequency curve*).

The notion of *relative frequency* helps us in describing statistical populations. A relative frequency is the ratio of the number of objects with a particular attribute to the total number of objects under consideration.

Example: In a cross between two varieties of garden pea (1st variety: yellow seeds; 2nd variety: green seeds), the second generation yielded 8,023 plants, 6,022 with yellow seeds and 2,001 with green seeds (Mendel, 1865).

The relative frequency of plants with yellow seeds is $\frac{6022}{8023}$ and that of plants with green seeds is $\frac{2001}{8023}$.

Step-angles

Step-angles arise at parallel lines which are intersected by a transversal. They lie on corresponding sides of the parallel lines and on the same side of the transversal, and are equal (see *Angle*).

Stereometry

Stereometry or solid geometry is the study of geometrical objects in three-dimensional space. The term stereometry is frequently confined to that part of solid geometry considered with the measurement of solid figures.

For some simple cases the volume can be calculated from a knowledge of the lengths of the edges of the solid, or of the radii and altitudes. But in general the *Integral calculus* (see *Infinitesimal calculus*) is required for the determination of the volume of a solid.

(For particular solids, see: *Cube, Rectangular solid, Prism, Pyramid, Cone, Conical frustrum, Sphere, Polyhedra, Platonic solids*.)

Stirling's formula

Stirling's formula provides the means for approximate evaluation of $n!$ for large n:

$$n! \approx n^n e^{-n} \sqrt{2\pi n}.$$

Straight line

The straight line is one of the basic elements of plane and of solid geometry. Properties of the straight line: a straight line is uniquely determined by two points. If three points lie on a straight line then we can say of one of the three points that it lies between the other two. A straight line is divided by any one of its points into two parts. A straight line is unbounded in two directions. Two straight lines which lie in one and the same plane have either one point (point of intersection) in common, or none; in the latter case they are said to be parallel. A straight line divides a plane into two parts. A straight line which does not lie wholly in a plane either has exactly one point in common with the plane (point of intersection, trace) or none at all; in the latter case the line is parallel to the plane.

Two straight lines which are not coplanar have no point in common. Such lines are either parallel or 'skew' with respect to each other.

Straight line segment

The totality of points which lie between two fixed points A and B on a straight line, together with the points A and B, form a straight line segment. A and B are called the end-points of the segment (Fig. 298).

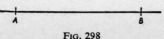

FIG. 298

411

Straight line segments, ratios of

The ratio of two straight line segments a and b (which need not lie on the same line) is written $a:b$ or $\frac{a}{b}$. If two such ratios $a:b$ and $c:d$ are equal to one another we have a relation of proportionality, $a:b = c:d$.

1. *First theorem on rays (first proportionality theorem).*
Given two rays deriving from a single point and cut by two parallel straight lines, the ratio of segments on the one ray is equal to the ratio of corresponding segments on the other (Fig. 299, $\frac{a}{b} = \frac{c}{d}$). Conversely, if two rays deriving from a single point are cut by two straight lines in such a way that segments cut off on one line bear the same ratio to one another as do corresponding segments on the other line, then the lines are parallel.

2. *Second theorem on rays (second proportionality theorem).*
Given two rays deriving from a single point and cut by two parallel straight lines, the ratio of segments cut off on the two parallels is the same as the ratio of segments cut off on either of the two rays, reckoned from the origin of the rays.

$$(\text{Fig. 299}) \ \frac{p}{q} = \frac{a + b}{a}; \quad (\text{Fig. 300}) \ \frac{p}{q} = \frac{a}{b}.$$

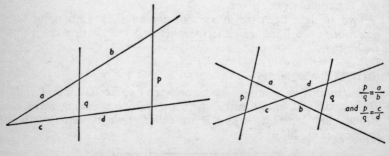

Fig. 299   Fig. 300

Given two parallel lines cutting three rays which proceed from the same point, the ratio of segments cut off on the one parallel is equal to the corresponding ratio on the other.

$$\text{(Fig. 301)} \quad \frac{\overline{AB}}{\overline{BC}} = \frac{\overline{A_1B_1}}{\overline{A_1C_1}}.$$

Constructions

To divide a segment $\overline{AB}$ in the ratio $m:n$.

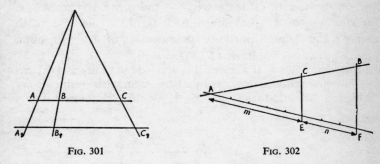

FIG. 301   FIG. 302

(a) *Inner division.* First solution (Fig. 302). Through A draw an arbitrary line; mark off on this, from A to E, m equal segments, and from E to F, n equal segments. If through E is drawn the line parallel to the join $\overline{FB}$ of F and B then

$$\overline{CA}:\overline{CB} = m:n.$$

Second solution (Fig. 303). Draw parallel lines through A and B and mark off on them from A and B respectively, in opposite directions, m and n segments of equal length. Then the join of E and F, the resulting end-points, divides the segment $\overline{AB}$ at the point C in the ratio $m:n$.

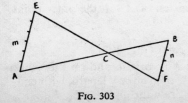

FIG. 303   FIG. 304

413

(b) *Outer division*. First solution (Fig. 304). Draw a ray with A as origin, and on this mark off, first m equal segments reaching to F, and then, from F, n equal segments in the opposite direction (towards A). Draw the line through F parallel to $\overline{EB}$. This cuts the extension of $\overline{AB}$ in the point D. We then have

$$\overline{AD}:\overline{BD} = m:n.$$

Second solution (Fig. 305). Draw parallel lines through A and B, and on them mark off respectively m and n equal segments, on the same side of $\overline{AB}$. The intersection, D, of the join of the end-points E and F thus formed with the extension of $\overline{AB}$, is the outer point of division. We have $\overline{AD}:\overline{BD} = m:n$.

Harmonic division. If a segment is divided internally and externally in equal ratios $m:n$ we say that the segment is harmonically divided in the ratio $m:n$ (Fig. 306). Draw through the end-points

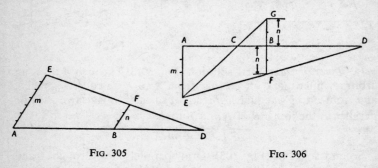

FIG. 305   FIG. 306

A and B two parallel lines, and mark off from A on the line through A m equal segments reaching to E. On the other line, mark off from B on each side n equal segments reaching to F and G. The line $\overline{EG}$ intersects the segment $\overline{AB}$ in the inner point of division, C. $\overline{EF}$ intersects the extension of $\overline{AB}$ in the outer point of division, D.

Division of a segment into n equal parts (Fig. 307)

Draw a ray, with the end-point A as origin, and on this mark off consecutively n equal segments, of arbitrary length, with end-points $E_1, E_2, \ldots, E_n = F$. Then draw through $E_1, E_2, E_3, \ldots,$

lines parallel to the join $\overline{FB}$. The segment $\overline{AB}$ is divided by these lines into n equal parts.

Construction of the fourth proportional (Fig. 308)

The fourth proportional of three given segments a, b and c is that segment, d, which satisfies the proportionality relation $a:b = c:d$. Take a double ray with origin S. Mark off on one ray, each measured from S, the segments a and b, and on the

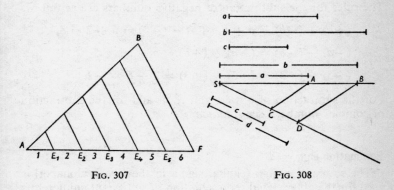

FIG. 307   FIG. 308

other ray, again from S, c. Join the end-point A of the segment a to the end-point C of the segment c, and draw through B the line parallel to $\overline{AC}$. This line cuts the other ray in the point D. D is the end-point of the required fourth proportional $\overline{SD}$ of a, b and c.

Subtraction

Subtraction is the second fundamental operation of arithmetic, the inverse of addition. The following terminology is used:

$$17 \qquad 9 \qquad 8$$
Minuend — Subtrahend = Difference

Subtraction can be carried out within the domain of the natural numbers only if the minuend is greater than the subtrahend. To

415

make subtraction universally possible, negative numbers must be introduced. In this way we arrive at the domain of *Integral numbers* (see art.).

Subtraction of relative numbers

The rules for the subtraction of positive numbers are the same as those for the subtraction of absolute numbers.

$$5 - (+2) = 5 - 2 = 3, \quad 3 - 7 = -4.$$

The rules for the subtraction of negative numbers are as follows

$$(+a) - (-b) = a + b, (+5) - (-3) = 5 + 3 = 8,$$

$$(-a) - (-b) = (-a) + (+b) = b - a,$$

$$(-5) - (-3) = (-5) + (+3) = 3 - 5 = -2.$$

For the subtraction of powers and roots and for the subtraction of complex numbers, see *Addition*.

Summation sign = Σ

The summation sign (capital sigma in the Greek alphabet) is used for the abbreviated representation of sums containing terms which are all of the same type; *e.g.* for the sum

$$S = 1 + 2 + 3 + 4 + 5 + 6 + \ldots + 100,$$

we can write

$$S = \sum_{k=1}^{100} k.$$

Thus the sign Σ here means that all numbers must be added which can be derived from the expression k by replacing k successively by all values lying within, and including, the summation limits 1 and 100.

Example: $S = \dfrac{1}{2} + \dfrac{2}{3} + \dfrac{3}{4} + \ldots + \dfrac{n}{n+1}$ can be abbreviated as

$$S = \sum_{k=1}^{n} \frac{k}{k+1}.$$

Here $\sum\limits_{k=1}^{n}$ means that values of k between 1 and n inclusive are to be successively substituted in the expression to be summed, $\dfrac{k}{k+1}$, and the resulting fractions added.

The summation sign can also be used to represent the sum of so-called infinite series (see *Infinite series*). In such cases, the upper summation limit will be ∞.

Example: The *geometric series* (see art.)

$$S = 1 + \frac{1}{2} + \frac{1}{4} + \frac{1}{8} + \dots$$

can be written

$$S = \sum_{k=0}^{\infty} \frac{1}{2^k}.$$

Supplementary angles

Two angles which add up to 180° (two right angles) are said to be supplementary angles, *e.g.* neighbouring angles in a parallelogram are supplementary. See Fig. 309.

$$\alpha + \beta = 180°, \ \beta + \gamma = 180°, \ \gamma + \delta = 180°, \ \delta + \alpha = 180°.$$

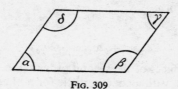

Fig. 309

Surfaces

A surface is a geometrical construct in space which can be regarded as derivable from a plane by a reversible transformation. If s and t are two variables which independently range over the intervals $a < t < b$, $c < s < d$ and $u(s, t)$, $v(s, t)$ and $w(s, t)$ are three functions of s and t which are defined (and continuous) in the intervals given for s and t, we can make a point of space correspond to each pair of values (s, t) by means of the equations

417

$x = u(s, t)$, $y = v(s, t)$, $z = w(s, t)$. The totality of all these points is called a (continuous) surface, and the three equations $x = u(s, t)$, $y = v(s, t)$, $z = w(s, t)$ are called a parametric representation of the surface. If in the above definition the intervals are bounded, the totality of points is called a surface-segment.

Example: If a_1, a_2, a_3, b_1, b_2, b_3, c_1, c_2, c_3 are any real numbers and s and t are two variables the functions

$$x = a_1 + a_2 s + a_3 t, \quad y = b_1 + b_2 s + b_3 t, \quad z = c_1 + c_2 s + c_3 t$$

for $-\infty < s < +\infty$ and $-\infty < t < +\infty$ represent a plane.

A sphere is a *closed surface*. Every set of points in space which can be obtained as the uniquely reversible and continuous image of a sphere is a closed surface.

The sphere with centre $O(x_m, y_m, z_m)$ and radius r has parametric representation

$$x = x_m + r \cos \lambda \cos \phi, \quad y = y_m + r \sin \lambda \cos \phi,$$

$$z = z_m + r \sin \phi;$$

where $0 \leq \lambda < 2\pi$ and $-\dfrac{\pi}{2} \leq \phi < \dfrac{\pi}{2}$.

Surfaces of the second order

A surface of the second order is represented by a functional equation of the form

$$F(x, y, z) = a_{11}x^2 + a_{22}y^2 + a_{33}z^2 + 2a_{12}xy + 2a_{13}xz$$
$$+ 2a_{23}yz + 2a_{14}x + 2a_{24}y + 2a_{34}z + a_{44} = 0.$$

The set of all surfaces of the second order can be divided into the following groups, with a characteristic form of equation for each.

1. *Ellipsoid* (Fig. 310)

$$\frac{x^2}{a^2} + \frac{y^2}{b^2} + \frac{z^2}{c^2} = 1.$$

Special cases:

(a) If $a^2 = b^2 = c^2 = R^2$, the equation becomes

$$x^2 + y^2 + z^2 = R^2,$$

i.e. the ellipsoid is a sphere.

(b) If $a^2 = b^2$, the equation becomes $\dfrac{x^2}{a^2} + \dfrac{y^2}{a^2} + \dfrac{z^2}{c^2} = 1$. This ellipsoid arises by rotation of the ellipse $\dfrac{x^2}{a^2} + \dfrac{z^2}{c^2} = 1$ about the z-axis, and is called, therefore, an ellipsoid of revolution.

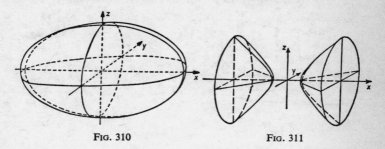

FIG. 310   FIG. 311

2. *Hyperboloid of two sheets* (Fig. 311).

$$\frac{x^2}{a^2} - \frac{y^2}{b^2} - \frac{z^2}{c^2} = 1.$$

Special case: if $b^2 = c^2$ we have a hyperboloid of revolution in two sheets,

$$\frac{x^2}{a^2} - \frac{y^2}{b^2} - \frac{z^2}{b^2} = 1.$$

This arises from the rotation of the hyperbola $\dfrac{x^2}{a^2} - \dfrac{y^2}{b^2} = 1$ about the x-axis.

3. *Hyperboloid of one sheet* (Fig. 312).

$$\frac{x^2}{a^2} + \frac{y^2}{b^2} - \frac{z^2}{c^2} = 1.$$

Special case: if $a^2 = b^2$ we have a hyperboloid of revolution in one sheet; it arises by rotation of the hyperbola $\dfrac{y^2}{b^2} - \dfrac{z^2}{c^2} = 1$ about the z-axis.

419

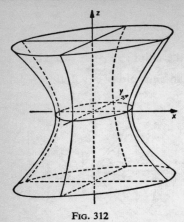

FIG. 312

FIG. 313

4. *Elliptical Double Cone* (Fig. 313).

$$\frac{x^2}{a^2} + \frac{y^2}{b^2} - \frac{z^2}{c^2} = 0.$$

The vertex of the cone is the origin, and the cone intersects the plane $z = c$ in the ellipse $\frac{x^2}{a^2} + \frac{y^2}{b^2} = 1$.

Special case: the right circular cone has the equation

$$\frac{x^2}{a^2} + \frac{y^2}{a^2} - \frac{z^2}{c^2} = 0.$$

5. *Elliptical Paraboloid* (Fig. 314).

$$\frac{x^2}{a^2} + \frac{y^2}{b^2} - 2z = 0.$$

Special case: If $a = b$, we have a paraboloid of revolution which arises by rotation of the parabola $y^2 = 2b^2z$ about the z-axis.

6. *Hyperbolic Paraboloid* (Fig. 315).

$$\frac{x^2}{a^2} - \frac{y^2}{b^2} - 2z = 0$$

(often referred to as a saddle-surface).

420

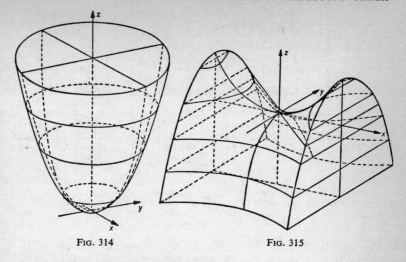

FIG. 314   FIG. 315

7. *Elliptical Cylinder* (Fig. 316).

$$\frac{x^2}{a^2} + \frac{y^2}{b^2} - 1 = 0.$$

Given an ellipse in the xy-plane, an elliptical cylinder is formed by the straight lines perpendicular to the xy-plane and passing through the ellipse. These lines are called generators or rulings of the cylinder.

Special case: the right circular cylinder whose generators run parallel to the z-axis, has the equation

$$\frac{x^2}{a^2} + \frac{y^2}{a^2} - 1 = 0.$$

8. *Hyperbolic Cylinder* (Fig. 317).

$$\frac{x^2}{a^2} - \frac{y^2}{b^2} - 1 = 0.$$

The generators of this cylinder are parallel to the z-axis and pass through the hyperbola $\frac{x^2}{a^2} - \frac{y^2}{b^2} = 1$ lying in the xy-plane.

421

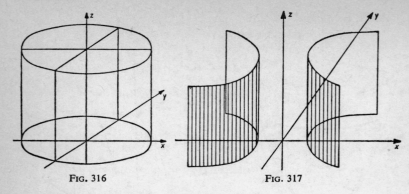

FIG. 316   FIG. 317

9. *Parabolic Cylinder* (Fig. 318).

$$x^2 - 2py = 0.$$

The generators of this cylinder pass through the parabola $x^2 - 2py = 0$ lying in the xy-plane, and are parallel to the z-axis.

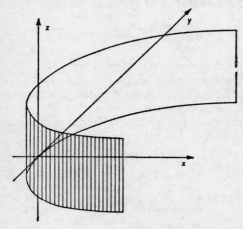

FIG. 318

Symmetry

The concept of symmetry includes various properties which can belong to plane or solid geometrical figures. We distinguish between (see individual articles)

A. In the plane:
    1. Axial symmetry
    2. *n*-fold symmetry
    3. Central symmetry (Point-symmetry)

B. In space:
    1. Symmetry with respect to a plane
    2. Symmetry with respect to a point (Central symmetry).

Symmetry, *n*-fold

n-fold symmetries are properties of special plane figures. A figure which is *n*-fold symmetric coincides with itself when rotated through an angle of $\dfrac{360°}{n}$ about a point, its *centre of symmetry*. *n* must be an integer.

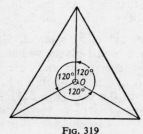

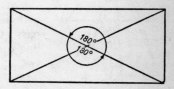

Fig. 319   Fig. 320

Example: 1. An equilateral triangle is *3-fold symmetric* with respect to its centroid, *O*. Thus if the triangle is rotated through 120°, 240° or 360° about *O* it becomes superposed on its original position (Fig. 319).

2. A parallelogram is *2-fold symmetric* about the point of intersection of its diagonals (Fig. 320). Rotations through 180° and through 360° produce superposition.

3. A regular *n*-agon is *n-fold symmetric* with respect to the centre of its circumcircle *O*. Rotations through the angles

$$\frac{360°}{n}, \frac{2 \cdot 360°}{n}, \frac{3 \cdot 360°}{n}, \ldots, \frac{(n-1) \cdot 360°}{n} \text{ and } \frac{n \cdot 360°}{n}$$

produce superposition.

n is the largest integer with the property that the figure is superposed on itself by rotation through $\dfrac{360°}{n}$. In such cases, rotations through angles $\dfrac{2 \cdot 360°}{n}$, $\dfrac{3 \cdot 360°}{n}$, ..., $\dfrac{(n-1)360°}{n}$ and $\dfrac{n}{n} \cdot 360°$ also produce superposition.

2-fold symmetric figures are also said to be centrally symmetric (see *Central symmetry*).

Symmetry with respect to a plane

Symmetry with respect to a plane E (the plane of symmetry) is a property which a solid geometrical figure may possess. The plane of symmetry E divides the figure into two halves such that the one part is obtained from the other by reflection in E.

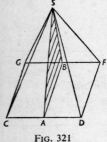

FIG. 321

Example: A square pyramid is symmetric with respect to each of the planes which pass through the vertex S and the line of intersection of the mid-points of two opposite sides of the base (Fig. 321).

Tangent

A tangent is a straight line which has a point in common (point of contact) with a given curve (of arbitrary form) and at this point has the same slope as the curve (see *Gradient, Circle*).

Tangent (tan)

The tangent function is a trigonometrical function. tan α is the ratio of the side opposite to the angle α to the side adjacent to α in a right-angled triangle (see *Trigonometry*):

$$\tan \alpha = \frac{\text{opposite side}}{\text{adjacent side}}.$$

Tangent hexagon

A tangent hexagon is a hexagon which circumscribes a circle or conic, its sides being tangents to the circle or conic (see *Brianchon's theorem*).

Tangent quadrilateral

A quadrilateral which possesses an inscribed circle is called a tangent quadrilateral. The four sides of the quadrilateral are tangents to the incircle. A quadrilateral is a tangent quadrilateral if and only if the sum of two opposite sides is equal to the sum of the other pair of opposite sides (Fig. 322). The isosceles kite-shaped quadrilateral, the rhombus and the square possess this property; in general isosceles trapeziums, parallelograms and rectangles do not.

$$a + c = b + d$$
$$a_2 = b_1 \qquad \underbrace{a_1 + a_2} + \underbrace{c_1 + c_2} = d_2 + \underbrace{b_1 + b_2} + d_1$$
$$b_2 = c_1$$
$$c_2 = d_1 \qquad a \quad + \quad c \quad = \quad b \quad + d$$
$$d_2 = a_1$$

Tangent theorem (geometry)

If a secant and a tangent of a circle intersect in a point P then the length of the tangent $\overline{PB}$ is the mean proportional (geometric mean) of the segments from P cut off by the circle on the secant.

$$\overline{PC} : \overline{PB} = \overline{PB} : \overline{PD} \quad \text{or} \quad (\overline{PB})^2 = \overline{PC} \cdot \overline{PD} \quad \text{(Fig. 323)}.$$

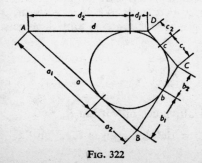

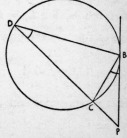

FIG. 322   FIG. 323

425

Tangent theorem (trigonometry)

The tangent theorem is a theorem of plane trigonometry. If a, b and c are the sides, and α, β and γ the angles of a triangle, then

$$\text{I. } \frac{a+b}{a-b} = \frac{\tan\dfrac{\alpha+\beta}{2}}{\tan\dfrac{\alpha-\beta}{2}} \qquad \text{II. } \frac{b+c}{b-c} = \frac{\tan\dfrac{\beta+\gamma}{2}}{\tan\dfrac{\beta-\gamma}{2}}$$

$$\text{III. } \frac{c+a}{c-a} = \frac{\tan\dfrac{\gamma+\alpha}{2}}{\tan\dfrac{\gamma-\alpha}{2}}.$$

Taylor's series

The Taylor series can be used to determine the development in power series of given functions. The Taylor series can be obtained from *Taylor's theorem*. By Taylor's theorem we can put

$$f(x) = f(a) + \frac{f'(a)}{1!}(x-a) + \frac{f''(a)}{2!}(x-a)^2 + \ldots$$

$$+ \frac{f^{(n)}(a)}{n!}(x-a)^n + R_n.$$

Taylor's formula gives $f(x)$ with increasing accuracy, the larger the n chosen, provided the remainder term R_n of the Taylor theorem for $f(x)$ at a fixed point $x = a$ tends to 0 as $n \to \infty$ (or, in symbols, $\lim_{n \to \infty} R_n = 0$). The given function $f(x)$ can then be represented by the power-series

$$f(x) = f(a) + \frac{x-a}{1!}f'(a) + \frac{f''(a)}{2!}(x-a)^2 + \ldots.$$

This power-series converges for all values of x if $\lim_{n \to \infty} R_n = 0$.

The Taylor series can be used to 'develop a given function $f(x)$ in powers of $(x - a)$'.

426

Putting $a = 0$ in the Taylor series we obtain as a special case the Maclaurin series:

$$f(x) = f(0) + \frac{f'(0)}{1!}\, x + \frac{f''(0)}{2!}\, x^2 + \frac{f'''(0)}{3!}\, x^3 + \ldots$$

Example: To develop $f(x) = e^x$ in powers of x (that is, with $a = 0$):

$$f(x) = e^x, \qquad f(0) = 1;$$

$$f'(x) = e^x, \qquad f'(0) = 1;$$

$$f''(x) = e^x, \qquad f''(0) = 1; \text{ and so on,}$$

so that

$$f(x) = 1 + \frac{1}{1!}\, x + \frac{1}{2!}\, x^2 + \frac{1}{3!}\, x^3 + \ldots$$

Taylor's theorem

Taylor's theorem concerns the error which appears if a function is approximated by an integral function of the nth degree.

$$f(x) = f(a) + \frac{f'(a)}{1!}\, (x - a) + \frac{f''(a)}{2!}\, (x - a)^2 + \ldots$$

$$+ \frac{f^{(n)}(a)}{n!}\, (x - a)^n + \frac{f^{(n+1)}(b)}{(n + 1)!}\, (x - a)^{n+1},$$

where $b = a + \theta(x - a)$ $(0 \leq \theta \leq 1)$ is a number between a and x, $f(x)$ the given function, and $f'(a), f''(a), \ldots, f^{(n)}(a)$, $f^{(n+1)}(a)$ the 1st, 2nd, $\ldots$, $(n + 1)$th derivatives of the given function at a. The term

$$R_n = \frac{f^{(n+1)}(b)}{(n + 1)!}\, (x - a)^{n+1}$$

is the *remainder term.*

Ten, powers of

Very large and very small numbers can be conveniently represented with the help of powers of ten. We have

$$10^1 = 10$$
$$10^2 = 100$$
$$10^3 = 1,000$$
$$10^4 = 10,000$$
$$10^5 = 100,000, \text{ and so on.}$$

The number 36,000,000,000 can be written briefly in the form

$$36,000,000,000 = 36 \times 10^9 = 3 \cdot 6 \times 10^{10} = 0 \cdot 36 \times 10^{11}.$$

In general the factor in front of the power of ten is taken to lie between 1 and 10. Powers of ten with negative exponents can be used to represent very small numbers. We have

$$10^{-1} = 0 \cdot 1 \quad = \frac{1}{10},$$

$$10^{-2} = 0 \cdot 01 \quad = \frac{1}{100},$$

$$10^{-3} = 0 \cdot 001 = \frac{1}{1,000}, \text{ and so on.}$$

Example of a small number:

Mass of the hydrogen atom: $1 \cdot 67 \times 10^{-24}$ gm.

Without using powers of ten this would have to be written: 0·000,000,000,000,000,000,000,001,67 gm.

Tetrahedron

A four-sided polyhedron. A regular tetrahedron is a regular three-sided pyramid in which the base-edges and side-edges are of equal length (see *Pyramid* and *Platonic solids*).

Thales, circle of (Thales of Miletus, probably 624–546 B.C.)

Theorem of Thales. If the vertex of an angle moves on a semi-circle, and the end-points of its arms remain at the end-points of the diameter, then the angle remains unaltered as a right angle. The semicircle or also the complete circle is referred to as the circle of Thales. The circumference angles on the diameter of a circle are right angles (see *Triangle*).

Third proportional

The solution of the proportional relation $b:a = a:x$ is referred to as the third proportional between the line-segments a and b. The third proportional is $x = \dfrac{a^2}{b}$ and can be constructed with the help of the first theorem on rays. By Fig. 324 we have:

$$\frac{\overline{SB}}{\overline{BA}} = \frac{b}{a} = \frac{\overline{SC}}{\overline{CD}} = \frac{a}{x}.$$

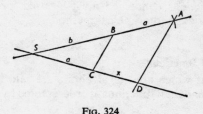

FIG. 324

Trace (trace-point, piercing point)

The point of intersection of a straight line and a plane is referred to as the trace of the line on the plane.

Trace-line

The line of intersection of two planes is referred to as a trace-line.

Transcendental curves

A curve is said to be transcendental if it is not an algebraic curve, *i.e.* if no algebraic equation can be found which represents the curve.

Transcendental curves are represented by *transcendental functions*.

Examples: Cycloid, Archimedes's spiral, logarithmic spiral, catenary, logarithmic curves, exponential curves, trigonometrical curves.

Transcendental equations

All non-algebraic equations are called transcendental. The simple transcendental equations either contain the unknown as an exponent (*exponential equations*) or the logarithm of the unknown (*logarithmic equations*) or a trigonometrical function of the unknown (*goniometric equations*).

No general procedure can be given for the solution of transcendental equations. Either the special properties of the transcendental functions concerned must be used, or one must fall back on numerical and graphical methods.

Transcendental functions

All functions which are not algebraic are said to be transcendental. Transcendental functions are represented by transcendenta. curves.

The transcendental functions used in elementary mathematics are

1. The exponential functions. The variable x occurs in the exponent, *e.g.* $y = a^x$, $y = e^x$, $y = e^{x^2}$.

2. The logarithmic functions (inverse functions of the exponential functions), *e.g.* $y = \log x$, $y = \ln x$, $y = \log (x^2 - 1)$.

3. The circular or trigonometric functions:

$$y = \sin x, y = \cos x, y = \tan x, y = \cot x, y = \sec x,$$

$$y = \operatorname{cosec} x.$$

4. The inverse trigonometric functions:

$$y = \sin^{-1} x, y = \cos^{-1} x, y = \tan^{-1} x, y = \cot^{-1} x,$$

$$y = \sec^{-1} x, y = \operatorname{cosec}^{-1} x.$$

5. The hyperbolic functions:

$$y = \sinh x, \ y = \cosh x, \ y = \tanh x, \ y = \coth x,$$
$$y = \operatorname{sech} x, \ y = \operatorname{cosech} x.$$

6. The inverse hyperbolic functions:

$$y = \sinh^{-1} x, \qquad y = \cosh^{-1} x,$$
$$y = \tanh^{-1} x, \qquad y = \coth^{-1} x,$$
$$y = \operatorname{sech}^{-1} x, \qquad y = \operatorname{cosech}^{-1} x.$$

Transcendental numbers

All *non-algebraic real numbers* (see *Algebraic numbers*) are called transcendental numbers, *e.g.* $e = 2 \cdot 718,281,828,459,045 \ldots$, $\pi = 3 \cdot 141,592,654 \ldots$. The existence of transcendental numbers was first proved by Joseph Liouville (1851). Georg Cantor showed (1874) that there are more transcendental than algebraic numbers; the set of all algebraic numbers is enumerable (like the integers), the set of transcendental numbers is not (see *Number*).

Transformation

A rule which associates with each point P of a space one or more points P' of the same space is said to be a transformation or mapping. The points P' are image points of P, and P is an inverse image point of P'.

See *Affine transformation*
   Area-preserving transformation
   Conformal transformation
   Continuous transformation
   Length-preserving transformation
   Linear transformation
   Perspective transformation
   Projective transformation
   Similarity transformation
   Single-valued transformation

Central perspective
Central projection
Parallel translation
Parallel projection
Reflection, affine
Reflection in a line
Reflection in a plane
Reflection in a point
Rigid motion
Rotation
Shear

431

Transversal

A straight line which intersects the sides of a triangle or their extensions is called a transversal of the triangle. If it passes through a vertex of the triangle it is called a *vertex-transversal*.

Trapezium

A quadrilateral with two sides parallel is called a trapezium. If the two non-parallel sides of the trapezium are equal, it is said to be isosceles (for further properties, see *Quadrilateral*).

Triangle

Nomenclature, numerical relations between sides and angles.

Definition and nomenclature

If three points in a plane which are not collinear are joined in pairs by straight-line segments, we obtain a triangle (Fig. 325). The three given points are called *vertices* (corners) of the triangle. The vertices of a triangle are usually denoted by capital letters of the Roman alphabet: A, B, C. The order of labelling is arbitrary, but the vertices are usually labelled alphabetically in anti-clockwise order (Fig. 326). The three-line-segments joining vertices are called the *sides* of the triangle. The sides of the triangle are denoted by small letters of the Roman alphabet a, b, c in such a way that the side labelled a lies opposite the vertex A, the side b opposite the vertex B, and the side c opposite the vertex C.

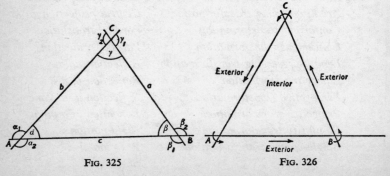

FIG. 325   FIG. 326

Each pair of neighbouring sides of a triangle form the arms of an *interior angle* of the triangle. The interior angles of the triangle are usually denoted by the small Greek letters α, β, γ, the angle α being at the vertex A, the angle β at the vertex B and the angle γ at the vertex C. If the sides of the triangle are extended beyond the vertices there are formed at each vertex three further angles. One of these three new angles is vertically opposite to the interior angle at the vertex. Both of the other angles are angles adjacent to the interior angle of the triangle, and are called *exterior angles* of the triangle. Each vertex has two exterior angles, equal to and vertically opposite each other. The exterior angles at the vertex A can be denoted by α_1 and α_2, at the vertex B by β_1 and β_2, and at the vertex C by γ_1 and γ_2. Thus the same letters are used as for the interior angles, but with suffixes, although obviously other labellings are possible. If we proceed round the triangle in the anti-clockwise sense then the *interior* of the triangle lies to our left and the *exterior* to our right (Fig. 326).

Numerical relations between the sides of a triangle

Two sides of a triangle are together always longer than the third:

$$a + b > c, \quad (\text{'>' means } greater\ than)$$
$$b + c > a,$$
$$c + a > b.$$

Numerical relations between the angles of a triangle

1. The sum of the interior angles of a triangle is 180°:

$$\alpha + \beta + \gamma = 180° \text{ (Fig. 327).}$$

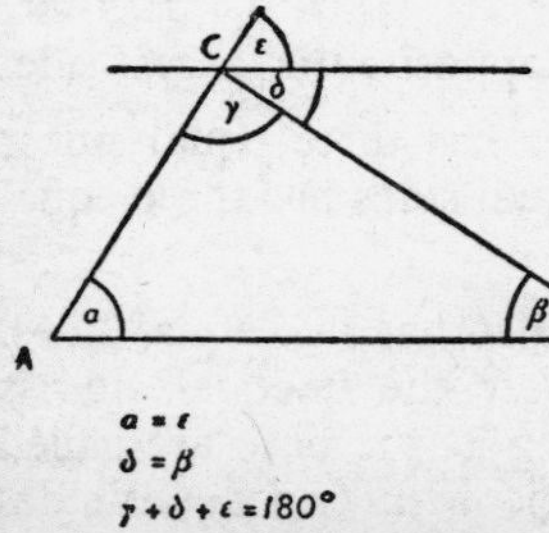

$$a = \epsilon$$
$$\delta = \beta$$
$$\gamma + \delta + \epsilon = 180°$$

Fig. 327

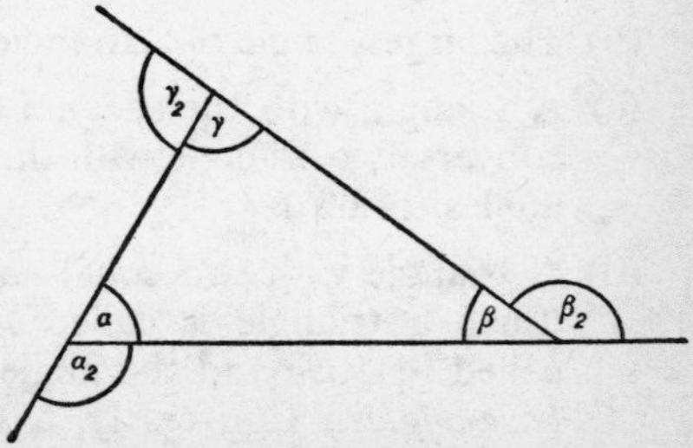

Fig. 328

433

2. (Consequences of 1.) Two angles of a triangle determine the third:

$$\gamma = 180° - (\alpha + \beta).$$

A triangle can possess at most one right angle (right-angled triangle). A triangle can possess at most one obtuse angle (obtuse-angled triangle). A triangle always has two acute angles.

3. Every exterior angle of a triangle is equal to the sum of the two interior angles not adjacent to it (Fig. 327).

4. The sum of the exterior angles of a triangle is 360°:

$$\alpha_2 + \beta_2 + \gamma_2 = 360° \text{ (Fig. 328).}$$

For $\alpha + \alpha_2 + \beta + \beta_2 + \gamma + \gamma_2 = 3 \times 180°,$

that is, $\alpha + \beta + \gamma + \alpha_2 + \beta_2 + \gamma_2 = 540°,$

or $180° + \alpha_2 + \beta_2 + \gamma_2 = 540°,$

so that $\alpha_2 + \beta_2 + \gamma_2 = 360°.$

Numerical relations between the sides of a triangle and its angles

1. The larger of two sides lies opposite the larger angle.
   If $a > b$ then $\alpha > \beta$.

2. Conversely, the larger of two angles lies opposite the larger side.
   If $\alpha > \beta$ then $a > b$.

3. (Following from 1. and 2.)

(a) The largest side of a triangle lies opposite the largest angle.

(b) The largest angle of a triangle lies opposite the largest side.

(c) A triangle with three equal angles has three equal sides; conversely a triangle with three equal sides has three equal angles (of 60°).

(d) A triangle with two equal angles also has two equal sides. (Such a triangle is called *isosceles*; the unequal side is called its *base* and the angles lying at the base are called *base-angles*.) Conversely, a triangle with two equal sides has two equal angles (the base-angles).

(e) In obtuse-angled triangles the largest side lies opposite the obtuse angle.

(f) In a right-angled triangle the side opposite the right angle is called the *hypotenuse*. The hypotenuse is the largest side.

(g) The angles adjacent to the largest side of a triangle must be acute.

Classification of triangles

(a) *Classification according to size of angles*

Acute-angled triangles	Triangles with three acute angles are called acute-angled (Fig. 329).
Right-angled triangles	Triangles with a right angle are called right-angled. Both the other angles must be acute (Fig. 330).

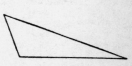

FIG. 329   FIG. 330   FIG. 331

Obtuse-angled triangles	Triangles with an obtuse angle are called obtuse-angled. Both the other angles must be acute (Fig. 331).

(b) *Classification according to size of sides*

Equilateral triangles	Triangles with three equal sides are called equilateral (Fig. 332).
Isosceles triangles	Triangles with two equal sides are called isosceles (Fig. 333).
Scalene triangles	Triangles with three unequal sides are called scalene (Fig. 334).

435

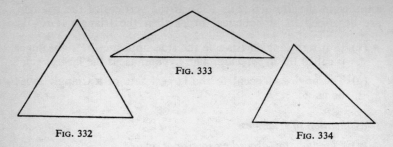

FIG. 332   FIG. 333   FIG. 334

(c) *Classification according to number of axes of symmetry*

No axis of symmetry — Triangles with no axis of symmetry are scalene (Fig. 335).

One axis of symmetry — Triangles with one axis of symmetry are isosceles (Fig. 336).

More than one axis of symmetry — Triangles with two axes of symmetry also have a third; such triangles are equilateral (Fig. 337).

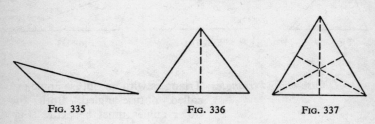

FIG. 335   FIG. 336   FIG. 337

Construction given sides and angles; congruence theorems

(a) *Three sides given* (abbreviation: *SSS*). If one side c is given, the two vertices A and B are determined. We know C is at distance b from A and a from B. Consequently the vertex C lies on the circle with radius b and centre A, and also on the circle with radius a and centre B. Since $a + b > c$ and $b + c > a$ these circles have two points of intersection, C_1 and C_2, and either will serve as the third vertex C of the triangle in question. The triangles ABC_1 and ABC_2 are the mirror-images of one another in the line $\overline{AB}$ (Fig. 338). If the vertices of the triangle are described in alphabetical order then the triangle ABC_1 is described in the anti-clockwise sense and the triangle ABC_2 in the clockwise sense. The two triangles are differently 'orientated'.

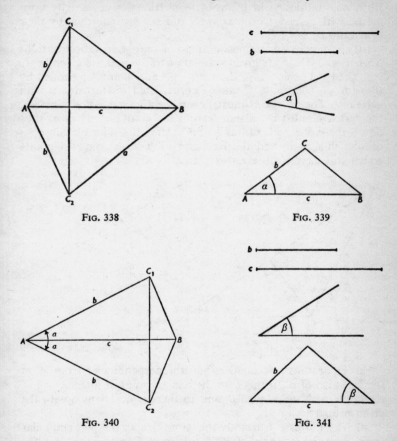

FIG. 338   FIG. 339

FIG. 340   FIG. 341

(b) Two sides and an angle given

(i) Two sides and their included angle given (abbreviation: SAS). If the sides given are b and c, the included angle is α. The side c determines the positions of the vertices A and B. The angle

α is now brought up to the side $\overline{AB}$ and given vertex A. The side b is drawn on the free arm of α. In this way the vertex C is also fixed (Fig. 339). In the drawing of the angle α there are two possibilities, since it can be drawn on either side of $\overline{AB}$ (Fig. 340). Both possibilities yield triangles. The triangles are axially symmetric with respect to the axis AB and are distinguished by their orientations.

(ii) Two sides and opposite angle of one given (abbreviation: *SSA*, Fig. 341). If the given sides are b and c and the given angle is β, then the positions of the vertices A and B are determined by the side c. The angle β can be constructed on the side c with vertex B. The vertex C must lie on the free arm of β; further, the vertex C must be distant b from the point A, and must thus lie on the circle with radius b and centre A. Under certain conditions this circle and the free arm of β have common points which will serve for the vertex C in question.

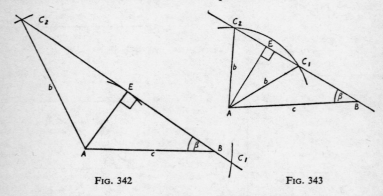

Fig. 342   Fig. 343

(α) The radius b is smaller than the perpendicular from A on the free arm of β. In this case there is no point of intersection of the circle with the arm of β, and so there is no triangle with the given properties.

(β) The radius b is exactly the same size as the perpendicular from A on the free arm of B. In this case, E (see Fig. 342) is the third vertex of the triangle. The triangle has a right angle at E.

(γ) The radius b is longer than the perpendicular from A on to the free arm of β, but smaller than c. The circle cuts the free arm of β in two points C_1 and C_2, and so in this case there are two different triangles ABC_1 and ABC_2 distinguished by the size of a (Fig. 343).

(δ) The radius b is longer than c. In this case again, the circle has two intersections with the straight line which has the direction of the free arm of β. These two points of intersection are separated by B. Only one point of intersection $C_2 = C$ comes into question, since the triangle must have the angle β. In this case there is exactly one triangle of the required type (Fig. 342).

(ε) $b = c$. The point of intersection differing from B gives a unique point C.

(c) *One side and two angles given*

(i) One side and the two angles adjacent to it given (abbreviation: *ASA*). If the side c with vertices A and B is given, then an

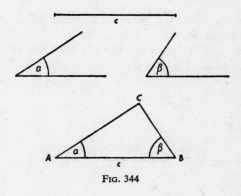

Fig. 344

angle which lies on this side yields a geometrical locus on which the third vertex must lie. The other adjacent angle yields a further locus for the vertex C. Thus the intersection of the two free arms of the angles is the third vertex. Provided the sum of the two given angles is less than 180°, there is always a point of intersection C (Fig. 344).

(ii) One side, one adjacent angle and the opposite angle given (abbreviation: *SAA*, Fig. 345). The third angle of the triangle can be calculated from the fact that the sum of the interior angles of the triangle must be 180° (Fig. 346). The sum of the two given angles must be less than 180°. When this is the case the triangle can be constructed as in (a) above (Fig. 347).

But the construction can also follow Fig. 345. The side c with end-points A and B is fixed, and the angle α is drawn adjacent to c and with vertex A. An arbitrary point C_1 is chosen on the free arm of α, and the angle γ is constructed with vertex C_1

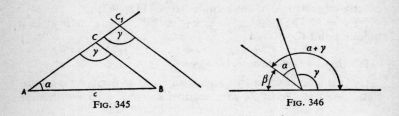

FIG. 345   FIG. 346

adjacent to the line $\overline{AC_1}$. Now the free arm of the angle γ does not pass through B, and so a line parallel to the free arm of γ is constructed so as to pass through B. This line cuts $\overline{AC_1}$ in the third vertex of the triangle, C.

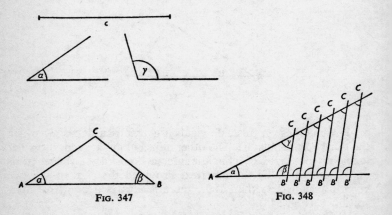

FIG. 347   FIG. 348

(d) *Three angles given* (abbreviation: *AAA*). If two angles of the triangle are given, say α and β, the third is determined by equation $\gamma = 180° - (\alpha + \beta)$. What we know of the three angles is therefore equivalent to a knowledge of only two independent elements. If α and β are given, let α be first laid out. An arbitrary point B can now be taken on one arm of α, and the angle β be constructed adjacent to this arm and with B as vertex. In this way arbitrarily many triangles can be constructed (Fig. 348). All such triangles possess the three given angles. As we see, the three angles are not sufficient to determine completely the construction of a triangle; for this at least one side must be given.

Summary: Three independent elements must be given for the construction of a triangle from sides and angles. The four principal cases which lead to unique solutions are set out below:

		Given:	Conditions:
1.	SSS	3 sides, a, b, c	$a + b > c$, $b + c > a$
2.	SAS	2 sides and the included angle, e.g. b, c, α.	$\alpha < 180°$
3.	SSA	2 sides and an opposite angle, e.g. b, c, β.	$\beta < 180°$ $b > c$ 1 triangle $b = c$ 1 triangle $\begin{cases} b < c, \ b > l, \text{ 2 triangles } (l \\ \text{the perpendicular from } A \\ \text{on the arm of } \beta) \end{cases}$ $b < c$, $b = l$ 1 triangle $b < c$, $b < l$ no triangle
4 (a)	ASA	1 side and 2 angles (adjacent angles), e.g. c, α, β.	$\alpha + \beta < 180°$
(b)	SAA	1 side, 1 adjacent and 1 opposite angle, e.g. c, α, γ.	$\alpha + \gamma < 180°$

Congruence of triangles

A triangle ABC is said to be congruent to a triangle $A_1B_1C_1$ if corresponding sides and angles can be made to coincide; if this is so we have

$$\overline{AB} = \overline{A_1B_1}, \ \overline{AC} = \overline{A_1C_1}, \ \overline{BC} = \overline{B_1C_1},$$

$$\alpha = \angle \ CAB = \alpha_1 = \angle \ C_1A_1B_1,$$

$$\beta = \angle \ ABC = \beta_1 = \angle \ A_1B_1C_1,$$

$$\gamma = \angle \ BCA = \gamma_1 = \angle \ B_1C_1A_1.$$

Symbolically: $\triangle \ ABC \cong \triangle \ A_1B_1C_1$; read: 'triangle ABC congruent to triangle $A_1B_1C_1$.'

(Congruent triangles coincide in shape and size.)

We have the following congruence theorems for triangles:

First congruence theorem for triangles

The triangle ABC is congruent to the triangle $A_1B_1C_1$ if two corresponding sides and their included angle coincide:

$$\triangle \ ABC \cong \triangle \ A_1B_1C_1 \ \text{if} \ \overline{AB} = \overline{A_1B_1}, \ \overline{AC} = \overline{A_1C_1}, \ \text{and} \ \alpha = \alpha_1.$$

Second congruence theorem for triangles

The triangle ABC is congruent to the triangle $A_1B_1C_1$ if one side and its two adjacent angles coincide:

$$\triangle \ ABC \cong \triangle \ A_1B_1C_1 \ \text{if} \ \overline{AB} = \overline{A_1B_1}, \ \alpha = \alpha_1 \ \text{and} \ \beta = \beta_1.$$

The same is true if one side, one adjacent and one opposite angle coincide:

$$\triangle \ ABC \cong \triangle A_1B_1C_1 \ \text{if} \ \overline{AB} = \overline{A_1B_1}, \ \alpha = \alpha_1 \ \text{and} \ \gamma = \gamma_1.$$

Third congruence theorem for triangles

If for two triangles ABC and $A_1B_1C_1$ all three pairs of corresponding sides coincide, then the triangles are congruent.

$$\triangle \ ABC \cong \triangle \ A_1B_1C_1 \ \text{if} \ \overline{AB} = \overline{A_1B_1}, \ \overline{AC} = \overline{A_1C_1} \ \text{and} \ \overline{BC} = \overline{B_1C_1}.$$

Fourth congruence theorem for triangles

If for two triangles ABC and $A_1B_1C_1$ two corresponding sides and the angle which lies opposite the larger of the two sides coincide, then the triangles are congruent.

$\triangle ABC \cong \triangle A_1B_1C_1$ if $\overline{AB} = \overline{A_1B_1}$, $\overline{AC} = \overline{A_1C_1}$ and (if $\overline{AC} > \overline{AB}$) $\beta = \beta_1$.

Transversals of a triangle

A straight line which cuts the sides of a triangle or their extensions is called a transversal. If the transversal passes through a vertex it is called a vertex-transversal.

Theorem of *Menelaos* (1st century A.D., Alexandria). Every

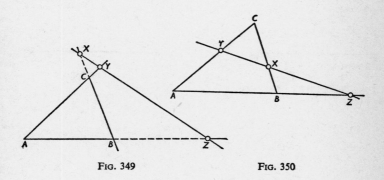

FIG. 349   FIG. 350

transversal cuts the sides of a triangle in such a way that the product of the three resulting *division-ratios* (see above)—taken in the same sense—is 1 (Figs. 349 and 350):

$$\frac{\overline{AZ}}{\overline{BZ}} \cdot \frac{\overline{BX}}{\overline{CX}} \cdot \frac{\overline{CY}}{\overline{AY}} = 1.$$

The proof is by means of ray-theorems.

Theorem of *Ceva* (1647–1736). Three concurrent vertex-transversals of a triangle cut the sides of the triangle in such a way that the product of three non-adjacent directed segments of sides equals the product of the three other segments (Figs. 351, 352):

$$\overline{AY}\,.\,\overline{BZ}\,.\,\overline{CX} = \overline{AZ}\,.\,\overline{BX}\,.\,\overline{CY}.$$

The proof is by means of the sine-theorem.

Theorem on the joins of the mid-points of sides of a triangle

If a line is drawn through the mid-point of one side of a triangle, parallel to a second, then it passes through the mid-point of the

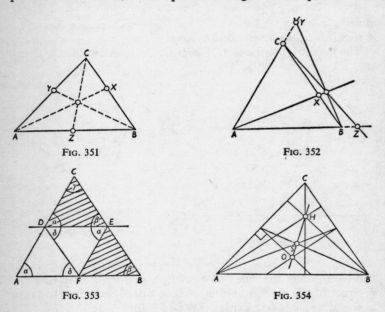

FIG. 351   FIG. 352

FIG. 353   FIG. 354

third side, and is half the length of the second side. If the mid-points of two sides of a triangle are joined by a straight line, then this line is parallel to the third side of the triangle and is half its length (Fig. 353). (Proof is by means of congruent triangles.)

Euler's line

In any triangle the orthocentre H (the point of intersection of altitudes), the centroid S (the point of intersection of lines joining vertices to mid-points of opposite sides), and the circumcentre O lie on a straight line, Euler's line, and we have $\overline{HS}:\overline{SO} = 2:1$ (Fig. 354).

Mid-perpendiculars of a triangle

A mid-perpendicular of a triangle is a straight line which is perpendicular to one side of the triangle and passes through the mid-point of that side. A triangle has three mid-perpendiculars m_a, m_b and m_c, one for each side (Fig. 355). The mid-perpendiculars of a triangle are concurrent in the centre of the circumscribed circle of the triangle (see below).

Bisectors of the sides of a triangle

The bisector of a side of a triangle is the line joining the mid-point of a side to the opposite vertex. A triangle possesses three side-bisectors, s_a, s_b, s_c (Fig. 356).

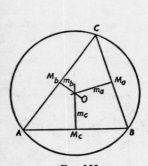

Fig. 355

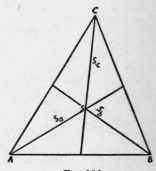

Fig. 356

The three side-bisectors of a triangle are concurrent in a point S, the centroid of the triangle; the side-bisectors are therefore also called centroid-lines. The centroid divides the side-bisectors in the ratio $2:1$.

Altitudes of a triangle

An altitude of a triangle is perpendicular to a side of the triangle and passes through the vertex of the triangle opposite to that side. An altitude need not necessarily lie inside the triangle. Every triangle has three altitudes, which are concurrent (see Figs. 357-9). In an acute-angled triangle the altitudes and their point of intersection lie inside the triangle (Fig. 357). In obtuse-

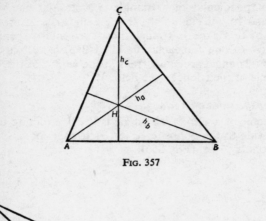

FIG. 357

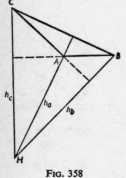

FIG. 358

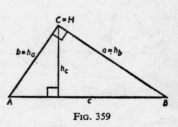

FIG. 359

angled triangles, two altitudes lie outside the triangle, and accordingly the point of intersection of altitudes also lies outside (Fig. 358). In right-angled triangles the altitudes belonging to the shorter sides coincide with those sides, and only the altitude h_c, belonging to the hypotenuse, lies within the triangle. In a right-angled triangle the point of intersection of altitudes is the vertex C of the right angle (Fig. 359).

446

Angle-bisectors of a triangle

The angle-bisectors of a triangle are the lines joining vertices to the opposite sides and bisecting the angles at the vertices. A triangle possesses three angle-bisectors, w_α, w_β, w_γ, one for each angle. The angle-bisectors of a triangle are concurrent in a point O which is the centre of the *inscribed circle* (see below) of the

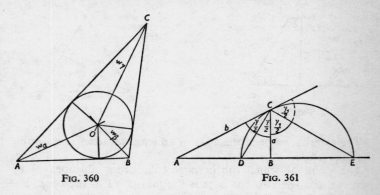

FIG. 360   FIG. 361

triangle (Fig. 360). An angle-bisector divides the opposite side in the ratio of the sides adjacent to the angle bisected (Fig. 361):

$$\frac{\overline{DA}}{\overline{DB}} = \frac{b}{a}.$$

The bisector of an exterior angle of a triangle divides the opposite side externally in the ratio of adjacent sides (see *Circle of Apollonius*) Fig. 361:

$$\frac{\overline{EA}}{\overline{EB}} = \frac{b}{a}.$$

The bisectors of an angle of a triangle and its exterior angle divide the opposite side harmonically (see *Harmonic ratio*).

Isosceles triangles, equilateral triangles, right-angled triangles

The isosceles triangle. A triangle with two sides of equal length is called isosceles. The unequal side is called the base of the

447

triangle. The vertex opposite it is called the apex of the triangle. The angles adjacent to the base are called base-angles. The perpendicular from the apex onto the base is called the axis of the triangle (Fig. 362). The base-angles are equal.

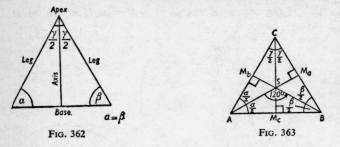

FIG. 362

FIG. 363

The external angle at the apex of an isosceles triangle is double the base-angle.

The point at which the perpendicular from the apex of an isosceles triangle cuts the base is the mid-point of the base. The perpendicular itself is the axis of symmetry of the triangle, it

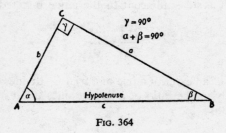

FIG. 364

bisects the angle at the apex, is the altitude associated with the base, the mid-perpendicular of the base, and its side-bisector. The perpendicular from the apex of an isosceles triangle onto the base divides the triangle into two congruent right-angled triangles.

The equilateral triangle. A triangle with three equal sides is called equilateral (Fig. 363). The interior angles of an equilateral triangle are all 60°, the exterior angles all 120°. The foot of the perpendicular from one vertex of an equilateral triangle onto the

448

opposite side is the mid-point of that side. The perpendicular is an axis of symmetry of the triangle and divides the triangle into two right-angled triangles. The perpendicular from one vertex onto the opposite side bisects the angle at the vertex and is side-bisector, altitude and mid-perpendicular of the opposite side. An equilateral triangle possesses three axes of symmetry, *viz.* the angle-bisectors of the three interior angles of the triangle. An equilateral triangle is centrally-symmetrical with respect to the point of intersection S of the three axes of symmetry ($=$ angle-bisectors) with angle of rotation 120° (*i.e.* a rotation of the triangle about S through an angle of 120° brings it into coincidence with itself).

The right-angled triangle. A triangle with one right angle is called a right-angled triangle (Fig. 364). The side of the triangle which lies opposite the right angle is called the hypotenuse. The

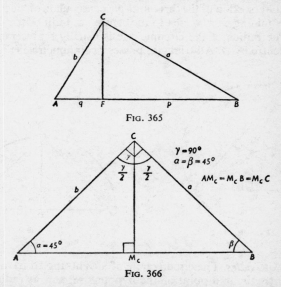

FIG. 365

FIG. 366

hypotenuse is always the largest side of a right-angled triangle. Since one angle of a right-angled triangle is 90° the remaining angles must add up to 90°, *i.e.* are complementary angles (Fig. 364). The perpendicular $\overline{CF}$ from the vertex C of the right angle divides the hypotenuse of the right-angled triangle into two parts p and q which are called the projections of the two shorter sides on the hypotenuse (Fig. 365).

The right-angled isosceles triangle. A triangle with one right angle and two equal sides is called right-angled isosceles. The angle at the vertex must be the right angle (Fig. 366). The foot, M_c, of the perpendicular from the apex onto the hypotenuse of the triangle bisects the hypotenuse. The perpendicular is half the length of the hypotenuse; it divides the triangle into two further right-angled isosceles triangles (Fig. 366).

Triangle and circle

1. *The circumcircle.* A circle which passes through the three vertices of a triangle is called the circumscribed circle or circumcircle of the triangle. The mid-point of the circumcircle is the point of intersection of the three mid-perpendiculars of the triangle. The lines joining each vertex to the centre are radii of the circumcircle. The radius of the circumcircle is usually represented by r and its centre by O. All triangles possess a circumcircle (Fig. 367).

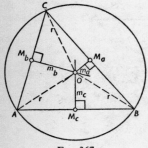

FIG. 367

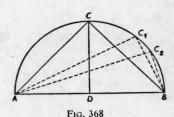

FIG. 368

Circle of Thales. The circumcircle of a right-angled triangle has as its centre the mid-point of the hypotenuse, and as radius half the length of the hypotenuse. It is called the *circle of Thales* (Thales of Miletus, *c*. 600 B.C.). The circle of Thales (half-circle of Thales) is the locus of points which are the vertices of right-angled triangles with the same hypotenuse c (Fig. 368).

All points C, C_1, C_2, etc., on the circle, taken together with the base, form right-angled triangles with a right angle at C, C_1, C_2, etc.

Proof: Since D is the centre of the circumcircle, $\overline{AD} = \overline{DB} = \overline{DC_1}$; since ADC_1, BDC_1, are isosceles triangles, $\alpha = \gamma_1$ and $\gamma_2 = \beta$; since δ_1 is an external angle of triangle BDC, $\delta_1 = \gamma_2 + \beta$, and similarly $\delta_2 = \alpha + \gamma_1$. That is, $\delta_1 = 2\gamma_2$ and $\delta_2 = 2\gamma_1$. Therefore, $\frac{1}{2}(\delta_1 + \delta_2) = \gamma_1 + \gamma_2$. But $\delta_1 + \delta_2$ equals two right angles, and so $\gamma_1 + \gamma_2$ equals one right angle, as required (Fig. 369).

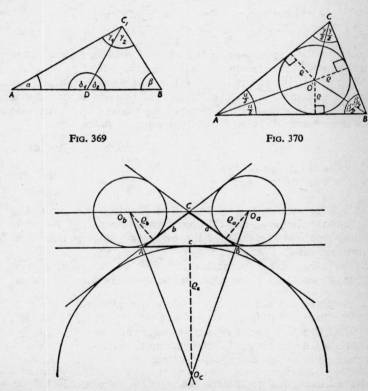

FIG. 369   FIG. 370

FIG. 371

2. *The incircle*. A circle is said to be inscribed in a triangle, or to be in the incircle of a triangle, if it touches all three sides of the triangle. The centre O' of the incircle is the intersection of the three angle-bisectors of the triangle. Each perpendicular from

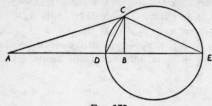

Fig. 372

the centre O' onto a side of the triangle yields a radius of the incircle, which is generally denoted by ρ (Fig. 370).

3. *The escribed circles* (Fig. 371). A circle which touches one side of a triangle and the extensions of the two other sides is called an ecircle or escribed circle of the triangle. Every triangle has three escribed circles. Their designation is as follows:

		Centre	Radius
Circle touches on the outside of the side:	a	O_a	ρ_a
	b	O_b	ρ_b
	c	O_c	ρ_c

Circle of Apollonius (Apollonius of Perga, *c*. 200 B.C.). The circle of Apollonius is a circle which serves to construct a triangle if one side and the ratio of the other two sides is given (see *Harmonic ratio*), Fig. 372.

Nine-point circle (Feuerbach's circle (Fig. 373)). The nine-point circle is a circle on whose perimeter lie the following nine points:

1. The three feet of the altitudes of the triangle H_a, H_b, H_c;
2. The three mid-points of the sides of the triangle M_a, M_b, M_c;
3. The three mid-points of the line-segments between the vertices of the triangle and the intersection of the altitudes (orthocentre) A_1, B_1, C_1.

The radius is equal to half the radius of the circumscribed circle. The centre is the mid-point of the line $\overline{OH}$ (O = centre of the circumscribed circle; $H =$ orthocentre of the triangle; $S =$ centroid) and forms with H, S and O four harmonic points. The nine-point circle touches the incircle and the three escribed circles.

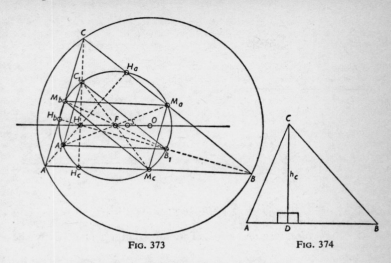

FIG. 373   FIG. 374

Construction of a triangle from given information

For the construction of a triangle from given information about sides and angles, see above (Fig. 374).

Individual problems

1. *Altitudes given.* An altitude divides a triangle into two right-angled triangles, and these triangles can be used to construct the required triangle.

2. *Bisectors of sides given.* The given bisectors form with the

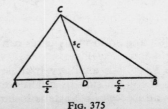

FIG. 375

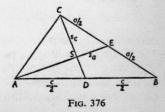

FIG. 376

halves of the associated sides sub-triangles which can serve for the construction of the complete triangle (Fig. 375). The sub-triangle which has as one vertex the centroid of the triangle can

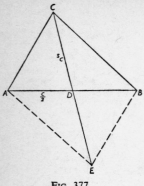

FIG. 377

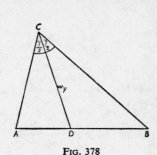

FIG. 378

also be used (Fig. 376). A parallelogram can often be used as an auxiliary figure (Fig. 377).

3. *Angle-bisectors are given.* The sub-triangles created by the

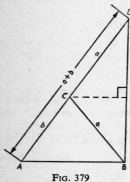

FIG. 379

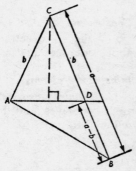

FIG. 380

angle-bisectors can be used (Fig. 378), and so in many cases can the circle of Apollonius (see *Triangle* and *Circle*).

4. *Sum or difference of two sides given.* An auxiliary triangle can be used with one side equal to the given sum or difference (Figs. 379 and 380). In the one case an isosceles triangle is to be

cut off from this triangle; in the other case an isosceles triangle is to be added.

5. *Sum of two angles given.* Note here that an exterior angle of a triangle is always equal to the sum of the non-adjacent interior angles (Fig. 381).

6. *Side and opposite angle given.* In these cases the opposite

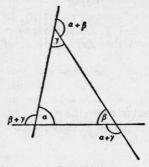

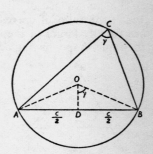

FIG. 381

FIG. 382

angle can be treated as circumference angle in a circle which has the side as chord. The sub-triangle AOB can be constructed by using the centre-angle (= double the circumference angle) and the given side (Fig. 382).

7. *Ratio of sides and an angle given.* Construction of a triangle by *similarity-method*. The shape of a triangle is determined by two ratios of pairs of sides, by two angles, or by one ratio of sides and an angle. If one of the above conditions is given for the construction of a triangle a triangle can first be constructed which is similar to the required triangle. For the construction of the triangle itself another linear measurement is then needed (Fig. 383).

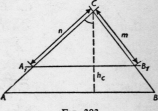

FIG. 383

Similarity of triangles

Two triangles $A_1B_1C_1$ and $A_2B_2C_2$ with sides $a_1b_1c_1$ and $a_2b_2c_2$ are called similar if their angles and *ratios* of corresponding sides coincide. That is, the statement 'two triangles are similar' implies the following six relations:

$$\alpha_1 = \alpha_2, \ \beta_1 = \beta_2, \ \gamma_1 = \gamma_2,$$
$$a_1 : b_1 = a_2 : b_2, \ b_1 : c_1 = b_2 : c_2 \text{ and } c_1 : a_1 = c_2 : a_2.$$

Symbolically: $A_1B_1C_1 \sim A_2B_2C_2$. Read: triangle $A_1B_1C_1$ similar to triangle $A_2B_2C_2$.

The congruence of triangles is a special case of similarity, in which the ratio of corresponding sides is 1:1, *i.e.* the triangles are equally large. In the case of similarity they need only be of the same shape, having equal angles.

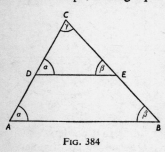

FIG. 384

Theorems concerning the similarity of triangles. If a line is drawn parallel to one side of a triangle within that triangle, the smaller triangle thus cut off is similar to the complete triangle.

Proof: Fig. 384. Since $\overline{DE}$ is parallel to $\overline{AB}$ the angles at A and D are step angles and so are equal, as are the angles at B and E. The triangles ABC and DEC therefore have equal angles. Again, since $\overline{DE}$ is parallel to $\overline{AB}$, by the first and second ray theorems (see below) applied to the double ray with vertex C:

$$\overline{CA} : \overline{CD} = \overline{CB} : \overline{CE},$$

so that

$$\overline{CA} : \overline{CB} = \overline{CD} : \overline{CE};$$

similarly

$$\overline{CA} : \overline{CD} = \overline{AB} : \overline{DE},$$

and also

$$\overline{CB} : \overline{CE} = \overline{AB} : \overline{DE},$$

so that

$$\overline{CA} : \overline{AB} = \overline{CD} : \overline{DE},$$

and

$$\overline{CD} : \overline{AB} = \overline{CE} : \overline{DE}.$$

The triangles ABC and DEC therefore coincide in respect of angles and ratios of sides and so are similar.

First Similarity Theorem. Two triangles $A_1B_1C_1$ and $A_2B_2C_2$ are similar if they coincide in respect of two angles. That is,

$$\triangle A_1B_1C_1 \sim \triangle A_2B_2C_2, \text{ if } \alpha_1 = \alpha_2 \text{ and } \beta_1 = \beta_2.$$

Proof: Fig. 385. Since the sum of the angles of a triangle is 180° the angles γ_1 and γ_2 must also coincide.

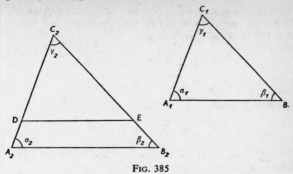

FIG. 385

Mark off now the segments $\overline{C_2D}$ and $\overline{C_2E}$ on $\overline{C_2A_2}$ and $\overline{C_2B_2}$ such that $\overline{C_2D} = \overline{C_1A_1}$ and $\overline{C_2E} = \overline{C_1B_1}$. The triangles $A_1B_1C_1$ and DEC_2 are congruent, and to establish the similarity of the triangles $A_1B_1C_1$ and $A_2B_2C_2$ we need only verify that the triangles $A_2B_2C_2$ and DEC_2 are similar. This follows immediately from the last result, since $\overline{DE}$ is parallel to $\overline{A_2B_2}$.

Second Similarity Theorem. Two triangles $A_1B_1C_1$ and $A_2B_2C_2$ are similar if they coincide in respect of the ratio of two sides and the angle included by these sides. That is,

$$\triangle A_1B_1C_1 \sim \triangle A_2B_2C_2 \text{ if } \overline{A_1C_1}:\overline{A_1B_1} = \overline{A_2C_2}:\overline{A_2B_2} \text{ and } \alpha_1 = \alpha_2.$$

Proof: Fig. 386. Given: $\alpha_1 = \alpha_2$, $\overline{A_1C_1}:\overline{A_1B_1} = \overline{A_2C_2}:\overline{A_2B_2}$.

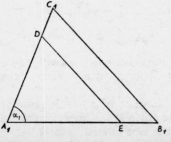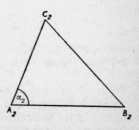

FIG. 386

457

Mark off on the side $\overline{A_1B_1}$ the segment $\overline{A_1E} = \overline{A_2B_2}$ and on the side $\overline{A_1C_1}$ the segment $\overline{A_1D} = \overline{A_2C_2}$. The triangle A_1ED is congruent to the triangle $A_2B_2C_2$ (2 sides and included angle coincidence), and we need only verify the similarity of the triangles $A_1B_1C_1$ and A_1ED. We are given

$$\overline{A_1C_1} : \overline{A_1B_1} = \overline{A_2C_2} : \overline{A_2B_2},$$

so that
$$\overline{A_1C_1} : \overline{A_2C_2} = \overline{A_1B_1} : \overline{A_2B_2},$$

and so by construction

$$\overline{A_1C_1} : \overline{A_1D} = \overline{A_1B_1} : \overline{A_1E}.$$

Therefore, by the converse of the first theorem on rays, $\overline{DE}$ is parallel to $\overline{C_1B_1}$, and so, as in the first similarity theorem, triangle A_1ED is similar to triangle $A_1B_1C_1$.

Third Similarity Theorem. Two triangles $A_1B_1C_1$ and $A_2B_2C_2$ are similar if they coincide in respect of the ratios of their three sides. That is,

$$\triangle A_1B_1C_1 \sim \triangle A_2B_2C_2$$

if
$$\overline{A_1B_1} : \overline{A_1C_1} = \overline{A_2B_2} : \overline{A_2C_2},$$

$$\overline{B_1C_1} : \overline{A_1C_1} = \overline{B_2C_2} : \overline{A_2C_2}$$

and
$$\overline{A_1B_1} : \overline{B_1C_1} = \overline{A_2B_2} : \overline{B_2C_2}.$$

Fourth Similarity Theorem. Two triangles $A_1B_1C_1$ and $A_2B_2C_2$ are similar if they coincide in respect of the ratio of two sides, and the angle opposite to the larger of these sides. If

$$\overline{A_1B_1} > \overline{A_1C_1},\ \gamma_1 = \gamma_2 \text{ and } \overline{A_1B_1} : \overline{A_1C_1} = \overline{A_2B_2} : \overline{A_2C_2}$$

then
$$\triangle A_1B_1C_1 \sim \triangle A_2B_2C_2.$$

Similarity of triangles with equal sides. All triangles with equal sides are similar, since they coincide in respect of their three angles.

Similarity of isosceles triangles. Isosceles triangles are similar if they coincide in respect of (a) the angle at the apex; or (b) the base-angles; or (c) the ratio of lateral side to base.

Similarity of right-angled triangles. Right-angled triangles are similar, if they coincide in respect of (a) one angle adjacent to the hypotenuse; or (b) the ratio of any two sides. All right-angled isosceles triangles are similar, since they coincide in respect of three angles.

Similarity within right-angled triangles. The altitude of a right-angled triangle divides the triangle into two sub-triangles which are similar to one another and to the original triangle (Fig 387). Because of the similarity of these triangles we have the following proportionalities:

(i) In a right-angled triangle the altitude is the geometric mean of the intercepts it makes on the hypotenuse (*i.e.* of the projections of the smaller sides on the hypotenuse): $q:h = h:p$, $h = \sqrt{pq}$ (Fig. 387). This relation is a consequence of the similarity of the triangles *AFC* and *CFB*.

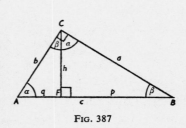

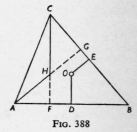

FIG. 387   FIG. 388

(ii) In a right-angled triangle each of the smaller sides is the geometric mean of the hypotenuse and the projection of the side onto the hypotenuse. $a = \sqrt{pc}$, $b = \sqrt{qc}$. These relations result from the similarity of the triangles *ABC* and *ACF* (or *CBF*) (Fig. 387).

Transversals in similar triangles. In similar triangles the ratios of any two corresponding lengths (such as altitudes, side-bisectors, angle-bisectors, radii of in- and excircles, mid-perpendiculars) are equal to the ratio of two corresponding sides.

Perimeter- and area-ratios in similar triangles. In the same way the perimeters of similar triangles are to each other as corresponding sides: $\angle_1:\angle_2 = a_1:a_2 = b_1:b_2 = c_1:c_2$.

The areas of similar triangles are to each other as the squares of corresponding sides: $\triangle_1:\triangle_2 = a_1^2:a_2^2 = b_1^2:b_2^2 = c_1^2:c_2^2$.

TRIANGLE

Ratios of segments in the triangle. Each *side-bisector* of a triangle is divided by the centroid in the ratio 1:2 (*i.e.* the segment adjacent to the vertex is twice as large as the segment on the opposite side). (See above, side-bisectors of a triangle.) The three *altitudes* of a triangle intersect in a single point, the orthocentre; they are to each other inversely as the sides on which they fall (see above, altitudes of a triangle):

$$h_a:h_b = b:a; \quad h_b:h_c = c:b.$$

The *segment of an altitude* adjacent to the vertex is double the length of the perpendicular from the centre of the circumcircle onto the corresponding side (Fig. 388).

The *bisector of an angle* of a triangle and the bisector of the associated external angle divide the opposite side of the triangle externally and internally in the ratio of the adjacent sides (see *Harmonic division*).

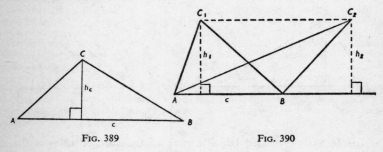

FIG. 389   FIG. 390

Area of a triangle, theorem of Pythagoras, etc.

The area of a triangle is calculated from the base g and the altitude h of the triangle as $\triangle = \frac{1}{2}gh$. Here the base can be taken as any of the three sides of the triangle; the altitude is the altitude projecting onto the chosen base. Thus we have

$$\triangle = \tfrac{1}{2}ch_c = \tfrac{1}{2}bh_b = \tfrac{1}{2}ah_a \text{ (Fig. 389)}.$$

From these formulae we at once get the theorem: triangles with equal base and equal altitude are equal in area (Fig. 390). See *Area, calculation of.*

Heron's Formula (Alexandria, 1st century A.D.). If

$$s = \tfrac{1}{2}(a + b + c)$$

then the area of the triangle is

$$\triangle = \sqrt{s \cdot (s - a) \cdot (s - b) \cdot (s - c)}.$$

Further formulae for calculating the area of a triangle:

1. Given the radius ρ of the inscribed circle and the sides:

$$\triangle = \rho \cdot s.$$

2. Given the radius r of the circumscribed circle and the sides:

$$\triangle = \frac{abc}{4r}.$$

3. Given two sides and their included angle

$$\triangle = \frac{ab \cdot \sin \gamma}{2} = \frac{bc \cdot \sin \alpha}{2} = \frac{ca \cdot \sin \beta}{2}.$$

4. Given the three angles and the radius of the circumscribed circle:

$$\triangle = 2r^2 \sin \alpha \sin \beta \sin \gamma.$$

Euclid's Theorem (Alexandria, 300 B.C.). In every right-angled triangle the square on one of the lesser sides is equal to the rectangle formed from the hypotenuse and the projection of the same side on the hypotenuse: $b^2 = cq$, or $a^2 = cp$.

Proof (Fig. 391): Triangle ABH is congruent (and so equal in area) to triangle ACD since:

1. $\overline{AH} = \overline{AC}$
2. $\overline{AB} = \overline{AD}$
3. $\angle HAB = 90° + \alpha = \angle CAD.$

The triangle AHC has the same base, $\overline{AH}$, and the same altitude, $\overline{AC}$, as the triangle AHB. These triangles are therefore equal in area. The triangles ACD and AFD have the same base $\overline{AD}$ and the same altitude $\overline{AF}$. These triangles too are therefore equal in area. We therefore have

$$\triangle HAC = \triangle HAB = \triangle CAD = \triangle FAD.$$

Now the area of the square $HACG$ is twice that of the triangle HAC, and the area of the rectangle $AFED$ is twice that of the

461

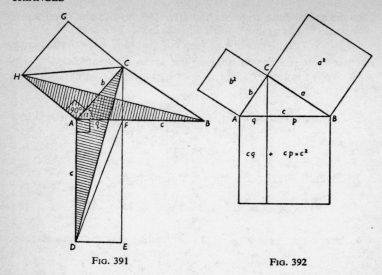

Fig. 391   Fig. 392

triangle *AFD*. But these two triangles are equal in area, and so the square and the rectangle are also equal in area.

The theorem of Pythagoras (Pythagoras of Samos, 6th century B.C.). In every right-angled triangle the square on the hypotenuse equals the sum of the squares on the other two sides; $a^2 + b^2 = c^2$.

1st proof: by Euclid's theorem $a^2 = cp$, $b^2 = cq$ (see Fig. 392), and so $a^2 + b^2 = cp + cq = c(p + q) = c^2$, as required.

2nd proof: In the left-hand half of Fig. 393 the large square has area $(a + b)^2$, that is $a^2 + b^2 + 2ab$. The four triangles on

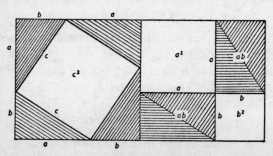

Fig. 393

the perimeter have together the area $2ab$, and so the inner square (of area c^2) has area $a^2 + b^2$. That is, $a^2 + b^2 = c^2$.

Altitude Theorem (Euclid). In a right-angled triangle the square on the altitude is equal to the rectangle formed by the segments of the hypotenuse cut off by the altitude: $h^2 = pq$ (Fig. 394).

Proof: By Pythagoras's theorem,

$$b^2 = h^2 + q^2;$$

by Euclid's theorem,

$$b^2 = cq = (p + q)q = pq + q^2.$$

Therefore, $\quad h^2 + q^2 = pq + q^2,$

that is, $\qquad\qquad h^2 = pq,$

as required.

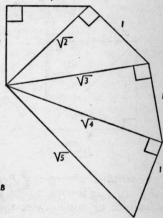

FIG. 394 $\qquad\qquad$ FIG. 395

Applications of the theorem of Pythagoras. By means of the theorem of Pythagoras, a square can be constructed whose area is the sum of the areas of two other squares. In particular a square can be constructed whose area is double that of a given square. The theorem can be also used to construct line-segments whose lengths are $\sqrt{2}$, $\sqrt{3}$, etc. (Fig. 395).

Calculations:

(a) Diagonal of square with side a:

$$a^2 + a^2 = d^2, \text{ by Pythagoras's theorem,}$$

that is, $\qquad\qquad 2a^2 = d^2,$

or $\qquad\qquad a\sqrt{2} = d$ (Fig. 396).

(b) Altitude and area of equilateral triangle with side a (Fig. 397): By Pythagoras's theorem,

$$h^2 = a^2 - \left(\frac{a}{2}\right)^2 = \frac{3}{4}a^2,$$

that is

$$h = \frac{a}{2}\sqrt{3}.$$

Therefore

$$\triangle = \frac{a}{2}h = \frac{a \cdot a}{2 \cdot 2}\sqrt{3} = \frac{a^2}{4}\sqrt{3}.$$

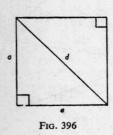

FIG. 396

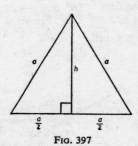

FIG. 397

Generalised theorem of Pythagoras. The square on a side of (any) triangle is equal to the sum of the squares on the other two sides plus or minus twice the rectangle formed by one of these sides and the projection of the other on it; the plus or minus sign is taken according as the first side lies opposite an acute or an obtuse angle.

Proof:

(i) for acute-angled triangles (Fig. 398).

By the theorem of Pythagoras applied to the triangles AFB and BFC:

$$c^2 = h^2 + p^2 \text{ and } a^2 = h^2 + q^2,$$

therefore

$$c^2 = a^2 - q^2 + p^2 = a^2 + p^2 + q^2 + 2pq - 2q^2 - 2pq,$$

that is,

$$c^2 = a^2 + (p + q)^2 - 2q(q + p).$$

But $q + p = b$, so that $c^2 = a^2 + b^2 - 2bq$, as required.

464

(ii) for obtuse-angled triangles (Fig. 399).

In the triangle AFB we have by the theorem of Pythagoras

$$c^2 = h^2 + (b + q)^2 = h^2 + b^2 + q^2 + 2bq.$$

But in the triangle BFC we have $a^2 = h^2 + q^2$, so that

$$c^2 = b^2 + a^2 + 2bq.$$

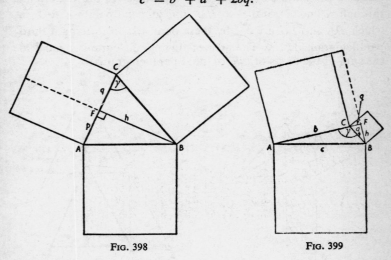

FIG. 398   FIG. 399

Projection theorem, theorem of Pappus, extension of theorem of Pythagoras

Projection theorem for triangles. The rectangle formed by one side of a triangle and the projection on it of a second side is equal to the rectangle formed by the second side and the projection of the first on the second.

Proof: (Fig. 400). The rectangle $ADEF$ has the same base $\overline{AD}$ and the same height $\overline{AF}$ as the parallelogram $ADMB$. These two figures therefore have equal areas. The parallelograms $ADMB$ and $ACNG$ are congruent (since they coincide in respect of two neighbouring sides and their included angle) and so have equal areas. The parallelogram $ACNG$ has the same base, $\overline{AC}$, and the same height, $\overline{AK}$, as the rectangle $AKHG$. The rectangle thus has the same area as the parallelogram $ACNG$. We therefore have

465

area $ADEF$ = area $ADMB$ = area $ACNG$ = area $AKHG$, that is, the rectangle $\overline{ADEF}$ is equal in area to the rectangle $\overline{AKHG}$.

Theorem of Pappus (Pappus of Alexandria, *c* 300 A.D.). Construct on two sides of a triangle ABC arbitrary parallelograms, $ACDE$ on the one and $BCFG$ on the other; continue the sides $\overline{DE}$ and $\overline{FG}$ until they intersect in the point H; draw the lines through A and B parallel to $\overline{HC}$, and join the points K to L in which $\overline{DE}$ and $\overline{FG}$ are cut by these parallels, so forming a third parallelogram $\overline{ABLK}$. The area of this parallelogram is equal to the sum of the areas of two original parallelograms.

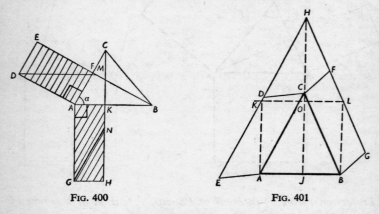

FIG. 400   FIG. 401

Proof: We have $\overline{AK} = \overline{CH} = \overline{BL}$; and these three segments are parallel (Fig. 401). Therefore $ABLK$ is a parallelogram. The area of the parallelogram $ACDE$ is equal to the area of the parallelogram $ACHK$ (base $\overline{AC}$ in common and height equal). Similarly, the area of the parallelogram $BCFG$ is equal to the area of the parallelogram $BCHL$; the area of the parallelogram $ACHK$ is equal to the area of the parallelogram $AJMK$; and the area of the parallelogram $BCHL$ is equal to the area of the parallelogram $BLMJ$. That is, area $ACDE$ = area $AJMK$, and area $BCFG$ = area $BLMJ$, and so the parallelograms $ACDE$ and $BCFG$ are together equal in area to the parallelogram $ABLK$.

Extension of the theorem of Pythagoras. If similar figures are constructed on the three sides of a right-angled triangle the area of the figure on the hypotenuse is equal to the sum of the areas of the figures on the other two sides (Figs. 402 and 403). The proof of this extension follows from the original theorem together with the similarity theorems, according to which the areas of similar figures vary as the squares of corresponding sides.

In particular we can take as similar figures the semicircles on the sides of the right-angled triangle. In this case the two smaller semicircles together are equal to the semicircle on the hypotenuse. It follows from this theorem that the two shaded crescents (crescents of Hippocrates) together have the same area as the triangle itself.

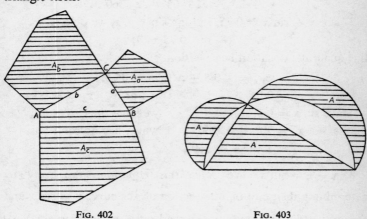

FIG. 402   FIG. 403

Trigonometric equations

Trigonometrical (conditional) equations contain the unknown as the argument of one or more trigonometrical functions. *E.g.*

$$\cos x = \frac{1}{2}, \sin^2 x + \sin x = \frac{3}{4}.$$

A trigonometrical equation may have infinitely many solutions:

$$\cos x = \frac{1}{2} \text{ has solutions } x = \frac{\pi}{3} + 2k\pi$$

and

$$x = \frac{5}{3}\pi + 2k\pi,$$

where

$$k = 0, \pm 1, \pm 2, \ldots.$$

467

There are also trigonometrical equations which have no real solutions, *e.g.* $\sin x = 2$.

In general only numerical or graphical methods can be used for the solution of such equations.

Examples:

1. $\sin (x + 30°) = 0\cdot81$. From the tables of the sine function, we obtain:
$$x_1 + 30° = 54° \, 6' + k \, . \, 360° \; (k = 0, \pm1, \pm2, \ldots).$$
Further, since $\sin \alpha = \sin (180° - \alpha)$, we have
$$x_2 + 30° = 125° \, 54' + k \, . \, 360°.$$

2. $\sin^2 x + \sin x = 0\cdot75$. Putting $\sin x = z$, we obtain
$$z^2 + z - 0\cdot75 = 0;$$
this quadratic equation has solution
$$z_{1,2} = -0\cdot5 \pm \sqrt{0\cdot25 + 0\cdot75}.$$

For $z_1 = 0\cdot5$ For $z_2 = -1\cdot5$
we have $\sin x = 0\cdot5$,   we have $\sin x = -1\cdot5$,
that is $x_1 = 30° + k \, . \, 360°$ which has no solutions.
and $x_2 = 150° + k \, . \, 360°$.

3. $x - \dfrac{2}{3} = \sin x$. We solve this equation graphically by determining the point of intersection of the curve $y = \sin x$ and the straight line $y = x - \dfrac{2}{3}$. We read off $x_1 = 2\cdot6$ (Fig. 404).

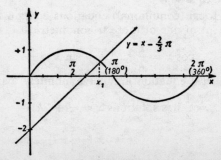

FIG. 404

468

4. If different trigonometrical functions are contained in the equation, then with the help of the fundamental trigonometrical identities we attempt to modify the equation so that only one angular function occurs in it. It may still happen that the same angular function with different arguments occurs; we then use the addition theorems to make all arguments equal.

Example 1:

$\tan 2x = -3 \tan x$. Since $\tan 2x = \dfrac{2 \tan x}{1 - \tan^2 x}$, we have

$\dfrac{2 \tan x}{1 - \tan^2 x} = -3 \tan x$. The equation is certainly satisfied when $\tan x = 0$, *i.e.* for $x = 0 + k \cdot 180°$; $k = 0, 1, 2, \ldots$.

If $\tan x \neq 0$, we may divide the equation through by $\tan x$ to obtain:

$$2 = (-3)(1 - \tan^2 x),$$

which gives after reordering:

$$\tan^2 x = \frac{5}{3}, \text{ i.e. } \tan x = \pm \frac{1}{3} \sqrt{15} = \pm 1 \cdot 291.$$

From the tables we have

$$x_1 = 52° \ 14' + k \cdot 180°, \quad k = 0, \pm 1, \pm 2, \ldots,$$

and $\qquad x_2 = 127° \ 46' + k \cdot 180°.$

Example 2:

$\sin 2x + \sin x = 0$. We use the identity $\sin 2x = 2 \sin x \cos x$ to transform the equation to $2 \sin x \cos x + \sin x = 0$. The left hand side can be written as a product:

$$\sin x \ (2 \cos x + 1) = 0.$$

The equation is satisfied if either the first or the second factor is zero.

I. $\sin x = 0$ gives the solutions $x_1 = k\pi$.

II. $2 \cos x + 1 = 0$ or $\cos x = -\dfrac{1}{2}$ gives the solutions

$$x_2 = 2 \frac{\pi}{3} + 2k\pi, \quad k = 0, \pm 1, \pm 2, \ldots,$$

and $\qquad x_3 = 4 \dfrac{\pi}{3} + 2k\pi.$

Trigonometrical series

The developments of the trigonometrical functions in power-series are known as trigonometrical series. *E.g.*

$$\sin x = x - \frac{x^3}{3!} + \frac{x^5}{5!} - \frac{x^7}{7!} + \ldots + (-1)^k \frac{x^{2k+1}}{(2k+1)!} + \ldots,$$

$$\cos x = 1 - \frac{x^2}{2!} + \frac{x^4}{4!} - \frac{x^6}{6!} + \ldots + (-1)^k \frac{x^{2k}}{(2k)!} + \ldots.$$

Both series converge for all values of x. The argument x is here in angular measure.

Trigonometrical tables

Trigonometrical tables contain the function values of the trigonometrical functions $\sin x$, $\cos x$, $\tan x$ and $\cot x$. The values of the argument are given either in degrees or radians, and additional tables are often provided for transforming from degrees to radians.

Tables of the logarithms of the trigonometrical functions are of use when frequent calculations are necessary. These contain the logarithms of $\sin x$, $\cos x$, $\tan x$ and $\cot x$. For technical reasons the tables have the peculiarity that the characteristic is increased by 10 with the exception of values of *log tan* from 45° to 89° 59′ 59″ and of *log cot* from 0° to 44° 59′ 59″. For actual tables, see *Table* 3.

Trigonometry (Greek, measurement of triangles)

Trigonometry is the part of mathematics which has to do with the calculation of elements of the triangle using the angular functions. At the basis of all such calculations is the right-angled triangle. All other triangles can be divided into two right-angled triangles by dropping an altitude from one vertex. Now if two right-angled triangles coincide in respect of one acute angle they are similar in shape; more precisely, the ratio of two corresponding sides in such triangles is the same. The ratio of two sides in a right-angled triangle is thus dependent only on the size of the acute angle and not on the lengths of the sides, *i.e.* it is a function of the angle (angular function). The various possible ratios of sides have individual names: sine (sin), cosine (cos), tangent (tan), secant (sec), cosecant (cosec), and cotangent (cot).

Explanation:

1. In a right-angled triangle ABC with angles α, β, $\gamma = 90°$, AC is called the side *adjacent* to α, BC is called the side *opposite* to α, AB is the hypotenuse (Fig. 405).

2. We define:
$$\sin \alpha = \frac{\text{opposite side}}{\text{hypotenuse}},$$

$$\cos \alpha = \frac{\text{adjacent side}}{\text{hypotenuse}},$$

$$\tan \alpha = \frac{\text{opposite side}}{\text{adjacent side}},$$

$$\cot \alpha = \frac{\text{adjacent side}}{\text{opposite side}}.$$

3. These are the most common angular functions. But the following are also frequently used:

$$\sec \alpha = \frac{\text{hypotenuse}}{\text{adjacent side}}; \qquad \operatorname{cosec} \alpha = \frac{\text{hypotenuse}}{\text{opposite side}}.$$

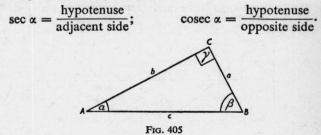

FIG. 405

Sine function and cosine function

The best insight into the manner in which the numerical value of a trigonometrical function varies with the angle α is obtained by means of the unit circle. An arbitrary radius of the unit circle is chosen as direction from which angles are measured, conventionally in the anti-clockwise sense. A second radius of the unit circle is drawn making the angle α with the initial direction. From the end-point of the second radius the perpendicular is dropped onto the first radius. This is to be taken as the side of the right-angled triangle opposite to the angle α, and the projection of the second radius on the first is to be its adjacent side. Since the hypotenuse is of unit length, in this figure the length of the perpendicular is equal to sin α and of the projection of the radius is cos α (Figs. 406 and 407).

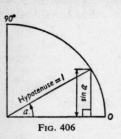

FIG. 406

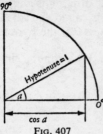

FIG. 407

Graphical representation of sine and cosine functions. Taking an arbitrary unit distance we mark off values of the angle α on the abscissa axis of a coordinate system in degrees or (better) in *angular measure* (see art.) and, taking as ordinate successive values for sin α, we obtain the curve for the function sin α (Fig. 408). Similarly we obtain the curve representing cos α (Fig. 408).

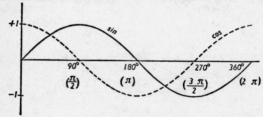

FIG. 408

The values of the sine function run from 0 to 1 as the size of the angle advances from 0° to 90°. In particular, sin 0° = 0 and sin 90° = 1. The values of the cosine function run from 1 to 0 as the size of the angle proceeds from 0° to 90°. In particular, cos 0° = 1 and cos 90° = 0.

Tangent and cotangent functions

The values of the tangent and cotangent functions can also be represented by means of the unit circle.

We draw the unit circle, choose the initial direction, lay out the radius which makes the angle α with the initial direction (measuring in the anti-clockwise sense) and draw the tangent at the end-point of the radius specified by the initial direction. On this tangent the extension of the second radius cuts off a segment which can be taken as the opposite side corresponding to the angle α (Fig. 409). Since in this case the adjacent side is of unit length, the segment of the tangent is equal to tan α.

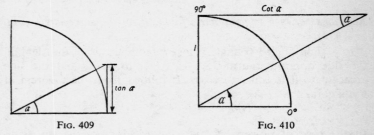

FIG. 409   FIG. 410

In order to represent the cotangent, we draw the tangent to the circle at the end-point of the radius which is perpendicular to the initial direction, thus obtaining a right-angled triangle in which the opposite side of the angle α is of unit length. The segment cut off on the tangent is cot α (Fig. 410).

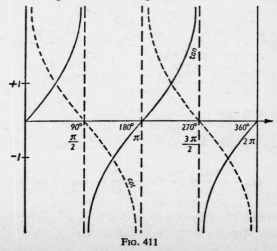

FIG. 411

473

Graphical representation of tangent and cotangent functions. The graphical representation of the tangent and cotangent functions is obtained as in the case of the sine function. As the angle α runs from 0° to 90°, the value of tan α passes from 0 to ∞, and of cot α from ∞ to 0. Here when we write tan 90° = ∞ we mean that larger and larger function values are obtained for tan α the nearer α approaches 90°, and similarly for cot α as α approaches 0°.

Relations between trigonometric functions of the same angle (Fig. 412)

In a right-angled triangle whose hypotenuse is of unit length, the side opposite the angle α is equal to sin α, and the side adjacent to it is equal to cos α. It follows from the theorem of Pythagoras that

$$(\sin \alpha)^2 + (\cos \alpha)^2 = 1.$$

In the case of powers of trigonometrical functions, so as to avoid ambiguity, it is customary to put the exponent next to and above the function symbol. Thus we write

$$\sin^2 \alpha + \cos^2 \alpha = 1.$$

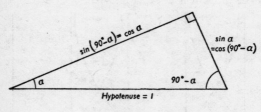

Fig. 412

Likewise from Fig. 412 the following relations can be obtained:

$$\tan \alpha = \frac{\sin \alpha}{\cos \alpha}, \ \cot \alpha = \frac{\cos \alpha}{\sin \alpha}, \ \tan \alpha = \frac{1}{\cot \alpha}.$$

The signs of the roots in the following table are given by the table of signs for trigonometrical functions (see p. 478).

	sin	cos	tan	cot
$\sin \alpha =$		$\sqrt{1 - \cos^2 \alpha}$	$\dfrac{\tan \alpha}{\sqrt{1 + \tan^2 \alpha}}$	$\dfrac{1}{\sqrt{1 + \cot^2 \alpha}}$
$\cos \alpha =$	$\sqrt{1 - \sin^2 \alpha}$		$\dfrac{1}{\sqrt{1 + \tan^2 \alpha}}$	$\dfrac{\cot \alpha}{\sqrt{1 + \cot^2 \alpha}}$
$\tan \alpha =$	$\dfrac{\sin \alpha}{\sqrt{1 - \sin^2 \alpha}}$	$\dfrac{\sqrt{1 - \cos^2 \alpha}}{\cos \alpha}$		$\dfrac{1}{\cot \alpha}$
$\cot \alpha =$	$\dfrac{\sqrt{1 - \sin^2 \alpha}}{\sin \alpha}$	$\dfrac{\cos \alpha}{\sqrt{1 - \cos^2 \alpha}}$	$\dfrac{1}{\tan \alpha}$	

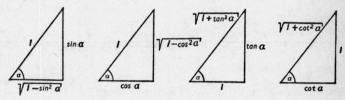

Fig. 413

Relations between functions of the angles α and $90° - \alpha$

The angles α and $90° - \alpha$ are said to be complementary with respect to one another. From Fig. 412 we get

$$\sin (90° - \alpha) = \cos \alpha,$$
$$\cos (90° - \alpha) = \sin \alpha,$$
$$\tan (90° - \alpha) = \cot \alpha,$$
$$\cot (90° - \alpha) = \tan \alpha.$$

Thus, in passing from an angle α to its complementary angle $90° - \alpha$, we pass from a trigonometrical function to its cofunction. Cosine is an abbreviation for 'complementary sine', *i.e.* sine of the complementary angle, and cotangent an abbreviation for 'complementary tangent', *i.e.* tangent of the complementary angle.

475

Easily calculated function values

From the isosceles and right-angled triangle of Fig. 414 we obtain

$$\sin 45° = \frac{a}{a\sqrt{2}} = \frac{1}{2}\sqrt{2}, \quad \tan 45° = \frac{a}{a} = 1,$$

$$\cos 45° = \frac{a}{a\sqrt{2}} = \frac{1}{2}\sqrt{2}, \quad \cot 45° = \frac{a}{a} = 1.$$

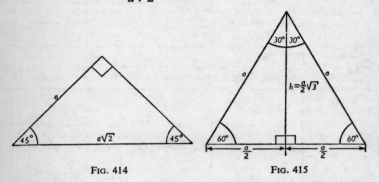

FIG. 414   FIG. 415

From the equilateral triangle of Fig. 415 we get

$$\sin 30° = \frac{\frac{a}{2}}{a} = \frac{1}{2}, \qquad\qquad \sin 60° = \frac{\frac{a}{2}\sqrt{3}}{a} = \frac{1}{2}\sqrt{3},$$

$$\cos 30° = \frac{\frac{a}{2}\sqrt{3}}{a} = \frac{1}{2}\sqrt{3}, \qquad \cos 60° = \frac{\frac{a}{2}}{a} = \frac{1}{2},$$

$$\tan 30° = \frac{\frac{a}{2}}{\frac{a}{2}\sqrt{3}} = \frac{1}{\sqrt{3}} = \frac{1}{3}\sqrt{3}, \quad \tan 60° = \frac{\frac{a}{2}\sqrt{3}}{\frac{a}{2}} = \sqrt{3},$$

$$\cot 30° = \frac{\frac{a}{2}\sqrt{3}}{\frac{a}{2}} = \sqrt{3}, \qquad \cot 60° = \frac{\frac{a}{2}}{\frac{a}{2}\sqrt{3}} = \frac{1}{\sqrt{3}} = \frac{1}{3}\sqrt{3}.$$

These results are summarised in the following table:

	0°	30°	45°	60°	90°
sin	0	$\frac{1}{2}$	$\frac{1}{2}\sqrt{2}$	$\frac{1}{2}\sqrt{3}$	1
cos	1	$\frac{1}{2}\sqrt{3}$	$\frac{1}{2}\sqrt{2}$	$\frac{1}{2}$	0
tan	0	$\frac{1}{3}\sqrt{3}$	1	$\sqrt{3}$	∞
cot	∞	$\sqrt{3}$	1	$\frac{1}{3}\sqrt{3}$	0

Trigonometrical functions for arbitrary angles

In order to extend the definition of the trigonometrical functions to angles of any size we again use the unit circle, as in the case of the definition for acute angles. We again fix an initial direction,

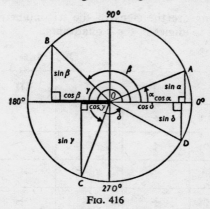

Fig. 416

and then lay out the angle from this in the anti-clockwise sense (Figs. 416 and 417). We now drop the perpendicular from the end of the second radius we have obtained onto the diameter containing the initial direction. The length of this perpendicular

477

(positive or negative) is then sin α, and the length of the projection, cos α (Fig. 416). The length of the intercept of the second radius on the tangent at the end-point of the initial direction is tan α; the length of the intercept on the tangent parallel to the initial direction is cot α (Fig. 417).

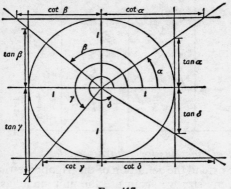

FIG. 417

The following are the signs of the trigonometrical functions corresponding to angles in the 4 quadrants:

Quadrant

		I	II	III	IV
	sin	+	+	−	−
Function	cos	+	−	−	+
	tan	+	−	+	−
	cot	+	−	+	−

From the definition, we obtain a function value for each of the trigonometrical functions corresponding to every angle. Angles can be given in either degrees or radians, the latter being best suited for graphical representation. The angle is plotted on the abscissa axis in radians and corresponding function values appear as ordinates (Figs. 418, 419, 420).

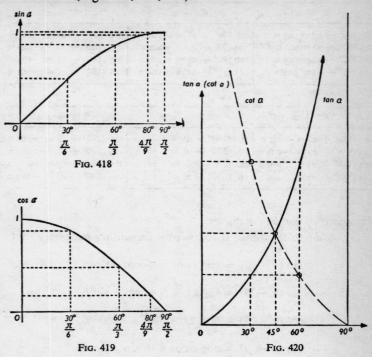

Fig. 418

Fig. 419

Fig. 420

Periodicity of the trigonometrical functions

The trigonometrical functions can be defined in the same way for angles greater than $2\pi = 360°$. We then have

$$\sin(\alpha + n \cdot 360°) = \sin \alpha,$$
$$\cos(\alpha + n \cdot 360°) = \cos \alpha,$$
$$\tan(\alpha + n \cdot 180°) = \tan \alpha,$$
$$\cot(\alpha + n \cdot 180°) = \cot \alpha.$$

The sine and cosine functions have the period $360°$ ($= 2\pi$).
The tangent and cotangent functions have the period $180°$ ($= \pi$).

Relations between trigonometrical functions of the angles α, 90° ± α, 180° ± α *and* 270° ± α

90° − α	90° + α	180° − α
sin (90° − α) = cos α	sin (90° + α) = cos α	sin (180° − α) = sin α
cos (90° − α) = sin α	cos (90° + α) = −sin α	cos (180° − α) = −cos α
tan (90° − α) = cot α	tan (90° + α) = −cot α	tan (180° − α) = −tan α
cot (90° − α) = tan α	cot (90° + α) = −tan α	cot (180° − α) = −cot α

180° + α	270° − α	270° + α
sin (180° + α) = −sin α	sin (270° − α) = −cos α	sin (270° + α) = −cos α
cos (180° + α) = −cos α	cos (270° − α) = −sin α	cos (270° + α) = sin α
tan (180° + α) = tan α	tan (270° − α) = cot α	tan (270° + α) = −cot α
cot (180° + α) = cot α	cot (270° − α) = tan α	cot (270° + α) = −tan α

Functions of compound angles

(1) *Addition theorems.* It follows by elementary geometry that

$$\sin (\alpha + \beta) = \sin \alpha \cos \beta + \cos \alpha \sin \beta,$$

$$\sin (\alpha - \beta) = \sin \alpha \cos \beta - \cos \alpha \sin \beta,$$

$$\cos (\alpha + \beta) = \cos \alpha \cos \beta - \sin \alpha \sin \beta,$$

$$\cos (\alpha - \beta) = \cos \alpha \cos \beta + \sin \alpha \sin \beta,$$

$$\tan (\alpha + \beta) = \frac{\tan \alpha + \tan \beta}{1 - \tan \alpha \tan \beta}, \quad \tan (\alpha - \beta) = \frac{\tan \alpha - \tan \beta}{1 + \tan \alpha \tan \beta},$$

$$\cot (\alpha + \beta) = \frac{\cot \alpha \cot \beta - 1}{\cot \beta + \cot \alpha}, \quad \cot (\alpha - \beta) = \frac{\cot \alpha \cot \beta + 1}{\cot \beta - \cot \alpha}.$$

(2) *Consequences of the addition theorems*

$$\sin 2\alpha = 2 \sin \alpha \cos \alpha, \quad \cos 2\alpha = \cos^2 \alpha - \sin^2 \alpha = 2 \cos^2 \alpha - 1$$
$$= 1 - 2 \sin^2 \alpha,$$

$$\tan 2\alpha = \frac{2 \tan \alpha}{1 - \tan^2 \alpha}, \qquad \cot 2\alpha = \frac{\cot^2 \alpha - 1}{2 \cot \alpha},$$

$$\sin \alpha = \sqrt{\frac{1 - \cos 2\alpha}{2}}; \qquad \cos \alpha = \sqrt{\frac{1 + \cos 2\alpha}{2}};$$

$$\tan \alpha = \sqrt{\frac{1 - \cos 2\alpha}{1 + \cos 2\alpha}} = \frac{\sin 2\alpha}{1 + \cos 2\alpha}.$$

Similarly,

$$\sin 3\alpha = 3 \sin \alpha - 4 \sin^3 \alpha; \quad \cos 3\alpha = 4 \cos^3 \alpha - 3 \cos \alpha;$$

$$\tan 3\alpha = \frac{3 \tan \alpha - \tan^3 \alpha}{1 - 3 \tan^2 \alpha}; \quad \cot 3\alpha = \frac{\cot^3 \alpha - 3 \cot \alpha}{3 \cot^2 \alpha - 1};$$

and

$$\sin n\alpha = \binom{n}{1} \cos^{n-1} \alpha \sin \alpha - \binom{n}{3} \cos^{n-3} \alpha \sin^3 \alpha$$

$$+ \binom{n}{5} \cos^{n-5} \alpha \sin^5 \alpha - \ldots,$$

$$\cos n\alpha = \cos^n \alpha - \binom{n}{2} \cos^{n-2} \alpha \sin^2 \alpha$$

$$+ \binom{n}{4} \cos^{n-4} \alpha \sin^4 \alpha - \ldots.$$

Sums and differences of the trigonometrical functions:

$$\sin \alpha + \sin \beta = 2 \sin \frac{\alpha + \beta}{2} \cdot \cos \frac{\alpha - \beta}{2},$$

$$\sin \alpha - \sin \beta = 2 \cos \frac{\alpha + \beta}{2} \cdot \sin \frac{\alpha - \beta}{2},$$

$$\cos \alpha + \cos \beta = 2 \cos \frac{\alpha + \beta}{2} \cdot \cos \frac{\alpha - \beta}{2},$$

481

$$\cos \alpha - \cos \beta = -2 \sin \frac{\alpha + \beta}{2} \cdot \sin \frac{\alpha - \beta}{2},$$

$$\cos \alpha + \sin \beta = 2 \sin \left(45° - \frac{\alpha - \beta}{2}\right) \sin \left(45° + \frac{\alpha + \beta}{2}\right),$$

$$\cos \alpha - \sin \beta = 2 \sin \left(45° - \frac{\alpha + \beta}{2}\right) \sin \left(45° + \frac{\alpha - \beta}{2}\right),$$

$$\cot \alpha \pm \tan \beta = \frac{\cos (\alpha \mp \beta)}{\sin \alpha \cos \beta},$$

$$\cos \alpha + \sin \alpha = \sqrt{2} \sin (45° + \alpha),$$

$$\cos \alpha - \sin \alpha = \sqrt{2} \cos (45° + \alpha),$$

$$\cot \alpha + \tan \alpha = \frac{2}{\sin 2\alpha}, \quad \cot \alpha - \tan \alpha = 2 \cot 2\alpha,$$

$$\frac{1 + \tan \alpha}{1 - \tan \alpha} = \tan (45° + \alpha), \quad \frac{\cot \alpha + 1}{\cot \alpha - 1} = \cot (45° - \alpha).$$

Trisection of an angle

The trisection of an angle of arbitrary size is not possible by use of ruler and compass only, although special angles can of course be trisected in this way (*e.g.* the angles 45°, 90° and 180° can be so trisected, since the angles 15°, 30° and 60° can be constructed by means of ruler and compass). Approximate constructions for the trisection of an arbitrary angle are however possible.

Truncated pyramid

The volume of a truncated pyramid is $V = \frac{1}{3}H(G + GG_1 + G_1)$ where G is the area of the base-surface and G_1 is the area of the upper-surface (Fig. 232).

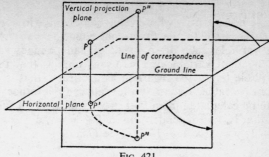

FIG. 421

Two-plane projection (Biorthogonal projection)

Two-plane projection is a mapping procedure of descriptive geometry. A given solid figure is projected by orthogonal parallel projection onto two mutually perpendicular image-planes, the top-view or horizontal projection plane, and the front-view or vertical projection plane. The line of intersection of the two image planes is called the *ground line*. Every figure thus has two image-figures. That in the horizontal plane is called the *plan*, and that in the vertical plane is called the *elevation*.

If we wish to carry out the construction of the two images in a single plane, we must rotate one of the planes about the ground line through 90°. This is generally done so that the part of the vertical projection plane lying above the ground line coincides with the part of the horizontal projection plane lying behind the ground line. The image of a point P in the plan is denoted by P' and the image in the elevation by P''. $P'P''$ is perpendicular to the ground line and is called the *line of correspondence* of the two images (Fig. 421).

Unit fractions

Fractions with numerator 1, *e.g.* $\frac{1}{1} = 1, \frac{1}{2}, \frac{1}{3}, \ldots$

Unit vector

A vector whose length is 1 is called a unit vector. For any vector **a**, a unit vector can be found which has the same direction as **a**, *viz.* the vector $\frac{\mathbf{a}}{|\mathbf{a}|}$ ($|\mathbf{a}|$ is the absolute value of **a** (see *Vector*)).

Variable

A variable is a quantity whose value can change, in contrast to a *constant* (see art.). In the functional equation $y = 7x - 1$, x and y are variables. We often speak of 'independent variables' and of 'dependent variables'. This usage implies that the value of one variable (*e.g.* x) is regarded as arbitrary, that is, x is an independent variable, and that the values of another variable (*e.g.* y) can be calculated from that of x by means of a functional equation, that is, y is dependent on x. E.g. $y = 7x - 1$.

For $x = 1$, $y = 7 \times 1 - 1 = 6$ (see *Function*).

Vector

A vector is a line-segment, in a plane or in three-dimensional space, which has a definite direction-sense and which can be arbitrarily displaced parallel to itself. Vectors are denoted either by letters of the alphabet in bold type or by placing an arrow over the line-segment concerned. If P_1 is the point of origin, and P_2 the end-point of the vector $\mathbf{R}$, the length of the segment P_1P_2 is called the absolute value, or magnitude, of the vector and is written $R = |\mathbf{R}|$. If the point of origin and the end-point of a vector are the same, the vector is the *null-vector*. The null-vector has length zero and is regarded as having no definite direction; it is written as $\mathbf{0}$. If (x_1, y_1, z_1) and (x_2, y_2, z_2) are the rectangular coordinates of the given points P_1 and P_2, the vector $\mathbf{R} = P_1P_2$ is uniquely specified by the coordinate-differences

$$x_2 - x_1, \, y_2 - y_1, \, z_2 - z_1$$

These differences are the *components* of the vector, and we write

$$\mathbf{R} = (x_2 - x_1, \, y_2 - y_1, \, z_2 - z_1).$$

The null vector has components $(0, 0, 0) = \mathbf{0}$.
Vectors regarded as in a plane have only two components.
Vectors in space have three components.
The length of a vector is calculated from its components by Pythagoras's theorem as follows:

$$R = |\mathbf{R}| = \sqrt{(x_2 - x_1)^2 + (y_2 - y_1)^2 + (z_2 - z_1)^2}.$$

Multiplication of a vector by a real number

To multiply a vector $\mathbf{R} = (x_2 - x_1, y_2 - y_1, z_2 - z_1)$ by a real number c, we multiply its length by c, leaving its direction unchanged if c is positive, and reversing it if c is negative. If the components of the vector are given, then

$$c\mathbf{R} = [c(x_2 - x_1), c(y_2 - y_1), c(z_2 - z_1)].$$

Thus multiplying a vector by c merely involves multiplying each component. The vector $-\mathbf{R}$ in particular, has the coordinates

$$-\mathbf{R} = [-(x_2 - x_1), -(y_2 - y_1), -(z_2 - z_1)].$$

If a vector is divided by its length we obtain a vector of length 1. Any vector of length 1 is called a *unit vector*. The vector $\dfrac{\mathbf{R}}{|\mathbf{R}|}$ has length 1, and is the unit vector associated with the vector $\mathbf{R}$. It has the same direction as $\mathbf{R}$.

A vector whose point of origin is fixed at a definite point is called a *bound vector*. In particular, so-called 'position vectors' are bound vectors, their initial positions being bound to the point of origin of the coordinate system. A position vector has as its components the coordinates of its end-point. The vectors whose points of origin are at the origin of the coordinate system and whose end-points are at the unit-points on the axes are called the unit coordinate vectors. In a plane these vectors are

$$\mathbf{i} = (1, 0), \mathbf{j} = (0, 1).$$

In three dimensions they are

$$\mathbf{i} = (1, 0, 0), \mathbf{j} = (0, 1, 0), \mathbf{k} = (0, 0, 1).$$

Addition of vectors (Fig. 422)

If $\mathbf{A} = (a_x, a_y, a_z)$ and $\mathbf{B} = (b_x, b_y, b_z)$ are two vectors, the vector with components $(a_x + b_x, a_y + b_y, a_z + b_z)$ is called the sum, $\mathbf{A} + \mathbf{B}$, of $\mathbf{A}$ and $\mathbf{B}$.

To construct the sum $\mathbf{A} + \mathbf{B}$ of two vectors, we move each vector parallel to itself till its point of origin coincides with the origin, O, of the coordinate system. $\mathbf{A}$ and $\mathbf{B}$ then form two sides of a parallelogram. The diagonal of this parallelogram which passes through the origin represents the vector $\mathbf{A} + \mathbf{B}$, O being taken as its point of origin.

Addition of vectors is commutative and associative. The difference $\mathbf{A} - \mathbf{B}$ of the vectors A and B is obtained by adding $(-\mathbf{B})$ to $\mathbf{A}$. It can be constructed by means of the same parallelogram used in constructing the sum, the difference being represented by the diagonal which does not pass through O (Fig. 423).

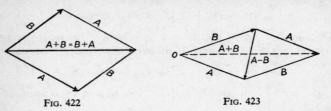

FIG. 422   FIG. 423

Representation of vectors by means of the vectors $\mathbf{i}$, $\mathbf{j}$, $\mathbf{k}$

Any vector in three dimensional space can be represented by the sum of multiples of the unit vectors, $\mathbf{i}$, $\mathbf{j}$, $\mathbf{k}$. The procedure in a plane is illustrated in Fig. 424. We have $\mathbf{A} = a_x\mathbf{i} + a_y\mathbf{j}$. The corresponding procedure in three dimensions is given in Fig. 425, $\mathbf{A} = a_x\mathbf{i} + a_y\mathbf{j} + a_z\mathbf{k}$; a_x, a_y and a_z are the components of the vector $\mathbf{A}$ in the directions $\mathbf{i}$, $\mathbf{j}$ and $\mathbf{k}$.

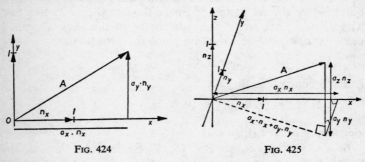

FIG. 424   FIG. 425

Scalar and vector products in two dimensions (Fig. 426)

Let $\mathbf{A} = (a_x, a_y)$ and $\mathbf{B} = (b_x, b_y)$ be two plane non-null vectors forming angles ϕ_a and ϕ_b with the positive x-direction. Then the components of these vectors are

$$a_x = |\mathbf{A}| \cos \phi_a, \quad b_x = |\mathbf{B}| \cos \phi_b;$$
$$a_y = |\mathbf{A}| \sin \phi_a, \quad b_y = |\mathbf{B}| \sin \phi_b.$$

The angle between the two vectors is $\phi = \phi_a - \phi_b$. Then

$$\cos\phi = \cos(\phi_a - \phi_b) = \cos\phi_a\cos\phi_b + \sin\phi_a\sin\phi_b$$

$$\sin\phi = \sin(\phi_a - \phi_b) = \sin\phi_a\cos\phi_b - \sin\phi_b\cos\phi_a,$$

or, in terms of the components of the vectors,

$$\cos\phi = \frac{a_x b_x + a_y b_y}{|\mathbf{A}| \cdot |\mathbf{B}|},$$

$$\sin\phi = \frac{a_x b_y - a_y b_x}{|\mathbf{A}| \cdot |\mathbf{B}|}.$$

The expression $a_x b_x + a_y b_y = |\mathbf{A}|\,|\mathbf{B}|\cos\phi$ is called the scalar, or inner, product of the two vectors. It is written $(\mathbf{A} \cdot \mathbf{B})$, $\mathbf{AB}$ or $\mathbf{A} \cdot \mathbf{B}$. The scalar product of two vectors is a numerical quantity (a scalar, or scalar quantity), and has no direction. The expression $a_x b_y - a_y b_x = |\mathbf{A}|\,|\mathbf{B}|\sin\phi$ is called the vector, or outer, product. It is written $[\mathbf{A}, \mathbf{B}] = [\mathbf{A}\,\mathbf{B}]$, $\mathbf{A} \wedge \mathbf{B}$ or $\mathbf{A} \times \mathbf{B}$. As we are considering vectors in a single plane this product also is a scalar.

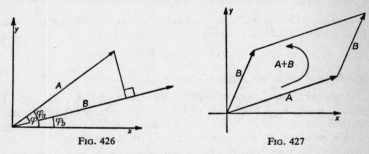

FIG. 426   FIG. 427

Geometrical interpretation of the scalar product. From the definition $\mathbf{AB} = |\mathbf{A}|\,|\mathbf{B}|\cos\phi = |\mathbf{A}| \cdot (|\mathbf{B}|\cos\phi)$ it follows that the scalar product of two vectors is equal to the product of their magnitudes and the cosine of the enclosed angle, or (equivalently) to the magnitude of one of the vectors multiplied by the length of the projection of the second vector on the first (or on the extension of the first).

Geometrical interpretation of the vector product. The vector product of two vectors $\mathbf{A}$ and $\mathbf{B}$ is equal to the area of the parallelogram associated with them. The result is positive if the vectors $\mathbf{A}$ and $\mathbf{B}$ follow one another in the anti-clockwise sense (Fig. 427).

Properties of the scalar product

1. Commutative law, $\mathbf{A} \cdot \mathbf{B} = \mathbf{B} \cdot \mathbf{A}$.
2. Linearity, $(c_1 \mathbf{A}) \cdot (c_2 \mathbf{B}) = c_1 c_2 (\mathbf{A} \cdot \mathbf{B})$.
3. Distributive law, $(\mathbf{A} + \mathbf{B}) \cdot \mathbf{D} = \mathbf{A} \cdot \mathbf{D} + \mathbf{B} \cdot \mathbf{D}$.
4. Product of unit coordinate vectors, $\mathbf{i} \cdot \mathbf{i} = \mathbf{i}^2 = \mathbf{j} \cdot \mathbf{j} = \mathbf{j}^2 = 1$, $\mathbf{i} \cdot \mathbf{j} = 0$.
5. The scalar product of two vectors is zero if the vectors are perpendicular to one another or if one vector is the null vector.
6. The scalar product of a vector with itself is equal to the square of its length,

$$\mathbf{A} \cdot \mathbf{A} = \mathbf{A}^2 = |\mathbf{A}|^2.$$

Properties of the vector product

1. Alternating law, $\mathbf{A} \wedge \mathbf{B} = -(\mathbf{B} \wedge \mathbf{A})$.
2. Linearity, $(c_1 \mathbf{A}) \wedge (c_2 \mathbf{B}) = c_1 c_2 (\mathbf{A} \wedge \mathbf{B})$.
3. Distributive law, $(\mathbf{A} + \mathbf{B}) \wedge \mathbf{D} = \mathbf{A} \wedge \mathbf{D} + \mathbf{B} \wedge \mathbf{D}$.
4. Product of unit coordinate vectors, $\mathbf{i} \wedge \mathbf{i} = 0$, $\mathbf{i} \wedge \mathbf{j} = 1$, $\mathbf{j} \wedge \mathbf{i} = -1$.
5. The vector product of two vectors is zero if the vectors are parallel or if one vector is the null vector,

$$c_1 \mathbf{A} \wedge c_2 \mathbf{A} = 0.$$

Products in three dimensions

Scalar product of two three-dimensional vectors. If $\mathbf{A} = (a_x, a_y, a_z)$ and $\mathbf{B} = (b_x, b_y, b_z)$ are two vectors in space then the numerical quantity $a_x b_x + a_y b_y + a_z b_z = |\mathbf{A}| \, |\mathbf{B}| \cos \phi$ is defined as the scalar product of the vectors $\mathbf{A}$ and $\mathbf{B}$. Here ϕ is the angle between the two vectors. The scalar product of two vectors in space has the same properties as the scalar product of vectors in a plane.

For the unit coordinate vectors we have

$$\mathbf{i} \cdot \mathbf{i} = \mathbf{j} \cdot \mathbf{j} = \mathbf{k} \cdot \mathbf{k} = 1, \, \mathbf{j} \cdot \mathbf{k} = \mathbf{k} \cdot \mathbf{i} = \mathbf{i} \cdot \mathbf{j} = 0.$$

Vector product of two three-dimensional vectors. The vector product of two three-dimensional vectors, $\mathbf{A} = (a_x, a_y, a_z)$ and $\mathbf{B} = (b_x, b_y, b_z)$, is the *vector* with components

$$(a_y b_z - a_z b_y, \, a_z b_x - a_x b_z, \, a_x b_y - a_y b_x),$$
$$\mathbf{A} \wedge \mathbf{B} = (a_y b_z - a_z b_y, \, a_z b_x - a_x b_z, \, a_x b_y - a_y b_x).$$

Geometrical interpretation. The vector product of two three-dimensional vectors **A** and **B** is a vector which is perpendicular to the plane formed by the two vectors and whose magnitude is equal to the area of the parallelogram specified by **A** and **B**.

Difference between plane and three-dimensional vector product

As long as only plane vectors (vectors with two components) are considered, the vector product of two vectors is taken to be a scalar. With three-dimensional vectors (vectors with three components) the vector product is a vector.

The properties of the vector product in the plane set out above hold also for the vector-product in space, and in addition we have for products of unit coordinate vectors in space the equations:

$$\mathbf{i} \wedge \mathbf{i} = \mathbf{j} \wedge \mathbf{j} = \mathbf{k} \wedge \mathbf{k} = 0,$$

$$\mathbf{i} \wedge \mathbf{j} = \mathbf{k}, \mathbf{j} \wedge \mathbf{i} = -\mathbf{k}; \mathbf{i} \wedge \mathbf{k} = -\mathbf{j}, \mathbf{k} \wedge \mathbf{i} = \mathbf{j}; \mathbf{j} \wedge \mathbf{k} = \mathbf{i}, \mathbf{k} \wedge \mathbf{j} = -\mathbf{i}.$$

Vector calculus

Vector calculus is the branch of mathematics comprising the mathematical theorems relating to calculation with vectors (see *Vector*).

Vertical

The vertical direction at a point on the earth's surface is the direction passing through the earth's centre. It may be determined by means of a plumb-line. In geometry two lines are said to be vertical or perpendicular with respect to one another if they form a right angle (see *Angle*).

Vertically opposite angles

Two angles which have a common vertex and whose arms together form in pairs two straight lines are said to be vertically opposite. In Fig. 428 α, γ and β, δ are pairs of vertically opposite angles. Vertically opposite angles are equal. Thus in Fig. 428 $\alpha = \gamma$, $\beta = \delta$ (see *Angle*).

FIG. 428

Volume, measurement of

In the metric system the theoretical unit of volume is the *stere* (one cubic metre = 1 kilolitre), the unit in common use being the litre which, for all practical purposes is one cubic decimetre.

In English measure the unit of volume is the (Imperial) gallon which equals 277·42 cubic inches = 4·546 litres. The U.S.A. gallon equals 231·00 cubic inches = 3·785 litres. Other English measures are related as follows:

$$4 \text{ gills} = 1 \text{ pint}$$

$$2 \text{ pints} = 1 \text{ quart}$$

$$4 \text{ quarts} = 1 \text{ gallon}$$

$$8 \text{ gallons} = 1 \text{ bushel.}$$

Weight, measurement of

The unit of weight in the metric system is the *kilogramme*, the standard kilogramme, established in 1889, being a solid cylinder of platinum-iridium preserved in Paris. The British and American *pounds*, though differing very slightly in their exact definition, can each be taken equal to 0·4536 kg. The definitions of some subsidiary units differ in British and American usage. We have

$$1 \text{ ton } = 20 \text{ hundredweight}$$

$$1 \text{ cwt.} = 4 \text{ quarters}$$

$$1 \text{ qr.} = 28 \text{ lb (British), } 25 \text{ lb (American)}$$

$$1 \text{ lb.} = 16 \text{ ounces}$$

$$1 \text{ oz.} = 16 \text{ drams.}$$

Thus 1 cwt. (British) = 112 lb.   1 cwt. (American) = 100 lb.

1 ton (British) = 2240 lb.   1 ton (American) = 2000 lb.

Zero

Zero is the number which can be added to (or subtracted from) another number a without a being altered thereby: $a + 0 = a$.

If a number is multiplied by zero, the result is zero: $a \times 0 = 0$. Division of a number by zero must be excluded if contradictions in the operation of the basic rules of arithmetic are to be avoided.

A zero symbol is used in all place-value systems. Number systems without place-values, *e.g.* the Roman, need have no zero symbol. See *Axioms of arithmetic, Division, Differential coefficient.*

MATHEMATICAL FORMULAE

I ARITHMETIC

1. Types of number

We distinguish the following types of number:

(1) *Natural* or positive integral numbers, *e.g.* 2, 6, 11.

(2) *Integral* numbers (positive and negative), *e.g.* −3, −1, 3, 8.

(3) *Rational* numbers, *i.e.* numbers which can be represented as the ratios of integral numbers.

(4) *Algebraic* numbers, *i.e.* numbers which are solutions of algebraic equations with integral coefficients (see p. 498 ff.).

(5) *Transcendental* numbers, *i.e.* numbers which are not solutions of algebraic equations with integral coefficients.

(6) *Real* numbers, which comprise all the above types of number. Every real number can be represented by an infinite decimal fraction. Non-rational real numbers are referred to as *irrational*.

The absolute value (modulus) of a number x, written $|x|$, is x if x is positive and $-x$ if x is negative.

For imaginary and complex numbers, see p. 497.

2. Addition and subtraction

(1)
$$a + b = b + a$$

$$(+a) + (+b) = a + b$$

$$(-a) + (+b) = -a + b = b - a$$

$$(+a) + (-b) = a - b = -b + a$$

$$a + (b + c) = (a + b) + c$$

$$a + (b - c) = (a + b) - c$$

(2)
$$a - b = -(b - a)$$

$$(+a) - (+b) = a - b$$

$$(+a) - (-b) = a + b$$

492

$$(-a) - (+b) = -a - b = -(a + b)$$
$$(-a) - (-b) = -a + b = b - a$$
$$a - (b + c) = a - b - c$$
$$a - (b - c) = a - b + c$$

(3)
$$\big|\, |a| - |b| \,\big| \leq |a + b| \leq |a| + |b|$$
$$\big|\, |a| - |b| \,\big| \leq |a - b| \leq |a| + |b|$$

2. *Multiplication and division*

(1)
$$a \cdot b = b \cdot a$$
$$(+a) \cdot (+b) = a \cdot b$$
$$(+a) \cdot (-b) = -a \cdot b$$
$$(-a) \cdot (+b) = -a \cdot b$$
$$(-a) \cdot (-b) = +a \cdot b$$

(2)
$$(a + b) \cdot c = a \cdot c + b \cdot c$$
$$(a - b) \cdot c = a \cdot c - b \cdot c$$
$$(a + b)(c + d) = ac + bc + ad + bd$$
$$(a + b)(c - d) = ac + bc - ad - bd$$
$$(a - b)(c + d) = ac - bc + ad - bd$$
$$(a - b)(c - d) = ac - bc - ad + bd$$

(3)
$$(a + b)(a + b) = (a + b)^2 = a^2 + 2ab + b^2$$
$$(a - b)(a - b) = (a - b)^2 = a^2 - 2ab + b^2$$
$$(a + b)(a - b) = a^2 - b^2$$

(4)
$$|a \cdot b| = |a| \cdot |b|$$

(5)
$$(a + b) \div c = a \div c + b \div c$$
$$(a - b) \div c = a \div c - b \div c$$
$$(+ab) \div (+a) = +b$$
$$(+ab) \div (-a) = -b$$

FORMULAE

$$(-ab) \div (+a) = -b$$
$$(-ab) \div (-a) = +b$$

(6) $$|a| \div |b| = |a \div b|$$

4. *Ratios and fractions*

The equation $a:b = c:d$ is a *proportion*.

If $$ad = bc$$

then

(1) $$a:c = b:d$$
$$d:b = c:a$$
$$b:a = d:c$$

(2) $$am:bm = c:d$$
$$am:b = cm:d$$
$$(a:m):(b:m) = c:d$$
$$(a:m):b = (c:m):d$$

(3) $$a:(a + b) = c:(c + d)$$
$$b:(a + b) = d:(c + d)$$
$$a:(a - b) = c:(c - d)$$
$$b:(a - b) = d:(c - d)$$

(4) $$(ma + nb):(mc + nd) = (pa + qb):(pc + qd)$$

The following are special cases of proportionality:

Continued proportion: $\qquad a:b = b:c$

Harmonic proportion: $\qquad (a - b):(c - d) = a:d$

Continued harmonic proportion: $(a - b):(b - d) = a:d$

We may write $a:b$ as a fraction $\frac{a}{b}$; thus, for example,

$$(a + b):c = (a + b) \div c = \frac{a + b}{c}$$

494

The following rules apply to calculation with fractions:

(1)
$$\frac{a}{b} = \frac{a \times m}{b \times m}; \qquad \frac{a}{b} = \frac{a \div m}{b \div m}$$

(2) If the fractions $\frac{a_1}{n_1}, \frac{a_2}{n_2}, \ldots, \frac{a_k}{n_k}$, have different denominators, a common denominator h may be found, namely, the (least) common multiple of $n_1, \ldots, n_k$.

(3) Addition and subtraction:

$$\frac{a}{b} + \frac{c}{d} = \frac{ad + cb}{bd} \quad (bd \text{ is the common denominator})$$

$$\frac{a}{b} + \frac{c}{d} - \frac{e}{f} = \frac{adf + bcf - bde}{bdf}$$

(4) Multiplication and division

$$\frac{a}{b} \cdot c = \frac{ac}{b}$$

$$\frac{a}{b} \cdot \frac{c}{d} = \frac{ac}{bd}$$

$$\frac{a}{b} \div c = \frac{a}{bc}$$

$$\frac{a}{b} \div \frac{c}{d} = \frac{ad}{bc}$$

5. *Powers and roots*

(1) If m is a positive integer then we define

$$a^m = a \times a \times \ldots \times a \ (m \text{ factors}),$$

$$a^{-m} = \frac{1}{a^m}, \ a^0 = 1. \ (a \text{ is the base}, \ m \text{ the exponent}, \ a^m \text{ '}a \text{ to the power } m\text{'.})$$

(2) For any integers m, r, it follows that:

$$a^m a^r = a^{(m+r)}$$

$$a^m \div a^r = a^{m-r}$$

$$(a \times b)^m = a^m \times b^m$$

$$(a \div b)^m = a^m \div b^m$$

$$(a^m)^r = a^{mr}$$

(3) Fractional exponents are defined so as to preserve relations (2): if m, n are integers, $a^{\frac{1}{n}} = \sqrt[n]{a}$, the nth root of a. Then

$$a^{\frac{m}{n}} = \sqrt[n]{a^m} = (\sqrt[n]{a})^m.$$

If m, n, r, s are positive or negative integers, roots are related as follows:

$$\sqrt[n]{a \cdot b} = \sqrt[n]{a} \cdot \sqrt[n]{b};$$

$$\sqrt[n]{a \div b} = \sqrt[n]{a} \div \sqrt[n]{b};$$

$$\sqrt[n]{a^r} = (\sqrt[n]{a})^r = \sqrt[m \cdot n]{a^{rm}};$$

$$\sqrt[n]{\sqrt[r]{a}} = \sqrt[nr]{a} = \sqrt[r]{\sqrt[n]{a}};$$

$$\sqrt[-n]{a^r} = \sqrt[n]{a^{-r}}; \quad a\sqrt[n]{b} = \sqrt[n]{a^n b}.$$

(4) Further:

$$a^{\frac{m}{n}} \cdot a^{\frac{r}{s}} = a^{\frac{m}{n} + \frac{r}{s}};$$

$$a^{\frac{m}{n}} \div a^{\frac{r}{s}} = a^{\frac{m}{n} - \frac{r}{s}};$$

$$(a \cdot b)^{\frac{m}{n}} = a^{\frac{m}{n}} \cdot b^{\frac{m}{n}};$$

$$(a \div b)^{\frac{m}{n}} = a^{\frac{m}{n}} \div b^{\frac{m}{n}};$$

$$\left(a^{\frac{m}{n}}\right)^{\frac{r}{s}} = a^{\frac{mr}{ns}}.$$

6. *Binomial coefficients*

(1) By $n!$ (n-factorial), we mean the product

$$n! = 1 \cdot 2 \cdot 3 \ldots (n-1) \cdot n, \quad n \text{ a positive integer,}$$

and define $0! = 1$.

(2) By the binomial coefficient $\binom{n}{r}$ (n over r) we understand the fraction

$$\binom{n}{r} = \frac{n(n-1)\ldots(n-r+1)}{r!} = \frac{n!}{(n-r)!r!}$$

(r and n integers, $1 \leq r \leq n$),

and define $\binom{n}{0} = 1$, $\binom{n}{r} = 0$ if $r > n$.

(3) Then:

$$\binom{n}{n} = 1$$

$$\binom{n}{r} = \binom{n}{n-r} = \frac{n!}{(n-r)!r!} \text{ if } r < n$$

$$\binom{n+1}{r+1} = \binom{n}{r} + \binom{n-1}{r} + \binom{n-2}{r} + \ldots + \binom{r}{r}$$

$$\binom{n+1}{r} = \binom{n}{r} + \binom{n}{r-1} = \binom{n}{r} \cdot \frac{n+1}{n-r+1}$$

$$\binom{m+n}{r} = \binom{m}{r}\binom{n}{0} + \binom{m}{r-1}\binom{n}{1} + \ldots + \binom{m}{1}\binom{n}{r-1}$$
$$+ \binom{m}{0}\binom{n}{r}$$

(4) The *binomial theorem* for positive integral n is as follows:

$$(a \pm b)^n = \binom{n}{0} a^n \pm \binom{n}{1} a^{n-1}b + \ldots + (\pm 1)^n \binom{n}{n} b^n$$

7. *Imaginary and complex numbers*

(1) The imaginary unit i is defined by the relation $i^2 = -1$. If a and b are real numbers we refer to

$y = ib$ as an imaginary number,

$z = a + ib$ as a complex number,

and $\bar{z} = a - ib$ as the associated conjugate complex number.

a is called the real part ($a = \mathrm{R}(z)$), b the imaginary part ($b = \mathrm{I}\,(z)$) of z.

(2) Then
$$i^3 = -i \qquad i^4 = +1 \qquad i^5 = i$$
$$i^{4n+2} = -1 \qquad i^{4n+3} = -i \qquad i^{4n+4} = +1 \qquad i^{4n+5} = i$$

(3) If $z_1 = a_1 + ib_1$, $z_2 = a_2 + ib_2$, then

$$z_1 \pm z_2 = (a_1 \pm a_2) + i(b_1 \pm b_2)$$

$$z_1 \cdot z_2 = (a_1 a_2 - b_1 b_2) + i(a_1 b_2 + a_2 b_1)$$

$$\frac{z_1}{z_2} = \frac{a_1 a_2 + b_1 b_2}{a_2^2 + b_2^2} + i\,\frac{a_2 b_1 - a_1 b_2}{a_2^2 + b_2^2}$$

(4) Further,

$$z \cdot \bar{z} = (a + ib)(a - ib) = a^2 + b^2 = |z|^2.$$

Also, if $r = +\sqrt{a^2 + b^2}$ and $\tan \phi = \dfrac{b}{a}$, then

$$z = a + ib = r\,(\cos \phi + i \sin \phi),$$
$$\bar{z} = a - ib = r\,(\cos \phi - i \sin \phi).$$

$r = |z|$ is called the absolute value of z, $\phi = \arg z$ the argument of z.

(5) De Moivre's Theorem: if m and n are integers ($n \neq 0$) then:

$$(\cos \phi \pm i \sin \phi)^{\frac{m}{n}} = \cos \frac{m}{n}\,(2k\pi + \phi) \pm i \sin \frac{m}{n}\,(2k\pi + \phi),$$

$$k = 0, \pm 1, \pm 2, \ldots$$

In particular

$$(\cos \phi \pm i \sin \phi)^m = \cos m\phi \pm i \sin m\phi,$$

and $(\cos \phi \pm i \sin \phi)^{\frac{1}{n}} = \cos \dfrac{\phi}{n} \pm i \sin \dfrac{\phi}{n}.$

II. ALGEBRA

An equation of the nth degree ($n \geq 1$) in the unknown x is an equation of the form

$$a_0 x^n + a_1 x^{n-1} + a_2 x^{n-2} + \ldots + a_{n-1} x + a_n = 0.$$

$a_0, a_1, \ldots, a_n$ are called coefficients of the equation; the n solutions $x = x_1, \ldots, x_n$ are called roots.

If the equation is brought into the form

$$f(x) = x^n + b_1 x^{n-1} + \ldots + b_n = 0,$$

where $\qquad b_k = \dfrac{a_k}{a_0},$

then $\qquad f(x) = (x - x_1)(x - x_2) \ldots (x - x_n).$

The coefficients b_k and the roots of the equation $f(x) = 0$ are related as follows:

$$b_1 = -(x_1 + x_2 + \ldots + x_n),$$

$$b_2 = x_1 x_2 + x_1 x_3 + \ldots + x_2 x_3 + \ldots + x_{n-1} x_n,$$

$$b_3 = -(x_1 x_2 x_3 + x_1 x_2 x_4 + \ldots + x_2 x_3 x_4 + \ldots$$
$$+ x_{n-2} x_{n-1} x_n),$$

$$\ldots \ldots \ldots$$

$$b_n = (-1)^n x_1 x_2 x_3 \ldots x_n.$$

Each of these expressions is a symmetric function of the roots, *i.e.* each remains unaltered under permutation of $x_1, x_2, \ldots, x_n$.

An algebraic equation with m unknowns, $y_1, y_2, \ldots, y_m$, is an equation of the form

$$F(y_1, y_2, \ldots, y_m) = 0,$$

where $F(y_1, \ldots, y_m)$ is the sum of terms of the form

$$a_{\alpha\beta\gamma \ldots \rho} \, y_1^{\alpha} y_2^{\beta} \ldots y_m^{\rho},$$

the coefficients $a_{\alpha\beta\gamma \ldots \rho}$ being arbitrary, and $\alpha, \beta, \ldots, \rho$ positive integers. The largest value taken by $\alpha + \beta + \ldots + \rho$ is the degree of the equation.

FORMULAE

1. *Equations with one unknown*

(1) *Linear equations.* An equation of the first degree in one unknown is of the form

$$ax + b = 0, \quad a \neq 0,$$

and has solution $x = \dfrac{-b}{a}$.

(2) *Quadratic equations.* An equation of the second degree in one unknown is of the form

$$ax^2 + bx + c = 0, \quad a \neq 0.$$

It has two solutions x_1 and x_2:

$$x_{1,2} = \frac{-b \pm \sqrt{b^2 - 4ac}}{2a}.$$

The solutions x_1 and x_2 are

real and different if $b^2 - 4ac > 0$,

real and equal if $b^2 - 4ac = 0$,

conjugate complex if $b^2 - 4ac < 0$.

(3) *Cubic equations.* A cubic equation is an equation of the form

$$ax^3 + bx^2 + cx + d = 0, \quad a \neq 0,$$

which, by the transformation

$$x = y - \frac{b}{3a},$$

can be brought to the standard form

$$y^3 + 3py + 2q = 0,$$

where

$$3p = -\frac{1}{3}\left(\frac{b}{a}\right)^2 + \frac{a}{c}; \quad 2q = \frac{2}{27}\left(\frac{b}{a}\right)^3 - \frac{1}{3}\frac{bc}{a^2} + \frac{d}{a}.$$

The cubic equation has

three real and different roots if $q^3 + p^3 < 0$,

three real solutions, of which at least two are equal, if

$$q^2 + p^3 = 0,$$

one real and two conjugate complex solutions if $q^2 + p^3 > 0$.

Then if

(α) $q^2 + p^3 \geq 0$ (Cardan's formula), putting

$$u = \sqrt[3]{-q + \sqrt{q^2 + p^3}},$$
$$v = \sqrt[3]{-q - \sqrt{q^2 + p^3}},$$

where the real roots are taken, we have as the solutions of the standard equation:

$$y_1 = u + v,$$

$$y_2 = -\frac{u + v}{2} + \frac{i}{2}\sqrt{3}(u - v),$$

$$y_3 = -\frac{u + v}{2} - \frac{i}{2}\sqrt{3}(u - v).$$

(β) $q^2 + p^3 \geq 0$ and $q \neq 0$, $p > 0$, putting

$$\tan \phi = \frac{\sqrt{p^3}}{q}, \ \tan \psi = \sqrt[3]{\tan \frac{\phi}{2}},$$

where $\qquad -\dfrac{\pi}{2} < \phi < \dfrac{\pi}{2}, \ -\dfrac{\pi}{4} < \psi < \dfrac{\pi}{4},$

we have the solutions

$$y_1 = -2\sqrt{p} \cot 2\psi,$$

$$y_2 = \sqrt{p}\left(\cot 2\psi + \frac{i\sqrt{3}}{\sin 2\psi}\right),$$

$$y_3 = \sqrt{p}\left(\cot 2\psi - \frac{i\sqrt{3}}{\sin 2\psi}\right).$$

(γ) $q^2 + p^3 \geq 0$ and $q \neq 0$, $p < 0$, putting

$$\sin \phi = \frac{\sqrt{-p^3}}{q}, \ \tan \psi = \sqrt[3]{\tan \frac{\phi}{2}},$$

where $\qquad -\dfrac{\pi}{2} < \phi < \dfrac{\pi}{2}, \ -\dfrac{\pi}{4} < \psi < \dfrac{\pi}{4},$

we have the solutions

$$y_1 = -2\sqrt{-p}\,\frac{1}{\sin 2\psi},$$

$$y_2 = \sqrt{-p}\left(\frac{1}{\sin 2\psi} + i\sqrt{3}\cot 2\psi\right),$$

$$y_3 = \sqrt{-p}\left(\frac{1}{\sin 2\psi} - i\sqrt{3}\cot 2\psi\right).$$

(δ) $q^2 + p^3 \leq 0$ (irreducible case), putting

$$\cos\phi = \frac{-q}{\sqrt{-p^3}}$$

we have the solutions

$$y_1 = 2\sqrt{-p}\,\cos\frac{\phi}{3},$$

$$y_2 = -2\sqrt{-p}\,\cos\left(\frac{\phi}{3} + 60°\right),$$

$$y_3 = -2\sqrt{-p}\,\cos\left(\frac{\phi}{3} - 60°\right).$$

(4) *Biquadratic equations.* A biquadratic or quartic equation is an equation of the form:

$$x^4 + ax^3 + bx^2 + cx + d = 0.$$

By the transformation

$$x = \xi - \frac{a}{4}$$

this can be reduced to the standard form

$$\xi^4 + p\xi^2 + q\xi + r = 0.$$

If we form the cubic resolvent

$$y^3 + \frac{p}{2}y^2 + \frac{p^2 - 4r}{16}y - \frac{q^2}{64} = 0$$

and determine its solutions y_1, y_2, y_3 (see p. 500), we may obtain the four solutions of the reduced equation from

$$\xi = \pm \sqrt{y_1} \pm \sqrt{y_2} \pm \sqrt{y_3},$$

where the signs are chosen so that

$$\sqrt{y_1} \cdot \sqrt{y_2} \cdot \sqrt{y_3} = -\frac{q}{8}.$$

2. *Equations with more than one unknown*

(1) *Determinants*

(α) A matrix with m rows and n columns is a system of $n \times m$ numbers a_{ik} written in the rectangular array

$$\mathbf{A} = \begin{pmatrix} a_{11} & a_{12} & \ldots a_{1n} \\ a_{21} & a_{22} & \ldots a_{2n} \\ \cdot & & \cdot \\ \cdot & & \cdot \\ \cdot & & \cdot \\ a_{m1} & a_{m2} & \ldots a_{mn} \end{pmatrix} = (a_{ik}).$$

The a_{ik} are called the elements of the matrix. If $n = m$, the matrix is said to be square. In what follows we confine ourselves to square matrices.

Product: If $\mathbf{A} = (a_{ik})$ and $\mathbf{B} = (b_{ik})$ are matrices with n rows and columns, the product matrix $\mathbf{A} . \mathbf{B}$ (in that order) is the matrix $\mathbf{C} = (c_{ik})$ such that

$$c_{ik} = \sum_1^n a_{is} b_{sk}.$$

Sum: If $\mathbf{A} = (a_{ik})$ and $\mathbf{B} = (b_{ik})$ are matrices with n rows and columns, the matrix $\mathbf{D}$ is called the sum of the matrices $\mathbf{A}$ and $\mathbf{B}$, $\mathbf{D} = \mathbf{A} + \mathbf{B}$, if

$$d_{ik} = a_{ik} + b_{ik}.$$

(β) The determinant Δ of the matrix $\mathbf{A} = (a_{ik})$, written

$$\Delta = \begin{vmatrix} a_{11} & a_{12} & a_{13} & \ldots a_{1n} \\ a_{21} & a_{22} & a_{23} & \ldots a_{2n} \\ \cdot & & & \cdot \\ \cdot & & & \cdot \\ \cdot & & & \cdot \\ a_{n1} & a_{n2} & a_{n3} & \ldots a_{nn} \end{vmatrix} = |\mathbf{A}|,$$

is the sum of all the products

$$\pm a_{1\alpha}a_{2\beta}a_{3\gamma} \cdots a_{n\rho}$$

which arise when α, β, γ, . . ., ρ are allowed to range through all permutations of the numbers 1, . . ., n. The positive or negative sign is taken according as α, β, γ, . . ., ρ is an even or odd permutation of 1, 2, . . ., n. In particular:

$$\begin{vmatrix} a_{11} & a_{12} \\ a_{21} & a_{22} \end{vmatrix} = a_{11}a_{22} - a_{12}a_{21}$$

and

$$\begin{vmatrix} a_{11} & a_{12} & a_{13} \\ a_{21} & a_{22} & a_{23} \\ a_{31} & a_{32} & a_{33} \end{vmatrix} = \begin{matrix} a_{11}a_{22}a_{33} + a_{21}a_{32}a_{13} + a_{31}a_{12}a_{23} \\ -a_{31}a_{22}a_{13} - a_{11}a_{32}a_{23} - a_{21}a_{12}a_{33}. \end{matrix}$$

(γ) We have the following theorems for determinants:

(i) If $\mathbf{A}' = (a_{ki})$ is the matrix obtained from $\mathbf{A} = (a_{ik})$ by interchanging rows and columns (the *transposed* matrix) and $|\mathbf{A}|$ denotes the determinant of $\mathbf{A}$, then:

$$|\mathbf{A}| = |\mathbf{A}'|.$$

Thus
$$\begin{vmatrix} a_{11} & a_{12} \\ a_{21} & a_{22} \end{vmatrix} = \begin{vmatrix} a_{11} & a_{21} \\ a_{12} & a_{22} \end{vmatrix}.$$

(ii) If two rows or two columns of a determinant are interchanged, odd permutations of α, β, γ, . . ., ρ, become even and *vice versa*, and so the sign of the determinant is altered.

E.g.
$$\begin{vmatrix} a_{11} & a_{12} \\ a_{21} & a_{22} \end{vmatrix} = - \begin{vmatrix} a_{12} & a_{11} \\ a_{22} & a_{21} \end{vmatrix}.$$

(iii) If all the elements of one row or of one column are multiplied by the same number, each term of the determinant and hence the determinant itself is multiplied by that number. Thus for example

$$\begin{vmatrix} ca_{11} & ca_{12} \\ a_{21} & a_{22} \end{vmatrix} = c \begin{vmatrix} a_{11} & a_{12} \\ a_{21} & a_{22} \end{vmatrix}.$$

(iv) If two rows or two columns are equal, interchange of these rows or columns leaves the value Δ of the determinant unaltered.

504

That is, by (ii), $\Delta = -\Delta$, and hence $\Delta = 0$. By (iii), the same applies when two rows or columns are proportional.

E.g.
$$\begin{vmatrix} a_{11} & ca_{11} \\ a_{21} & ca_{21} \end{vmatrix} = 0$$

(v) If every element of one row or column is the sum of two numbers, the determinant can be written as the sum of two determinants, *e.g.*

$$\begin{vmatrix} a_{11} + \alpha_{11} & a_{12} \\ a_{21} + \alpha_{21} & a_{22} \end{vmatrix} = \begin{vmatrix} a_{11} & a_{12} \\ a_{21} & a_{22} \end{vmatrix} + \begin{vmatrix} \alpha_{11} & a_{12} \\ \alpha_{21} & a_{22} \end{vmatrix}.$$

(vi) By (iv) and (v), the value of a determinant is unaltered if to each element of a row (or column) is added a constant multiple of the corresponding element of another row (or column).

E.g.
$$\begin{vmatrix} a_{11} & a_{12} + ca_{11} \\ a_{21} & a_{22} + ca_{21} \end{vmatrix} = \begin{vmatrix} a_{11} & a_{12} \\ a_{21} & a_{22} \end{vmatrix}.$$

(vii) Product theorem. It follows from the way $\mathbf{A} \cdot \mathbf{B}$ is defined that

$$|\mathbf{A} \cdot \mathbf{B}| = |\mathbf{A}| \times |\mathbf{B}|.$$

(viii) By the cofactor A_{ik} of the element a_{ik} of a determinant is meant the determinant, prefixed by the sign $(-1)^{i+k}$, obtained by deleting the ith row and the kth column of $|\mathbf{A}|$. We then have:

$$\Delta = \sum_{i=1}^{n} a_{ik}A_{ik} = \sum_{k=1}^{n} a_{ik}A_{ik}.$$

(ix) If all elements of a determinant of the $(n + r)$th degree common to n columns and r rows vanish, the determinant can be separated into the product of two determinants of degrees n and r:

$$\begin{vmatrix} a_{11} \ldots a_{1n} & b_{11} \ldots b_{1r} \\ \ldots\ldots\ldots & \ldots\ldots\ldots \\ a_{n1} \ldots a_{nn} & b_{n1} \ldots b_{nr} \\ \ldots\ldots\ldots & \ldots\ldots\ldots \\ 0 \ldots\ldots 0 & c_{11} \ldots c_{1r} \\ \ldots\ldots\ldots & \ldots\ldots\ldots \\ 0 \ldots\ldots 0 & c_{r1} \ldots c_{rr} \end{vmatrix} = \begin{vmatrix} a_{11} \ldots a_{1n} \\ \ldots\ldots\ldots \\ a_{n1} \ldots a_{nn} \end{vmatrix} \cdot \begin{vmatrix} c_{11} \ldots c_{1r} \\ \ldots\ldots\ldots \\ c_{r1} \ldots c_{rr} \end{vmatrix}$$

(2) *Systems of linear equations*

(α) The system of linear equations of the *n*th order

$$a_{11}x_1 + a_{12}x_2 + \ldots + a_{1n}x_n = \alpha_1$$
$$a_{21}x_1 + a_{22}x_2 + \ldots + a_{2n}x_n = \alpha_2$$
$$\ldots\ldots\ldots\ldots\ldots\ldots\ldots\ldots\ldots\ldots\ldots\ldots$$
$$a_{n1}x_1 + a_{n2}x_2 + \ldots + a_{nn}x_n = \alpha_n$$

with unknowns x_1, x_2, . . ., x_n, possesses exactly one set of solutions if

$$\Delta = \begin{vmatrix} a_{11} & a_{12} \ldots a_{1n} \\ a_{21} & a_{22} \ldots a_{2n} \\ \ldots\ldots\ldots\ldots\ldots \\ a_{n1} & a_{n2} \ldots a_{nn} \end{vmatrix} \neq 0,$$

namely

$$x_k = \frac{\sum_{i=1}^{n} A_{ik}\alpha_i}{\Delta} \qquad (k = 1, 2, \ldots, n).$$

(β) If the system of equations is homogeneous, *i.e.* if

$$\alpha_1 = \alpha_2 = \ldots = \alpha_n = 0,$$

then a necessary and sufficient condition that the only solution is

$$x_1 = x_2 = \ldots = x_n = 0 \text{ is } \Delta \neq 0.$$

(γ) The system of *m* equations in *n* unknowns:

$$a_{11}x_1 + a_{12}x_2 + \ldots + a_{1n}x_n = \alpha_1$$
$$a_{21}x_1 + a_{22}x_2 + \ldots + a_{2n}x_n = \alpha_2$$
$$\ldots\ldots\ldots\ldots\ldots\ldots\ldots\ldots\ldots\ldots\ldots\ldots$$
$$a_{m1}x_1 + a_{m2}x_2 + \ldots + a_{mn}x_n = \alpha_m$$

is soluble if and only if the two matrices

$$\begin{pmatrix} a_{11} \ldots a_{1n} & \alpha_1 \\ \ldots\ldots\ldots\ldots\ldots \\ a_{m1} \ldots a_{mn} & \alpha_m \end{pmatrix} \text{ and } \begin{pmatrix} a_{11} \ldots a_{1n} \\ \ldots\ldots\ldots \\ a_{m1} \ldots a_{mn} \end{pmatrix}$$

have the same *rank*. A matrix **A** has rank *r* if all determinants of the $(r + 1)$th order, but not all determinants of the *r*th order, formed by elimination of rows and columns of **A**, vanish.

III. APPLICATIONS

1. *Compound interest*

(1) The ratio of two numbers a and b can be expressed as the percentage $p = 100 \dfrac{a}{b}$. We say that a is p per cent (or $p\%$) of b; 91 is 26% of 350.

(2) The proportional increase of an initial capital sum a during an interest period is referred to as the interest-rate p (expressed as a percentage). The factor q by which the initial capital must be multiplied to obtain the final capital is therefore

$$q = 1 + \frac{p}{100}.$$

The capital sum resulting after n interest periods is

$$b = a\left(1 + \frac{p}{100}\right)^n.$$

(3) If the capital is increased or diminished at the end of each interest period by the amount r, we have

$$b = aq^n \pm r\frac{q^n - 1}{q - 1}.$$

(4) If the amount contributed by r is paid at the end of each interest period, the sum arising at the end of the nth period is

$$R_n = \frac{r(q^n - 1)}{q - 1}.$$

If r is paid at the beginning of the interest-period

$$R_n = rq\frac{q^n - 1}{q - 1}.$$

(5) The initial capital required for an annuity r paid at the end of each of n interest-periods is

$$A_n = r\frac{q^n - 1}{(q - 1)q^n} = \frac{r}{q - 1}\left(1 - \frac{1}{q^n}\right).$$

For a perpetual annuity

$$A_\infty = \frac{r}{q-1}.$$

(6) A capital sum a is to be amortised in n interest periods by payment of a fixed instalment at the end of each interest period. If p is the rate of interest (as a percentage) and p_1 is the amortisation rate (as a percentage), then the condition for the capital to be extinguished after n interest-periods is

$$\left(1 + \frac{p}{100}\right)^n = \frac{p}{p_1} + 1.$$

2. Probability and Statistics

(1) *The notion of probability.* If A, B are definite events and $A \wedge B$ (both A and B), $A \vee B$ (at least one of A and B) and $\bar{A}$ (not A) are associated events, the probability $P(A)$ of the event A may be introduced through the following axioms:

(i) $P(A)$ is a real function with

$$0 \le P(A) \le 1;$$

(ii) If E is an event which invariably occurs, then:

$$P(E) = 1;$$

(iii) If the events A and B are exclusive then

$$P(A \vee B) = P(A) + P(B);$$

(iv) If $A_1, A_2, \ldots, A_\infty$ are events which are pairwise exclusive then:

$$P(A_1 \vee A_2 \vee \ldots) = \sum_{i=1}^{\infty} P(A_i).$$

(2) *Elementary theorems*

(i) $\qquad P(A \wedge B) + P(A \vee B) = P(A) + P(B),$

(ii) $\qquad\qquad\qquad P(\bar{A}) = 1 - P(A),$

(iii) $\qquad\qquad P(A \wedge B) = P(A)P(B),$

if A and B are independent events.

(iv) Let A and B be events such that if B occurs, A always occurs; then if $P(A)$ and $P(B)$ are the probabilities of the individual events, the probability of the occurrence of B given that A has already occurred is:

$$P(B|A) = \frac{P(B)}{P(A)}.$$

(3) *Statistics.* Suppose an individual event can occur in k different ways as $A_1, \ldots, A_k$ with probabilities $P(A_1), \ldots, P(A_k)$, and that N independent trials take place. The probability that of the N resulting events, n_1 are of type A_1, n_2 of type A_2, etc., is:

$$P(n_1, n_2, \ldots, n_k) = \frac{N!}{n_1! n_2! \ldots n_k!} P(A_1)^{n_1} P(A_2)^{n_2} \ldots P(A_k)^{n_k},$$

where $\qquad N = \sum_{j=1}^{k} n_j.$

In particular, the probability that of the N events n are of type A_1 is

$$P(n) = \binom{N}{n} p^n q^{N-n} \quad \text{(Newton's formula)},$$

where $P(A_1) = p$, and $q = 1 - p$.

If N is large compared with 1 (written $N \gg 1$), this gives

$$P(n) = \frac{1}{\sqrt{2\pi Npq}} e^{-\frac{(n-Np)^2}{2Npq}} \quad \text{(Laplace's formula)},$$

and if $p \ll 1$ and $\dfrac{n}{N} \ll 1$,

$$P(n) = \frac{e^{-Np}(Np)^n}{n!} \quad \text{(Poisson's formula)}.$$

(4) *Deviations.* The quantities

$$s = n - \bar{n} \quad \text{and} \quad \delta = \frac{n - \bar{n}}{\bar{n}},$$

where $\qquad \bar{n} = \sum_{n=1}^{N} nP(n) = Np,$

are called the absolute and relative deviations.

(i) Average absolute deviation:

$$|\bar{s}| = 2P(\nu)\left(\bar{n} - \frac{\nu\bar{n}}{N}\right),$$

where $\nu = [\bar{n}]$ is the largest integer less than or equal to $\bar{n}$.

(ii) Average relative deviation:

$$|\bar{\delta}| = 2P(\nu)\left(1 - \frac{\nu}{N}\right).$$

(iii) Mean absolute deviation:

$$\overline{s^2} = \overline{n^2} - \bar{n}^2 = Npq = \bar{n}q.$$

(iv) Mean relative deviation:

$$\overline{\delta^2} = \frac{q}{\bar{n}}.$$

In particular, if $p \ll 1$ and $N \gg 1$, and since $pN = \bar{n}$,

$$P(n) = \frac{e^{-\bar{n}}\bar{n}^n}{n!} \quad \text{(Poisson's Law)},$$

and we have

$$\overline{s^2} = \bar{n} \text{ and } \overline{\delta^2} = \frac{1}{\bar{n}}.$$

If N and $\bar{n}$ are so large that δ is effectively continuous, and without $p \ll 1$, then the probability that δ lies between δ and $\delta + d\delta$ is given by

$$P(\delta)d\delta = \sqrt{\frac{\bar{n}}{2\pi q}}\, e^{-\frac{\bar{n}}{2q}\delta^2}\, d\delta \quad \text{(Gauss's Law)},$$

and we have

$$|\bar{\delta}| = \sqrt{\frac{2q}{\pi\bar{n}}},\ \overline{\delta^2} = \frac{q}{\bar{n}}.$$

3. *Combinatory analysis*

(1) *Permutations*

(i) The number of permutations of n different elements is

$$p(n) = n!$$

(ii) If of the n elements groups of α_1, α_2, . . ., α_k elements are indistinguishable amongst themselves,

$$p(n; \alpha_1, \ldots, \alpha_k) = \frac{n!}{\alpha_1! \alpha_2! \ldots \alpha_k!}.$$

(iii) The number of permutations of n elements taken k at a time without repetition is

$$p(n; k) = \binom{n}{k} k!$$

(iv) The number of permutations of n elements taken k at a time with repetition is

$$\tilde{p}(n; k) = n^k.$$

(2) *Combinations*

(i) The number of k-fold combinations of n elements taken without repetition is

$$c(n; k) = \binom{n}{k}.$$

(ii) The number of k-fold combinations of n elements, with repetition allowed is

$$\tilde{c}(n; k) = \binom{n + k - 1}{k}.$$

4. *Interpolation formulae*

(1) *The problem.* Suppose n different values x_1, x_2, . . ., x_n of a variable x are given and associated with them are the numbers y_1, y_2, . . ., y_n (not necessarily all different). We require a polynomial $G(x)$ such that for each $x = x_k$, $y = G(x)$ takes the corresponding value y_k. By the general theorems (see p. 499 ff.) there is exactly one rational integral function which is of at most the $(n-1)$th degree, and which, for the given values of x, takes the corresponding values of y. To determine this function for a given concrete problem either the interpolation formula of Lagrange or that of Newton can be used.

(2) *Lagrange's Interpolation Formula.* The function

$$g_1(x) = \frac{(x - x_2)(x - x_3) \ldots (x - x_n)}{(x_1 - x_2)(x_1 - x_3) \ldots (x_1 - x_n)}$$

takes the values 1, 0, . . ., 0 for $x_1, x_2, \ldots, x_n$, the given values of x. By cyclic permutation of the indices we can construct the functions $g_2(x), g_3(x), \ldots, g_n(x)$ which for the given values of x take the values

$$0, 1, 0, \ldots, 0$$
$$0, 0, 1, \ldots, 0$$
$$\cdots\cdots\cdots\cdots$$
$$0, 0, 0, \ldots, 1$$

The function

$$G(x) = y_1 g_1(x) + y_2 g_2(x) + \ldots + y_n g_n(x)$$

then has the property that it takes the values $y_1, y_2, \ldots, y_n$ at the given values of x, and it is a polynomial of the $(n-1)$th degree.

(3) *Newton's Interpolation Formula.* Let $c_1, c_2, \ldots, c_{n-1}$ be constants. Then the function

$$\begin{aligned}
G(x) = y_1 &+ c_1(x - x_1) \\
&+ c_2(x - x_1)(x - x_2) \\
&+ c_3(x - x_1)(x - x_2)(x - x_3) \\
&\cdots\cdots\cdots\cdots\cdots\cdots\cdots \\
&+ c_{n-1}(x - x_1) \ldots (x - x_{n-1})
\end{aligned}$$

is at most of the $(n-1)$th degree, and for $x = x_1$ has the value y_1. We can now determine c_1 so that $y_2 = G(x_2)$, independently of the values of $c_2, \ldots, c_{n-1}$, *viz.*

$$c_1 = \frac{y_2 - y_1}{x_2 - x_1}.$$

The constant c_2 is determined so that $y_3 = G(x_3)$, and so on. Finally we determine c_{n-1} by the requirement $y_n = G(x_n)$. If the constants determined by this method are substituted in the function $G(x)$, this function has all the required properties.

The Newton procedure has the advantage that we can solve the problem step by step. If, for example, it is shown that in determining three constants c_1, c_2, c_3, the function $G(x)$ approximates, with a sufficient degree of accuracy, to the values y_k for the remaining $n - 3$ values of x, then we can cut short the procedure and put the remaining constants equal to zero, so using a polynomial of the 3rd degree.

IV. GEOMETRY AND TRIGONOMETRY

A. Plane Geometry

1. *General theorems*

(1) *The Triangle*

(i) $\alpha + \beta + \gamma = 180°$ (Fig. 429).

(ii) The angle bisector w_γ divides the side c in the ratio $p:q = a:b$ (Fig. 429).

(iii) The altitudes h_a, h_b, h_c and the sides a, b, c (Fig. 429) are related as follows:

$$h_a:h_b:h_c = \frac{1}{a}:\frac{1}{b}:\frac{1}{c} = bc:ac:ab.$$

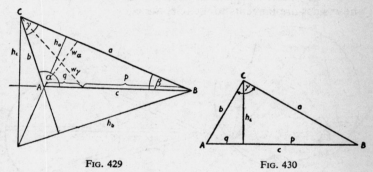

FIG. 429   FIG. 430

(iv) In a right-angled triangle (Fig. 430) we have

$$a^2 = pc,$$
$$b^2 = qc,$$
$$h_c^2 = pq,$$

and
$$a^2 + b^2 = c^2,$$

(the so-called Theorem of Pythagoras).

(v) More generally, if similar figures with areas $A(a)$, $A(b)$, $A(c)$, are constructed on the three sides of a right-angled triangle, then $A(a) + A(b) = A(c)$.

(2) *The Circle*

Notation: O = centre of the circle; t = tangent; α', β', α'' = angles at circumference; μ = angle at centre; α, β = angles between chord and tangent (Fig. 431).

We have the following theorems:

(i) All angles at the circumference on the same arc are equal:

$$\alpha' = \alpha'' = \alpha''' \ldots;$$

(ii) $$\mu = 2\alpha' = 2\alpha'';$$

(iii) $$\alpha = \alpha', \beta = \beta'.$$

(iv) If s is a diameter, $\alpha' = 90°$ (Theorem of Thales).

(v) The sums of opposite pairs of angles in a quadrilateral inscribed in a circle are equal.

(vi) The sums of opposite pairs of sides of a quadrilateral whose sides are tangents to a circle, are equal.

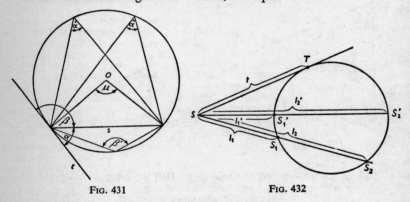

FIG. 431   FIG. 432

(vii) Secant-tangent theorem (Fig. 432):

$$t^2 = l_1 l_2 = l_1' l_2'.$$

2. *Properties of polygons*

(2) *Irregular polygons*

(i) Triangle:

Notation: a, b, c = sides; α, β, γ = angles; h_a, h_b, h_c = altitudes; r = radius of circumscribed circle; ρ = radius of inscribed circle; ρ_a, ρ_b, ρ_c = radii of escribed circles; m_a, m_b, m_c = medians;

w_α, w_β, w_γ = bisectors of interior angles; w'_α, w'_β, w'_γ = bisectors of exterior angles; t_a, t_b, t_c = intercepts formed on sides by points of contact of the inscribed circle; $\triangle$ = area; $s = \dfrac{a + b + c}{2}$.

Right-angled triangle ($\gamma = 90°$)

$$a^2 + b^2 = c^2, \qquad \triangle = \frac{ab}{2},$$

$$h_c = \frac{ab}{c}, \qquad r = \frac{c}{2},$$

$$\rho_a = \frac{a + c - b}{2},$$

$$\rho_b = \frac{b + c - a}{2}, \quad \rho_c = \frac{a + b + c}{2}, \quad \rho = \frac{a + b - c}{2}.$$

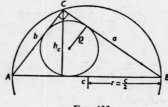

Fig. 433

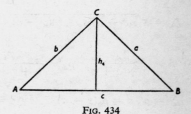

Fig. 434

Isosceles triangle ($a = b$)

$$\triangle = \frac{c}{4} \sqrt{4a^2 - c^2},$$

$$h_a = h_b = \frac{2\triangle}{a},$$

$$h_c = \frac{1}{2} \sqrt{4a^2 - c^2} = \rho_a = \rho_b,$$

$$\rho = \frac{c(2a - c)}{4h_c}, \quad \rho_c = \frac{c(2a + c)}{4h_c}, \quad r = \frac{a^2}{2h_c}.$$

515

FORMULAE

General triangle

If p is the projection of b on a, q the projection of a on b, then:

$$ap = bq$$
$$c^2 = a^2 + b^2 + 2bq, \text{ if } \gamma > 90°$$
$$c^2 = a^2 + b^2 - 2bq, \text{ if } \gamma < 90°.$$

If a_c and b_c are the projections of a and b on c, then:

$$a^2 - b^2 = a_c^2 - b_c^2.$$

Further,

$$p = \frac{a^2 + b^2 - c^2}{2a}, \qquad q = \frac{a^2 + b^2 - c^2}{2b},$$

$$h_a = \frac{bc}{2r}, \qquad r = \frac{abc}{4\triangle}, \qquad \triangle = \frac{ah_a}{2},$$

$$\triangle = \sqrt{s(s-a)(s-b)(s-c)} = \frac{1}{4}\sqrt{4a^2b^2 - (a^2 + b^2 - c^2)^2},$$

$$\rho = \frac{2\triangle}{a+b+c}, \quad \rho_a = \frac{2\triangle}{b+c-a}, \quad \frac{1}{\rho} = \frac{1}{\rho_a} + \frac{1}{\rho_b} + \frac{1}{\rho_c},$$

$$\triangle = \rho \cdot s = \rho_a(s-a), \qquad \triangle^2 = \rho\rho_a\rho_b\rho_c,$$

$$\rho_a + \rho_b + \rho_c = \rho + 4r,$$

$$m_a = \sqrt{\frac{1}{2}\left(b^2 + c^2 - \frac{1}{2}a^2\right)},$$

$$m_a^2 + m_b^2 + m_c^2 = \frac{3}{4}(a^2 + b^2 + c^2),$$

$$w_\alpha = \frac{1}{b+c}\sqrt{bc(a+b+c)(-a+b+c)},$$

$$w_\alpha' = \frac{1}{b-c}\sqrt{bc(a+b-c)(a-b+c)}.$$

(ii) Parallelogram:

Notation: a, b = sides; h_a, h_b = altitudes; d_1, d_2 = diagonals; A = area.

Then $\qquad A = ah_a = bh_b,$

and $\qquad d_{1,2} = \sqrt{a^2 + b^2 \pm 2a\sqrt{b^2 - h_a^2}}.$

If $a = b$ then d_1 is perpendicular to d_2.

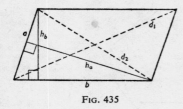

Fig. 435

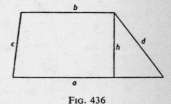

Fig. 436

(iii) Trapezium:

Notation: a, b = parallel sides; c, d = non-parallel sides;

$$h = \text{altitude}; A = \text{area}; s = \frac{a + b + c + d}{2}.$$

Then $\quad A = \dfrac{(a + b)h}{2},$

and $\qquad h = \dfrac{2}{a - b} \sqrt{s(s - a + b)(s - c)(s - d)}.$

(iv) Inscribed quadrilateral:

Notation: a, b, c, d = sides; r = radius of circumscribed circle;

A = area; d_1, d_2 = diagonals; $s = \dfrac{a + b + c + d}{2}.$

Then $\qquad A = \sqrt{(s - a)(s - b)(s - c)(s - d)},$

$$r = \frac{1}{4A} \sqrt{(ab + cd)(ac + bd)(ad + bc)},$$

517

$$d_2 = \sqrt{\frac{(ab + cd)(ac + bd)}{ad + bc}},$$

and $\qquad d_1 d_2 = ac + bd$ (Ptolemy's theorem).

If a further circle can be inscribed in the quadrilateral, then

$$A = \sqrt{abcd}.$$

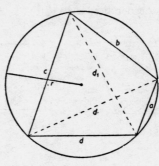

FIG. 437

(2) *Regular polygons*

Notation: $a =$ length of side; $r =$ radius of circumscribed circle; $\rho =$ radius of inscribed circle; $d =$ diagonal; $A =$ area. If n is the number of sides, then the central angle associated with a side is $\dfrac{360°}{n}$, and the interior angle is $\left(180 - \dfrac{360}{n}\right)°$.

(i) Triangle:

$$h = \frac{a}{2}\sqrt{3} = \frac{3r}{2} = 3\rho \quad (h = \text{altitude})$$

$$r = \frac{2}{3}h = \frac{a}{3}\sqrt{3} = 2\rho$$

$$\rho = \frac{h}{3} = \frac{a}{6}\sqrt{3} = \frac{r}{2}$$

$$\triangle = \frac{a^2}{4}\sqrt{3} = \frac{h^2}{3}\sqrt{3} = \frac{3r^2}{4}\sqrt{3} = 3\rho^2\sqrt{3}$$

(ii) Square:

$$r = \frac{a}{2} \sqrt{2} = \rho\sqrt{2}$$

$$\rho = \frac{a}{2} = \frac{r}{2} \sqrt{2}$$

$$A = a^2 = 2r^2 = 4\rho^2$$

(iii) Pentagon:

$$r = \frac{a}{10} \sqrt{50 + 10\sqrt{5}} = \rho(\sqrt{5} - 1)$$

$$\rho = \frac{a}{10} \sqrt{25 + 10\sqrt{5}} = \frac{r}{4}(\sqrt{5} + 1)$$

$$a = \frac{r}{2} \sqrt{10 - 2\sqrt{5}} = 2\rho \sqrt{5 - 2\sqrt{5}}$$

$$d = \frac{a}{2}(\sqrt{5} + 1) = \frac{r}{2} \sqrt{10 + 2\sqrt{5}} = \rho \sqrt{10 - 2\sqrt{5}}$$

$$A = \frac{a^2}{4} \sqrt{25 + 10\sqrt{5}} = \frac{5r^2}{8} \sqrt{10 + 2\sqrt{5}} = 5\rho^2 \sqrt{5 - 2\sqrt{5}}$$

(iv) Hexagon:

$$r = a = \frac{2}{3} \rho\sqrt{3}$$

$$\rho = \frac{a}{2} \sqrt{3} = \frac{r}{2} \sqrt{3}$$

$$A = \frac{3a^2}{2} \sqrt{3} = \frac{3r^2}{2} \sqrt{3} = 2\rho^2\sqrt{3}$$

(v) Octagon:

$$r = \frac{a}{2} \sqrt{4 + 2\sqrt{2}} = \rho \sqrt{4 - 2\sqrt{2}}$$

$$\rho = \frac{a}{2}(\sqrt{2} + 1) = \frac{r}{2} \sqrt{2 + \sqrt{2}}$$

519

FORMULAE

$$a = r\sqrt{2 - \sqrt{2}} = 2\rho(\sqrt{2} - 1)$$

$$A = 2a^2(\sqrt{2} + 1) = 2r^2\sqrt{2} = 8\rho^2(\sqrt{2} - 1)$$

(vi) Decagon:

$$r = \frac{a}{2}(\sqrt{5} + 1) = \frac{\rho}{5}\sqrt{50 - 10\sqrt{5}}$$

$$\rho = \frac{a}{2}\sqrt{5 + 2\sqrt{5}} = \frac{r}{4}\sqrt{10 + 2\sqrt{5}}$$

$$a = \frac{r}{2}(\sqrt{5} - 1) = \frac{2\rho}{5}\sqrt{25 - 10\sqrt{5}}$$

$$A = \frac{5a^2}{2}\sqrt{5 + 2\sqrt{5}} = \frac{5r^2}{4}\sqrt{10 - 2\sqrt{5}} = 2\rho^2\sqrt{25 - 10\sqrt{5}}$$

(vii) Circle:

r = radius; l = circumference; $\pi = 3{\cdot}1415\ldots$.

$$l = 2\pi r$$

$$A = \pi r^2$$

The arc-length for angle β is $\frac{\pi r}{180}\beta$, and the area of sector with angle β is $\frac{\pi r^2}{360}\beta$.

B. Solid geometry

A polyhedron is a body bounded by plane surfaces. It is convex if the interior angles formed by adjacent planes are less than 180°. A polyhedron is regular if its surfaces are regular congruent polygons and if the same number of polygons meet at each vertex.

If v is the number of vertices, s the number of surfaces, e the number of edges and a the number of angles between the edges, then for any convex polyhedron:

$$v + s = e + 2 \quad \text{(Euler's polyhedron theorem)}$$

and $\qquad 2e = a$.

520

1. *General polyhedra and other solids*

Notation: V = volume; S = total surface; A = lateral surface; S_b = base surface; S_u = upper surface; h = altitude; r_b = base-circle radius; r_u = upper surface-circle radius; R = radius of sphere; a, b, c = edges; d = diagonal; s = generator; m = median-section.

(1) *Prism*

$$V = hS_b$$

Regular prism (Fig. 438; base-edge a)

$$V = \frac{1}{4} a^2 h\sqrt{3}$$

$$S = a\left(\frac{a}{2}\sqrt{3} + 3h\right)$$

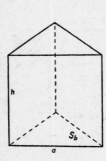

FIG. 438

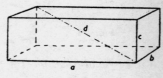

FIG. 439

(2) *Rectangular solid* (Fig. 439)

$$V = abc$$
$$S = 2(ab + bc + ca)$$
$$d = \sqrt{a^2 + b^2 + c^2}$$

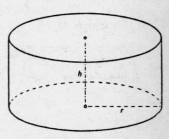

FIG. 440

(3) *Circular cylinder*

General circular cylinder: $V = \pi r^2 h$

Right circular cylinder: $A = 2\pi rh$
(Fig. 440)

$$S = 2\pi r(h + r)$$

521

(4) *Pyramid*

$$V = S_b \cdot \frac{h}{3}$$

Regular four-sided right pyramid (Fig. 441; base edge *a*)

$$V = \frac{a^2}{3} h$$

$$S = a^2 + 2a \sqrt{h^2 + \frac{a^2}{4}}$$

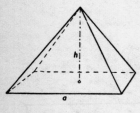

Fig. 441

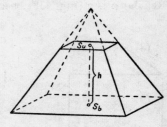

Fig. 442

(5) *Pyramid frustrum* (Fig. 442)

$$V = \frac{h}{3} (S_b + \sqrt{S_b S_u} + S_u)$$

(6) *Circular cone*

General circular cone: $\qquad V = \frac{1}{3} \pi r^2 h$

Right circular cone (Fig. 443): $A = \pi r s$

$$S = \pi r (s + r)$$

$$s = \sqrt{r^2 + h^2}$$

(7) *Frustrum of cone*

General circular cone: $\qquad V = \frac{\pi h}{3} (r_b^2 + r_b r_u + r_u^2)$

Right circular cone (Fig. 444): $A = (r_b + r_u) \pi s$

522

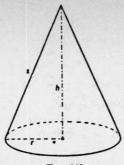

Fig. 443

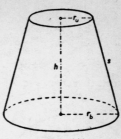

Fig. 444

(8) *Prismatoid*

$$V = \frac{h}{6}(S_b + S_u + 4m)$$

(9) *Obliquely-cut right three-sided prism*

$$V = S_b \frac{a + b + c}{3}$$

(10) *Sphere*

$$V = \frac{4}{3}\pi R^3; \quad S = 4\pi R^2$$

Spherical zone between two parallel planes (Fig. 445) at distance h:

$$V = \frac{\pi h}{3}(3r_b^2 + 3r_u^2 + h^2)$$

$$S = \pi(r_b^2 + 2Rh + r_u^2)$$

$$A = 2\pi Rh$$

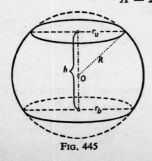

Fig. 445

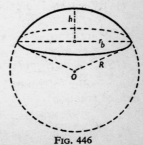

Fig. 446

Spherical segment with altitude h (Fig. 446):

$$V = \frac{\pi h}{6}(3r_b^2 + h^2)$$

$$S = \pi(2r_b^2 + h^2)$$

$$A = 2\pi Rh = \pi(r_b^2 + h^2)$$

Spherical sector (Fig. 447; r = radius, h = altitude):

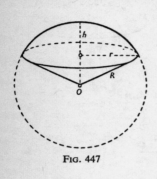

$$V = \frac{2}{3}\pi R^2 h$$

$$S = \pi R(r + 2h)$$

Spherical wedge (α = angle formed by boundary planes):

$$V = \pi R^3 \left(\frac{\alpha}{270°}\right)$$

(11) *Ellipsoid* (semi-axes a, b, c)

$$V = \frac{4}{3}\pi abc$$

Fig. 447

(12) *Ellipsoid of revolution*

$$V = \frac{4}{3}\pi ab^2 \quad (2a = \text{axis of rotation}).$$

(13) *Paraboloid of revolution*

$$V = \frac{1}{2}\pi r^2 h$$

(14) *Truncated paraboloid of revolution*

$$V = \frac{1}{2}\pi(r_b^2 + r_u^2)h$$

(15) *Anchor ring (Torus)*

r = radius of rotated circle, R = distance of its centre from axis of rotation:

$$V = 2\pi^2 r^2 R$$

$$S = 4\pi^2 r R$$

2. *Regular polyhedra*

There are only 5 regular convex polyhedra, the 'Platonic' solids. *Notation:* R = radius of circumscribed sphere; r = radius of inscribed sphere; a = edge.

(1) *Tetrahedron* (Fig. 448; 4 equilateral triangles)

$$V = \frac{a^3}{12}\sqrt{2} \qquad S = a^2\sqrt{3}$$

$$R = \frac{a}{4}\sqrt{6} \qquad r = \frac{a}{12}\sqrt{6}$$

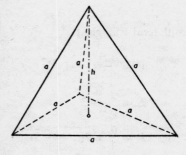

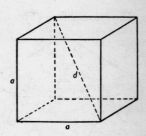

FIG. 448

FIG. 449

(2) *Cube* (Fig. 449; 6 squares)

$$V = a^3 \qquad S = 6a^2$$

$$R = \frac{a}{2}\sqrt{3} \qquad r = \frac{a}{2}$$

(3) *Octahedron* (Fig. 450; 8 equilateral triangles)

$$V = \frac{a^3}{3}\sqrt{2} \qquad S = 2a^2\sqrt{3}$$

$$R = \frac{a}{2}\sqrt{2} \qquad r = \frac{a}{6}\sqrt{6}$$

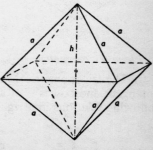

FIG. 450

525

(4) *Dodecahedron* (Fig. 451; 12 regular pentagons)

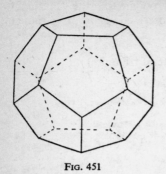

$$V = \frac{a^3}{4}(15 + 7\sqrt{5})$$

$$S = 3a^2 \sqrt{5(5 + 2\sqrt{5})}$$

$$R = \frac{a}{4}(1 + \sqrt{5})\sqrt{3}$$

$$r = \frac{a}{4} \sqrt{\frac{50 + 22\sqrt{5}}{5}}$$

FIG. 451

(5) *Icosahedron* (Fig. 452; 20 equilateral triangles)

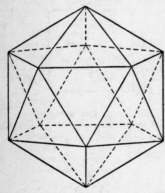

$$V = \frac{5a^3}{12}(3 + \sqrt{5})$$

$$S = 5a^2\sqrt{3}$$

$$R = \frac{a}{4} \sqrt{2(5 + \sqrt{5})}$$

$$r = \frac{a}{2} \sqrt{\frac{7 + 3\sqrt{5}}{6}}$$

FIG. 452

C. Trigonometry

1. *Plane trigonometry*

(i) The trigonometrical functions sine, cosine, tangent, secant, cotangent and cosecant of an (acute) angle α are defined by the following relations in a right-angled triangle (Fig. 453):

$$\sin \alpha = \frac{a}{c} \qquad \cos \alpha = \frac{b}{c} \qquad \tan \alpha = \frac{a}{b}$$

$$\csc \alpha = \frac{c}{a} \qquad \sec \alpha = \frac{c}{b} \qquad \cot \alpha = \frac{b}{a}$$

(See also p. 471 ff.)

The angular functions $\sin \alpha$, $\cos \alpha$, $\tan \alpha$, $\cot \alpha$ can be represented by the segments marked in Fig. 454, where the circle has unit radius. The four quadrants are denoted by I, II, III, IV.

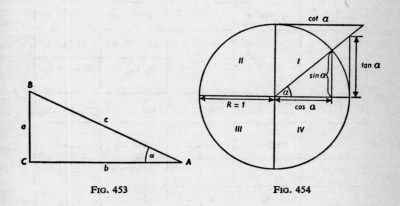

FIG. 453   FIG. 454

(ii) The signs of the trigonometrical functions in the 4 quadrants are

	sin	cos	tan	cot
I	+	+	+	+
II	+	−	−	−
III	−	−	+	+
IV	−	+	−	−

The angular functions in the four quadrants are related as follows:

	sin	cos	tan	cot
$-\alpha$	$-\sin\alpha$	$\cos\alpha$	$-\tan\alpha$	$-\cot\alpha$
$90° \pm \alpha$	$\cos\alpha$	$\mp\sin\alpha$	$\mp\cot\alpha$	$\mp\tan\alpha$
$180° \pm \alpha$	$\mp\sin\alpha$	$-\cos\alpha$	$\pm\tan\alpha$	$\pm\cot\alpha$
$270° \pm \alpha$	$-\cos\alpha$	$\pm\sin\alpha$	$\mp\cot\alpha$	$\mp\tan\alpha$
$360° \pm \alpha$	$\pm\sin\alpha$	$\cos\alpha$	$\pm\tan\alpha$	$\pm\cot\alpha$

(iii) Values of the trigonometrical functions of special angles:

α	$\sin\alpha$	$\cos\alpha$	$\tan\alpha$	$\cot\alpha$
$0°$	0	1	0	$\pm\infty$
$30°$	$\frac{1}{2}$	$\frac{1}{2}\sqrt{3}$	$\frac{1}{3}\sqrt{3}$	$\sqrt{3}$
$45°$	$\frac{1}{2}\sqrt{2}$	$\frac{1}{2}\sqrt{2}$	1	1
$60°$	$\frac{1}{2}\sqrt{3}$	$\frac{1}{2}$	$\sqrt{3}$	$\frac{1}{3}\sqrt{3}$
$90°$	1	0	$\pm\infty$	0
$180°$	0	-1	0	$\pm\infty$
$270°$	-1	0	$\pm\infty$	0
$360°$	0	1	0	$\pm\infty$

(iv) Relations between angle and arc-length in a circle of unit radius:

The arc-length associated with the angle α is

$$\text{arc } \alpha = 2\pi \frac{\alpha}{360} \quad (\alpha \text{ measured in degrees})$$

α	$1°$	$30°$	$45°$	$60°$	$90°$	$180°$	$270°$	$360°$
arc α	$\dfrac{\pi}{180}$	$\dfrac{\pi}{6}$	$\dfrac{\pi}{4}$	$\dfrac{\pi}{3}$	$\dfrac{\pi}{2}$	π	$\dfrac{3\pi}{2}$	2π
Numerical value	0·017	0·524	0·785	1·05	1·57	3·14	4·71	6·28

(v) In a general triangle, not necessarily right-angled (Fig. 455), the following theorems hold:

(1) *Sine theorem*

$$\frac{a}{b} = \frac{\sin \alpha}{\sin \beta}, \quad \frac{a}{c} = \frac{\sin \alpha}{\sin \gamma}, \quad \frac{b}{c} = \frac{\sin \beta}{\sin \gamma}.$$

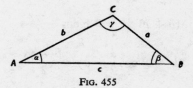

FIG. 455

(2) *Cosine theorem*

$$a^2 = b^2 + c^2 - 2bc \cos \alpha,$$
$$b^2 = a^2 + c^2 - 2ac \cos \beta,$$
$$c^2 = a^2 + b^2 - 2ab \cos \gamma.$$

(3) *Tangent theorem*

$$\frac{a-b}{a+b} = \frac{\tan \dfrac{\alpha - \beta}{2}}{\tan \dfrac{\alpha + \beta}{2}}; \quad \frac{a-c}{a+c} = \frac{\tan \dfrac{\alpha - \gamma}{2}}{\tan \dfrac{\alpha + \gamma}{2}}; \quad \frac{b-c}{b+c} = \frac{\tan \dfrac{\beta - \gamma}{2}}{\tan \dfrac{\beta + \gamma}{2}}.$$

(4) *Cotangent theorem*

If $\quad s = \dfrac{a + b + c}{2}\quad$ and $\quad \rho = \sqrt{\dfrac{(s - a)(s - b)(s - c)}{s}}$,

then:

$$\cot \frac{\alpha}{2} = \frac{s - a}{\rho}; \quad \cot \frac{\beta}{2} = \frac{s - b}{\rho}; \quad \cot \frac{\gamma}{2} = \frac{s - c}{\rho}.$$

(5) *Area of triangle*

$$\triangle = \frac{1}{2}\, ab \sin \gamma = \frac{1}{2}\, ca \sin \beta = \frac{1}{2}\, bc \sin \alpha.$$

(6) *Radius of circumscribed circle*

$$r = \frac{a}{2 \sin \alpha} = \frac{b}{2 \sin \beta} = \frac{c}{2 \sin \gamma}.$$

(7) *Radius of inscribed circle*

$$\rho = (s - a) \tan \frac{\alpha}{2} = (s - b) \tan \frac{\beta}{2} = (s - c) \tan \frac{\gamma}{2}.$$

(8) *Mollweide equations*

$$(b + c) \sin \frac{\alpha}{2} = a \cos \frac{\beta - \gamma}{2},$$

$$(b - c) \cos \frac{\alpha}{2} = a \sin \frac{\beta - \gamma}{2}.$$

(9) *Altitude formulae*

$$h_a = b \sin \gamma = c \sin \beta,$$

$$h_b = c \sin \alpha = a \sin \gamma,$$

$$h_c = a \sin \beta = b \sin \alpha.$$

(10) *Projection theorem*

$$a = b \cos \gamma + c \cos \beta,$$

$$b = a \cos \gamma + c \cos \alpha,$$

$$c = a \cos \beta + b \cos \alpha.$$

(vi) Connections between trigonometric functions:

$$\sin^2 \alpha + \cos^2 \alpha = 1,$$

$$\tan \alpha = \frac{\sin \alpha}{\cos \alpha} = \frac{1}{\cot \alpha},$$

$$\cot \alpha = \frac{\cos \alpha}{\sin \alpha} = \frac{1}{\tan \alpha},$$

$$\frac{1}{\cos^2 \alpha} = 1 + \tan^2 \alpha; \quad \frac{1}{\sin^2 \alpha} = 1 + \cot^2 \alpha.$$

	$\sin \alpha$	$\cos \alpha$	$\tan \alpha$	$\cot \alpha$
$\sin \alpha$		$\sqrt{1 - \cos^2 \alpha}$	$\dfrac{\tan \alpha}{\sqrt{1 + \tan^2 \alpha}}$	$\dfrac{1}{\sqrt{1 + \cot^2 \alpha}}$
$\cos \alpha$	$\sqrt{1 - \sin^2 \alpha}$		$\dfrac{1}{\sqrt{1 + \tan^2 \alpha}}$	$\dfrac{\cot \alpha}{\sqrt{1 + \cot^2 \alpha}}$
$\tan \alpha$	$\dfrac{\sin \alpha}{\sqrt{1 - \sin^2 \alpha}}$	$\dfrac{\sqrt{1 - \cos^2 \alpha}}{\cos \alpha}$		$\dfrac{1}{\cot \alpha}$
$\cot \alpha$	$\dfrac{\sqrt{1 - \sin^2 \alpha}}{\sin \alpha}$	$\dfrac{\cos \alpha}{\sqrt{1 - \cos^2 \alpha}}$	$\dfrac{1}{\tan \alpha}$	

(vii) Addition theorems for trigonometrical functions:
(1) *Addition theorems*

$$\sin (\alpha \pm \beta) = \sin \alpha \cos \beta \pm \cos \alpha \sin \beta$$

$$\cos (\alpha \pm \beta) = \cos \alpha \cos \beta \mp \sin \alpha \sin \beta$$

$$\tan (\alpha \pm \beta) = \frac{\tan \alpha \pm \tan \beta}{1 \mp \tan \alpha \tan \beta}$$

$$\cot (\alpha \pm \beta) = \frac{\cot \alpha \cot \beta \mp 1}{\cot \beta \pm \cot \alpha}$$

(2) *Sums and differences of functions*

$$\sin \alpha + \sin \beta = 2 \sin \frac{\alpha + \beta}{2} \cos \frac{\alpha - \beta}{2}$$

$$\sin \alpha - \sin \beta = 2 \cos \frac{\alpha + \beta}{2} \sin \frac{\alpha - \beta}{2}$$

$$\cos \alpha + \cos \beta = 2 \cos \frac{\alpha + \beta}{2} \cos \frac{\alpha - \beta}{2}$$

$$\cos \alpha - \cos \beta = -2 \sin \frac{\alpha + \beta}{2} \sin \frac{\alpha - \beta}{2}$$

$$\cos \alpha \pm \sin \beta = 2 \sin \left(45° - \frac{\alpha \mp \beta}{2} \right) \sin \left(45° + \frac{\alpha \pm \beta}{2} \right)$$

$$\cot \alpha \pm \tan \beta = \frac{\cos (\alpha \mp \beta)}{\sin \alpha \cos \beta}$$

2. *Spherical Trigonometry* (see p. 406; Figs. 292, 293)

(1) *The right-angled spherical triangle* (c = hypotenuse)

$$\cos c = \cos a \cos b$$
$$\cos c = \cot \alpha \cot \beta \qquad\qquad 90° < \alpha + \beta < 270°$$

$$\left. \begin{array}{l} \cos \alpha = \cos a \sin \beta \\ \cos \beta = \cos b \sin \alpha \end{array} \right\} \qquad -90° < \alpha - \beta < +90°$$

$$\left. \begin{array}{l} \sin \alpha = \dfrac{\sin a}{\sin c}; \quad \sin \beta = \dfrac{\sin b}{\sin c} \\[2mm] \cos \alpha = \dfrac{\tan b}{\tan c}; \quad \cos \beta = \dfrac{\tan a}{\tan c} \end{array} \right\} \begin{array}{l} \sin a \leqq \sin c \\[2mm] \sin b \leqq \sin c \end{array}$$

$$\tan \alpha = \frac{\tan a}{\sin b}; \quad \tan \beta = \frac{\tan b}{\sin a}.$$

(2) *The oblique spherical triangle*

(i) Sine theorem:

$$\sin a : \sin b : \sin c = \sin \alpha : \sin \beta : \sin \gamma$$

(a) Side-cosine theorem:

$$\cos a = \cos b \cos c + \sin b \sin c \cos \alpha$$
$$\cos b = \cos c \cos a + \sin c \sin a \cos \beta$$
$$\cos c = \cos a \cos b + \sin a \sin b \cos \gamma$$

(b) Angle-cosine theorem:

$$\cos \alpha = -\cos \beta \cos \gamma + \sin \beta \sin \gamma \cos a$$
$$\cos \beta = -\cos \gamma \cos \alpha + \sin \gamma \sin \alpha \cos b$$
$$\cos \gamma = -\cos \alpha \cos \beta + \sin \alpha \sin \beta \cos c$$

(ii) Altitude formulae:

$$\sin a \sin \beta = \sin b \sin \alpha = \sin h_c$$
$$\sin b \sin \gamma = \sin c \sin \beta = \sin h_a$$
$$\sin c \sin \alpha = \sin a \sin \gamma = \sin h_b$$

(iii)

$$\sin a \cos \beta = \cos b \sin c - \sin b \cos c \cos \alpha$$
$$\sin a \cos \gamma = \cos c \sin b - \sin c \cos b \cos \alpha$$
$$\sin \alpha \cos b = \cos \beta \sin \gamma + \sin \beta \cos \gamma \cos a$$
$$\sin \alpha \cos c = \cos \gamma \sin \beta + \sin \gamma \cos \beta \cos a$$

(iv) Delambre's and Gauss's equations:

$$\sin \frac{\alpha}{2} \sin \frac{b+c}{2} = \sin \frac{a}{2} \cos \frac{\beta-\gamma}{2}$$

$$\sin \frac{\alpha}{2} \cos \frac{b+c}{2} = \cos \frac{a}{2} \cos \frac{\beta+\gamma}{2}$$

$$\cos \frac{\alpha}{2} \sin \frac{b-c}{2} = \sin \frac{a}{2} \sin \frac{\beta-\gamma}{2}$$

$$\cos \frac{\alpha}{2} \cos \frac{b-c}{2} = \cos \frac{a}{2} \sin \frac{\beta+\gamma}{2}$$

(v) Napier's equations:

$$\tan \frac{b+c}{2} \cos \frac{\beta+\gamma}{2} = \tan \frac{a}{2} \cos \frac{\beta-\gamma}{2}$$

$$\tan \frac{\beta+\gamma}{2} \cos \frac{b+c}{2} = \cot \frac{\alpha}{2} \cos \frac{b-c}{2}$$

533

$$\tan \frac{b - c}{2} \sin \frac{\beta + \gamma}{2} = \tan \frac{a}{2} \sin \frac{\beta - \gamma}{2}$$

$$\tan \frac{\beta - \gamma}{2} \sin \frac{b + c}{2} = \cot \frac{\alpha}{2} \sin \frac{b - c}{2}$$

(vi) If $\dfrac{a + b + c}{2} = s$, $\dfrac{\alpha + \beta + \gamma}{2} = \sigma$,

then

$$\sin \frac{\alpha}{2} = \sqrt{\frac{\sin (s - b) \cdot \sin (s - c)}{\sin b \cdot \sin c}}, \quad \cos \frac{\alpha}{2} = \sqrt{\frac{\sin s \cdot \sin (s - a)}{\sin b \cdot \sin c}},$$

$$\sin \frac{a}{2} = \sqrt{\frac{- \cos \sigma \cos (\sigma - \alpha)}{\sin \beta \sin \gamma}}, \quad \cos \frac{a}{2} = \sqrt{\frac{\cos (\sigma - \beta) \cos (\sigma - \gamma)}{\sin \beta \sin \gamma}}.$$

(vii) If $S = \sqrt[+]{\sin s \cdot \sin (s - a) \cdot \sin (s - b) \cdot \sin (s - c)}$,

then $\sin \alpha = \dfrac{2S}{\sin b \sin c}$.

If $\quad \Sigma = \sqrt[+]{- \cos \sigma \cdot \cos (\sigma - \alpha) \cdot \cos (\sigma - \beta) \cdot \cos (\sigma - \gamma)}$,

then $\sin a = \dfrac{2\Sigma}{\sin \beta \cdot \sin \gamma}$.

(viii) If $k = \sqrt[+]{\dfrac{\sin (s - a) \cdot \sin (s - b) \cdot \sin (s - c)}{\sin s}}$,

then $\cot \dfrac{\alpha}{2} = \dfrac{\sin (s - a)}{k}$.

If $\quad \kappa = \sqrt[+]{\dfrac{\cos (\sigma - \alpha) \cdot \cos (\sigma - \beta) \cdot \cos (\sigma - \gamma)}{- \cos \sigma}}$,

then $\tan \dfrac{a}{2} = \dfrac{\cos (\sigma - \alpha)}{\kappa}$.

(ix) If $\varepsilon = \alpha + \beta + \gamma - 180°$ (spherical excess),

then $\tan \dfrac{\varepsilon}{4} = \sqrt[+]{\tan \dfrac{s}{2} \tan \dfrac{s-a}{2} \tan \dfrac{s-b}{2} \tan \dfrac{s-c}{2}}$,

and $\tan \left(\dfrac{\alpha}{2} - \dfrac{\varepsilon}{4} \right) = \sqrt[+]{\dfrac{\tan \dfrac{s-b}{2} \tan \dfrac{s-c}{2}}{\tan \dfrac{s}{2} \tan \dfrac{s-a}{2}}}.$

If $\qquad d = 360° - (a + b + c)$ (spherical defect),
then

$\tan \dfrac{d}{4} = \sqrt[+]{- \tan \left(45° + \dfrac{\sigma}{2} \right) \tan \left(45° - \dfrac{\sigma - \alpha}{2} \right) \times}$

$$\tan \left(45° - \dfrac{\sigma - \beta}{2} \right) \tan \left(45° - \dfrac{\sigma - \gamma}{2} \right),$$

and $\tan \left(\dfrac{a}{2} - \dfrac{d}{4} \right) = \sqrt[+]{\dfrac{\tan \dfrac{\sigma - \beta}{2} \tan \dfrac{\sigma - \gamma}{2}}{\tan \dfrac{\sigma}{2} \tan \dfrac{\sigma - \alpha}{2}}}.$

(x) Spherical in-circle radius ρ:

given by $\tan \rho = k$.

(xi) Area of spherical triangle:

given by $\triangle = R^2 \operatorname{arc} \varepsilon = r^2 \varepsilon$ (ε in radians).

(xii) Area of spherical lune with angle α (radius of sphere R):

given by $\triangle = 2R^2 \operatorname{arc} \alpha = 2R^2 \alpha$ (α in radians).

V. ANALYTICAL GEOMETRY

A. Analytical geometry of the plane

x, y are the rectangular cartesian coordinates of a point $P = P(x, y)$, x being the abscissa and y the ordinate.

1. *Transformation of coordinates*

(i) Parallel translation of the (x, y)-system:

$$x = a + x' \qquad x' = x - a;$$
$$y = b + y' \qquad y' = y - b.$$

The (x, y)-system passes over into the (x', y')-system by parallel displacement of the axes so that the point (a, b) becomes the new origin.

(ii) Rotations and parallel translation of the (x, y)-system:

$$x = a + x' \cos \alpha - y' \sin \alpha;$$
$$x' = (x - a) \cos \alpha + (y - b) \sin \alpha;$$
$$y = b + x' \sin \alpha + y' \cos \alpha;$$
$$y' = -(x - a) \sin \alpha + (y - b) \cos \alpha.$$

2. *Relations between coordinates of points*

(i) The distance d between two points $P_1(x_1, y_1)$ and $P_2(x_2, y_2)$ is

$$d = \sqrt{(x_1 - x_2)^2 + (y_1 - y_2)^2}.$$

(ii) The coordinates (x, y) of the point $P(x, y)$ which divides the segment $\overrightarrow{P_1 P_2}$ in the ratio $m:n$ are

$$x = \frac{nx_1 + mx_2}{m + n}, \quad y = \frac{ny_1 + my_2}{m + n},$$

where (x_1, y_1) and (x_2, y_2) are the coordinates of P_1 and P_2.

(iii) The area $\triangle$ of the triangle with vertices $P_1(x_1, y_1)$, $P_2(x_2, y_2)$, $P_3(x_3, y_3)$ is

$$\triangle = \tfrac{1}{2}\{x_1(y_2 - y_3) + x_2(y_3 - y_1) + x_3(y_1 - y_2)\}.$$

(iv) The area A of a polygon with n sides and vertices $P_1(x_1, y_1)$, . . ., $P_n(x_n, y_n)$ is

$$A = \tfrac{1}{2}\{x_1(y_2 - y_n) + x_2(y_3 - y_1) + x_3(y_4 - y_2) + \cdots$$
$$+ x_n(y_1 - y_{n-1})\}.$$

3. *Equation of a straight line*

Let $m = \tan \phi$ be the gradient of the straight line relative to the x-axis and α the angle between the x-axis and the positive direction of the normal to the line. Let $(a, 0)$ and $(0, b)$ be the points of intersection of the line with the x- and y-axes respectively. The perpendicular p from the origin onto the straight line is taken as positive or negative according as its direction is or is not that of the normal.

(i) General form:

$$Ax + By + C = 0 \qquad (A, B \text{ not both zero})$$

Then $a = -\dfrac{C}{A}, \quad b = -\dfrac{C}{B}, \quad m = -\dfrac{A}{B}, \quad p = -\dfrac{C}{\sqrt{A^2 + B^2}},$

$$\sin \alpha = \frac{B}{\sqrt{A^2 + B^2}}, \quad \cos \alpha = \frac{A}{\sqrt{A^2 + B^2}}.$$

(ii) Hessian normal form:

$$x \cos \alpha + y \sin \alpha - p = 0$$

(iii) Straight line through the point (x_0, y_0) with gradient m:

$$y - y_0 = m(x - x_0)$$

(iv) Intercept equation:

$$\frac{x}{a} + \frac{y}{b} = 1 \qquad (a \neq 0, b \neq 0)$$

(v) Straight line through the points $P_1(x_1, y_1)$ and $P_2(x_2, y_2)$:

$$\frac{y - y_1}{x - x_1} = \frac{y_2 - y_1}{x_2 - x_1}$$

537

(vi) Equation of the straight line through the point $P_1(x_1, y_1)$ and forming angle θ with the straight line $Ax + By + C = 0$:

$$y - y_1 = \frac{B \tan \theta - A}{A \tan \theta + B}(x - x_1)$$

(vii) Distance d_1 of the point $P_1(x_1, y_1)$ from the straight line $Ax + By + C = 0$:

$$d_1 = \frac{Ax_1 + By_1 + C}{\sqrt{A^2 + B^2}}$$

(viii) Point of intersection $P_0(x_0, y_0)$ of the two straight lines $A_1 x + B_1 y + C_1 = 0$, $A_2 x + B_2 y + C_2 = 0$ $(A_1 A_2 \neq A_2 B_1)$:

$$x_0 = \frac{B_1 C_2 - B_2 C_1}{A_1 B_2 - A_2 B_1}, \quad y_0 = \frac{C_1 A_2 - C_2 A_1}{A_1 B_2 - A_2 B_1}$$

Angle θ between the two straight lines

$$A_1 x + B_1 y + C_1 = 0; \quad A_2 x + B_2 y + C_2 = 0:$$

$$\tan \theta = \frac{A_1 B_2 - A_2 B_1}{A_1 A_2 + B_1 B_2} = \frac{m_2 - m_1}{m_1 m_2 + 1}$$

(ix) Three straight lines

$$a_{i1} x + a_{i2} y + a_{i3} = 0 \quad (i = 1, 2, 3)$$

are concurrent if

$$|a_{ik}| = 0.$$

4. Conic sections

(1) *The general equation of the second degree.* The general equation

$$a_{11} x^2 + 2a_{12} xy + a_{22} y^2 + 2a_{13} x + 2a_{23} y + a_{33} = 0$$

represents a conic section (curve of the second order). We distinguish the following cases:

(i) Proper conic-sections, when $A = |a_{ik}| \neq 0$:

    (a) Real ellipse: $A_{33} > 0$; a_{11} and A with same sign.

    (b) Imaginary ellipse: $A_{33} > 0$; a_{11} and A with different signs.

(c) Circle: $A_{33} > 0$; $a_{11} = a_{22}$; $a_{12} = 0$ (rectangular coordinates).

(d) Parabola: $A_{33} = 0$.

(e) Hyperbola: $A_{33} < 0$.

(ii) Degenerate conic sections, when $A = 0$:

(a) Real pair of straight lines, with finite point of intersection: $A_{33} < 0$.

(b) Pair of parallel straight lines: $A_{33} = 0$,
real if $A_{11} < 0$ or $A_{22} < 0$,
coincident if $A_{11} = 0$ or $A_{22} = 0$,
imaginary if $A_{11} > 0$ or $A_{22} > 0$.

(c) Imaginary pair of straight lines with real, finite point of intersection: $A_{33} > 0$.

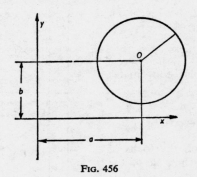

Fig. 456

(2) *The circle* (Fig. 456)

(i) General equation:

$$x^2 + y^2 + 2Ax + 2By + C = 0$$

(ii) Coordinates of centre (a, b), radius r:

$$(x - a)^2 + (y - b)^2 = r^2$$

(iii) Centre at origin:

$$x^2 + y^2 = r^2$$

(iv) Centre lying on x-axis at point $(a, 0)$, origin lying on circle (vertex equation):

$$y^2 = 2ax - x^2$$

(v) Circle through the three points $P_1(x_1, y_1)$, $P_2(x_2, y_2)$, $P_3(x_3, y_3)$:

$$\begin{vmatrix} x^2 + y^2 & x & y & 1 \\ x_1^2 + y_1^2 & x_1 & y_1 & 1 \\ x_2^2 + y_2^2 & x_2 & y_2 & 1 \\ x_3^2 + y_3^2 & x_3 & y_3 & 1 \end{vmatrix} = 0$$

(vi) Tangent through the point $P_1(x_1, y_1)$, where (a, b) is the centre of the circle and r the radius:

$$(x - a)(x_1 - a) + (y - b)(y_1 - b) = r^2$$

(3) *The parabola* (Fig. 457). Vertex-equation:

$$y^2 = 2px$$

Equation in polar coordinates (ρ, θ):

$$\rho = \frac{p}{1 + \cos \theta}$$

(In this equation the focus of the parabola is the pole of the coordinate system.)

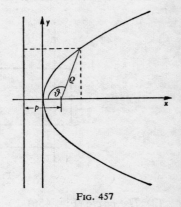

FIG. 457

(i) Tangents through the point $P_1(x_1, y_1)$:

$$y - y_1 = \frac{y_1 \pm \sqrt{y_1^2 - 2px_1}}{2x_1} (x - x_1)$$

(ii) Tangent with gradient m:

$$v - mx = \frac{p}{2m}$$

540

(iii) Normal at the point $P_1(x_1, y_1)$:

$$p(y - y_1) + y_1(x - x_1) = 0$$

(iv) Length of the focal line from the point $P_1(x_1, y_1)$:

$$r = x_1 + \frac{p}{2}$$

(v) Area of the segment cut off by the chord with end-points $P_1(x_1, y_1)$ and $P_2(x_2, y_2)$:

$$A = \frac{(y_1 - y_2)^2}{12p}$$

(4) *The ellipse* (Fig. 458). Equation referred to principal axes:

$$\frac{x^2}{a^2} + \frac{y^2}{b^2} = 1$$

where the lengths of the major and minor axes are $2a$ and $2b$ respectively.

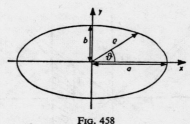

Fig. 458

Polar equation, relative to centre as pole:

$$\rho^2 = \frac{b^2}{1 - \varepsilon^2 \cos^2 \theta} \quad \left(\varepsilon = \text{numerical eccentricity} = \frac{e}{a} \right)$$

(i) Tangents to the ellipse through the point $P_1(x_1, y_1)$:

$$y - y_1 = \frac{-x_1 y_1 \pm \sqrt{b^2 x_1^2 + a^2 y_1^2 - a^2 b^2}}{a^2 - x_1^2} (x - x_1)$$

Tangents with gradient $m = \tan \phi$:

$$y - mx = \pm \sqrt{m^2 a^2 + b^2}$$

541

(ii) Normal through the point $P_1(x_1, y_1)$:

$$y - y_1 = \frac{a^2 y_1}{b^2 x_1}(x - x_1)$$

(iii) Abscissae of the foci (linear eccentricity):

$$e_1 = +\sqrt{a^2 - b^2}, \quad e_2 = -\sqrt{a^2 - b^2}$$

(iv) Focal lengths of the point ($P_1(x_1, y_1)$:

$$r_1 = a + x_1\varepsilon, \quad r_2 = a - x_1\varepsilon$$

(v) Area of the elliptical zone between the minor axis and parallel chord at distance x_1:

$$A = \frac{b}{a}\left(x_1\sqrt{a^2 - x_1^2} + a^2 \sin^{-1}\frac{x_1}{a}\right)$$

(vi) Area of the whole ellipse:

$$A = \pi ab$$

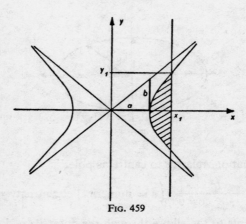

Fig. 459

(5) *Hyperbola* (Fig. 459). Equation referred to principal axes:

$$\frac{x^2}{a^2} - \frac{y^2}{b^2} = 1$$

where the lengths of the major and minor axes are $2a$ and $2b$ respectively.

Polar equation, relative to centre as pole:

$$\rho^2 = \frac{b^2}{1 - \varepsilon^2 \cos^2 \theta}$$

$$\left(\varepsilon = \text{numerical eccentricity} = \frac{e}{a}\right).$$

(i) Tangents from the point $P_1(x_1, y_1)$ to the hyperbola:

$$y - y_1 = \frac{-x_1 y_1 \pm \sqrt{-b^2 x_1^2 + a^2 y_1^2 + a^2 b^2}}{a^2 - x_1^2} (x - x_1).$$

Tangents with gradient m:

$$y - mx = \pm \sqrt{m^2 a^2 - b^2}.$$

(ii) Normal through the point $P_1(x_1, y_1)$:

$$y - y_1 = -\frac{a^2 y_1}{b^2 x_1} (x - x_1).$$

(iii) Asymptotes of the hyperbola:

$$\frac{x}{a} + \frac{y}{b} = 0; \quad \frac{x}{a} - \frac{y}{b} = 0.$$

(iv) Abscissae of foci (linear eccentricity):

$$e_1 = +\sqrt{a^2 + b^2}; \quad e_2 = -\sqrt{a^2 + b^2}.$$

(v) Focal lengths of the point $P_1(x_1, y_1)$:

$$r_1 = a + x_1 \varepsilon; \quad r_2 = -(a - x_1 \varepsilon).$$

(vi) Area of the segment of the hyperbola cut off by the chord $x = x_1$:

$$A = x_1 y_1 - ab \ln \left(\frac{x_1}{a} + \frac{y_1}{b}\right) \quad (x_1 \geq a).$$

B. Analytical geometry of three dimensions

x, y, z are the rectangular cartesian coordinates of a point $P(x, y, z)$. The axes conventionally form a right-handed system, i.e. regarded from the positive z-axis, the y-axis stands at a positive angle $90°$ relative to the x-axis. Where more suitable three-dimensional polar coordinates r, θ, ϕ are used instead.

543

1. Transformation of coordinates

(1) *Parallel translation of the (x, y, z)-system*

$$x = a + x' \qquad x' = x - a$$
$$y = b + y' \qquad y' = y - b$$
$$z = c + z' \qquad z' = z - c.$$

The (x, y, z)-system passes over into the (x', y', z')-system by parallel displacement of the axes so that the point (a, b, c) becomes the new origin.

(2) *Rotation and parallel displacement of the (x, y, z)-system.* The (x, y, z)-system passes over into the (x', y', z')-system by parallel displacement of the axes so that the point (a, b, c) becomes the new origin, followed by a rotation of the axes. If the cosines of the angles between the (x', y', z') and (x, y, z) axes are denoted by

	x	y	z
x'	α_1	β_1	γ_1
y'	α_2	β_2	γ_2
z'	α_3	β_3	$\gamma_3,$

then we have:

$$x = a + \alpha_1 x' + \alpha_2 y' + \alpha_3 z'$$
$$y = b + \beta_1 x' + \beta_2 y' + \beta_3 z'$$
$$z = c + \gamma_1 x' + \gamma_2 y' + \gamma_3 z'$$
$$x' = \alpha_1(x - a) + \beta_1(y - b) + \gamma_1(z - c)$$
$$y' = \alpha_2(x - a) + \beta_2(y - b) + \gamma_2(z - c)$$
$$z' = \alpha_3(x - a) + \beta_3(y - b) + \gamma_3(z - c).$$

The α_i, β_i, γ_i are related as follows:

$$\sum_k \alpha_k^2 = \sum_k \beta_k^2 = \sum_k \gamma_k^2 = \alpha_i^2 + \beta_i^2 + \gamma_i^2 = 1,$$

$$\sum_k \alpha_k \beta_k = \sum_k \beta_k \gamma_k = \sum_k \gamma_k \alpha_k = \alpha_i \alpha_j + \beta_i \beta_j + \gamma_i \gamma_j = 0$$

$$(i, j, k = 1, 2, 3) \qquad (i \neq j).$$

2. Relations between the coordinates of points

(i) The distance d between two points $P_1(x_1, y_1, z_1)$ and $P_2(x_2, y_2, z_2)$ is

$$d = \sqrt{(x_1 - x_2)^2 + (y_1 - y_2)^2 + (z_1 - z_2)^2}.$$

(ii) The coordinates of the point $P(x, y, z)$ which divides the segment $\overrightarrow{P_1 P_2}$ in the ratio $m{:}n$ are

$$x = \frac{mx_2 + nx_1}{m + n}, \quad y = \frac{my_2 + ny_1}{m + n}, \quad z = \frac{mz_2 + nz_1}{m + n}.$$

(iii) The area $\triangle$ of a triangle with vertices $P_1(x_1, y_1, z_1)$, $P_2(x_2, y_2, z_2)$, $P_3(x_3, y_3, z_3)$ is

$$\triangle = -\frac{1}{2d} \begin{vmatrix} x_1 & y_1 & z_1 \\ x_2 & y_2 & z_2 \\ x_3 & y_3 & z_3 \end{vmatrix},$$

where d is the distance of the plane of the triangle from the origin.

(iv) The volume V of the tetrahedron with vertices $P_i(x_i, y_i, z_i)$, $i = 1, 2, 3, 4$:

$$V = \frac{1}{6} \begin{vmatrix} x_1 & y_1 & z_1 & 1 \\ x_2 & y_2 & z_2 & 1 \\ x_3 & y_3 & z_3 & 1 \\ x_4 & y_4 & z_4 & 1 \end{vmatrix}.$$

3. The plane

A plane is thought of as having a fixed normal associated with it. We regard the positive side of the plane as that side into which the positive direction of the normal is directed. α, β, γ denote the positive angles ($\leq 180°$), which the normal makes with the axes. a, b, c denote the intercepts of the plane with the axes. The perpendicular p from O onto the plane is positive if it has the same direction as the normal, and negative if not.

(i) General equation:

$$Ax + By + Cz + D = 0.$$

545

Then

$$a = -\frac{D}{A}; \quad b = -\frac{D}{B}, \quad c = -\frac{D}{C}, \quad p = -\frac{D}{\sqrt{A^2 + B^2 + C^2}},$$

$$\cos\alpha = -\frac{p}{D}A, \quad \cos\beta = -\frac{p}{D}B, \quad \cos\gamma = -\frac{p}{D}C.$$

The sign of the root establishes the direction of the fixed normal.

(ii) Hessian normal form:

$$x\cos\alpha + y\cos\beta + z\cos\gamma - p = 0.$$

(iii) Intercept equation:

$$\frac{x}{a} + \frac{y}{b} + \frac{z}{c} - 1 = 0.$$

(iv) Planes through the point $P_0(x_0, y_0, z_0)$:

$$A(x - x_0) + B(y - y_0) + C(z - z_0) = 0.$$

(v) Plane through the points $P_1(x_1, y_1, z_1)$; $P_2(x_2, y_2, z_2)$; $P_3(x_3, y_3, z_3)$:

$$\begin{vmatrix} x & y & z & 1 \\ x_1 & y_1 & z_1 & 1 \\ x_2 & y_2 & z_2 & 1 \\ x_3 & y_3 & z_3 & 1 \end{vmatrix} = 0.$$

The distance d_1 of the point $P_1(x_1, y_1, z_1)$ from the plane

$$Ax + By + Cz + D = 0:$$

$$d_1 = \frac{Ax_1 + By_1 + Cz_1 + D}{\sqrt{A^2 + B^2 + C^2}}.$$

The angle θ, in which the planes

$$A_1x + B_1y + C_1z + D_1 = 0$$

$$A_2x + B_2y + C_2z + D_2 = 0$$

intersect:

$$\cos\theta = \frac{A_1A_2 + B_1B_2 + C_1C_2}{\sqrt{A_1^2 + B_1^2 + C_1^2}\sqrt{A_2^2 + B_2^2 + C_2^2}}.$$

The coordinates of the point of intersection of the planes

$$A_1 x + B_1 y + C_1 z + D_1 = 0$$
$$A_2 x + B_2 y + C_2 z + D_2 = 0$$
$$A_3 x + B_3 y + C_3 z + D_3 = 0:$$

$$x = \frac{1}{D} \begin{vmatrix} -D_1 & B_1 & C_1 \\ -D_2 & B_2 & C_2 \\ -D_3 & B_3 & C_3 \end{vmatrix} \qquad y = \frac{1}{D} \begin{vmatrix} A_1 & -D_1 & C_1 \\ A_2 & -D_2 & C_2 \\ A_3 & -D_3 & C_3 \end{vmatrix}$$

$$z = \frac{1}{D} \begin{vmatrix} A_1 & B_1 & -D_1 \\ A_2 & B_2 & -D_2 \\ A_3 & B_3 & -D_3 \end{vmatrix} \qquad D = \begin{vmatrix} A_1 & B_1 & C_1 \\ A_2 & B_2 & C_2 \\ A_3 & B_3 & C_3 \end{vmatrix}.$$

4. The straight line

A straight line is determined by two independent equations of the first degree in x, y, z.

(i) General form:

$$A_1 x + B_1 y + C_1 z + D_1 = 0$$
$$A_2 x + B_2 y + C_2 z + D_2 = 0$$

(straight line as intersection of two planes).

(ii) Simple form:

$$y = mx + b$$
$$z = nx + c$$

(straight line as intersection of two planes, one of which is perpendicular to the (x, y)-plane, the other perpendicular to the (x, z)-plane).

(iii) Straight line through the point $P_1(x_1, y_1, z_1)$ with direction α, β, γ:

$$\frac{x - x_1}{\cos \alpha} = \frac{y - y_1}{\cos \beta} = \frac{z - z_1}{\cos \gamma}.$$

(iv) Straight line through two points $P_1(x_1, y_1, z_1)$ and $P_2(x_2, y_2, z_2)$:

$$\frac{x - x_1}{x_2 - x_1} = \frac{y - y_1}{y_2 - y_1} = \frac{z - z_1}{z_2 - z_1}.$$

Angles α, β, γ between the straight line defined by the planes

$$A_1 x + B_1 y + C_1 z + D_1 = 0$$

$$A_2 x + B_2 y + C_2 z + D_2 = 0$$

and the axes are given by:

$$\cos \alpha = \frac{1}{N} \begin{vmatrix} B_1 & C_1 \\ B_2 & C_2 \end{vmatrix} \quad \cos \beta = \frac{1}{N} \begin{vmatrix} C_1 & A_1 \\ C_2 & A_2 \end{vmatrix} \quad \cos \gamma = \frac{1}{N} \begin{vmatrix} A_1 & B_1 \\ A_2 & B_2 \end{vmatrix}$$

where

$$N^2 = \begin{vmatrix} B_1 & C_1 \\ B_2 & C_2 \end{vmatrix}^2 + \begin{vmatrix} C_1 & A_1 \\ C_2 & A_2 \end{vmatrix}^2 + \begin{vmatrix} A_1 & B_1 \\ A_2 & B_2 \end{vmatrix}^2,$$

and N may be either positive or negative.

Angle θ between two straight lines with directions α_1, β_1, γ_1 and α_2, β_2, γ_2 is given by:

$$\cos \theta = \cos \alpha_1 \cos \alpha_2 + \cos \beta_1 \cos \beta_2 + \cos \gamma_1 \cos \gamma_2.$$

Shortest distance d between the two straight lines

$$\frac{x - x_1}{\cos \alpha_1} = \frac{y - y_1}{\cos \beta_1} = \frac{z - z_1}{\cos \gamma_1}; \quad \frac{x - x_2}{\cos \alpha_2} = \frac{y - y_2}{\cos \beta_2} = \frac{z - z_2}{\cos \gamma_2}:$$

$$d = \frac{1}{\sin \theta} \begin{vmatrix} x_1 - x_2 & \cos \alpha_1 & \cos \alpha_2 \\ y_1 - y_2 & \cos \beta_1 & \cos \beta_2 \\ z_1 - z_2 & \cos \gamma_1 & \cos \gamma_2 \end{vmatrix}.$$

5. *Surfaces of the second order*

(1) *The general equation of the second degree*. The general equation:

$$a_{11}x^2 + 2a_{12}xy + a_{22}y^2 + 2a_{13}xz + 2a_{23}yz + a_{33}z^2$$
$$+ 2a_{14}x + 2a_{24}y + 2a_{34}z + a_{44} = 0$$

represents a surface of the second order.

We distinguish the following cases:

I. Proper Surfaces: $A \neq 0$

		$A > 0$		$A < 0$
		$A'_{44}, A'A''_{44} > 0$	$A'_{44}, A'A_{44}$ not both > 0	
$A_{44} \neq 0$	$A'_{44} > 0$ $A_{44}A''_{44} > 0$	Imag. ellipsoid		Ellipsoid
	$A_{44}, A_{44}A''_{44}$ not both > 0		Hyperboloid of one sheet	Hyperboloid of two sheets
$A_{44} = 0,$ $A'_{44} \neq 0$	$A'_{44} > 0$			Elliptical paraboloid
	$A'_{44} < 0$		Hyperbolic paraboloid	

II. Degenerate surfaces: $A = 0$

		$A' \neq 0$		$A' = 0, A'' \neq 0$		$A' = 0$ $A'' = 0$ $A''' \neq 0$
		$A'_{44} > 0$ $A'A''_{44} > 0$	$A_4, A'A''_{44}$ not both > 0	$A'' > 0$	$A'' < 0$	
$A_{44} \neq 0$	$A'_{44} > 0$ $A_{44}A''_{44} > 0$	Imag. ell. cone				
	$A'_{44}, A_{44}A''_{44},$ not both > 0		Ellipt. cone			
$A_{44} = 0,$ $A'_{44} \neq 0$	$A'_{44} > 0$	Imag. ell. cylinder	Ellipt. cylinder	Imag. pair of planes		
	$A'_{44} < 0$		Hyperb. cylinder		Real pair of planes	
$A_{44} = 0, A'_{44} = 0,$ $A''_{44} \neq 0$			Parabol. cylinder	Imag. parallel pair of planes	Real pair of parallel planes	Double-plane

where

$$A'_{44} = \begin{vmatrix} a_{11} & a_{12} \\ a_{21} & a_{22} \end{vmatrix} + \begin{vmatrix} a_{22} & a_{23} \\ a_{32} & a_{33} \end{vmatrix} + \begin{vmatrix} a_{33} & a_{31} \\ a_{13} & a_{11} \end{vmatrix}$$

$$A''_{44} = a_{11} + a_{22} + a_{33}$$

$$A' = A_{11} + A_{22} + A_{33} + A_{44}$$

$$A'' = \begin{vmatrix} a_{11} & a_{12} \\ a_{21} & a_{22} \end{vmatrix} + \begin{vmatrix} a_{11} & a_{13} \\ a_{31} & a_{33} \end{vmatrix} + \begin{vmatrix} a_{11} & a_{14} \\ a_{41} & a_{44} \end{vmatrix} + \begin{vmatrix} a_{22} & a_{23} \\ a_{32} & a_{33} \end{vmatrix}$$

$$+ \begin{vmatrix} a_{22} & a_{24} \\ a_{42} & a_{44} \end{vmatrix} + \begin{vmatrix} a_{33} & a_{34} \\ a_{43} & a_{44} \end{vmatrix}$$

$$A''' = a_{11} + a_{22} + a_{33} + a_{44}.$$

(2) *Particular surfaces of the second order.* The general equation of the second degree can be brought, by suitable coordinate transformations, to the normal forms appropriate to the particular surfaces of the second order.

(i) Real ellipsoid:

$$\frac{x^2}{a^2} + \frac{y^2}{b^2} + \frac{z^2}{c^2} = 1$$

(referred to principal axes).

(ii) Hyperboloid of one sheet:

$$\frac{x^2}{a^2} + \frac{y^2}{b^2} - \frac{z^2}{c^2} = 1$$

(referred to principal axes).

Asymptotic cone:

$$\frac{x^2}{a^2} + \frac{y^2}{b^2} - \frac{z^2}{c^2} = 0.$$

(iii) Hyperboloid of two sheets:

$$\frac{x^2}{a^2} + \frac{y^2}{b^2} - \frac{z^2}{c^2} + 1 = 0$$

(referred to principal axes).

Asymptotic cone:

$$\frac{x^2}{a^2} + \frac{y^2}{b^2} - \frac{z^2}{c^2} = 0.$$

(iv) Elliptical paraboloid:

$$\frac{x^2}{a} + \frac{y^2}{b} = 2z$$

(a and b have the same sign).

(v) Hyperbolic paraboloid:

$$\frac{x^2}{a} - \frac{y^2}{b} = 2z$$

(a, b positive).

(vi) Real cone:

$$\frac{x^2}{a^2} + \frac{y^2}{b^2} - \frac{z^2}{c^2} = 0.$$

(vii) Imaginary cone:

$$\frac{x^2}{a^2} + \frac{y^2}{b^2} + \frac{z^2}{c^2} = 0.$$

(viii) Elliptical cylinder:

$$\frac{x^2}{a^2} + \frac{y^2}{b^2} = 1.$$

(ix) Hyperbolic cylinder:

$$\frac{x^2}{a^2} - \frac{y^2}{b^2} = 1.$$

(x) Parabolic cylinder:

$$\frac{x^2}{a^2} - \frac{2y}{b} = 0.$$

C. Vector calculus

1. *Definitions*

(i) A *scalar* is a function of the position-coordinates (x, y, z) which associates a numerical value with every point. In what follows scalars are denoted by small greek letters.

(ii) A *vector* is a function of the position-coordinates (x, y, z) which associates an absolute value *and* a direction with every point. Vectors are sometimes indicated by arrows. Two vectors are regarded as equal if lengths and directions can be made to coincide by parallel translation. We shall denote vectors by small latin letters in heavy type, **a**, **b**, **c**, and the corresponding absolute values $|\mathbf{a}|$, $|\mathbf{b}|$, $|\mathbf{c}|$, by a, b, c.

(iii) *Components* of a vector: suppose we have a rectangular coordinate system (x, y, z) and vectors **i**, **j**, **k** each with absolute value 1 (unit vectors), whose directions coincide respectively with the directions of the coordinate axes. Then a vector **a** can be uniquely represented in the form

$$\mathbf{a} = a_x \mathbf{i} + a_y \mathbf{j} + a_z \mathbf{k}$$

where a_x, a_y, a_z are real numbers, the components of the vector **a**. We also write

$$\mathbf{a} = \begin{pmatrix} a_x \\ a_y \\ a_z \end{pmatrix}.$$

2. *Vector Algebra*

(1) *Sum of two vectors.* The sum of two vectors

$$\mathbf{a} + \mathbf{b} = \mathbf{c}$$

is a vector **c** which depends on the summands **a** and **b** in such a way that it is represented both in length and direction by the diagonal of the parallelogram, two of whose sides proceeding from the same point as the diagonal are represented by **a** and **b**. In terms of components:

$$a_x + b_x = c_x$$
$$a_y + b_y = c_y$$
$$a_z + b_z = c_z.$$

The following rules hold for sums:

$$\mathbf{a} + \mathbf{b} = \mathbf{b} + \mathbf{a}$$
$$(\mathbf{a} + \mathbf{b}) + \mathbf{c} = \mathbf{a} + (\mathbf{b} + \mathbf{c}).$$

(2) *Product of a vector and a scalar.* The product $\phi\mathbf{a}$ of a vector and a scalar is taken to be the vector

$$\mathbf{b} = \phi\mathbf{a}$$

with absolute value $b = a\phi$ and the same direction as $\mathbf{a}$. In terms of components

$$b_x = \phi a_x$$
$$b_y = \phi a_y$$
$$b_z = \phi a_z.$$

(3) *The scalar product of two vectors.* The scalar or inner product $\mathbf{a} . \mathbf{b}$ of two vectors $\mathbf{a}$ and $\mathbf{b}$ is a scalar of magnitude

$$\mathbf{a} . \mathbf{b} = ab \cos \phi$$

where ϕ is the angle between the directions of $\mathbf{a}$ and $\mathbf{b}$. In terms of components:

$$\mathbf{a} . \mathbf{b} = a_x b_x + a_y b_y + a_z b_z$$

we have:

$$\mathbf{a} . \mathbf{b} = \mathbf{b} . \mathbf{a}$$
$$(\mathbf{a} + \mathbf{b}) . \mathbf{c} = \mathbf{a} . \mathbf{c} + \mathbf{b} . \mathbf{c}$$
$$(\lambda\mathbf{a}) . \mathbf{b} = \lambda(\mathbf{a} . \mathbf{b})$$
$$\mathbf{a}^2 = |\mathbf{a}|^2 = \mathbf{a} . \mathbf{a}$$
$$\mathbf{j} . \mathbf{k} = \mathbf{k} . \mathbf{i} = \mathbf{i} . \mathbf{j} = 0.$$

If $\mathbf{a} . \mathbf{b} = 0$, the vectors are perpendicular to one another.

(4) *The vector product.* By the vector or outer product $\mathbf{a} \wedge \mathbf{b}$ of two vectors $\mathbf{a}$ and $\mathbf{b}$ is meant the vector

$$\mathbf{c} = \mathbf{a} \wedge \mathbf{b}$$

which is perpendicular to the plane determined by $\mathbf{a}$ and $\mathbf{b}$ (the vectors $\mathbf{a}$, $\mathbf{b}$, $\mathbf{c}$ forming a right-handed system) and of magnitude

$$c = |\mathbf{a} \wedge \mathbf{b}| = ab \sin \phi$$

553

where ϕ is again the angle between **a** and **b**. In terms of components

$$c_x = (\mathbf{a} \wedge \mathbf{b})_x = a_y b_z - a_z b_y$$
$$c_y = (\mathbf{a} \wedge \mathbf{b})_y = a_z b_x - a_x b_z$$
$$c_z = (\mathbf{a} \wedge \mathbf{b})_z = a_x b_y - a_y b_x.$$

We have:

(i)
$$\mathbf{a} \wedge \mathbf{b} = -\mathbf{b} \wedge \mathbf{a}$$
$$(\mathbf{a} + \mathbf{b}) \wedge \mathbf{c} = (\mathbf{a} \wedge \mathbf{c}) + (\mathbf{b} \wedge \mathbf{c})$$
$$(\lambda \mathbf{a} \wedge \mathbf{b}) = (\mathbf{a} \wedge \lambda \mathbf{b}) = \lambda(\mathbf{a} \wedge \mathbf{b})$$
$$\mathbf{i} \wedge \mathbf{i} = \mathbf{j} \wedge \mathbf{j} = \mathbf{k} \wedge \mathbf{k} = 0$$
$$\mathbf{i} \wedge \mathbf{j} = \mathbf{k}; \quad \mathbf{j} \wedge \mathbf{k} = \mathbf{i}; \quad \mathbf{k} \wedge \mathbf{i} = \mathbf{j}.$$

(ii)
$$\mathbf{a} \cdot (\mathbf{b} \wedge \mathbf{c}) = \mathbf{b} \cdot (\mathbf{c} \wedge \mathbf{a}) = \mathbf{c} \cdot (\mathbf{a} \wedge \mathbf{b})$$
$$\mathbf{a} \wedge (\mathbf{b} \wedge \mathbf{c}) = \mathbf{b}(\mathbf{ac}) - \mathbf{c}(\mathbf{ab})$$
$$(\mathbf{a} \wedge \mathbf{b})(\mathbf{c} \wedge \mathbf{d}) = \mathbf{a}[\mathbf{b} \wedge (\mathbf{c} \wedge \mathbf{d})] = (\mathbf{ac})(\mathbf{bd}) - (\mathbf{bc})(\mathbf{ad})$$
$$\mathbf{a} \wedge (\mathbf{b} \wedge \mathbf{c}) + \mathbf{b} \wedge (\mathbf{c} \wedge \mathbf{a}) + \mathbf{c} \wedge (\mathbf{a} \wedge \mathbf{b}) = 0$$
$$(\mathbf{a} \wedge \mathbf{b}) \wedge (\mathbf{c} \wedge \mathbf{d}) = \mathbf{c}[(\mathbf{a} \wedge \mathbf{b})\mathbf{d}] - \mathbf{d}[(\mathbf{a} \wedge \mathbf{b})\mathbf{c}].$$

(iii) $\mathbf{a} \cdot (\mathbf{b} \wedge \mathbf{c})$ is the volume of the parallelepiped defined by the three vectors **a**, **b**, **c**. If $\mathbf{a} \wedge \mathbf{b} = 0$, the vectors **a** and **b** are parallel.

Separation of a vector **a** into two components of which one is parallel to, the other perpendicular to, an arbitrary unit vector **e**:

$$\mathbf{a} = \mathbf{e}(\mathbf{e} \cdot \mathbf{a}) + \mathbf{e} \wedge (\mathbf{a} \wedge \mathbf{e}).$$

The vectors **a**, **b**, **c** proceeding from a point form a tetrahedron with volume

$$V = \frac{1}{6}\mathbf{c} \cdot (\mathbf{a} \wedge \mathbf{b}).$$

3. *Vector analysis*

(1) *Gradient*. Let $\phi = \phi(x, y, z)$ be a scalar. Then the gradient of ϕ is defined as the vector

$$\operatorname{grad} \phi = \mathbf{i} \frac{\partial \phi}{\partial x} + \mathbf{j} \frac{\partial \phi}{\partial y} + \mathbf{k} \frac{\partial \phi}{\partial z}.$$

Using the vector operator

$$\nabla = \mathbf{i}\frac{\partial}{\partial x} + \mathbf{j}\frac{\partial}{\partial y} + \mathbf{k}\frac{\partial}{\partial z},$$

the gradient can be expressed in the form

$$\text{grad } \phi = \nabla\phi.$$

We have

$$\nabla(\phi + \psi) = \nabla\phi + \nabla\psi$$

$$\nabla(\phi\psi) = \phi\nabla\psi + \psi\nabla\phi.$$

(2) *Divergence.* The divergence of a vector $\mathbf{a}$ is defined as the scalar

$$\text{div } \mathbf{a} = \frac{\partial a_x}{\partial x} + \frac{\partial a_y}{\partial y} + \frac{\partial a_z}{\partial z}.$$

Using the vector operator ∇,

$$\text{div } \mathbf{a} = \nabla\mathbf{a},$$

the inner product of ∇ and $\mathbf{a}$. By twice applying ∇ to the scalar, we obtain:

$$\nabla(\nabla\phi) = \text{div grad } \phi = \frac{\partial^2\phi}{\partial x^2} + \frac{\partial^2\phi}{\partial y^2} + \frac{\partial^2\phi}{\partial z^2} = \triangle\phi,$$

where $\nabla\nabla$ is written as $\triangle$.

We have

$$\nabla(\mathbf{a} + \mathbf{b}) = \nabla\mathbf{a} + \nabla\mathbf{b}$$

$$\triangle(\phi + \psi) = \triangle\phi + \triangle\psi.$$

(3) *Curl.* The curl of a vector $\mathbf{a}$, curl $\mathbf{a}$, denotes the vector with components:

$$(\text{curl } \mathbf{a})_x = \frac{\partial a_z}{\partial y} - \frac{\partial a_y}{\partial z}$$

$$(\text{curl } \mathbf{a})_y = \frac{\partial a_x}{\partial z} - \frac{\partial a_z}{\partial x}$$

$$(\text{curl } \mathbf{a})_z = \frac{\partial a_y}{\partial x} - \frac{\partial a_x}{\partial y}.$$

Using the vector operator ∇, we can write

$$\text{curl } \mathbf{a} = \nabla \wedge \mathbf{a}.$$

We have

$$\nabla \wedge (\mathbf{a} + \mathbf{b}) = (\nabla \wedge \mathbf{a}) + (\nabla \wedge \mathbf{b}).$$

(4) *Relations between grad, div and curl*

$$\text{div } (\mathbf{a}\phi) = \phi \text{ div } \mathbf{a} + \mathbf{a} \text{ grad } \phi$$

$$\text{curl } (\mathbf{a}\phi) = \phi \text{ curl } \mathbf{a} - \mathbf{a} \wedge \text{grad } \phi$$

$$\text{div } (\mathbf{a} \wedge \mathbf{b}) = \mathbf{b} \text{ curl } \mathbf{a} - \mathbf{a} \text{ curl } \mathbf{b}$$

$$\text{curl } (\mathbf{a} \wedge \mathbf{b}) = (\mathbf{b} \text{ grad}) \mathbf{a} - (\mathbf{a} \text{ grad}) \mathbf{b} + \mathbf{a} \text{ div } \mathbf{b} - \mathbf{b} \text{ div } \mathbf{a}$$

$$\text{grad } (\mathbf{ab}) = (\mathbf{b} \text{ grad}) \mathbf{a} + (\mathbf{a} \text{ grad } \mathbf{b}) + \mathbf{a} \wedge \text{curl } \mathbf{b} + \mathbf{b} \wedge \text{curl } \mathbf{a}$$

$$\text{curl grad } \phi = 0$$

$$\text{div curl } \mathbf{a} = 0$$

$$\text{curl } (\text{curl } \mathbf{a}) = \text{grad } (\text{div } \mathbf{a}) - \triangle \mathbf{a}.$$

Using ∇ these formulae become:

$$\nabla (\mathbf{a}\phi) = \phi \nabla \mathbf{a} + \mathbf{a} \nabla \phi$$

$$\nabla \wedge (\mathbf{a}\phi) = \phi (\nabla \wedge \mathbf{a}) - (\mathbf{a} \wedge \nabla \phi)$$

$$\nabla (\mathbf{a} \wedge \mathbf{b}) = \mathbf{b} (\nabla \wedge \mathbf{a}) - \mathbf{a} (\nabla \wedge \mathbf{b})$$

$$\nabla \wedge (\mathbf{a} \wedge \mathbf{b}) = (\mathbf{b}\nabla)\mathbf{a} - (\mathbf{a}\nabla)\mathbf{b} + \mathbf{a}(\nabla \mathbf{b}) - \mathbf{b}(\nabla \mathbf{a})$$

$$\nabla (\mathbf{ab}) = (\mathbf{b}\nabla)\mathbf{a} + (\mathbf{a}\nabla)\mathbf{b} + \mathbf{a} \wedge (\nabla \wedge \mathbf{b}) + \mathbf{b} \wedge (\nabla \wedge \mathbf{a})$$

$$\nabla \wedge (\nabla \phi) = 0$$

$$\nabla (\nabla \wedge \mathbf{a}) = 0$$

$$\nabla \wedge (\nabla \wedge \mathbf{a}) = \nabla (\nabla \mathbf{a}) - \triangle \mathbf{a}.$$

VI. SPECIAL FUNCTIONS

In this section we deal with the properties of special functions which are of particular significance in geometry and physics. In the individual cases we shall give

(a) the definition of the function concerned, as the solution of a differential equation, or in terms of other functions;

(b) important representations as a series, an integral or a product;

(c) functional equations, addition-theorems, differential coefficients, orthogonality relations, asymptotic behaviour at significant points;

(d) relations with other functions discussed here.

1. Exponential functions

The exponential function $\exp(x) = e^x$ is the simplest integral transcendental function without finite poles or zeros.

(1) *Differential equation*

$$y'(x) - y(x) = 0$$

where
$$y(0) = 1.$$

(2) *Development as series*

$$\exp(x) = 1 + \frac{x}{1!} + \frac{x^2}{2!} + \frac{x^3}{3!} + \ldots$$

where $-\infty < x < +\infty$.

Limit

$$\exp(x) = \lim_{n \to \infty} \left(1 + \frac{x}{n}\right)^n = \lim_{n \to \infty} \frac{1}{\left(1 - \frac{x}{n}\right)^n}$$

(3) *Differential coefficient:*

$$\frac{d}{dx} e^x = e^x$$

Addition theorem:

$$\exp(x + y) = \exp(x) \cdot \exp(y)$$

(Because of the addition theorem we may write $\exp(x) = e^x$.)

Special values:

$$\exp(1) = \lim_{n \to \infty} \left(1 + \frac{1}{n}\right)^n = e = 2 \cdot 718281 \ldots$$

$$\exp(\pm 2\pi i) = 1; \quad \exp(\pm \pi i) = -1.$$

2. *Logarithmic functions*

(1) The natural logarithm $f(x) = \ln x$ is defined as the inverse function of the exponential function, *i.e.* by the relation

$$e^{\ln x} = \ln e^x = x$$

(2) *Representation as series*

$$\ln(1 + x) = \frac{x}{1} - \frac{x^2}{2} + \frac{x^3}{3} - \frac{x^4}{4} + \ldots,$$

where $-1 < x \leq +1$.

$$\ln(1 - x) = -\frac{x}{1} - \frac{x^2}{2} - \frac{x^3}{3} - \frac{x^4}{4} - \ldots,$$

where $-1 \leq x < +1$.

$$\ln(a + x) = \ln a + 2\left\{\frac{x}{2a + x} + \frac{1}{3}\left(\frac{x}{2a + x}\right)^3 \right.$$
$$\left. + \frac{1}{5}\left(\frac{x}{2a + x}\right)^5 + \ldots\right\},$$

where $0 < a < \infty$, $-a < x < \infty$.

$$\ln x = 2\left\{\frac{x - 1}{x + 1} + \frac{1}{3}\left(\frac{x - 1}{x + 1}\right)^3 + \frac{1}{5}\left(\frac{x - 1}{x + 1}\right)^5 + \ldots\right\},$$

where $0 < x < \infty$.

Representation as integral: $\quad \ln x = \displaystyle\int_1^x \frac{dt}{t}$

Differential coefficient: $\quad \dfrac{d}{dx} \ln x = \dfrac{1}{x}$

Functional equation: $\ln xy = \ln x + \ln y$

Limit: $\ln x = \lim\limits_{\varepsilon \to 0} \dfrac{x^\varepsilon - 1}{\varepsilon}$ $(x > 0)$

Singularities: $\ln x$ has essential singularities (branch-points of infinite order) and is therefore infinitely multiple-valued. The function-values in the individual branches are separated by multiples of $2\pi i$.

3. *Hyperbolic functions*

(1) *Definitions*

$$\sinh x = \frac{e^x - e^{-x}}{2} \qquad \cosh x = \frac{e^x + e^{-x}}{2}$$

$$\tanh x = \frac{e^x - e^{-x}}{e^x + e^{-x}} \qquad \coth x = \frac{e^x + e^{-x}}{e^x - e^{-x}}$$

$\sinh x$ and $\cosh x$ are solutions of the differential equation

$$y''(x) - y(x) = 0.$$

(2) *Representation as series*

$$\sinh x = x + \frac{x^3}{3!} + \frac{x^5}{5!} + \ldots, \quad |x| < \infty$$

$$\cosh x = 1 + \frac{x^2}{2!} + \frac{x^4}{4!} + \ldots, \quad |x| < \infty$$

$$\tanh x = x - \frac{x^3}{3} + \frac{2}{15}x^5 - \frac{17}{315}x^7 + \ldots, \quad |x| < \frac{\pi}{2}$$

$$= \sum_{n=1}^{\infty} (-1)^{n-1} \frac{2^{2n}(2^{2n} - 1)B_n}{(2n)!} x^{2n-1}$$

$$x \coth x = 1 + \frac{1}{3}x^2 - \frac{1}{45}x^4 + \frac{2}{945}x^6 - \ldots, \quad |x| < \pi$$

$$= 1 + \sum_{n=1}^{\infty} (-1)^{n-1} \frac{2^{2n}B_n}{(2n)!} x^{2n}$$

(the B_n are *Bernoulli's numbers*, see p. 580).

559

Differential coefficients:

$$\frac{d}{dx} \sinh x = \cosh x \qquad \frac{d}{dx} \cosh x = \sinh x$$

$$\frac{d}{dx} \tanh x = \frac{1}{\cosh^2 x} \qquad \frac{d}{dx} \coth x = -\frac{1}{\sinh^2 x}$$

(3) The hyperbolic functions are related as follows:

$$\cosh^2 x - \sinh^2 x = 1 \qquad \tanh x = \frac{\sinh x}{\cosh x} = \frac{1}{\coth x}$$

$$\sinh \left(x + \frac{i\pi}{2} \right) = i \cosh x \qquad \cosh \left(x + \frac{i\pi}{2} \right) = i \sinh x$$

$$\sinh (-x) = -\sinh x \qquad \cosh (-x) = +\cosh x$$

$$\tanh (-x) = -\tanh x \qquad \coth (-x) = -\coth x$$

$$\cosh x = \sqrt{1 + \sinh^2 x} = \frac{1}{\sqrt{1 - \tanh^2 x}} = \frac{\coth x}{\sqrt{\coth^2 x - 1}}$$

$$\sinh x = \sqrt{\cosh^2 x - 1} = \frac{\tanh x}{\sqrt{1 - \tanh^2 x}} = \frac{1}{\sqrt{\coth^2 x - 1}}$$

$$\tanh x = \frac{\sinh x}{\sqrt{1 + \sinh^2 x}} = \frac{\sqrt{\cosh^2 x - 1}}{\cosh x} = \frac{1}{\coth x}$$

$$\coth x = \frac{\sqrt{1 + \sinh^2 x}}{\sinh x} = \frac{\cosh x}{\sqrt{\cosh^2 x - 1}} = \frac{1}{\tanh x}$$

(4) *Addition theorems:*

$$\sinh (x \pm y) = \sinh x \cosh y \pm \cosh x \sinh y$$

$$\cosh (x \pm y) = \cosh x \cosh y \pm \sinh x \sinh y$$

$$\tanh (x \pm y) = \frac{\tanh x \pm \tanh y}{1 \pm \tanh x \tanh y}$$

$$\coth (x \pm y) = \frac{\coth x \coth y \pm 1}{\coth y \pm \coth x}$$

Functions of double arguments:

$$\sinh 2x = 2 \cosh x \, . \, \sinh x$$

$$\cosh 2x = \cosh^2 x + \sinh^2 x$$

$$\tanh 2x = \frac{2 \tanh x}{1 + \tanh^2 x}$$

$$\coth 2x = \frac{\coth^2 x + 1}{2 \coth x}$$

Function of half arguments:

$$\sinh \frac{x}{2} = \sqrt{\frac{\cosh x - 1}{2}}$$

$$\cosh \frac{x}{2} = \sqrt{\frac{\cosh x + 1}{2}}$$

$$\tanh \frac{x}{2} = \frac{\sinh x}{\cosh x + 1} = \frac{\cosh x - 1}{\sinh x}$$

$$\coth \frac{x}{2} = \frac{\sinh x}{\cosh x - 1} = \frac{\cosh x + 1}{\sinh x}$$

Sums and differences of the functions:

$$\sinh x \pm \sinh y = 2 \sinh \frac{x \pm y}{2} \cosh \frac{x \mp y}{2}$$

$$\cosh x + \cosh y = 2 \cosh \frac{x + y}{2} \cosh \frac{x - y}{2}$$

$$\cosh x - \cosh y = 2 \sinh \frac{x + y}{2} \sinh \frac{x - y}{2}$$

$$\tanh x \pm \tanh y = \frac{\sinh (x \pm y)}{\cosh x \cosh y}$$

$$\coth x \pm \coth y = \frac{\sinh (y \pm x)}{\sinh x \sinh y}$$

561

Products of the functions:

$$2 \sinh nx \sinh mx = \cosh (n + m)x - \cosh (n - m)x$$

$$2 \cosh nx \cosh mx = \cosh (n + m)x + \cosh (n - m)x$$

$$2 \sinh nx \cosh mx = \sinh (n + m)x + \sinh (n - m)x$$

(5) *Connections with trigonometric functions* (see below)

$$\sinh x = -i \sin ix \qquad \cosh x = \cos ix$$

$$\tanh x = -i \tan ix \qquad \coth x = +i \cot ix$$

4. *Trigonometric functions*

(1) The trigonometric functions can be defined as follows:

$$\sin x = \frac{e^{ix} - e^{-ix}}{2i} \qquad \cos x = \frac{e^{ix} + e^{-ix}}{2}$$

$$\tan x = \frac{-i(e^{ix} - e^{-ix})}{e^{ix} + e^{-ix}} \qquad \cot x = \frac{i(e^{ix} + e^{-ix})}{e^{ix} - e^{-ix}}.$$

$\sin x$ and $\cos x$ are both solutions of the differential equation

$$y''(x) + y(x) = 0.$$

(2) *Development as series*

$$\sin x = \frac{x}{1!} - \frac{x^3}{3!} + \frac{x^5}{5!} - \ldots, \quad |x| < \infty$$

$$\cos x = 1 - \frac{x^2}{2!} + \frac{x^4}{4!} - \frac{x^6}{6!} + \ldots, \quad |x| < \infty$$

$$\tan x = \sum_{n=1}^{\infty} \frac{2^{2n}(2^{2n} - 1)}{(2n)!} B_n x^{2n-1}, \quad |x| < \frac{\pi}{2}$$

$$x \cot x = 1 - \sum_{n=1}^{\infty} \frac{2^{2n}}{(2n)!} B_n x^{2n}, \quad |x| < \pi$$

(the B_n are *Bernoulli's numbers*, see p. 580).

Representation as product:

$$\sin \pi x = \pi x \prod_{k=1}^{\infty} \left(1 - \frac{x^2}{k^2}\right)$$

Differential coefficients:

$$\frac{d}{dx} \sin x = \cos x \qquad \frac{d}{dx} \cos x = - \sin x$$

$$\frac{d}{dx} \tan x = \frac{1}{\cos^2 x} \qquad \frac{d}{dx} \cot x = - \frac{1}{\sin^2 x}$$

(3) The trigonometric functions are related as follows:

$$\sin^2 x + \cos^2 x = 1 \qquad \tan x = \frac{\sin x}{\cos x} = \frac{1}{\cot x}$$

$$\sin (x + \pi/2) = \cos x \qquad \cos (x + \pi/2) = - \sin x$$

$$\sin (-x) = - \sin x \qquad \cos (-x) = + \cos x$$

$$\tan (-x) = - \tan x \qquad \cot (-x) = - \cot x$$

$$\sin x = \sqrt{1 - \cos^2 x} = \frac{\tan x}{\sqrt{1 + \tan^2 x}} = \frac{1}{\sqrt{1 + \cot^2 x}}$$

$$\cos x = \sqrt{1 - \sin^2 x} = \frac{1}{\sqrt{1 + \tan^2 x}} = \frac{\cot x}{\sqrt{1 + \cot^2 x}}$$

$$\tan x = \frac{\sin x}{\sqrt{1 - \sin^2 x}} = \frac{\sqrt{1 - \cos^2 x}}{\cos x} = \frac{1}{\cot x}$$

$$\cot x = \frac{\sqrt{1 - \sin^2 x}}{\sin x} = \frac{\cos x}{\sqrt{1 - \cos^2 x}} = \frac{1}{\tan x}$$

Addition theorems:

$$\sin (x \pm y) = \sin x \cos y \pm \cos x \sin y$$

$$\cos (x \pm y) = \cos x \cos y \mp \sin x \sin y$$

$$\tan (x \pm y) = \frac{\tan x \pm \tan y}{1 \mp \tan x \tan y}$$

$$\cot (x \pm y) = \frac{\cot x \cot y \mp 1}{\cot y \pm \cot x}$$

563

Functions of double argument:

$$\sin 2x = 2 \sin x \cos x = \frac{2 \tan x}{1 + \tan^2 x}$$

$$\cos 2x = \cos^2 x - \sin^2 x = \frac{1 - \tan^2 x}{1 + \tan^2 x}$$

$$\tan 2x = \frac{2 \tan x}{1 - \tan^2 x}$$

$$\cot 2x = \frac{\cot^2 x - 1}{2 \cot x}$$

Functions of half argument:

$$\sin \frac{x}{2} = \sqrt{\frac{1 - \cos x}{2}}$$

$$\cos \frac{x}{2} = \sqrt{\frac{1 + \cos x}{2}}$$

$$\tan \frac{x}{2} = \frac{\sin x}{1 + \cos x} = \frac{1 - \cos x}{\sin x}$$

$$\cot \frac{x}{2} = \frac{\sin x}{1 - \cos x} = \frac{1 + \cos x}{\sin x}$$

Sums and differences of the functions:

$$\sin x \pm \sin y = 2 \sin \frac{x \pm y}{2} \cos \frac{x \mp y}{2}$$

$$\cos x + \cos y = 2 \cos \frac{x + y}{2} \cos \frac{x - y}{2}$$

$$\cos x - \cos y = -2 \sin \frac{x + y}{2} \sin \frac{x - y}{2}$$

$$\tan x \pm \tan y = \frac{\sin (x \pm y)}{\cos x \cos y}$$

$$\cot x \pm \cot y = \frac{\sin (y \pm x)}{\sin x \sin y}$$

Products of the functions:

$$2 \sin nx \sin mx = \cos (n - m)x - \cos (n + m)x$$

$$2 \cos nx \cos mx = \cos (n - m)x + \cos (n + m)x$$

$$2 \sin nx \cos mx = \sin (n - m)x + \sin (n + m)x$$

Special values:

$$\sin (n \cdot \pi) = 0 \qquad \sin (\pi/2 \cdot n) = (-1)^{\frac{n-1}{2}}$$

$$\cos (n \cdot \pi) = (-1)^n \qquad \cos (\pi/2 \cdot n) = 0$$

$$(n = 0, 1, \ldots) \qquad\qquad (n = 1, 3, \ldots)$$

(4) *Connections with hyperbolic functions*

$$\sin x = -i \sinh ix \qquad \tan x = -i \tanh ix$$

$$\cos x = \cosh ix \qquad \cot x = +i \coth ix$$

5. *Inverse trigonometric and hyperbolic functions*

(1) *Definitions*

$$\sin^{-1} x, \quad \cos^{-1} x, \quad \tan^{-1} x, \quad \cot^{-1} x$$

$$\sinh^{-1} x, \quad \cosh^{-1} x, \quad \tanh^{-1} x, \quad \coth^{-1} x$$

are defined as the inverse functions of the trigonometric and hyperbolic functions. Thus

$$\sin (\sin^{-1} x) = \sin^{-1} (\sin x) = x$$

$$\cos (\cos^{-1} x) = \cos^{-1} (\cos x) = x$$

$$\tan (\tan^{-1} x) = \tan (\tan^{-1} x) = x$$

$$\cot (\cot^{-1} x) = \cot^{-1} (\cot x) = x$$

$$\sinh (\sinh^{-1} x) = \sinh^{-1} (\sinh x) = x$$

$$\cosh (\cosh^{-1} x) = \cosh^{-1} (\cosh x) = x$$

$$\tanh (\tanh^{-1} x) = \tanh (\tanh^{-1} x) = x$$

$$\coth (\coth^{-1} x) = \coth (\coth^{-1} x) = x.$$

(2) *Representation as series*

$$\sin^{-1} x = x + \frac{1}{2}\frac{x^3}{3} + \frac{1}{2}\cdot\frac{3}{4}\frac{x^5}{5} + \ldots, \quad |x| \le 1$$

$$\tan^{-1} x = x - \frac{x^3}{3} + \frac{x^5}{5} - \frac{x^7}{7} + \ldots, \quad |x| \le 1$$

$$\tanh^{-1} x = \coth^{-1}\frac{1}{x} = x + \frac{x^3}{3} + \frac{x^5}{5} + \ldots, \quad |x| < 1$$

(3) *Differential coefficients*

$$\frac{d}{dx}\sin^{-1} x = \frac{1}{\sqrt{1 - x^2}}, \quad -1 < x < +1,$$

where the sign of the root is positive if $-\pi/2 < \sin^{-1} x < \pi/2$.

$$\frac{d}{dx}\cos^{-1} x = -\frac{1}{\sqrt{1 - x^2}}, \quad -1 < x < +1,$$

where the sign of the root is positive if $0 < \cos^{-1} x < \pi$.

$$\frac{d}{dx}\tan^{-1} x = -\frac{d}{dx}\cot^{-1} x = \frac{1}{1 + x^2} \text{ for all } x.$$

$$\frac{d(\sinh^{-1} x)}{dx} = \frac{1}{\sqrt{x^2 + 1}}; \quad \frac{d(\cosh^{-1} x)}{dx} = \frac{1}{\sqrt{x^2 - 1}}$$

$$\frac{d}{dx}\tanh^{-1} x = \frac{d\coth^{-1} x}{dx} = \frac{1}{1 - x^2}$$

Sums and differences of the functions:

$$\sin^{-1} x \pm \sin^{-1} y = \sin^{-1}(x\sqrt{1 - y^2} \pm y\sqrt{1 - x^2})$$

$$= \cos^{-1}(\sqrt{1 - x^2}\sqrt{1 - y^2} \mp xy)$$

$$\cos^{-1} x \pm \cos^{-1} y = \sin^{-1}(y\sqrt{1 - x^2} \pm x\sqrt{1 - y^2})$$

$$= \cos^{-1}(xy \mp \sqrt{1 - x^2}\sqrt{1 - y^2})$$

$$\tan^{-1} x \pm \tan^{-1} y = \tan^{-1}\frac{x \pm y}{1 \mp xy}$$

$$\sinh^{-1} x \pm \sinh^{-1} y = \sinh^{-1} (x\sqrt{y^2 + 1} \pm y\sqrt{x^2 + 1})$$
$$= \cosh^{-1} (\sqrt{x^2 + 1} \sqrt{y^2 + 1} \pm xy)$$
$$\cosh^{-1} x \pm \cosh^{-1} y = \sinh^{-1} (y\sqrt{x^2 - 1} \pm x\sqrt{y^2 - 1})$$
$$= \cosh^{-1} (xy \pm \sqrt{x^2 - 1} \sqrt{y^2 - 1})$$
$$\tanh^{-1} x \pm \tanh^{-1} y = \tanh^{-1} \frac{x \pm y}{1 \pm xy}$$

Special values:

$$\tan^{-1} 1 = \pi/4 = 1 - \frac{1}{3} + \frac{1}{5} - \frac{1}{7} + \ldots$$

(Leibniz's series).

Singularities: The functions each possess infinitely many values for a given argument. On each branch lie two branch-points of the first order whose branch-intersections run to ∞.

(4) *Representation by means of logarithms*

$$\sin^{-1} x = +i \ln (-ix + \sqrt{1 - x^2})$$
$$\cos^{-1} x = +i \ln (x + i \sqrt{1 - x^2})$$
$$\tan^{-1} x = \frac{-i}{2} \ln \frac{1 + ix}{1 - ix}$$
$$\cot^{-1} x = \frac{-i}{2} \ln \frac{ix - 1}{ix + 1}$$
$$\sinh^{-1} x = \ln (x + \sqrt{x^2 + 1})$$
$$\cosh^{-1} x = \ln (x + \sqrt{x^2 - 1})$$
$$\tanh^{-1} x = \frac{1}{2} \ln \frac{1 + x}{1 - x}$$
$$\coth^{-1} x = \frac{1}{2} \ln \frac{x + 1}{x - 1}$$

6. The Γ-function

(1) The function $\Gamma(x)$ is a meromorphic function of x with simple poles at $x = -n$ $(n = 0, 1, 2, \ldots)$ and residues $(-1)^n/n!$.

It is uniquely defined by the following conditions:

  (i) $\Gamma(x + 1) = x\Gamma(x)$,
  (ii) $\Gamma(x)$ is real and positive when x is real and positive,
  (iii) for real, positive x, $[\Gamma'(x)]^2 < \Gamma(x)\,\Gamma''(x)$,
  (iv) $\Gamma(1) = 1$.

(2) *Representation as integral*

$$\Gamma(x) = \int_0^\infty e^{-t}t^{x-1}\,dt = \int_0^1 \left(\ln\frac{1}{t}\right)^{x-1}dt \qquad (R(x) > 0)$$

$$\Gamma(x) = \int_1^\infty e^{-t}t^{x-1}\,dt + \sum_{n=0}^\infty \frac{(-1)^n}{n!(x+n)} \qquad x \text{ arbitrary}$$

Representation as product:

$$\frac{1}{\Gamma(x)} = xe^{Cx}\prod_1^\infty \left(1 + \frac{x}{n}\right)e^{-\frac{x}{n}}$$

where $\quad C = \lim_{m\to\infty}\left(\sum_{l=1}^m \frac{1}{l} - \ln m\right) = 0.577215\ldots$

(C is called *Euler's constant*).

Representation as limit:

$$\Gamma(x + 1) = \lim_{n\to\infty} \frac{1.2.3\ldots n.n^x}{(x+1)(x+2)\ldots(x+n)}$$

(3) *Functional equations*

$$\Gamma(x + 1) = x\Gamma(x)$$

$$\Gamma(x)\,\Gamma(1 - x) = \frac{\pi}{\sin \pi x}$$

$$\Gamma\left(\frac{1}{2} + x\right)\Gamma\left(\frac{1}{2} - x\right) = \frac{\pi}{\cos \pi x}$$

Asymptotic behaviour (Stirling's formula):

$$\Gamma(x) = e^{(x-\frac{1}{2})\ln x - x}\sqrt{2\pi}\left\{1 + \frac{1}{12x} + \frac{1}{288x^2} + O(x^{-3})\right\}$$

Special values:

$$\Gamma(n + 1) = n! \qquad (n = 0, 1, 2, \ldots)$$

$$\Gamma\left(\frac{1}{2}\right) = \sqrt{\pi}$$

$$\Gamma(1) = \Gamma(2) = 1$$

7. *The δ-function*

(1) The δ-function is not a function in the usual sense, being only defined as a distribution. In using $\delta(x)$, therefore, a certain amount of caution is needed. The δ-function satisfies the conditions:

(i) $\delta(x - t) = 0$ for $x \neq t$.

(ii) $\int_{-\infty}^{\infty} \delta(x - t)\, dt = 1$.

(2) *Fourier-representation*

$$\delta(x - t) = \frac{1}{2\pi} \int_{-\infty}^{\infty} e^{iz(x-t)}\, dz$$

Series representation

If $\phi_n(x)$ is a complete orthonormal system $\delta(x - t)$ can be represented by the series

$$\delta(x - t) = \sum_{n=0}^{\infty} \phi_n^*(x)\phi_n(t)$$

Representation as limit:

$$\delta(x - t) = \frac{1}{\sqrt{\pi}} \lim_{\varepsilon \to 0} \left[\frac{1}{\sqrt{\varepsilon}} e^{-\frac{(x-t)^2}{\varepsilon}} \right]$$

$$\delta(x - t) = \frac{1}{\pi} \lim_{\varepsilon \to 0} \left[\frac{\varepsilon}{\varepsilon^2 + (x - t)^2} \right]$$

$$\delta(x - t) = \frac{1}{\pi} \lim_{n \to \infty} \left[\frac{\sin n(x - t)}{x - t} \right]$$

$$\delta(x - t) = \frac{1}{i\pi} \lim_{n \to \infty} \left[\frac{e^{in(x-t)}}{x - t} \right]$$

Special properties of $\delta(x)$:

$$\delta(x) = \delta(-x) = \delta^*(x); \quad \delta(x) = 0, \quad x \neq 0$$

$$a\delta(x) = \delta\left(\frac{x}{a}\right); \quad x\delta(x) = 0; \quad f(x)\delta(x) = f(0)\delta(x)$$

$$(a \pm x)\delta(x) = f(a)\delta(x); \quad \int_{-\infty}^{+\infty} f(t)\delta(x-t)dt = f(x)$$

$$\int_{-\infty}^{+\infty} \delta(x-t)\delta(s-t)dt = \delta(x-t)$$

Differentiation of the function:

$$\delta'(x) = -\frac{1}{x}\,\delta(x) = -\delta'(-x)$$

$$\delta''(x) = \frac{2}{x^2}\,\delta(x); \quad \frac{d^n}{dx^n}\,\delta(x) = (-1)^n \frac{n!}{x^n}\,\delta(x)$$

We have the following formulae for the differential coefficients of $\delta(x)$:

$$\int_{-\infty}^{+\infty} f(t)\delta'(x-t)dt = f'(x), \text{ if } f'(x) \text{ is continuous for } t = x$$

$$\int_{-\infty}^{+\infty} \delta'(x-t)\delta(s-t) = \delta'(x-s)$$

$$\int_{-\infty}^{+\infty} f(x)\frac{\partial^n}{\partial x^n}\,\delta(t-x)dt = (-1)^n \frac{d^n}{dx^n} f(x),$$

$$\text{if } f^{(n)}(t) \text{ is continuous for } t = x$$

(3) *Decomposition into $\delta_+(z) + \delta_-(z)$.* As a function of the complex variable z, $\delta(z)$ has poles of the first order at $i\varepsilon$ and $-i\varepsilon$, with residues $+\frac{1}{2\pi i}$ and $-\frac{1}{2\pi i}$. We can split $\delta(z)$ into a sum of two functions, each of which has only one pole:

$$\delta(z) = \delta_+(z) + \delta_-(z)$$

where

$$\delta_+(z) = \frac{1}{2}\left[\delta(z) - P\frac{1}{i\pi z}\right] = \frac{1}{2\pi}\int_{-0}^{+\infty} ds\, e^{-isz}$$

$$= + \frac{1}{2\pi i}\lim_{\varepsilon \to 0}\frac{1}{(z - i\varepsilon)}$$

$$\delta_-(z) = \frac{1}{2}\left[\delta(z) + P\frac{1}{i\pi z}\right] = \frac{1}{2\pi}\int_{-0}^{+\infty} ds\, e^{-isz}$$

$$= - \frac{1}{2\pi i}\lim_{\varepsilon \to 0}\frac{1}{z + i\varepsilon}.$$

The following relations hold between $\delta_+(z)$ and $\delta_-(z)$:

$$\delta_+(z) = \delta_-(-z) = \delta_-^*(z) = (\delta_-(z^*))^*$$
$$\delta_-(z) = \delta_+(-z) = \delta_+^*(z) = (\delta_+(z^*))^*.$$

VII. SERIES AND EXPANSIONS IN SERIES

1. *General*

(1) The formal sum of infinitely many terms

$$\sum_{\nu=1}^{\infty} u_\nu = u_1 + u_2 + \ldots$$

is called an infinite series. If the partial-sums

$$s_n = \sum_{\nu=1}^{n} u_\nu$$

tend to a finite limit

$$s = \lim_{n \to \infty} s_n,$$

the series is said to be convergent; otherwise it is said to be divergent. The limiting value s of a convergent series is defined to be its sum, and we write

$$s = \sum_{\nu=1}^{\infty} u_\nu.$$

$\sum_{\nu=1}^{\infty} u_\nu$ is said to be absolutely convergent if $\sum_{\nu=1}^{\infty} |u_\nu|$ is also convergent; otherwise it is said to be conditionally convergent.

(2) A power-series is a series of the form

$$P(x) = \sum_{\nu=0}^{\infty} a_\nu x^\nu = a_0 + a_1 x + a_2 x^2 + \ldots,$$

where the a_ν are constants and x is variable. For every power series there exists a value $\rho \geq 0$, such that $P(x)$ is absolutely convergent for all $|x| < \rho$ and divergent for all $|x| > \rho$. ρ is called the radius of convergence, and the interval $-\rho < x < +\rho$ the interval of convergence. We have:

$$\rho = \left(\overline{\lim_{n \to \infty}} \; \sqrt[n]{|a_n|} \right)^{-1}$$

or

$$\rho = \lim_{n \to \infty} \left| \frac{a_n}{a_{n+1}} \right|.$$

A power-series $P(x)$ represents a function of x within its interval of convergence. It may be differentiated term by term within this interval. In what follows the interval of convergence will usually be given in the form $[-a < x < a]$.

(3) If $f(x)$ is differentiable $(n + 1)$ times in the interval $(x, x + h)$, then we have Taylor's formula

$$f(x + h) = f(x) + \frac{h}{1!}f'(x) + \frac{h^2}{2!}f''(x) + \ldots + \frac{h^n}{n!}f^{(n)}(x)$$
$$+ \frac{h^{n+1}}{(n + 1)!}f^{(n+1)}(x + \theta h),$$

where $0 < \theta < 1$. The last term is the remainder-term. If this tends to 0 as n tends to infinity, we obtain from Taylor's formula the Taylor series. Other forms of the remainder terms are:

$$R_{n+1} = \frac{h^{n+1}(1 - \theta)^n}{n!}f^{(n+1)}(x + \theta h),$$

and

$$R_{n+1} = \frac{1}{n!}\int_o^h f^{(n+1)}(x + t)(h - t)^n \, dt.$$

If we put $x = 0$ and $h = \xi$, we obtain Maclaurin's formula or series:

$$f(\xi) = f(0) + \frac{\xi}{1!}f'(0) + \ldots + \frac{\xi^n}{n!}f^{(n)}(0)$$
$$+ \frac{\xi^{n+1}}{(n + 1)!}f^{(n+1)}(\theta\xi), \qquad 0 < \theta < 1.$$

(4) *Tests of convergence*

(i) If $|u_n| < C|v_n|$, where C is a constant independent of n, and if v_n is the nth term of the sequence $\sum_{n=0}^{\infty} v_n$ which is known to be absolutely convergent, then $\sum_{n=0}^{\infty} u_n$ is absolutely convergent.

(ii) $\sum_{n=0}^{\infty} u_n$ is absolutely convergent if

$$\lim_{n \to \infty} |u_n|^{1/n} < 1 \qquad \text{(Cauchy's test)}.$$

573

(iii) If for all $n > N$, where N is a fixed number

$$\left| \frac{u_{n+1}}{u_n} \right| \le \rho < 1,$$

then $\sum_{n=0}^{\infty} u_n$ is absolutely convergent (d'Alembert's test).

(iv) $\sum_{n=0}^{\infty} u_n$ is convergent if

$$\lim_{n \to \infty} n \left(\frac{u_{n+1}}{u_n} - 1 \right) < -1$$

(Raabe's test).

(v) $\sum_{n=0}^{\infty} u_n$ is convergent if

$$\lim_{n \to \infty} \left\{ n \left(\frac{u_{n+1}}{u_n} - 1 \right) + 1 \right\} \ln n < -1.$$

2. *Series for known functions*

The intervals of convergence for the following series are given (where necessary) in square brackets.

$(1 + x)^{\alpha}$ is convergent for real x $[-1 < x < +1]$.

$$(1 + x)^{\frac{n}{m}} = 1 + \frac{n}{m} x - \frac{n(m - n)}{2! \, m^2} x^2 + \frac{n(m - n)(2m - n)}{3! \, m^3} x^3$$

$$- \ldots + (-1)^{k+1} \frac{n(m - n)(2m - n) \ldots [(k - 1)m - n]}{k! \, m^k} x^k$$

$$+ \ldots.$$

$$(1 + x)^{-1} = 1 - x + x^2 - x^3 + x^4 - \ldots.$$

$$(1 + x)^{-2} = 1 - 2x + 3x^2 - 4x^3 + 5x^4 - \ldots.$$

$$\sqrt{1 + x} = 1 + \frac{1}{2} x - \frac{1 \cdot 1}{2 \cdot 4} x^2 + \frac{1 \cdot 1 \cdot 3}{2 \cdot 4 \cdot 6} x^3 - \frac{1 \cdot 1 \cdot 3 \cdot 5}{2 \cdot 4 \cdot 6 \cdot 8} x^4$$

$$+ \ldots.$$

$$\frac{1}{\sqrt{1 + x}} = 1 - \frac{1}{2} x + \frac{1 \cdot 3}{2 \cdot 4} x^2 - \frac{1 \cdot 3 \cdot 5}{2 \cdot 4 \cdot 6} x^3 + \frac{1 \cdot 3 \cdot 5 \cdot 7}{2 \cdot 4 \cdot 6 \cdot 8} x^4$$

$$- \ldots.$$

$$(1 + x)^{1/3} = 1 + \frac{1}{3}x - \frac{1 \cdot 2}{3 \cdot 6}x^2 + \frac{1 \cdot 2 \cdot 5}{3 \cdot 6 \cdot 9}x^3 - \frac{1 \cdot 2 \cdot 5 \cdot 8}{3 \cdot 6 \cdot 9 \cdot 12}x^4$$
$$+ \dots$$

$$(1 + x)^{-1/3} = 1 - \frac{1}{3}x + \frac{1 \cdot 4}{3 \cdot 6}x^2 - \frac{1 \cdot 4 \cdot 7}{3 \cdot 6 \cdot 9}x^3 + \frac{1 \cdot 4 \cdot 7 \cdot 10}{3 \cdot 6 \cdot 9 \cdot 12}x^4$$
$$- \dots$$

$$(1 + x)^{3/2} = 1 + \frac{3}{2}x + \frac{3 \cdot 1}{2 \cdot 4}x^2 - \frac{3 \cdot 1 \cdot 1}{2 \cdot 4 \cdot 6}x^3 + \frac{3 \cdot 1 \cdot 1 \cdot 3}{2 \cdot 4 \cdot 6 \cdot 8}x^4$$
$$- \frac{3 \cdot 1 \cdot 1 \cdot 3 \cdot 5}{2 \cdot 4 \cdot 6 \cdot 8 \cdot 10}x^5 + \dots$$

$$(1 + x)^{-3/2} = 1 - \frac{3}{2}x + \frac{3 \cdot 5}{2 \cdot 4}x^2 - \frac{3 \cdot 5 \cdot 7}{2 \cdot 4 \cdot 6}x^3 + \dots$$

$$(1 + x)^{1/4} = 1 + \frac{1}{4}x - \frac{3}{32}x^2 + \frac{7}{128}x^3 - \frac{77}{2048}x^4 + \dots$$

$$(1 + x)^{-1/4} = 1 - \frac{1}{4}x + \frac{5}{32}x^2 - \frac{15}{128}x^3 + \frac{195}{2048}x^4 - \dots$$

$$(1 + x)^{1/5} = 1 + \frac{1}{5}x - \frac{2}{25}x^2 + \frac{6}{125}x^3 - \frac{21}{625}x^4 + \dots$$

$$(1 + x)^{-1/5} = 1 - \frac{1}{5}x + \frac{3}{25}x^2 - \frac{11}{125}x^3 + \frac{44}{625}x^4 - \dots$$

$$(1 + x)^{1/6} = 1 + \frac{1}{6}x - \frac{5}{72}x^2 + \frac{55}{1296}x^3 - \frac{935}{31104}x^4 + \dots$$

$$(1 + x)^{-1/6} = 1 - \frac{1}{6}x + \frac{7}{72}x^2 - \frac{91}{1296}x^3 + \frac{1729}{31104}x^4 - \dots$$

$$\frac{x}{1 - x} = \frac{x}{1 + x} + \frac{2x^2}{1 + x^2} + \frac{4x^4}{1 + x^4} + \frac{8x^8}{1 + x^8} + \dots \quad [x^2 < 1].$$

$$\frac{x}{1-x} = \frac{x}{1-x^2} + \frac{x^2}{1-x^4} + \frac{x^4}{1-x^8} + \dots \qquad [x^2 < 1].$$

$$\frac{1}{x-1} = \frac{1}{x+1} + \frac{2}{x^2+1} + \frac{4}{x^4+1} + \dots \qquad [x^2 > 1].$$

In the following series, B_n are Bernoulli's numbers (see p. 580) and E_n Euler's numbers (see p. 580).

$$\sin x = x - \frac{x^3}{3!} + \frac{x^5}{5!} - \frac{x^7}{7!} + \dots$$

$$= \sum_{n=0}^{\infty} (-1)^n \frac{x^{2n+1}}{(2n+1)!} \qquad [x^2 < \infty].$$

$$\cos x = 1 - \frac{x^2}{2!} + \frac{x^4}{4!} - \frac{x^6}{6!} + \dots$$

$$= \sum_{n=0}^{\infty} (-1)^n \frac{x^{2n}}{(2n)!} \qquad [x^2 < \infty].$$

$$\tan x = x + \frac{1}{3} x^3 + \frac{2}{15} x^5 + \frac{17}{315} x^7 + \frac{62}{2835} x^9 + \dots$$

$$= \sum_{n=1}^{\infty} \frac{2^{2n}(2^{2n} - 1)}{(2n)!} B_n x^{2n-1} \qquad \left[x^2 < \frac{\pi^2}{4} \right].$$

$$\cot x = \frac{1}{x} - \frac{x}{3} - \frac{1}{45} x^3 - \frac{2}{945} x^5 - \frac{1}{4725} x^7 - \dots$$

$$= \frac{1}{x} - \sum_{n=1}^{\infty} \frac{2^{2n} B_n}{(2n)!} x^{2n-1} \qquad [0 < x^2 < \pi^2].$$

$$\sec x = 1 + \frac{1}{2!} x^2 + \frac{5}{4!} x^4 + \frac{61}{6!} x^6 + \dots$$

$$= \sum_{n=0}^{\infty} \frac{E_n}{(2n)!} x^{2n} \qquad \left[x^2 < \frac{\pi^2}{4} \right].$$

$$\operatorname{cosec} x = \frac{1}{x} + \frac{1}{3!}x + \frac{7}{3.5!}x^3 + \frac{31}{3.7!}x^5 + \ldots$$

$$= \frac{1}{x} + \sum_{n=0}^{\infty} \frac{2(2^{2n+1} - 1)}{(2n+2)!} B_{n+1} x^{2n+1} \qquad [x^2 < \pi^2].$$

$$\sin^{-1} x = x + \frac{1}{2.3}x^3 + \frac{1.3}{2.4.5}x^5 + \frac{1.3.5}{2.4.6.7}x^7 + \ldots$$

$$= \sum_{n=0}^{\infty} \frac{(2n)!}{2^{2n}(n!)^2(2n+1)} x^{2n+1} \qquad [x^2 \leq 1].$$

$$\tan^{-1} x = x - \frac{1}{3}x^3 + \frac{1}{5}x^5 - \frac{1}{7}x^7 + \ldots$$

$$= \sum_{n=0}^{\infty} (-1)^n \frac{x^{2n+1}}{2n+1} \qquad [x^2 \leq 1].$$

$$\tan^{-1} x = \frac{x}{1+x^2} \left\{ 1 + \frac{2}{3}\frac{x^2}{1+x^2} + \frac{2.4}{3.5}\left(\frac{x^2}{1+x^2}\right)^2 + \ldots \right\}$$

$$= \frac{x}{1+x^2} \sum_{n=0}^{\infty} \frac{2^{2n}(n!)^2}{(2n+1)!} \left(\frac{x^2}{1+x^2}\right)^n \qquad x^2 < \infty.$$

$$\tan^{-1} x = \frac{\pi}{2} - \frac{1}{x} + \frac{1}{3x^3} - \frac{1}{5x^5} + \frac{1}{7x^7} - \ldots$$

$$= \frac{\pi}{2} - \sum_{n=0}^{\infty} (-1)^n \frac{1}{(2n+1)x^{2n+1}} \qquad [x^2 \geq 1].$$

$$\sec^{-1} x = \frac{\pi}{2} - \frac{1}{x} - \frac{1}{2.3}\frac{1}{x^3} - \frac{1.3}{2.4.5}\frac{1}{x^5} - \frac{1.3.5}{2.4.6.7}\frac{1}{x^7} - \ldots$$

$$= \frac{\pi}{2} - \sum_{n=0}^{\infty} \frac{(2n)!}{2^{2n}(n!)^2(2n+1)} x^{-2n-1} \qquad [x > 1]$$

$$\sinh x = x + \frac{x^3}{3!} + \frac{x^5}{5!} + \frac{x^7}{7!} + \ldots = \sum_{n=0}^{\infty} \frac{x^{2n+1}}{(2n+1)!} \quad [x^2 < \infty].$$

577

$$\cosh x = 1 + \frac{x^2}{2!} + \frac{x^4}{4!} + \frac{x^6}{6!} + \ldots = \sum_{n=0}^{\infty} \frac{x^{2n}}{(2n)!} \qquad [x^2 < \infty].$$

$$\tanh x = x - \frac{1}{3}x^3 + \frac{2}{15}x^5 - \frac{17}{315}x^7 + \ldots$$

$$= \sum_{n=1}^{\infty} (-1)^{n-1} \frac{2^{2n}(2^{2n}-1)}{(2n)!} B_n x^{2n-1} \qquad \left[x^2 < \frac{\pi^2}{4}\right].$$

$$x \coth x = 1 + \frac{1}{3}x^2 - \frac{1}{45}x^4 + \frac{2}{945}x^6 - \ldots$$

$$= 1 + \sum_{n=1}^{\infty} (-1)^{n-1} \frac{2^{2n}B_n}{(2n)!} x^{2n} \qquad [x^2 < \pi^2].$$

$$\sinh^{-1} x = x - \frac{1}{2 \cdot 3}x^3 + \frac{1 \cdot 3}{2 \cdot 4 \cdot 5}x^5 - \ldots$$

$$= \sum_{n=0}^{\infty} (-1)^n \frac{(2n)!}{2^{2n}(n!)^2(2n+1)} x^{2n+1} \qquad [x^2 < 1].$$

$$\sinh^{-1} x = \ln 2x + \frac{1}{2}\frac{1}{2x^2} - \frac{1 \cdot 3}{2 \cdot 4}\frac{1}{4x^4} + \ldots$$

$$= \ln 2x + \sum_{n=1}^{\infty} (-1)^n \frac{(2n)!}{2^{2n}(n!)^2 2n} x^{-2n} \qquad [x^2 > 1].$$

$$\cosh^{-1} x = \ln 2x - \frac{1}{2}\frac{1}{2x^2} - \frac{1 \cdot 3}{2 \cdot 4}\frac{1}{4x^4} - \ldots$$

$$= \ln 2x - \sum_{n=1}^{\infty} \frac{(2n)!}{2^{2n}(n!)^2 2n} x^{-2n} \qquad [x^2 > 1].$$

$$\tanh^{-1} x = x + \frac{1}{3}x^3 + \frac{1}{5}x^5 + \frac{1}{7}x^7 + \ldots$$

$$= \sum_{n=0}^{\infty} \frac{x^{2n+1}}{2n+1} \qquad [x^2 < 1].$$

$$\sinh^{-1}\frac{1}{x} = \frac{1}{x} - \frac{1}{2}\frac{1}{3x^3} + \frac{1 \cdot 3}{2 \cdot 4}\frac{1}{5x^5} - \cdots$$

$$= \sum_{n=0}^{\infty}(-1)^n \frac{(2n)!}{2^{2n}(n!)^2(2n+1)}x^{-2n-1} \qquad [x^2 > 1].$$

$$\cosh^{-1}\frac{1}{x} = \ln\frac{2}{x} - \frac{1}{2}\frac{x^2}{2} - \frac{1 \cdot 3}{2 \cdot 4}\frac{x^4}{4} - \cdots$$

$$= \ln\frac{2}{x} - \sum_{n=1}^{\infty}\frac{(2n)!}{2^{2n}(n!)^2 2n}x^{2n} \qquad [x^2 < 1].$$

$$\sinh^{-1}\frac{1}{x} = \ln\frac{2}{x} + \frac{1}{2}\frac{x^2}{2} - \frac{1 \cdot 3}{2 \cdot 4}\frac{x^4}{4} + \cdots$$

$$= \ln\frac{2}{x} + \sum_{n=1}^{\infty}(-1)^n \frac{(2n)!}{2^{2n}(n!)^2 2n}x^{2n} \qquad [x^2 < 1].$$

$$\tanh^{-1}\frac{1}{x} = \frac{1}{x} + \frac{1}{3x^3} + \frac{1}{5x^5} + \cdots = \sum_{n=0}^{\infty}\frac{x^{-2n-1}}{2n+1} \qquad [x^2 > 1].$$

3. Numerical series

Writing $S_n = \dfrac{1}{1^n} + \dfrac{1}{2^n} + \dfrac{1}{3^n} + \dfrac{1}{4^n} + \cdots = \sum\limits_{k=1}^{\infty}\dfrac{1}{k^n}$, we have:

$$S_1 = \infty$$

$$S_2 = \frac{\pi^2}{6} = 1 \cdot 6449340668 \ldots$$

$$S_3 = \frac{\pi^3}{25 \cdot 79436 \ldots} = 1 \cdot 2020569032 \ldots$$

$$S_4 = \frac{\pi^4}{90} = 1 \cdot 0823232337 \ldots$$

$$S_5 = \frac{\pi^5}{295 \cdot 1215} = 1 \cdot 0369277551 \ldots$$

$$S_6 = \frac{\pi^6}{945} = 1 \cdot 0173430620 \ldots$$

$$S_7 = \frac{\pi^7}{2995 \cdot 286 \ldots} = 1 \cdot 0083492774 \ldots$$

$$S_8 = \frac{\pi^8}{9450} = 1 \cdot 0040773562 \ldots$$

$$S_9 = \frac{\pi^9}{29749 \cdot 35 \ldots} = 1 \cdot 0020083928 \ldots$$

$$S_{10} = 1 \cdot 0009945751 \ldots$$

Bernoulli's Numbers

$$\frac{2^{2n-1}\pi^{2n}}{(2n)!} B_n = \frac{1}{1^{2n}} + \frac{1}{2^{2n}} + \frac{1}{3^{2n}} + \frac{1}{4^{2n}} + \ldots = \sum_{k=1}^{\infty} \frac{1}{k^{2n}}.$$

$$\frac{(2^{2n}-1)\pi^{2n}}{2(2n)!} B_n = \frac{1}{1^{2n}} + \frac{1}{3^{2n}} + \frac{1}{5^{2n}} + \frac{1}{7^{2n}} + \ldots$$

$$= \sum_{k=0}^{\infty} \frac{1}{(2k+1)^{2n}}.$$

$$\frac{(2^{2n-1}-1)\pi^{2n}}{(2n)!} B_n = \frac{1}{1^{2n}} - \frac{1}{2^{2n}} + \frac{1}{3^{2n}} - \frac{1}{4^{2n}} + \ldots$$

$$= \sum_{k=1}^{\infty} (-1)^{n-1} \frac{1}{k^{2n}}.$$

$$B_1 = \frac{1}{6}, \qquad\qquad B_6 = \frac{691}{2730},$$

$$B_2 = \frac{1}{30}, \qquad\qquad B_7 = \frac{7}{6},$$

$$B_3 = \frac{1}{42}, \qquad\qquad B_8 = \frac{3617}{510},$$

$$B_4 = \frac{1}{30}, \qquad\qquad B_9 = \frac{43867}{798},$$

$$B_5 = \frac{5}{66}, \qquad\qquad B_{10} = \frac{174611}{330}.$$

Euler's Numbers

$$\frac{\pi^{2n+1}}{2^{2n+2}(2n)!} E_n = 1 - \frac{1}{3^{2n+1}} + \frac{1}{5^{2n+1}} - \frac{1}{7^{2n+1}} + \cdots$$

$$= \sum_{k=1}^{\infty} (-1)^{k-1} \frac{1}{(2k-1)^{2n+1}}.$$

$E_1 = 1,$ $E_4 = 1385,$

$E_2 = 5,$ $E_5 = 50521,$

$E_3 = 61,$ $E_6 = 2702765.$

VIII. DIFFERENTIAL CALCULUS

1. *The differential coefficient*

The *differential coefficient*, or derivative, $\dfrac{df(x)}{dx} = f'(x)$ of a function $f(x)$, is the limiting value

$$f'(x) = \lim_{h \to 0} \frac{f(x+h) - f(x)}{h}.$$

If $f'(x)$ exists at the point x, then $f(x)$ is said to be differentiable there. The function is then also continuous at that point. If the differentiation process is repeated, the higher derivatives of $f(x)$ are obtained.

$$\frac{d}{dx}\left(\frac{df(x)}{dx}\right) = \frac{d^2f(x)}{dx^2} = f''(x); \quad \frac{d}{dx}\left(\frac{d^2f(x)}{dx^2}\right) = \frac{d^3f(x)}{dx^3} = f'''(x), \text{ etc.}$$

If a function $z = f(x, y)$ depends on two variables x and y, two *partial derivatives* can be formed. Regarding, *e.g.*, y as constant and $f(x, y)$ accordingly as a function of x alone, the partial derivative of the function with respect to x, denoted by $\dfrac{\partial z}{\partial x}$, $\dfrac{\partial f(x, y)}{\partial x}$ or $f_x(x, y)$, is:

$$\frac{\partial z}{\partial x} = \lim_{h \to 0} \frac{f(x+h, y) - f(x, y)}{h};$$

and similarly

$$\frac{\partial z}{\partial y} = \lim_{k \to 0} \frac{f(x, y+k) - f(y)}{k}.$$

$$dz = \frac{\partial z}{\partial x}\,dx + \frac{\partial z}{\partial y}\,dy$$

is the total differential of z.

By repetition of the process, we obtain the higher partial derivatives

$$f_{xx} = \frac{\partial^2 z}{\partial x^2}, \; f_{xy} = \frac{\partial^2 z}{\partial x \partial y}, \; f_{yy} = \frac{\partial^2 z}{\partial y^2}, \; f_{xxx} = \frac{\partial^3 z}{\partial x^3}, \; f_{xxy} = \frac{\partial^3 z}{\partial x^2 \partial y}, \text{ etc.}$$

2. *Rules for differentiation*

(1) If $f(x)$ and $g(x)$ are differentiable functions of the variable x, then

$$\frac{d}{dx}\left(f(x) \pm g(x)\right) = \frac{d}{dx}f(x) \pm \frac{d}{dx}g(x),$$

$$\frac{d}{dx}\left(f(x) \cdot g(x)\right) = g(x)\frac{d}{dx}f(x) + f(x)\frac{d}{dx}g(x),$$

$$\frac{d}{dx}\left(\frac{f(x)}{g(x)}\right) = \frac{f'(x)g(x) - g'(x)f(x)}{g(x)^2}.$$

For the nth derivative $\dfrac{d^n f(x)}{dx^n} = f^{(n)}(x)$ we have:

$$\frac{d^n}{dx^n}\left(f(x)g(x)\right) = f^{(n)}(x)g(x) + \binom{n}{1}f^{(n-1)}(x)g^{(1)}(x) + \cdots$$
$$+ f(x)g^{(n)}(x).$$

(2) If $y = f(u)$ and $u = g(x)$ are differentiable in the domain under consideration then

$$\frac{dy}{dx} = \frac{dy}{du}\frac{du}{dx} = f'(u)g'(x).$$

The higher derivatives are:

$$\frac{d^2y}{dx^2} = \frac{d^2y}{du^2}\left(\frac{du}{dx}\right)^2 + \frac{dy}{du}\frac{d^2u}{dx^2},$$

$$\frac{d^3y}{dx^3} = \frac{d^3y}{du^3}\left(\frac{du}{dx}\right)^3 + 3\frac{d^2y}{du^2}\frac{du}{dx}\frac{d^2u}{dx^2} + \frac{dy}{du}\frac{d^3u}{dx^3}, \text{ etc.}$$

(3) If $y = f(x)$, $x = g(y)$ are inverse functions and $\dfrac{dx}{dy} \neq 0$, then

$$\frac{dy}{dx} = \frac{1}{\dfrac{dx}{dy}}, \quad \frac{d^2y}{dx^2} = \frac{-\dfrac{d^2x}{dy^2}}{\left(\dfrac{dx}{dy}\right)^3}, \text{ etc.}$$

(4) If the interdependence of the variables x and y is given in the implicit form $f(x, y) = 0$, then

$$df = \frac{\partial f}{\partial x}\, dx + \frac{\partial f}{\partial y}\, dy = 0$$

and, if $\dfrac{\partial f}{\partial y} \neq 0$,

$$\frac{dy}{dx} = -\frac{\dfrac{\partial f}{\partial x}}{\dfrac{\partial f}{\partial y}} = -\frac{f_x}{f_y},$$

$$\frac{d^2y}{dx^2} = -\frac{f_{xx}f_y^2 - 2f_{xy}f_xf_y + f_{yy}f_x^2}{f_y^3}, \quad \text{etc.}$$

(5) *Differentiation of integrals*

(i) Differentiation with respect to an integral-limit:

$$\frac{d}{dx}\int_a^r f(t)\, dt = -\frac{d}{dx}\int_x^a f(t)\, dt = f(x)$$

(ii) Differentiation with respect to a parameter, where the limits $a \leq t \leq b$ are independent of x:

$$\frac{d}{dx}\int_a^b f(x, t)\, dt = \int_a^b \frac{\partial}{\partial x}f(x, t)\, dt$$

(iii) Differentiation with respect to a parameter x where the limits $a = a(x)$ and $b = b(x)$ are also dependent on this parameter:

$$\frac{d}{dx}\int_{a(x)}^{b(x)} f(x, t)\, dt = b'(x)f(x, b) - a'(x)f(x, a) + \int_a^b \frac{\partial}{\partial x}f(x, t)\, dt$$

3. *Special cases of differentiation*

$$\frac{da}{dx} = 0 \ (a \text{ constant})$$

$$\frac{dx^n}{dx} = nx^{n-1}; \ \frac{dx}{dx} = 1$$

$$\frac{da^x}{dx} = a^x \ln a; \quad \frac{de^x}{dx} = e^x$$

$$\frac{d \log_a x}{dx} = \frac{1}{x} \log_a e; \quad \frac{d \ln x}{dx} = \frac{1}{x}$$

$$\frac{d \sin x}{dx} = \cos x$$

$$\frac{d \cos x}{dx} = -\sin x$$

$$\frac{d \tan x}{dx} = \frac{1}{\cos^2 x}$$

$$\frac{d \cot x}{dx} = -\frac{1}{\sin^2 x}$$

$$\frac{d}{dx} \sin^{-1} x = \frac{1}{\sqrt{1 - x^2}}, \quad -1 < x < +1$$

$$\left(\text{where the sign of the root is positive if } -\frac{\pi}{2} < \sin^{-1} x < +\frac{\pi}{2} \right)$$

$$\frac{d}{dx} \cos^{-1} x = -\frac{1}{\sqrt{1 - x^2}} \quad \text{if } -1 < x < +1$$

(where the sign of the root is positive, $0 < \cos^{-1} x < \pi$)

$$\frac{d}{dx} \tan^{-1} x = \frac{1}{1 + x^2}, \quad -\frac{\pi}{2} < \tan^{-1} x < \frac{\pi}{2}$$

$$\frac{d}{dx} \cot^{-1} x = -\frac{1}{1 + x^2}, \quad 0 < \cot^{-1} x < \pi$$

$$\frac{d}{dx} \sinh x = \cosh x$$

$$\frac{d}{dx} \cosh x = \sinh x$$

$$\frac{d}{dx} \tanh x = \frac{1}{\cosh^2 x}$$

$$\frac{d}{dx} \coth x = -\frac{1}{\sinh^2 x}$$

$$\frac{d}{dx} \sinh^{-1} x = \frac{1}{\sqrt{x^2 + 1}}$$

$$\frac{d}{dx} \cosh^{-1} x = \pm \frac{1}{\sqrt{x^2 - 1}}$$

$$\frac{d}{dx} \tanh^{-1} x = \frac{d\,(\coth^{-1} x)}{dx} = \frac{1}{1 - x^2}$$

IX. INTEGRAL CALCULUS

A. General formulae

Definition of the indefinite integral. The function $F(x)$ is an indefinite integral of $f(x)$, and written

$$F(x) = \int f(x)\, dx,$$

if

$$d\frac{F(x)}{dx} = F'(x) = f(x).$$

Since $F(x) + C$ is also an indefinite integral (C any constant) we write generally

$$\int f(x)\, dx = F(x) + C.$$

Definition of the definite integral. If $f(x)$ is continuous in the interval $a = x_0 \leq x \leq x_n = b$, which is divided by the points $x_1, \ldots, x_{n-1}$ into n sub-intervals such that the length of each interval tends to 0 as n tends to ∞, then there exists, independently of the special subdivision chosen, the limiting value

$$G(a, b) = \lim_{n \to \infty} \sum_{i=1}^{n} f(\xi_i)(x_i - x_{i-1}),$$

where ξ_i satisfies the condition $x_{i-1} \leq \xi_i \leq x_i$.

If

$$\int f(x)\, dx = F(x) + C,$$

then

$$G(a, b) = \int_b^a f(x)\, dx = F(b) - F(a).$$

The connection with the indefinite integral arises here if the upper limit $b = \xi$ is variable. In this case:

$$\int_a^\xi f(x)\, dx = F(\xi) - F(a) = F(\xi) + C,$$

a function of the upper limit. Since

$$\frac{d}{d\xi} \int_a^\xi f(x)\, dx = F'(\xi) = f(\xi),$$

$F(\xi)$ is an indefinite integral of $f(\xi)$.

FORMULAE

(1) $$\int Cf(x)\,dx = C\int f(x)\,dx,$$

where C is independent of x.

(2) $$\int [f(x) \pm g(x)]\,dx = \int f(x)\,dx \pm \int g(x)\,dx.$$

(3) Integration by parts:

$$\int f(x)G(x)\,dx = F(x)G(x) - \int F(x)g(x)\,dx,$$

where $F'(x) = f(x)$ and $G'(x) = g(x)$.

(4) Integration by substitution:

$$\int f(x)\,dx = \int f(g(y))g'(y)\,dy,$$

where x is put equal to $g(y)$.

(5) $$\int_a^b f(x)\,dx = -\int_b^a f(x)\,dx.$$

$$\int_a^b [f(x) \pm g(x)]\,dx = \int_a^b f(x)\,dx \pm \int_a^b g(x)\,dx.$$

$$\int_a^b f(x)\,dx = \int_a^c f(x)\,dx + \int_c^b f(x)\,dx.$$

$$\int_a^b u\,dv = u(b)v(b) - u(a)v(a) - \int_a^b v\,du.$$

(6) Suppose $t = t(x)$ is one-valued in $a \le x \le b$ and $t(a) = \alpha$, $t(b) = \beta$. Suppose the inverse function $x = \phi(t)$ is also one-valued in $\alpha \le t \le \beta$, and that $t(x)$ and $\phi(t)$ have continuous derivatives in the intervals under consideration. Then:

$$\int_a^b f(x)\,dx = \int_\alpha^\beta f(\phi(t))\,\phi'(t)\,dt.$$

B. Indefinite integrals

1. *Rational Integrands*

(1) $\displaystyle\int (a_0 + a_1 x + a_2 x^2 + \ldots + a_n x^n)\, dx = a_0 x + \frac{a_1}{2} x^2$
$$+ \frac{a_2}{3} x^3 + \ldots + \frac{a_n}{n+1} x^{n+1} + C.$$

(2) $\displaystyle\int (ax + b)^n\, dx = \frac{(ax+b)^{n+1}}{(n+1)a} + C, \quad n \neq -1.$

(3) $\displaystyle\int \frac{dx}{(x-a)^k} = \frac{-1}{k-1} \cdot \frac{1}{(x-a)^{k-1}} + C, \quad k \neq 1.$

(4) $\displaystyle\int \frac{dx}{ax+b} = \frac{1}{a} \ln C(ax+b).$

(5) $\displaystyle\int \frac{ax+b}{cx+d}\, dx = \frac{ax+b}{c} + \frac{-ad+bc}{c^2} \ln(cx+d) + C.$

(6) $\displaystyle\int \frac{dx}{(ax+b)(cx+d)} = \frac{1}{ad-bc} \ln \frac{ax+b}{cx+d} + C.$

(7) $\displaystyle\int \frac{dx}{a^2 x^2 + b^2} = \frac{1}{ab} \tan^{-1} \frac{ax}{b} + C_1$
$$= \frac{1}{ab} \sin^{-1} \frac{ax}{\sqrt{a^2 x^2 + b^2}} + C_2.$$

(8) $\displaystyle\int \frac{x}{x^2+a^2}\, dx = \frac{1}{2} \ln C(x^2+a^2).$

(9) $\displaystyle\int \frac{x}{(x^2+a^2)^{k+1}}\, dx = \frac{-1}{2k(x^2+a^2)^k} + C.$

(10) $\displaystyle\int \frac{dx}{x^2+a^2} = \frac{1}{a} \tan^{-1} \frac{x}{a} + C.$

(11) $\displaystyle\int \frac{dx}{x(x^2+a^2)} = \frac{1}{2a^2} \ln \frac{x^2}{x^2+a^2} + C.$

$$(12) \quad \int \frac{dx}{a^2 x^2 - b^2} = \frac{1}{2ab} \ln C \frac{ax - b}{ax + b}.$$

$$(13) \quad \int \frac{x}{x^2 - a^2} \, dx = \frac{1}{2} \ln C(x^2 - a^2).$$

$$(14) \quad \int \frac{dx}{x \pm 1} = \ln C(x \pm 1).$$

$$(15) \quad \int \frac{dx}{x^2 + 1} = \tan^{-1} x + C_1 = -\tan^{-1} \frac{1}{x} + C_2$$
$$= -\cot^{-1} x + C_3.$$

2. Algebraic Integrands

$$(16) \quad \int \sqrt[n]{ax + b} \, dx = \frac{n}{(n + 1)a} (ax + b)^{1 + 1/n} + C.$$

$$(17) \quad \int \frac{dx}{\sqrt[n]{ax + b}} = \frac{n}{(n - 1)a} (ax + b)^{1 - 1/n} + C.$$

$$(18) \quad \int (ax + b)^{p/n} \, dx = \frac{n}{(n + p)a} (ax + b)^{1 + p/n} + C,$$
$$p = \pm 1, \pm 2, \ldots \text{ (but } p \neq -n).$$

$$(19) \quad {}^* \int \sqrt{X} \, dx = \left(\frac{x}{2} + \frac{b}{2a} \right) \sqrt{X}$$
$$+ \frac{ac - b^2}{2a\sqrt{a}} \ln C_1 \left(\frac{ax + b}{\sqrt{a}} + \sqrt{X} \right), \quad \text{for } a > 0.$$

$$(20) \quad {}^* \int \frac{dx}{\sqrt{X}} = \begin{cases} \dfrac{1}{\sqrt{a}} \ln C_1 \left(\dfrac{ax + b}{\sqrt{a}} + \sqrt{X} \right), & \text{for } a > 0; \\[2ex] \dfrac{-1}{\sqrt{-a}} \sin^{-1} \dfrac{ax + b}{\sqrt{b^2 - ac}} + C_2, & \text{for } a < 0; \\[2ex] \dfrac{1}{\sqrt{a}} \ln C_3(ax + b), & \text{for } b^2 - ac = 0. \end{cases}$$

$^* = ax^2 + 2b x + Xc.$

(21) $^*\displaystyle\int \frac{x}{X^{3/2}}\,dx = \frac{-1}{ac-b^2}\,\frac{bx+c}{\sqrt{X}} + C.$

(22) $^*\displaystyle\int \frac{dx}{X^{3/2}} = \frac{1}{ac-b^2}\,\frac{ax+b}{\sqrt{X}} + C.$

(23) $\displaystyle\int \frac{x^2}{\sqrt{x^2+a^2}}\,dx = \frac{x}{2}\sqrt{x^2+a^2} - \frac{a^2}{2}\ln C\!\left(x+\sqrt{x^2+a^2}\right).$

(24) $\displaystyle\int \frac{dx}{x^2\sqrt{x^2+a^2}} = -\frac{1}{a^2}\frac{\sqrt{x^2+a^2}}{x} + C.$

(25) $\displaystyle\int x\sqrt{x^2+a^2}\,dx = \frac{1}{3}(x^2+a^2)^{3/2} + C.$

(26) $\displaystyle\int x^2\sqrt{x^2+a^2}\,dx = \frac{x}{8}(2x^2+a^2)\sqrt{x^2+a^2}$

$$-\frac{a^4}{8}\ln C(x+\sqrt{x^2+a^2}).$$

(27) $\displaystyle\int \frac{\sqrt{x^2+a^2}}{x}\,dx = \sqrt{x^2+a^2} + \frac{a}{2}\ln C\,\frac{\sqrt{x^2+a^2}-a}{\sqrt{x^2+a^2}+a}.$

(28) $\displaystyle\int \frac{dx}{x\sqrt{x^2-a^2}} = \frac{-1}{a}\sin^{-1}\frac{a}{|x|} + C,\ |x| \ge a > 0.$

(29) $\displaystyle\int \frac{dx}{\sqrt{a^2-x^2}} = \sin^{-1}\frac{x}{|a|} + C = \tan^{-1}\frac{x}{\sqrt{a^2-x^2}} + C.$

(30) $\displaystyle\int \frac{x}{\sqrt{a^2-x^2}}\,dx = -\sqrt{a^2-x^2} + C.$

3. Transcendental Integrands

(31) $\displaystyle\int e^{\lambda x}\,dx = \frac{1}{\lambda}e^{\lambda x} + C.$

$^*\ X = ax^2 + 2bx + c.$

(32) $\displaystyle\int a^x \, dx = \frac{a^x}{\ln a} + C.$

(33) $\displaystyle\int \frac{dx}{ae^{\lambda x} + b} = \frac{x}{b} - \frac{1}{b\lambda} \ln (ae^{\lambda x} + b) + C, \quad b \neq 0.$

(34) $\displaystyle\int \frac{dx}{ae^{\lambda x} + be^{-\lambda x}} = \frac{1}{\lambda\sqrt{ab}} \tan^{-1} \sqrt{\frac{a}{b}}\, e^{\lambda x} + C, \quad \text{for } ab > 0.$

(35) $\displaystyle\int xe^{-x^2} \, dx = \frac{-1}{2} e^{-x^2} + C.$

(36) $\displaystyle\int \ln x \, dx = x \ln x - x + C.$

(37) $\displaystyle\int \sin x \, dx = - \cos x + C.$

(38) $\displaystyle\int \cos x \, dx = \sin x + C.$

(39) $\displaystyle\int \sin^2 x \, dx = \frac{-1}{2} \sin x \cos x + \frac{x}{2} + C.$

(40) $\displaystyle\int \frac{dx}{\sin x} = \ln \tan \frac{x}{2} + C.$

(41) $\displaystyle\int \frac{dx}{\sin^2 x} = - \cot x + C.$

(42) $\displaystyle\int \cos^2 x \, dx = \frac{1}{2} \sin x \cos x + \frac{x}{2} + C.$

(43) $\displaystyle\int \frac{dx}{\cos^2 x} = \tan x + C.$

(44) $\displaystyle\int \tan x \, dx = - \ln \cos x + C.$

(45) $\displaystyle\int \tan^2 x \, dx = \tan x - x + C.$

(46) $\displaystyle\int \cot x \, dx = \ln \sin x + C.$

(47) $\displaystyle\int \cot^2 x \, dx = -\cot x + C.$

(48) $\displaystyle\int \sinh x \, dx = \cosh x + C.$

(49) $\displaystyle\int \cosh x \, dx = \sinh x + C.$

(50) $\displaystyle\int \frac{dx}{\sinh x} = \ln \tanh \frac{x}{2} + C = \ln \frac{\cosh x - 1}{\sinh x} + C.$

(51) $\displaystyle\int \frac{dx}{\sinh^2 x} = -\coth x + C.$

(52) $\displaystyle\int \frac{dx}{\cosh x} = \sin^{-1}(\tanh x) + C = \cos^{-1}\frac{1}{\cosh x} + C_1$

$\qquad\qquad = \tan^{-1}(\sinh x) + C_2.$

(53) $\displaystyle\int \frac{dx}{\cosh^2 x} = \tanh x + C.$

(54) $\displaystyle\int \sinh^{-1}\frac{x}{a} \, dx = x \sinh^{-1}\frac{x}{a} - \sqrt{x^2 + a^2} + C.$

(55) $\displaystyle\int \cosh^{-1}\frac{x}{a} \, dx = x \cosh^{-1}\frac{x}{a} - \sqrt{x^2 - a^2} + C.$

(56) $\displaystyle\int x \sinh^{-1}\frac{x}{a} \, dx = \frac{2x^2 + a^2}{4} \sinh^{-1}\frac{x}{a} - \frac{x}{4}\sqrt{x^2 + a^2} + C.$

(57) $\displaystyle\int x \cosh^{-1}\frac{x}{a} \, dx = \frac{2x^2 - a^2}{4} \cosh^{-1}\frac{x}{a} - \frac{x}{4}\sqrt{x^2 - a^2} + C.$

C. Definite Integrals

1. *Rational Integrands*

(1) $\displaystyle\int_0^\infty \frac{dx}{(ax^2 + 2bx + c)^n}$

$$= \frac{(-1)^{n-1}}{(n-1)!} \frac{\partial^{n-1}}{\partial c^{n-1}} \left[\frac{1}{\sqrt{ac - b^2}} \cot^{-1} \frac{b}{\sqrt{ac - b^2}} \right],$$

$$a > 0, \ ac > b^2.$$

(2) $\displaystyle\int_0^\infty \frac{x^{p-1}}{ax^n + b} \, dx = \frac{\pi}{nb \sin \dfrac{p\pi}{n}} \left(\frac{b}{a}\right)^{\frac{p}{n}},$

$$n > p = 1, 2, \ldots; \ ab > 0.$$

(3) $\displaystyle\int_0^1 \frac{x^{m-1} - x^{n-m-1}}{1 - x^n} \, dx = \frac{\pi}{n} \cot \frac{m\pi}{n},$

$$m, n = 1, 2, \ldots; \ m \le n - 1.$$

(4) $\displaystyle\int_0^\infty \frac{x^{m-1} - x^{p-1}}{x^n - 1} \, dx = \frac{\pi}{n} \left[\cot \frac{p\pi}{n} - \cot \frac{m\pi}{n} \right],$

$$m, n, p = 1, 2, \ldots; \ n > m, \ n > p.$$

(5) $\displaystyle\int_0^\infty \frac{dx}{(x^2 + a^2)(x + b)^n}$

$$= \frac{(-1)^{n-1}}{(n-1)!} \cdot \frac{\partial^{n-1}}{\partial b^{n-1}} \left\{ \frac{1}{a^2 + b^2} \left(\frac{b\pi}{2a} - \ln \frac{b}{a} \right) \right\},$$

$$n = 1, 2, \ldots; \ a > 0, \ b > 0.$$

(6) $\displaystyle\int_0^\infty \frac{Ax^2 + 2Bx + C}{(ax^2 + b)(cx^2 + d)} \, dx$

$$= \frac{B}{ad - bc} \ln \frac{ad}{bc} + \frac{(A\sqrt{bd} + C\sqrt{ac})\pi}{2\sqrt{abcd}\,(\sqrt{ad} + \sqrt{bc})},$$

$$a, b, c, d > 0, \ ad \ne bc.$$

2. Algebraic Integrands

(7) $\displaystyle\int_0^\infty \frac{dx}{(ax^2 + 2bx + c)\sqrt{x}} = \frac{\pi}{\sqrt{2c(\sqrt{ac} + b)}},$

$$a > 0, \ b > 0, \ ac > b^2.$$

(8) $\displaystyle\int_0^\infty \frac{\sqrt{x}\,dx}{ax^2 + 2bx + c} = \frac{\pi}{\sqrt{2a(\sqrt{ac} + b)}},$

$$a > 0, \ b > 0, \ ac > b^2.$$

(9) $\displaystyle\int_a^b \frac{dx}{(cx + d)\sqrt{(x - a)(b - x)}} = \frac{\pi}{\sqrt{(ac + d)(bc + d)}},$

$$ac + d > 0, \ bc + d > 0.$$

(10) $\displaystyle\int_a^b \frac{\sqrt{(x - a)(b - x)}}{cx + d}\,dx = \frac{\pi}{2c^2}\,[\sqrt{ac + d} - \sqrt{bc + d}]^2,$

$$c \neq 0, \ ac + d > 0, \ bc + d > 0.$$

(11) $\displaystyle\int_0^a \frac{dx}{\sqrt{x^2 + a^2}} = \ln(1 + \sqrt{2}).$

(12) $\displaystyle\int_0^a \frac{x\,dx}{\sqrt{x^2 + a^2}} = a(\sqrt{2} - 1).$

(13) $\displaystyle\int_0^a \frac{x^2\,dx}{\sqrt{x^2 + a^2}} = \frac{a^2}{2}\,(\sqrt{2} - \ln(1 + \sqrt{2})).$

3. Transcendental Integrands

(14) $\displaystyle\int_a^b \frac{e^{\lambda x}}{\gamma + \delta e^{\lambda x}}\,dx = \frac{1}{\lambda\delta}\ln\frac{\gamma + \delta e^{\lambda b}}{\gamma + \delta e^{\lambda a}},$

$$\lambda\delta \neq 0, \ (\gamma + \delta e^{\lambda b})(\gamma + \delta e^{\lambda a}) > 0.$$

(15) $\displaystyle\int_0^\infty \frac{dx}{\sqrt{ae^{\lambda x} + b}} = \begin{cases} \dfrac{1}{\lambda\sqrt{b}}\ln\dfrac{\sqrt{a + b} + \sqrt{b}}{\sqrt{a + b} - \sqrt{b}}, & \lambda, a, b > 0, \\[2ex] \dfrac{2}{\lambda\sqrt{-b}}\tan^{-1}\dfrac{\sqrt{-b}}{\sqrt{a + b}}, & \end{cases}$

$$\lambda > 0, \ 0 < -b < a.$$

(16) $\displaystyle\int_0^\infty \frac{dx}{e^{\lambda x} + e^{-\lambda x}} = \frac{\pi}{4\lambda}, \quad \lambda > 0.$

(17) $\displaystyle\int_0^1 \frac{x\,e^x}{(x+1)^2}\,dx = \frac{e-2}{2}.$

(18) $\displaystyle\int_0^\infty \frac{e^{-\alpha x} - e^{-\beta x}}{x}\,dx = \ln\frac{\beta}{\alpha},$ $\qquad\qquad \alpha, \beta > 0.$

(19) $\displaystyle\int_0^\infty \frac{x}{e^x - 1}\,dx = \frac{\pi^2}{6}.$

(20) $\displaystyle\int_0^\infty \frac{x}{e^x + 1}\,dx = \frac{\pi^2}{12}.$ $\qquad$ (21) $\displaystyle\int_0^\infty e^{-x^2}\,dx = \frac{\sqrt{\pi}}{2}.$

(22) $\displaystyle\int_{-\infty}^\infty e^{-\lambda x^2}\,dx = 2\int_0^\infty e^{-\lambda x^2}\,dx = \sqrt{\frac{\pi}{\lambda}},$ $\qquad \lambda > 0.$

(23) $\displaystyle\int_{-\infty}^\infty e^{-(ax^2 + 2bx + c)}\,dx = \sqrt{\frac{\pi}{a}}\,e^{\frac{b^2 - ac}{a}},$ $\qquad a > 0.$

(24) $\displaystyle\int_{-\infty}^\infty e^{-(ax^2 + 2bx + c)}\,x\,dx = \frac{-b}{a}\sqrt{\frac{\pi}{a}}\,e^{\frac{b^2 - ac}{a}},$ $\qquad a > 0.$

(25) $\displaystyle\int_{-\infty}^\infty e^{-(ax^2 + 2bx + c)}\,x^2\,dx = \frac{a + 2b^2}{2a^2}\sqrt{\frac{\pi}{a}}\,e^{\frac{b^2 - ac}{a}},$ $\qquad a > 0.$

(26) $\displaystyle\int_0^1 (\ln x)^k\,dx = e^{\pi i k}\,\Gamma(k + 1),$ $\qquad k > -1.$

(27) $\displaystyle\int_0^1 \sqrt{\ln\frac{1}{x}}\,dx = \frac{\sqrt{\pi}}{2}.$ $\qquad$ (28) $\displaystyle\int_0^1 \frac{dx}{\sqrt{\ln\frac{1}{x}}} = \sqrt{\pi}.$

(29) $\displaystyle\int_0^1 \frac{\ln x}{x - 1}\,dx = \frac{\pi^2}{6}.$ $\qquad$ (30) $\displaystyle\int_0^1 \frac{\ln x}{x^2 - 1}\,dx = \frac{\pi^2}{8}.$

(31) $\displaystyle\int_0^1 \frac{\ln x}{x + 1}\,dx = -\frac{\pi^2}{12}.$ $\qquad$ (32) $\displaystyle\int_0^1 \frac{x \ln x}{x + 1}\,dx = \frac{\pi^2}{12} - 1.$

(33) $\displaystyle\int_0^\infty e^{-x} \ln x \, dx = -C$

(C is Euler's constant, 0·577215665 . . .).

(34) $\displaystyle\int_0^\infty e^{-\lambda x^2} \ln x \, dx = -\frac{1}{4}\sqrt{\frac{\pi}{\lambda}}\,(C + \ln 4\lambda), \qquad\qquad \lambda > 0.$

(35) $\displaystyle\int_0^\pi f(\sin x) \cos x \, dx = 0.$

(36) $\displaystyle\int_{-\pi/2}^{\pi/2} f(\cos x) \sin x \, dx = 0.$

(37) $\displaystyle\int_0^{\pi/2} \frac{dx}{a + b \sin x} = \begin{cases} \dfrac{1}{\sqrt{a^2 - b^2}} \cos^{-1}\dfrac{b}{a}, & a > |b|, \\[3mm] \dfrac{1}{\sqrt{b^2 - a^2}} \ln\left|\dfrac{b + \sqrt{b^2 - a^2}}{a}\right|, & \\[3mm] & |b| < |a|. \end{cases}$

(38) $\displaystyle\int_0^{\pi/2} \frac{dx}{a + b \cos x} = \int_0^{\pi/2} \frac{dx}{a + b \sin x}.$

(39) $\displaystyle\int_0^{\pi/2} \sin ax \, dx = \frac{1 - \cos\dfrac{a\pi}{2}}{a}, \qquad\qquad a \neq 0.$

(40) $\displaystyle\int_0^{\pi/2} \cos ax \, dx = \frac{1}{a} \sin\frac{a\pi}{2}, \qquad\qquad a \neq 0.$

(41) $\displaystyle\int_0^1 {\sin^{-1} \atop \cos^{-1}} px \, dx = {\cos^{-1} \atop \sin^{-1}} p \mp \frac{1 - \sqrt{1 - p^2}}{p}, \qquad 0 \leq p \leq 1.$

(42) $\displaystyle\int_0^a \sin^{-1}\frac{x}{a} \, dx = a\left(\frac{\pi}{2} - 1\right), \qquad\qquad a \neq 0.$

(43) $\displaystyle\int_0^a \cos^{-1}\frac{x}{a} \, dx = a, \quad a \neq 0.$ (44) $\displaystyle\int_0^1 \sin^{-1} x \, \frac{dx}{x} = \frac{\pi}{2} \ln 2.$

(45) $\displaystyle\int_0^1 \begin{matrix}\tan^{-1}\\\cot^{-1}\end{matrix} (px)\, dx = \begin{matrix}\tan^{-1}\\\cot^{-1}\end{matrix} p \mp \frac{1}{2p} \ln(1 + p^2).$

(46) $\displaystyle\int_0^a \begin{matrix}\tan^{-1}\\\cot^{-1}\end{matrix} \left(\frac{x}{a}\right) dx = \frac{a\pi}{4} \mp \frac{a}{2}\ln 2.$

(47) $\displaystyle\int_0^\infty \frac{\sinh ax}{\sinh bx}\, dx = \frac{\pi}{2b}\tan\frac{a\pi}{2b},$ \hfill $b > |a|.$

(48) $\displaystyle\int_0^\infty \frac{\cosh ax}{\cosh bx}\, dx = \frac{\pi}{2b\cos\dfrac{a\pi}{2b}},$ \hfill $b > |a|.$

(49) $\displaystyle\int_0^\infty \frac{dx}{\cosh bx} = \frac{\pi}{2b},$ \hfill $b > 0.$

(50) $\displaystyle\int_0^\infty \sinh^{-1} x\, \frac{dx}{x^{k+1}} = \frac{\Gamma\left(\dfrac{k}{2}\right)\Gamma\left(\dfrac{1-k}{2}\right)}{2k\sqrt{\pi}},$ \hfill $0 < k < 1.$

(51) $\displaystyle\int_1^\infty \cosh^{-1} x\, \frac{dx}{x^{k+1}} = \frac{\sqrt{\pi}\,\Gamma\left(\dfrac{k}{2}\right)}{2k\,\Gamma\left(\dfrac{k+1}{2}\right)},$ \hfill $k > 0.$

(52) $\displaystyle\int_0^a \tanh^{-1}\frac{x}{a}\, dx = a\ln 2.$

(53) $\displaystyle\int_a^\infty \coth^{-1}\frac{x}{a}\frac{dx}{x} = \frac{\pi^2}{8},$ \hfill $a > 0.$

MATHEMATICAL TABLES

———

TABLE 1
Powers, square-roots, and cube-roots
of x = 1·00 to x = 10·00

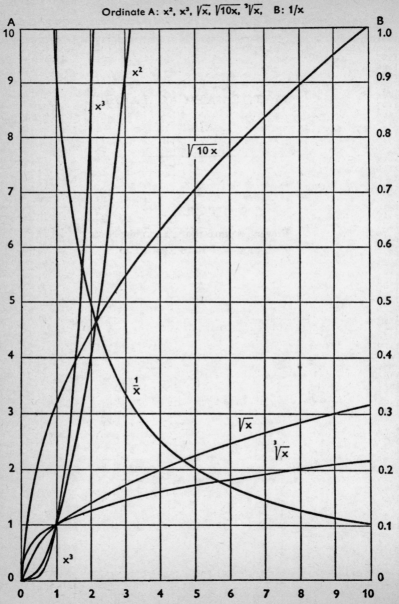

Graph for Table 1

Ordinate A: x^2, x^3, $\sqrt{x}$, $\sqrt{10x}$, $\sqrt[3]{x}$,   B: $1/x$

x	x^2	x^3	$\dfrac{1}{x}$	$\sqrt{x}$	$\sqrt{10x}$	$\sqrt[3]{x}$
1.00	1.0000	1.000	1.00000	1.0000	3.162	1.0000
1.01	1.0201	1.030	0.99010	1.0050	3.178	1.0033
1.02	1.0404	1.061	0.98039	1.0100	3.194	1.0066
1.03	1.0609	1.093	0.97087	1.0149	3.209	1.0099
1.04	1.0816	1.125	0.96154	1.0198	3.225	1.0132
1.05	1.1025	1.158	0.95238	1.0247	3.240	1.0164
1.06	1.1236	1.191	0.94340	1.0296	3.256	1.0196
1.07	1.1449	1.225	0.93458	1.0344	3.271	1.0228
1.08	1.1664	1.260	0.92593	1.0392	3.286	1.0260
1.09	1.1881	1.295	0.91743	1.0440	3.302	1.0291
1.10	1.2100	1.331	0.90909	1.0488	3.317	1.0323
1.11	1.2321	1.368	0.90090	1.0536	3.332	1.0354
1.12	1.2544	1.405	0.89286	1.0583	3.347	1.0385
1.13	1.2769	1.443	0.88496	1.0630	3.362	1.0416
1.14	1.2996	1.482	0.87719	1.0677	3.376	1.0446
1.15	1.3225	1.521	0.86957	1.0724	3.391	1.0477
1.16	1.3456	1.561	0.86207	1.0770	3.406	1.0507
1.17	1.3689	1.602	0.85470	1.0817	3.421	1.0537
1.18	1.3924	1.643	0.84746	1.0863	3.435	1.0567
1.19	1.4161	1.685	0.84034	1.0909	3.450	1.0597
1.20	1.4400	1.728	0.83333	1.0954	3.464	1.0627
1.21	1.4641	1.772	0.82645	1.1000	3.479	1.0656
1.22	1.4884	1.816	0.81967	1.1045	3.493	1.0685
1.23	1.5129	1.861	0.81301	1.1091	3.507	1.0714
1.24	1.5376	1.907	0.80645	1.1136	3.521	1.0743
1.25	1.5625	1.953	0.80000	1.1180	3.536	1.0772
1.26	1.5876	2.000	0.79365	1.1225	3.550	1.0801
1.27	1.6129	2.048	0.78740	1.1269	3.564	1.0829
1.28	1.6384	2.097	0.78125	1.1314	3.578	1.0858
1.29	1.6641	2.147	0.77519	1.1358	3.592	1.0886
1.30	1.6900	2.197	0.76923	1.1402	3.606	1.0914
1.31	1.7161	2.248	0.76336	1.1446	3.619	1.0942
1.32	1.7424	2.300	0.75758	1.1489	3.633	1.0970
1.33	1.7689	2.353	0.75186	1.1533	3.647	1.0997
1.34	1.7956	2.406	0.74627	1.1576	3.661	1.1025
1.35	1.8225	2.460	0.74074	1.1619	3.674	1.1052
1.36	1.8496	2.515	0.73529	1.1662	3.688	1.1079
1.37	1.8769	2.571	0.72993	1.1705	3.701	1.1106
1.38	1.9044	2.628	0.72464	1.1747	3.715	1.1133
1.39	1.9321	2.686	0.71942	1.1790	3.728	1.1160
1.40	1.9600	2.744	0.71429	1.1832	3.742	1.1187
1.41	1.9881	2.803	0.70922	1.1874	3.755	1.1213
1.42	2.0164	2.863	0.70423	1.1916	3.768	1.1240
1.43	2.0449	2.924	0.69930	1.1958	3.782	1.1266
1.44	2.0736	2.986	0.69444	1.2000	3.795	1.1292
1.45	2.1025	3.049	0.68966	1.2042	3.808	1.1319
1.46	2.1316	3.112	0.68493	1.2083	3.821	1.1344
1.47	2.1609	3.177	0.68027	1.2124	3.834	1.1370
1.48	2.1904	3.242	0.67568	1.2166	3.847	1.1396
1.49	2.2201	3.308	0.67114	1.2207	3.860	1.1422
1.50	2.2500	3.375	0.66667	1.2247	3.873	1.1447
x	x^2	x^3	$\dfrac{1}{x}$	$\sqrt{x}$	$\sqrt{10x}$	$\sqrt[3]{x}$

x	x^2	x^3	$\dfrac{1}{x}$	$\sqrt{x}$	$\sqrt{10x}$	$\sqrt[3]{x}$
1.50	2.2500	3.375	0.66667	1.2247	3.873	1.1447
1.51	2.2801	3.443	0.66225	1.2288	3.886	1.1473
1.52	2.3104	3.512	0.65789	1.2329	3.899	1.1498
1.53	2.3409	3.582	0.65359	1.2369	3.912	1.1523
1.54	2.3716	3.652	0.64935	1.2410	3.924	1.1548
1.55	2.4025	3.724	0.64516	1.2450	3.937	1.1573
1.56	2.4336	3.796	0.64103	1.2490	3.950	1.1598
1.57	2.4649	3.870	0.63694	1.2530	3.962	1.1623
1.58	2.4964	3.944	0.63291	1.2570	3.975	1.1647
1.59	2.5281	4.020	0.62893	1.2610	3.987	1.1672
1.60	2.5600	4.096	0.62500	1.2649	4.000	1.1696
1.61	2.5921	4.173	0.62112	1.2689	4.012	1.1720
1.62	2.6244	4.252	0.61728	1.2728	4.025	1.1745
1.63	2.6569	4.331	0.61350	1.2767	4.037	1.1769
1.64	2.6896	4.411	0.60976	1.2806	4.050	1.1793
1.65	2.7225	4.492	0.60606	1.2845	4.062	1.1817
1.66	2.7556	4.574	0.60241	1.2884	4.074	1.1840
1.67	2.7889	4.657	0.59880	1.2923	4.087	1.1864
1.68	2.8224	4.742	0.59524	1.2961	4.099	1.1888
1.69	2.8561	4.827	0.59172	1.3000	4.111	1.1911
1.70	2.8900	4.913	0.58824	1.3038	4.123	1.1935
1.71	2.9241	5.000	0.58480	1.3077	4.135	1.1958
1.72	2.9584	5.088	0.58140	1.3115	4.147	1.1981
1.73	2.9929	5.178	0.57803	1.3153	4.159	1.2005
1.74	3.0276	5.268	0.57471	1.3191	4.171	1.2028
1.75	3.0625	5.359	0.57143	1.3229	4.183	1.2051
1.76	3.0976	5.452	0.56818	1.3266	4.195	1.2074
1.77	3.1329	5.545	0.56497	1.3304	4.207	1.2096
1.78	3.1684	5.640	0.56180	1.3342	4.219	1.2119
1.79	3.2041	5.735	0.55866	1.3379	4.231	1.2142
1.80	3.2400	5.832	0.55556	1.3416	4.243	1.2164
1.81	3.2761	5.930	0.55249	1.3454	4.254	1.2187
1.82	3.3124	6.029	0.54945	1.3491	4.266	1.2209
1.83	3.3489	6.128	0.54645	1.3528	4.278	1.2232
1.84	3.3856	6.230	0.54348	1.3565	4.290	1.2254
1.85	3.4225	6.332	0.54054	1.3601	4.301	1.2276
1.86	3.4596	6.435	0.53763	1.3638	4.313	1.2298
1.87	3.4969	6.539	0.53476	1.3675	4.324	1.2320
1.88	3.5344	6.645	0.53191	1.3711	4.336	1.2342
1.89	3.5721	6.751	0.52910	1.3748	4.347	1.2364
1.90	3.6100	6.859	0.52632	1.3784	4.359	1.2386
1.91	3.6481	6.968	0.52356	1.3820	4.370	1.2407
1.92	3.6864	7.078	0.52083	1.3856	4.382	1.2429
1.93	3.7249	7.189	0.51813	1.3892	4.393	1.2450
1.94	3.7636	7.301	0.51546	1.3928	4.405	1.2472
1.95	3.8025	7.415	0.51282	1.3964	4.416	1.2493
1.96	3.8416	7.530	0.51020	1.4000	4.427	1.2515
1.97	3.8809	7.645	0.50761	1.4036	4.438	1.2536
1.98	3.9204	7.762	0.50505	1.4071	4.450	1.2557
1.99	3.9601	7.881	0.50251	1.4107	4.461	1.2578
2.00	4.0000	8.000	0.50000	1.4142	4.472	1.2599
x	x^2	x^3	$\dfrac{1}{x}$	$\sqrt{x}$	$\sqrt{10x}$	$\sqrt[3]{x}$

x	x^2	x^3	$\frac{1}{x}$	$\sqrt{x}$	$\sqrt{10x}$	$\sqrt[3]{x}$
2.00	4.0000	8.000	0.50000	1.4142	4.472	1.2599
2.01	4.0401	8.121	0.49751	1.4177	4.483	1.2620
2.02	4.0804	8.242	0.49505	1.4213	4.494	1.2641
2.03	4.1209	8.365	0.49261	1.4248	4.506	1.2662
2.04	4.1616	8.490	0.49020	1.4283	4.517	1.2683
2.05	4.2025	8.615	0.48780	1.4318	4.528	1.2703
2.06	4.2436	8.742	0.48544	1.4353	4.539	1.2724
2.07	4.2849	8.870	0.48309	1.4387	4.550	1.2745
2.08	4.3264	8.999	0.48077	1.4422	4.561	1.2765
2.09	4.3681	9.129	0.47847	1.4457	4.572	1.2785
2.10	4.4100	9.261	0.47619	1.4491	4.583	1.2806
2.11	4.4521	9.394	0.47393	1.4526	4.593	1.2826
2.12	4.4944	9.528	0.47170	1.4560	4.604	1.2846
2.13	4.5369	9.664	0.46948	1.4595	4.615	1.2866
2.14	4.5796	9.800	0.46729	1.4629	4.626	1.2887
2.15	4.6225	9.938	0.46512	1.4663	4.637	1.2907
2.16	4.6656	10.078	0.46296	1.4697	4.648	1.2927
2.17	4.7089	10.218	0.46083	1.4731	4.658	1.2947
2.18	4.7524	10.360	0.45872	1.4765	4.669	1.2966
2.19	4.7961	10.503	0.45662	1.4799	4.680	1.2986
2.20	4.8400	10.648	0.45455	1.4832	4.690	1.3006
2.21	4.8841	10.794	0.45249	1.4866	4.701	1.3026
2.22	4.9284	10.941	0.45045	1.4900	4.712	1.3045
2.23	4.9729	11.090	0.44843	1.4933	4.722	1.3065
2.24	5.0176	11.239	0.44643	1.4967	4.733	1.3084
2.25	5.0625	11.391	0.44444	1.5000	4.743	1.3104
2.26	5.1076	11.543	0.44248	1.5033	4.754	1.3123
2.27	5.1529	11.697	0.44053	1.5067	4.764	1.3142
2.28	5.1984	11.852	0.43860	1.5100	4.775	1.3162
2.29	5.2441	12.009	0.43668	1.5133	4.785	1.3181
2.30	5.2900	12.167	0.43478	1.5166	4.796	1.3200
2.31	5.3361	12.326	0.43290	1.5199	4.806	1.3219
2.32	5.3824	12.487	0.43103	1.5232	4.817	1.3238
2.33	5.4289	12.649	0.42918	1.5264	4.827	1.3257
2.34	5.4756	12.813	0.42735	1.5297	4.837	1.3276
2.35	5.5225	12.978	0.42553	1.5330	4.848	1.3295
2.36	5.5696	13.144	0.42373	1.5362	4.858	1.3314
2.37	5.6169	13.312	0.42194	1.5395	4.868	1.3333
2.38	5.6644	13.481	0.42017	1.5427	4.879	1.3351
2.39	5.7121	13.652	0.41841	1.5460	4.889	1.3370
2.40	5.7600	13.824	0.41667	1.5492	4.899	1.3389
2.41	5.8081	13.998	0.41494	1.5524	4.909	1.3407
2.42	5.8564	14.172	0.41322	1.5556	4.919	1.3426
2.43	5.9049	14.349	0.41152	1.5588	4.930	1.3444
2.44	5.9536	14.527	0.40984	1.5620	4.940	1.3463
2.45	6.0025	14.706	0.40816	1.5652	4.950	1.3481
2.46	6.0516	14.887	0.40650	1.5684	4.960	1.3499
2.47	6.1009	15.069	0.40486	1.5716	4.970	1.3518
2.48	6.1504	15.253	0.40323	1.5748	4.980	1.3536
2.49	6.2001	15.438	0.40161	1.5780	4.990	1.3554
2.50	6.2500	15.625	0.40000	1.5811	5.000	1.3572
x	x^2	x^3	$\frac{1}{x}$	$\sqrt{x}$	$\sqrt{10x}$	$\sqrt[3]{x}$

x	x^2	x^3	$\frac{1}{x}$	$\sqrt{x}$	$\sqrt{10x}$	$\sqrt[3]{x}$
2.50	6.2500	15.625	0.40000	1.5811	5.000	1.3572
2.51	6.3001	15.813	0.39841	1.5843	5.010	1.3590
2.52	6.3504	16.003	0.39683	1.5875	5.020	1.3608
2.53	6.4009	16.194	0.39526	1.5906	5.030	1.3626
2.54	6.4516	16.387	0.39370	1.5937	5.040	1.3644
2.55	6.5025	16.581	0.39216	1.5969	5.050	1.3662
2.56	6.5536	16.777	0.39063	1.6000	5.060	1.3680
2.57	6.6049	16.975	0.38911	1.6031	5.070	1.3698
2.58	6.6564	17.174	0.38760	1.6062	5.079	1.3715
2.59	6.7081	17.374	0.38610	1.6093	5.089	1.3733
2.60	6.7600	17.576	0.38462	1.6125	5.099	1.3751
2.61	6.8121	17.780	0.38314	1.6155	5.109	1.3768
2.62	6.8644	17.985	0.38168	1.6186	5.119	1.3786
2.63	6.9169	18.191	0.38023	1.6217	5.128	1.3803
2.64	6.9696	18.400	0.37879	1.6248	5.138	1.3821
2.65	7.0225	18.610	0.37736	1.6279	5.148	1.3838
2.66	7.0756	18.821	0.37594	1.6310	5.158	1.3856
2.67	7.1289	19.034	0.37453	1.6340	5.167	1.3873
2.68	7.1824	19.249	0.37313	1.6371	5.177	1.3890
2.69	7.2361	19.465	0.37175	1.6401	5.187	1.3908
2.70	7.2900	19.683	0.37037	1.6432	5.196	1.3925
2.71	7.3441	19.903	0.36900	1.6462	5.206	1.3942
2.72	7.3984	20.124	0.36765	1.6492	5.215	1.3959
2.73	7.4529	20.346	0.36630	1.6523	5.225	1.3976
2.74	7.5076	20.571	0.36496	1.6553	5.235	1.3993
2.75	7.5625	20.797	0.36364	1.6583	5.244	1.4010
2.76	7.6176	21.025	0.36232	1.6613	5.254	1.4027
2.77	7.6729	21.254	0.36101	1.6643	5.263	1.4044
2.78	7.7284	21.485	0.35971	1.6673	5.273	1.4061
2.79	7.7841	21.718	0.35842	1.6703	5.282	1.4078
2.80	7.8400	21.952	0.35714	1.6733	5.292	1.4095
2.81	7.8961	22.188	0.35587	1.6763	5.301	1.4111
2.82	7.9524	22.426	0.35461	1.6793	5.310	1.4128
2.83	8.0089	22.665	0.35336	1.6823	5.320	1.4145
2.84	8.0656	22.906	0.35211	1.6852	5.329	1.4161
2.85	8.1225	23.149	0.35088	1.6882	5.339	1.4178
2.86	8.1796	23.394	0.34965	1.6912	5.348	1.4195
2.87	8.2369	23.640	0.34843	1.6941	5.357	1.4211
2.88	8.2944	23.888	0.34722	1.6971	5.367	1.4228
2.89	8.3521	24.138	0.34602	1.7000	5.376	1.4244
2.90	8.4100	24.389	0.34483	1.7029	5.385	1.4260
2.91	8.4681	24.642	0.34364	1.7059	5.394	1.4277
2.92	8.5264	24.897	0.34247	1.7088	5.404	1.4293
2.93	8.5849	25.154	0.34130	1.7117	5.413	1.4309
2.94	8.6436	25.412	0.34014	1.7146	5.422	1.4326
2.95	8.7025	25.672	0.33898	1.7176	5.431	1.4342
2.96	8.7616	25.934	0.33784	1.7205	5.441	1.4358
2.97	8.8209	26.198	0.33670	1.7234	5.450	1.4374
2.98	8.8804	26.464	0.33557	1.7263	5.459	1.4390
2.99	8.9401	26.731	0.33445	1.7292	5.468	1.4406
3.00	9.0000	27.000	0.33333	1.7321	5.477	1.4422
x	x^2	x^3	$\frac{1}{x}$	$\sqrt{x}$	$\sqrt{10x}$	$\sqrt[3]{x}$

x	x^2	x^3	$\frac{1}{x}$	$\sqrt{x}$	$\sqrt{10x}$	$\sqrt[3]{x}$
3.00	9.0000	27.000	0.33333	1.7321	5.477	1.4422
3.01	9.0601	27.271	0.33223	1.7349	5.486	1.4439
3.02	9.1204	27.544	0.33113	1.7378	5.495	1.4454
3.03	9.1809	27.818	0.33003	1.7407	5.505	1.4470
3.04	9.2416	28.094	0.32895	1.7436	5.514	1.4486
3.05	9.3025	28.373	0.32787	1.7464	5.523	1.4502
3.06	9.3636	28.653	0.32680	1.7493	5.532	1.4518
3.07	9.4249	28.934	0.32573	1.7521	5.541	1.4534
3.08	9.4864	29.218	0.32468	1.7550	5.550	1.4550
3.09	9.5481	29.504	0.32362	1.7578	5.559	1.4565
3.10	9.6100	29.791	0.32258	1.7607	5.568	1.4581
3.11	9.6721	30.080	0.32154	1.7635	5.577	1.4597
3.12	9.7344	30.371	0.32051	1.7664	5.586	1.4612
3.13	9.7969	30.664	0.31949	1.7692	5.595	1.4628
3.14	9.8596	30.959	0.31847	1.7720	5.604	1.4643
3.15	9.9225	31.256	0.31746	1.7748	5.612	1.4659
3.16	9.9856	31.554	0.31646	1.7776	5.621	1.4674
3.17	10.0489	31.855	0.31546	1.7804	5.630	1.4690
3.18	10.1124	32.157	0.31447	1.7833	5.639	1.4705
3.19	10.1761	32.462	0.31348	1.7861	5.648	1.4721
3.20	10.2400	32.768	0.31250	1.7889	5.657	1.4736
3.21	10.3041	33.076	0.31153	1.7916	5.666	1.4751
3.22	10.3684	33.386	0.31056	1.7944	5.675	1.4767
3.23	10.4329	33.698	0.30960	1.7972	5.683	1.4782
3.24	10.4976	34.012	0.30864	1.8000	5.692	1.4797
3.25	10.5625	34.328	0.30769	1.8028	5.701	1.4812
3.26	10.6276	34.646	0.30675	1.8055	5.710	1.4828
3.27	10.6929	34.966	0.30581	1.8083	5.718	1.4843
3.28	10.7584	35.288	0.30488	1.8111	5.727	1.4858
3.29	10.8241	35.611	0.30395	1.8138	5.736	1.4873
3.30	10.8900	35.937	0.30303	1.8166	5.745	1.4888
3.31	10.9561	36.265	0.30211	1.8193	5.753	1.4903
3.32	11.0224	36.594	0.30120	1.8221	5.762	1.4918
3.33	11.0889	36.926	0.30030	1.8248	5.771	1.4933
3.34	11.1556	37.260	0.29940	1.8276	5.779	1.4948
3.35	11.2225	37.595	0.29851	1.8303	5.788	1.4963
3.36	11.2896	37.933	0.29762	1.8330	5.797	1.4978
3.37	11.3569	38.273	0.29674	1.8358	5.805	1.4993
3.38	11.4244	38.614	0.29586	1.8385	5.814	1.5007
3.39	11.4921	38.958	0.29499	1.8412	5.822	1.5022
3.40	11.5600	39.304	0.29412	1.8439	5.831	1.5037
3.41	11.6281	39.652	0.29326	1.8466	5.840	1.5052
3.42	11.6964	40.002	0.29240	1.8493	5.848	1.5066
3.43	11.7649	40.354	0.29155	1.8520	5.857	1.5081
3.44	11.8336	40.708	0.29070	1.8547	5.865	1.5096
3.45	11.9025	41.064	0.28986	1.8574	5.874	1.5110
3.46	11.9716	41.422	0.28902	1.8601	5.882	1.5125
3.47	12.0409	41.782	0.28818	1.8628	5.891	1.5139
3.48	12.1104	42.144	0.28736	1.8655	5.899	1.5154
3.49	12.1801	42.509	0.28653	1.8682	5.908	1.5168
3.50	12.2500	42.875	0.28571	1.8708	5.916	1.5183
x	x^2	x^3	$\frac{1}{x}$	$\sqrt{x}$	$\sqrt{10x}$	$\sqrt[3]{x}$

x	x^2	x^3	$\frac{1}{x}$	$\sqrt{x}$	$\sqrt{10x}$	$\sqrt[3]{x}$
3.50	12.2500	42.875	0.28571	1.8708	5.916	1.5183
3.51	12.3201	43.244	0.28490	1.8735	5.925	1.5197
3.52	12.3904	43.614	0.28409	1.8762	5.933	1.5212
3.53	12.4609	43.987	0.28329	1.8788	5.941	1.5226
3.54	12.5316	44.362	0.28249	1.8815	5.950	1.5241
3.55	12.6025	44.739	0.28169	1.8841	5.958	1.5255
3.56	12.6736	45.118	0.28090	1.8868	5.967	1.5269
3.57	12.7449	45.499	0.28011	1.8894	5.975	1.5283
3.58	12.8164	45.883	0.27933	1.8921	5.983	1.5298
3.59	12.8881	46.268	0.27855	1.8947	5.992	1.5312
3.60	12.9600	46.656	0.27778	1.8974	6.000	1.5326
3.61	13.0321	47.046	0.27701	1.9000	6.008	1.5340
3.62	13.1044	47.438	0.27624	1.9026	6.017	1.5355
3.63	13.1769	47.832	0.27548	1.9053	6.025	1.5369
3.64	13.2496	48.229	0.27473	1.9079	6.033	1.5383
3.65	13.3225	48.627	0.27397	1.9105	6.042	1.5397
3.66	13.3956	49.028	0.27322	1.9131	6.050	1.5411
3.67	13.4689	49.431	0.27248	1.9157	6.058	1.5425
3.68	13.5424	49.836	0.27174	1.9183	6.066	1.5439
3.69	13.6161	50.243	0.27100	1.9209	6.075	1.5453
3.70	13.6900	50.653	0.27027	1.9235	6.083	1.5467
3.71	13.7641	51.065	0.26954	1.9261	6.091	1.5481
3.72	13.8384	51.479	0.26882	1.9287	6.099	1.5495
3.73	13.9129	51.895	0.26810	1.9313	6.107	1.5508
3.74	13.9876	52.314	0.26738	1.9339	6.116	1.5522
3.75	14.0625	52.734	0.26667	1.9365	6.124	1.5536
3.76	14.1376	53.157	0.26596	1.9391	6.132	1.5550
3.77	14.2129	53.583	0.26525	1.9416	6.140	1.5564
3.78	14.2884	54.010	0.26455	1.9442	6.148	1.5577
3.79	14.3641	54.440	0.26385	1.9468	6.156	1.5591
3.80	14.4400	54.872	0.26316	1.9494	6.164	1.5605
3.81	14.5161	55.306	0.26247	1.9519	6.173	1.5619
3.82	14.5924	55.743	0.26178	1.9545	6.181	1.5632
3.83	14.6689	56.182	0.26110	1.9570	6.189	1.5646
3.84	14.7456	56.623	0.26042	1.9596	6.197	1.5659
3.85	14.8225	57.067	0.25974	1.9621	6.205	1.5673
3.86	14.8996	57.512	0.25907	1.9647	6.213	1.5687
3.87	14.9769	57.961	0.25840	1.9672	6.221	1.5700
3.88	15.0544	58.411	0.25773	1.9698	6.229	1.5714
3.89	15.1321	58.864	0.25707	1.9723	6.237	1.5727
3.90	15.2100	59.319	0.25641	1.9748	6.245	1.5741
3.91	15.2881	59.776	0.25575	1.9774	6.253	1.5754
3.92	15.3664	60.236	0.25510	1.9799	6.261	1.5767
3.93	15.4449	60.698	0.25445	1.9824	6.269	1.5781
3.94	15.5236	61.163	0.25381	1.9849	6.277	1.5794
3.95	15.6025	61.630	0.25316	1.9875	6.285	1.5808
3.96	15.6816	62.099	0.25253	1.9900	6.293	1.5821
3.97	15.7609	62.571	0.25189	1.9925	6.301	1.5834
3.98	15.8404	63.045	0.25126	1.9950	6.309	1.5848
3.99	15.9201	63.521	0.25063	1.9975	6.317	1.5861
4.00	16.0000	64.000	0.25000	2.0000	6.325	1.5874
x	x^2	x^3	$\frac{1}{x}$	$\sqrt{x}$	$\sqrt{10x}$	$\sqrt[3]{x}$

x	x^2	x^3	$\dfrac{1}{x}$	$\sqrt{x}$	$\sqrt{10x}$	$\sqrt[3]{x}$
4.00	16.0000	64.000	0.25000	2.0000	6.325	1.5874
4.01	16.0801	64.481	0.24938	2.0025	6.332	1.5887
4.02	16.1604	64.965	0.24876	2.0050	6.340	1.5900
4.03	16.2409	65.451	0.24814	2.0075	6.348	1.5914
4.04	16.3216	65.939	0.24752	2.0100	6.356	1.5927
4.05	16.4025	66.430	0.24691	2.0125	6.364	1.5940
4.06	16.4836	66.923	0.24631	2.0149	6.372	1.5953
4.07	16.5649	67.419	0.24570	2.0174	6.380	1.5966
4.08	16.6464	67.917	0.24510	2.0199	6.387	1.5979
4.09	16.7281	68.418	0.24450	2.0224	6.395	1.5992
4.10	16.8100	68.921	0.24390	2.0248	6.403	1.6005
4.11	16.8921	69.427	0.24331	2.0273	6.411	1.6018
4.12	16.9744	69.935	0.24272	2.0298	6.419	1.6031
4.13	17.0569	70.445	0.24213	2.0322	6.427	1.6044
4.14	17.1396	70.958	0.24155	2.0347	6.434	1.6057
4.15	17.2225	71.473	0.24096	2.0372	6.442	1.6070
4.16	17.3056	71.991	0.24038	2.0396	6.450	1.6083
4.17	17.3889	72.512	0.23981	2.0421	6.458	1.6096
4.18	17.4724	73.035	0.23923	2.0445	6.465	1.6109
4.19	17.5561	73.560	0.23866	2.0469	6.473	1.6121
4.20	17.6400	74.088	0.23810	2.0494	6.481	1.6134
4.21	17.7241	74.618	0.23753	2.0518	6.488	1.6147
4.22	17.8084	75.151	0.23697	2.0543	6.496	1.6160
4.23	17.8929	75.687	0.23641	2.0567	6.504	1.6173
4.24	17.9776	76.225	0.23585	2.0591	6.512	1.6185
4.25	18.0625	76.766	0.23529	2.0616	6.519	1.6198
4.26	18.1476	77.309	0.23474	2.0640	6.527	1.6211
4.27	18.2329	77.854	0.23419	2.0664	6.535	1.6223
4.28	18.3184	78.403	0.23364	2.0688	6.542	1.6236
4.29	18.4041	78.954	0.23310	2.0712	6.550	1.6249
4.30	18.4900	79.507	0.23256	2.0736	6.557	1.6261
4.31	18.5761	80.063	0.23202	2.0761	6.565	1.6274
4.32	18.6624	80.622	0.23148	2.0785	6.573	1.6287
4.33	18.7489	81.183	0.23095	2.0809	6.580	1.6299
4.34	18.8356	81.747	0.23041	2.0833	6.588	1.6312
4.35	18.9225	82.313	0.22989	2.0857	6.595	1.6324
4.36	19.0096	82.882	0.22936	2.0881	6.603	1.6337
4.37	19.0969	83.453	0.22883	2.0905	6.611	1.6349
4.38	19.1844	84.028	0.22831	2.0928	6.618	1.6362
4.39	19.2721	84.605	0.22779	2.0952	6.626	1.6374
4.40	19.3600	85.184	0.22727	2.0976	6.633	1.6386
4.41	19.4481	85.766	0.22676	2.1000	6.641	1.6399
4.42	19.5364	86.351	0.22624	2.1024	6.648	1.6411
4.43	19.6249	86.938	0.22573	2.1048	6.656	1.6424
4.44	19.7136	87.528	0.22523	2.1071	6.663	1.6436
4.45	19.8025	88.121	0.22472	2.1095	6.671	1.6448
4.46	19.8916	88.717	0.22422	2.1119	6.678	1.6461
4.47	19.9809	89.315	0.22371	2.1142	6.686	1.6473
4.48	20.0704	89.915	0.22321	2.1166	6.693	1.6485
4.49	20.1601	90.519	0.22272	2.1190	6.701	1.6497
4.50	20.2500	91.125	0.22222	2.1213	6.708	1.6510
x	x^2	x^3	$\dfrac{1}{x}$	$\sqrt{x}$	$\sqrt{10x}$	$\sqrt[3]{x}$

x	x^2	x^3	$\frac{1}{x}$	$\sqrt{x}$	$\sqrt{10x}$	$\sqrt[3]{x}$
4.50	20.2500	91.125	0.22222	2.1213	6.708	1.6510
4.51	20.3401	91.734	0.22173	2.1237	6.716	1.6522
4.52	20.4304	92.345	0.22124	2.1260	6.723	1.6534
4.53	20.5209	92.960	0.22075	2.1284	6.731	1.6546
4.54	20.6116	93.577	0.22026	2.1307	6.738	1.6558
4.55	20.7025	94.196	0.21978	2.1331	6.745	1.6571
4.56	20.7936	94.819	0.21930	2.1354	6.753	1.6583
4.57	20.8849	95.444	0.21882	2.1378	6.760	1.6595
4.58	20.9764	96.072	0.21834	2.1401	6.768	1.6607
4.59	21.0681	96.703	0.21786	2.1424	6.775	1.6619
4.60	21.1600	97.336	0.21739	2.1448	6.782	1.6631
4.61	21.2521	97.972	0.21692	2.1471	6.790	1.6643
4.62	21.3444	98.611	0.21645	2.1494	6.797	1.6655
4.63	21.4369	99.253	0.21598	2.1517	6.804	1.6667
4.64	21.5296	99.897	0.21552	2.1541	6.812	1.6679
4.65	21.6225	100.545	0.21505	2.1564	6.819	1.6691
4.66	21.7156	101.195	0.21459	2.1587	6.826	1.6703
4.67	21.8089	101.848	0.21413	2.1610	6.834	1.6715
4.68	21.9024	102.503	0.21368	2.1633	6.841	1.6727
4.69	21.9961	103.162	0.21322	2.1656	6.848	1.6739
4.70	22.0900	103.823	0.21277	2.1679	6.856	1.6751
4.71	22.1841	104.487	0.21231	2.1703	6.863	1.6763
4.72	22.2784	105.154	0.21186	2.1726	6.870	1.6774
4.73	22.3729	105.824	0.21142	2.1749	6.877	1.6786
4.74	22.4676	106.496	0.21097	2.1772	6.885	1.6798
4.75	22.5625	107.172	0.21053	2.1794	6.892	1.6810
4.76	22.6576	107.850	0.21008	2.1817	6.899	1.6822
4.77	22.7529	108.531	0.20964	2.1840	6.907	1.6833
4.78	22.8484	109.215	0.20921	2.1863	6.914	1.6845
4.79	22.9441	109.902	0.20877	2.1886	6.921	1.6857
4.80	23.0400	110.592	0.20833	2.1909	6.928	1.6869
4.81	23.1361	111.285	0.20790	2.1932	6.935	1.6880
4.82	23.2324	111.980	0.20747	2.1954	6.943	1.6892
4.83	23.3289	112.679	0.20704	2.1977	6.950	1.6904
4.84	23.4256	113.380	0.20661	2.2000	6.957	1.6915
4.85	23.5225	114.084	0.20619	2.2023	6.964	1.6927
4.86	23.6196	114.791	0.20576	2.2045	6.971	1.6939
4.87	23.7169	115.501	0.20534	2.2068	6.979	1.6950
4.88	23.8144	116.214	0.20492	2.2091	6.986	1.6962
4.89	23.9121	116.930	0.20450	2.2113	6.993	1.6973
4.90	24.0100	117.649	0.20408	2.2136	7.000	1.6985
4.91	24.1081	118.371	0.20367	2.2159	7.007	1.6997
4.92	24.2064	119.095	0.20325	2.2181	7.014	1.7008
4.93	24.3049	119.823	0.20284	2.2204	7.021	1.7020
4.94	24.4036	120.554	0.20243	2.2226	7.029	1.7031
4.95	24.5025	121.287	0.20202	2.2249	7.036	1.7043
4.96	24.6016	122.024	0.20161	2.2271	7.043	1.7054
4.97	24.7009	122.763	0.20121	2.2293	7.050	1.7065
4.98	24.8004	123.506	0.20080	2.2316	7.057	1.7077
4.99	24.9001	124.251	0.20040	2.2338	7.064	1.7088
5.00	25.0000	125.000	0.20000	2.2361	7.071	1.7100
x	x^2	x^3	$\frac{1}{x}$	$\sqrt{x}$	$\sqrt{10x}$	$\sqrt[3]{x}$

x	x^2	x^3	$\frac{1}{x}$	$\sqrt{x}$	$\sqrt{10x}$	$\sqrt[3]{x}$
5.00	25.0000	125.000	0.20000	2.2361	7.071	1.7100
5.01	25.1001	125.752	0.19960	2.2383	7.078	1.7111
5.02	25.2004	126.506	0.19920	2.2405	7.085	1.7123
5.03	25.3009	127.264	0.19881	2.2428	7.092	1.7134
5.04	25.4016	128.024	0.19841	2.2450	7.099	1.7145
5.05	25.5025	128.788	0.19802	2.2472	7.106	1.7157
5.06	25.6036	129.554	0.19763	2.2494	7.113	1.7168
5.07	25.7049	130.324	0.19724	2.2517	7.120	1.7179
5.08	25.8064	131.097	0.19685	2.2539	7.127	1.7190
5.09	25.9081	131.872	0.19646	2.2561	7.134	1.7202
5.10	26.0100	132.651	0.19608	2.2583	7.141	1.7213
5.11	26.1121	133.433	0.19569	2.2605	7.148	1.7224
5.12	26.2144	134.218	0.19531	2.2627	7.155	1.7235
5.13	26.3169	135.006	0.19493	2.2650	7.162	1.7247
5.14	26.4196	135.797	0.19455	2.2672	7.169	1.7258
5.15	26.5225	136.591	0.19417	2.2694	7.176	1.7269
5.16	26.6256	137.388	0.19380	2.2716	7.183	1.7280
5.17	26.7289	138.188	0.19342	2.2738	7.190	1.7291
5.18	26.8324	138.992	0.19305	2.2760	7.197	1.7303
5.19	26.9361	139.798	0.19268	2.2782	7.204	1.7314
5.20	27.0400	140.608	0.19231	2.2804	7.211	1.7325
5.21	27.1441	141.421	0.19194	2.2825	7.218	1.7336
5.22	27.2484	142.237	0.19157	2.2847	7.225	1.7347
5.23	27.3529	143.056	0.19120	2.2869	7.232	1.7358
5.24	27.4576	143.878	0.19084	2.2891	7.239	1.7369
5.25	27.5625	144.703	0.19048	2.2913	7.246	1.7380
5.26	27.6676	145.532	0.19011	2.2935	7.253	1.7391
5.27	27.7729	146.363	0.18975	2.2956	7.259	1.7402
5.28	27.8784	147.198	0.18939	2.2978	7.266	1.7413
5.29	27.9841	148.036	0.18904	2.3000	7.273	1.7424
5.30	28.0900	148.877	0.18868	2.3022	7.280	1.7435
5.31	28.1961	149.721	0.18832	2.3043	7.287	1.7446
5.32	28.3024	150.569	0.18797	2.3065	7.294	1.7457
5.33	28.4089	151.419	0.18762	2.3087	7.301	1.7468
5.34	28.5156	152.273	0.18727	2.3108	7.308	1.7479
5.35	28.6225	153.130	0.18692	2.3130	7.314	1.7490
5.36	28.7296	153.991	0.18657	2.3152	7.321	1.7501
5.37	28.8369	154.854	0.18622	2.3173	7.328	1.7512
5.38	28.9444	155.721	0.18587	2.3195	7.335	1.7522
5.39	29.0521	156.591	0.18553	2.3216	7.342	1.7533
5.40	29.1600	157.464	0.18519	2.3238	7.348	1.7544
5.41	29.2681	158.340	0.18484	2.3259	7.355	1.7555
5.42	29.3764	159.220	0.18450	2.3281	7.362	1.7566
5.43	29.4849	160.103	0.18416	2.3302	7.369	1.7577
5.44	29.5936	160.989	0.18382	2.3324	7.376	1.7587
5.45	29.7025	161.879	0.18349	2.3345	7.382	1.7598
5.46	29.8116	162.771	0.18315	2.3367	7.389	1.7609
5.47	29.9209	163.667	0.18282	2.3388	7.396	1.7620
5.48	30.0304	164.567	0.18248	2.3409	7.403	1.7630
5.49	30.1401	165.469	0.18215	2.3431	7.409	1.7641
5.50	30.2500	166.375	0.18182	2.3452	7.416	1.7652
x	x^2	x^3	$\frac{1}{x}$	$\sqrt{x}$	$\sqrt{10x}$	$\sqrt[3]{x}$

x	x^2	x^3	$\frac{1}{x}$	$\sqrt{x}$	$\sqrt{10x}$	$\sqrt[3]{x}$
5.50	30.2500	166.375	0.18182	2.3452	7.416	1.7652
5.51	30.3601	167.284	0.18149	2.3473	7.423	1.7662
5.52	30.4704	168.197	0.18116	2.3495	7.430	1.7673
5.53	30.5809	169.112	0.18083	2.3516	7.436	1.7684
5.54	30.6916	170.031	0.18051	2.3537	7.443	1.7694
5.55	30.8025	170.954	0.18018	2.3558	7.450	1.7705
5.56	30.9136	171.880	0.17986	2.3580	7.457	1.7716
5.57	31.0249	172.809	0.17953	2.3601	7.463	1.7726
5.58	31.1364	173.741	0.17921	2.3622	7.470	1.7737
5.59	31.2481	174.677	0.17889	2.3643	7.477	1.7748
5.60	31.3600	175.616	0.17857	2.3664	7.483	1.7758
5.61	31.4721	176.558	0.17825	2.3685	7.490	1.7769
5.62	31.5844	177.504	0.17794	2.3707	7.497	1.7779
5.63	31.6969	178.454	0.17762	2.3728	7.503	1.7790
5.64	31.8096	179.406	0.17730	2.3749	7.510	1.7800
5.65	31.9225	180.362	0.17699	2.3770	7.517	1.7811
5.66	32.0356	181.321	0.17668	2.3791	7.523	1.7821
5.67	32.1489	182.284	0.17637	2.3812	7.530	1.7832
5.68	32.2624	183.250	0.17606	2.3833	7.537	1.7842
5.69	32.3761	184.220	0.17575	2.3854	7.543	1.7853
5.70	32.4900	185.193	0.17544	2.3875	7.550	1.7863
5.71	32.6041	186.169	0.17513	2.3896	7.556	1.7874
5.72	32.7184	187.149	0.17483	2.3917	7.563	1.7884
5.73	32.8329	188.133	0.17452	2.3937	7.570	1.7894
5.74	32.9476	189.119	0.17422	2.3958	7.576	1.7905
5.75	33.0625	190.109	0.17391	2.3979	7.583	1.7915
5.76	33.1776	191.103	0.17361	2.4000	7.589	1.7926
5.77	33.2929	192.100	0.17331	2.4021	7.596	1.7936
5.78	33.4084	193.101	0.17301	2.4042	7.603	1.7946
5.79	33.5241	194.105	0.17271	2.4062	7.609	1.7957
5.80	33.6400	195.112	0.17241	2.4083	7.616	1.7967
5.81	33.7561	196.123	0.17212	2.4104	7.622	1.7977
5.82	33.8724	197.137	0.17182	2.4125	7.629	1.7988
5.83	33.9889	198.155	0.17153	2.4145	7.635	1.7998
5.84	34.1056	199.177	0.17123	2.4166	7.642	1.8008
5.85	34.2225	200.202	0.17094	2.4187	7.649	1.8018
5.86	34.3396	201.230	0.17065	2.4207	7.655	1.8029
5.87	34.4569	202.262	0.17036	2.4228	7.662	1.8039
5.88	34.5744	203.297	0.17007	2.4249	7.668	1.8049
5.89	34.6921	204.336	0.16978	2.4269	7.675	1.8059
5.90	34.8100	205.379	0.16949	2.4290	7.681	1.8070
5.91	34.9281	206.425	0.16920	2.4310	7.688	1.8080
5.92	35.0464	207.475	0.16892	2.4331	7.694	1.8090
5.93	35.1649	208.528	0.16863	2.4352	7.701	1.8100
5.94	35.2836	209.585	0.16835	2.4372	7.707	1.8110
5.95	35.4025	210.645	0.16807	2.4393	7.714	1.8121
5.96	35.5216	211.709	0.16779	2.4413	7.720	1.8131
5.97	35.6409	212.776	0.16750	2.4434	7.727	1.8141
5.98	35.7604	213.847	0.16722	2.4454	7.733	1.8151
5.99	35.8801	214.922	0.16694	2.4474	7.740	1.8161
6.00	36.0000	216.000	0.16667	2.4495	7.746	1.8171
x	x^2	x^3	$\frac{1}{x}$	$\sqrt{x}$	$\sqrt{10x}$	$\sqrt[3]{x}$

x	x^2	x^3	$\frac{1}{x}$	$\sqrt{x}$	$\sqrt{10x}$	$\sqrt[3]{x}$
6.00	36.0000	216.000	0.16667	2.4495	7.746	1.8171
6.01	36.1201	217.082	0.16639	2.4515	7.752	1.8181
6.02	36.2404	218.167	0.16611	2.4536	7.759	1.8191
6.03	36.3609	219.256	0.16584	2.4556	7.765	1.8201
6.04	36.4816	220.349	0.16556	2.4576	7.772	1.8211
6.05	36.6025	221.445	0.16529	2.4597	7.778	1.8222
6.06	36.7236	222.545	0.16502	2.4617	7.785	1.8232
6.07	36.8449	223.649	0.16474	2.4637	7.791	1.8242
6.08	36.9664	224.756	0.16447	2.4658	7.797	1.8252
6.09	37.0881	225.867	0.16420	2.4678	7.804	1.8262
6.10	37.2100	226.981	0.16393	2.4698	7.810	1.8272
6.11	37.3321	228.099	0.16367	2.4718	7.817	1.8282
6.12	37.4544	229.221	0.16340	2.4739	7.823	1.8292
6.13	37.5769	230.346	0.16313	2.4759	7.829	1.8302
6.14	37.6996	231.476	0.16287	2.4779	7.836	1.8311
6.15	37.8225	232.608	0.16260	2.4799	7.842	1.8321
6.16	37.9456	233.745	0.16234	2.4819	7.849	1.8331
6.17	38.0689	234.885	0.16207	2.4839	7.855	1.8341
6.18	38.1924	236.029	0.16181	2.4860	7.861	1.8351
6.19	38.3161	237.177	0.16155	2.4880	7.868	1.8361
6.20	38.4400	238.328	0.16129	2.4900	7.874	1.8371
6.21	38.5641	239.483	0.16103	2.4920	7.880	1.8381
6.22	38.6884	240.642	0.16077	2.4940	7.887	1.8391
6.23	38.8129	241.804	0.16051	2.4960	7.893	1.8400
6.24	38.9376	242.971	0.16026	2.4980	7.899	1.8410
6.25	39.0625	244.141	0.16000	2.5000	7.906	1.8420
6.26	39.1876	245.314	0.15974	2.5020	7.912	1.8430
6.27	39.3129	246.492	0.15949	2.5040	7.918	1.8440
6.28	39.4384	247.673	0.15924	2.5060	7.925	1.8450
6.29	39.5641	248.858	0.15898	2.5080	7.931	1.8459
6.30	39.6900	250.047	0.15873	2.5100	7.937	1.8469
6.31	39.8161	251.240	0.15848	2.5120	7.944	1.8479
6.32	39.9424	252.436	0.15823	2.5140	7.950	1.8489
6.33	40.0689	253.636	0.15798	2.5159	7.956	1.8498
6.34	40.1956	254.840	0.15773	2.5179	7.962	1.8508
6.35	40.3225	256.048	0.15748	2.5199	7.969	1.8518
6.36	40.4496	257.259	0.15723	2.5219	7.975	1.8528
6.37	40.5769	258.475	0.15699	2.5239	7.981	1.8537
6.38	40.7044	259.694	0.15674	2.5259	7.987	1.8547
6.39	40.8321	260.917	0.15649	2.5278	7.994	1.8557
6.40	40.9600	262.144	0.15625	2.5298	8.000	1.8566
6.41	41.0881	263.375	0.15601	2.5318	8.006	1.8576
6.42	41.2164	264.609	0.15576	2.5338	8.012	1.8586
6.43	41.3449	265.848	0.15552	2.5357	8.019	1.8595
6.44	41.4736	267.090	0.15528	2.5377	8.025	1.8605
6.45	41.6025	268.336	0.15504	2.5397	8.031	1.8615
6.46	41.7316	269.586	0.15480	2.5417	8.037	1.8624
6.47	41.8609	270.840	0.15456	2.5436	8.044	1.8634
6.48	41.9904	272.098	0.15432	2.5456	8.050	1.8643
6.49	42.1201	273.359	0.15408	2.5475	8.056	1.8653
6.50	42.2500	274.625	0.15385	2.5495	8.062	1.8663
x	x^2	x^3	$\frac{1}{x}$	$\sqrt{x}$	$\sqrt{10x}$	$\sqrt[3]{x}$

x	x^2	x^3	$\dfrac{1}{x}$	$\sqrt{x}$	$\sqrt{10x}$	$\sqrt[3]{x}$
6.50	42.2500	274.625	0.15385	2.5495	8.062	1.8663
6.51	42.3801	275.894	0.15361	2.5515	8.068	1.8672
6.52	42.5104	277.168	0.15337	2.5534	8.075	1.8682
6.53	42.6409	278.445	0.15314	2.5554	8.081	1.8691
6.54	42.7716	279.726	0.15291	2.5573	8.087	1.8701
6.55	42.9025	281.011	0.15267	2.5593	8.093	1.8710
6.56	43.0336	282.300	0.15244	2.5612	8.099	1.8720
6.57	43.1649	283.593	0.15221	2.5632	8.106	1.8729
6.58	43.2964	284.890	0.15198	2.5652	8.112	1.8739
6.59	43.4281	286.191	0.15175	2.5671	8.118	1.8748
6.60	43.5600	287.496	0.15152	2.5690	8.124	1.8758
6.61	43.6921	288.805	0.15129	2.5710	8.130	1.8767
6.62	43.8244	290.118	0.15106	2.5729	8.136	1.8777
6.63	43.9569	291.434	0.15083	2.5749	8.142	1.8786
6.64	44.0896	292.755	0.15060	2.5768	8.149	1.8796
6.65	44.2225	294.080	0.15038	2.5788	8.155	1.8805
6.66	44.3556	295.408	0.15015	2.5807	8.161	1.8814
6.67	44.4889	296.741	0.14993	2.5826	8.167	1.8824
6.68	44.6224	298.078	0.14970	2.5846	8.173	1.8833
6.69	44.7561	299.418	0.14948	2.5865	8.179	1.8843
6.70	44.8900	300.763	0.14925	2.5884	8.185	1.8852
6.71	45.0241	302.112	0.14903	2.5904	8.191	1.8861
6.72	45.1584	303.464	0.14881	2.5923	8.198	1.8871
6.73	45.2929	304.821	0.14859	2.5942	8.204	1.8880
6.74	45.4276	306.182	0.14837	2.5962	8.210	1.8889
6.75	45.5625	307.547	0.14815	2.5981	8.216	1.8899
6.76	45.6976	308.916	0.14793	2.6000	8.222	1.8908
6.77	45.8329	310.289	0.14771	2.6019	8.228	1.8917
6.78	45.9684	311.666	0.14749	2.6038	8.234	1.8927
6.79	46.1041	313.047	0.14728	2.6058	8.240	1.8936
6.80	46.2400	314.432	0.14706	2.6077	8.246	1.8945
6.81	46.3761	315.821	0.14684	2.6096	8.252	1.8955
6.82	46.5124	317.215	0.14663	2.6115	8.258	1.8964
6.83	46.6489	318.612	0.14641	2.6134	8.264	1.8973
6.84	46.7856	320.014	0.14620	2.6153	8.270	1.8982
6.85	46.9225	321.419	0.14599	2.6173	8.276	1.8992
6.86	47.0596	322.829	0.14577	2.6192	8.283	1.9001
6.87	47.1969	324.243	0.14556	2.6211	8.289	1.9010
6.88	47.3344	325.661	0.14535	2.6230	8.295	1.9019
6.89	47.4721	327.083	0.14514	2.6249	8.301	1.9029
6.90	47.6100	328.509	0.14493	2.6268	8.307	1.9038
6.91	47.7481	329.939	0.14472	2.6287	8.313	1.9047
6.92	47.8864	331.374	0.14451	2.6306	8.319	1.9056
6.93	48.0249	332.813	0.14430	2.6325	8.325	1.9065
6.94	48.1636	334.255	0.14409	2.6344	8.331	1.9075
6.95	48.3025	335.702	0.14388	2.6363	8.337	1.9084
6.96	48.4416	337.154	0.14368	2.6382	8.343	1.9093
6.97	48.5809	338.609	0.14347	2.6401	8.349	1.9102
6.98	48.7204	340.068	0.14327	2.6420	8.355	1.9111
6.99	48.8601	341.532	0.14306	2.6439	8.361	1.9120
7.00	49.0000	343.000	0.14286	2.6458	8.367	1.9129
x	x^2	x^3	$\dfrac{1}{x}$	$\sqrt{x}$	$\sqrt{10x}$	$\sqrt[3]{x}$

x	x^2	x^3	$\frac{1}{x}$	$\sqrt{x}$	$\sqrt{10x}$	$\sqrt[3]{x}$
7.00	49.0000	343.000	0.14286	2.6458	8.367	1.9129
7.01	49.1401	344.472	0.14265	2.6476	8.373	1.9138
7.02	49.2804	345.948	0.14245	2.6495	8.379	1.9148
7.03	49.4209	347.429	0.14225	2.6514	8.385	1.9157
7.04	49.5616	348.914	0.14205	2.6533	8.390	1.9166
7.05	49.7025	350.403	0.14184	2.6552	8.396	1.9175
7.06	49.8436	351.896	0.14164	2.6571	8.402	1.9184
7.07	49.9849	353.393	0.14144	2.6589	8.408	1.9193
7.08	50.1264	354.895	0.14124	2.6608	8.414	1.9202
7.09	50.2681	356.401	0.14104	2.6627	8.420	1.9211
7.10	50.4100	357.911	0.14085	2.6646	8.426	1.9220
7.11	50.5521	359.425	0.14065	2.6665	8.432	1.9229
7.12	30.6944	360.944	0.14045	2.6683	8.438	1.9238
7.13	50.8369	362.467	0.14025	2.6702	8.444	1.9247
7.14	50.9796	363.994	0.14006	2.6721	8.450	1.9256
7.15	51.1225	365.526	0.13986	2.6739	8.456	1.9265
7.16	51.2656	367.062	0.13966	2.6758	8.462	1.9274
7.17	51.4089	368.602	0.13947	2.6777	8.468	1.9283
7.18	51.5524	370.146	0.13928	2.6796	8.473	1.9292
7.19	51.6961	371.695	0.13908	2.6814	8.479	1.9301
7.20	51.8400	373.248	0.13889	2.6833	8.485	1.9310
7.21	51.9841	374.805	0.13870	2.6851	8.491	1.9319
7.22	52.1284	376.367	0.13850	2.6870	8.497	1.9328
7.23	52.2729	377.933	0.13831	2.6889	8.503	1.9337
7.24	52.4176	379.503	0.13812	2.6907	8.509	1.9345
7.25	52.5625	381.078	0.13793	2.6926	8.515	1.9354
7.26	52.7076	382.657	0.13774	2.6944	8.521	1.9363
7.27	52.8529	384.241	0.13755	2.6963	8.526	1.9372
7.28	52.9984	385.828	0.13736	2.6981	8.532	1.9381
7.29	53.1441	387.420	0.13717	2.7000	8.538	1.9390
7.30	53.2900	389.017	0.13699	2.7019	8.544	1.9399
7.31	53.4361	390.618	0.13680	2.7037	8.550	1.9408
7.32	53.5824	392.223	0.13661	2.7055	8.556	1.9416
7.33	53.7289	393.833	0.13643	2.7074	8.562	1.9425
7.34	53.8756	395.447	0.13624	2.7092	8.567	1.9434
7.35	54.0225	397.065	0.13605	2.7111	8.573	1.9443
7.36	54.1696	398.688	0.13587	2.7129	8.579	1.9452
7.37	54.3169	400.316	0.13569	2.7148	8.585	1.9461
7.38	54.4644	401.947	0.13550	2.7166	8.591	1.9469
7.39	54.6121	403.583	0.13532	2.7185	8.597	1.9478
7.40	54.7600	405.224	0.13514	2.7203	8.602	1.9487
7.41	54.9081	406.869	0.13495	2.7221	8.608	1.9496
7.42	55.0564	408.518	0.13477	2.7240	8.614	1.9504
7.43	55.2049	410.172	0.13459	2.7258	8.620	1.9513
7.44	55.3536	411.831	0.13441	2.7276	8.626	1.9522
7.45	55.5025	413.494	0.13423	2.7295	8.631	1.9531
7.46	55.6516	415.161	0.13405	2.7313	8.637	1.9539
7.47	55.8009	416.833	0.13387	2.7331	8.643	1.9548
7.48	55.9504	418.509	0.13369	2.7350	8.649	1.9557
7.49	56.1001	420.190	0.13351	2.7368	8.654	1.9566
7.50	56.2500	421.875	0.13333	2.7386	8.660	1.9574
x	x^2	x^3	$\frac{1}{x}$	$\sqrt{x}$	$\sqrt{10x}$	$\sqrt[3]{x}$

x	x^2	x^3	$\frac{1}{x}$	$\sqrt{x}$	$\sqrt{10x}$	$\sqrt[3]{x}$
7.50	56.2500	421.875	0.13333	2.7386	8.660	1.9574
7.51	56.4001	423.565	0.13316	2.7404	8.666	1.9583
7.52	56.5504	425.259	0.13298	2.7423	8.672	1.9592
7.53	56.7009	426.958	0.13280	2.7441	8.678	1.9600
7.54	56.8516	428.661	0.13263	2.7459	8.683	1.9609
7.55	57.0025	430.369	0.13245	2.7477	8.689	1.9618
7.56	57.1536	432.081	0.13228	2.7495	8.695	1.9626
7.57	57.3049	433.798	0.13210	2.7514	8.701	1.9635
7.58	57.4564	435.520	0.13193	2.7532	8.706	1.9644
7.59	57.6081	437.245	0.13175	2.7550	8.712	1.9652
7.60	57.7600	438.976	0.13158	2.7568	8.718	1.9661
7.61	57.9121	440.711	0.13141	2.7586	8.724	1.9670
7.62	58.0644	442.451	0.13123	2.7604	8.729	1.9678
7.63	58.2169	444.195	0.13106	2.7622	8.735	1.9687
7.64	58.3696	445.944	0.13089	2.7641	8.741	1.9695
7.65	58.5225	447.697	0.13072	2.7659	8.746	1.9704
7.66	58.6756	449.455	0.13055	2.7677	8.752	1.9713
7.67	58.8289	451.218	0.13038	2.7695	8.758	1.9721
7.68	58.9824	452.985	0.13021	2.7713	8.764	1.9730
7.69	59.1361	454.757	0.13004	2.7731	8.769	1.9738
7.70	59.2900	456.533	0.12987	2.7749	8.775	1.9747
7.71	59.4441	458.314	0.12970	2.7767	8.781	1.9755
7.72	59.5984	460.100	0.12953	2.7785	8.786	1.9764
7.73	59.7529	461.890	0.12937	2.7803	8.792	1.9772
7.74	59.9076	463.685	0.12920	2.7821	8.798	1.9781
7.75	60.0625	465.484	0.12903	2.7839	8.803	1.9789
7.76	60.2176	467.289	0.12887	2.7857	8.809	1.9798
7.77	60.3729	469.097	0.12870	2.7875	8.815	1.9806
7.78	60.5284	470.911	0.12853	2.7893	8.820	1.9815
7.79	60.6841	472.729	0.12837	2.7911	8.826	1.9823
7.80	60.8400	474.552	0.12821	2.7928	8.832	1.9832
7.81	60.9961	476.380	0.12804	2.7946	8.837	1.9840
7.82	61.1524	478.212	0.12788	2.7964	8.843	1.9849
7.83	61.3089	480.049	0.12771	2.7982	8.849	1.9857
7.84	61.4656	481.890	0.12755	2.8000	8.854	1.9866
7.85	61.6225	483.737	0.12739	2.8018	8.860	1.9874
7.86	61.7796	485.588	0.12723	2.8036	8.866	1.9883
7.87	61.9369	487.443	0.12706	2.8054	8.871	1.9891
7.88	62.0944	489.304	0.12690	2.8071	8.877	1.9899
7.89	62.2521	491.169	0.12674	2.8089	8.883	1.9908
7.90	62.4100	493.039	0.12658	2.8107	8.888	1.9916
7.91	62.5681	494.914	0.12642	2.8125	8.894	1.9925
7.92	62.7264	496.793	0.12626	2.8142	8.899	1.9933
7.93	62.8849	498.677	0.12610	2.8160	8.905	1.9941
7.94	63.0436	500.566	0.12594	2.8178	8.911	1.9950
7.95	63.2025	502.460	0.12579	2.8196	8.916	1.9958
7.96	63.3616	504.358	0.12563	2.8213	8.922	1.9967
7.97	63.5209	506.262	0.12547	2.8231	8.927	1.9975
7.98	63.6804	508.170	0.12531	2.8249	8.933	1.9983
7.99	63.8401	510.082	0.12516	2.8267	8.939	1.9992
8.00	64.0000	512.000	0.12500	2.8284	8.944	2.0000
x	x^2	x^3	$\frac{1}{x}$	$\sqrt{x}$	$\sqrt{10x}$	$\sqrt[3]{x}$

x	x^2	x^3	$\frac{1}{x}$	$\sqrt{x}$	$\sqrt{10x}$	$\sqrt[3]{x}$
8.00	64.0000	512.000	0.12500	2.8284	8.944	2.0000
8.01	64.1601	513.922	0.12484	2.8302	8.950	2.0008
8.02	64.3204	515.850	0.12469	2.8320	8.955	2.0017
8.03	64.4809	517.782	0.12453	2.8337	8.961	2.0025
8.04	64.6416	519.718	0.12438	2.8355	8.967	2.0033
8.05	64.8025	521.660	0.12422	2.8373	8.972	2.0042
8.06	64.9636	523.607	0.12407	2.8390	8.978	2.0050
8.07	65.1249	525.558	0.12392	2.8408	8.983	2.0058
8.08	65.2864	527.514	0.12376	2.8425	8.989	2.0066
8.09	65.4481	529.475	0.12361	2.8443	8.994	2.0075
8.10	65.6100	531.441	0.12346	2.8460	9.000	2.0083
8.11	65.7721	533.412	0.12330	2.8478	9.006	2.0091
8.12	65.9344	535.387	0.12315	2.8496	9.011	2.0100
8.13	66.0969	537.368	0.12300	2.8513	9.017	2.0108
8.14	66.2596	539.353	0.12285	2.8531	9.022	2.0116
8.15	66.4225	541.343	0.12270	2.8548	9.028	2.0124
8.16	66.5856	543.338	0.12255	2.8566	9.033	2.0132
8.17	66.7489	545.339	0.12240	2.8583	9.039	2.0141
8.18	66.9124	547.343	0.12225	2.8601	9.044	2.0149
8.19	67.0761	549.353	0.12210	2.8618	9.050	2.0157
8.20	67.2400	551.368	0.12195	2.8636	9.055	2.0165
8.21	67.4041	553.388	0.12180	2.8653	9.061	2.0173
8.22	67.5684	555.412	0.12165	2.8671	9.066	2.0182
8.23	67.7329	557.442	0.12151	2.8688	9.072	2.0190
8.24	67.8976	559.476	0.12136	2.8705	9.077	2.0198
8.25	68.0625	561.516	0.12121	2.8723	9.083	2.0206
8.26	68.2276	563.560	0.12107	2.8740	9.088	2.0214
8.27	68.3929	565.609	0.12092	2.8758	9.094	2.0223
8.28	68.5584	567.664	0.12077	2.8775	9.099	2.0231
8.29	68.7241	569.723	0.12063	2.8792	9.105	2.0239
8.30	68.8900	571.787	0.12048	2.8810	9.110	2.0247
8.31	69.0561	573.856	0.12034	2.8827	9.116	2.0255
8.32	69.2224	575.930	0.12019	2.8844	9.121	2.0263
8.33	69.3889	578.010	0.12005	2.8862	9.127	2.0271
8.34	69.5556	580.094	0.11990	2.8879	9.132	2.0279
8.35	69.7225	582.183	0.11976	2.8896	9.138	2.0288
8.36	69.8896	584.277	0.11962	2.8914	9.143	2.0296
8.37	70.0569	586.376	0.11947	2.8931	9.149	2.0304
8.38	70.2244	588.480	0.11933	2.8948	9.154	2.0312
8.39	70.3921	590.590	0.11919	2.8965	9.160	2.0320
8.40	70.5600	592.704	0.11905	2.8983	9.165	2.0328
8.41	70.7281	594.823	0.11891	2.9000	9.171	2.0336
8.42	70.8964	596.948	0.11876	2.9017	9.176	2.0344
8.43	71.0649	599.077	0.11862	2.9034	9.182	2.0352
8.44	71.2336	601.212	0.11848	2.9052	9.187	2.0360
8.45	71.4025	603.351	0.11834	2.9069	9.192	2.0368
8.46	71.5716	605.496	0.11820	2.9086	9.198	2.0376
8.47	71.7409	607.645	0.11806	2.9103	9.203	2.0384
8.48	71.9104	609.800	0.11792	2.9120	9.209	2.0392
8.49	72.0801	611.960	0.11779	2.9138	9.214	2.0400
8.50	72.2500	614.125	0.11765	2.9155	9.220	2.0408
x	x^2	x^3	$\frac{1}{x}$	$\sqrt{x}$	$\sqrt{10x}$	$\sqrt[3]{x}$

x	x^2	x^3	$\dfrac{1}{x}$	$\sqrt{x}$	$\sqrt{10x}$	$\sqrt[3]{x}$
8.50	72.2500	614.125	0.11765	2.9155	9.220	2.0408
8.51	72.4201	616.295	0.11751	2.9172	9.225	2.0416
8.52	72.5904	618.470	0.11737	2.9189	9.230	2.0424
8.53	72.7609	620.650	0.11723	2.9206	9.236	2.0432
8.54	72.9316	622.836	0.11710	2.9223	9.241	2.0440
8.55	73.1025	625.026	0.11696	2.9240	9.247	2.0448
8.56	73.2736	627.222	0.11682	2.9257	9.252	2.0456
8.57	73.4449	629.423	0.11669	2.9275	9.257	2.0464
8.58	73.6164	631.629	0.11655	2.9292	9.263	2.0472
8.59	73.7881	633.840	0.11641	2.9309	9.268	2.0480
8.60	73.9600	636.056	0.11628	2.9326	9.274	2.0488
8.61	74.1321	638.277	0.11614	2.9343	9.279	2.0496
8.62	74.3044	640.504	0.11601	2.9360	9.284	2.0504
8.63	74.4769	642.736	0.11587	2.9377	9.290	2.0512
8.64	74.6496	644.973	0.11574	2.9394	9.295	2.0520
8.65	74.8225	647.215	0.11561	2.9411	9.301	2.0528
8.66	74.9956	649.462	0.11547	2.9428	9.306	2.0536
8.67	75.1689	651.714	0.11534	2.9445	9.311	2.0543
8.68	75.3424	653.972	0.11521	2.9462	9.317	2.0551
8.69	75.5161	656.235	0.11507	2.9479	9.322	2.0559
8.70	75.6900	658.503	0.11494	2.9496	9.327	2.0567
8.71	75.8641	660.776	0.11481	2.9513	9.333	2.0575
8.72	76.0384	663.055	0.11468	2.9530	9.338	2.0583
8.73	76.2129	665.339	0.11455	2.9547	9.343	2.0591
8.74	76.3876	667.628	0.11442	2.9563	9.349	2.0599
8.75	76.5625	669.922	0.11429	2.9580	9.354	2.0606
8.76	76.7376	672.221	0.11416	2.9597	9.359	2.0614
8.77	76.9129	674.526	0.11403	2.9614	9.365	2.0622
8.78	77.0884	676.836	0.11390	2.9631	9.370	2.0630
8.79	77.2641	679.151	0.11377	2.9648	9.375	2.0638
8.80	77.4400	681.472	0.11364	2.9665	9.381	2.0646
8.81	77.6161	683.798	0.11351	2.9682	9.386	2.0653
8.82	77.7924	686.129	0.11338	2.9698	9.391	2.0661
8.83	77.9689	688.465	0.11325	2.9715	9.397	2.0669
8.84	78.1456	690.807	0.11312	2.9732	9.402	2.0677
8.85	78.3225	693.154	0.11299	2.9749	9.407	2.0685
8.86	78.4996	695.506	0.11287	2.9766	9.413	2.0692
8.87	78.6769	697.864	0.11274	2.9783	9.418	2.0700
8.88	78.8544	700.227	0.11261	2.9799	9.423	2.0708
8.89	79.0321	702.595	0.11249	2.9816	9.429	2.0716
8.90	79.2100	704.969	0.11236	2.9833	9.434	2.0724
8.91	79.3881	707.348	0.11223	2.9850	9.439	2.0731
8.92	79.5664	709.732	0.11211	2.9866	9.445	2.0739
8.93	79.7449	712.122	0.11198	2.9883	9.450	2.0747
8.94	79.9236	714.517	0.11186	2.9900	9.455	2.0755
8.95	80.1025	716.917	0.11173	2.9917	9.460	2.0762
8.96	80.2816	719.323	0.11161	2.9933	9.466	2.0770
8.97	80.4609	721.734	0.11148	2.9950	9.471	2.0778
8.98	80.6404	724.151	0.11136	2.9967	9.476	2.0785
8.99	80.8201	726.573	0.11123	2.9983	9.482	2.0793
9.00	81.0000	729.000	0.11111	3.0000	9.487	2.0801
x	x^2	x^3	$\dfrac{1}{x}$	$\sqrt{x}$	$\sqrt{10x}$	$\sqrt[3]{x}$

x	x^2	x^3	$\frac{1}{x}$	$\sqrt{x}$	$\sqrt{10x}$	$\sqrt[3]{x}$
9.00	81.0000	729.000	0.11111	3.0000	9.487	2.0801
9.01	81.1801	731.433	0.11099	3.0017	9.492	2.0809
9.02	81.3604	733.871	0.11086	3.0033	9.497	2.0816
9.03	81.5409	736.314	0.11074	3.0050	9.503	2.0824
9.04	81.7216	738.763	0.11062	3.0067	9.508	2.0832
9.05	81.9025	741.218	0.11050	3.0083	9.513	2.0839
9.06	82.0836	743.677	0.11038	3.0100	9.518	2.0847
9.07	82.2649	746.143	0.11025	3.0116	9.524	2.0855
9.08	82.4464	748.613	0.11013	3.0133	9.529	2.0862
9.09	82.6281	751.089	0.11001	3.0150	9.534	2.0870
9.10	82.8100	753.571	0.10989	3.0166	9.539	2.0878
9.11	82.9921	756.058	0.10977	3.0183	9.545	2.0885
9.12	83.1744	758.551	0.10965	3.0199	9.550	2.0893
9.13	83.3569	761.048	0.10953	3.0216	9.555	2.0901
9.14	83.5396	763.552	0.10941	3.0232	9.560	2.0908
9.15	83.7225	766.061	0.10929	3.0249	9.566	2.0916
9.16	83.9056	768.575	0.10917	3.0265	9.571	2.0923
9.17	84.0889	771.095	0.10905	3.0282	9.576	2.0931
9.18	84.2724	773.621	0.10893	3.0299	9.581	2.0939
9.19	84.4561	776.152	0.10881	3.0315	9.586	2.0946
9.20	84.6400	778.688	0.10870	3.0332	9.592	2.0954
9.21	84.8241	781.230	0.10858	3.0348	9.597	2.0961
9.22	85.0084	783.777	0.10846	3.0364	9.602	2.0969
9.23	85.1929	786.330	0.10834	3.0381	9.607	2.0977
9.24	85.3776	788.889	0.10823	3.0397	9.612	2.0984
9.25	85.5625	791.453	0.10811	3.0414	9.618	2.0992
9.26	85.7476	794.023	0.10799	3.0430	9.623	2.0999
9.27	85.9329	796.598	0.10787	3.0447	9.628	2.1007
9.28	86.1184	799.179	0.10776	3.0463	9.633	2.1014
9.29	86.3041	801.765	0.10764	3.0480	9.638	2.1022
9.30	86.4900	804.357	0.10753	3.0496	9.644	2.1029
9.31	86.6761	806.954	0.10741	3.0512	9.649	2.1037
9.32	86.8624	809.558	0.10730	3.0529	9.654	2.1045
9.33	87.0489	812.166	0.10718	3.0545	9.659	2.1052
9.34	87.2356	814.781	0.10707	3.0561	9.664	2.1060
9.35	87.4225	817.400	0.10695	3.0578	9.670	2.1067
9.36	87.6096	820.026	0.10684	3.0594	9.675	2.1075
9.37	87.7969	822.657	0.10672	3.0610	9.680	2.1082
9.38	87.9844	825.294	0.10661	3.0627	9.685	2.1090
9.39	88.1721	827.936	0.10650	3.0643	9.690	2.1097
9.40	88.3600	830.584	0.10638	3.0659	9.695	2.1105
9.41	88.5481	833.238	0.10627	3.0676	9.701	2.1112
9.42	88.7364	835.897	0.10616	3.0692	9.706	2.1120
9.43	88.9249	838.562	0.10604	3.0708	9.711	2.1127
9.44	89.1136	841.232	0.10593	3.0725	9.716	2.1134
9.45	89.3025	843.909	0.10582	3.0741	9.721	2.1142
9.46	89.4916	846.591	0.10571	3.0757	9.726	2.1149
9.47	89.6809	849.278	0.10560	3.0773	9.731	2.1157
9.48	89.8704	851.971	0.10549	3.0790	9.737	2.1164
9.49	90.0601	854.670	0.10537	3.0806	9.742	2.1172
9.50	90.2500	857.375	0.10526	3.0822	9.747	2.1179
x	x^2	x^3	$\frac{1}{x}$	$\sqrt{x}$	$\sqrt{10x}$	$\sqrt[3]{x}$

x	x^2	x^3	$\dfrac{1}{x}$	$\sqrt{x}$	$\sqrt{10x}$	$\sqrt[3]{x}$
9.50	90.2500	857.375	0.10526	3.0822	9.747	2.1179
9.51	90.4401	860.085	0.10515	3.0838	9.752	2.1187
9.52	90.6304	862.801	0.10504	3.0854	9.757	2.1194
9.53	90.8209	865.523	0.10493	3.0871	9.762	2.1201
9.54	91.0116	868.251	0.10482	3.0887	9.767	2.1209
9.55	91.2025	870.984	0.10471	3.0903	9.772	2.1216
9.56	91.3936	873.723	0.10460	3.0919	9.778	2.1224
9.57	91.5849	876.467	0.10449	3.0935	9.783	2.1231
9.58	91.7764	879.218	0.10438	3.0952	9.788	2.1238
9.59	91.9681	881.974	0.10428	3.0968	9.793	2.1246
9.60	92.1600	884.736	0.10417	3.0984	9.798	2.1253
9.61	92.3521	887.504	0.10406	3.1000	9.803	2.1261
9.62	92.5444	890.277	0.10395	3.1016	9.808	2.1268
9.63	92.7369	893.056	0.10384	3.1032	9.813	2.1275
9.64	92.9296	895.841	0.10373	3.1048	9.818	2.1283
9.65	93.1225	898.632	0.10363	3.1064	9.823	2.1290
9.66	93.3156	901.429	0.10352	3.1081	9.829	2.1297
9.67	93.5089	904.231	0.10341	3.1097	9.834	2.1305
9.68	93.7024	907.039	0.10331	3.1113	9.839	2.1312
9.69	93.8961	909.853	0.10320	3.1129	9.844	2.1319
9.70	94.0900	912.673	0.10309	3.1145	9.849	2.1327
9.71	94.2841	915.499	0.10299	3.1161	9.854	2.1334
9.72	94.4784	918.330	0.10288	3.1177	9.859	2.1341
9.73	94.6729	921.167	0.10277	3.1193	9.864	2.1349
9.74	94.8676	924.010	0.10267	3.1209	9.869	2.1356
9.75	95.0625	926.859	0.10256	3.1225	9.874	2.1363
9.76	95.2576	929.714	0.10246	3.1241	9.879	2.1371
9.77	95.4529	932.575	0.10235	3.1257	9.884	2.1378
9.78	95.6484	935.441	0.10225	3.1273	9.889	2.1385
9.79	95.8441	938.314	0.10215	3.1289	9.894	2.1392
9.80	96.0400	941.192	0.10204	3.1305	9.899	2.1400
9.81	96.2361	944.076	0.10194	3.1321	9.905	2.1407
9.82	96.4324	946.966	0.10183	3.1337	9.910	2.1414
9.83	96.6289	949.862	0.10173	3.1353	9.915	2.1422
9.84	96.8256	952.764	0.10163	3.1369	9.920	2.1429
9.85	97.0225	955.672	0.10152	3.1385	9.925	2.1436
9.86	97.2196	958.585	0.10142	3.1401	9.930	2.1443
9.87	97.4169	961.505	0.10132	3.1417	9.935	2.1451
9.88	97.6144	964.430	0.10121	3.1432	9.940	2.1458
9.89	97.8121	967.362	0.10111	3.1448	9.945	2.1465
9.90	98.0100	970.299	0.10101	3.1464	9.950	2.1472
9.91	98.2081	973.242	0.10091	3.1480	9.955	2.1480
9.92	98.4064	976.191	0.10081	3.1496	9.960	2.1487
9.93	98.6049	979.147	0.10070	3.1512	9.965	2.1494
9.94	98.8036	982.108	0.10060	3.1528	9.970	2.1501
9.95	99.0025	985.075	0.10050	3.1544	9.975	2.1508
9.96	99.2016	988.048	0.10040	3.1559	9.980	2.1516
9.97	99.4009	991.027	0.10030	3.1575	9.985	2.1523
9.98	99.6004	994.012	0.10020	3.1591	9.990	2.1530
9.99	99.8001	997.003	0.10010	3.1607	9.995	2.1537
10.00	100.0000	1000.000	0.10000	3.1623	10.000	2.1544
x	x^2	x^3	$\dfrac{1}{x}$	$\sqrt{x}$	$\sqrt{10x}$	$\sqrt[3]{x}$

TABLE 2

Five-figure tables of common logarithms from N = 100 to N = 1000

Graph for Table 2

log N

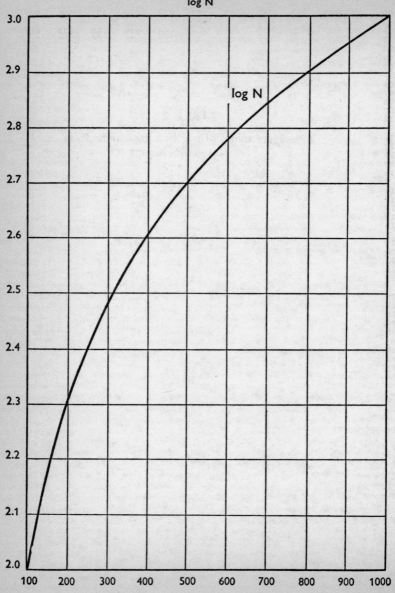

N	0	1	2	3	4	5	6	7	8	9
100	00 000	043	087	130	173	217	260	303	346	389
101	00 432	475	518	561	604	647	689	732	775	817
102	00 860	903	945	988	*030	*072	*115	*157	*199	*242
103	01 284	326	368	410	452	494	536	578	620	662
104	01 703	745	787	828	870	912	953	995	*036	*078
105	02 119	160	202	243	284	325	366	407	449	490
106	02 531	572	612	653	694	735	776	816	857	898
107	02 938	979	*019	*060	*100	*141	*181	*222	*262	*302
108	03 342	383	423	463	503	543	583	623	663	703
109	03 743	782	822	862	902	941	981	*021	*060	*100
110	04 139	179	218	258	297	336	376	415	454	493
111	04 532	571	610	650	689	727	766	805	844	883
112	04 922	961	999	*038	*077	*115	*154	*192	*231	*269
113	05 308	346	385	423	461	500	538	576	614	652
114	05 690	729	767	805	843	881	918	956	994	*032
115	06 070	108	145	183	221	258	296	333	371	408
116	06 446	483	521	558	595	633	670	707	744	781
117	06 819	856	893	930	967	*004	*041	*078	*115	*151
118	07 188	225	262	298	335	372	408	445	482	518
119	07 555	591	628	664	700	737	773	809	846	882
120	07 918	954	990	*027	*063	*099	*135	*171	*207	*243
121	08 279	314	350	386	422	458	493	529	565	600
122	08 636	672	707	743	778	814	849	884	920	955
123	08 991	*026	*061	*096	*132	*167	*202	*237	*272	*307
124	09 342	377	412	447	482	517	552	587	621	656
125	09 691	726	760	795	830	864	899	934	968	*003
126	10 037	072	106	140	175	209	243	278	312	346
127	10 380	415	449	483	517	551	585	619	653	687
128	10 721	755	789	823	857	890	924	958	992	*025
129	11 059	093	126	160	193	227	261	294	327	361
130	11 394	428	461	494	528	561	594	628	661	694
131	11 727	760	793	826	860	893	926	959	992	*024
132	12 057	090	123	156	189	222	254	287	320	352
133	12 385	418	450	483	516	548	581	613	646	678
134	12 710	743	775	808	840	872	905	937	969	*001
135	13 033	066	098	130	162	194	226	258	290	322
136	13 354	386	418	450	481	513	545	577	609	640
137	13 672	704	735	767	799	830	862	893	925	956
138	13 988	*019	*051	*082	*114	*145	*176	*208	*239	*270
139	14 301	333	364	395	426	457	489	520	551	582
140	14 613	644	675	706	737	768	799	829	860	891
141	14 922	953	983	*014	*045	*076	*106	*137	*168	*198
142	15 229	259	290	320	351	381	412	442	473	503
143	15 534	564	594	625	655	685	715	746	776	806
144	15 836	866	897	927	957	987	*017	*047	*077	*107
145	16 137	167	197	227	256	286	316	346	376	406
146	16 435	465	495	524	554	584	613	643	673	702
147	16 732	761	791	820	850	879	909	938	967	997
148	17 026	056	085	114	143	173	202	231	260	289
149	17 319	348	377	406	435	464	493	522	551	580
150	17 609	638	667	696	725	754	782	811	840	869

| N | 0 | 1 | 2 | 3 | 4 | 5 | 6 | 7 | 8 | 9 |

N	0	1	2	3	4	5	6	7	8	9
150	17 609	638	667	696	725	754	782	811	840	869
151	17 898	926	955	984	*013	*041	*070	*099	*127	*156
152	18 184	213	241	270	298	327	355	384	412	441
153	18 469	498	526	554	583	611	639	667	696	724
154	18 752	780	808	837	865	893	921	949	977	*005
155	19 033	061	089	117	145	173	201	229	257	285
156	19 312	340	368	396	424	451	479	507	535	562
157	19 590	618	645	673	700	728	756	783	811	838
158	19 866	893	921	948	976	*003	*030	*058	*085	*112
159	20 140	167	194	222	249	276	303	330	358	385
160	20 412	439	466	493	520	548	575	602	629	656
161	20 683	710	737	763	790	817	844	871	898	925
162	20 952	978	*005	*032	*059	*085	*112	*139	*165	*192
163	21 219	245	272	299	325	352	378	405	431	458
164	21 484	511	537	564	590	617	643	669	696	722
165	21 748	775	801	827	854	880	906	932	958	985
166	22 011	037	063	089	115	141	167	194	220	246
167	22 272	298	324	350	376	401	427	453	479	505
168	22 531	557	583	608	634	660	686	712	737	763
169	22 789	814	840	866	891	917	943	968	994	*019
170	23 045	070	096	121	147	172	198	223	249	274
171	23 300	325	350	376	401	426	452	477	502	528
172	23 553	578	603	629	654	679	704	729	754	779
173	23 805	830	855	880	905	930	955	980	*005	*030
174	24 055	080	105	130	155	180	204	229	254	279
175	24 304	329	353	378	403	428	452	477	502	527
176	24 551	576	601	625	650	674	699	724	748	773
177	24 797	822	846	871	895	920	944	969	993	*018
178	25 042	066	091	115	139	164	188	212	237	26?
179	25 285	310	334	358	382	406	431	455	479	50?
180	25 527	551	575	600	624	648	672	696	720	744
181	25 768	792	816	840	864	888	912	935	959	983
182	26 007	031	055	079	102	126	150	174	198	221
183	26 245	269	293	316	340	364	387	411	435	458
184	26 482	505	529	553	576	600	623	647	670	694
185	26 717	741	764	788	811	834	858	881	905	928
186	26 951	975	998	*021	*045	*068	*091	*114	*138	*161
187	27 184	207	231	254	277	300	323	346	370	393
188	27 416	439	462	485	508	531	554	577	600	623
189	27 646	669	692	715	738	761	784	807	830	852
190	27 875	898	921	944	967	989	*012	*035	*058	*081
191	28 103	126	149	171	194	217	240	262	285	307
192	28 330	353	375	398	421	443	466	488	511	533
193	28 556	578	601	623	646	668	691	713	735	758
194	28 780	803	825	847	870	892	914	937	959	981
195	29 003	026	048	070	092	115	137	159	181	203
196	29 226	248	270	292	314	336	358	380	403	425
197	29 447	469	491	513	535	557	579	601	623	645
198	29 667	688	710	732	754	776	798	820	842	863
199	29 885	907	929	951	973	994	*016	*038	*060	*081
200	30 103	125	146	168	190	211	233	255	276	298
N	0	1	2	3	4	5	6	7	8	9

N	0	1	2	3	4	5	6	7	8	9
200	30 103	125	146	168	190	211	233	255	276	298
201	30 320	341	363	384	406	428	449	471	492	514
202	30 535	557	578	600	621	643	664	685	707	728
203	30 750	771	792	814	835	856	878	899	920	942
204	30 963	984	*006	*027	*048	*069	*091	*112	*133	*154
205	31 175	197	218	239	260	281	302	323	345	366
206	31 387	408	429	450	471	492	513	534	555	576
207	31 597	618	639	660	681	702	723	744	765	785
208	31 806	827	848	869	890	911	931	952	973	994
209	32 015	035	056	077	098	118	139	160	181	201
210	32 222	243	263	284	305	325	346	366	387	408
211	32 428	449	469	490	510	531	552	572	593	613
212	32 634	654	675	695	715	736	756	777	797	818
213	32 838	858	879	899	919	940	960	980	*001	*021
214	33 041	062	082	102	122	143	163	183	203	224
215	33 244	264	284	304	325	345	365	385	405	425
216	33 445	465	486	506	526	546	566	586	606	626
217	33 646	666	686	706	726	746	766	786	806	826
218	33 846	866	885	905	925	945	965	985	*005	*025
219	34 044	064	084	104	124	143	163	183	203	223
220	34 242	262	282	301	321	341	361	380	400	420
221	34 439	459	479	498	518	537	557	577	596	616
222	34 635	655	674	694	713	733	753	772	792	811
223	34 830	850	869	889	908	928	947	967	986	*005
224	35 025	044	064	083	102	122	141	160	180	199
225	35 218	238	257	276	295	315	334	353	372	392
226	35 411	430	449	468	488	507	526	545	564	583
227	35 603	622	641	660	679	698	717	736	755	774
228	35 793	813	832	851	870	889	908	927	946	965
229	35 984	*003	*021	*040	*059	*078	*097	*116	*135	*154
230	36 173	192	211	229	248	267	286	305	324	342
231	36 361	380	399	418	436	455	474	493	511	530
232	36 549	568	586	605	624	642	661	680	698	717
233	36 736	754	773	791	810	829	847	866	884	903
234	36 922	940	959	977	996	*014	*033	*051	*070	*088
235	37 107	125	144	162	181	199	218	236	254	273
236	37 291	310	328	346	365	383	401	420	438	457
237	37 475	493	511	530	548	566	585	603	621	639
238	37 658	676	694	712	731	749	767	785	803	822
239	37 840	858	876	894	912	931	949	967	985	*003
240	38 021	039	057	075	093	112	130	148	166	184
241	38 202	220	238	256	274	292	310	328	346	364
242	38 382	399	417	435	453	471	489	507	525	543
243	38 561	578	596	614	632	650	668	686	703	721
244	38 739	757	775	792	810	828	846	863	881	899
245	38 917	934	952	970	987	*005	*023	*041	*058	*076
246	39 094	111	129	146	164	182	199	217	235	252
247	39 270	287	305	322	340	358	375	393	410	428
248	39 445	463	480	498	515	533	550	568	585	602
249	39 620	637	655	672	690	707	724	742	759	777
250	39 794	811	829	846	863	881	898	915	933	950
N	0	1	2	3	4	5	6	7	8	9

N	0	1	2	3	4	5	6	7	8	9
250	39 794	811	829	846	863	881	898	915	933	950
251	39 967	985	*002	*019	*037	*054	*071	*088	*106	*123
252	40 140	157	175	192	209	226	243	261	278	295
253	40 312	329	346	364	381	398	415	432	449	466
254	40 483	500	518	535	552	569	586	603	620	637
255	40 654	671	688	705	722	739	756	773	790	807
256	40 824	841	858	875	892	909	926	943	960	976
257	40 993	*010	*027	*044	*061	*078	*095	*111	*128	*145
258	41 162	179	196	212	229	246	263	280	296	313
259	41 330	347	363	380	397	414	430	447	464	481
260	41 497	514	531	547	564	581	597	614	631	647
261	41 664	681	697	714	731	747	764	780	797	814
262	41 830	847	863	880	896	913	929	946	963	979
263	41 996	*012	*029	*045	*062	*078	*095	*111	*127	*144
264	42 160	177	193	210	226	243	259	275	292	308
265	42 325	341	357	374	390	406	423	439	455	472
266	42 488	504	521	537	553	570	586	602	619	635
267	42 651	667	684	700	716	732	749	765	781	797
268	42 813	830	846	862	878	894	911	927	943	959
269	42 975	991	*008	*024	*040	*056	*072	*088	*104	*120
270	43 136	152	169	185	201	217	233	249	265	281
271	43 297	313	329	345	361	377	393	409	425	441
272	43 457	473	489	505	521	537	553	569	584	600
273	43 616	632	648	664	680	696	712	727	743	759
274	43 775	791	807	823	838	854	870	886	902	917
275	43 933	949	965	981	996	*012	*028	*044	*059	*075
276	44 091	107	122	138	154	170	185	201	217	232
277	44 248	264	279	295	311	326	342	358	373	389
278	44 404	420	436	451	467	483	498	514	529	545
279	44 560	576	592	607	623	638	654	669	685	700
280	44 716	731	747	762	778	793	809	824	840	855
281	44 871	886	902	917	932	948	963	979	994	*010
282	45 025	040	056	071	086	102	117	133	148	163
283	45 179	194	209	225	240	255	271	286	301	317
284	45 332	347	362	378	393	408	423	439	454	469
285	45 484	500	515	530	545	561	576	591	606	621
286	45 637	652	667	682	697	712	728	743	758	773
287	45 788	803	818	834	849	864	879	894	909	924
288	45 939	954	969	984	*000	*015	*030	*045	*060	*075
289	46 090	105	120	135	150	165	180	195	210	225
290	46 240	255	270	285	300	315	330	345	359	374
291	46 389	404	419	434	449	464	479	494	509	523
292	46 538	553	568	583	598	613	627	642	657	672
293	46 687	702	716	731	746	761	776	790	805	820
294	46 835	850	864	879	894	909	923	938	953	967
295	46 982	997	*012	*026	*041	*056	*070	*085	*100	*114
296	47 129	144	159	173	188	202	217	232	246	261
297	47 276	290	305	319	334	349	363	378	392	407
298	47 422	436	451	465	480	494	509	524	538	553
299	47 567	582	596	611	625	640	654	669	683	698
300	47 712	727	741	756	770	784	799	813	828	842
N	0	1	2	3	4	5	6	7	8	9

N	0	1	2	3	4	5	6	7	8	9
300	47 712	727	741	756	770	784	799	813	828	842
301	47 857	871	885	900	914	929	943	958	972	986
302	48 001	015	029	044	058	073	087	101	116	130
303	48 144	159	173	187	202	216	230	244	259	273
304	48 287	302	316	330	344	359	373	387	401	416
305	48 430	444	458	473	487	501	515	530	544	558
306	48 572	586	601	615	629	643	657	671	686	700
307	48 714	728	742	756	770	785	799	813	827	841
308	48 855	869	883	897	911	926	940	954	968	982
309	48 996	*010	*024	*038	*052	*066	*080	*094	*108	*122
310	49 136	150	164	178	192	206	220	234	248	262
311	49 276	290	304	318	332	346	360	374	388	402
312	49 415	429	443	457	471	485	499	513	527	541
313	49 554	568	582	596	610	624	638	651	665	679
314	49 693	707	721	734	748	762	776	790	803	817
315	49 831	845	859	872	886	900	914	927	941	955
316	49 969	982	996	*010	*024	*037	*051	*065	*079	*092
317	50 106	120	133	147	161	174	188	202	215	229
318	50 243	256	270	284	297	311	325	338	352	365
319	50 379	393	406	420	433	447	461	474	488	501
320	50 515	529	542	556	569	583	596	610	623	637
321	50 651	664	678	691	705	718	732	745	759	772
322	50 786	799	813	826	840	853	866	880	893	907
323	50 920	934	947	961	974	987	*001	*014	*028	*041
324	51 055	068	081	095	108	121	135	148	162	175
325	51 188	202	215	228	242	255	268	282	295	308
326	51 322	335	348	362	375	388	402	415	428	441
327	51 455	468	481	495	508	521	534	548	561	574
328	51 587	601	614	627	640	654	667	680	693	706
329	51 720	733	746	759	772	786	799	812	825	838
330	51 851	865	878	891	904	917	930	943	957	970
331	51 983	996	*009	*022	*035	*048	*061	*075	*088	*101
332	52 114	127	140	153	166	179	192	205	218	231
333	52 244	257	270	284	297	310	323	336	349	362
334	52 375	388	401	414	427	440	453	466	479	492
335	52 504	517	530	543	556	569	582	595	608	621
336	52 634	647	660	673	686	699	711	724	737	750
337	52 763	776	789	802	815	827	840	853	866	879
338	52 892	905	917	930	943	956	969	982	994	*007
339	53 020	033	046	058	071	084	097	110	122	135
340	53 148	161	173	186	199	212	224	237	250	263
341	53 275	288	301	314	326	339	352	364	377	390
342	53 403	415	428	441	453	466	479	491	504	517
343	53 529	542	555	567	580	593	605	618	631	643
344	53 656	668	681	694	706	719	732	744	757	769
345	53 782	794	807	820	832	845	857	870	882	895
346	53 908	920	933	945	958	970	983	995	*008	*020
347	54 033	045	058	070	083	095	108	120	133	145
348	54 158	170	183	195	208	220	233	245	258	270
349	54 283	295	307	320	332	345	357	370	382	394
350	54 407	419	432	444	456	469	481	494	506	518
N	0	1	2	3	4	5	6	7	8	9

N	0	1	2	3	4	5	6	7	8	9
350	54 407	419	432	444	456	469	481	494	506	518
351	54 531	543	555	568	580	593	605	617	630	642
352	54 654	667	679	691	704	716	728	741	753	765
353	54 777	790	802	814	827	839	851	864	876	888
354	54 900	913	925	937	949	962	974	986	998	*011
355	55 023	035	047	060	072	084	096	108	121	133
356	55 145	157	169	182	194	206	218	230	242	255
357	55 267	279	291	303	315	328	340	352	364	376
358	55 388	400	413	425	437	449	461	473	485	497
359	55 509	522	534	546	558	570	582	594	606	618
360	55 630	642	654	666	678	691	703	715	727	739
361	55 751	763	775	787	799	811	823	835	847	859
362	55 871	883	895	907	919	931	943	955	967	979
363	55 991	*003	*015	*027	*038	*050	*062	*074	*086	*098
364	56 110	122	134	146	158	170	182	194	205	217
365	56 229	241	253	265	277	289	301	312	324	336
366	56 348	360	372	384	396	407	419	431	443	455
367	56 467	478	490	502	514	526	538	549	561	573
368	56 585	597	608	620	632	644	656	667	679	691
369	56 703	714	726	738	750	761	773	785	797	808
370	56 820	832	844	855	867	879	891	902	914	926
371	56 937	949	961	972	984	996	*008	*019	*031	*043
372	57 054	066	078	089	101	113	124	136	148	159
373	57 171	183	194	206	217	229	241	252	264	276
374	57 287	299	310	322	334	345	357	368	380	392
375	57 403	415	426	438	449	461	473	484	496	507
376	57 519	530	542	553	565	576	588	600	611	623
377	57 634	646	657	669	680	692	703	715	726	738
378	57 749	761	772	784	795	807	818	830	841	852
379	57 864	875	887	898	910	921	933	944	955	967
380	57 978	990	*001	*013	*024	*035	*047	*058	*070	*081
381	58 092	104	115	127	138	149	161	172	184	195
382	58 206	218	229	240	252	263	274	286	297	309
383	58 320	331	343	354	365	377	388	399	410	422
384	58 433	444	456	467	478	490	501	512	524	535
385	58 546	557	569	580	591	602	614	625	636	647
386	58 659	670	681	692	704	715	726	737	749	760
387	58 771	782	794	805	816	827	838	850	861	872
388	58 883	894	906	917	928	939	950	961	973	984
389	58 995	*006	*017	*028	*040	*051	*062	*073	*084	*095
390	59 106	118	129	140	151	162	173	184	195	207
391	59 218	229	240	251	262	273	284	295	306	318
392	59 329	340	351	362	373	384	395	406	417	428
393	59 439	450	461	472	483	494	506	517	528	539
394	59 550	561	572	583	594	605	616	627	638	649
395	59 660	671	682	693	704	715	726	737	748	759
396	59 770	780	791	802	813	824	835	846	857	868
397	59 879	890	901	912	923	934	945	956	966	977
398	59 988	999	*010	*021	*032	*043	*054	*065	*076	*086
399	60 097	108	119	130	141	152	163	173	184	195
400	60 206	217	228	239	249	260	271	282	293	304
N	0	1	2	3	4	5	6	7	8	9

N	0	1	2	3	4	5	6	7	8	9
400	60 206	217	228	239	249	260	271	282	293	304
401	60 314	325	336	347	358	369	379	390	401	412
402	60 423	433	444	455	466	477	487	498	509	520
403	60 531	541	552	563	574	584	595	606	617	627
404	60 638	649	660	670	681	692	703	713	724	735
405	60 746	756	767	778	788	799	810	821	831	842
406	60 853	863	874	885	895	906	917	927	938	949
407	60 959	970	981	991	*002	*013	*023	*034	*045	*055
408	61 066	077	087	098	109	119	130	140	151	162
409	61 172	183	194	204	215	225	236	247	257	268
410	61 278	289	300	310	321	331	342	352	363	374
411	61 384	395	405	416	426	437	448	458	469	479
412	61 490	500	511	521	532	542	553	563	574	584
413	61 595	606	616	627	637	648	658	669	679	690
414	61 700	711	721	731	742	752	763	773	784	794
415	61 805	815	826	836	847	857	868	878	888	899
416	61 909	920	930	941	951	962	972	982	993	*003
417	62 014	024	034	045	055	066	076	086	097	107
418	62 118	128	138	149	159	170	180	190	201	211
419	62 221	232	242	252	263	273	284	294	304	315
420	62 325	335	346	356	366	377	387	397	408	418
421	62 428	439	449	459	469	480	490	500	511	521
422	62 531	542	552	562	572	583	593	603	613	624
423	62 634	644	655	665	675	685	696	706	716	726
424	62 737	747	757	767	778	788	798	808	818	829
425	62 839	849	859	870	880	890	900	910	921	931
426	62 941	951	961	972	982	992	*002	*012	*022	*033
427	63 043	053	063	073	083	094	104	114	124	134
428	63 144	155	165	175	185	195	205	215	225	236
429	63 246	256	266	276	286	296	306	317	327	337
430	63 347	357	367	377	387	397	407	417	428	438
431	63 448	458	468	478	488	498	508	518	528	538
432	63 548	558	568	579	589	599	609	619	629	639
433	63 649	659	669	679	689	699	709	719	729	739
434	63 749	759	769	779	789	799	809	819	829	839
435	63 849	859	869	879	889	899	909	919	929	939
436	63 949	959	969	979	988	998	*008	*018	*028	*038
437	64 048	058	068	078	088	098	108	118	128	137
438	64 147	157	167	177	187	197	207	217	227	237
439	64 246	256	266	276	286	296	306	316	326	335
440	64 345	355	365	375	385	395	404	414	424	434
441	64 444	454	464	473	483	493	503	513	523	532
442	64 542	552	562	572	582	591	601	611	621	631
443	64 640	650	660	670	680	689	699	709	719	729
444	64 738	748	758	768	777	787	797	807	816	826
445	64 836	846	856	865	875	885	895	904	914	924
446	64 933	943	953	963	972	982	992	*002	*011	*021
447	65 031	040	050	060	070	079	089	099	108	118
448	65 128	137	147	157	167	176	186	196	205	215
449	65 225	234	244	254	263	273	283	292	302	312
450	65 321	331	341	350	360	369	379	389	398	408

N	0	1	2	3	4	5	6	7	8	9
450	65 321	331	341	350	360	369	379	389	398	408
451	65 418	427	437	447	456	466	475	485	495	504
452	65 514	523	533	543	552	562	571	581	591	600
453	65 610	619	629	639	648	658	667	677	686	696
454	65 706	715	725	734	744	753	763	772	782	792
455	65 801	811	820	830	839	849	858	868	877	887
456	65 896	906	916	925	935	944	954	963	973	982
457	65 992	*001	*011	*020	*030	*039	*049	*058	*068	*077
458	66 087	096	106	115	124	134	143	153	162	172
459	66 181	191	200	210	219	229	238	247	257	266
460	66 276	285	295	304	314	323	332	342	351	361
461	66 370	380	389	398	408	417	427	436	445	455
462	66 464	474	483	492	502	511	521	530	539	549
463	66 558	567	577	586	596	605	614	624	633	642
464	66 652	661	671	680	689	699	708	717	727	736
465	66 745	755	764	773	783	792	801	811	820	829
466	66 839	848	857	867	876	885	894	904	913	922
467	66 932	941	950	960	969	978	987	997	*006	*015
468	67 025	034	043	052	062	071	080	089	099	108
469	67 117	127	136	145	154	164	173	182	191	201
470	67 210	219	228	237	247	256	265	274	284	293
471	67 302	311	321	330	339	348	357	367	376	385
472	67 394	403	413	422	431	440	449	459	468	477
473	67 486	495	504	514	523	532	541	550	560	569
474	67 578	587	596	605	614	624	633	642	651	660
475	67 669	679	688	697	706	715	724	733	742	752
476	67 761	770	779	788	797	806	815	825	834	843
477	67 852	861	870	879	888	897	906	916	925	934
478	67 943	952	961	970	979	988	997	*006	*015	*024
479	68 034	043	052	061	070	079	088	097	106	115
480	68 124	133	142	151	160	169	178	187	196	205
481	68 215	224	233	242	251	260	269	278	287	296
482	68 305	314	323	332	341	350	359	368	377	386
483	68 395	404	413	422	431	440	449	458	467	476
484	68 485	494	502	511	520	529	538	547	556	565
485	68 574	583	592	601	610	619	628	637	646	655
486	68 664	673	681	690	699	708	717	726	735	744
487	68 753	762	771	780	789	797	806	815	824	833
488	68 842	851	860	869	878	886	895	904	913	922
489	68 931	940	949	958	966	975	984	993	*002	*011
490	69 020	028	037	046	055	064	073	082	090	099
491	69 108	117	126	135	144	152	161	170	179	188
492	69 197	205	214	223	232	241	249	258	267	276
493	69 285	294	302	311	320	329	338	346	355	364
494	69 373	381	390	399	408	417	425	434	443	452
495	69 461	469	478	487	496	504	513	522	531	539
496	69 548	557	566	574	583	592	601	609	618	627
497	69 636	644	653	662	671	679	688	697	705	714
498	69 723	732	740	749	758	767	775	784	793	801
499	69 810	819	827	836	845	854	862	871	880	888
500	69 897	906	914	923	932	940	949	958	966	975
N	0	1	2	3	4	5	6	7	8	9

LG N

N	0	1	2	3	4	5	6	7	8	9
500	69 897	906	914	923	932	940	949	958	966	975
501	69 984	992	*001	*010	*018	*027	*036	*044	*053	*062
502	70 070	079	088	096	105	114	122	131	140	148
503	70 157	165	174	183	191	200	209	217	226	234
504	70 243	252	260	269	278	286	295	303	312	321
505	70 329	338	346	355	364	372	381	389	398	406
506	70 415	424	432	441	449	458	467	475	484	492
507	70 501	509	518	526	535	544	552	561	569	578
508	70 586	595	603	612	621	629	638	646	655	663
509	70 672	680	689	697	706	714	723	731	740	749
510	70 757	766	774	783	791	800	808	817	825	834
511	70 842	851	859	868	876	885	893	902	910	919
512	70 927	935	944	952	961	969	978	986	995	*003
513	71 012	020	029	037	046	054	063	071	079	088
514	71 096	105	113	122	130	139	147	155	164	172
515	71 181	189	198	206	214	223	231	240	248	257
516	71 265	273	282	290	299	307	315	324	332	341
517	71 349	357	366	374	383	391	399	408	416	425
518	71 433	441	450	458	466	475	483	492	500	508
519	71 517	525	533	542	550	559	567	575	584	592
520	71 600	609	617	625	634	642	650	659	667	675
521	71 684	692	700	709	717	725	734	742	750	759
522	71 767	775	784	792	800	809	817	825	834	842
523	71 850	858	867	875	883	892	900	908	917	925
524	71 933	941	950	958	966	975	983	991	999	*008
525	72 016	024	032	041	049	057	066	074	082	090
526	72 099	107	115	123	132	140	148	156	165	173
527	72 181	189	198	206	214	222	230	239	247	255
528	72 263	272	280	288	296	304	313	321	329	337
529	72 346	354	362	370	378	387	395	403	411	419
530	72 428	436	444	452	460	469	477	485	493	501
531	72 509	518	526	534	542	550	558	567	575	583
532	72 591	599	607	616	624	632	640	648	656	665
533	72 673	681	689	697	705	713	722	730	738	746
534	72 754	762	770	779	787	795	803	811	819	827
535	72 835	843	852	860	868	876	884	892	900	908
536	72 916	925	933	941	949	957	965	973	981	989
537	72 997	*006	*014	*022	*030	*038	*046	*054	*062	*070
538	73 078	086	094	102	111	119	127	135	143	151
539	73 159	167	175	183	191	199	207	215	223	231
540	73 239	247	255	263	272	280	288	296	304	312
541	73 320	328	336	344	352	360	368	376	384	392
542	73 400	408	416	424	432	440	448	456	464	472
543	73 480	488	496	504	512	520	528	536	544	552
544	73 560	568	576	584	592	600	608	616	624	632
545	73 640	648	656	664	672	679	687	695	703	711
546	73 719	727	735	743	751	759	767	775	783	791
547	73 799	807	815	823	830	838	846	854	862	870
548	73 878	886	894	902	910	918	926	933	941	949
549	73 957	965	973	981	989	997	*005	*013	*020	*028
550	74 036	044	052	060	068	076	084	092	099	107
N	0	1	2	3	4	5	6	7	8	9

N	0	1	2	3	4	5	6	7	8	9
550	74 036	044	052	060	068	076	084	092	099	107
551	74 115	123	131	139	147	155	162	170	178	186
552	74 194	202	210	218	225	233	241	249	257	265
553	74 273	280	288	296	304	312	320	327	335	343
554	74 351	359	367	374	382	390	398	406	414	421
555	74 429	437	445	453	461	468	476	484	492	500
556	74 507	515	523	531	539	547	554	562	570	578
557	74 586	593	601	609	617	624	632	640	648	656
558	74 663	671	679	687	695	702	710	718	726	733
559	74 741	749	757	764	772	780	788	796	803	811
560	74 819	827	834	842	850	858	865	873	881	889
561	74 896	904	912	920	927	935	943	950	958	966
562	74 974	981	989	997	*005	*012	*020	*028	*035	*043
563	75 051	059	066	074	082	089	097	105	113	120
564	75 128	136	143	151	159	166	174	182	189	197
565	75 205	213	220	228	236	243	251	259	266	274
566	75 282	289	297	305	312	320	328	335	343	351
567	75 358	366	374	381	389	397	404	412	420	427
568	75 435	442	450	458	465	473	481	488	496	504
569	75 511	519	526	534	542	549	557	565	572	580
570	75 587	595	603	610	618	626	633	641	648	656
571	75 664	671	679	686	694	702	709	717	724	732
572	75 740	747	755	762	770	778	785	793	800	808
573	75 815	823	831	838	846	853	861	868	876	884
574	75 891	899	906	914	921	929	937	944	952	959
575	75 967	974	982	989	997	*005	*012	*020	*027	*035
576	76 042	050	057	065	072	080	087	095	103	110
577	76 118	125	133	140	148	155	163	170	178	185
578	76 193	200	208	215	223	230	238	245	253	260
579	76 268	275	283	290	298	305	313	320	328	335
580	76 343	350	358	365	373	380	388	395	403	410
581	76 418	425	433	440	448	455	462	470	477	485
582	76 492	500	507	515	522	530	537	545	552	559
583	76 567	574	582	589	597	604	612	619	626	634
584	76 641	649	656	664	671	678	686	693	701	708
585	76 716	723	730	738	745	753	760	768	775	782
586	76 790	797	805	812	819	827	834	842	849	856
587	76 864	871	879	886	893	901	908	916	923	930
588	76 938	945	953	960	967	975	982	989	997	*004
589	77 012	019	026	034	041	048	056	063	070	078
590	77 085	093	100	107	115	122	129	137	144	151
591	77 159	166	173	181	188	195	203	210	217	225
592	77 232	240	247	254	262	269	276	283	291	298
593	77 305	313	320	327	335	342	349	357	364	371
594	77 379	386	393	401	408	415	422	430	437	444
595	77 452	459	466	474	481	488	495	503	510	517
596	77 525	532	539	546	554	561	568	576	583	590
597	77 597	605	612	619	627	634	641	648	656	663
598	77 670	677	685	692	699	706	714	721	728	735
599	77 743	750	757	764	772	779	786	793	801	808
600	77 815	822	830	837	844	851	859	866	873	880
N	0	1	2	3	4	5	6	7	8	9

N	0	1	2	3	4	5	6	7	8	9
600	77 815	822	830	837	844	851	859	866	873	880
601	77 887	895	902	909	916	924	931	938	945	952
602	77 960	967	974	981	988	996	*003	*010	*017	*025
603	78 032	039	046	053	061	068	075	082	089	097
604	78 104	111	118	125	132	140	147	154	161	168
605	78 176	183	190	197	204	211	219	226	233	240
606	78 247	254	262	269	276	283	290	297	305	312
607	78 319	326	333	340	347	355	362	369	376	383
608	78 390	398	405	412	419	426	433	440	447	455
609	78 462	469	476	483	490	497	504	512	519	526
610	78 533	540	547	554	561	569	576	583	590	597
611	78 604	611	618	625	633	640	647	654	661	668
612	78 675	682	689	696	704	711	718	725	732	739
613	78 746	753	760	767	774	781	789	796	803	810
614	78 817	824	831	838	845	852	859	866	873	880
615	78 888	895	902	909	916	923	930	937	944	951
616	78 958	965	972	979	986	993	*000	*007	*014	*021
617	79 029	036	043	050	057	064	071	078	085	092
618	79 099	106	113	120	127	134	141	148	155	162
619	79 169	176	183	190	197	204	211	218	225	232
620	79 239	246	253	260	267	274	281	288	295	302
621	79 309	316	323	330	337	344	351	358	365	372
622	79 379	386	393	400	407	414	421	428	435	442
623	79 449	456	463	470	477	484	491	498	505	511
624	79 518	525	532	539	546	553	560	567	574	581
625	79 588	595	602	609	616	623	630	637	644	650
626	79 657	664	671	678	685	692	699	706	713	720
627	79 727	734	741	748	754	761	768	775	782	789
628	79 796	803	810	817	824	831	837	844	851	858
629	79 865	872	879	886	893	900	906	913	920	927
630	79 934	941	948	955	962	969	975	982	989	996
631	80 003	010	017	024	030	037	044	051	058	065
632	80 072	079	085	092	099	106	113	120	127	134
633	80 140	147	154	161	168	175	182	188	195	202
634	80 209	216	223	229	236	243	250	257	264	271
635	80 277	284	291	298	305	312	318	325	332	339
636	80 346	353	359	366	373	380	387	393	400	407
637	80 414	421	428	434	441	448	455	462	468	475
638	80 482	489	496	502	509	516	523	530	536	543
639	80 550	557	564	570	577	584	591	598	604	611
640	80 618	625	632	638	645	652	659	665	672	679
641	80 686	693	699	706	713	720	726	733	740	747
642	80 754	760	767	774	781	787	794	801	808	814
643	80 821	828	835	841	848	855	862	868	875	882
644	80 889	895	902	909	916	922	929	936	943	949
645	80 956	963	969	976	983	990	996	*003	*010	*017
646	81 023	030	037	043	050	057	064	070	077	084
647	81 090	097	104	111	117	124	131	137	144	151
648	81 158	164	171	178	184	191	198	204	211	218
649	81 224	231	238	245	251	258	265	271	278	285
650	81 291	298	305	311	318	325	331	338	345	351
N	0	1	2	3	4	5	6	7	8	9

N	0	1	2	3	4	5	6	7	8	9
650	81 291	298	305	311	318	325	331	338	345	351
651	81 358	365	371	378	385	391	398	405	411	418
652	81 425	431	438	445	451	458	465	471	478	485
653	81 491	498	505	511	518	525	531	538	544	551
654	81 558	564	571	578	584	591	598	604	611	617
655	81 624	631	637	644	651	657	664	671	677	684
656	81 690	697	704	710	717	723	730	737	743	750
657	81 757	763	770	776	783	790	796	803	809	816
658	81 823	829	836	842	849	856	862	869	875	882
659	81 889	895	902	908	915	921	928	935	941	948
660	81 954	961	968	974	981	987	994	*000	*007	*014
661	82 020	027	033	040	046	053	060	066	073	079
662	82 086	092	099	105	112	119	125	132	138	145
663	82 151	158	164	171	178	184	191	197	204	210
664	82 217	223	230	236	243	249	256	263	269	276
665	82 282	289	295	302	308	315	321	328	334	341
666	82 347	354	360	367	373	380	387	393	400	406
667	82 413	419	426	432	439	445	452	458	465	471
668	82 478	484	491	497	504	510	517	523	530	536
669	82 543	549	556	562	569	575	582	588	595	601
670	82 607	614	620	627	633	640	646	653	659	666
671	82 672	679	685	692	698	705	711	718	724	730
672	82 737	743	750	756	763	769	776	782	789	795
673	82 802	808	814	821	827	834	840	847	853	860
674	82 866	872	879	885	892	898	905	911	918	924
675	82 930	937	943	950	956	963	969	975	982	988
676	82 995	*001	*008	*014	*020	*027	*033	*040	*046	*052
677	83 059	065	072	078	085	091	097	104	110	117
678	83 123	129	136	142	149	155	161	168	174	181
679	83 187	193	200	206	213	219	225	232	238	245
680	83 251	257	264	270	276	283	289	296	302	308
681	83 315	321	327	334	340	347	353	359	366	372
682	83 378	385	391	398	404	410	417	423	429	436
683	83 442	448	455	461	467	474	480	487	493	499
684	83 506	512	518	525	531	537	544	550	556	563
685	83 569	575	582	588	594	601	607	613	620	626
686	83 632	639	645	651	658	664	670	677	683	689
687	83 696	702	708	715	721	727	734	740	746	753
688	83 759	765	771	778	784	790	797	803	809	816
689	83 822	828	835	841	847	853	860	866	872	879
690	83 885	891	897	904	910	916	923	929	935	942
691	83 948	954	960	967	973	979	985	992	998	*004
692	84 011	017	023	029	036	042	048	055	061	067
693	84 073	080	086	092	098	105	111	117	123	130
694	84 136	142	148	155	161	167	173	180	186	192
695	84 198	205	211	217	223	230	236	242	248	255
696	84 261	267	273	280	286	292	298	305	311	317
697	84 323	330	336	342	348	354	361	367	373	379
698	84 386	392	398	404	410	417	423	429	435	442
699	84 448	454	460	466	473	479	485	491	497	504
700	84 510	516	522	528	535	541	547	553	559	566

N	0	1	2	3	4	5	6	7	8	9

N	0	1	2	3	4	5	6	7	8	9
700	84 510	516	522	528	535	541	547	553	559	566
701	84 572	578	584	590	597	603	609	615	621	628
702	84 634	640	646	652	658	665	671	677	683	689
703	84 696	702	708	714	720	726	733	739	745	751
704	84 757	763	770	776	782	788	794	800	807	813
705	84 819	825	831	837	844	850	856	862	868	874
706	84 880	887	893	899	905	911	917	924	930	936
707	84 942	948	954	960	967	973	979	985	991	997
708	85 003	009	016	022	028	034	040	046	052	058
709	85 065	071	077	083	089	095	101	107	114	120
710	85 126	132	138	144	150	156	163	169	175	181
711	85 187	193	199	205	211	217	224	230	236	242
712	85 248	254	260	266	272	278	285	291	297	303
713	85 309	315	321	327	333	339	345	352	358	364
714	85 370	376	382	388	394	400	406	412	418	425
715	85 431	437	443	449	455	461	467	473	479	485
716	85 491	497	503	509	516	522	528	534	540	546
717	85 552	558	564	570	576	582	588	594	600	606
718	85 612	618	625	631	637	643	649	655	661	667
719	85 673	679	685	691	697	703	709	715	721	727
720	85 733	739	745	751	757	763	769	775	781	788
721	85 794	800	806	812	818	824	830	836	842	848
722	85 854	860	866	872	878	884	890	896	902	908
723	85 914	920	926	932	938	944	950	956	962	968
724	85 974	980	986	992	998	*004	*010	*016	*022	*028
725	86 034	040	046	052	058	064	070	076	082	088
726	86 094	100	106	112	118	124	130	136	141	147
727	86 153	159	165	171	177	183	189	195	201	207
728	86 213	219	225	231	237	243	249	255	261	267
729	86 273	279	285	291	297	303	308	314	320	326
730	86 332	338	344	350	356	362	368	374	380	386
731	86 392	398	404	410	415	421	427	433	439	445
732	86 451	457	463	469	475	481	487	493	499	504
733	86 510	516	522	528	534	540	546	552	558	564
734	86 570	576	581	587	593	599	605	611	617	623
735	86 629	635	641	646	652	658	664	670	676	682
736	86 688	694	700	705	711	717	723	729	735	741
737	86 747	753	759	764	770	776	782	788	794	800
738	86 806	812	817	823	829	835	841	847	853	859
739	86 864	870	876	882	888	894	900	906	911	917
740	86 923	929	935	941	947	953	958	964	970	976
741	86 982	988	994	999	*005	*011	*017	*023	*029	*035
742	87 040	046	052	058	064	070	075	081	087	093
743	87 099	105	111	116	122	128	134	140	146	151
744	87 157	163	169	175	181	186	192	198	204	210
745	87 216	221	227	233	239	245	251	256	262	268
746	87 274	280	286	291	297	303	309	315	320	326
747	87 332	338	344	349	355	361	367	373	379	384
748	87 390	396	402	408	413	419	425	431	437	442
749	87 448	454	460	466	471	477	483	489	495	500
750	87 506	512	518	523	529	535	541	547	552	558

N	0	1	2	3	4	5	6	7	8	9

N	0	1	2	3	4	5	6	7	8	9
750	87 506	512	518	523	529	535	541	547	552	558
751	87 564	570	576	581	587	593	599	604	610	616
752	87 622	628	633	639	645	651	656	662	668	674
753	87 679	685	691	697	703	708	714	720	726	731
754	87 737	743	749	754	760	766	772	777	783	789
755	87 795	800	806	812	818	823	829	835	841	846
756	87 852	858	864	869	875	881	887	892	898	904
757	87 910	915	921	927	933	938	944	950	955	961
758	87 967	973	978	984	990	996	*001	*007	*013	*018
759	88 024	030	036	041	047	053	058	064	070	076
760	88 081	087	093	098	104	110	116	121	127	133
761	88 138	144	150	156	161	167	173	178	184	190
762	88 195	201	207	213	218	224	230	235	241	247
763	88 252	258	264	270	275	281	287	292	298	304
764	88 309	315	321	326	332	338	343	349	355	360
765	88 366	372	377	383	389	395	400	406	412	417
766	88 423	429	434	440	446	451	457	463	468	474
767	88 480	485	491	497	502	508	513	519	525	530
768	88 536	542	547	553	559	564	570	576	581	587
769	88 593	598	604	610	615	621	627	632	638	643
770	88 649	655	660	666	672	677	683	689	694	700
771	88 705	711	717	722	728	734	739	745	750	756
772	88 762	767	773	779	784	790	795	801	807	812
773	88 818	824	829	835	840	846	852	857	863	868
774	88 874	880	885	891	897	902	908	913	919	925
775	88 930	936	941	947	953	958	964	969	975	981
776	88 986	992	997	*003	*009	*014	*020	*025	*031	*037
777	89 042	048	053	059	064	070	076	081	087	092
778	89 098	104	109	115	120	126	131	137	143	148
779	89 154	159	165	170	176	182	187	193	198	204
780	89 209	215	221	226	232	237	243	248	254	260
781	89 265	271	276	282	287	293	298	304	310	315
782	89 321	326	332	337	343	348	354	360	365	371
783	89 376	382	387	393	398	404	409	415	421	426
784	89 432	437	443	448	454	459	465	470	476	481
785	89 487	492	498	504	509	515	520	526	531	537
786	89 542	548	553	559	564	570	575	581	586	592
787	89 597	603	609	614	620	625	631	636	642	647
788	89 653	658	664	669	675	680	686	691	697	702
789	89 708	713	719	724	730	735	741	746	752	757
790	89 763	768	774	779	785	790	796	801	807	812
791	89 818	823	829	834	840	845	851	856	862	867
792	89 873	878	883	889	894	900	905	911	916	922
793	89 927	933	938	944	949	955	960	966	971	977
794	89 982	988	993	998	*004	*009	*015	*020	*026	*031
795	90 037	042	048	053	059	064	069	075	080	086
796	90 091	097	102	108	113	119	124	129	135	140
797	90 146	151	157	162	168	173	179	184	189	195
798	90 200	206	211	217	222	227	233	238	244	249
799	90 255	260	266	271	276	282	287	293	298	304
800	90 309	314	320	325	331	336	342	347	352	358
N	0	1	2	3	4	5	6	7	8	9

N	0	1	2	3	4	5	6	7	8	9
800	90 309	314	320	325	331	336	342	347	352	358
801	90 363	369	374	380	385	390	396	401	407	412
802	90 417	423	428	434	439	445	450	455	461	466
803	90 472	477	482	488	493	499	504	509	515	520
804	90 526	531	536	542	547	553	558	563	569	574
805	90 580	585	590	596	601	607	612	617	623	628
806	90 634	639	644	650	655	660	666	671	677	682
807	90 687	693	698	703	709	714	720	725	730	736
808	90 741	747	752	757	763	768	773	779	784	789
809	90 795	800	806	811	816	822	827	832	838	843
810	90 849	854	859	865	870	875	881	886	891	897
811	90 902	907	913	918	924	929	934	940	945	950
812	90 956	961	966	972	977	982	988	993	998	*004
813	91 009	014	020	025	030	036	041	046	052	057
814	91 062	068	073	078	084	089	094	100	105	110
815	91 116	121	126	132	137	142	148	153	158	164
816	91 169	174	180	185	190	196	201	206	212	217
817	91 222	228	233	238	243	249	254	259	265	270
818	91 275	281	286	291	297	302	307	312	318	323
819	91 328	334	339	344	350	355	360	365	371	376
820	91 381	387	392	397	403	408	413	418	424	429
821	91 434	440	445	450	455	461	466	471	477	482
822	91 487	492	498	503	508	514	519	524	529	535
823	91 540	545	551	556	561	566	572	577	582	587
824	91 593	598	603	609	614	619	624	630	635	640
825	91 645	651	656	661	666	672	677	682	687	693
826	91 698	703	709	714	719	724	730	735	740	745
827	91 751	756	761	766	772	777	782	787	793	798
828	91 803	808	814	819	824	829	834	840	845	850
829	91 855	861	866	871	876	882	887	892	897	903
830	91 908	913	918	924	929	934	939	944	950	955
831	91 960	965	971	976	981	986	991	997	*002	*007
832	92 012	018	023	028	033	038	044	049	054	059
833	92 065	070	075	080	085	091	096	101	106	111
834	92 117	122	127	132	137	143	148	153	158	163
835	92 169	174	179	184	189	195	200	205	210	215
836	92 221	226	231	236	241	247	252	257	262	267
837	92 273	278	283	288	293	298	304	309	314	319
838	92 324	330	335	340	345	350	355	361	366	371
839	92 376	381	387	392	397	402	407	412	418	423
840	92 428	433	438	443	449	454	459	464	469	474
841	92 480	485	490	495	500	505	511	516	521	526
842	92 531	536	542	547	552	557	562	567	572	578
843	92 583	588	593	598	603	609	614	619	624	629
844	92 634	639	645	650	655	660	665	670	675	681
845	92 686	691	696	701	706	711	716	722	727	732
846	92 737	742	747	752	758	763	768	773	778	783
847	92 788	793	799	804	809	814	819	824	829	834
848	92 840	845	850	855	860	865	870	875	881	886
849	92 891	896	901	906	911	916	921	927	932	937
850	92 942	947	952	957	962	967	973	978	983	988
N	0	1	2	3	4	5	6	7	8	9

N	0	1	2	3	4	5	6	7	8	9
850	92 942	947	952	957	962	967	973	978	983	988
851	92 993	998	*003	*008	*013	*018	*024	*029	*034	*039
852	93 044	049	054	059	064	069	075	080	085	090
853	93 095	100	105	110	115	120	125	131	136	141
854	93 146	151	156	161	166	171	176	181	186	192
855	93 197	202	207	212	217	222	227	232	237	242
856	93 247	252	258	263	268	273	278	283	288	293
857	93 298	303	308	313	318	323	328	334	339	344
858	93 349	354	359	364	369	374	379	384	389	394
859	93 399	404	409	414	420	425	430	435	440	445
860	93 450	455	460	465	470	475	480	485	490	495
861	93 500	505	510	515	520	526	531	536	541	546
862	93 551	556	561	566	571	576	581	586	591	596
863	93 601	606	611	616	621	626	631	636	641	646
864	93 651	656	661	666	671	676	682	687	692	697
865	93 702	707	712	717	722	727	732	737	742	747
866	93 752	757	762	767	772	777	782	787	792	797
867	93 802	807	812	817	822	827	832	837	842	847
868	93 852	857	862	867	872	877	882	887	892	897
869	93 902	907	912	917	922	927	932	937	942	947
870	93 952	957	962	967	972	977	982	987	992	997
871	94 002	007	012	017	022	027	032	037	042	047
872	94 052	057	062	067	072	077	082	086	091	096
873	94 101	106	111	116	121	126	131	136	141	146
874	94 151	156	161	166	171	176	181	186	191	196
875	94 201	206	211	216	221	226	231	236	240	245
876	94 250	255	260	265	270	275	280	285	290	295
877	94 300	305	310	315	320	325	330	335	340	345
878	94 349	354	359	364	369	374	379	384	389	394
879	94 399	404	409	414	419	424	429	433	438	443
880	94 448	453	458	463	468	473	478	483	488	493
881	94 498	503	507	512	517	522	527	532	537	542
882	94 547	552	557	562	567	571	576	581	586	591
883	94 596	601	606	611	616	621	626	630	635	640
884	94 645	650	655	660	665	670	675	680	685	689
885	94 694	699	704	709	714	719	724	729	734	738
886	94 743	748	753	758	763	768	773	778	783	787
887	94 792	797	802	807	812	817	822	827	832	836
888	94 841	846	851	856	861	866	871	876	880	885
889	94 890	895	900	905	910	915	919	924	929	934
890	94 939	944	949	954	959	963	968	973	978	983
891	94 988	993	998	*002	*007	*012	*017	*022	*027	*032
892	95 036	041	046	051	056	061	066	071	075	080
893	95 085	090	095	100	105	109	114	119	124	129
894	95 134	139	143	148	153	158	163	168	173	177
895	95 182	187	192	197	202	207	211	216	221	226
896	95 231	236	240	245	250	255	260	265	270	274
897	95 279	284	289	294	299	303	308	313	318	323
898	95 328	332	337	342	347	352	357	361	366	371
899	95 376	381	386	390	395	400	405	410	415	419
900	95 424	429	434	439	444	448	453	458	463	468
N	0	1	2	3	4	5	6	7	8	9

N	0	1	2	3	4	5	6	7	8	9
900	95 424	429	434	439	444	448	453	458	463	468
901	95 472	477	482	487	492	497	501	506	511	516
902	95 521	525	530	535	540	545	550	554	559	564
903	95 569	574	578	583	588	593	598	602	607	612
904	95 617	622	626	631	636	641	646	650	655	660
905	95 665	670	674	679	684	689	694	698	703	708
906	95 713	718	722	727	732	737	742	746	751	756
907	95 761	766	770	775	780	785	789	794	799	804
908	95 809	813	818	823	828	832	837	842	847	852
909	95 856	861	866	871	875	880	885	890	895	899
910	95 904	909	914	918	923	928	933	938	942	947
911	95 952	957	961	966	971	976	980	985	990	995
912	95 999	*004	*009	*014	*019	*023	*028	*033	*038	*042
913	96 047	052	057	061	066	071	076	080	085	090
914	96 095	099	104	109	114	118	123	128	133	137
915	96 142	147	152	156	161	166	171	175	180	185
916	96 190	194	199	204	209	213	218	223	227	232
917	96 237	242	246	251	256	261	265	270	275	280
918	96 284	289	294	298	303	308	313	317	322	327
919	96 332	336	341	346	350	355	360	365	369	374
920	96 379	384	388	393	398	402	407	412	417	421
921	96 426	431	435	440	445	450	454	459	464	468
922	96 473	478	483	487	492	497	501	506	511	515
923	96 520	525	530	534	539	544	548	553	558	562
924	96 567	572	577	581	586	591	595	600	605	609
925	96 614	619	624	628	633	638	642	647	652	656
926	96 661	666	670	675	680	685	689	694	699	703
927	96 708	713	717	722	727	731	736	741	745	750
928	96 755	759	764	769	774	778	783	788	792	797
929	96 802	806	811	816	820	825	830	834	839	844
930	96 848	853	858	862	867	872	876	881	886	890
931	96 895	900	904	909	914	918	923	928	932	937
932	96 942	946	951	956	960	965	970	974	979	984
933	96 988	993	997	*002	*007	*011	*016	*021	*025	*030
934	97 035	039	044	049	053	058	063	067	072	077
935	97 081	086	090	095	100	104	109	114	118	123
936	97 128	132	137	142	146	151	155	160	165	169
937	97 174	179	183	188	192	197	202	206	211	216
938	97 220	225	230	234	239	243	248	253	257	262
939	97 267	271	276	280	285	290	294	299	304	308
940	97 313	317	322	327	331	336	340	345	350	354
941	97 359	364	368	373	377	382	387	391	396	400
942	97 405	410	414	419	424	428	433	437	442	447
943	97 451	456	460	465	470	474	479	483	488	493
944	97 497	502	506	511	516	520	525	529	534	539
945	97 543	548	552	557	562	566	571	575	580	585
946	97 589	594	598	603	607	612	617	621	626	630
947	97 635	640	644	649	653	658	663	667	672	676
948	97 681	685	690	695	699	704	708	713	717	722
949	97 727	731	736	740	745	749	754	759	763	768
950	97 772	777	782	786	791	795	800	804	809	813
N	0	1	2	3	4	5	6	7	8	9

N	0	1	2	3	4	5	6	7	8	9
950	97 772	777	782	786	791	795	800	804	809	813
951	97 818	823	827	832	836	841	845	850	855	859
952	97 864	868	873	877	882	886	891	896	900	905
953	97 909	914	918	923	928	932	937	941	946	950
954	97 955	959	964	968	973	978	982	987	991	996
955	98 000	005	009	014	019	023	028	032	037	041
956	98 046	050	055	059	064	068	073	078	082	087
957	98 091	096	100	105	109	114	118	123	127	132
958	98 137	141	146	150	155	159	164	168	173	177
959	98 182	186	191	195	200	204	209	214	218	223
960	98 227	232	236	241	245	250	254	259	263	268
961	98 272	277	281	286	290	295	299	304	308	313
962	98 318	322	327	331	336	340	345	349	354	358
963	98 363	367	372	376	381	385	390	394	399	403
964	98 408	412	417	421	426	430	435	439	444	448
965	98 453	457	462	466	471	475	480	484	489	493
966	98 498	502	507	511	516	520	525	529	534	538
967	98 543	547	552	556	561	565	570	574	579	583
968	98 588	592	597	601	605	610	614	619	623	628
969	98 632	637	641	646	650	655	659	664	668	673
970	98 677	682	686	691	695	700	704	709	713	717
971	98 722	726	731	735	740	744	749	753	758	762
972	98 767	771	776	780	784	789	793	798	802	807
973	98 811	816	820	825	829	834	838	843	847	851
974	98 856	860	865	869	874	878	883	887	892	896
975	98 900	905	909	914	918	923	927	932	936	941
976	98 945	949	954	958	963	967	972	976	981	985
977	98 989	994	998	*003	*007	*012	*016	*021	*025	*029
978	99 034	038	043	047	052	056	061	065	069	074
979	99 078	083	087	092	096	100	105	109	114	118
980	99 123	127	131	136	140	145	149	154	158	162
981	99 167	171	176	180	185	189	193	198	202	207
982	99 211	216	220	224	229	233	238	242	247	251
983	99 255	260	264	269	273	277	282	286	291	295
984	99 300	304	308	313	317	322	326	330	335	339
985	99 344	348	352	357	361	366	370	374	379	383
986	99 388	392	396	401	405	410	414	419	423	427
987	99 432	436	441	445	449	454	458	463	467	471
988	99 476	480	484	489	493	498	502	506	511	515
989	99 520	524	528	533	537	542	546	550	555	559
990	99 564	568	572	577	581	585	590	594	599	603
991	99 607	612	616	621	625	629	634	638	642	647
992	99 651	656	660	664	669	673	677	682	686	691
993	99 695	699	704	708	712	717	721	726	730	734
994	99 739	743	747	752	756	760	765	769	774	778
995	99 782	787	791	795	800	804	808	813	817	822
996	99 826	830	835	839	843	848	852	856	861	865
997	99 870	874	878	883	887	891	896	900	904	909
998	99 913	917	922	926	930	935	939	944	948	952
999	99 957	961	965	970	974	978	983	987	991	996
1000	00 000	004	009	013	017	022	026	030	035	039

N	0	1	2	3	4	5	6	7	8	9

TABLE 3

Trigonometrical functions
ϕ **the central angle of the unit circle.**
x = 0·000 to x = 0·800

Graph for Table 3
Trigonometrical functions

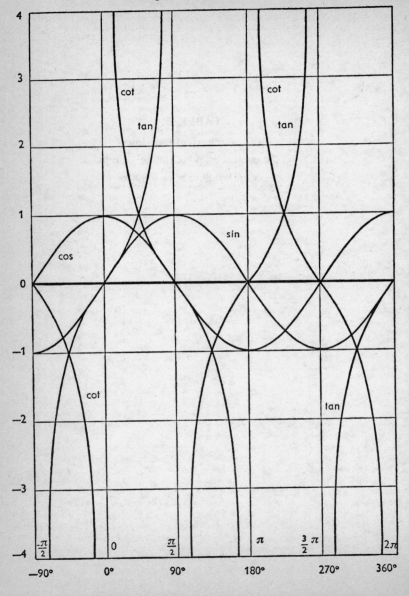

x	φ	sin x	cos x	tan x	cot x
0.000	0° 00′ 00.00″	0.00000	1.00000	0.00000	∞
0.001	0 03 26.26	0.00100	1.00000	0.00100	1000.00
0.002	0 06 52.53	0.00200	1.00000	0.00200	499.999
0.003	0 10 18.79	0.00300	1.00000	0.00300	333.332
0.004	0 13 45.06	0.00400	0.99999	0.00400	249.999
0.005	0 17 11.32	0.00500	0.99999	0.00500	199.998
0.006	0 20 37.59	0.00600	0.99998	0.00600	166.665
0.007	0 24 03.85	0.00700	0.99998	0.00700	142.855
0.008	0 27 30.12	0.00800	0.99997	0.00800	124.997
0.009	0 30 56.38	0.00900	0.99996	0.00900	111.108
0.010	0 34 22.65	0.01000	0.99995	0.01000	99.9967
0.011	0 37 48.91	0.01100	0.99994	0.01100	90.9054
0.012	0 41 15.18	0.01200	0.99993	0.01200	83.3293
0.013	0 44 41.44	0.01300	0.99992	0.01300	76.9187
0.014	0 48 07.71	0.01400	0.99990	0.01400	71.4239
0.015	0 51 33.97	0.01500	0.99989	0.01500	66.6617
0.016	0 55 00.24	0.01600	0.99987	0.01600	62.4947
0.017	0 58 26.50	0.01700	0.99986	0.01700	58.8179
0.018	1 01 52.77	0.01800	0.99984	0.01800	55.5496
0.019	1 05 19.03	0.01900	0.99982	0.01900	52.6252
0.020	1 08 45.30	0.02000	0.99980	0.02000	49.9933
0.021	1 12 11.56	0.02100	0.99978	0.02100	47.6120
0.022	1 15 37.83	0.02200	0.99976	0.02200	45.4472
0.023	1 19 04.09	0.02300	0.99974	0.02300	43.4706
0.024	1 22 30.36	0.02400	0.99971	0.02400	41.6587
0.025	1 25 56.62	0.02500	0.99969	0.02501	39.9917
0.026	1 29 22.88	0.02600	0.99966	0.02601	38.4529
0.027	1 32 49.15	0.02700	0.99964	0.02701	37.0280
0.028	1 36 15.41	0.02800	0.99961	0.02801	35.7050
0.029	1 39 41.68	0.02900	0.99958	0.02901	34.4731
0.030	1 43 07.94	0.03000	0.99955	0.03001	33.3233
0.031	1 46 34.21	0.03100	0.99952	0.03101	32.2477
0.032	1 50 00.47	0.03199	0.99949	0.03201	31.2393
0.033	1 53 26.74	0.03299	0.99946	0.03301	30.2920
0.034	1 56 53.00	0.03399	0.99942	0.03401	29.4004
0.035	2 00 19.27	0.03499	0.99939	0.03501	28.5598
0.036	2 03 45.53	0.03599	0.99935	0.03602	27.7658
0.037	2 07 11.80	0.03699	0.99932	0.03702	27.0147
0.038	2 10 38.06	0.03799	0.99928	0.03802	26.3031
0.039	2 14 04.33	0.03899	0.99924	0.03902	25.6280
0.040	2 17 30.59	0.03999	0.99920	0.04002	24.9867
0.041	2 20 56.86	0.04099	0.99916	0.04102	24.3766
0.042	2 24 23.12	0.04199	0.99912	0.04202	23.7955
0.043	2 27 49.39	0.04299	0.99908	0.04303	23.2415
0.044	2 31 15.65	0.04399	0.99903	0.04403	22.7126
0.045	2 34 41.92	0.04498	0.99899	0.04503	22.2072
0.046	2 38 08.18	0.04598	0.99894	0.04603	21.7238
0.047	2 41 34.45	0.04698	0.99890	0.04703	21.2609
0.048	2 45 00.71	0.04798	0.99885	0.04804	20.8173
0.049	2 48 26.98	0.04898	0.99880	0.04904	20.3918
0.050	2 51 53.24	0.04998	0.99875	0.05004	19.9833

x	φ	sin x	cos x	tan x	cot x

x	φ	sin x	cos x	tan x	cot x
0.050	2° 51′ 53.24″	0.04998	0.99875	0.05004	19.9833
0.051	2 55 19.51	0.05098	0.99870	0.05104	19.5908
0.052	2 58 45.77	0.05198	0.99865	0.05205	19.2134
0.053	3 02 12.03	0.05298	0.99860	0.05305	18.8503
0.054	3 05 38.30	0.05397	0.99854	0.05405	18.5005
0.055	3 09 04.56	0.05497	0.99849	0.05506	18.1635
0.056	3 12 30.83	0.05597	0.99843	0.05606	17.8385
0.057	3 15 57.09	0.05697	0.99838	0.05706	17.5249
0.058	3 19 23.36	0.05797	0.99832	0.05807	17.2220
0.059	3 22 49.62	0.05897	0.99826	0.05907	16.9295
0.060	3 26 15.89	0.05996	0.99820	0.06007	16.6467
0.061	3 29 42.15	0.06096	0.99814	0.06108	16.3731
0.062	3 33 08.42	0.06196	0.99808	0.06208	16.1084
0.063	3 36 34.68	0.06296	0.99802	0.06308	15.8520
0.064	3 40 00.95	0.06396	0.99795	0.06409	15.6037
0.065	3 43 27.21	0.06495	0.99789	0.06509	15.3629
0.066	3 46 53.48	0.06595	0.99782	0.06610	15.1295
0.067	3 50 19.74	0.06695	0.99776	0.06710	14.9030
0.068	3 53 46.01	0.06795	0.99769	0.06811	14.6832
0.069	3 57 12.27	0.06895	0.99762	0.06911	14.4697
0.070	4 00 38.54	0.06994	0.99755	0.07011	14.2624
0.071	4 04 04.80	0.07094	0.99748	0.07112	14.0608
0.072	4 07 31.07	0.07194	0.99741	0.07212	13.8649
0.073	4 10 57.33	0.07294	0.99734	0.07313	13.6742
0.074	4 14 23.60	0.07393	0.99726	0.07414	13.4888
0.075	4 17 49.86	0.07493	0.99719	0.07514	13.3083
0.076	4 21 16.13	0.07593	0.99711	0.07615	13.1326
0.077	4 24 42.39	0.07692	0.99704	0.07715	12.9613
0.078	4 28 08.65	0.07792	0.99696	0.07816	12.7945
0.079	4 31 34.92	0.07892	0.99688	0.07916	12.6319
0.080	4 35 01.18	0.07991	0.99680	0.08017	12.4733
0.081	4 38 27.45	0.08091	0.99672	0.08118	12.3187
0.082	4 41 53.71	0.08191	0.99664	0.08218	12.1678
0.083	4 45 19.98	0.08290	0.99656	0.08319	12.0205
0.084	4 48 46.24	0.08390	0.99647	0.08420	11.8767
0.085	4 52 12.51	0.08490	0.99639	0.08521	11.7364
0.086	4 55 38.77	0.08589	0.99630	0.08621	11.5992
0.087	4 59 05.04	0.08689	0.99622	0.08722	11.4652
0.088	5 02 31.30	0.08789	0.99613	0.08823	11.3343
0.089	5 05 57.57	0.08888	0.99604	0.08924	11.2063
0.090	5 09 23.83	0.08988	0.99595	0.09024	11.0811
0.091	5 12 50.10	0.09087	0.99586	0.09125	10.9587
0.092	5 16 16.36	0.09187	0.99577	0.09226	10.8389
0.093	5 19 42.63	0.09287	0.99568	0.09327	10.7217
0.094	5 23 08.89	0.09386	0.99559	0.09428	10.6069
0.095	5 26 35.16	0.09486	0.99549	0.09529	10.4946
0.096	5 30 01.42	0.09585	0.99540	0.09630	10.3846
0.097	5 33 27.69	0.09685	0.99530	0.09731	10.2769
0.098	5 36 53.95	0.09784	0.99520	0.09831	10.1714
0.099	5 40 20.22	0.09884	0.99510	0.09932	10.0680
0.100	5 43 46.48	0.09983	0.99500	0.10033	9.96664
x	φ	sin x	cos x	tan x	cot x

x	φ	sin x	cos x	tan x	cot x
0.100	5° 43' 46.48"	0.09983	0.99500	0.10033	9.96664
0.101	5 47 12.75	0.10083	0.99490	0.10134	9.86730
0.102	5 50 39.01	0.10182	0.99480	0.10236	9.76990
0.103	5 54 05.28	0.10282	0.99470	0.10337	9.67438
0.104	5 57 31.54	0.10381	0.99460	0.10438	9.58069
0.105	6 00 57.80	0.10481	0.99449	0.10539	9.48878
0.106	6 04 24.07	0.10580	0.99439	0.10640	9.39860
0.107	6 07 50.33	0.10680	0.99428	0.10741	9.31010
0.108	6 11 16.60	0.10779	0.99417	0.10842	9.22323
0.109	6 14 42.86	0.10878	0.99407	0.10943	9.13795
0.110	6 18 09.13	0.10978	0.99396	0.11045	9.05421
0.111	6 21 35.39	0.11077	0.99385	0.11146	8.97198
0.112	6 25 01.66	0.11177	0.99373	0.11247	8.89121
0.113	6 28 27.92	0.11276	0.99362	0.11348	8.81186
0.114	6 31 54.19	0.11375	0.99351	0.11450	8.73390
0.115	6 35 20.45	0.11475	0.99339	0.11551	8.65729
0.116	6 38 46.72	0.11574	0.99328	0.11652	8.58199
0.117	6 42 12.98	0.11673	0.99316	0.11754	8.50797
0.118	6 45 39.25	0.11773	0.99305	0.11855	8.43521
0.119	6 49 05.51	0.11872	0.99293	0.11956	8.36366
0.120	6 52 31.78	0.11971	0.99281	0.12058	8.29329
0.121	6 55 58.04	0.12070	0.99269	0.12159	8.22409
0.122	6 59 24.31	0.12170	0.99257	0.12261	8.15601
0.123	7 02 50.57	0.12269	0.99245	0.12362	8.08904
0.124	7 06 16.84	0.12368	0.99232	0.12464	8.02314
0.125	7 09 43.10	0.12467	0.99220	0.12566	7.95829
0.126	7 13 09.37	0.12567	0.99207	0.12667	7.89446
0.127	7 16 35.63	0.12666	0.99195	0.12769	7.83164
0.128	7 20 01.90	0.12765	0.99182	0.12870	7.76979
0.129	7 23 28.16	0.12864	0.99169	0.12972	7.70889
0.130	7 26 54.42	0.12963	0.99156	0.13074	7.64893
0.131	7 30 20.69	0.13063	0.99143	0.13175	7.58987
0.132	7 33 46.95	0.13162	0.99130	0.13277	7.53171
0.133	7 37 13.22	0.13261	0.99117	0.13379	7.47441
0.134	7 40 39.48	0.13360	0.99104	0.13481	7.41797
0.135	7 44 05.75	0.13459	0.99090	0.13583	7.36235
0.136	7 47 32.01	0.13558	0.99077	0.13684	7.30755
0.137	7 50 58.28	0.13657	0.99063	0.13786	7.25355
0.138	7 54 24.54	0.13756	0.99049	0.13888	7.20032
0.139	7 57 50.81	0.13855	0.99036	0.13990	7.14785
0.140	8 01 17.07	0.13954	0.99022	0.14092	7.09613
0.141	8 04 43.34	0.14053	0.99008	0.14194	7.04514
0.142	8 08 09.60	0.14152	0.98993	0.14296	6.99486
0.143	8 11 35.87	0.14251	0.98979	0.14398	6.94528
0.144	8 15 02.13	0.14350	0.98965	0.14500	6.89638
0.145	8 18 28.40	0.14449	0.98951	0.14602	6.84815
0.146	8 21 54.66	0.14548	0.98936	0.14705	6.80058
0.147	8 25 20.93	0.14647	0.98921	0.14807	6.75365
0.148	8 28 47.19	0.14746	0.98907	0.14909	6.70735
0.149	8 32 13.46	0.14845	0.98892	0.15011	6.66167
0.150	8 35 39.72	0.14944	0.98877	0.15114	6.61659
x	φ	sin x	cos x	tan x	cot x

x	φ	sin x	cos x	tan x	cot x
0.150	8° 35' 39.72"	0.14944	0.98877	0.15114	6.61659
0.151	8 39 05.99	0.15043	0.98862	0.15216	6.57211
0.152	8 42 32.25	0.15142	0.98847	0.15318	6.52820
0.153	8 45 58.52	0.15240	0.98832	0.15421	6.48487
0.154	8 49 24.78	0.15339	0.98817	0.15523	6.44209
0.155	8 52 51.04	0.15438	0.98801	0.15625	6.39986
0.156	8 56 17.31	0.15537	0.98786	0.15728	6.35817
0.157	8 59 43.57	0.15636	0.98770	0.15830	6.31701
0.158	9 03 09.84	0.15734	0.98754	0.15933	6.27636
0.159	9 06 36.10	0.15833	0.98739	0.16035	6.23622
0.160	9 10 02.37	0.15932	0.98723	0.16138	6.19658
0.161	9 13 28.63	0.16031	0.98707	0.16241	6.15742
0.162	9 16 54.90	0.16129	0.98691	0.16343	6.11874
0.163	9 20 21.16	0.16228	0.98674	0.16446	6.08054
0.164	9 23 47.43	0.16327	0.98658	0.16549	6.04280
0.165	9 27 13.69	0.16425	0.98642	0.16651	6.00551
0.166	9 30 39.96	0.16524	0.98625	0.16754	5.96866
0.167	9 34 06.22	0.16622	0.98609	0.16857	5.93225
0.168	9 37 32.49	0.16721	0.98592	0.16960	5.89628
0.169	9 40 58.75	0.16820	0.98575	0.17063	5.86072
0.170	9 44 25.02	0.16918	0.98558	0.17166	5.82558
0.171	9 47 51.28	0.17017	0.98542	0.17269	5.79084
0.172	9 51 17.55	0.17115	0.98524	0.17372	5.75651
0.173	9 54 43.81	0.17214	0.98507	0.17475	5.72256
0.174	9 58 10.08	0.17312	0.98490	0.17578	5.68901
0.175	10 01 36.34	0.17411	0.98473	0.17681	5.65583
0.176	10 05 02.61	0.17509	0.98455	0.17784	5.62303
0.177	10 08 28.87	0.17608	0.98438	0.17887	5.59059
0.178	10 11 55.14	0.17706	0.98420	0.17990	5.55852
0.179	10 15 21.40	0.17805	0.98402	0.18094	5.52680
0.180	10 18 47.67	0.17903	0.98384	0.18197	5.49543
0.181	10 22 13.93	0.18001	0.98366	0.18300	5.46440
0.182	10 25 40.19	0.18100	0.98348	0.18404	5.43370
0.183	10 29 06.46	0.18198	0.98330	0.18507	5.40334
0.184	10 32 32.72	0.18296	0.98312	0.18611	5.37331
0.185	10 35 58.99	0.18395	0.98294	0.18714	5.34360
0.186	10 39 25.25	0.18493	0.98275	0.18818	5.31420
0.187	10 42 51.52	0.18591	0.98257	0.18921	5.28511
0.188	10 46 17.78	0.18689	0.98238	0.19025	5.25633
0.189	10 49 44.05	0.18788	0.98219	0.19128	5.22785
0.190	10 53 10.31	0.18886	0.98200	0.19232	5.19967
0.191	10 56 36.58	0.18984	0.98181	0.19336	5.17178
0.192	11 00 02.84	0.19082	0.98162	0.19439	5.14418
0.193	11 03 29.11	0.19180	0.98143	0.19543	5.11685
0.194	11 06 55.37	0.19279	0.98124	0.19647	5.08981
0.195	11 10 21.64	0.19377	0.98105	0.19751	5.06304
0.196	11 13 47.90	0.19475	0.98085	0.19855	5.03654
0.197	11 17 14.17	0.19573	0.98066	0.19959	5.01030
0.198	11 20 40.43	0.19671	0.98046	0.20063	4.98433
0.199	11 24 06.70	0.19769	0.98026	0.20167	4.95862
0.200	11 27 32.96	0.19867	0.98007	0.20271	4.93315
x	φ	sin x	cos x	tan x	cot x

x	φ	sin x	cos x	tan x	cot x
0.200	11°27′32.96″	0.19867	0.98007	0.20271	4.93315
0.201	11 30 59.23	0.19965	0.97987	0.20375	4.90794
0.202	11 34 25.49	0.20063	0.97967	0.20479	4.88298
0.203	11 37 51.76	0.20161	0.97947	0.20584	4.85826
0.204	11 41 18.02	0.20259	0.97926	0.20688	4.83377
0.205	11 44 44.29	0.20357	0.97906	0.20792	4.80952
0.206	11 48 10.55	0.20455	0.97886	0.20896	4.78551
0.207	11 51 36.81	0.20552	0.97865	0.21001	4.76172
0.208	11 55 03.08	0.20650	0.97845	0.21105	4.73816
0.209	11 58 29.34	0.20748	0.97824	0.21210	4.71482
0.210	12 01 55.61	0.20846	0.97803	0.21314	4.69170
0.211	12 05 21.87	0.20944	0.97782	0.21419	4.66879
0.212	12 08 48.14	0.21042	0.97761	0.21523	4.64610
0.213	12 12 14.40	0.21139	0.97740	0.21628	4.62362
0.214	12 15 40.67	0.21237	0.97719	0.21733	4.60135
0.215	12 19 06.93	0.21335	0.97698	0.21838	4.57927
0.216	12 22 33.20	0.21432	0.97676	0.21942	4.55740
0.217	12 25 59.46	0.21530	0.97655	0.22047	4.53573
0.218	12 29 25.73	0.21628	0.97633	0.22152	4.51426
0.219	12 32 51.99	0.21725	0.97612	0.22257	4.49298
0.220	12 36 18.26	0.21823	0.97590	0.22362	4.47188
0.221	12 39 44.52	0.21921	0.97568	0.22467	4.45098
0.222	12 43 10.79	0.22018	0.97546	0.22572	4.43026
0.223	12 46 37.05	0.22116	0.97524	0.22677	4.40972
0.224	12 50 03.32	0.22213	0.97502	0.22782	4.38937
0.225	12 53 29.58	0.22311	0.97479	0.22888	4.36919
0.226	12 56 55.85	0.22408	0.97457	0.22993	4.34919
0.227	13 00 22.11	0.22506	0.97435	0.23098	4.32936
0.228	13 03 48.38	0.22603	0.97412	0.23203	4.30970
0.229	13 07 14.64	0.22700	0.97389	0.23309	4.29021
0.230	13 10 40.91	0.22798	0.97367	0.23414	4.27089
0.231	13 14 07.17	0.22895	0.97344	0.23520	4.25173
0.232	13 17 33.44	0.22992	0.97321	0.23625	4.23273
0.233	13 20 59.70	0.23090	0.97298	0.23731	4.21390
0.234	13 24 25.96	0.23187	0.97275	0.23837	4.19522
0.235	13 27 52.23	0.23284	0.97251	0.23942	4.17670
0.236	13 31 18.49	0.23382	0.97228	0.24048	4.15833
0.237	13 34 44.76	0.23479	0.97205	0.24154	4.14011
0.238	13 38 11.02	0.23576	0.97181	0.24260	4.12205
0.239	13 41 37.29	0.23673	0.97158	0.24366	4.10413
0.240	13 45 03.55	0.23770	0.97134	0.24472	4.08636
0.241	13 48 29.82	0.23867	0.97110	0.24578	4.06873
0.242	13 51 56.08	0.23964	0.97086	0.24684	4.05125
0.243	13 55 22.35	0.24062	0.97062	0.24790	4.03391
0.244	13 58 48.61	0.24159	0.97038	0.24896	4.01670
0.245	14 02 14.88	0.24256	0.97014	0.25002	3.99964
0.246	14 05 41.14	0.24353	0.96989	0.25109	3.98271
0.247	14 09 07.41	0.24450	0.96965	0.25215	3.96591
0.248	14 12 33.67	0.24547	0.96941	0.25321	3.94925
0.249	14 15 59.94	0.24643	0.96916	0.25428	3.93272
0.250	14 19 26.20	0.24740	0.96891	0.25534	3.91632
x	φ	sin x	cos x	tan x	cot x

x	φ	sin x	cos x	tan x	cot x
0.250	14° 19′ 26.20″	0.24740	0.96891	0.25534	3.91632
0.251	14 22 52.47	0.24837	0.96866	0.25641	3.90004
0.252	14 26 18.73	0.24934	0.96842	0.25747	3.88390
0.253	14 29 45.00	0.25031	0.96817	0.25854	3.86787
0.254	14 33 11.26	0.25128	0.96792	0.25961	3.85197
0.255	14 36 37.53	0.25225	0.96766	0.26067	3.83620
0.256	14 40 03.79	0.25321	0.96741	0.26174	3.82054
0.257	14 43 30.06	0.25418	0.96716	0.26281	3.80500
0.258	14 46 56.32	0.25515	0.96690	0.26388	3.78958
0.259	14 50 22.58	0.25611	0.96665	0.26495	3.77428
0.260	14 53 48.85	0.25708	0.96639	0.26602	3.75909
0.261	14 57 15.11	0.25805	0.96613	0.26709	3.74402
0.262	15 00 41.38	0.25901	0.96587	0.26816	3.72906
0.263	15 04 07.64	0.25998	0.96561	0.26924	3.71421
0.264	15 07 33.91	0.26094	0.96535	0.27031	3.69947
0.265	15 11 00.17	0.26191	0.96509	0.27138	3.68484
0.266	15 14 26.44	0.26287	0.96483	0.27246	3.67031
0.267	15 17 52.70	0.26384	0.96457	0.27353	3.65589
0.268	15 21 18.97	0.26480	0.96430	0.27461	3.64158
0.269	15 24 45.23	0.26577	0.96404	0.27568	3.62737
0.270	15 28 11.50	0.26673	0.96377	0.27676	3.61326
0.271	15 31 37.76	0.26770	0.96350	0.27784	3.59926
0.272	15 35 04.03	0.26866	0.96324	0.27891	3.58535
0.273	15 38 30.29	0.26962	0.96297	0.27999	3.57155
0.274	15 41 56.56	0.27058	0.96270	0.28107	3.55784
0.275	15 45 22.82	0.27155	0.96243	0.28215	3.54423
0.276	15 48 49.09	0.27251	0.96215	0.28323	3.53072
0.277	15 52 15.35	0.27347	0.96188	0.28431	3.51730
0.278	15 55 41.62	0.27443	0.96161	0.28539	3.50397
0.279	15 59 07.88	0.27539	0.96133	0.28647	3.49074
0.280	16 02 34.15	0.27636	0.96106	0.28755	3.47760
0.281	16 06 00.41	0.27732	0.96078	0.28864	3.46456
0.282	16 09 26.68	0.27828	0.96050	0.28972	3.45160
0.283	16 12 52.94	0.27924	0.96022	0.29081	3.43873
0.284	16 16 19.20	0.28020	0.95994	0.29189	3.42595
0.285	16 19 45.47	0.28116	0.95966	0.29298	3.41325
0.286	16 23 11.73	0.28212	0.95938	0.29406	3.40065
0.287	16 26 38.00	0.28308	0.95910	0.29515	3.38812
0.288	16 30 04.26	0.28404	0.95881	0.29624	3.37569
0.289	16 33 30.53	0.28499	0.95853	0.29732	3.36333
0.290	16 36 56.79	0.28595	0.95824	0.29841	3.35106
0.291	16 40 23.06	0.28691	0.95796	0.29950	3.33887
0.292	16 43 49.32	0.28787	0.95767	0.30059	3.32677
0.293	16 47 15.59	0.28883	0.95738	0.30168	3.31474
0.294	16 50 41.85	0.28978	0.95709	0.30277	3.30279
0.295	16 54 08.12	0.29074	0.95680	0.30387	3.29092
0.296	16 57 34.38	0.29170	0.95651	0.30496	3.27913
0.297	17 01 00.65	0.29265	0.95622	0.30605	3.26742
0.298	17 04 26.91	0.29361	0.95593	0.30715	3.25578
0.299	17 07 53.18	0.29456	0.95563	0.30824	3.24422
0.300	17 11 19.44	0.29552	0.95534	0.30934	3.23273
x	φ	sin x	cos x	tan x	cot x

x	φ	sin x	cos x	tan x	cot x
0.300	17° 11 19.44″	0.29552	0.95534	0.30934	3.23273
0.301	17 14 45.71	0.29648	0.95504	0.31043	3.22131
0.302	17 18 11.97	0.29743	0.95474	0.31153	3.20997
0.303	17 21 38.24	0.29838	0.95445	0.31263	3.19871
0.304	17 25 04.50	0.29934	0.95415	0.31372	3.18751
0.305	17 28 30.77	0.30029	0.95385	0.31482	3.17639
0.306	17 31 57.03	0.30125	0.95355	0.31592	3.16533
0.307	17 35 23.30	0.30220	0.95324	0.31702	3.15435
0.308	17 38 49.56	0.30315	0.95294	0.31812	3.14343
0.309	17 42 15.83	0.30411	0.95264	0.31923	3.13258
0.310	17 45 42.09	0.30506	0.95233	0.32033	3.12180
0.311	17 49 08.35	0.30601	0.95203	0.32143	3.11109
0.312	17 52 34.62	0.30696	0.95172	0.32253	3.10045
0.313	17 56 00.88	0.30791	0.95141	0.32364	3.08987
0.314	17 59 27.15	0.30887	0.95111	0.32474	3.07935
0.315	18 02 53.41	0.30982	0.95080	0.32585	3.06890
0.316	18 06 19.68	0.31077	0.95049	0.32696	3.05852
0.317	18 09 45.94	0.31172	0.95017	0.32806	3.04819
0.318	18 13 12.21	0.31267	0.94986	0.32917	3.03793
0.319	18 16 38.47	0.31362	0.94955	0.33028	3.02773
0.320	18 20 04.74	0.31457	0.94924	0.33139	3.01760
0.321	18 23 31.00	0.31552	0.94892	0.33250	3.00752
0.322	18 26 57.27	0.31646	0.94860	0.33361	2.99751
0.323	18 30 23.53	0.31741	0.94829	0.33472	2.98755
0.324	18 33 49.80	0.31836	0.94797	0.33583	2.97766
0.325	18 37 16.06	0.31931	0.94765	0.33695	2.96782
0.326	18 40 42.33	0.32026	0.94733	0.33806	2.95804
0.327	18 44 08.59	0.32120	0.94701	0.33918	2.94832
0.328	18 47 34.86	0.32215	0.94669	0.34029	2.93865
0.329	18 51 01.12	0.32310	0.94637	0.34141	2.92905
0.330	18 54 27.39	0.32404	0.94604	0.34252	2.91950
0.331	18 57 53.65	0.32499	0.94572	0.34364	2.91000
0.332	19 01 19.92	0.32593	0.94539	0.34476	2.90056
0.333	19 04 46.18	0.32688	0.94507	0.34588	2.89117
0.334	19 08 12.45	0.32782	0.94474	0.34700	2.88184
0.335	19 11 38.71	0.32877	0.94441	0.34812	2.87256
0.336	19 15 04.97	0.32971	0.94408	0.34924	2.86334
0.337	19 18 31.24	0.33066	0.94375	0.35037	2.85417
0.338	19 21 57.50	0.33160	0.94342	0.35149	2.84505
0.339	19 25 23.77	0.33254	0.94309	0.35261	2.83598
0.340	19 28 50.03	0.33349	0.94275	0.35374	2.82696
0.341	19 32 16.30	0.33443	0.94242	0.35486	2.81799
0.342	19 35 42.56	0.33537	0.94209	0.35599	2.80908
0.343	19 39 08.83	0.33631	0.94175	0.35712	2.80021
0.344	19 42 35.09	0.33726	0.94141	0.35824	2.79140
0.345	19 46 01.36	0.33820	0.94108	0.35937	2.78263
0.346	19 49 27.62	0.33914	0.94074	0.36050	2.77391
0.347	19 52 53.89	0.34008	0.94040	0.36163	2.76524
0.348	19 56 20.15	0.34102	0.94006	0.36276	2.75662
0.349	19 59 46.42	0.34196	0.93972	0.36390	2.74804
0.350	20 03 12.68	0.34290	0.93937	0.36503	2.73951
x	φ	sin x	cos x	tan x	cot x

x	φ	sin x	cos x	tan x	cot x
0.350	20° 03' 12.68"	0.34290	0.93937	0.36503	2.73951
0.351	20 06 38.95	0.34384	0.93903	0.36616	2.73103
0.352	20 10 05.21	0.34478	0.93869	0.36730	2.72259
0.353	20 13 31.48	0.34571	0.93834	0.36843	2.71421
0.354	20 16 57.74	0.34665	0.93799	0.36957	2.70586
0.355	20 20 24.01	0.34759	0.93765	0.37071	2.69756
0.356	20 23 50.27	0.34853	0.93730	0.37184	2.68931
0.357	20 27 16.54	0.34946	0.93695	0.37298	2.68110
0.358	20 30 42.80	0.35040	0.93660	0.37412	2.67293
0.359	20 34 09.07	0.35134	0.93625	0.37526	2.66481
0.360	20 37 35.33	0.35227	0.93590	0.37640	2.65673
0.361	20 41 01.60	0.35321	0.93554	0.37754	2.64869
0.362	20 44 27.86	0.35415	0.93519	0.37869	2.64070
0.363	20 47 54.12	0.35508	0.93484	0.37983	2.63274
0.364	20 51 20.39	0.35601	0.93448	0.38098	2.62483
0.365	20 54 46.65	0.35695	0.93412	0.38212	2.61696
0.366	20 58 12.92	0.35788	0.93377	0.38327	2.60914
0.367	21 01 39.18	0.35882	0.93341	0.38442	2.60135
0.368	21 05 05.45	0.35975	0.93305	0.38556	2.59360
0.369	21 08 31.71	0.36068	0.93269	0.38671	2.58590
0.370	21 11 57.98	0.36162	0.93233	0.38786	2.57823
0.371	21 15 24.24	0.36255	0.93197	0.38901	2.57060
0.372	21 18 50.51	0.36348	0.93160	0.39017	2.56301
0.373	21 22 16.77	0.36441	0.93124	0.39132	2.55546
0.374	21 25 43.04	0.36534	0.93087	0.39247	2.54795
0.375	21 29 09.30	0.36627	0.93051	0.39363	2.54048
0.376	21 32 35.57	0.36720	0.93014	0.39478	2.53304
0.377	21 36 01.83	0.36813	0.92977	0.39594	2.52565
0.378	21 39 28.10	0.36906	0.92940	0.39710	2.51829
0.379	21 42 54.36	0.36999	0.92904	0.39825	2.51096
0.380	21 46 20.63	0.37092	0.92866	0.39941	2.50368
0.381	21 49 46.89	0.37185	0.92829	0.40057	2.49643
0.382	21 53 13.16	0.37278	0.92792	0.40173	2.48921
0.383	21 56 39.42	0.37370	0.92755	0.40290	2.48203
0.384	22 00 05.69	0.37463	0.92717	0.40406	2.47489
0.385	22 03 31.95	0.37556	0.92680	0.40522	2.46778
0.386	22 06 58.22	0.37649	0.92642	0.40639	2.46071
0.387	22 10 24.48	0.37741	0.92605	0.40755	2.45367
0.388	22 13 50.74	0.37834	0.92567	0.40872	2.44667
0.389	22 17 17.01	0.37926	0.92529	0.40989	2.43970
0.390	22 20 43.27	0.38019	0.92491	0.41105	2.43276
0.391	22 24 09.54	0.38111	0.92453	0.41222	2.42586
0.392	22 27 35.80	0.38204	0.92415	0.41339	2.41900
0.393	22 31 02.07	0.38296	0.92376	0.41457	2.41216
0.394	22 34 28.33	0.38388	0.92338	0.41574	2.40536
0.395	22 37 54.60	0.38481	0.92300	0.41691	2.39859
0.396	22 41 20.86	0.38573	0.92261	0.41809	2.39185
0.397	22 44 47.13	0.38665	0.92223	0.41926	2.38515
0.398	22 48 13.39	0.38758	0.92184	0.42044	2.37847
0.399	22 51 39.66	0.38850	0.92145	0.42161	2.37183
0.400	22 55 05.92	0.38942	0.92106	0.42279	2.36522
x	φ	sin x	cos x	tan x	cot x

x	φ	sin x	cos x	tan x	cot x
0.400	22° 55' 05.92"	0.38942	0.92106	0.42279	2.36522
0.401	22 58 32.19	0.39034	0.92067	0.42397	2.35864
0.402	23 01 58.45	0.39126	0.92028	0.42515	2.35210
0.403	23 05 24.72	0.39218	0.91989	0.42633	2.34558
0.404	23 08 50.98	0.39310	0.91950	0.42752	2.33909
0.405	23 12 17.25	0.39402	0.91910	0.42870	2.33264
0.406	23 15 43.51	0.39494	0.91871	0.42988	2.32621
0.407	23 19 09.78	0.39586	0.91831	0.43107	2.31981
0.408	23 22 36.04	0.39677	0.91792	0.43226	2.31345
0.409	23 26 02.31	0.39769	0.91752	0.43344	2.30711
0.410	23 29 28.57	0.39861	0.91712	0.43463	2.30080
0.411	23 32 54.84	0.39953	0.91672	0.43582	2.29452
0.412	23 36 21.10	0.40044	0.91632	0.43701	2.28827
0.413	23 39 47.36	0.40136	0.91592	0.43820	2.28205
0.414	23 43 13.63	0.40227	0.91552	0.43940	2.27586
0.415	23 46 39.89	0.40319	0.91512	0.44059	2.26969
0.416	23 50 06.16	0.40410	0.91471	0.44178	2.26355
0.417	23 53 32.42	0.40502	0.91431	0.44298	2.25744
0.418	23 56 58.69	0.40593	0.91390	0.44418	2.25136
0.419	24 00 24.95	0.40685	0.91350	0.44537	2.24531
0.420	24 03 51.22	0.40776	0.91309	0.44657	2.23928
0.421	24 07 17.48	0.40867	0.91268	0.44777	2.23328
0.422	24 10 43.75	0.40959	0.91227	0.44897	2.22730
0.423	24 14 10.01	0.41050	0.91186	0.45018	2.22136
0.424	24 17 36.28	0.41141	0.91145	0.45138	2.21543
0.425	24 21 02.54	0.41232	0.91104	0.45258	2.20954
0.426	24 24 28.81	0.41323	0.91063	0.45379	2.20367
0.427	24 27 55.07	0.41414	0.91021	0.45500	2.19783
0.428	24 31 21.34	0.41505	0.90980	0.45620	2.19201
0.429	24 34 47.60	0.41596	0.90938	0.45741	2.18622
0.430	24 38 13.87	0.41687	0.90897	0.45862	2.18045
0.431	24 41 40.13	0.41778	0.90855	0.45983	2.17471
0.432	24 45 06.40	0.41869	0.90813	0.46104	2.16899
0.433	24 48 32.66	0.41960	0.90771	0.46226	2.16330
0.434	24 51 58.93	0.42050	0.90729	0.46347	2.15763
0.435	24 55 25.19	0.42141	0.90687	0.46469	2.15199
0.436	24 58 51.46	0.42232	0.90645	0.46590	2.14637
0.437	25 02 17.72	0.42322	0.90603	0.46712	2.14077
0.438	25 05 43.99	0.42413	0.90560	0.46834	2.13520
0.439	25 09 10.25	0.42503	0.90518	0.46956	2.12966
0.440	25 12 36.51	0.42594	0.90475	0.47078	2.12413
0.441	25 16 02.78	0.42684	0.90433	0.47200	2.11863
0.442	25 19 29.04	0.42775	0.90390	0.47323	2.11315
0.443	25 22 55.31	0.42865	0.90347	0.47445	2.10770
0.444	25 26 21.57	0.42956	0.90304	0.47568	2.10227
0.445	25 29 47.84	0.43046	0.90261	0.47690	2.09686
0.446	25 33 14.10	0.43136	0.90218	0.47813	2.09148
0.447	25 36 40.37	0.43226	0.90175	0.47936	2.08611
0.448	25 40 06.63	0.43316	0.90132	0.48059	2.08077
0.449	25 43 32.90	0.43406	0.90088	0.48182	2.07545
0.450	25 46 59.16	0.43497	0.90045	0.48306	2.07016
x	φ	sin x	cos x	tan x	cot x

x	φ	sin x	cos x	tan x	cot x
0.450	25° 46' 59.16"	0.43497	0.90045	0.48306	2.07016
0.451	25 50 25.43	0.43587	0.90001	0.48429	2.06488
0.452	25 53 51.69	0.43677	0.89958	0.48552	2.05963
0.453	25 57 17.96	0.43766	0.89914	0.48676	2.05440
0.454	26 00 44.22	0.43856	0.89870	0.48800	2.04919
0.455	26 04 10.49	0.43946	0.89826	0.48924	2.04400
0.456	26 07 36.75	0.44036	0.89782	0.49048	2.03883
0.457	26 11 03.02	0.44126	0.89738	0.49172	2.03369
0.458	26 14 29.28	0.44216	0.89694	0.49296	2.02856
0.459	26 17 55.55	0.44305	0.89650	0.49420	2.02346
0.460	26 21 21.81	0.44395	0.89605	0.49545	2.01837
0.461	26 24 48.08	0.44484	0.89561	0.49669	2.01331
0.462	26 28 14.34	0.44574	0.89516	0.49794	2.00827
0.463	26 31 40.61	0.44663	0.89472	0.49919	2.00324
0.464	26 35 06.87	0.44753	0.89427	0.50044	1.99824
0.465	26 38 33.13	0.44842	0.89382	0.50169	1.99326
0.466	26 41 59.40	0.44932	0.89337	0.50294	1.98829
0.467	26 45 25.66	0.45021	0.89292	0.50420	1.98335
0.468	26 48 51.93	0.45110	0.89247	0.50545	1.97843
0.469	26 52 18.19	0.45199	0.89202	0.50671	1.97352
0.470	26 55 44.46	0.45289	0.89157	0.50797	1.96864
0.471	26 59 10.72	0.45378	0.89111	0.50922	1.96377
0.472	27 02 36.99	0.45467	0.89066	0.51048	1.95892
0.473	27 06 03.25	0.45556	0.89021	0.51175	1.95410
0.474	27 09 29.52	0.45645	0.88975	0.51301	1.94929
0.475	27 12 55.78	0.45734	0.88929	0.51427	1.94450
0.476	27 16 22.05	0.45823	0.88883	0.51554	1.93972
0.477	27 19 48.31	0.45912	0.88838	0.51680	1.93497
0.478	27 23 14.58	0.46000	0.88792	0.51807	1.93024
0.479	27 26 40.84	0.46089	0.88746	0.51934	1.92552
0.480	27 30 07.11	0.46178	0.88699	0.52061	1.92082
0.481	27 33 33.37	0.46267	0.88653	0.52188	1.91614
0.482	27 36 59.64	0.46355	0.88607	0.52316	1.91148
0.483	27 40 25.90	0.46444	0.88561	0.52443	1.90683
0.484	27 43 52.17	0.46532	0.88514	0.52571	1.90221
0.485	27 47 18.43	0.46621	0.88467	0.52698	1.89760
0.486	27 50 44.70	0.46709	0.88421	0.52826	1.89300
0.487	27 54 10.96	0.46798	0.88374	0.52954	1.88843
0.488	27 57 37.23	0.46886	0.88327	0.53082	1.88387
0.489	28 01 03.49	0.46974	0.88280	0.53210	1.87933
0.490	28 04 29.76	0.47063	0.88233	0.53339	1.87481
0.491	28 07 56.02	0.47151	0.88186	0.53467	1.87030
0.492	28 11 22.28	0.47239	0.88139	0.53596	1.86581
0.493	28 14 48.55	0.47327	0.88092	0.53725	1.86134
0.494	28 18 14.81	0.47415	0.88044	0.53854	1.85688
0.495	28 21 41.08	0.47503	0.87997	0.53983	1.85244
0.496	28 25 07.34	0.47591	0.87949	0.54112	1.84802
0.497	28 28 33.61	0.47679	0.87902	0.54241	1.84361
0.498	28 31 59.87	0.47767	0.87854	0.54371	1.83922
0.499	28 35 26.14	0.47855	0.87806	0.54500	1.83485
0.500	28 38 52.40	0.47943	0.87758	0.54630	1.83049
x	φ	sin x	cos x	tan x	cot x

x	φ	sin x	cos x	tan x	cot x
0.500	28° 38' 52.40"	0.47943	0.87758	0.54630	1.83049
0.501	28 42 18.67	0.48030	0.87710	0.54760	1.82614
0.502	28 45 44.93	0.48118	0.87662	0.54890	1.82182
0.503	28 49 11.20	0.48206	0.87614	0.55020	1.81751
0.504	28 52 37.46	0.48293	0.87566	0.55151	1.81321
0.505	28 56 03.73	0.48381	0.87517	0.55281	1.80893
0.506	28 59 29.99	0.48468	0.87469	0.55412	1.80467
0.507	29 02 56.26	0.48556	0.87421	0.55543	1.80042
0.508	29 06 22.52	0.48643	0.87372	0.55674	1.79618
0.509	29 09 48.79	0.48730	0.87323	0.55805	1.79197
0.510	29 13 15.05	0.48818	0.87274	0.55936	1.78776
0.511	29 16 41.32	0.48905	0.87226	0.56067	1.78357
0.512	29 20 07.58	0.48992	0.87177	0.56199	1.77940
0.513	29 23 33.85	0.49079	0.87128	0.56330	1.77524
0.514	29 27 00.11	0.49166	0.87078	0.56462	1.77110
0.515	29 30 26.38	0.49253	0.87029	0.56594	1.76697
0.516	29 33 52.64	0.49340	0.86980	0.56726	1.76285
0.517	29 37 18.90	0.49427	0.86931	0.56859	1.75875
0.518	29 40 45.17	0.49514	0.86881	0.56991	1.75467
0.519	29 44 11.43	0.49601	0.86832	0.57123	1.75059
0.520	29 47 37.70	0.49688	0.86782	0.57256	1.74654
0.521	29 51 03.96	0.49775	0.86732	0.57389	1.74249
0.522	29 54 30.23	0.49861	0.86682	0.57522	1.73846
0.523	29 57 56.49	0.49948	0.86632	0.57655	1.73445
0.524	30 01 22.76	0.50035	0.86582	0.57789	1.73045
0.525	30 04 49.02	0.50121	0.86532	0.57922	1.72646
0.526	30 08 15.29	0.50208	0.86482	0.58056	1.72249
0.527	30 11 41.55	0.50294	0.86432	0.58189	1.71853
0.528	30 15 07.82	0.50381	0.86382	0.58323	1.71458
0.529	30 18 34.08	0.50467	0.86331	0.58457	1.71065
0.530	30 22 00.35	0.50553	0.86281	0.58592	1.70673
0.531	30 25 26.61	0.50640	0.86230	0.58726	1.70282
0.532	30 28 52.88	0.50726	0.86179	0.58861	1.69893
0.533	30 32 19.14	0.50812	0.86129	0.58995	1.69505
0.534	30 35 45.41	0.50898	0.86078	0.59130	1.69118
0.535	30 39 11.67	0.50984	0.86027	0.59265	1.68733
0.536	30 42 37.94	0.51070	0.85976	0.59401	1.68349
0.537	30 46 04.20	0.51156	0.85925	0.59536	1.67966
0.538	30 49 30.47	0.51242	0.85874	0.59671	1.67584
0.539	30 52 56.73	0.51328	0.85822	0.59807	1.67204
0.540	30 56 23.00	0.51414	0.85771	0.59943	1.66825
0.541	30 59 49.26	0.51499	0.85719	0.60079	1.66448
0.542	31 03 15.52	0.51585	0.85668	0.60215	1.66071
0.543	31 06 41.79	0.51671	0.85616	0.60351	1.65696
0.544	31 10 08.05	0.51756	0.85565	0.60488	1.65322
0.545	31 13 34.32	0.51842	0.85513	0.60625	1.64949
0.546	31 17 00.58	0.51927	0.85461	0.60762	1.64578
0.547	31 20 26.85	0.52013	0.85409	0.60899	1.64208
0.548	31 23 53.11	0.52098	0.85357	0.61036	1.63839
0.549	31 27 19.38	0.52183	0.85305	0.61173	1.63471
0.550	31 30 45.64	0.52269	0.85252	0.61311	1.63104
x	φ	sin x	cos x	tan x	cot x

x	φ	sin x	cos x	tan x	cot x
0.550	31° 30′ 45.64″	0.52269	0.85252	0.61311	1.63104
0.551	31 34 11.91	0.52354	0.85200	0.61448	1.62739
0.552	31 37 38.17	0.52439	0.85148	0.61586	1.62374
0.553	31 41 04.44	0.52524	0.85095	0.61724	1.62011
0.554	31 44 30.70	0.52609	0.85043	0.61862	1.61650
0.555	31 47 56.97	0.52694	0.84990	0.62001	1.61289
0.556	31 51 23.23	0.52779	0.84937	0.62139	1.60929
0.557	31 54 49.50	0.52864	0.84884	0.62278	1.60571
0.558	31 58 15.76	0.52949	0.84832	0.62417	1.60214
0.559	32 01 42.03	0.53034	0.84779	0.62556	1.59857
0.560	32 05 08.29	0.53119	0.84726	0.62695	1.59502
0.561	32 08 34.56	0.53203	0.84672	0.62834	1.59149
0.562	32 12 00.82	0.53288	0.84619	0.62974	1.58796
0.563	32 15 27.09	0.53373	0.84566	0.63114	1.58444
0.564	32 18 53.35	0.53457	0.84512	0.63254	1.58094
0.565	32 22 19.62	0.53542	0.84459	0.63394	1.57744
0.566	32 25 45.88	0.53626	0.84405	0.63534	1.57396
0.567	32 29 12.15	0.53710	0.84352	0.63674	1.57049
0.568	32 32 38.41	0.53795	0.84298	0.63815	1.56703
0.569	32 36 04.67	0.53879	0.84244	0.63956	1.56358
0.570	32 39 30.94	0.53963	0.84190	0.64097	1.56014
0.571	32 42 57.20	0.54047	0.84136	0.64238	1.55671
0.572	32 46 23.47	0.54131	0.84082	0.64479	1.55329
0.573	32 49 49.73	0.54216	0.84028	0.64521	1.54988
0.574	32 53 16.00	0.54300	0.83974	0.64663	1.54649
0.575	32 56 42.26	0.54383	0.83919	0.64805	1.54310
0.576	33 00 08.53	0.54467	0.83865	0.64947	1.53973
0.577	33 03 34.79	0.54551	0.83810	0.65089	1.53636
0.578	33 07 01.06	0.54635	0.83756	0.65231	1.53300
0.579	33 10 27.32	0.54719	0.83701	0.65374	1.52966
0.580	33 13 53.59	0.54802	0.83646	0.65517	1.52633
0.581	33 17 19.85	0.54886	0.83591	0.65660	1.52300
0.582	33 20 46.12	0.54970	0.83536	0.65803	1.51969
0.583	33 24 12.38	0.55053	0.83481	0.65946	1.51638
0.584	33 27 38.65	0.55137	0.83426	0.66090	1.51309
0.585	33 31 04.91	0.55220	0.83371	0.66234	1.50980
0.586	33 34 31.18	0.55303	0.83316	0.66378	1.50653
0.587	33 37 57.44	0.55387	0.83261	0.66522	1.50326
0.588	33 41 23.71	0.55470	0.83205	0.66666	1.50001
0.589	33 44 49.97	0.55553	0.83150	0.66811	1.49676
0.590	33 48 16.24	0.55636	0.83094	0.66956	1.49353
0.591	33 51 42.50	0.55719	0.83038	0.67100	1.49030
0.592	33 55 08.77	0.55802	0.82983	0.67246	1.48709
0.593	33 58 35.03	0.55885	0.82927	0.67391	1.48388
0.594	34 02 01.29	0.55968	0.82871	0.67536	1.48068
0.595	34 05 27.56	0.56051	0.82815	0.67682	1.47749
0.596	34 08 53.82	0.56134	0.82759	0.67828	1.47432
0.597	34 12 20.09	0.56216	0.82703	0.67974	1.47115
0.598	34 15 46.35	0.56299	0.82646	0.68120	1.46799
0.599	34 19 12.62	0.56382	0.82590	0.68267	1.46484
0.600	34 22 38.88	0.56464	0.82534	0.68414	1.46170
x	φ	sin x	cos x	tan x	cot x

x	φ	sin x	cos x	tan x	cot x
0.600	34° 22′ 38.88″	0.56464	0.82534	0.68414	1.46170
0.601	34 26 05.15	0.56547	0.82477	0.68561	1.45856
0.602	34 29 31.41	0.56629	0.82420	0.68708	1.45544
0.603	34 32 57.68	0.56712	0.82364	0.68855	1.45233
0.604	34 36 23.94	0.56794	0.82307	0.69003	1.44922
0.605	34 39 50.21	0.56876	0.82250	0.69150	1.44613
0.606	34 43 16.47	0.56958	0.82193	0.69298	1.44304
0.607	34 46 42.74	0.57041	0.82136	0.69446	1.43996
0.608	34 50 09.00	0.57123	0.82079	0.69595	1.43689
0.609	34 53 35.27	0.57205	0.82022	0.69743	1.43383
0.610	34 57 01.53	0.57287	0.81965	0.69892	1.43078
0.611	35 00 27.80	0.57369	0.81907	0.70041	1.42774
0.612	35 03 54.06	0.57451	0.81850	0.70190	1.42470
0.613	35 07 20.33	0.57532	0.81793	0.70339	1.42168
0.614	35 10 46.59	0.57614	0.81735	0.70489	1.41866
0.615	35 14 12.86	0.57696	0.81677	0.70639	1.41565
0.616	35 17 39.12	0.57778	0.81620	0.70789	1.41265
0.617	35 21 05.39	0.57859	0.81562	0.70939	1.40966
0.618	35 24 31.65	0.57941	0.81504	0.71089	1.40668
0.619	35 27 57.92	0.58022	0.81446	0.71240	1.40370
0.620	35 31 24.18	0.58104	0.81388	0.71391	1.40074
0.621	35 34 50.44	0.58185	0.81330	0.71542	1.39778
0.622	35 38 16.71	0.58266	0.81271	0.71693	1.39483
0.623	35 41 42.97	0.58347	0.81213	0.71845	1.39189
0.624	35 45 09.24	0.58429	0.81155	0.71996	1.38896
0.625	35 48 35.50	0.58510	0.81096	0.72148	1.38603
0.626	35 52 01.77	0.58591	0.81038	0.72301	1.38311
0.627	35 55 28.03	0.58672	0.80979	0.72453	1.38021
0.628	35 58 54.30	0.58753	0.80920	0.72606	1.37730
0.629	36 02 20.56	0.58834	0.80862	0.72758	1.37441
0.630	36 05 46.83	0.58914	0.80803	0.72911	1.37153
0.631	36 09 13.09	0.58995	0.80744	0.73065	1.36865
0.632	36 12 39.36	0.59076	0.80685	0.73218	1.36578
0.633	36 16 05.62	0.59157	0.80626	0.73372	1.36292
0.634	36 19 31.89	0.59237	0.80566	0.73526	1.36006
0.635	36 22 58.15	0.59318	0.80507	0.73680	1.35722
0.636	36 26 24.42	0.59398	0.80448	0.73834	1.35438
0.637	36 29 50.68	0.59479	0.80388	0.73989	1.35155
0.638	36 33 16.95	0.59559	0.80329	0.74144	1.34873
0.639	36 36 43.21	0.59639	0.80269	0.74299	1.34591
0.640	36 40 09.48	0.59720	0.80210	0.74454	1.34310
0.641	36 43 35.74	0.59800	0.80150	0.74610	1.34030
0.642	36 47 02.01	0.59880	0.80090	0.74766	1.33751
0.643	36 50 28.27	0.59960	0.80030	0.74922	1.33473
0.644	36 53 54.54	0.60040	0.79970	0.75078	1.33195
0.645	36 57 20.80	0.60120	0.79910	0.75234	1.32918
0.646	37 00 47.06	0.60200	0.79850	0.75391	1.32642
0.647	37 04 13.33	0.60280	0.79790	0.75548	1.32366
0.648	37 07 39.59	0.60359	0.79729	0.75705	1.32091
0.649	37 11 05.86	0.60439	0.79669	0.75863	1.31817
0.650	37 14 32.12	0.60519	0.79608	0.76020	1.31544

x	φ	sin x	cos x	tan x	cot x

x	φ	sin x	cos x	tan x	cot x
0.650	37° 14′ 32.12″	0.60519	0.79608	0.76020	1.31544
0.651	37 17 58.39	0.60598	0.79548	0.76178	1.31271
0.652	37 21 24.65	0.60678	0.79487	0.76337	1.30999
0.653	37 24 50.92	0.60757	0.79426	0.76495	1.30728
0.654	37 28 17.18	0.60837	0.79366	0.76654	1.30457
0.655	37 31 43.45	0.60916	0.79305	0.76812	1.30187
0.656	37 35 09.71	0.60995	0.79244	0.76972	1.29918
0.657	37 38 35.98	0.61074	0.79183	0.77131	1.29650
0.658	37 42 02.24	0.61154	0.79122	0.77291	1.29382
0.659	37 45 28.51	0.61233	0.79060	0.77450	1.29115
0.660	37 48 54.77	0.61312	0.78999	0.77610	1.28849
0.661	37 52 21.04	0.61391	0.78938	0.77771	1.28583
0.662	37 55 47.30	0.61470	0.78876	0.77931	1.28318
0.663	37 59 13.57	0.61548	0.78815	0.78092	1.28054
0.664	38 02 39.83	0.61627	0.78753	0.78253	1.27790
0.665	38 06 06.10	0.61706	0.78692	0.78415	1.27527
0.666	38 09 32.36	0.61785	0.78630	0.78576	1.27265
0.667	38 12 58.63	0.61863	0.78568	0.78738	1.27003
0.668	38 16 24.89	0.61942	0.78506	0.78900	1.26742
0.669	38 19 51.16	0.62020	0.78444	0.79063	1.26482
0.670	38 23 17.42	0.62099	0.78382	0.79225	1.26222
0.671	38 26 43.68	0.62177	0.78320	0.79388	1.25963
0.672	38 30 09.95	0.62255	0.78258	0.79551	1.25705
0.673	38 33 36.21	0.62333	0.78196	0.79715	1.25447
0.674	38 37 02.48	0.62412	0.78133	0.79879	1.25190
0.675	38 40 28.74	0.62490	0.78071	0.80042	1.24934
0.676	38 43 55.01	0.62568	0.78008	0.80207	1.24678
0.677	38 47 21.27	0.62646	0.77946	0.80371	1.24423
0.678	38 50 47.54	0.62724	0.77883	0.80536	1.24168
0.679	38 54 13.80	0.62802	0.77820	0.80701	1.23914
0.680	38 57 40.07	0.62879	0.77757	0.80866	1.23661
0.681	39 01 06.33	0.62957	0.77694	0.81032	1.23409
0.682	39 04 32.60	0.63035	0.77631	0.81197	1.23157
0.683	39 07 58.86	0.63112	0.77568	0.81364	1.22905
0.684	39 11 25.13	0.63190	0.77505	0.81530	1.22654
0.685	39 14 51.39	0.63267	0.77442	0.81696	1.22404
0.686	39 18 17.66	0.63345	0.77379	0.81863	1.22155
0.687	39 21 43.92	0.63422	0.77315	0.82031	1.21906
0.688	39 25 10.19	0.63499	0.77252	0.82198	1.21658
0.689	39 28 36.45	0.63577	0.77188	0.82366	1.21410
0.690	39 32 02.72	0.63654	0.77125	0.82534	1.21163
0.691	39 35 28.98	0.63731	0.77061	0.82702	1.20916
0.692	39 38 55.25	0.63808	0.76997	0.82870	1.20670
0.693	39 42 21.51	0.63885	0.76933	0.83039	1.20425
0.694	39 45 47.78	0.63962	0.76869	0.83208	1.20180
0.695	39 49 14.04	0.64039	0.76805	0.83378	1.19936
0.696	39 52 40.31	0.64115	0.76741	0.83547	1.19693
0.697	39 56 06.57	0.64192	0.76677	0.83717	1.19450
0.698	39 59 32.83	0.64269	0.76613	0.83888	1.19207
0.699	40 02 59.10	0.64345	0.76549	0.84058	1.18965
0.700	40 06 25.36	0.64422	0.76484	0.84229	1.18724
x	φ	sin x	cos x	cot x

x	φ	sin x	cos x	tan x	cot x
0.700	40° 06' 25.36"	0.64422	0.76484	0.84229	1.18724
0.701	40 09 51.63	0.64498	0.76420	0.84400	1.18484
0.702	40 13 17.89	0.64575	0.76355	0.84571	1.18243
0.703	40 16 44.16	0.64651	0.76291	0.84743	1.18004
0.704	40 20 10.42	0.64727	0.76226	0.84915	1.17765
0.705	40 23 36.69	0.64803	0.76161	0.85087	1.17527
0.706	40 27 02.95	0.64880	0.76096	0.85260	1.17289
0.707	40 30 29.22	0.64956	0.76031	0.85433	1.17051
0.708	40 33 55.48	0.65032	0.75966	0.85606	1.16815
0.709	40 37 21.75	0.65108	0.75901	0.85779	1.16578
0.710	40 40 48.01	0.65183	0.75836	0.85953	1.16343
0.711	40 44 14.28	0.65259	0.75771	0.86127	1.16108
0.712	40 47 40.54	0.65335	0.75706	0.86301	1.15873
0.713	40 51 06.81	0.65411	0.75640	0.86476	1.15639
0.714	40 54 33.07	0.65486	0.75575	0.86651	1.15406
0.715	40 57 59.34	0.65562	0.75509	0.86826	1.15173
0.716	41 01 25.60	0.65637	0.75444	0.87002	1.14940
0.717	41 04 51.87	0.65713	0.75378	0.87177	1.14709
0.718	41 08 18.13	0.65788	0.75312	0.87354	1.14477
0.719	41 11 44.40	0.65863	0.75246	0.87530	1.14247
0.720	41 15 10.66	0.65938	0.75181	0.87707	1.14016
0.721	41 18 36.93	0.66014	0.75115	0.87884	1.13787
0.722	41 22 03.19	0.66089	0.75049	0.88061	1.13557
0.723	41 25 29.45	0.66164	0.74982	0.88239	1.13329
0.724	41 28 55.72	0.66239	0.74916	0.88417	1.13100
0.725	41 32 21.98	0.66314	0.74850	0.88595	1.12873
0.726	41 35 48.25	0.66388	0.74784	0.88774	1.12646
0.727	41 39 14.51	0.66463	0.74717	0.88953	1.12419
0.728	41 42 40.78	0.66538	0.74651	0.89132	1.12193
0.729	41 46 07.04	0.66612	0.74584	0.89312	1.11967
0.730	41 49 33.31	0.66687	0.74517	0.89492	1.11742
0.731	41 52 59.57	0.66761	0.74451	0.89672	1.11518
0.732	41 56 25.84	0.66836	0.74384	0.89853	1.11293
0.733	41 59 52.10	0.66910	0.74317	0.90033	1.11070
0.734	42 03 18.37	0.66984	0.74250	0.90215	1.10847
0.735	42 06 44.63	0.67059	0.74183	0.90396	1.10624
0.736	42 10 10.90	0.67133	0.74116	0.90578	1.10402
0.737	42 13 37.16	0.67207	0.74049	0.90760	1.10180
0.738	42 17 03.43	0.67281	0.73982	0.90943	1.09959
0.739	42 20 29.69	0.67355	0.73914	0.91126	1.09738
0.740	42 23 55.96	0.67429	0.73847	0.91309	1.09518
0.741	42 27 22.22	0.67503	0.73779	0.91492	1.09299
0.742	42 30 48.49	0.67576	0.73712	0.91676	1.09079
0.743	42 34 14.75	0.67650	0.73644	0.91861	1.08861
0.744	42 37 41.02	0.67724	0.73577	0.92045	1.08642
0.745	42 41 07.28	0.67797	0.73509	0.92230	1.08425
0.746	42 44 33.55	0.67871	0.73441	0.92415	1.08207
0.747	42 47 59.81	0.67944	0.73373	0.92601	1.07990
0.748	42 51 26.08	0.68017	0.73305	0.92787	1.07774
0.749	42 54 52.34	0.68091	0.73237	0.92973	1.07558
0.750	42 58 18.60	0.68164	0.73169	0.93160	1.07343
x	φ	sin x	cos x	tan x	cot x

x	φ	sin x	cos x	tan x	cot x
0.750	42° 58′ 18.60″	0.68164	0.73169	0.93160	1.07343
0.751	43 01 44.87	0.68237	0.73101	0.93347	1.07128
0.752	43 05 11.13	0.68310	0.73032	0.93534	1.06913
0.753	43 08 37.40	0.68383	0.72964	0.93722	1.06699
0.754	43 12 03.66	0.68456	0.72896	0.93910	1.06485
0.755	43 15 29.93	0.68529	0.72827	0.94098	1.06272
0.756	43 18 56.19	0.68602	0.72759	0.94287	1.06060
0.757	43 22 22.46	0.68674	0.72690	0.94476	1.05847
0.758	43 25 48.72	0.68747	0.72621	0.94665	1.05635
0.759	43 29 14.99	0.68820	0.72552	0.94855	1.05424
0.760	43 32 41.25	0.68892	0.72484	0.95045	1.05213
0.761	43 36 07.52	0.68965	0.72415	0.95236	1.05003
0.762	43 39 33.78	0.69037	0.72346	0.95427	1.04793
0.763	43 43 00.05	0.69109	0.72277	0.95618	1.04583
0.764	43 46 26.31	0.69182	0.72207	0.95809	1.04374
0.765	43 49 52.58	0.69254	0.72138	0.96001	1.04165
0.766	43 53 18.84	0.69326	0.72069	0.96194	1.03957
0.767	43 56 45.11	0.69398	0.72000	0.96386	1.03749
0.768	44 00 11.37	0.69470	0.71930	0.96580	1.03542
0.769	44 03 37.64	0.69542	0.71861	0.96773	1.03335
0.770	44 07 03.90	0.69614	0.71791	0.96967	1.03128
0.771	44 10 30.17	0.69685	0.71721	0.97161	1.02922
0.772	44 13 56.43	0.69757	0.71652	0.97356	1.02716
0.773	44 17 22.70	0.69829	0.71582	0.97551	1.02511
0.774	44 20 48.96	0.69900	0.71512	0.97746	1.02306
0.775	44 24 15.22	0.69972	0.71442	0.97942	1.02102
0.776	44 27 41.49	0.70043	0.71372	0.98138	1.01898
0.777	44 31 07.75	0.70114	0.71302	0.98334	1.01694
0.778	44 34 34.02	0.70186	0.71232	0.98531	1.01491
0.779	44 38 00.28	0.70257	0.71162	0.98728	1.01288
0.780	44 41 26.55	0.70328	0.71091	0.98926	1.01086
0.781	44 44 52.81	0.70399	0.71021	0.99124	1.00884
0.782	44 48 19.08	0.70470	0.70951	0.99323	1.00682
0.783	44 51 45.34	0.70541	0.70880	0.99522	1.00481
0.784	44 55 11.61	0.70612	0.70809	0.99721	1.00280
0.785	44 58 37.87	0.70683	0.70739	0.99920	1.00080
0.786	45 02 04.14	0.70753	0.70668	1.00120	0.99880
0.787	45 05 30.40	0.70824	0.70597	1.00321	0.99680
0.788	45 08 56.67	0.70894	0.70526	1.00522	0.99481
0.789	45 12 22.93	0.70965	0.70456	1.00723	0.99282
0.790	45 15 49.20	0.71035	0.70385	1.00925	0.99084
0.791	45 19 15.46	0.71106	0.70313	1.01127	0.98886
0.792	45 22 41.73	0.71176	0.70242	1.01329	0.98688
0.793	45 26 07.99	0.71246	0.70171	1.01532	0.98491
0.794	45 29 34.26	0.71316	0.70100	1.01735	0.98294
0.795	45 33 00.52	0.71386	0.70028	1.01939	0.98098
0.796	45 36 26.79	0.71456	0.69957	1.02143	0.97902
0.797	45 39 53.05	0.71526	0.69886	1.02348	0.97706
0.798	45 43 19.32	0.71596	0.69814	1.02553	0.97511
0.799	45 46 45.58	0.71666	0.69742	1.02758	0.97316
0.800	45 50 11.84	0.71736	0.69671	1.02964	0.97121
x	φ	sin x	cos x	tan x	cot x

TABLE 4

Exponential functions
Natural logarithms
Hyperbolic functions
from x = 0·000 to x = 1·650

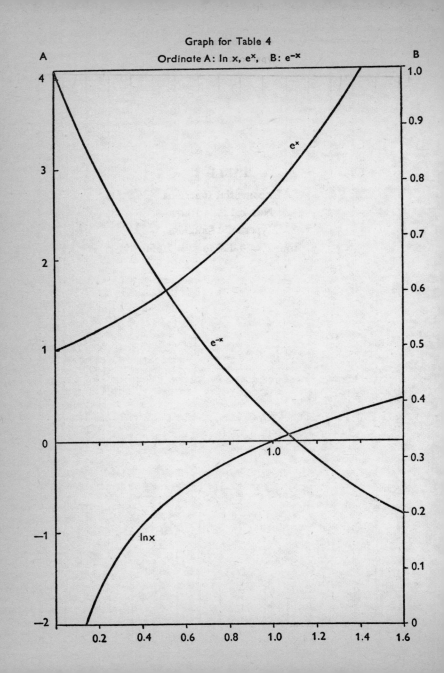

Graph for Table 4
Ordinate A: ln x, e^x,   B: e^{-x}

Graph for Table 4

Hyperbolic functions

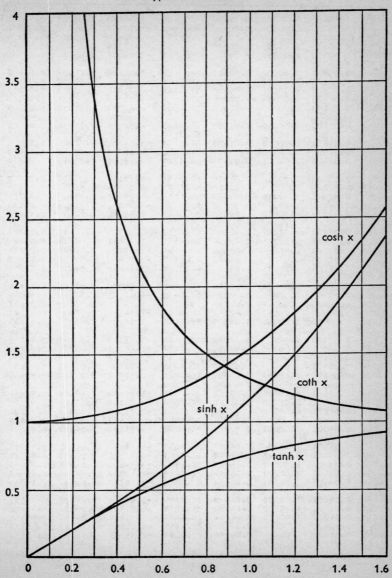

x	sinh x	cosh x	tanh x	coth x	ln x	e^x	e^−x
0.000	0.00000	1.00000	0.00000	∞	− ∞	1.00000	1.00000
0.001	0.00100	1.00000	0.00100	1000.00	−6.90776	1.00100	0.99900
0.002	0.00200	1.00000	0.00200	500.001	−6.21461	1.00200	0.99800
0.003	0.00300	1.00000	0.00300	333.334	−5.80914	1.00300	0.99700
0.004	0.00400	1.00001	0.00400	250.001	−5.52146	1.00401	0.99601
0.005	0.00500	1.00001	0.00500	200.002	−5.29832	1.00501	0.99501
0.006	0.00600	1.00002	0.00600	166.669	−5.11600	1.00602	0.99402
0.007	0.00700	1.00002	0.00700	142.859	−4.96185	1.00702	0.99302
0.008	0.00800	1.00003	0.00800	125.003	−4.82831	1.00803	0.99203
0.009	0.00900	1.00004	0.00900	111.114	−4.71053	1.00904	0.99104
0.010	0.01000	1.00005	0.01000	100.003	−4.60517	1.01005	0.99005
0.011	0.01100	1.00006	0.01100	90.9128	−4.50986	1.01106	0.98906
0.012	0.01200	1.00007	0.01200	83.3373	−4.42285	1.01207	0.98807
0.013	0.01300	1.00008	0.01300	76.9274	−4.34281	1.01308	0.98708
0.014	0.01400	1.00010	0.01400	71.4332	−4.26870	1.01410	0.98610
0.015	0.01500	1.00011	0.01500	66.6717	−4.19971	1.01511	0.98511
0.016	0.01600	1.00013	0.01600	62.5053	−4.13517	1.01613	0.98413
0.017	0.01700	1.00014	0.01700	58.8292	−4.07454	1.01715	0.98314
0.018	0.01800	1.00016	0.01800	55.5616	−4.01738	1.01816	0.98216
0.019	0.01900	1.00018	0.01900	52.6379	−3.96332	1.01918	0.98118
0.020	0.02000	1.00020	0.02000	50.0067	−3.91202	1.02020	0.98020
0.021	0.02100	1.00022	0.02100	47.6260	−3.86323	1.02122	0.97922
0.022	0.02200	1.00024	0.02200	45.4619	−3.81671	1.02224	0.97824
0.023	0.02300	1.00026	0.02300	43.4859	−3.77226	1.02327	0.97726
0.024	0.02400	1.00029	0.02400	41.6747	−3.72970	1.02429	0.97629
0.025	0.02500	1.00031	0.02499	40.0083	−3.68888	1.02532	0.97531
0.026	0.02600	1.00034	0.02599	38.4702	−3.64966	1.02634	0.97434
0.027	0.02700	1.00036	0.02699	37.0460	−3.61192	1.02737	0.97336
0.028	0.02800	1.00039	0.02799	35.7236	−3.57555	1.02840	0.97239
0.029	0.02900	1.00042	0.02899	34.4924	−3.54046	1.02942	0.97142
0.030	0.03000	1.00045	0.02999	33.3433	−3.50656	1.03045	0.97045
0.031	0.03100	1.00048	0.03099	32.2684	−3.47377	1.03149	0.96948
0.032	0.03201	1.00051	0.03199	31.2607	−3.44202	1.03252	0.96851
0.033	0.03301	1.00054	0.03299	30.3140	−3.41125	1.03355	0.96754
0.034	0.03401	1.00058	0.03399	29.4231	−3.38139	1.03458	0.96657
0.035	0.03501	1.00061	0.03499	28.5831	−3.35241	1.03562	0.96561
0.036	0.03601	1.00065	0.03598	27.7898	−3.32424	1.03666	0.96464
0.037	0.03701	1.00068	0.03698	27.0394	−3.29684	1.03769	0.96368
0.038	0.03801	1.00072	0.03798	26.3285	−3.27017	1.03873	0.96271
0.039	0.03901	1.00076	0.03898	25.6540*	−3.24419	1.03977	0.96175
0.040	0.04001	1.00080	0.03998	25.0133	−3.21888	1.04081	0.96079
0.041	0.04101	1.00084	0.04098	24.4039	−3.19418	1.04185	0.95983
0.042	0.04201	1.00088	0.04198	23.8235	−3.17009	1.04289	0.95887
0.043	0.04301	1.00092	0.04297	23.2701	−3.14656	1.04394	0.95791
0.044	0.04401	1.00097	0.04397	22.7419	−3.12357	1.04498	0.95695
0.045	0.04502	1.00101	0.04497	22.2372	−3.10109	1.04603	0.95600
0.046	0.04602	1.00106	0.04597	21.7545	−3.07911	1.04707	0.95504
0.047	0.04702	1.00110	0.04697	21.2923	−3.05761	1.04812	0.95409
0.048	0.04802	1.00115	0.04796	20.8493	−3.03655	1.04917	0.95313
0.049	0.04902	1.00120	0.04896	20.4245	−3.01593	1.05022	0.95218
0.050	0.05002	1.00125	0.04996	20.0167	−2.99573	1.05127	0.95123
x	sinh x	cosh x	tanh x	coth x	ln x	e^x	e^−x

x	sinh x	cosh x	tanh x	coth x	ln x	e^x	e^-x
0.050	0.05002	1.00125	0.04996	20.0167	-2.99573	1.05127	0.95123
0.051	0.05102	1.00130	0.05096	19.6248	-2.97593	1.05232	0.95028
0.052	0.05202	1.00135	0.05195	19.2481	-2.95651	1.05338	0.94933
0.053	0.05302	1.00140	0.05295	18.8856	-2.93746	1.05443	0.94838
0.054	0.05403	1.00146	0.05395	18.5365	-2.91877	1.05548	0.94743
0.055	0.05503	1.00151	0.05494	18.2001	-2.90042	1.05654	0.94649
0.056	0.05603	1.00157	0.05594	17.8758	-2.88240	1.05760	0.94554
0.057	0.05703	1.00162	0.05694	17.5629	-2.86470	1.05866	0.94459
0.058	0.05803	1.00168	0.05794	17.2607	-2.84731	1.05971	0.94365
0.059	0.05903	1.00174	0.05893	16.9688	-2.83022	1.06078	0.94271
0.060	0.06004	1.00180	0.05993	16.6867	-2.81341	1.06184	0.94176
0.061	0.06104	1.00186	0.06092	16.4138	-2.79688	1.06290	0.94082
0.062	0.06204	1.00192	0.06192	16.1497	-2.78062	1.06396	0.93988
0.063	0.06304	1.00199	0.06292	15.8940	-2.76462	1.06503	0.93894
0.064	0.06404	1.00205	0.06391	15.6463	-2.74887	1.06609	0.93800
0.065	0.06505	1.00211	0.06491	15.4063	-2.73337	1.06716	0.93707
0.066	0.06605	1.00218	0.06590	15.1735	-2.71810	1.06823	0.93613
0.067	0.06705	1.00225	0.06690	14.9477	-2.70306	1.06930	0.93520
0.068	0.06805	1.00231	0.06790	14.7285	-2.68825	1.07037	0.93426
0.069	0.06905	1.00238	0.06889	14.5157	-2.67365	1.07144	0.93333
0.070	0.07006	1.00245	0.06989	14.3090	-2.65926	1.07251	0.93239
0.071	0.07106	1.00252	0.07088	14.1082	-2.64508	1.07358	0.93146
0.072	0.07206	1.00259	0.07188	13.9129	-2.63109	1.07466	0.93053
0.073	0.07306	1.00267	0.07287	13.7230	-2.61730	1.07573	0.92960
0.074	0.07407	1.00274	0.07387	13.5382	-2.60369	1.07681	0.92867
0.075	0.07507	1.00281	0.07486	13.3583	-2.59027	1.07788	0.92774
0.076	0.07607	1.00289	0.07585	13.1832	-2.57702	1.07896	0.92682
0.077	0.07708	1.00297	0.07685	13.0127	-2.56395	1.08004	0.92589
0.078	0.07808	1.00304	0.07784	12.8465	-2.55105	1.08112	0.92496
0.079	0.07908	1.00312	0.07884	12.6846	-2.53831	1.08220	0.92404
0.080	0.08009	1.00320	0.07983	12.5267	-2.52573	1.08329	0.92312
0.081	0.08109	1.00328	0.08082	12.3727	-2.51331	1.08437	0.92219
0.082	0.08209	1.00336	0.08182	12.2224	-2.50104	1.08546	0.92127
0.083	0.08310	1.00345	0.08281	12.0758	-2.48891	1.08654	0.92035
0.084	0.08410	1.00353	0.08380	11.9327	-2.47694	1.08763	0.91943
0.085	0.08510	1.00361	0.08480	11.7930	-2.46510	1.08872	0.91851
0.086	0.08611	1.00370	0.08579	11.6566	-2.45341	1.08981	0.91759
0.087	0.08711	1.00379	0.08678	11.5232	-2.44185	1.09090	0.91668
0.088	0.08811	1.00387	0.08777	11.3930	-2.43042	1.09199	0.91576
0.089	0.08912	1.00396	0.08877	11.2656	-2.41912	1.09308	0.91485
0.090	0.09012	1.00405	0.08976	11.1411	-2.40795	1.09417	0.91393
0.091	0.09113	1.00414	0.09075	11.0193	-2.39690	1.09527	0.91302
0.092	0.09213	1.00423	0.09174	10.9002	-2.38597	1.09636	0.91211
0.093	0.09313	1.00433	0.09273	10.7837	-2.37516	1.09746	0.91119
0.094	0.09414	1.00442	0.09372	10.6696	-2.36446	1.09856	0.91028
0.095	0.09514	1.00452	0.09472	10.5580	-2.35388	1.09966	0.90937
0.096	0.09615	1.00461	0.09571	10.4486	-2.34341	1.10076	0.90846
0.097	0.09715	1.00471	0.09670	10.3416	-2.33304	1.10186	0.90756
0.098	0.09816	1.00481	0.09769	10.2367	-2.32279	1.10296	0.90665
0.099	0.09916	1.00490	0.09868	10.1340	-2.31264	1.10407	0.90574
0.100	0.10017	1.00500	0.09967	10.0333	-2.30259	1.10517	0.90484
x	sinh x	cosh x	tanh x	coth x	ln x	e^x	e^-x

x	sinh x	cosh x	tanh x	coth x	ln x	e^x	e^{-x}
0.100	0.10017	1.00500	0.09967	10.0333	-2.30259	1.10517	0.90484
0.101	0.10117	1.00510	0.10066	9.93463	-2.29263	1.10628	0.90393
0.102	0.10218	1.00521	0.10165	9.83790	-2.28278	1.10738	0.90303
0.103	0.10318	1.00531	0.10264	9.74305	-2.27303	1.10849	0.90213
0.104	0.10419	1.00541	0.10363	9.65003	-2.26336	1.10960	0.90123
0.105	0.10519	1.00552	0.10462	9.55878	-2.25379	1.11071	0.90032
0.106	0.10620	1.00562	0.10560	9.46927	-2.24432	1.11182	0.89942
0.107	0.10720	1.00573	0.10659	9.38143	-2.23493	1.11293	0.89853
0.108	0.10821	1.00584	0.10758	9.29523	-2.22562	1.11405	0.89763
0.109	0.10922	1.00595	0.10857	9.21062	-2.21641	1.11516	0.89673
0.110	0.11022	1.00606	0.10956	9.12755	-2.20727	1.11628	0.89583
0.111	0.11123	1.00617	0.11055	9.04598	-2.19823	1.11739	0.89494
0.112	0.11223	1.00628	0.11153	8.96587	-2.18926	1.11851	0.89404
0.113	0.11324	1.00639	0.11252	8.88719	-2.18037	1.11963	0.89315
0.114	0.11425	1.00651	0.11351	8.80990	-2.17156	1.12075	0.89226
0.115	0.11525	1.00662	0.11450	8.73395	-2.16282	1.12187	0.89137
0.116	0.11626	1.00674	0.11548	8.65932	-2.15417	1.12300	0.89048
0.117	0.11727	1.00685	0.11647	8.58597	-2.14558	1.12412	0.88959
0.118	0.11827	1.00697	0.11746	8.51387	-2.13707	1.12524	0.88870
0.119	0.11928	1.00709	0.11844	8.44299	-2.12863	1.12637	0.88781
0.120	0.12029	1.00721	0.11943	8.37329	-2.12026	1.12750	0.88692
0.121	0.12130	1.00733	0.12041	8.30476	-2.11196	1.12862	0.88603
0.122	0.12230	1.00745	0.12140	8.23735	-2.10373	1.12975	0.88515
0.123	0.12331	1.00757	0.12238	8.17104	-2.09557	1.13088	0.88426
0.124	0.12432	1.00770	0.12337	8.10581	-2.08747	1.13202	0.88338
0.125	0.12533	1.00782	0.12435	8.04162	-2.07944	1.13315	0.88250
0.126	0.12633	1.00795	0.12534	7.97846	-2.07147	1.13428	0.88161
0.127	0.12734	1.00808	0.12632	7.91630	-2.06357	1.13542	0.88073
0.128	0.12835	1.00820	0.12731	7.85512	-2.05573	1.13655	0.87985
0.129	0.12936	1.00833	0.12829	7.79489	-2.04794	1.13769	0.87897
0.130	0.13037	1.00846	0.12927	7.73559	-2.04022	1.13883	0.87810
0.131	0.13138	1.00859	0.13026	7.67720	-2.03256	1.13997	0.87722
0.132	0.13238	1.00872	0.13124	7.61971	-2.02495	1.14111	0.87634
0.133	0.13339	1.00886	0.13222	7.56308	-2.01741	1.14225	0.87547
0.134	0.13440	1.00899	0.13320	7.50730	-2.00992	1.14339	0.87459
0.135	0.13541	1.00913	0.13419	7.45235	-2.00248	1.14454	0.87372
0.136	0.13642	1.00926	0.13517	7.39822	-1.99510	1.14568	0.87284
0.137	0.13743	1.00940	0.13615	7.34488	-1.98777	1.14683	0.87197
0.138	0.13844	1.00954	0.13713	7.29232	-1.98050	1.14798	0.87110
0.139	0.13945	1.00968	0.13811	7.24052	-1.97328	1.14912	0.87023
0.140	0.14046	1.00982	0.13909	7.18946	-1.96611	1.15027	0.86936
0.141	0.14147	1.00996	0.14007	7.13914	-1.95900	1.15142	0.86849
0.142	0.14248	1.01010	0.14105	7.08952	-1.95193	1.15258	0.86762
0.143	0.14349	1.01024	0.14203	7.04061	-1.94491	1.15373	0.86675
0.144	0.14450	1.01039	0.14301	6.99238	-1.93794	1.15488	0.86589
0.145	0.14551	1.01053	0.14399	6.94482	-1.93102	1.15604	0.86502
0.146	0.14652	1.01068	0.14497	6.89791	-1.92415	1.15720	0.86416
0.147	0.14753	1.01082	0.14595	6.85165	-1.91732	1.15835	0.86329
0.148	0.14854	1.01097	0.14693	6.80602	-1.91054	1.15951	0.86243
0.149	0.14955	1.01112	0.14791	6.76100	-1.90381	1.16067	0.86157
0.150	0.15056	1.01127	0.14889	6.71659	-1.89712	1.16183	0.86071
x	sinh x	cosh x	tanh x	coth x	ln x	e^x	e^{-x}

x	sinh x	cosh x	tanh x	coth x	ln x	e^x	e^-x
0.150	0.15056	1.01127	0.14889	6.71659	-1.89712	1.16183	0.86071
0.151	0.15157	1.01142	0.14986	6.67277	-1.89048	1.16300	0.85985
0.152	0.15259	1.01157	0.15084	6.62954	-1.88387	1.16416	0.85899
0.153	0.15360	1.01173	0.15182	6.58687	-1.87732	1.16532	0.85813
0.154	0.15461	1.01188	0.15279	6.54476	-1.87080	1.16649	0.85727
0.155	0.15562	1.01204	0.15377	6.50320	-1.86433	1.16766	0.85642
0.156	0.15663	1.01219	0.15475	6.46217	-1.85790	1.16883	0.85556
0.157	0.15765	1.01235	0.15572	6.42167	-1.85151	1.17000	0.85470
0.158	0.15866	1.01251	0.15670	6.38169	-1.84516	1.17117	0.85385
0.159	0.15967	1.01267	0.15767	6.34222	-1.83885	1.17234	0.85300
0.160	0.16068	1.01283	0.15865	6.30324	-1.83258	1.17351	0.85214
0.161	0.16170	1.01299	0.15962	6.26475	-1.82635	1.17468	0.85129
0.162	0.16271	1.01315	0.16060	6.22675	-1.82016	1.17586	0.85044
0.163	0.16372	1.01331	0.16157	6.18921	-1.81401	1.17704	0.84959
0.164	0.16474	1.01348	0.16255	6.15213	-1.80789	1.17821	0.84874
0.165	0.16575	1.01364	0.16352	6.11551	-1.80181	1.17939	0.84789
0.166	0.16676	1.01381	0.16449	6.07933	-1.79577	1.18057	0.84705
0.167	0.16778	1.01398	0.16546	6.04359	-1.78976	1.18175	0.84620
0.168	0.16879	1.01415	0.16644	6.00828	-1.78379	1.18294	0.84535
0.169	0.16981	1.01431	0.16741	5.97339	-1.77786	1.18412	0.84451
0.170	0.17082	1.01448	0.16838	5.93891	-1.77196	1.18530	0.84366
0.171	0.17183	1.01466	0.16935	5.90484	-1.76609	1.18649	0.84282
0.172	0.17285	1.01483	0.17032	5.87117	-1.76026	1.18768	0.84198
0.173	0.17386	1.01500	0.17129	5.83790	-1.75446	1.18887	0.84114
0.174	0.17488	1.01518	0.17227	5.80501	-1.74870	1.19006	0.84030
0.175	0.17589	1.01535	0.17324	5.77250	-1.74297	1.19125	0.83946
0.176	0.17691	1.01553	0.17420	5.74036	-1.73727	1.19244	0.83862
0.177	0.17793	1.01571	0.17517	5.70859	-1.73161	1.19363	0.83778
0.178	0.17894	1.01588	0.17614	5.67719	-1.72597	1.19483	0.83694
0.179	0.17996	1.01606	0.17711	5.64613	-1.72037	1.19602	0.83611
0.180	0.18097	1.01624	0.17808	5.61543	-1.71480	1.19722	0.83527
0.181	0.18199	1.01643	0.17905	5.58506	-1.70926	1.19842	0.83444
0.182	0.18301	1.01661	0.18002	5.55504	-1.70375	1.19961	0.83360
0.183	0.18402	1.01679	0.18098	5.52535	-1.69827	1.20081	0.83277
0.184	0.18504	1.01698	0.18195	5.49598	-1.69282	1.20202	0.83194
0.185	0.18606	1.01716	0.18292	5.46693	-1.68740	1.20322	0.83110
0.186	0.18707	1.01735	0.18388	5.43820	-1.68201	1.20442	0.83027
0.187	0.18809	1.01754	0.18485	5.40978	-1.67665	1.20563	0.82944
0.188	0.18911	1.01772	0.18582	5.38167	-1.67131	1.20683	0.82861
0.189	0.19013	1.01791	0.18678	5.35386	-1.66601	1.20804	0.82779
0.190	0.19115	1.01810	0.18775	5.32634	-1.66073	1.20925	0.82696
0.191	0.19216	1.01830	0.18871	5.29911	-1.65548	1.21046	0.82613
0.192	0.19318	1.01849	0.18967	5.27218	-1.65026	1.21167	0.82531
0.193	0.19420	1.01868	0.19064	5.24552	-1.64507	1.21288	0.82448
0.194	0.19522	1.01888	0.19160	5.21914	-1.63990	1.21410	0.82366
0.195	0.19624	1.01907	0.19257	5.19304	-1.63476	1.21531	0.82283
0.196	0.19726	1.01927	0.19353	5.16721	-1.62964	1.21653	0.82201
0.197	0.19828	1.01947	0.19449	5.14164	-1.62455	1.21774	0.82119
0.198	0.19930	1.01967	0.19545	5.11633	-1.61949	1.21896	0.82037
0.199	0.20032	1.01987	0.19641	5.09128	-1.61445	1.22018	0.81955
0.200	0.20134	1.02007	0.19738	5.06649	-1.60944	1.22140	0.81873
x	sinh x	cosh x	tanh x	coth x	ln x	e^x	e^-x

x	sinh x	cosh x	tanh x	coth x	ln x	e^x	e^−x
0.200	0.20134	1.02007	0.19738	5.06649	−1.60944	1.22140	0.81873
0.201	0.20236	1.02027	0.19834	5.04194	−1.60445	1.22262	0.81791
0.202	0.20338	1.02047	0.19930	5.01765	−1.59949	1.22385	0.81709
0.203	0.20440	1.02068	0.20026	4.99359	−1.59455	1.22507	0.81628
0.204	0.20542	1.02088	0.20122	4.96977	−1.58964	1.22630	0.81546
0.205	0.20644	1.02109	0.20218	4.94619	−1.58475	1.22753	0.81465
0.206	0.20746	1.02129	0.20313	4.92284	−1.57988	1.22875	0.81383
0.207	0.20848	1.02150	0.20409	4.89972	−1.57504	1.22998	0.81302
0.208	0.20950	1.02171	0.20505	4.87683	−1.57022	1.23121	0.81221
0.209	0.21052	1.02192	0.20601	4.85415	−1.56542	1.23244	0.81140
0.210	0.21155	1.02213	0.20697	4.83170	−1.56065	1.23368	0.81058
0.211	0.21257	1.02234	0.20792	4.80946	−1.55590	1.23491	0.80977
0.212	0.21359	1.02256	0.20888	4.78744	−1.55117	1.23615	0.80896
0.213	0.21461	1.02277	0.20984	4.76562	−1.54646	1.23738	0.80816
0.214	0.21564	1.02299	0.21079	4.74401	−1.54178	1.23862	0.80735
0.215	0.21666	1.02320	0.21175	4.72261	−1.53712	1.23986	0.80654
0.216	0.21768	1.02342	0.21270	4.70141	−1.53248	1.24110	0.80574
0.217	0.21871	1.02364	0.21366	4.68040	−1.52786	1.24234	0.80493
0.218	0.21973	1.02386	0.21461	4.65959	−1.52326	1.24359	0.80413
0.219	0.22075	1.02408	0.21556	4.63898	−1.51868	1.24483	0.80332
0.220	0.22178	1.02430	0.21652	4.61855	−1.51413	1.24608	0.80252
0.221	0.22280	1.02452	0.21747	4.59831	−1.50959	1.24732	0.80172
0.222	0.22383	1.02474	0.21842	4.57826	−1.50508	1.24857	0.80092
0.223	0.22485	1.02497	0.21938	4.55839	−1.50058	1.24982	0.80011
0.224	0.22588	1.02519	0.22033	4.53870	−1.49611	1.25107	0.79932
0.225	0.22690	1.02542	0.22128	4.51919	−1.49165	1.25232	0.79852
0.226	0.22793	1.02565	0.22223	4.49986	−1.48722	1.25358	0.79772
0.227	0.22895	1.02588	0.22318	4.48069	−1.48281	1.25483	0.79692
0.228	0.22998	1.02610	0.22413	4.46170	−1.47841	1.25609	0.79612
0.229	0.23101	1.02634	0.22508	4.44288	−1.47403	1.25734	0.79533
0.230	0.23203	1.02657	0.22603	4.42422	−1.46968	1.25860	0.79453
0.231	0.23306	1.02680	0.22698	4.40573	−1.46534	1.25986	0.79374
0.232	0.23409	1.02703	0.22793	4.38740	−1.46102	1.26112	0.79295
0.233	0.23511	1.02727	0.22887	4.36923	−1.45672	1.26238	0.79215
0.234	0.23614	1.02750	0.22982	4.35122	−1.45243	1.26364	0.79136
0.235	0.23717	1.02774	0.23077	4.33337	−1.44817	1.26491	0.79057
0.236	0.23820	1.02798	0.23171	4.31566	−1.44392	1.26617	0.78978
0.237	0.23922	1.02822	0.23266	4.29812	−1.43970	1.26744	0.78899
0.238	0.24025	1.02846	0.23361	4.28072	−1.43548	1.26871	0.78820
0.239	0.24128	1.02870	0.23455	4.26347	−1.43129	1.26998	0.78741
0.240	0.24231	1.02894	0.23550	4.24636	−1.42712	1.27125	0.78663
0.241	0.24334	1.02918	0.23644	4.22940	−1.42296	1.27252	0.78584
0.242	0.24437	1.02943	0.23738	4.21258	−1.41882	1.27379	0.78506
0.243	0.24540	1.02967	0.23833	4.19591	−1.41469	1.27507	0.78427
0.244	0.24643	1.02992	0.23927	4.17937	−1.41059	1.27634	0.78349
0.245	0.24746	1.03016	0.24021	4.16297	−1.40650	1.27762	0.78270
0.246	0.24849	1.03041	0.24115	4.14671	−1.40242	1.27890	0.78192
0.247	0.24952	1.03066	0.24210	4.13058	−1.39837	1.28018	0.78114
0.248	0.25055	1.03091	0.24304	4.11459	−1.39433	1.28146	0.78036
0.249	0.25158	1.03116	0.24398	4.09872	−1.39030	1.28274	0.77958
0.250	0.25261	1.03141	0.24492	4.08299	−1.38629	1.28403	0.77880
x	sinh x	cosh x	tanh x	coth x	ln x	e^x	e^−x

x	sinh x	cosh x	tanh x	coth x	ln x	eˣ	e⁻ˣ
0.250	0.25261	1.03141	0.24492	4.08299	−1.38629	1.28403	0.77880
0.251	0.25364	1.03167	0.24586	4.06738	−1.38230	1.28531	0.77802
0.252	0.25468	1.03192	0.24680	4.05190	−1.37833	1.28660	0.77724
0.253	0.25571	1.03218	0.24774	4.03654	−1.37437	1.28788	0.77647
0.254	0.25674	1.03243	0.24868	4.02131	−1.37042	1.28917	0.77569
0.255	0.25777	1.03269	0.24961	4.00620	−1.36649	1.29046	0.77492
0.256	0.25881	1.03295	0.25055	3.99121	−1.36258	1.29175	0.77414
0.257	0.25984	1.03321	0.25149	3.97634	−1.35868	1.29305	0.77337
0.258	0.26087	1.03347	0.25242	3.96159	−1.35480	1.29434	0.77260
0.259	0.26191	1.03373	0.25336	3.94695	−1.35093	1.29563	0.77182
0.260	0.26294	1.03399	0.25430	3.93243	−1.34707	1.29693	0.77105
0.261	0.26397	1.03425	0.25523	3.91803	−1.34323	1.29823	0.77028
0.262	0.26501	1.03452	0.25617	3.90373	−1.33941	1.29953	0.76951
0.263	0.26604	1.03478	0.25710	3.88955	−1.33560	1.30083	0.76874
0.264	0.26708	1.03505	0.25803	3.87547	−1.33181	1.30213	0.76797
0.265	0.26811	1.03532	0.25897	3.86151	−1.32803	1.30343	0.76721
0.266	0.26915	1.03559	0.25990	3.84765	−1.32426	1.30474	0.76644
0.267	0.27018	1.03586	0.26083	3.83390	−1.32051	1.30604	0.76567
0.268	0.27122	1.03613	0.26176	3.82025	−1.31677	1.30735	0.76491
0.269	0.27226	1.03640	0.26269	3.80671	−1.31304	1.30866	0.76414
0.270	0.27329	1.03667	0.26362	3.79327	−1.30933	1.30996	0.76338
0.271	0.27433	1.03695	0.26456	3.77993	−1.30564	1.31128	0.76262
0.272	0.27537	1.03722	0.26548	3.76669	−1.30195	1.31259	0.76185
0.273	0.27640	1.03750	0.26641	3.75355	−1.29828	1.31390	0.76109
0.274	0.27744	1.03777	0.26734	3.74051	−1.29463	1.31521	0.76033
0.275	0.27848	1.03805	0.26827	3.72757	−1.29098	1.31653	0.75957
0.276	0.27952	1.03833	0.26920	3.71472	−1.28735	1.31785	0.75881
0.277	0.28056	1.03861	0.27013	3.70197	−1.28374	1.31917	0.75805
0.278	0.28159	1.03889	0.27105	3.68932	−1.28013	1.32049	0.75730
0.279	0.28263	1.03917	0.27198	3.67675	−1.27654	1.32181	0.75654
0.280	0.28367	1.03946	0.27291	3.66428	−1.27297	1.32313	0.75578
0.281	0.28471	1.03974	0.27383	3.65190	−1.26940	1.32445	0.75503
0.282	0.28575	1.04003	0.27476	3.63960	−1.26585	1.32578	0.75427
0.283	0.28679	1.04031	0.27568	3.62740	−1.26231	1.32711	0.75352
0.284	0.28783	1.04060	0.27660	3.61529	−1.25878	1.32843	0.75277
0.285	0.28887	1.04089	0.27753	3.60326	−1.25527	1.32976	0.75201
0.286	0.28991	1.04118	0.27845	3.59132	−1.25176	1.33109	0.75126
0.287	0.29096	1.04147	0.27937	3.57947	−1.24827	1.33242	0.75051
0.288	0.29200	1.04176	0.28029	3.56770	−1.24479	1.33376	0.74976
0.289	0.29304	1.04205	0.28121	3.55601	−1.24133	1.33509	0.74901
0.290	0.29408	1.04235	0.28213	3.54440	−1.23787	1.33643	0.74826
0.291	0.29512	1.04264	0.28305	3.53288	−1.23443	1.33776	0.74752
0.292	0.29617	1.04294	0.28397	3.52144	−1.23100	1.33910	0.74677
0.293	0.29721	1.04323	0.28489	3.51008	−1.22758	1.34044	0.74602
0.294	0.29825	1.04353	0.28581	3.49880	−1.22418	1.34178	0.74528
0.295	0.29930	1.04383	0.28673	3.48760	−1.22078	1.34313	0.74453
0.296	0.30034	1.04413	0.28765	3.47647	−1.21740	1.34447	0.74379
0.297	0.30139	1.04443	0.28856	3.46543	−1.21402	1.34582	0.74304
0.298	0.30243	1.04473	0.28948	3.45445	−1.21066	1.34716	0.74230
0.299	0.30348	1.04503	0.29040	3.44356	−1.20731	1.34851	0.74156
0.300	0.30452	1.04534	0.29131	3.43274	−1.20397	1.34986	0.74082

x	sinh x	cosh x	tanh x	coth x	ln x	eˣ	e⁻ˣ

x	sinh x	cosh x	tanh x	coth x	ln x	e^x	e^-x
0.300	0.30452	1.04534	0.29131	3.43274	-1.20397	1.34986	0.74082
0.301	0.30557	1.04564	0.29223	3.42199	-1.20065	1.35121	0.74008
0.302	0.30661	1.04595	0.29314	3.41132	-1.19733	1.35256	0.73934
0.303	0.30766	1.04626	0.29406	3.40072	-1.19402	1.35391	0.73860
0.304	0.30870	1.04656	0.29497	3.39019	-1.19073	1.35527	0.73786
0.305	0.30975	1.04687	0.29588	3.37973	-1.18744	1.35663	0.73712
0.306	0.31080	1.04718	0.29679	3.36934	-1.18417	1.35798	0.73639
0.307	0.31185	1.04750	0.29771	3.35903	-1.18091	1.35934	0.73565
0.308	0.31289	1.04781	0.29862	3.34878	-1.17766	1.36070	0.73492
0.309	0.31394	1.04812	0.29953	3.33860	-1.17441	1.36206	0.73418
0.310	0.31499	1.04844	0.30044	3.32848	-1.17118	1.36343	0.73345
0.311	0.31604	1.04875	0.30135	3.31844	-1.16796	1.36479	0.73271
0.312	0.31709	1.04907	0.30226	3.30846	-1.16475	1.36615	0.73198
0.313	0.31814	1.04939	0.30316	3.29855	-1.16155	1.36752	0.73125
0.314	0.31919	1.04970	0.30407	3.28870	-1.15836	1.36889	0.73052
0.315	0.32024	1.05002	0.30498	3.27892	-1.15518	1.37026	0.72979
0.316	0.32129	1.05034	0.30589	3.26920	-1.15201	1.37163	0.72906
0.317	0.32234	1.05067	0.30679	3.25954	-1.14885	1.37300	0.72833
0.318	0.32339	1.05099	0.30770	3.24995	-1.14570	1.37438	0.72760
0.319	0.32444	1.05131	0.30860	3.24042	-1.14256	1.37575	0.72688
0.320	0.32549	1.05164	0.30951	3.23095	-1.13943	1.37713	0.72615
0.321	0.32654	1.05196	0.31041	3.22154	-1.13631	1.37851	0.72542
0.322	0.32759	1.05229	0.31131	3.21219	-1.13320	1.37988	0.72470
0.323	0.32865	1.05262	0.31222	3.20290	-1.13010	1.38127	0.72397
0.324	0.32970	1.05295	0.31312	3.19367	-1.12701	1.38265	0.72325
0.325	0.33075	1.05328	0.31402	3.18450	-1.12393	1.38403	0.72253
0.326	0.33181	1.05361	0.31492	3.17539	-1.12086	1.38542	0.72181
0.327	0.33286	1.05394	0.31582	3.16633	-1.11780	1.38680	0.72108
0.328	0.33391	1.05428	0.31672	3.15734	-1.11474	1.38819	0.72036
0.329	0.33497	1.05461	0.31762	3.14840	-1.11170	1.38958	0.71964
0.330	0.33602	1.05495	0.31852	3.13951	-1.10866	1.39097	0.71892
0.331	0.33708	1.05528	0.31942	3.13068	-1.10564	1.39236	0.71821
0.332	0.33813	1.05562	0.32032	3.12191	-1.10262	1.39375	0.71749
0.333	0.33919	1.05596	0.32121	3.11319	-1.09961	1.39515	0.71677
0.334	0.34024	1.05630	0.32211	3.10453	-1.09661	1.39654	0.71605
0.335	0.34130	1.05664	0.32301	3.09591	-1.09362	1.39794	0.71534
0.336	0.34236	1.05698	0.32390	3.08736	-1.09064	1.39934	0.71462
0.337	0.34342	1.05732	0.32480	3.07885	-1.08767	1.40074	0.71391
0.338	0.34447	1.05767	0.32569	3.07040	-1.08471	1.40214	0.71320
0.339	0.34553	1.05801	0.32658	3.06200	-1.08176	1.40354	0.71248
0.340	0.34659	1.05836	0.32748	3.05365	-1.07881	1.40495	0.71177
0.341	0.34765	1.05871	0.32837	3.04535	-1.07587	1.40635	0.71106
0.342	0.34871	1.05905	0.32926	3.03710	-1.07294	1.40776	0.71035
0.343	0.34977	1.05940	0.33015	3.02890	-1.07002	1.40917	0.70964
0.344	0.35082	1.05975	0.33104	3.02075	-1.06711	1.41058	0.70893
0.345	0.35188	1.06011	0.33193	3.01265	-1.06421	1.41199	0.70822
0.346	0.35295	1.06046	0.33282	3.00460	-1.06132	1.41340	0.70751
0.347	0.35401	1.06081	0.33371	2.99659	-1.05843	1.41482	0.70681
0.348	0.35507	1.06117	0.33460	2.98864	-1.05555	1.41623	0.70610
0.349	0.35613	1.06152	0.33549	2.98073	-1.05268	1.41765	0.70539
0.350	0.35719	1.06188	0.33638	2.97287	-1.04982	1.41907	0.70469
x	sinh x	cosh x	tanh x	coth x	ln x	e^x	e^-x

x	sinh x	cosh x	tanh x	coth x	ln x	e^x	e^-x
0.350	0.35719	1.06188	0.33638	2.97287	-1.04982	1.41907	0.70469
0.351	0.35825	1.06224	0.33726	2.96505	-1.04697	1.42049	0.70398
0.352	0.35931	1.06259	0.33815	2.95728	-1.04412	1.42191	0.70328
0.353	0.36038	1.06295	0.33903	2.94956	-1.04129	1.42333	0.70258
0.354	0.36144	1.06332	0.33992	2.94188	-1.03846	1.42476	0.70187
0.355	0.36250	1.06368	0.34080	2.93425	-1.03564	1.42618	0.70117
0.356	0.36357	1.06404	0.34169	2.92666	-1.03282	1.42761	0.70047
0.357	0.36463	1.06440	0.34257	2.91912	-1.03002	1.42904	0.69977
0.358	0.36570	1.06477	0.34345	2.91162	-1.02722	1.43047	0.69907
0.359	0.36676	1.06514	0.34433	2.90417	-1.02443	1.43190	0.69837
0.360	0.36783	1.06550	0.34521	2.89675	-1.02165	1.43333	0.69768
0.361	0.36889	1.06587	0.34609	2.88938	-1.01888	1.43476	0.69698
0.362	0.36996	1.06624	0.34697	2.88206	-1.01611	1.43620	0.69628
0.363	0.37102	1.06661	0.34785	2.87477	-1.01335	1.43764	0.69559
0.364	0.37209	1.06698	0.34873	2.86753	-1.01060	1.43907	0.69489
0.365	0.37316	1.06736	0.34961	2.86033	-1.00786	1.44051	0.69420
0.366	0.37423	1.06773	0.35049	2.85316	-1.00512	1.44196	0.69350
0.367	0.37529	1.06810	0.35136	2.84604	-1.00239	1.44340	0.69281
0.368	0.37636	1.06848	0.35224	2.83896	-0.99967	1.44484	0.69212
0.369	0.37743	1.06886	0.35312	2.83192	-0.99696	1.44629	0.69143
0.370	0.37850	1.06923	0.35399	2.82492	-0.99425	1.44773	0.69073
0.371	0.37957	1.06961	0.35487	2.81796	-0.99155	1.44918	0.69004
0.372	0.38064	1.06999	0.35574	2.81104	-0.98886	1.45063	0.68935
0.373	0.38171	1.07037	0.35661	2.80416	-0.98618	1.45208	0.68867
0.374	0.38278	1.07076	0.35749	2.79732	-0.98350	1.45354	0.68798
0.375	0.38385	1.07114	0.35836	2.79051	-0.98083	1.45499	0.68729
0.376	0.38492	1.07152	0.35923	2.78374	-0.97817	1.45645	0.68660
0.377	0.38599	1.07191	0.36010	2.77701	-0.97551	1.45790	0.68592
0.378	0.38707	1.07230	0.36097	2.77032	-0.97286	1.45936	0.68523
0.379	0.38814	1.07268	0.36184	2.76366	-0.97022	1.46082	0.68455
0.380	0.38921	1.07307	0.36271	2.75704	-0.96758	1.46228	0.68386
0.381	0.39028	1.07346	0.36358	2.75046	-0.96496	1.46375	0.68318
0.382	0.39136	1.07385	0.36444	2.74391	-0.96233	1.46521	0.68250
0.383	0.39243	1.07425	0.36531	2.73740	-0.95972	1.46668	0.68181
0.384	0.39351	1.07464	0.36618	2.73093	-0.95711	1.46815	0.68113
0.385	0.39458	1.07503	0.36704	2.72449	-0.95451	1.46961	0.68045
0.386	0.39566	1.07543	0.36791	2.71808	-0.95192	1.47108	0.67977
0.387	0.39673	1.07582	0.36877	2.71171	-0.94933	1.47256	0.67909
0.388	0.39781	1.07622	0.36963	2.70537	-0.94675	1.47403	0.67841
0.389	0.39889	1.07662	0.37050	2.69907	-0.94418	1.47550	0.67773
0.390	0.39996	1.07702	0.37136	2.69280	-0.94161	1.47698	0.67706
0.391	0.40104	1.07742	0.37222	2.68657	-0.93905	1.47846	0.67638
0.392	0.40212	1.07782	0.37308	2.68037	-0.93649	1.47994	0.67570
0.393	0.40319	1.07822	0.37394	2.67420	-0.93395	1.48142	0.67503
0.394	0.40427	1.07863	0.37480	2.66807	-0.93140	1.48290	0.67435
0.395	0.40535	1.07903	0.37566	2.66196	-0.92887	1.48438	0.67368
0.396	0.40643	1.07944	0.37652	2.65589	-0.92634	1.48587	0.67301
0.397	0.40751	1.07984	0.37738	2.64986	-0.92382	1.48736	0.67233
0.398	0.40859	1.08025	0.37824	2.64385	-0.92130	1.48884	0.67166
0.399	0.40967	1.08066	0.37909	2.63788	-0.91879	1.49033	0.67099
0.400	0.41075	1.08107	0.37995	2.63193	-0.91629	1.49182	0.67032

x	sinh x	cosh x	tanh x	coth x	ln x	e^x	e^-x

| x | sinh x | cosh x | tanh x | coth x | ln x | eˣ | e⁻ˣ |

x	sinh x	cosh x	tanh x	coth x	ln x	e^x	e^{-x}
0.400	0.41075	1.08107	0.37995	2.63193	-0.91629	1.49182	0.67032
0.401	0.41183	1.08148	0.38080	2.62602	-0.91379	1.49332	0.66965
0.402	0.41292	1.08190	0.38166	2.62014	-0.91130	1.49481	0.66898
0.403	0.41400	1.08231	0.38251	2.61429	-0.90882	1.49631	0.66831
0.404	0.41508	1.08272	0.38337	2.60847	-0.90634	1.49780	0.66764
0.405	0.41616	1.08314	0.38422	2.60268	-0.90387	1.49930	0.66698
0.406	0.41725	1.08356	0.38507	2.59692	-0.90140	1.50080	0.66631
0.407	0.41833	1.08397	0.38592	2.59119	-0.89894	1.50230	0.66564
0.408	0.41941	1.08439	0.38677	2.58549	-0.89649	1.50381	0.66498
0.409	0.42050	1.08481	0.38762	2.57982	-0.89404	1.50531	0.66431
0.410	0.42158	1.08523	0.38847	2.57418	-0.89160	1.50682	0.66365
0.411	0.42267	1.08566	0.38932	2.56857	-0.88916	1.50833	0.66299
0.412	0.42376	1.08608	0.39017	2.56299	-0.88673	1.50983	0.66232
0.413	0.42484	1.08650	0.39102	2.55743	-0.88431	1.51135	0.66166
0.414	0.42593	1.08693	0.39186	2.55191	-0.88189	1.51286	0.66100
0.415	0.42702	1.08736	0.39271	2.54641	-0.87948	1.51437	0.66034
0.416	0.42810	1.08778	0.39356	2.54094	-0.87707	1.51589	0.65968
0.417	0.42919	1.08821	0.39440	2.53550	-0.87467	1.51740	0.65902
0.418	0.43028	1.08864	0.39524	2.53008	-0.87227	1.51892	0.65836
0.419	0.43137	1.08907	0.39609	2.52469	-0.86988	1.52044	0.65770
0.420	0.43246	1.08950	0.39693	2.51933	-0.86750	1.52196	0.65705
0.421	0.43355	1.08994	0.39777	2.51400	-0.86512	1.52348	0.65639
0.422	0.43464	1.09037	0.39861	2.50869	-0.86275	1.52501	0.65573
0.423	0.43573	1.09081	0.39945	2.50341	-0.86038	1.52653	0.65508
0.424	0.43682	1.09124	0.40029	2.49816	-0.85802	1.52806	0.65442
0.425	0.43791	1.09168	0.40113	2.49293	-0.85567	1.52959	0.65377
0.426	0.43900	1.09212	0.40197	2.48773	-0.85332	1.53112	0.65312
0.427	0.44009	1.09256	0.40281	2.48255	-0.85097	1.53265	0.65246
0.428	0.44119	1.09300	0.40365	2.47740	-0.84863	1.53419	0.65181
0.429	0.44228	1.09344	0.40449	2.47228	-0.84630	1.53572	0.65116
0.430	0.44337	1.09388	0.40532	2.46718	-0.84397	1.53726	0.65051
0.431	0.44447	1.09433	0.40616	2.46210	-0.84165	1.53880	0.64986
0.432	0.44556	1.09477	0.40699	2.45705	-0.83933	1.54034	0.64921
0.433	0.44666	1.09522	0.40783	2.45203	-0.83702	1.54188	0.64856
0.434	0.44775	1.09567	0.40866	2.44703	-0.83471	1.54342	0.64791
0.435	0.44885	1.09611	0.40949	2.44205	-0.83241	1.54496	0.64726
0.436	0.44995	1.09656	0.41032	2.43710	-0.83011	1.54651	0.64662
0.437	0.45104	1.09701	0.41115	2.43217	-0.82782	1.54806	0.64597
0.438	0.45214	1.09747	0.41199	2.42727	-0.82554	1.54960	0.64533
0.439	0.45324	1.09792	0.41282	2.42239	-0.82326	1.55116	0.64468
0.440	0.45434	1.09837	0.41364	2.41754	-0.82098	1.55271	0.64404
0.441	0.45543	1.09883	0.41447	2.41270	-0.81871	1.55426	0.64339
0.442	0.45653	1.09928	0.41530	2.40789	-0.81645	1.55582	0.64275
0.443	0.45763	1.09974	0.41613	2.40311	-0.81419	1.55737	0.64211
0.444	0.45873	1.10020	0.41695	2.39834	-0.81193	1.55893	0.64147
0.445	0.45983	1.10066	0.41778	2.39360	-0.80968	1.56049	0.64082
0.446	0.46093	1.10112	0.41861	2.38888	-0.80744	1.56205	0.64018
0.447	0.46204	1.10158	0.41943	2.38419	-0.80520	1.56361	0.63954
0.448	0.46314	1.10204	0.42025	2.37952	-0.80296	1.56518	0.63890
0.449	0.46424	1.10251	0.42108	2.37486	-0.80073	1.56674	0.63827
0.450	0.46534	1.10297	0.42190	2.37024	-0.79851	1.56831	0.63763

| x | sinh x | cosh x | tanh x | coth x | ln x | e^x | e^{-x} |

x	sinh x	cosh x	tanh x	coth x	ln x	eˣ	e⁻ˣ
0.450	0.46534	1.10297	0.42190	2.37024	-0.79851	1.56831	0.63763
0.451	0.46645	1.10344	0.42272	2.36563	-0.79629	1.56988	0.63699
0.452	0.46755	1.10390	0.42354	2.36104	-0.79407	1.57145	0.63635
0.453	0.46865	1.10437	0.42436	2.35648	-0.79186	1.57302	0.63572
0.454	0.46976	1.10484	0.42518	2.35194	-0.78966	1.57460	0.63508
0.455	0.47086	1.10531	0.42600	2.34742	-0.78746	1.57617	0.63445
0.456	0.47197	1.10578	0.42682	2.34292	-0.78526	1.57775	0.63381
0.457	0.47307	1.10625	0.42764	2.33844	-0.78307	1.57933	0.63318
0.458	0.47418	1.10673	0.42845	2.33398	-0.78089	1.58091	0.63255
0.459	0.47529	1.10720	0.42927	2.32954	-0.77871	1.58249	0.63192
0.460	0.47640	1.10768	0.43008	2.32513	-0.77653	1.58407	0.63128
0.461	0.47750	1.10816	0.43090	2.32073	-0.77436	1.58566	0.63065
0.462	0.47861	1.10863	0.43171	2.31635	-0.77219	1.58725	0.63002
0.463	0.47972	1.10911	0.43253	2.31200	-0.77003	1.58883	0.62939
0.464	0.48083	1.10959	0.43334	2.30766	-0.76787	1.59042	0.62876
0.465	0.48194	1.11007	0.43415	2.30335	-0.76572	1.59201	0.62814
0.466	0.48305	1.11056	0.43496	2.29905	-0.76357	1.59361	0.62751
0.467	0.48416	1.11104	0.43577	2.29478	-0.76143	1.59520	0.62688
0.468	0.48527	1.11153	0.43658	2.29052	-0.75929	1.59680	0.62625
0.469	0.48638	1.11201	0.43739	2.28628	-0.75715	1.59839	0.62563
0.470	0.48750	1.11250	0.43820	2.28207	-0.75502	1.59999	0.62500
0.471	0.48861	1.11299	0.43901	2.27787	-0.75290	1.60159	0.62438
0.472	0.48972	1.11348	0.43981	2.27369	-0.75078	1.60320	0.62375
0.473	0.49084	1.11397	0.44062	2.26953	-0.74866	1.60480	0.62313
0.474	0.49195	1.11446	0.44143	2.26539	-0.74655	1.60641	0.62251
0.475	0.49306	1.11495	0.44223	2.26126	-0.74444	1.60801	0.62189
0.476	0.49418	1.11544	0.44303	2.25716	-0.74234	1.60962	0.62126
0.477	0.49530	1.11594	0.44384	2.25308	-0.74024	1.61123	0.62064
0.478	0.49641	1.11643	0.44464	2.24901	-0.73814	1.61285	0.62002
0.479	0.49753	1.11693	0.44544	2.24496	-0.73605	1.61446	0.61940
0.480	0.49865	1.11743	0.44624	2.24093	-0.73397	1.61607	0.61878
0.481	0.49976	1.11793	0.44704	2.23692	-0.73189	1.61769	0.61816
0.482	0.50088	1.11843	0.44784	2.23292	-0.72981	1.61931	0.61755
0.483	0.50200	1.11893	0.44864	2.22894	-0.72774	1.62093	0.61693
0.484	0.50312	1.11943	0.44944	2.22498	-0.72567	1.62255	0.61631
0.485	0.50424	1.11994	0.45024	2.22104	-0.72361	1.62418	0.61570
0.486	0.50536	1.12044	0.45104	2.21712	-0.72155	1.62580	0.61508
0.487	0.50648	1.12095	0.45183	2.21321	-0.71949	1.62743	0.61447
0.488	0.50760	1.12145	0.45263	2.20932	-0.71744	1.62905	0.61385
0.489	0.50872	1.12196	0.45342	2.20545	-0.71539	1.63068	0.61324
0.490	0.50984	1.12247	0.45422	2.20159	-0.71335	1.63232	0.61263
0.491	0.51097	1.12298	0.45501	2.19776	-0.71131	1.63395	0.61201
0.492	0.51209	1.12349	0.45580	2.19393	-0.70928	1.63558	0.61140
0.493	0.51321	1.12401	0.45659	2.19013	-0.70725	1.63722	0.61079
0.494	0.51434	1.12452	0.45739	2.18634	-0.70522	1.63886	0.61018
0.495	0.51546	1.12503	0.45818	2.18257	-0.70320	1.64050	0.60957
0.496	0.51659	1.12555	0.45897	2.17881	-0.70118	1.64214	0.60896
0.497	0.51771	1.12607	0.45975	2.17507	-0.69917	1.64378	0.60835
0.498	0.51884	1.12659	0.46054	2.17135	-0.69716	1.64543	0.60774
0.499	0.51997	1.12711	0.46133	2.16764	-0.69515	1.64707	0.60714
0.500	0.52110	1.12763	0.46212	2.16395	-0.69315	1.64872	0.60653
x	sinh x	cosh x	tanh x	coth x	ln x	eˣ	e⁻ˣ

x	sinh x	cosh x	tanh x	coth x	ln x	e^x	e^-x
0.500	0.52110	1.12763	0.46212	2.16395	-0.69315	1.64872	0.60653
0.501	0.52222	1.12815	0.46290	2.16028	-0.69115	1.65037	0.60592
0.502	0.52335	1.12867	0.46369	2.15662	-0.68916	1.65202	0.60532
0.503	0.52448	1.12919	0.46447	2.15298	-0.68717	1.65367	0.60471
0.504	0.52561	1.12972	0.46526	2.14935	-0.68518	1.65533	0.60411
0.505	0.52674	1.13025	0.46604	2.14574	-0.68320	1.65699	0.60351
0.506	0.52787	1.13077	0.46682	2.14214	-0.68122	1.65864	0.60290
0.507	0.52900	1.13130	0.46760	2.13856	-0.67924	1.66030	0.60230
0.508	0.53013	1.13183	0.46839	2.13499	-0.67727	1.66196	0.60170
0.509	0.53127	1.13236	0.46917	2.13144	-0.67531	1.66363	0.60110
0.510	0.53240	1.13289	0.46995	2.12791	-0.67334	1.66529	0.60050
0.511	0.53353	1.13343	0.47072	2.12439	-0.67139	1.66696	0.59990
0.512	0.53466	1.13396	0.47150	2.12088	-0.66943	1.66863	0.59930
0.513	0.53580	1.13450	0.47228	2.11739	-0.66748	1.67029	0.59870
0.514	0.53693	1.13503	0.47306	2.11391	-0.66553	1.67197	0.59810
0.515	0.53807	1.13557	0.47383	2.11045	-0.66359	1.67364	0.59750
0.516	0.53920	1.13611	0.47461	2.10701	-0.66165	1.67531	0.59690
0.517	0.54034	1.13665	0.47538	2.10357	-0.65971	1.67699	0.59631
0.518	0.54148	1.13719	0.47615	2.10016	-0.65778	1.67867	0.59571
0.519	0.54262	1.13773	0.47693	2.09675	-0.65585	1.68035	0.59512
0.520	0.54375	1.13827	0.47770	2.09336	-0.65393	1.68203	0.59452
0.521	0.54489	1.13882	0.47847	2.08999	-0.65201	1.68371	0.59393
0.522	0.54603	1.13936	0.47924	2.08663	-0.65009	1.68540	0.59333
0.523	0.54717	1.13991	0.48001	2.08328	-0.64817	1.68708	0.59274
0.524	0.54831	1.14046	0.48078	2.07995	-0.64626	1.68877	0.59215
0.525	0.54945	1.14101	0.48155	2.07663	-0.64436	1.69046	0.59156
0.526	0.55059	1.14156	0.48232	2.07332	-0.64245	1.69215	0.59096
0.527	0.55173	1.14211	0.48308	2.07003	-0.64055	1.69384	0.59037
0.528	0.55288	1.14266	0.48385	2.06675	-0.63866	1.69554	0.58978
0.529	0.55402	1.14321	0.48462	2.06349	-0.63677	1.69723	0.58919
0.530	0.55516	1.14377	0.48538	2.06024	-0.63488	1.69893	0.58860
0.531	0.55631	1.14432	0.48615	2.05700	-0.63299	1.70063	0.58802
0.532	0.55745	1.14488	0.48691	2.05377	-0.63111	1.70233	0.58743
0.533	0.55860	1.14544	0.48767	2.05056	-0.62923	1.70404	0.58684
0.534	0.55974	1.14600	0.48843	2.04736	-0.62736	1.70574	0.58626
0.535	0.56089	1.14656	0.48919	2.04418	-0.62549	1.70745	0.58567
0.536	0.56204	1.14712	0.48995	2.04101	-0.62362	1.70916	0.58508
0.537	0.56318	1.14768	0.49071	2.03785	-0.62176	1.71087	0.58450
0.538	0.56433	1.14825	0.49147	2.03470	-0.61990	1.71258	0.58391
0.539	0.56548	1.14881	0.49223	2.03157	-0.61804	1.71429	0.58333
0.540	0.56663	1.14938	0.49299	2.02845	-0.61619	1.71601	0.58275
0.541	0.56778	1.14994	0.49374	2.02534	-0.61434	1.71772	0.58217
0.542	0.56893	1.15051	0.49450	2.02224	-0.61249	1.71944	0.58158
0.543	0.57008	1.15108	0.49526	2.01916	-0.61065	1.72116	0.58100
0.544	0.57123	1.15165	0.49601	2.01609	-0.60881	1.72288	0.58042
0.545	0.57238	1.15223	0.49676	2.01303	-0.60697	1.72461	0.57984
0.546	0.57354	1.15280	0.49752	2.00998	-0.60514	1.72633	0.57926
0.547	0.57469	1.15337	0.49827	2.00695	-0.60331	1.72806	0.57868
0.548	0.57584	1.15395	0.49902	2.00393	-0.60148	1.72979	0.57810
0.549	0.57700	1.15452	0.49977	2.00092	-0.59966	1.73152	0.57753
0.550	0.57815	1.15510	0.50052	1.99792	-0.59784	1.73325	0.57695
x	sinh x	cosh x	tanh x	coth x	ln x	e^x	e^-x

x	sinh x	cosh x	tanh x	coth x	ln x	e^x	e^−x
0.550	0.57815	1.15510	0.50052	1.99792	−0.59784	1.73325	0.57695
0.551	0.57931	1.15568	0.50127	1.99494	−0.59602	1.73499	0.57637
0.552	0.58046	1.15626	0.50202	1.99196	−0.59421	1.73672	0.57580
0.553	0.58162	1.15684	0.50277	1.98900	−0.59240	1.73846	0.57522
0.554	0.58278	1.15742	0.50351	1.98605	−0.59059	1.74020	0.57465
0.555	0.58393	1.15801	0.50426	1.98311	−0.58879	1.74194	0.57407
0.556	0.58509	1.15859	0.50500	1.98018	−0.58699	1.74368	0.57350
0.557	0.58625	1.15918	0.50575	1.97727	−0.58519	1.74543	0.57293
0.558	0.58741	1.15976	0.50649	1.97436	−0.58340	1.74717	0.57235
0.559	0.58857	1.16035	0.50724	1.97147	−0.58161	1.74892	0.57178
0.560	0.58973	1.16094	0.50798	1.96859	−0.57982	1.75067	0.57121
0.561	0.59089	1.16153	0.50872	1.96572	−0.57803	1.75242	0.57064
0.562	0.59205	1.16212	0.50946	1.96286	−0.57625	1.75418	0.57007
0.563	0.59322	1.16272	0.51020	1.96002	−0.57448	1.75593	0.56950
0.564	0.59438	1.16331	0.51094	1.95718	−0.57270	1.75769	0.56893
0.565	0.59554	1.16390	0.51168	1.95435	−0.57093	1.75945	0.56836
0.566	0.59671	1.16450	0.51242	1.95154	−0.56916	1.76121	0.56779
0.567	0.59787	1.16510	0.51315	1.94874	−0.56740	1.76297	0.56722
0.568	0.59904	1.16570	0.51389	1.94595	−0.56563	1.76473	0.56666
0.569	0.60020	1.16630	0.51462	1.94316	−0.56387	1.76650	0.56609
0.570	0.60137	1.16690	0.51536	1.94039	−0.56212	1.76827	0.56553
0.571	0.60254	1.16750	0.51609	1.93763	−0.56037	1.77004	0.56496
0.572	0.60371	1.16810	0.51683	1.93489	−0.55862	1.77181	0.56440
0.573	0.60487	1.16871	0.51756	1.93215	−0.55687	1.77358	0.56383
0.574	0.60604	1.16931	0.51829	1.92942	−0.55513	1.77535	0.56327
0.575	0.60721	1.16992	0.51902	1.92670	−0.55339	1.77713	0.56270
0.576	0.60838	1.17053	0.51975	1.92399	−0.55165	1.77891	0.56214
0.577	0.60955	1.17113	0.52048	1.92130	−0.54991	1.78069	0.56158
0.578	0.61073	1.17174	0.52121	1.91861	−0.54818	1.78247	0.56102
0.579	0.61190	1.17236	0.52194	1.91594	−0.54645	1.78425	0.56046
0.580	0.61307	1.17297	0.52267	1.91327	−0.54473	1.78604	0.55990
0.581	0.61424	1.17358	0.52339	1.91061	−0.54300	1.78783	0.55934
0.582	0.61542	1.17420	0.52412	1.90797	−0.54128	1.78961	0.55878
0.583	0.61659	1.17481	0.52484	1.90533	−0.53957	1.79140	0.55822
0.584	0.61777	1.17543	0.52557	1.90271	−0.53785	1.79320	0.55766
0.585	0.61894	1.17605	0.52629	1.90009	−0.53614	1.79499	0.55711
0.586	0.62012	1.17667	0.52701	1.89749	−0.53444	1.79679	0.55655
0.587	0.62130	1.17729	0.52773	1.89489	−0.53273	1.79858	0.55599
0.588	0.62247	1.17791	0.52846	1.89231	−0.53103	1.80038	0.55544
0.589	0.62365	1.17853	0.52918	1.88973	−0.52933	1.80219	0.55488
0.590	0.62483	1.17916	0.52990	1.88716	−0.52763	1.80399	0.55433
0.591	0.62601	1.17978	0.53061	1.88461	−0.52594	1.80579	0.55377
0.592	0.62719	1.18041	0.53133	1.88206	−0.52425	1.80760	0.55322
0.593	0.62837	1.18104	0.53205	1.87952	−0.52256	1.80941	0.55267
0.594	0.62955	1.18167	0.53277	1.87700	−0.52088	1.81122	0.55211
0.595	0.63073	1.18230	0.53348	1.87448	−0.51919	1.81303	0.55156
0.596	0.63192	1.18293	0.53420	1.87197	−0.51751	1.81484	0.55101
0.597	0.63310	1.18356	0.53491	1.86947	−0.51584	1.81666	0.55046
0.598	0.63428	1.18419	0.53562	1.86698	−0.51416	1.81848	0.54991
0.599	0.63547	1.18483	0.53634	1.86450	−0.51249	1.82030	0.54936
0.600	0.63665	1.18547	0.53705	1.86203	−0.51083	1.82212	0.54881

x	sinh x	cosh x	tanh x	coth x	ln x	e^x	e^−x

x	sinh x	cosh x	tanh x	coth x	ln x	e^x	e^{-x}
0.600	0.63665	1.18547	0.53705	1.86203	-0.51083	1.82212	0.54881
0.601	0.63784	1.18610	0.53776	1.85956	-0.50916	1.82394	0.54826
0.602	0.63903	1.18674	0.53847	1.85711	-0.50750	1.82577	0.54772
0.603	0.64021	1.18738	0.53918	1.85467	-0.50584	1.82759	0.54717
0.604	0.64140	1.18802	0.53989	1.85223	-0.50418	1.82942	0.54662
0.605	0.64259	1.18866	0.54060	1.84980	-0.50253	1.83125	0.54607
0.606	0.64378	1.18931	0.54131	1.84739	-0.50088	1.83308	0.54553
0.607	0.64497	1.18995	0.54201	1.84498	-0.49923	1.83492	0.54498
0.608	0.64616	1.19060	0.54272	1.84258	-0.49758	1.83675	0.54444
0.609	0.64735	1.19124	0.54342	1.84019	-0.49594	1.83859	0.54389
0.610	0.64854	1.19189	0.54413	1.83781	-0.49430	1.84043	0.54335
0.611	0.64973	1.19254	0.54483	1.83543	-0.49266	1.84227	0.54281
0.612	0.65093	1.19319	0.54553	1.83307	-0.49102	1.84412	0.54227
0.613	0.65212	1.19384	0.54624	1.83071	-0.48939	1.84596	0.54172
0.614	0.65331	1.19449	0.54694	1.82837	-0.48776	1.84781	0.54118
0.615	0.65451	1.19515	0.54764	1.82603	-0.48613	1.84966	0.54064
0.616	0.65570	1.19580	0.54834	1.82370	-0.48451	1.85151	0.54010
0.617	0.65690	1.19646	0.54904	1.82137	-0.48289	1.85336	0.53956
0.618	0.65810	1.19712	0.54973	1.81906	-0.48127	1.85521	0.53902
0.619	0.65929	1.19778	0.55043	1.81676	-0.47965	1.85707	0.53848
0.620	0.66049	1.19844	0.55113	1.81446	-0.47804	1.85893	0.53794
0.621	0.66169	1.19910	0.55182	1.81217	-0.47642	1.86079	0.53741
0.622	0.66289	1.19976	0.55252	1.80989	-0.47482	1.86265	0.53687
0.623	0.66409	1.20042	0.55321	1.80762	-0.47321	1.86451	0.53633
0.624	0.66529	1.20109	0.55391	1.80536	-0.47160	1.86638	0.53580
0.625	0.66649	1.20175	0.55460	1.80310	-0.47000	1.86825	0.53526
0.626	0.66769	1.20242	0.55529	1.80086	-0.46840	1.87012	0.53473
0.627	0.66890	1.20309	0.55598	1.79862	-0.46681	1.87199	0.53419
0.628	0.67010	1.20376	0.55667	1.79639	-0.46522	1.87386	0.53366
0.629	0.67130	1.20443	0.55736	1.79416	-0.46362	1.87573	0.53312
0.630	0.67251	1.20510	0.55805	1.79195	-0.46204	1.87761	0.53259
0.631	0.67371	1.20577	0.55874	1.78974	-0.46045	1.87949	0.53206
0.632	0.67492	1.20645	0.55943	1.78754	-0.45887	1.88137	0.53153
0.633	0.67613	1.20712	0.56011	1.78535	-0.45728	1.88325	0.53100
0.634	0.67734	1.20780	0.56080	1.78317	-0.45571	1.88514	0.53047
0.635	0.67854	1.20848	0.56149	1.78099	-0.45413	1.88702	0.52994
0.636	0.67975	1.20916	0.56217	1.77882	-0.45256	1.88891	0.52941
0.637	0.68096	1.20984	0.56285	1.77666	-0.45099	1.89080	0.52888
0.638	0.68217	1.21052	0.56354	1.77451	-0.44942	1.89269	0.52835
0.639	0.68338	1.21120	0.56422	1.77236	-0.44785	1.89459	0.52782
0.640	0.68459	1.21189	0.56490	1.77023	-0.44629	1.89648	0.52729
0.641	0.68581	1.21257	0.56558	1.76810	-0.44473	1.89838	0.52677
0.642	0.68702	1.21326	0.56626	1.76597	-0.44317	1.90028	0.52624
0.643	0.68823	1.21395	0.56694	1.76386	-0.44161	1.90218	0.52571
0.644	0.68945	1.21463	0.56762	1.76175	-0.44006	1.90408	0.52519
0.645	0.69066	1.21532	0.56829	1.75965	-0.43850	1.90599	0.52466
0.646	0.69188	1.21602	0.56897	1.75756	-0.43696	1.90789	0.52414
0.647	0.69309	1.21671	0.56965	1.75547	-0.43541	1.90980	0.52361
0.648	0.69431	1.21740	0.57032	1.75340	-0.43386	1.91171	0.52309
0.649	0.69553	1.21810	0.57100	1.75132	-0.43232	1.91363	0.52257
0.650	0.69675	1.21879	0.57167	1.74926	-0.43078	1.91554	0.52205
x	sinh x	cosh x	tanh x	coth x	ln x	e^x	e^{-x}

x	sinh x	cosh x	tanh x	coth x	ln x	e^x	e^-x
0.650	0.69675	1.21879	0.57167	1.74926	-0.43078	1.91554	0.52205
0.651	0.69797	1.21949	0.57234	1.74720	-0.42925	1.91746	0.52152
0.652	0.69919	1.22019	0.57301	1.74516	-0.42771	1.91938	0.52100
0.653	0.70041	1.22089	0.57369	1.74311	-0.42618	1.92130	0.52048
0.654	0.70163	1.22159	0.57436	1.74108	-0.42465	1.92322	0.51996
0.655	0.70285	1.22229	0.57503	1.73905	-0.42312	1.92514	0.51944
0.656	0.70407	1.22300	0.57570	1.73703	-0.42159	1.92707	0.51892
0.657	0.70530	1.22370	0.57636	1.73502	-0.42007	1.92900	0.51840
0.658	0.70652	1.22441	0.57703	1.73301	-0.41855	1.93093	0.51789
0.659	0.70775	1.22511	0.57770	1.73101	-0.41703	1.93286	0.51737
0.660	0.70897	1.22582	0.57836	1.72902	-0.41552	1.93479	0.51685
0.661	0.71020	1.22653	0.57903	1.72703	-0.41400	1.93673	0.51633
0.662	0.71142	1.22724	0.57969	1.72505	-0.41249	1.93867	0.51582
0.663	0.71265	1.22795	0.58036	1.72308	-0.41098	1.94061	0.51530
0.664	0.71388	1.22867	0.58102	1.72111	-0.40947	1.94255	0.51479
0.665	0.71511	1.22938	0.58168	1.71915	-0.40797	1.94449	0.51427
0.666	0.71634	1.23010	0.58234	1.71720	-0.40647	1.94644	0.51376
0.667	0.71757	1.23081	0.58300	1.71526	-0.40497	1.94838	0.51325
0.668	0.71880	1.23153	0.58366	1.71332	-0.40347	1.95033	0.51273
0.669	0.72003	1.23225	0.58432	1.71139	-0.40197	1.95228	0.51222
0.670	0.72126	1.23297	0.58498	1.70946	-0.40048	1.95424	0.51171
0.671	0.72250	1.23369	0.58564	1.70754	-0.39899	1.95619	0.51120
0.672	0.72373	1.23442	0.58629	1.70563	-0.39750	1.95815	0.51069
0.673	0.72497	1.23514	0.58695	1.70372	-0.39601	1.96011	0.51018
0.674	0.72620	1.23587	0.58760	1.70182	-0.39453	1.96207	0.50967
0.675	0.72744	1.23659	0.58826	1.69993	-0.39304	1.96403	0.50916
0.676	0.72868	1.23732	0.58891	1.69804	-0.39156	1.96600	0.50865
0.677	0.72991	1.23805	0.58957	1.69616	-0.39008	1.96796	0.50814
0.678	0.73115	1.23878	0.59022	1.69429	-0.38861	1.96993	0.50763
0.679	0.73239	1.23951	0.59087	1.69242	-0.38713	1.97190	0.50712
0.680	0.73363	1.24025	0.59152	1.69056	-0.38566	1.97388	0.50662
0.681	0.73487	1.24098	0.59217	1.68871	-0.38419	1.97585	0.50611
0.682	0.73611	1.24172	0.59282	1.68686	-0.38273	1.97783	0.50560
0.683	0.73735	1.24245	0.59347	1.68502	-0.38126	1.97981	0.50510
0.684	0.73860	1.24319	0.59411	1.68318	-0.37980	1.98179	0.50459
0.685	0.73984	1.24393	0.59476	1.68135	-0.37834	1.98377	0.50409
0.686	0.74109	1.24467	0.59541	1.67953	-0.37688	1.98576	0.50359
0.687	0.74233	1.24541	0.59605	1.67771	-0.37542	1.98774	0.50308
0.688	0.74358	1.24616	0.59670	1.67590	-0.37397	1.98973	0.50258
0.689	0.74482	1.24690	0.59734	1.67409	-0.37251	1.99172	0.50208
0.690	0.74607	1.24765	0.59798	1.67229	-0.37106	1.99372	0.50158
0.691	0.74732	1.24839	0.59862	1.67050	-0.36962	1.99571	0.50107
0.692	0.74857	1.24914	0.59927	1.66871	-0.36817	1.99771	0.50057
0.693	0.74982	1.24989	0.59991	1.66693	-0.36673	1.99971	0.50007
0.694	0.75107	1.25064	0.60055	1.66515	-0.36528	2.00171	0.49957
0.695	0.75232	1.25139	0.60118	1.66338	-0.36384	2.00371	0.49907
0.696	0.75357	1.25214	0.60182	1.66162	-0.36241	2.00571	0.49858
0.697	0.75482	1.25290	0.60246	1.65986	-0.36097	2.00772	0.49808
0.698	0.75607	1.25365	0.60310	1.65811	-0.35954	2.00973	0.49758
0.699	0.75733	1.25441	0.60373	1.65636	-0.35810	2.01174	0.49708
0.700	0.75858	1.25517	0.60437	1.65462	-0.35667	2.01375	0.49659

x	sinh x	cosh x	tanh x	coth x	ln x	e^x	e^-x

x	sinh x	cosh x	tanh x	coth x	ln x	eˣ	e⁻ˣ
0.700	0.75858	1.25517	0.60437	1.65462	-0.35667	2.01375	0.49659
0.701	0.75984	1.25593	0.60500	1.65289	-0.35525	2.01577	0.49609
0.702	0.76110	1.25669	0.60564	1.65116	-0.35382	2.01778	0.49559
0.703	0.76235	1.25745	0.60627	1.64943	-0.35240	2.01980	0.49510
0.704	0.76361	1.25821	0.60690	1.64772	-0.35098	2.02182	0.49460
0.705	0.76487	1.25898	0.60753	1.64600	-0.34956	2.02385	0.49411
0.706	0.76613	1.25974	0.60816	1.64430	-0.34814	2.02587	0.49361
0.707	0.76739	1.26051	0.60879	1.64260	-0.34672	2.02790	0.49312
0.708	0.76865	1.26128	0.60942	1.64090	-0.34531	2.02993	0.49263
0.709	0.76991	1.26205	0.61005	1.63921	-0.34390	2.03196	0.49214
0.710	0.77117	1.26282	0.61068	1.63753	-0.34249	2.03399	0.49164
0.711	0.77244	1.26359	0.61130	1.63585	-0.34108	2.03603	0.49115
0.712	0.77370	1.26436	0.61193	1.63418	-0.33968	2.03806	0.49066
0.713	0.77497	1.26514	0.61255	1.63251	-0.33827	2.04010	0.49017
0.714	0.77623	1.26591	0.61318	1.63085	-0.33687	2.04214	0.48968
0.715	0.77750	1.26669	0.61380	1.62919	-0.33547	2.04419	0.48919
0.716	0.77876	1.26747	0.61443	1.62754	-0.33408	2.04623	0.48870
0.717	0.78003	1.26825	0.61505	1.62589	-0.33268	2.04828	0.48821
0.718	0.78130	1.26903	0.61567	1.62425	-0.33129	2.05033	0.48773
0.719	0.78257	1.26981	0.61629	1.62261	-0.32989	2.05238	0.48724
0.720	0.78384	1.27059	0.61691	1.62098	-0.32850	2.05443	0.48675
0.721	0.78511	1.27138	0.61753	1.61936	-0.32712	2.05649	0.48627
0.722	0.78638	1.27216	0.61815	1.61774	-0.32573	2.05855	0.48578
0.723	0.78766	1.27295	0.61876	1.61612	-0.32435	2.06061	0.48529
0.724	0.78893	1.27374	0.61938	1.61452	-0.32296	2.06267	0.48481
0.725	0.79020	1.27453	0.62000	1.61291	-0.32158	2.06473	0.48432
0.726	0.79148	1.27532	0.62061	1.61131	-0.32021	2.06680	0.48384
0.727	0.79275	1.27611	0.62123	1.60972	-0.31883	2.06886	0.48336
0.728	0.79403	1.27690	0.62184	1.60813	-0.31745	2.07093	0.48287
0.729	0.79531	1.27770	0.62245	1.60655	-0.31608	2.07301	0.48239
0.730	0.79659	1.27849	0.62307	1.60497	-0.31471	2.07508	0.48191
0.731	0.79786	1.27929	0.62368	1.60339	-0.31334	2.07716	0.48143
0.732	0.79914	1.28009	0.62429	1.60183	-0.31197	2.07923	0.48095
0.733	0.80042	1.28089	0.62490	1.60026	-0.31061	2.08132	0.48047
0.734	0.80171	1.28169	0.62551	1.59870	-0.30925	2.08340	0.47999
0.735	0.80299	1.28249	0.62611	1.59715	-0.30788	2.08548	0.47951
0.736	0.80427	1.28330	0.62672	1.59560	-0.30653	2.08757	0.47903
0.737	0.80555	1.28410	0.62733	1.59406	-0.30517	2.08966	0.47855
0.738	0.80684	1.28491	0.62794	1.59252	-0.30381	2.09175	0.47807
0.739	0.80812	1.28572	0.62854	1.59099	-0.30246	2.09384	0.47759
0.740	0.80941	1.28652	0.62915	1.58946	-0.30111	2.09594	0.47711
0.741	0.81070	1.28733	0.62975	1.58793	-0.29975	2.09803	0.47664
0.742	0.81199	1.28815	0.63035	1.58642	-0.29841	2.10013	0.47616
0.743	0.81327	1.28896	0.63095	1.58490	-0.29706	2.10223	0.47568
0.744	0.81456	1.28977	0.63156	1.58339	-0.29571	2.10434	0.47521
0.745	0.81585	1.29059	0.63216	1.58189	-0.29437	2.10644	0.47473
0.746	0.81714	1.29140	0.63276	1.58039	-0.29303	2.10855	0.47426
0.747	0.81844	1.29222	0.63336	1.57889	-0.29169	2.11066	0.47379
0.748	0.81973	1.29304	0.63395	1.57740	-0.29035	2.11277	0.47331
0.749	0.82102	1.29386	0.63455	1.57592	-0.28902	2.11488	0.47284
0.750	0.82232	1.29468	0.63515	1.57443	-0.28768	2.11700	0.47237

x	sinh x	cosh x	tanh x	coth x	ln x	eˣ	e⁻ˣ

x	sinh x	cosh x	tanh x	coth x	ln x	e^x	e^-x
0.750	0.82232	1.29468	0.63515	1.57443	-0.28768	2.11700	0.47237
0.751	0.82361	1.29551	0.63575	1.57296	-0.28635	2.11912	0.47189
0.752	0.82491	1.29633	0.63634	1.57149	-0.28502	2.12124	0.47142
0.753	0.82620	1.29716	0.63694	1.57002	-0.28369	2.12336	0.47095
0.754	0.82750	1.29798	0.63753	1.56856	-0.28236	2.12548	0.47048
0.755	0.82880	1.29881	0.63812	1.56710	-0.28104	2.12761	0.47001
0.756	0.83010	1.29964	0.63871	1.56564	-0.27971	2.12974	0.46954
0.757	0.83140	1.30047	0.63931	1.56419	-0.27839	2.13187	0.46907
0.758	0.83270	1.30130	0.63990	1.56275	-0.27707	2.13400	0.46860
0.759	0.83400	1.30214	0.64049	1.56131	-0.27575	2.13614	0.46813
0.760	0.83530	1.30297	0.64108	1.55988	-0.27444	2.13828	0.46767
0.761	0.83661	1.30381	0.64167	1.55844	-0.27312	2.14042	0.46720
0.762	0.83791	1.30464	0.64225	1.55702	-0.27181	2.14256	0.46673
0.763	0.83922	1.30548	0.64284	1.55560	-0.27050	2.14470	0.46627
0.764	0.84052	1.30632	0.64343	1.55418	-0.26919	2.14685	0.46580
0.765	0.84183	1.30716	0.64401	1.55276	-0.26788	2.14899	0.46533
0.766	0.84314	1.30801	0.64460	1.55136	-0.26657	2.15114	0.46487
0.767	0.84445	1.30885	0.64518	1.54995	-0.26527	2.15330	0.46440
0.768	0.84576	1.30970	0.64576	1.54855	-0.26397	2.15545	0.46394
0.769	0.84707	1.31054	0.64635	1.54716	-0.26266	2.15761	0.46348
0.770	0.84838	1.31139	0.64693	1.54576	-0.26136	2.15977	0.46301
0.771	0.84969	1.31224	0.64751	1.54438	-0.26007	2.16193	0.46255
0.772	0.85100	1.31309	0.64809	1.54299	-0.25877	2.16409	0.46209
0.773	0.85231	1.31394	0.64867	1.54161	-0.25748	2.16626	0.46163
0.774	0.85363	1.31479	0.64925	1.54024	-0.25618	2.16842	0.46116
0.775	0.85494	1.31565	0.64983	1.53887	-0.25489	2.17059	0.46070
0.776	0.85626	1.31650	0.65040	1.53750	-0.25360	2.17276	0.46024
0.777	0.85758	1.31736	0.65098	1.53614	-0.25231	2.17494	0.45978
0.778	0.85889	1.31822	0.65156	1.53478	-0.25103	2.17711	0.45932
0.779	0.86021	1.31908	0.65213	1.53343	-0.24974	2.17929	0.45886
0.780	0.86153	1.31994	0.65271	1.53208	-0.24846	2.18147	0.45841
0.781	0.86285	1.32080	0.65328	1.53074	-0.24718	2.18365	0.45795
0.782	0.86417	1.32166	0.65385	1.52940	-0.24590	2.18584	0.45749
0.783	0.86550	1.32253	0.65443	1.52806	-0.24462	2.18803	0.45703
0.784	0.86682	1.32340	0.65500	1.52673	-0.24335	2.19022	0.45658
0.785	0.86814	1.32426	0.65557	1.52540	-0.24207	2.19241	0.45612
0.786	0.86947	1.32513	0.65614	1.52407	-0.24080	2.19460	0.45566
0.787	0.87079	1.32600	0.65671	1.52275	-0.23953	2.19680	0.45521
0.788	0.87212	1.32687	0.65727	1.52143	-0.23826	2.19899	0.45475
0.789	0.87345	1.32775	0.65784	1.52012	-0.23699	2.20119	0.45430
0.790	0.87478	1.32862	0.65841	1.51881	-0.23572	2.20340	0.45384
0.791	0.87610	1.32950	0.65898	1.51751	-0.23446	2.20560	0.45339
0.792	0.87743	1.33037	0.65954	1.51621	-0.23319	2.20781	0.45294
0.793	0.87877	1.33125	0.66011	1.51491	-0.23193	2.21002	0.45249
0.794	0.88010	1.33213	0.66067	1.51362	-0.23067	2.21223	0.45203
0.795	0.88143	1.33301	0.66123	1.51233	-0.22941	2.21444	0.45158
0.796	0.88276	1.33389	0.66179	1.51104	-0.22816	2.21666	0.45113
0.797	0.88410	1.33478	0.66236	1.50976	-0.22690	2.21887	0.45068
0.798	0.88543	1.33566	0.66292	1.50848	-0.22565	2.22109	0.45023
0.799	0.88677	1.33655	0.66348	1.50721	-0.22439	2.22332	0.44978
0.800	0.88811	1.33743	0.66404	1.50594	-0.22314	2.22554	0.44933
x	sinh x	cosh x	tanh x	coth x	ln x	e^x	e^-x

x	sinh x	cosh x	tanh x	coth x	ln x	e^x	e^-x
0.800	0.88811	1.33743	0.66404	1.50594	−0.22314	2.22554	0.44933
0.801	0.88944	1.33832	0.66460	1.50467	−0.22189	2.22777	0.44888
0.802	0.89078	1.33921	0.66515	1.50341	−0.22065	2.23000	0.44843
0.803	0.89212	1.34011	0.66571	1.50215	−0.21940	2.23223	0.44798
0.804	0.89346	1.34100	0.66627	1.50090	−0.21816	2.23446	0.44754
0.805	0.89480	1.34189	0.66682	1.49965	−0.21691	2.23670	0.44709
0.806	0.89615	1.34279	0.66738	1.49840	−0.21567	2.23893	0.44664
0.807	0.89749	1.34368	0.66793	1.49716	−0.21443	2.24117	0.44619
0.808	0.89883	1.34458	0.66849	1.49592	−0.21319	2.24342	0.44575
0.809	0.90018	1.34548	0.66904	1.49468	−0.21196	2.24566	0.44530
0.810	0.90152	1.34638	0.66959	1.49345	−0.21072	2.24791	0.44486
0.811	0.90287	1.34729	0.67014	1.49222	−0.20949	2.25016	0.44441
0.812	0.90422	1.34819	0.67069	1.49100	−0.20825	2.25241	0.44397
0.813	0.90557	1.34909	0.67124	1.48978	−0.20702	2.25466	0.44353
0.814	0.90692	1.35000	0.67179	1.48856	−0.20579	2.25692	0.44308
0.815	0.90827	1.35091	0.67234	1.48734	−0.20457	2.25918	0.44264
0.816	0.90962	1.35182	0.67289	1.48613	−0.20334	2.26144	0.44220
0.817	0.91097	1.35273	0.67343	1.48493	−0.20212	2.26370	0.44175
0.818	0.91232	1.35364	0.67398	1.48372	−0.20089	2.26596	0.44131
0.819	0.91368	1.35455	0.67453	1.48252	−0.19967	2.26823	0.44087
0.820	0.91503	1.35547	0.67507	1.48133	−0.19845	2.27050	0.44043
0.821	0.91639	1.35638	0.67561	1.48014	−0.19723	2.27277	0.43999
0.822	0.91775	1.35730	0.67616	1.47895	−0.19601	2.27505	0.43955
0.823	0.91910	1.35822|	0.67670	1.47776	−0.19480	2.27732	0.43911
0.824	0.92046	1.35914	0.67724	1.47658	−0.19358	2.27960	0.43867
0.825	0.92182	1.36006	0.67778	1.47540	−0.19237	2.28188	0.43823
0.826	0.92318	1.36098	0.67832	1.47423	−0.19116	2.28416	0.43780
0.827	0.92454	1.36190	0.67886	1.47305	−0.18995	2.28645	0.43736
0.828	0.92591	1.36283	0.67940	1.47189	−0.18874	2.28874	0.43692
0.829	0.92727	1.36376	0.67994	1.47072	−0.18754	2.29103	0.43649
0.830	0.92863	1.36468	0.68048	1.46956	−0.18633	2.29332	0.43605
0.831	0.93000	1.36561	0.68101	1.46840	−0.18513	2.29561	0.43561
0.832	0.93137	1.36654	0.68155	1.46725	−0.18392	2.29791	0.43518
0.833	0.93273	1.36748	0.68208	1.46610	−0.18272	2.30021	0.43474
0.834	0.93410	1.36841	0.68262	1.46495	−0.18152	2.30251	0.43431
0.835	0.93547	1.36934	0.68315	1.46380	−0.18032	2.30481	0.43387
0.836	0.93684	1.37028	0.68368	1.46266	−0.17913	2.30712	0.43344
0.837	0.93821	1.37122	0.68422	1.46153	−0.17793	2.30943	0.43301
0.838	0.93958	1.37216	0.68475	1.46039	−0.17674	2.31174	0.43257
0.839	0.94095	1.37310	0.68528	1.45926	−0.17554	2.31405	0.43214
0.840	0.94233	1.37404	0.68581	1.45813	−0.17435	2.31637	0.43171
0.841	0.94370	1.37498	0.68634	1.45701	−0.17316	2.31868	0.43128
0.842	0.94508	1.37593	0.68687	1.45589	−0.17198	2.32100	0.43085
0.843	0.94645	1.37687	0.68739	1.45477	−0.17079	2.32333	0.43042
0.844	0.94783	1.37782	0.68792	1.45365	−0.16960	2.32565	0.42999
0.845	0.94921	1.37877	0.68845	1.45254	−0.16842	2.32798	0.42956
0.846	0.95059	1.37972	0.68897	1.45143	−0.16724	2.33031	0.42913
0.847	0.95197	1.38067	0.68950	1.45033	−0.16605	2.33264	0.42870
0.848	0.95335	1.38162	0.69002	1.44923	−0.16487	2.33497	0.42827
0.849	0.95473	1.38258	0.69055	1.44813	−0.16370	2.33731	0.42784
0.850	0.95612	1.38353	0.69107	1.44703	−0.16252	2.33965	0.42741
x	sinh x	cosh x	tanh x	coth x	ln x	e^x	e^-x

x	sinh x	cosh x	tanh x	coth x	ln x	e^x	e^-x
0.850	0.95612	1.38353	0.69107	1.44703	-0.16252	2.33965	0.42741
0.851	0.95750	1.38449	0.69159	1.44594	-0.16134	2.34199	0.42699
0.852	0.95888	1.38545	0.69211	1.44485	-0.16017	2.34433	0.42656
0.853	0.96027	1.38641	0.69263	1.44377	-0.15900	2.34668	0.42613
0.854	0.96166	1.38737	0.69315	1.44268	-0.15782	2.34902	0.42571
0.855	0.96305	1.38833	0.69367	1.44160	-0.15665	2.35137	0.42528
0.856	0.96443	1.38929	0.69419	1.44053	-0.15548	2.35373	0.42486
0.857	0.96582	1.39026	0.69471	1.43945	-0.15432	2.35608	0.42443
0.858	0.96721	1.39122	0.69523	1.43838	-0.15315	2.35844	0.42401
0.859	0.96861	1.39219	0.69574	1.43731	-0.15199	2.36080	0.42359
0.860	0.97000	1.39316	0.69626	1.43625	-0.15082	2.36316	0.42316
0.861	0.97139	1.39413	0.69677	1.43519	-0.14966	2.36553	0.42274
0.862	0.97279	1.39510	0.69729	1.43413	-0.14850	2.36789	0.42232
0.863	0.97418	1.39608	0.69780	1.43308	-0.14734	2.37026	0.42189
0.864	0.97558	1.39705	0.69831	1.43202	-0.14618	2.37263	0.42147
0.865	0.97698	1.39803	0.69882	1.43097	-0.14503	2.37501	0.42105
0.866	0.97838	1.39901	0.69934	1.42993	-0.14387	2.37738	0.42063
0.867	0.97978	1.39999	0.69985	1.42888	-0.14272	2.37976	0.42021
0.868	0.98118	1.40097	0.70036	1.42784	-0.14156	2.38214	0.41979
0.869	0.98258	1.40195	0.70087	1.42681	-0.14041	2.38453	0.41937
0.870	0.98398	1.40293	0.70137	1.42577	-0.13926	2.38691	0.41895
0.871	0.98538	1.40392	0.70188	1.42474	-0.13811	2.38930	0.41853
0.872	0.98679	1.40490	0.70239	1.42371	-0.13697	2.39169	0.41811
0.873	0.98819	1.40589	0.70290	1.42269	-0.13582	2.39408	0.41770
0.874	0.98960	1.40688	0.70340	1.42166	-0.13467	2.39648	0.41728
0.875	0.99101	1.40787	0.70391	1.42065	-0.13353	2.39888	0.41686
0.876	0.99242	1.40886	0.70441	1.41963	-0.13239	2.40128	0.41645
0.877	0.99382	1.40985	0.70491	1.41861	-0.13125	2.40368	0.41603
0.878	0.99523	1.41085	0.70542	1.41760	-0.13011	2.40608	0.41561
0.879	0.99665	1.41184	0.70592	1.41660	-0.12897	2.40849	0.41520
0.880	0.99806	1.41284	0.70642	1.41559	-0.12783	2.41090	0.41478
0.881	0.99947	1.41384	0.70692	1.41459	-0.12670	2.41331	0.41437
0.882	1.00089	1.41484	0.70742	1.41359	-0.12556	2.41573	0.41395
0.883	1.00230	1.41584	0.70792	1.41259	-0.12443	2.41814	0.41354
0.884	1.00372	1.41684	0.70842	1.41160	-0.12330	2.42056	0.41313
0.885	1.00514	1.41785	0.70892	1.41061	-0.12217	2.42298	0.41271
0.886	1.00655	1.41886	0.70941	1.40962	-0.12104	2.42541	0.41230
0.887	1.00797	1.41986	0.70991	1.40863	-0.11991	2.42784	0.41189
0.888	1.00939	1.42087	0.71040	1.40765	-0.11878	2.43026	0.41148
0.889	1.01081	1.42188	0.71090	1.40667	-0.11766	2.43270	0.41107
0.890	1.01224	1.42289	0.71139	1.40569	-0.11653	2.43513	0.41066
0.891	1.01366	1.42391	0.71189	1.40472	-0.11541	2.43757	0.41025
0.892	1.01508	1.42492	0.71238	1.40374	-0.11429	2.44000	0.40984
0.893	1.01651	1.42594	0.71287	1.40278	-0.11317	2.44245	0.40943
0.894	1.01794	1.42695	0.71336	1.40181	-0.11205	2.44489	0.40902
0.895	1.01936	1.42797	0.71385	1.40085	-0.11093	2.44734	0.40861
0.896	1.02079	1.42899	0.71434	1.39988	-0.10981	2.44978	0.40820
0.897	1.02222	1.43001	0.71483	1.39893	-0.10870	2.45224	0.40779
0.898	1.02365	1.43104	0.71532	1.39797	-0.10759	2.45469	0.40738
0.899	1.02508	1.43206	0.71581	1.39702	-0.10647	2.45714	0.40698
0.900	1.02652	1.43309	0.71630	1.39607	-0.10536	2.45960	0.40657
x	sinh x	cosh x	tanh x	coth x	ln x	e^x	e^-x

x	sinh x	cosh x	tanh x	coth x	ln x	e^x	e^-x
0.900	1.02652	1.43309	0.71630	1.39607	-0.10536	2.45960	0.40657
0.901	1.02795	1.43411	0.71678	1.39512	-0.10425	2.46206	0.40616
0.902	1.02938	1.43514	0.71727	1.39417	-0.10314	2.46453	0.40576
0.903	1.03082	1.43617	0.71776	1.39323	-0.10203	2.46699	0.40535
0.904	1.03226	1.43720	0.71824	1.39229	-0.10093	2.46946	0.40495
0.905	1.03370	1.43824	0.71872	1.39136	-0.09982	2.47193	0.40454
0.906	1.03513	1.43927	0.71921	1.39042	-0.09872	2.47441	0.40414
0.907	1.03657	1.44031	0.71969	1.38949	-0.09761	2.47688	0.40373
0.908	1.03801	1.44134	0.72017	1.38856	-0.09651	2.47936	0.40333
0.909	1.03946	1.44238	0.72065	1.38763	-0.09541	2.48184	0.40293
0.910	1.04090	1.44342	0.72113	1.38671	-0.09431	2.48432	0.40252
0.911	1.04234	1.44446	0.72161	1.38579	-0.09321	2.48681	0.40212
0.912	1.04379	1.44551	0.72209	1.38487	-0.09212	2.48930	0.40172
0.913	1.04523	1.44655	0.72257	1.38395	-0.09102	2.49179	0.40132
0.914	1.04668	1.44760	0.72305	1.38304	-0.08992	2.49428	0.40092
0.915	1.04813	1.44865	0.72352	1.38213	-0.08883	2.49678	0.40052
0.916	1.04958	1.44969	0.72400	1.38122	-0.08774	2.49927	0.40012
0.917	1.05103	1.45075	0.72448	1.38031	-0.08665	2.50177	0.39972
0.918	1.05248	1.45180	0.72495	1.37941	-0.08556	2.50428	0.39932
0.919	1.05393	1.45285	0.72542	1.37850	-0.08447	2.50678	0.39892
0.920	1.05539	1.45390	0.72590	1.37761	-0.08338	2.50929	0.39852
0.921	1.05684	1.45496	0.72637	1.37671	-0.08230	2.51180	0.39812
0.922	1.05830	1.45602	0.72684	1.37581	-0.08121	2.51431	0.39772
0.923	1.05975	1.45708	0.72731	1.37492	-0.08013	2.51683	0.39733
0.924	1.06121	1.45814	0.72778	1.37403	-0.07904	2.51935	0.39693
0.925	1.06267	1.45920	0.72825	1.37315	-0.07796	2.52187	0.39653
0.926	1.06413	1.46026	0.72872	1.37226	-0.07688	2.52439	0.39614
0.927	1.06559	1.46133	0.72919	1.37138	-0.07580	2.52692	0.39574
0.928	1.06705	1.46239	0.72966	1.37050	-0.07472	2.52945	0.39534
0.929	1.06851	1.46346	0.73013	1.36962	-0.07365	2.53198	0.39495
0.930	1.06998	1.46453	0.73059	1.36875	-0.07257	2.53451	0.39455
0.931	1.07144	1.46560	0.73106	1.36788	-0.07150	2.53704	0.39416
0.932	1.07291	1.46667	0.73152	1.36701	-0.07042	2.53958	0.39377
0.933	1.07438	1.46775	0.73199	1.36614	-0.06935	2.54212	0.39337
0.934	1.07584	1.46882	0.73245	1.36527	-0.06828	2.54467	0.39298
0.935	1.07731	1.46990	0.73292	1.36441	-0.06721	2.54721	0.39259
0.936	1.07878	1.47098	0.73338	1.36355	-0.06614	2.54976	0.39219
0.937	1.08026	1.47206	0.73384	1.36269	-0.06507	2.55231	0.39180
0.938	1.08173	1.47314	0.73430	1.36184	-0.06401	2.55487	0.39141
0.939	1.08320	1.47422	0.73476	1.36098	-0.06294	2.55742	0.39102
0.940	1.08468	1.47530	0.73522	1.36013	-0.06188	2.55998	0.39063
0.941	1.08615	1.47639	0.73568	1.35928	-0.06081	2.56254	0.39024
0.942	1.08763	1.47748	0.73614	1.35844	-0.05975	2.56511	0.38985
0.943	1.08911	1.47857	0.73660	1.35759	-0.05869	2.56767	0.38946
0.944	1.09059	1.47966	0.73705	1.35675	-0.05763	2.57024	0.38907
0.945	1.09207	1.48075	0.73751	1.35591	-0.05657	2.57281	0.38868
0.946	1.09355	1.48184	0.73797	1.35507	-0.05551	2.57539	0.38829
0.947	1.09503	1.48293	0.73842	1.35424	-0.05446	2.57796	0.38790
0.948	1.09651	1.48403	0.73888	1.35341	-0.05340	2.58054	0.38752
0.949	1.09800	1.48513	0.73933	1.35258	-0.05235	2.58313	0.38713
0.950	1.09948	1.48623	0.73978	1.35175	-0.05129	2.58571	0.38674
x	sinh x	cosh x	tanh x	coth x	ln x	e^x	e^-x

x	sinh x	cosh x	tanh x	coth x	ln x	e^x	e^−x
0.950	1.09948	1.48623	0.73978	1.35175	−0.05129	2.58571	0.38674
0.951	1.10097	1.48733	0.74024	1.35092	−0.05024	2.58830	0.38635
0.952	1.10246	1.48843	0.74069	1.35010	−0.04919	2.59089	0.38597
0.953	1.10395	1.48953	0.74114	1.34928	−0.04814	2.59348	0.38558
0.954	1.10544	1.49064	0.74159	1.34846	−0.04709	2.59607	0.38520
0.955	1.10693	1.49174	0.74204	1.34764	−0.04604	2.59867	0.38481
0.956	1.10842	1.49285	0.74249	1.34682	−0.04500	2.60127	0.38443
0.957	1.10991	1.49396	0.74294	1.34601	−0.04395	2.60387	0.38404
0.958	1.11141	1.49507	0.74338	1.34520	−0.04291	2.60648	0.38366
0.959	1.11291	1.49618	0.74383	1.34439	−0.04186	2.60909	0.38328
0.960	1.11440	1.49729	0.74428	1.34359	−0.04082	2.61170	0.38289
0.961	1.11590	1.49841	0.74472	1.34278	−0.03978	2.61431	0.38251
0.962	1.11740	1.49953	0.74517	1.34198	−0.03874	2.61693	0.38213
0.963	1.11890	1.50064	0.74561	1.34118	−0.03770	2.61954	0.38175
0.964	1.12040	1.50176	0.74606	1.34038	−0.03666	2.62216	0.38136
0.965	1.12190	1.50289	0.74650	1.33959	−0.03563	2.62479	0.38098
0.966	1.12341	1.50401	0.74694	1.33879	−0.03459	2.62741	0.38060
0.967	1.12491	1.50513	0.74738	1.33800	−0.03356	2.63004	0.38022
0.968	1.12642	1.50626	0.74782	1.33721	−0.03252	2.63267	0.37984
0.969	1.12792	1.50739	0.74826	1.33643	−0.03149	2.63531	0.37946
0.970	1.12943	1.50851	0.74870	1.33564	−0.03046	2.63794	0.37908
0.971	1.13094	1.50964	0.74914	1.33486	−0.02943	2.64058	0.37870
0.972	1.13245	1.51078	0.74958	1.33408	−0.02840	2.64323	0.37833
0.973	1.13396	1.51191	0.75002	1.33330	−0.02737	2.64587	0.37795
0.974	1.13547	1.51304	0.75046	1.33252	−0.02634	2.64852	0.37757
0.975	1.13699	1.51418	0.75089	1.33175	−0.02532	2.65117	0.37719
0.976	1.13850	1.51532	0.75133	1.33097	−0.02429	2.65382	0.37682
0.977	1.14002	1.51646	0.75176	1.33020	−0.02327	2.65647	0.37644
0.978	1.14154	1.51760	0.75220	1.32944	−0.02225	2.65913	0.37606
0.979	1.14305	1.51874	0.75263	1.32867	−0.02122	2.66179	0.37569
0.980	1.14457	1.51988	0.75307	1.32791	−0.02020	2.66446	0.37531
0.981	1.14609	1.52103	0.75350	1.32714	−0.01918	2.66712	0.37494
0.982	1.14761	1.52218	0.75393	1.32638	−0.01816	2.66979	0.37456
0.983	1.14914	1.52332	0.75436	1.32562	−0.01715	2.67246	0.37419
0.984	1.15066	1.52447	0.75479	1.32487	−0.01613	2.67514	0.37381
0.985	1.15219	1.52563	0.75522	1.32411	−0.01511	2.67781	0.37344
0.986	1.15371	1.52678	0.75565	1.32336	−0.01410	2.68049	0.37307
0.987	1.15524	1.52793	0.75608	1.32261	−0.01309	2.68317	0.37269
0.988	1.15677	1.52909	0.75651	1.32186	−0.01207	2.68586	0.37232
0.989	1.15830	1.53025	0.75694	1.32112	−0.01106	2.68854	0.37195
0.990	1.15983	1.53141	0.75736	1.32037	−0.01005	2.69123	0.37158
0.991	1.16136	1.53257	0.75779	1.31963	−0.00904	2.69393	0.37121
0.992	1.16289	1.53373	0.75821	1.31889	−0.00803	2.69662	0.37083
0.993	1.16443	1.53489	0.75864	1.31815	−0.00702	2.69932	0.37046
0.994	1.16596	1.53606	0.75906	1.31741	−0.00602	2.70202	0.37009
0.995	1.16750	1.53722	0.75949	1.31668	−0.00501	2.70472	0.36972
0.996	1.16904	1.53839	0.75991	1.31595	−0.00401	2.70743	0.36935
0.997	1.17058	1.53956	0.76033	1.31522	−0.00300	2.71014	0.36898
0.998	1.17212	1.54073	0.76075	1.31449	−0.00200	2.71285	0.36862
0.999	1.17366	1.54191	0.76117	1.31376	−0.00100	2.71556	0.36825
1.000	1.17520	1.54308	0.76159	1.31304	0.00000	2.71828	0.36788

x	sinh x	cosh x	tanh x	coth x	ln x	e^x	e^−x

x	sinh x	cosh x	tanh x	coth x	ln x	eˣ	e⁻ˣ
1.000	1.17520	1.54308	0.76159	1.31304	0.00000	2.71828	0.36788
1.001	1.17674	1.54426	0.76201	1.31231	0.00100	2.72100	0.36751
1.002	1.17829	1.54543	0.76243	1.31159	0.00200	2.72372	0.36714
1.003	1.17984	1.54661	0.76285	1.31087	0.00300	2.72645	0.36678
1.004	1.18138	1.54779	0.76327	1.31015	0.00399	2.72918	0.36641
1.005	1.18293	1.54898	0.76369	1.30944	0.00499	2.73191	0.36604
1.006	1.18448	1.55016	0.76410	1.30872	0.00598	2.73464	0.36568
1.007	1.18603	1.55134	0.76452	1.30801	0.00698	2.73738	0.36531
1.008	1.18758	1.55253	0.76493	1.30730	0.00797	2.74012	0.36495
1.009	1.18914	1.55372	0.76535	1.30660	0.00896	2.74286	0.36458
1.010	1.19069	1.55491	0.76576	1.30589	0.00995	2.74560	0.36422
1.011	1.19225	1.55610	0.76618	1.30518	0.01094	2.74835	0.36385
1.012	1.19380	1.55729	0.76659	1.30448	0.01193	2.75110	0.36349
1.013	1.19536	1.55849	0.76700	1.30378	0.01292	2.75385	0.36313
1.014	1.19692	1.55969	0.76741	1.30308	0.01390	2.75661	0.36277
1.015	1.19848	1.56088	0.76782	1.30238	0.01489	2.75936	0.36240
1.016	1.20004	1.56208	0.76823	1.30169	0.01587	2.76212	0.36204
1.017	1.20160	1.56328	0.76864	1.30100	0.01686	2.76489	0.36168
1.018	1.20317	1.56449	0.76905	1.30030	0.01784	2.76765	0.36132
1.019	1.20473	1.56569	0.76946	1.29961	0.01882	2.77042	0.36096
1.020	1.20630	1.56689	0.76987	1.29893	0.01980	2.77319	0.36059
1.021	1.20787	1.56810	0.77027	1.29824	0.02078	2.77597	0.36023
1.022	1.20944	1.56931	0.77068	1.29756	0.02176	2.77875	0.35987
1.023	1.21101	1.57052	0.77109	1.29687	0.02274	2.78153	0.35951
1.024	1.21258	1.57173	0.77149	1.29619	0.02372	2.78431	0.35916
1.025	1.21415	1.57295	0.77190	1.29551	0.02469	2.78710	0.35880
1.026	1.21572	1.57416	0.77230	1.29484	0.02567	2.78988	0.35844
1.027	1.21730	1.57538	0.77270	1.29416	0.02664	2.79268	0.35808
1.028	1.21887	1.57660	0.77310	1.29349	0.02762	2.79547	0.35772
1.029	1.22045	1.57782	0.77351	1.29281	0.02859	2.79827	0.35736
1.030	1.22203	1.57904	0.77391	1.29214	0.02956	2.80107	0.35701
1.031	1.22361	1.58026	0.77431	1.29147	0.03053	2.80387	0.35665
1.032	1.22519	1.58148	0.77471	1.29081	0.03150	2.80667	0.35629
1.033	1.22677	1.58271	0.77511	1.29014	0.03247	2.80948	0.35594
1.034	1.22836	1.58394	0.77551	1.28948	0.03343	2.81229	0.35558
1.035	1.22994	1.58517	0.77591	1.28882	0.03440	2.81511	0.35523
1.036	1.23153	1.58640	0.77630	1.28816	0.03537	2.81792	0.35487
1.037	1.23311	1.58763	0.77670	1.28750	0.03633	2.82074	0.35452
1.038	1.23470	1.58886	0.77710	1.28684	0.03730	2.82356	0.35416
1.039	1.23629	1.59010	0.77749	1.28619	0.03826	2.82639	0.35381
1.040	1.23788	1.59134	0.77789	1.28553	0.03922	2.82922	0.35345
1.041	1.23947	1.59257	0.77828	1.28488	0.04018	2.83205	0.35310
1.042	1.24107	1.59381	0.77868	1.28423	0.04114	2.83488	0.35275
1.043	1.24266	1.59506	0.77907	1.28358	0.04210	2.83772	0.35240
1.044	1.24426	1.59630	0.77946	1.28293	0.04306	2.84056	0.35204
1.045	1.24585	1.59755	0.77985	1.28229	0.04402	2.84340	0.35169
1.046	1.24745	1.59879	0.78025	1.28165	0.04497	2.84624	0.35134
1.047	1.24905	1.60004	0.78064	1.28100	0.04593	2.84909	0.35099
1.048	1.25065	1.60129	0.78103	1.28036	0.04688	2.85194	0.35064
1.049	1.25225	1.60254	0.78142	1.27973	0.04784	2.85479	0.35029
1.050	1.25386	1.60379	0.78181	1.27909	0.04879	2.85765	0.34994

x	sinh x	cosh x	tanh x	coth x	ln x	eˣ	e⁻ˣ

x	sinh x	cosh x	tanh x	coth x	ln x	e^x	e^-x
1.050	1.25386	1.60379	0.78181	1.27909	0.04879	2.85765	0.34994
1.051	1.25546	1.60505	0.78219	1.27845	0.04974	2.86051	0.34959
1.052	1.25707	1.60631	0.78258	1.27782	0.05069	2.86337	0.34924
1.053	1.25867	1.60756	0.78297	1.27719	0.05164	2.86624	0.34889
1.054	1.26028	1.60882	0.78336	1.27656	0.05259	2.86910	0.34854
1.055	1.26189	1.61008	0.78374	1.27593	0.05354	2.87198	0.34819
1.056	1.26350	1.61135	0.78413	1.27530	0.05449	2.87485	0.34784
1.057	1.26511	1.61261	0.78451	1.27468	0.05543	2.87772	0.34750
1.058	1.26673	1.61388	0.78490	1.27405	0.05638	2.88060	0.34715
1.059	1.26834	1.61514	0.78528	1.27343	0.05733	2.88349	0.34680
1.060	1.26996	1.61641	0.78566	1.27281	0.05827	2.88637	0.34646
1.061	1.27157	1.61768	0.78605	1.27219	0.05921	2.88926	0.34611
1.062	1.27319	1.61896	0.78643	1.27157	0.06015	2.89215	0.34576
1.063	1.27481	1.62023	0.78681	1.27096	0.06110	2.89504	0.34542
1.064	1.27643	1.62151	0.78719	1.27034	0.06204	2.89794	0.34507
1.065	1.27806	1.62278	0.78757	1.26973	0.06297	2.90084	0.34473
1.066	1.27968	1.62406	0.78795	1.26912	0.06391	2.90374	0.34438
1.067	1.28130	1.62534	0.78833	1.26851	0.06485	2.90665	0.34404
1.068	1.28293	1.62662	0.78871	1.26790	0.06579	2.90955	0.34370
1.069	1.28456	1.62791	0.78908	1.26729	0.06672	2.91247	0.34335
1.070	1.28619	1.62919	0.78946	1.26669	0.06766	2.91538	0.34301
1.071	1.28782	1.63048	0.78984	1.26608	0.06859	2.91830	0.34267
1.072	1.28945	1.63177	0.79021	1.26548	0.06953	2.92122	0.34232
1.073	1.29108	1.63306	0.79059	1.26488	0.07046	2.92414	0.34198
1.074	1.29271	1.63435	0.79096	1.26428	0.07139	2.92706	0.34164
1.075	1.29435	1.63565	0.79134	1.26368	0.07232	2.92999	0.34130
1.076	1.29598	1.63694	0.79171	1.26309	0.07325	2.93292	0.34096
1.077	1.29762	1.63824	0.79208	1.26249	0.07418	2.93586	0.34062
1.078	1.29926	1.63954	0.79246	1.26190	0.07511	2.93880	0.34028
1.079	1.30090	1.64084	0.79283	1.26131	0.07603	2.94174	0.33994
1.080	1.30254	1.64214	0.79320	1.26072	0.07696	2.94468	0.33960
1.081	1.30418	1.64344	0.79357	1.26013	0.07789	2.94763	0.33926
1.082	1.30583	1.64475	0.79394	1.25954	0.07881	2.95057	0.33892
1.083	1.30747	1.64605	0.79431	1.25896	0.07973	2.95353	0.33858
1.084	1.30912	1.64736	0.79468	1.25837	0.08066	2.95648	0.33824
1.085	1.31077	1.64867	0.79505	1.25779	0.08158	2.95944	0.33790
1.086	1.31242	1.64998	0.79541	1.25721	0.08250	2.96240	0.33756
1.087	1.31407	1.65130	0.79578	1.25663	0.08342	2.96536	0.33723
1.088	1.31572	1.65261	0.79615	1.25605	0.08434	2.96833	0.33689
1.089	1.31737	1.65393	0.79651	1.25547	0.08526	2.97130	0.33655
1.090	1.31903	1.65525	0.79688	1.25490	0.08618	2.97427	0.33622
1.091	1.32068	1.65657	0.79724	1.25432	0.08709	2.97725	0.33588
1.092	1.32234	1.65789	0.79761	1.25375	0.08801	2.98023	0.33554
1.093	1.32400	1.65921	0.79797	1.25318	0.08893	2.98321	0.33521
1.094	1.32566	1.66053	0.79833	1.25261	0.08984	2.98619	0.33487
1.095	1.32732	1.66186	0.79870	1.25204	0.09075	2.98918	0.33454
1.096	1.32898	1.66319	0.79906	1.25147	0.09167	2.99217	0.33421
1.097	1.33065	1.66452	0.79942	1.25091	0.09258	2.99517	0.33387
1.098	1.33231	1.66585	0.79978	1.25034	0.09349	2.99816	0.33354
1.099	1.33398	1.66718	0.80014	1.24978	0.09440	3.00116	0.33320
1.100	1.33565	1.66852	0.80050	1.24922	0.09531	3.00417	0.33287

x	sinh x	cosh x	tanh x	coth x	ln x	e^x	e^-x

x	sinh x	cosh x	tanh x	coth x	ln x	e^x	e^-x
1·100	1·33565	1·66852	0·80050	1·24922	0·09531	3·00417	0·33287
1·101	1·33732	1·66986	0·80086	1·24866	0·09622	3·00717	0·33254
1·102	1·33899	1·67119	0·80122	1·24810	0·09713	3·01018	0·33221
1·103	1·34066	1·67253	0·80157	1·24755	0·09803	3·01319	0·33187
1·104	1·34233	1·67387	0·80193	1·24699	0·09894	3·01621	0·33154
1·105	1·34401	1·67522	0·80229	1·24644	0·09985	3·01922	0·33121
1·106	1·34568	1·67656	0·80264	1·24588	0·10075	3·02225	0·33088
1·107	1·34736	1·67791	0·80300	1·24533	0·10165	3·02527	0·33055
1·108	1·34904	1·67926	0·80335	1·24478	0·10256	3·02830	0·33022
1·109	1·35072	1·68061	0·80371	1·24423	0·10346	3·03133	0·32989
1·110	1·35240	1·68196	0·80406	1·24368	0·10436	3·03436	0·32956
1·111	1·35408	1·68331	0·80442	1·24314	0·10526	3·03739	0·32923
1·112	1·35577	1·68467	0·80477	1·24259	0·10616	3·04043	0·32890
1·113	1·35745	1·68602	0·80512	1·24205	0·10706	3·04348	0·32857
1·114	1·35914	1·68738	0·80547	1·24151	0·10796	3·04652	0·32824
1·115	1·36083	1·68874	0·80582	1·24097	0·10885	3·04957	0·32792
1·116	1·36252	1·69010	0·80617	1·24043	0·10975	3·05262	0·32759
1·117	1·36421	1·69147	0·80652	1·23989	0·11065	3·05567	0·32726
1·118	1·36590	1·69283	0·80687	1·23935	0·11154	3·05873	0·32693
1·119	1·36759	1·69420	0·80722	1·23882	0·11244	3·06179	0·32661
1·120	1·36929	1·69557	0·80757	1·23828	0·11333	3·06485	0·32628
1·121	1·37098	1·69694	0·80792	1·23775	0·11422	3·06792	0·32595
1·122	1·37268	1·69831	0·80826	1·23722	0·11511	3·07099	0·32563
1·123	1·37438	1·69968	0·80861	1·23669	0·11600	3·07406	0·32530
1·124	1·37608	1·70106	0·80896	1·23616	0·11689	3·07714	0·32498
1·125	1·37778	1·70243	0·80930	1·23563	0·11778	3·08022	0·32465
1·126	1·37949	1·70381	0·80965	1·23511	0·11867	3·08330	0·32433
1·127	1·38119	1·70519	0·80999	1·23458	0·11956	3·08638	0·32400
1·128	1·38290	1·70658	0·81033	1·23406	0·12045	3·08947	0·32368
1·129	1·38460	1·70796	0·81068	1·23354	0·12133	3·09256	0·32336
1·130	1·38631	1·70934	0·81102	1·23302	0·12222	3·09566	0·32303
1·131	1·38802	1·71073	0·81136	1·23250	0·12310	3·09875	0·32271
1·132	1·38973	1·71212	0·81170	1·23198	0·12399	3·10185	0·32239
1·133	1·39145	1·71351	0·81204	1·23146	0·12487	3·10496	0·32207
1·134	1·39316	1·71490	0·81238	1·23095	0·12575	3·10806	0·32174
1·135	1·39488	1·71630	0·81272	1·23043	0·12663	3·11117	0·32142
1·136	1·39659	1·71769	0·81306	1·22992	0·12751	3·11429	0·32110
1·137	1·39831	1·71909	0·81340	1·22941	0·12839	3·11740	0·32078
1·138	1·40003	1·72049	0·81374	1·22889	0·12927	3·12052	0·32046
1·139	1·40175	1·72189	0·81408	1·22838	0·13015	3·12364	0·32014
1·140	1·40347	1·72329	0·81441	1·22788	0·13103	3·12677	0·31982
1·141	1·40520	1·72470	0·81475	1·22737	0·13191	3·12990	0·31950
1·142	1·40692	1·72610	0·81509	1·22686	0·13278	3·13303	0·31918
1·143	1·40865	1·72751	0·81542	1·22636	0·13366	3·13616	0·31886
1·144	1·41038	1·72892	0·81576	1·22586	0·13453	3·13930	0·31854
1·145	1·41211	1·73033	0·81609	1·22535	0·13540	3·14244	0·31822
1·146	1·41384	1·73175	0·81642	1·22485	0·13628	3·14559	0·31791
1·147	1·41557	1·73316	0·81676	1·22435	0·13715	3·14873	0·31759
1·148	1·41731	1·73458	0·81709	1·22385	0·13802	3·15188	0·31727
1·149	1·41904	1·73599	0·81742	1·22336	0·13889	3·15504	0·31695
1·150	1·42078	1·73741	0·81775	1·22286	0·13976	3·15819	0·31664

x	sinh x	cosh x	tanh x	coth x	ln x	e^x	e^-x

x	sinh x	cosh x	tanh x	coth x	ln x	eˣ	e⁻ˣ
1.150	1.42078	1.73741	0.81775	1.22286	0.13976	3.15819	0.31664
1.151	1.42252	1.73884	0.81809	1.22237	0.14063	3.16135	0.31632
1.152	1.42426	1.74026	0.81842	1.22187	0.14150	3.16452	0.31600
1.153	1.42600	1.74168	0.81875	1.22138	0.14237	3.16768	0.31569
1.154	1.42774	1.74311	0.81907	1.22089	0.14323	3.17085	0.31537
1.155	1.42948	1.74454	0.81940	1.22040	0.14410	3.17402	0.31506
1.156	1.43123	1.74597	0.81973	1.21991	0.14497	3.17720	0.31474
1.157	1.43297	1.74740	0.82006	1.21942	0.14583	3.18038	0.31443
1.158	1.43472	1.74884	0.82039	1.21894	0.14669	3.18356	0.31411
1.159	1.43647	1.75027	0.82071	1.21845	0.14756	3.18674	0.31380
1.160	1.43822	1.75171	0.82104	1.21797	0.14842	3.18993	0.31349
1.161	1.43998	1.75315	0.82137	1.21748	0.14928	3.19312	0.31317
1.162	1.44173	1.75459	0.82169	1.21700	0.15014	3.19632	0.31286
1.163	1.44349	1.75603	0.82202	1.21652	0.15100	3.19952	0.31255
1.164	1.44524	1.75748	0.82234	1.21604	0.15186	3.20272	0.31223
1.165	1.44700	1.75892	0.82266	1.21557	0.15272	3.20592	0.31192
1.166	1.44876	1.76037	0.82299	1.21509	0.15358	3.20913	0.31161
1.167	1.45052	1.76182	0.82331	1.21461	0.15444	3.21234	0.31130
1.168	1.45228	1.76327	0.82363	1.21414	0.15529	3.21556	0.31099
1.169	1.45405	1.76472	0.82395	1.21366	0.15615	3.21877	0.31068
1.170	1.45581	1.76618	0.82427	1.21319	0.15700	3.22199	0.31037
1.171	1.45758	1.76764	0.82459	1.21272	0.15786	3.22522	0.31006
1.172	1.45935	1.76909	0.82491	1.21225	0.15871	3.22844	0.30975
1.173	1.46112	1.77056	0.82523	1.21178	0.15956	3.23167	0.30944
1.174	1.46289	1.77202	0.82555	1.21131	0.16042	3.23491	0.30913
1.175	1.46466	1.77348	0.82587	1.21085	0.16127	3.23814	0.30882
1.176	1.46644	1.77495	0.82619	1.21038	0.16212	3.24138	0.30851
1.177	1.46821	1.77641	0.82650	1.20992	0.16297	3.24463	0.30820
1.178	1.46999	1.77788	0.82682	1.20945	0.16382	3.24787	0.30789
1.179	1.47177	1.77935	0.82714	1.20899	0.16467	3.25112	0.30759
1.180	1.47355	1.78083	0.82745	1.20853	0.16551	3.25437	0.30728
1.181	1.47533	1.78230	0.82777	1.20807	0.16636	3.25763	0.30697
1.182	1.47711	1.78378	0.82808	1.20761	0.16721	3.26089	0.30666
1.183	1.47890	1.78526	0.82840	1.20715	0.16805	3.26415	0.30636
1.184	1.48068	1.78673	0.82871	1.20670	0.16890	3.26742	0.30605
1.185	1.48247	1.78822	0.82902	1.20624	0.16974	3.27069	0.30575
1.186	1.48426	1.78970	0.82933	1.20579	0.17059	3.27396	0.30544
1.187	1.48605	1.79119	0.82965	1.20533	0.17143	3.27723	0.30514
1.188	1.48784	1.79267	0.82996	1.20488	0.17227	3.28051	0.30483
1.189	1.48964	1.79416	0.83027	1.20443	0.17311	3.28380	0.30453
1.190	1.49143	1.79565	0.83058	1.20398	0.17395	3.28708	0.30422
1.191	1.49323	1.79714	0.83089	1.20353	0.17479	3.29037	0.30392
1.192	1.49502	1.79864	0.83120	1.20308	0.17563	3.29366	0.30361
1.193	1.49682	1.80013	0.83151	1.20264	0.17647	3.29696	0.30331
1.194	1.49862	1.80163	0.83182	1.20219	0.17731	3.30026	0.30301
1.195	1.50043	1.80313	0.83212	1.20175	0.17815	3.30356	0.30270
1.196	1.50223	1.80463	0.83243	1.20130	0.17898	3.30686	0.30240
1.197	1.50404	1.80614	0.83274	1.20086	0.17982	3.31017	0.30210
1.198	1.50584	1.80764	0.83304	1.20042	0.18065	3.31348	0.30180
1.199	1.50765	1.80915	0.83335	1.19998	0.18149	3.31680	0.30150
1.200	1.50946	1.81066	0.83365	1.19954	0.18232	3.32012	0.30119

x	sinh x	cosh x	tanh x	coth x	ln x	eˣ	e⁻ˣ

x	sinh x	cosh x	tanh x	coth x	ln x	e^x	e^-x
1.200	1.50946	1.81066	0.83365	1.19954	0.18232	3.32012	0.30119
1.201	1.51127	1.81217	0.83396	1.19910	0.18315	3.32344	0.30089
1.202	1.51309	1.81368	0.83426	1.19866	0.18399	3.32676	0.30059
1.203	1.51490	1.81519	0.83457	1.19823	0.18482	3.33009	0.30029
1.204	1.51672	1.81671	0.83487	1.19779	0.18565	3.33342	0.29999
1.205	1.51853	1.81823	0.83517	1.19736	0.18648	3.33676	0.29969
1.206	1.52035	1.81974	0.83548	1.19692	0.18731	3.34010	0.29939
1.207	1.52217	1.82127	0.83578	1.19649	0.18814	3.34344	0.29909
1.208	1.52400	1.82279	0.83608	1.19606	0.18897	3.34678	0.29879
1.209	1.52582	1.82431	0.83638	1.19563	0.18979	3.35013	0.29850
1.210	1.52764	1.82584	0.83668	1.19520	0.19062	3.35348	0.29820
1.211	1.52947	1.82737	0.83698	1.19477	0.19145	3.35684	0.29790
1.212	1.53130	1.82890	0.83728	1.19435	0.19227	3.36020	0.29760
1.213	1.53313	1.83043	0.83758	1.19392	0.19310	3.36356	0.29730
1.214	1.53496	1.83197	0.83788	1.19349	0.19392	3.36693	0.29701
1.215	1.53679	1.83350	0.83817	1.19307	0.19474	3.37029	0.29671
1.216	1.53863	1.83504	0.83847	1.19265	0.19557	3.37367	0.29641
1.217	1.54046	1.83658	0.83877	1.19223	0.19639	3.37704	0.29612
1.218	1.54230	1.83812	0.83906	1.19181	0.19721	3.38042	0.29582
1.219	1.54414	1.83966	0.83936	1.19139	0.19803	3.38380	0.29553
1.220	1.54598	1.84121	0.83965	1.19097	0.19885	3.38719	0.29523
1.221	1.54782	1.84276	0.83995	1.19055	0.19967	3.39058	0.29494
1.222	1.54966	1.84430	0.84024	1.19013	0.20049	3.39397	0.29464
1.223	1.55151	1.84586	0.84054	1.18972	0.20131	3.39736	0.29435
1.224	1.55336	1.84741	0.84083	1.18930	0.20212	3.40076	0.29405
1.225	1.55520	1.84896	0.84112	1.18889	0.20294	3.40417	0.29376
1.226	1.55705	1.85052	0.84142	1.18847	0.20376	3.40757	0.29346
1.227	1.55891	1.85208	0.84171	1.18806	0.20457	3.41098	0.29317
1.228	1.56076	1.85364	0.84200	1.18765	0.20539	3.41439	0.29288
1.229	1.56261	1.85520	0.84229	1.18724	0.20620	3.41781	0.29259
1.230	1.56447	1.85676	0.84258	1.18683	0.20701	3.42123	0.29229
1.231	1.56633	1.85833	0.84287	1.18642	0.20783	3.42465	0.29200
1.232	1.56819	1.85989	0.84316	1.18602	0.20864	3.42808	0.29171
1.233	1.57005	1.86146	0.84345	1.18561	0.20945	3.43151	0.29142
1.234	1.57191	1.86303	0.84374	1.18521	0.21026	3.43494	0.29113
1.235	1.57377	1.86461	0.84402	1.18480	0.21107	3.43838	0.29083
1.236	1.57564	1.86618	0.84431	1.18440	0.21188	3.44182	0.29054
1.237	1.57750	1.86776	0.84460	1.18400	0.21269	3.44526	0.29025
1.238	1.57937	1.86934	0.84488	1.18359	0.21350	3.44871	0.28996
1.239	1.58124	1.87092	0.84517	1.18319	0.21430	3.45216	0.28967
1.240	1.58311	1.87250	0.84546	1.18279	0.21511	3.45561	0.28938
1.241	1.58499	1.87408	0.84574	1.18240	0.21592	3.45907	0.28909
1.242	1.58686	1.87567	0.84603	1.18200	0.21672	3.46253	0.28881
1.243	1.58874	1.87726	0.84631	1.18160	0.21753	3.46600	0.28852
1.244	1.59062	1.87885	0.84659	1.18121	0.21833	3.46946	0.28823
1.245	1.59250	1.88044	0.84688	1.18081	0.21914	3.47293	0.28794
1.246	1.59438	1.88203	0.84716	1.18042	0.21994	3.47641	0.28765
1.247	1.59626	1.88363	0.84744	1.18002	0.22074	3.47989	0.28737
1.248	1.59815	1.88522	0.84772	1.17963	0.22154	3.48337	0.28708
1.249	1.60003	1.88682	0.84800	1.17924	0.22234	3.48685	0.28679
1.250	1.60192	1.88842	0.84828	1.17885	0.22314	3.49034	0.28650
x	sinh x	cosh x	tanh x	coth x	ln x	e^x	e^-x

x	sinh x	cosh x	tanh x	coth x	ln x	e^x	e^-x
1.250	1.60192	1.88842	0.84828	1.17885	0.22314	3.49034	0.28650
1.251	1.60381	1.89003	0.84856	1.17846	0.22394	3.49384	0.28622
1.252	1.60570	1.89163	0.84884	1.17807	0.22474	3.49733	0.28593
1.253	1.60759	1.89324	0.84912	1.17769	0.22554	3.50083	0.28565
1.254	1.60949	1.89485	0.84940	1.17730	0.22634	3.50433	0.28536
1.255	1.61138	1.89646	0.84968	1.17691	0.22714	3.50784	0.28508
1.256	1.61328	1.89807	0.84996	1.17653	0.22793	3.51135	0.28479
1.257	1.61518	1.89968	0.85023	1.17615	0.22873	3.51486	0.28451
1.258	1.61708	1.90130	0.85051	1.17576	0.22952	3.51838	0.28422
1.259	1.61898	1.90292	0.85079	1.17538	0.23032	3.52190	0.28394
1.260	1.62088	1.90454	0.85106	1.17500	0.23111	3.52542	0.28365
1.261	1.62279	1.90616	0.85134	1.17462	0.23191	3.52895	0.28337
1.262	1.62470	1.90778	0.85161	1.17424	0.23270	3.53248	0.28309
1.263	1.62660	1.90941	0.85189	1.17386	0.23349	3.53601	0.28280
1.264	1.62851	1.91104	0.85216	1.17348	0.23428	3.53955	0.28252
1.265	1.63043	1.91267	0.85244	1.17311	0.23507	3.54309	0.28224
1.266	1.63234	1.91430	0.85271	1.17273	0.23586	3.54664	0.28196
1.267	1.63426	1.91593	0.85298	1.17236	0.23665	3.55019	0.28168
1.268	1.63617	1.91757	0.85325	1.17198	0.23744	3.55374	0.28139
1.269	1.63809	1.91920	0.85353	1.17161	0.23823	3.55729	0.28111
1.270	1.64001	1.92084	0.85380	1.17124	0.23902	3.56085	0.28083
1.271	1.64193	1.92248	0.85407	1.17087	0.23980	3.56442	0.28055
1.272	1.64386	1.92413	0.85434	1.17050	0.24059	3.56798	0.28027
1.273	1.64578	1.92577	0.85461	1.17013	0.24138	3.57155	0.27999
1.274	1.64771	1.92742	0.85488	1.16976	0.24216	3.57512	0.27971
1.275	1.64964	1.92907	0.85515	1.16939	0.24295	3.57870	0.27943
1.276	1.65157	1.93072	0.85542	1.16902	0.24373	3.58228	0.27915
1.277	1.65350	1.93237	0.85568	1.16866	0.24451	3.58587	0.27887
1.278	1.65543	1.93402	0.85595	1.16829	0.24530	3.58945	0.27859
1.279	1.65736	1.93568	0.85622	1.16793	0.24608	3.59304	0.27832
1.280	1.65930	1.93734	0.85648	1.16756	0.24686	3.59664	0.27804
1.281	1.66124	1.93900	0.85675	1.16720	0.24764	3.60024	0.27776
1.282	1.66318	1.94066	0.85702	1.16684	0.24842	3.60384	0.27748
1.283	1.66512	1.94233	0.85728	1.16648	0.24920	3.60745	0.27720
1.284	1.66706	1.94399	0.85755	1.16612	0.24998	3.61106	0.27693
1.285	1.66901	1.94566	0.85781	1.16576	0.25076	3.61467	0.27665
1.286	1.67096	1.94733	0.85808	1.16540	0.25154	3.61828	0.27637
1.287	1.67290	1.94900	0.85834	1.16504	0.25231	3.62190	0.27610
1.288	1.67485	1.95068	0.85860	1.16468	0.25309	3.62553	0.27582
1.289	1.67680	1.95235	0.85886	1.16433	0.25387	3.62916	0.27555
1.290	1.67876	1.95403	0.85913	1.16397	0.25464	3.63279	0.27527
1.291	1.68071	1.95571	0.85939	1.16362	0.25542	3.63642	0.27500
1.292	1.68267	1.95739	0.85965	1.16326	0.25619	3.64006	0.27472
1.293	1.68463	1.95907	0.85991	1.16291	0.25697	3.64370	0.27445
1.294	1.68659	1.96076	0.86017	1.16256	0.25774	3.64735	0.27417
1.295	1.68855	1.96245	0.86043	1.16221	0.25851	3.65100	0.27390
1.296	1.69051	1.96414	0.86069	1.16186	0.25928	3.65465	0.27362
1.297	1.69248	1.96583	0.86095	1.16151	0.26005	3.65831	0.27335
1.298	1.69444	1.96752	0.86121	1.16116	0.26082	3.66197	0.27308
1.299	1.69641	1.96922	0.86147	1.16081	0.26159	3.66563	0.27280
1.300	1.69838	1.97091	0.86172	1.16047	0.26236	3.66930	0.27253

x	sinh x	cosh x	tanh x	coth x	ln x	e^x	e^-x

x	sinh x	cosh x	tanh x	coth x	ln x	eˣ	e⁻ˣ
1.300	1.69838	1.97091	0.86172	1.16047	0.26236	3.66930	0.27253
1.301	1.70035	1.97261	0.86198	1.16012	0.26313	3.67297	0.27226
1.302	1.70233	1.97431	0.86224	1.15977	0.26390	3.67664	0.27199
1.303	1.70430	1.97602	0.86249	1.15943	0.26467	3.68032	0.27172
1.304	1.70628	1.97772	0.86275	1.15909	0.26544	3.68400	0.27144
1.305	1.70826	1.97943	0.86300	1.15874	0.26620	3.68769	0.27117
1.306	1.71024	1.98114	0.86326	1.15840	0.26697	3.69138	0.27090
1.307	1.71222	1.98285	0.86351	1.15806	0.26773	3.69507	0.27063
1.308	1.71420	1.98456	0.86377	1.15772	0.26850	3.69877	0.27036
1.309	1.71619	1.98628	0.86402	1.15738	0.26926	3.70247	0.27009
1.310	1.71818	1.98800	0.86428	1.15704	0.27003	3.70617	0.26982
1.311	1.72017	1.98972	0.86453	1.15670	0.27079	3.70988	0.26955
1.312	1.72216	1.99144	0.86478	1.15636	0.27155	3.71359	0.26928
1.313	1.72415	1.99316	0.86503	1.15603	0.27231	3.71731	0.26901
1.314	1.72614	1.99489	0.86528	1.15569	0.27308	3.72103	0.26874
1.315	1.72814	1.99661	0.86554	1.15535	0.27384	3.72475	0.26847
1.316	1.73014	1.99834	0.86579	1.15502	0.27460	3.72848	0.26821
1.317	1.73214	2.00007	0.86604	1.15469	0.27536	3.73221	0.26794
1.318	1.73414	2.00181	0.86629	1.15435	0.27612	3.73594	0.26767
1.319	1.73614	2.00354	0.86654	1.15402	0.27687	3.73968	0.26740
1.320	1.73814	2.00528	0.86678	1.15369	0.27763	3.74342	0.26714
1.321	1.74015	2.00702	0.86703	1.15336	0.27839	3.74717	0.26687
1.322	1.74216	2.00876	0.86728	1.15303	0.27915	3.75092	0.26660
1.323	1.74417	2.01050	0.86753	1.15270	0.27990	3.75467	0.26634
1.324	1.74618	2.01225	0.86778	1.15237	0.28066	3.75843	0.26607
1.325	1.74819	2.01399	0.86802	1.15204	0.28141	3.76219	0.26580
1.326	1.75021	2.01574	0.86827	1.15172	0.28217	3.76595	0.26554
1.327	1.75222	2.01749	0.86851	1.15139	0.28292	3.76972	0.26527
1.328	1.75424	2.01925	0.86876	1.15107	0.28367	3.77349	0.26501
1.329	1.75626	2.02100	0.86900	1.15074	0.28443	3.77726	0.26474
1.330	1.75828	2.02276	0.86925	1.15042	0.28518	3.78104	0.26448
1.331	1.76031	2.02452	0.86949	1.15009	0.28593	3.78483	0.26421
1.332	1.76233	2.02628	0.86974	1.14977	0.28668	3.78861	0.26395
1.333	1.76436	2.02804	0.86998	1.14945	0.28743	3.79240	0.26369
1.334	1.76639	2.02981	0.87022	1.14913	0.28818	3.79620	0.26342
1.335	1.76842	2.03158	0.87047	1.14881	0.28893	3.80000	0.26316
1.336	1.77045	2.03335	0.87071	1.14849	0.28968	3.80380	0.26290
1.337	1.77249	2.03512	0.87095	1.14817	0.29043	3.80760	0.26263
1.338	1.77452	2.03689	0.87119	1.14785	0.29118	3.81141	0.26237
1.339	1.77656	2.03867	0.87143	1.14754	0.29192	3.81523	0.26211
1.340	1.77860	2.04044	0.87167	1.14722	0.29267	3.81904	0.26185
1.341	1.78064	2.04222	0.87191	1.14690	0.29342	3.82286	0.26158
1.342	1.78268	2.04401	0.87215	1.14659	0.29416	3.82669	0.26132
1.343	1.78473	2.04579	0.87239	1.14628	0.29491	3.83052	0.26106
1.344	1.78677	2.04758	0.87263	1.14596	0.29565	3.83435	0.26080
1.345	1.78882	2.04936	0.87287	1.14565	0.29639	3.83819	0.26054
1.346	1.79087	2.05115	0.87311	1.14534	0.29714	3.84203	0.26028
1.347	1.79293	2.05294	0.87334	1.14503	0.29788	3.84587	0.26002
1.348	1.79498	2.05474	0.87358	1.14471	0.29862	3.84972	0.25976
1.349	1.79704	2.05653	0.87382	1.14440	0.29936	3.85357	0.25950
1.350	1.79909	2.05833	0.87405	1.14410	0.30010	3.85743	0.25924
x	sinh x	cosh x	tanh x	coth x	ln x	eˣ	e⁻ˣ

x	sinh x	cosh x	tanh x	coth x	ln x	eˣ	e⁻ˣ
1.350	1.79909	2.05833	0.87405	1.14410	0.30010	3.85743	0.25924
1.351	1.80115	2.06013	0.87429	1.14379	0.30085	3.86128	0.25898
1.352	1.80321	2.06194	0.87452	1.14348	0.30158	3.86515	0.25872
1.353	1.80528	2.06374	0.87476	1.14317	0.30232	3.86902	0.25846
1.354	1.80734	2.06555	0.87499	1.14286	0.30306	3.87289	0.25821
1.355	1.80941	2.06735	0.87523	1.14256	0.30380	3.87676	0.25795
1.356	1.81148	2.06916	0.87546	1.14225	0.30454	3.88064	0.25769
1.357	1.81355	2.07098	0.87570	1.14195	0.30528	3.88452	0.25743
1.358	1.81562	2.07279	0.87593	1.14165	0.30601	3.88841	0.25717
1.359	1.81769	2.07461	0.87616	1.14134	0.30675	3.89230	0.25692
1.360	1.81977	2.07643	0.87639	1.14104	0.30748	3.89619	0.25666
1.361	1.82184	2.07825	0.87662	1.14074	0.30822	3.90009	0.25640
1.362	1.82392	2.08007	0.87686	1.14044	0.30895	3.90399	0.25615
1.363	1.82600	2.08190	0.87709	1.14014	0.30969	3.90790	0.25589
1.364	1.82809	2.08372	0.87732	1.13984	0.31042	3.91181	0.25564
1.365	1.83017	2.08555	0.87755	1.13954	0.31115	3.91572	0.25538
1.366	1.83226	2.08738	0.87778	1.13924	0.31189	3.91964	0.25513
1.367	1.83435	2.08922	0.87801	1.13894	0.31262	3.92356	0.25487
1.368	1.83644	2.09105	0.87824	1.13865	0.31335	3.92749	0.25462
1.369	1.83853	2.09289	0.87846	1.13835	0.31408	3.93142	0.25436
1.370	1.84062	2.09473	0.87869	1.13805	0.31481	3.93535	0.25411
1.371	1.84272	2.09657	0.87892	1.13776	0.31554	3.93929	0.25385
1.372	1.84482	2.09841	0.87915	1.13747	0.31627	3.94323	0.25360
1.373	1.84691	2.10026	0.87937	1.13717	0.31700	3.94717	0.25335
1.374	1.84902	2.10211	0.87960	1.13688	0.31773	3.95112	0.25309
1.375	1.85112	2.10396	0.87983	1.13659	0.31845	3.95508	0.25284
1.376	1.85322	2.10581	0.88005	1.13630	0.31918	3.95903	0.25259
1.377	1.85533	2.10766	0.88028	1.13601	0.31991	3.96299	0.25233
1.378	1.85744	2.10952	0.88050	1.13571	0.32063	3.96696	0.25208
1.379	1.85955	2.11138	0.88073	1.13543	0.32136	3.97093	0.25183
1.380	1.86166	2.11324	0.88095	1.13514	0.32208	3.97490	0.25158
1.381	1.86378	2.11510	0.88117	1.13485	0.32281	3.97888	0.25133
1.382	1.86589	2.11697	0.88140	1.13456	0.32353	3.98286	0.25108
1.383	1.86801	2.11883	0.88162	1.13427	0.32426	3.98684	0.25082
1.384	1.87013	2.12070	0.88184	1.13399	0.32498	3.99083	0.25057
1.385	1.87225	2.12257	0.88207	1.13370	0.32570	3.99483	0.25032
1.386	1.87437	2.12445	0.88229	1.13342	0.32642	3.99882	0.25007
1.387	1.87650	2.12632	0.88251	1.13313	0.32714	4.00282	0.24982
1.388	1.87863	2.12820	0.88273	1.13285	0.32786	4.00683	0.24957
1.389	1.88076	2.13008	0.88295	1.13257	0.32858	4.01084	0.24932
1.390	1.88289	2.13196	0.88317	1.13228	0.32930	4.01485	0.24908
1.391	1.88502	2.13385	0.88339	1.13200	0.33002	4.01887	0.24883
1.392	1.88716	2.13573	0.88361	1.13172	0.33074	4.02289	0.24858
1.393	1.88929	2.13762	0.88383	1.13144	0.33146	4.02691	0.24833
1.394	1.89143	2.13951	0.88405	1.13116	0.33218	4.03094	0.24808
1.395	1.89357	2.14140	0.88427	1.13088	0.33289	4.03497	0.24783
1.396	1.89571	2.14330	0.88448	1.13060	0.33361	4.03901	0.24759
1.397	1.89786	2.14520	0.88470	1.13032	0.33433	4.04305	0.24734
1.398	1.90000	2.14709	0.88492	1.13005	0.33504	4.04710	0.24709
1.399	1.90215	2.14900	0.88514	1.12977	0.33576	4.05115	0.24684
1.400	1.90430	2.15090	0.88535	1.12949	0.33647	4.05520	0.24660
x	sinh x	cosh x	tanh x	coth x	ln x	eˣ	e⁻ˣ

x	sinh x	cosh x	tanh x	coth x	ln x	e^x	e^-x
1.400	1.90430	2.15090	0.88535	1.12949	0.33647	4.05520	0.24660
1.401	1.90645	2.15280	0.88557	1.12922	0.33719	4.05926	0.24635
1.402	1.90861	2.15471	0.88578	1.12894	0.33790	4.06332	0.24610
1.403	1.91076	2.15662	0.88600	1.12867	0.33861	4.06738	0.24586
1.404	1.91292	2.15853	0.88621	1.12840	0.33933	4.07145	0.24561
1.405	1.91508	2.16045	0.88643	1.12812	0.34004	4.07553	0.24537
1.406	1.91724	2.16236	0.88664	1.12785	0.34075	4.07960	0.24512
1.407	1.91940	2.16428	0.88686	1.12758	0.34146	4.08369	0.24488
1.408	1.92157	2.16620	0.88707	1.12731	0.34217	4.08777	0.24463
1.409	1.92374	2.16812	0.88728	1.12704	0.34288	4.09186	0.24439
1.410	1.92591	2.17005	0.88749	1.12677	0.34359	4.09596	0.24414
1.411	1.92808	2.17198	0.88771	1.12650	0.34430	4.10005	0.24390
1.412	1.93025	2.17391	0.88792	1.12623	0.34501	4.10416	0.24366
1.413	1.93242	2.17584	0.88813	1.12596	0.34572	4.10826	0.24341
1.414	1.93460	2.17777	0.88834	1.12569	0.34642	4.11237	0.24317
1.415	1.93678	2.17971	0.88855	1.12543	0.34713	4.11649	0.24293
1.416	1.93896	2.18164	0.88876	1.12516	0.34784	4.12061	0.24268
1.417	1.94114	2.18358	0.88897	1.12490	0.34854	4.12473	0.24244
1.418	1.94333	2.18553	0.88918	1.12463	0.34925	4.12885	0.24220
1.419	1.94551	2.18747	0.88939	1.12437	0.34995	4.13299	0.24196
1.420	1.94770	2.18942	0.88960	1.12410	0.35066	4.13712	0.24171
1.421	1.94989	2.19137	0.88981	1.12384	0.35136	4.14126	0.24147
1.422	1.95209	2.19332	0.89002	1.12358	0.35206	4.14540	0.24123
1.423	1.95428	2.19527	0.89022	1.12331	0.35277	4.14955	0.24099
1.424	1.95648	2.19723	0.89043	1.12305	0.35347	4.15370	0.24075
1.425	1.95867	2.19918	0.89064	1.12279	0.35417	4.15786	0.24051
1.426	1.96087	2.20114	0.89084	1.12253	0.35487	4.16202	0.24027
1.427	1.96308	2.20310	0.89105	1.12227	0.35557	4.16618	0.24003
1.428	1.96528	2.20507	0.89126	1.12201	0.35627	4.17035	0.23979
1.429	1.96749	2.20704	0.89146	1.12175	0.35697	4.17452	0.23955
1.430	1.96970	2.20900	0.89167	1.12150	0.35767	4.17870	0.23931
1.431	1.97191	2.21097	0.89187	1.12124	0.35837	4.18288	0.23907
1.432	1.97412	2.21295	0.89208	1.12098	0.35907	4.18706	0.23883
1.433	1.97633	2.21492	0.89228	1.12072	0.35977	4.19125	0.23859
1.434	1.97855	2.21690	0.89248	1.12047	0.36047	4.19545	0.23835
1.435	1.98076	2.21888	0.89269	1.12021	0.36116	4.19965	0.23812
1.436	1.98298	2.22086	0.89289	1.11996	0.36186	4.20385	0.23788
1.437	1.98521	2.22285	0.89309	1.11971	0.36256	4.20805	0.23764
1.438	1.98743	2.22483	0.89329	1.11945	0.36325	4.21226	0.23740
1.439	1.98966	2.22682	0.89350	1.11920	0.36395	4.21648	0.23716
1.440	1.99188	2.22881	0.89370	1.11895	0.36464	4.22070	0.23693
1.441	1.99411	2.23080	0.89390	1.11869	0.36534	4.22492	0.23669
1.442	1.99635	2.23280	0.89410	1.11844	0.36603	4.22915	0.23645
1.443	1.99858	2.23480	0.89430	1.11819	0.36672	4.23338	0.23622
1.444	2.00082	2.23680	0.89450	1.11794	0.36742	4.23761	0.23598
1.445	2.00305	2.23880	0.89470	1.11769	0.36811	4.24185	0.23575
1.446	2.00529	2.24080	0.89490	1.11744	0.36880	4.24610	0.23551
1.447	2.00753	2.24281	0.89510	1.11720	0.36949	4.25034	0.23528
1.448	2.00978	2.24482	0.89530	1.11695	0.37018	4.25460	0.23504
1.449	2.01202	2.24683	0.89549	1.11670	0.37087	4.25885	0.23480
1.450	2.01427	2.24884	0.89569	1.11645	0.37156	4.26311	0.23457

x	sinh x	cosh x	tanh x	coth x	ln x	e^x	e^-x

x	sinh x	cosh x	tanh x	coth x	ln x	e^x	e^{-x}
1.450	2.01427	2.24884	0.89569	1.11645	0.37156	4.26311	0.23457
1.451	2.01652	2.25086	0.89589	1.11621	0.37225	4.26738	0.23434
1.452	2.01877	2.25288	0.89609	1.11596	0.37294	4.27165	0.23410
1.453	2.02103	2.25490	0.89628	1.11572	0.37363	4.27592	0.23387
1.454	2.02328	2.25692	0.89648	1.11547	0.37432	4.28020	0.23363
1.455	2.02554	2.25894	0.89668	1.11523	0.37501	4.28448	0.23340
1.456	2.02780	2.26097	0.89687	1.11499	0.37569	4.28877	0.23317
1.457	2.03006	2.26300	0.89707	1.11474	0.37638	4.29306	0.23293
1.458	2.03233	2.26503	0.89726	1.11450	0.37707	4.29736	0.23270
1.459	2.03459	2.26706	0.89746	1.11426	0.37775	4.30166	0.23247
1.460	2.03686	2.26910	0.89765	1.11402	0.37844	4.30596	0.23224
1.461	2.03913	2.27114	0.89785	1.11378	0.37912	4.31027	0.23200
1.462	2.04140	2.27318	0.89804	1.11354	0.37981	4.31458	0.23177
1.463	2.04368	2.27522	0.89823	1.11330	0.38049	4.31890	0.23154
1.464	2.04595	2.27726	0.89843	1.11306	0.38117	4.32322	0.23131
1.465	2.04823	2.27931	0.89862	1.11282	0.38186	4.32754	0.23108
1.466	2.05051	2.28136	0.89881	1.11258	0.38254	4.33187	0.23085
1.467	2.05280	2.28341	0.89900	1.11234	0.38322	4.33621	0.23062
1.468	2.05508	2.28547	0.89920	1.11211	0.38390	4.34055	0.23039
1.469	2.05737	2.28752	0.89939	1.11187	0.38458	4.34489	0.23016
1.470	2.05965	2.28958	0.89958	1.11163	0.38526	4.34924	0.22993
1.471	2.06195	2.29164	0.89977	1.11140	0.38594	4.35359	0.22970
1.472	2.06424	2.29370	0.89996	1.11116	0.38662	4.35794	0.22947
1.473	2.06653	2.29577	0.90015	1.11093	0.38730	4.36230	0.22924
1.474	2.06883	2.29784	0.90034	1.11069	0.38798	4.36667	0.22901
1.475	2.07113	2.29991	0.90053	1.11046	0.38866	4.37104	0.22878
1.476	2.07343	2.30198	0.90072	1.11023	0.38934	4.37541	0.22855
1.477	2.07573	2.30405	0.90090	1.11000	0.39001	4.37979	0.22832
1.478	2.07804	2.30613	0.90109	1.10976	0.39069	4.38417	0.22809
1.479	2.08034	2.30821	0.90128	1.10953	0.39137	4.38855	0.22787
1.480	2.08265	2.31029	0.90147	1.10930	0.39204	4.39295	0.22764
1.481	2.08497	2.31238	0.90166	1.10907	0.39272	4.39734	0.22741
1.482	2.08728	2.31446	0.90184	1.10884	0.39339	4.40174	0.22718
1.483	2.08959	2.31655	0.90203	1.10861	0.39407	4.40614	0.22696
1.484	2.09191	2.31864	0.90221	1.10838	0.39474	4.41055	0.22673
1.485	2.09423	2.32073	0.90240	1.10816	0.39541	4.41497	0.22650
1.486	2.09655	2.32283	0.90259	1.10793	0.39609	4.41938	0.22628
1.487	2.09888	2.32493	0.90277	1.10770	0.39676	4.42380	0.22605
1.488	2.10120	2.32703	0.90296	1.10747	0.39743	4.42823	0.22582
1.489	2.10353	2.32913	0.90314	1.10725	0.39810	4.43266	0.22560
1.490	2.10586	2.33123	0.90332	1.10702	0.39878	4.43710	0.22537
1.491	2.10819	2.33334	0.90351	1.10680	0.39945	4.44153	0.22515
1.492	2.11053	2.33545	0.90369	1.10657	0.40012	4.44598	0.22492
1.493	2.11286	2.33756	0.90388	1.10635	0.40079	4.45043	0.22470
1.494	2.11520	2.33968	0.90406	1.10612	0.40146	4.45488	0.22447
1.495	2.11754	2.34179	0.90424	1.10590	0.40213	4.45934	0.22425
1.496	2.11989	2.34391	0.90442	1.10568	0.40279	4.46380	0.22402
1.497	2.12223	2.34603	0.90460	1.10546	0.40346	4.46826	0.22380
1.498	2.12458	2.34816	0.90479	1.10523	0.40413	4.47273	0.22358
1.499	2.12693	2.35028	0.90497	1.10501	0.40480	4.47721	0.22335
1.500	2.12928	2.35241	0.90515	1.10479	0.40547	4.48169	0.22313
x	sinh x	cosh x	tanh x	coth x	ln x	e^x	e^{-x}

x	sinh x	cosh x	tanh x	coth x	ln x	eˣ	e⁻ˣ
1.500	2.12928	2.35241	0.90515	1.10479	0.40547	4.48169	0.22313
1.501	2.13163	2.35454	0.90533	1.10457	0.40613	4.48617	0.22291
1.502	2.13399	2.35667	0.90551	1.10435	0.40680	4.49066	0.22268
1.503	2.13635	2.35881	0.90569	1.10413	0.40746	4.49515	0.22246
1.504	2.13871	2.36095	0.90587	1.10391	0.40813	4.49965	0.22224
1.505	2.14107	2.36309	0.90605	1.10369	0.40879	4.50415	0.22202
1.506	2.14343	2.36523	0.90623	1.10348	0.40946	4.50866	0.22180
1.507	2.14580	2.36737	0.90641	1.10326	0.41012	4.51317	0.22157
1.508	2.14817	2.36952	0.90658	1.10304	0.41078	4.51769	0.22135
1.509	2.15054	2.37167	0.90676	1.10283	0.41145	4.52221	0.22113
1.510	2.15291	2.37382	0.90694	1.10261	0.41211	4.52673	0.22091
1.511	2.15529	2.37597	0.90712	1.10239	0.41277	4.53126	0.22069
1.512	2.15766	2.37813	0.90729	1.10218	0.41343	4.53579	0.22047
1.513	2.16004	2.38029	0.90747	1.10196	0.41409	4.54033	0.22025
1.514	2.16242	2.38245	0.90765	1.10175	0.41476	4.54487	0.22003
1.515	2.16481	2.38461	0.90782	1.10154	0.41542	4.54942	0.21981
1.516	2.16719	2.38678	0.90800	1.10132	0.41608	4.55397	0.21959
1.517	2.16958	2.38895	0.90817	1.10111	0.41673	4.55853	0.21937
1.518	2.17197	2.39112	0.90835	1.10090	0.41739	4.56309	0.21915
1.519	2.17436	2.39329	0.90852	1.10069	0.41805	4.56766	0.21893
1.520	2.17676	2.39547	0.90870	1.10048	0.41871	4.57223	0.21871
1.521	2.17915	2.39765	0.90887	1.10027	0.41937	4.57680	0.21849
1.522	2.18155	2.39983	0.90905	1.10005	0.42003	4.58138	0.21827
1.523	2.18395	2.40201	0.90922	1.09984	0.42068	4.58596	0.21806
1.524	2.18636	2.40419	0.90939	1.09964	0.42134	4.59055	0.21784
1.525	2.18876	2.40638	0.90957	1.09943	0.42199	4.59514	0.21762
1.526	2.19117	2.40857	0.90974	1.09922	0.42265	4.59974	0.21740
1.527	2.19358	2.41076	0.90991	1.09901	0.42331	4.60434	0.21719
1.528	2.19599	2.41296	0.91008	1.09880	0.42396	4.60895	0.21697
1.529	2.19840	2.41516	0.91025	1.09860	0.42461	4.61356	0.21675
1.530	2.20082	2.41736	0.91042	1.09839	0.42527	4.61818	0.21654
1.531	2.20324	2.41956	0.91060	1.09818	0.42592	4.62280	0.21632
1.532	2.20566	2.42176	0.91077	1.09798	0.42657	4.62742	0.21610
1.533	2.20808	2.42397	0.91094	1.09777	0.42723	4.63205	0.21589
1.534	2.21051	2.42618	0.91111	1.09757	0.42788	4.63669	0.21567
1.535	2.21293	2.42839	0.91128	1.09736	0.42853	4.64133	0.21546
1.536	2.21536	2.43060	0.91145	1.09716	0.42918	4.64597	0.21524
1.537	2.21780	2.43282	0.91161	1.09695	0.42983	4.65062	0.21503
1.538	2.22023	2.43504	0.91178	1.09675	0.43048	4.65527	0.21481
1.539	2.22267	2.43726	0.91195	1.09655	0.43113	4.65993	0.21460
1.540	2.22510	2.43949	0.91212	1.09635	0.43178	4.66459	0.21438
1.541	2.22755	2.44171	0.91229	1.09614	0.43243	4.66926	0.21417
1.542	2.22999	2.44394	0.91246	1.09594	0.43308	4.67393	0.21395
1.543	2.23243	2.44617	0.91262	1.09574	0.43373	4.67861	0.21374
1.544	2.23488	2.44841	0.91279	1.09554	0.43438	4.68329	0.21353
1.545	2.23733	2.45064	0.91296	1.09534	0.43502	4.68797	0.21331
1.546	2.23978	2.45288	0.91312	1.09514	0.43567	4.69266	0.21310
1.547	2.24224	2.45512	0.91329	1.09494	0.43632	4.69736	0.21289
1.548	2.24469	2.45736	0.91345	1.09474	0.43696	4.70206	0.21267
1.549	2.24715	2.45961	0.91362	1.09455	0.43761	4.70676	0.21246
1.550	2.24961	2.46186	0.91379	1.09435	0.43825	4.71147	0.21225

x	sinh x	cosh x	tanh x	coth x	ln x	eˣ	e⁻ˣ

x	sinh x	cosh x	tanh x	coth x	ln x	e^x	e^-x
1.550	2.24961	2.46186	0.91379	1.09435	0.43825	4.71147	0.21225
1.551	2.25207	2.46411	0.91395	1.09415	0.43890	4.71618	0.21204
1.552	2.25454	2.46636	0.91411	1.09395	0.43954	4.72090	0.21182
1.553	2.25701	2.46862	0.91428	1.09376	0.44019	4.72563	0.21161
1.554	2.25948	2.47088	0.91444	1.09356	0.44083	4.73035	0.21140
1.555	2.26195	2.47314	0.91461	1.09337	0.44148	4.73509	0.21119
1.556	2.26442	2.47540	0.91477	1.09317	0.44212	4.73982	0.21098
1.557	2.26690	2.47767	0.91493	1.09298	0.44276	4.74457	0.21077
1.558	2.26938	2.47993	0.91510	1.09278	0.44340	4.74931	0.21056
1.559	2.27186	2.48221	0.91526	1.09259	0.44404	4.75406	0.21035
1.560	2.27434	2.48448	0.91542	1.09239	0.44469	4.75882	0.21014
1.561	2.27683	2.48675	0.91558	1.09220	0.44533	4.76358	0.20993
1.562	2.27932	2.48903	0.91574	1.09201	0.44597	4.76835	0.20972
1.563	2.28181	2.49131	0.91591	1.09182	0.44661	4.77312	0.20951
1.564	2.28430	2.49360	0.91607	1.09162	0.44725	4.77789	0.20930
1.565	2.28679	2.49588	0.91623	1.09143	0.44789	4.78267	0.20909
1.566	2.28929	2.49817	0.91639	1.09124	0.44852	4.78746	0.20888
1.567	2.29179	2.50046	0.91655	1.09105	0.44916	4.79225	0.20867
1.568	2.29429	2.50275	0.91671	1.09086	0.44980	4.79704	0.20846
1.569	2.29680	2.50505	0.91687	1.09067	0.45044	4.80184	0.20825
1.570	2.29930	2.50735	0.91703	1.09048	0.45108	4.80665	0.20805
1.571	2.30181	2.50965	0.91718	1.09029	0.45171	4.81146	0.20784
1.572	2.30432	2.51195	0.91734	1.09010	0.45235	4.81627	0.20763
1.573	2.30683	2.51426	0.91750	1.08992	0.45298	4.82109	0.20742
1.574	2.30935	2.51656	0.91766	1.08973	0.45362	4.82591	0.20721
1.575	2.31187	2.51887	0.91782	1.08954	0.45426	4.83074	0.20701
1.576	2.31439	2.52119	0.91797	1.08935	0.45489	4.83557	0.20680
1.577	2.31691	2.52350	0.91813	1.08917	0.45552	4.84041	0.20659
1.578	2.31943	2.52582	0.91829	1.08898	0.45616	4.84526	0.20639
1.579	2.32196	2.52814	0.91845	1.08880	0.45679	4.85010	0.20618
1.580	2.32449	2.53047	0.91860	1.08861	0.45742	4.85496	0.20598
1.581	2.32702	2.53279	0.91876	1.08843	0.45806	4.85981	0.20577
1.582	2.32956	2.53512	0.91891	1.08824	0.45869	4.86468	0.20556
1.583	2.33209	2.53745	0.91907	1.08806	0.45932	4.86954	0.20536
1.584	2.33463	2.53978	0.91922	1.08787	0.45995	4.87441	0.20515
1.585	2.33717	2.54212	0.91938	1.08769	0.46058	4.87929	0.20495
1.586	2.33972	2.54446	0.91953	1.08751	0.46122	4.88417	0.20474
1.587	2.34226	2.54680	0.91969	1.08733	0.46185	4.88906	0.20454
1.588	2.34481	2.54914	0.91984	1.08714	0.46248	4.89395	0.20433
1.589	2.34736	2.55149	0.92000	1.08696	0.46310	4.89885	0.20413
1.590	2.34991	2.55384	0.92015	1.08678	0.46373	4.90375	0.20393
1.591	2.35247	2.55619	0.92030	1.08660	0.46436	4.90866	0.20372
1.592	2.35502	2.55854	0.92046	1.08642	0.46499	4.91357	0.20352
1.593	2.35758	2.56090	0.92061	1.08624	0.46562	4.91848	0.20331
1.594	2.36015	2.56326	0.92076	1.08606	0.46625	4.92340	0.20311
1.595	2.36271	2.56562	0.92091	1.08588	0.46687	4.92833	0.20291
1.596	2.36528	2.56798	0.92106	1.08570	0.46750	4.93326	0.20271
1.597	2.36785	2.57035	0.92122	1.08552	0.46813	4.93820	0.20250
1.598	2.37042	2.57272	0.92137	1.08534	0.46875	4.94314	0.20230
1.599	2.37299	2.57509	0.92152	1.08517	0.46938	4.94808	0.20210
1.600	2.37557	2.57746	0.92167	1.08499	0.47000	4.95303	0.20190
x	sinh x	cosh x	tanh x	coth x	ln x	e^x	e^-x

x	sinh x	cosh x	tanh x	coth x	ln x	eˣ	e⁻ˣ
1.600	2.37557	2.57746	0.92167	1.08499	0.47000	4.95303	0.20190
1.601	2.37815	2.57984	0.92182	1.08481	0.47063	4.95799	0.20169
1.602	2.38073	2.58222	0.92197	1.08464	0.47125	4.96295	0.20149
1.603	2.38331	2.58460	0.92212	1.08446	0.47188	4.96791	0.20129
1.604	2.38590	2.58699	0.92227	1.08428	0.47250	4.97288	0.20109
1.605	2.38849	2.58937	0.92242	1.08411	0.47312	4.97786	0.20089
1.606	2.39108	2.59176	0.92257	1.08393	0.47375	4.98284	0.20069
1.607	2.39367	2.59416	0.92272	1.08376	0.47437	4.98783	0.20049
1.608	2.39626	2.59655	0.92286	1.08358	0.47499	4.99282	0.20029
1.609	2.39886	2.59895	0.92301	1.08341	0.47561	4.99781	0.20009
1.610	2.40146	2.60135	0.92316	1.08324	0.47623	5.00281	0.19989
1.611	2.40406	2.60375	0.92331	1.08306	0.47686	5.00782	0.19969
1.612	2.40667	2.60616	0.92346	1.08289	0.47748	5.01283	0.19949
1.613	2.40928	2.60857	0.92360	1.08272	0.47810	5.01784	0.19929
1.614	2.41189	2.61098	0.92375	1.08255	0.47872	5.02286	0.19909
1.615	2.41450	2.61339	0.92390	1.08237	0.47933	5.02789	0.19889
1.616	2.41711	2.61581	0.92404	1.08220	0.47995	5.03292	0.19869
1.617	2.41973	2.61822	0.92419	1.08203	0.48057	5.03795	0.19849
1.618	2.42235	2.62064	0.92433	1.08186	0.48119	5.04299	0.19829
1.619	2.42497	2.62307	0.92448	1.08169	0.48181	5.04804	0.19810
1.620	2.42760	2.62549	0.92462	1.08152	0.48243	5.05309	0.19790
1.621	2.43022	2.62792	0.92477	1.08135	0.48304	5.05815	0.19770
1.622	2.43285	2.63035	0.92491	1.08118	0.48366	5.06321	0.19750
1.623	2.43548	2.63279	0.92506	1.08101	0.48428	5.06827	0.19731
1.624	2.43812	2.63523	0.92520	1.08084	0.48489	5.07334	0.19711
1.625	2.44075	2.63767	0.92535	1.08068	0.48551	5.07842	0.19691
1.626	2.44339	2.64011	0.92549	1.08051	0.48612	5.08350	0.19671
1.627	2.44603	2.64255	0.92563	1.08034	0.48674	5.08859	0.19652
1.628	2.44868	2.64500	0.92578	1.08017	0.48735	5.09368	0.19632
1.629	2.45132	2.64745	0.92592	1.08001	0.48797	5.09877	0.19613
1.630	2.45397	2.64990	0.92606	1.07984	0.48858	5.10387	0.19593
1.631	2.45662	2.65236	0.92620	1.07968	0.48919	5.10898	0.19573
1.632	2.45928	2.65482	0.92635	1.07951	0.48981	5.11409	0.19554
1.633	2.46193	2.65728	0.92649	1.07935	0.49042	5.11921	0.19534
1.634	2.46459	2.65974	0.92663	1.07918	0.49103	5.12433	0.19515
1.635	2.46725	2.66221	0.92677	1.07902	0.49164	5.12946	0.19495
1.636	2.46992	2.66467	0.92691	1.07885	0.49225	5.13459	0.19476
1.637	2.47258	2.66715	0.92705	1.07869	0.49287	5.13973	0.19456
1.638	2.47525	2.66962	0.92719	1.07852	0.49348	5.14487	0.19437
1.639	2.47792	2.67210	0.92733	1.07836	0.49409	5.15002	0.19417
1.640	2.48059	2.67457	0.92747	1.07820	0.49470	5.15517	0.19398
1.641	2.48327	2.67706	0.92761	1.07804	0.49531	5.16033	0.19379
1.642	2.48595	2.67954	0.92775	1.07787	0.49592	5.16549	0.19359
1.643	2.48863	2.68203	0.92789	1.07771	0.49652	5.17066	0.19340
1.644	2.49131	2.68452	0.92803	1.07755	0.49713	5.17583	0.19321
1.645	2.49400	2.68701	0.92817	1.07739	0.49774	5.18101	0.19301
1.646	2.49669	2.68951	0.92831	1.07723	0.49835	5.18619	0.19282
1.647	2.49938	2.69200	0.92844	1.07707	0.49896	5.19138	0.19263
1.648	2.50207	2.69451	0.92858	1.07691	0.49956	5.19658	0.19243
1.649	2.50477	2.69701	0.92872	1.07675	0.50017	5.20178	0.19224
1.650	2.50746	2.69951	0.92886	1.07659	0.50078	5.20698	0.19205
x	sinh x	cosh x	tanh x	coth x	ln x	eˣ	e⁻ˣ

TABLE 5

Trigonometrical functions
Degrees in terms of radians
Range: $\phi = 0°$ to $\phi = 90°$

φ	x	sin φ	cos φ	tan φ	cot φ	x	φ
00° 00′	0.0000	0.0000	1.0000	0.0000	∞	1.5708	00′ 90°
06	0.0017	0.0017	1.0000	0.0017	572.96	1.5691	54
12	0.0035	0.0035	1.0000	0.0035	286.48	1.5673	48
18	0.0052	0.0052	1.0000	0.0052	190.98	1.5656	42
24	0.0070	0.0070	1.0000	0.0070	143.24	1.5638	36
30	0.0087	0.0087	1.0000	0.0087	114.59	1.5621	30
36	0.0105	0.0105	0.9999	0.0105	95.49	1.5603	24
42	0.0122	0.0122	0.9999	0.0122	81.85	1.5586	18
48	0.0140	0.0140	0.9999	0.0140	71.62	1.5568	12
54	0.0157	0.0157	0.9999	0.0157	63.66	1.5551	06
01 00	0.0175	0.0175	0.9998	0.0175	57.29	1.5533	00 89
06	0.0192	0.0192	0.9998	0.0192	52.08	1.5516	54
12	0.0209	0.0209	0.9998	0.0209	47.74	1.5499	48
18	0.0227	0.0227	0.9997	0.0227	44.07	1.5481	42
24	0.0244	0.0244	0.9997	0.0244	40.92	1.5464	36
30	0.0262	0.0262	0.9997	0.0262	38.19	1.5446	30
36	0.0279	0.0279	0.9996	0.0279	35.80	1.5429	24
42	0.0297	0.0297	0.9996	0.0297	33.69	1.5411	18
48	0.0314	0.0314	0.9995	0.0314	31.82	1.5394	12
54	0.0332	0.0332	0.9995	0.0332	30.14	1.5376	06
02 00	0.0349	0.0349	0.9994	0.0349	28.64	1.5359	00 88
06	0.0367	0.0366	0.9993	0.0367	27.27	1.5341	54
12	0.0384	0.0384	0.9993	0.0384	26.03	1.5324	48
18	0.0401	0.0401	0.9992	0.0402	24.90	1.5307	42
24	0.0419	0.0419	0.9991	0.0419	23.86	1.5289	36
30	0.0436	0.0436	0.9990	0.0437	22.90	1.5272	30
36	0.0454	0.0454	0.9990	0.0454	22.02	1.5254	24
42	0.0471	0.0471	0.9989	0.0472	21.20	1.5237	18
48	0.0489	0.0488	0.9988	0.0489	20.45	1.5219	12
54	0.0506	0.0506	0.9987	0.0507	19.74	1.5202	06
03 00	0.0524	0.0523	0.9986	0.0524	19.08	1.5184	00 87
06	0.0541	0.0541	0.9985	0.0542	18.46	1.5167	54
12	0.0559	0.0558	0.9984	0.0559	17.89	1.5149	48
18	0.0576	0.0576	0.9983	0.0577	17.34	1.5132	42
24	0.0593	0.0593	0.9982	0.0594	16.83	1.5115	36
30	0.0611	0.0610	0.9981	0.0612	16.35	1.5097	30
36	0.0628	0.0628	0.9980	0.0629	15.89	1.5080	24
42	0.0646	0.0645	0.9979	0.0647	15.46	1.5062	18
48	0.0663	0.0663	0.9978	0.0664	15.06	1.5045	12
54	0.0681	0.0680	0.9977	0.0682	14.67	1.5027	06
04 00	0.0698	0.0698	0.9976	0.0699	14.30	1.5010	00 86
06	0.0716	0.0715	0.9974	0.0717	13.95	1.4992	54
12	0.0733	0.0732	0.9973	0.0734	13.62	1.4975	48
18	0.0750	0.0750	0.9972	0.0752	13.30	1.4957	42
24	0.0768	0.0767	0.9971	0.0769	13.00	1.4940	36
30	0.0785	0.0785	0.9969	0.0787	12.71	1.4923	30
36	0.0803	0.0802	0.9968	0.0805	12.43	1.4905	24
42	0.0820	0.0819	0.9966	0.0822	12.16	1.4888	18
48	0.0838	0.0837	0.9965	0.0840	11.91	1.4870	12
54	0.0855	0.0854	0.9963	0.0857	11.66	1.4853	06
05 00	0.0873	0.0872	0.9962	0.0875	11.43	1.4835	00 85
φ	x	cos φ	sin φ	cot φ	tan φ	x	φ

φ	x	sin φ	cos φ	tan φ	cot φ	x	φ
05° 00′	0.0873	0.0872	0.9962	0.0875	11.430	1.4835	00′ 85°
06	0.0890	0.0889	0.9960	0.0892	11.205	1.4818	54
12	0.0908	0.0906	0.9959	0.0910	10.988	1.4800	48
18	0.0925	0.0924	0.9957	0.0928	10.780	1.4783	42
24	0.0942	0.0941	0.9956	0.0945	10.579	1.4765	36
30	0.0960	0.0958	0.9954	0.0963	10.385	1.4748	30
36	0.0977	0.0976	0.9952	0.0981	10.199	1.4731	24
42	0.0995	0.0993	0.9951	0.0998	10.019	1.4713	18
48	0.1012	0.1011	0.9949	0.1016	9.845	1.4696	12
54	0.1030	0.1028	0.9947	0.1033	9.677	1.4678	06
06 00	0.1047	0.1045	0.9945	0.1051	9.514	1.4661	00 84
06	0.1065	0.1063	0.9943	0.1069	9.357	1.4643	54
12	0.1082	0.1080	0.9942	0.1086	9.205	1.4626	48
18	0.1100	0.1097	0.9940	0.1104	9.058	1.4608	42
24	0.1117	0.1115	0.9938	0.1122	8.915	1.4591	36
30	0.1134	0.1132	0.9936	0.1139	8.777	1.4573	30
36	0.1152	0.1149	0.9934	0.1157	8.643	1.4556	24
42	0.1169	0.1167	0.9932	0.1175	8.513	1.4539	18
48	0.1187	0.1184	0.9930	0.1192	8.386	1.4521	12
54	0.1204	0.1201	0.9928	0.1210	8.264	1.4504	06
07 00	0.1222	0.1219	0.9925	0.1228	8.144	1.4486	00 83
06	0.1239	0.1236	0.9923	0.1246	8.028	1.4469	54
12	0.1257	0.1253	0.9921	0.1263	7.916	1.4451	48
18	0.1274	0.1271	0.9919	0.1281	7.806	1.4434	42
24	0.1292	0.1288	0.9917	0.1299	7.700	1.4416	36
30	0.1309	0.1305	0.9914	0.1317	7.596	1.4399	30
36	0.1326	0.1323	0.9912	0.1334	7.495	1.4382	24
42	0.1344	0.1340	0.9910	0.1352	7.396	1.4364	18
48	0.1361	0.1357	0.9907	0.1370	7.300	1.4347	12
54	0.1379	0.1374	0.9905	0.1388	7.207	1.4329	06
08 00	0.1396	0.1392	0.9903	0.1405	7.115	1.4312	00 82
06	0.1414	0.1409	0.9900	0.1423	7.026	1.4294	54
12	0.1431	0.1426	0.9898	0.1441	6.940	1.4277	48
18	0.1449	0.1444	0.9895	0.1459	6.855	1.4259	42
24	0.1466	0.1461	0.9893	0.1477	6.772	1.4242	36
30	0.1484	0.1478	0.9890	0.1495	6.691	1.4224	30
36	0.1501	0.1495	0.9888	0.1512	6.612	1.4207	24
42	0.1518	0.1513	0.9885	0.1530	6.535	1.4190	18
48	0.1536	0.1530	0.9882	0.1548	6.460	1.4172	12
54	0.1553	0.1547	0.9880	0.1566	6.386	1.4155	06
09 00	0.1571	0.1564	0.9877	0.1584	6.314	1.4137	00 81
06	0.1588	0.1582	0.9874	0.1602	6.243	1.4120	54
12	0.1606	0.1599	0.9871	0.1620	6.174	1.4102	48
18	0.1623	0.1616	0.9869	0.1638	6.107	1.4085	42
24	0.1641	0.1633	0.9866	0.1655	6.041	1.4067	36
30	0.1658	0.1650	0.9863	0.1673	5.976	1.4050	30
36	0.1676	0.1668	0.9860	0.1691	5.912	1.4032	24
42	0.1693	0.1685	0.9857	0.1709	5.850	1.4015	18
48	0.1710	0.1702	0.9854	0.1727	5.789	1.3998	12
54	0.1728	0.1719	0.9851	0.1745	5.730	1.3980	06
10 00	0.1745	0.1736	0.9848	0.1763	5.671	1.3963	00 80
φ	x	cos φ	sin φ	cot φ	tan φ	x	φ

φ	x	sin φ	cos φ	tan φ	cot φ	x	φ
10° 00′	0.1745	0.1736	0.9848	0.1763	5.671	1.3963	00′ 80°
06	0.1763	0.1754	0.9845	0.1781	5.614	1.3945	54
12	0.1780	0.1771	0.9842	0.1799	5.558	1.3928	48
18	0.1798	0.1788	0.9839	0.1817	5.503	1.3910	42
24	0.1815	0.1805	0.9836	0.1835	5.449	1.3893	36
30	0.1833	0.1822	0.9833	0.1853	5.396	1.3875	30
36	0.1850	0.1840	0.9829	0.1871	5.343	1.3858	24
42	0.1868	0.1857	0.9826	0.1890	5.292	1.3840	18
48	0.1885	0.1874	0.9823	0.1908	5.242	1.3823	12
54	0.1902	0.1891	0.9820	0.1926	5.193	1.3806	06
11 00	0.1920	0.1908	0.9816	0.1944	5.145	1.3788	00 79
06	0.1937	0.1925	0.9813	0.1962	5.097	1.3771	54
12	0.1955	0.1942	0.9810	0.1980	5.050	1.3753	48
18	0.1972	0.1959	0.9806	0.1998	5.005	1.3736	42
24	0.1990	0.1977	0.9803	0.2016	4.959	1.3718	36
30	0.2007	0.1994	0.9799	0.2035	4.915	1.3701	30
36	0.2025	0.2011	0.9796	0.2053	4.872	1.3683	24
42	0.2042	0.2028	0.9792	0.2071	4.829	1.3666	18
48	0.2059	0.2045	0.9789	0.2089	4.787	1.3648	12
54	0.2077	0.2062	0.9785	0.2107	4.745	1.3631	06
12 00	0.2094	0.2079	0.9781	0.2126	4.705	1.3614	00 78
06	0.2112	0.2096	0.9778	0.2144	4.665	1.3596	54
12	0.2129	0.2113	0.9774	0.2162	4.625	1.3579	48
18	0.2147	0.2130	0.9770	0.2180	4.586	1.3561	42
24	0.2164	0.2147	0.9767	0.2199	4.548	1.3544	36
30	0.2182	0.2164	0.9763	0.2217	4.511	1.3526	30
36	0.2199	0.2181	0.9759	0.2235	4.474	1.3509	24
42	0.2217	0.2198	0.9755	0.2254	4.437	1.3491	18
48	0.2234	0.2215	0.9751	0.2272	4.402	1.3474	12
54	0.2251	0.2233	0.9748	0.2290	4.366	1.3456	06
13 00	0.2269	0.2250	0.9744	0.2309	4.331	1.3439	00 77
06	0.2286	0.2267	0.9740	0.2327	4.297	1.3422	54
12	0.2304	0.2284	0.9736	0.2345	4.264	1.3404	48
18	0.2321	0.2300	0.9732	0.2364	4.230	1.3387	42
24	0.2339	0.2317	0.9728	0.2382	4.198	1.3369	36
30	0.2356	0.2334	0.9724	0.2401	4.165	1.3352	30
36	0.2374	0.2351	0.9720	0.2419	4.134	1.3334	24
42	0.2391	0.2368	0.9715	0.2438	4.102	1.3317	18
48	0.2409	0.2385	0.9711	0.2456	4.071	1.3299	12
54	0.2426	0.2402	0.9707	0.2475	4.041	1.3282	06
14 00	0.2443	0.2419	0.9703	0.2493	4.011	1.3265	00 76
06	0.2461	0.2436	0.9699	0.2512	3.981	1.3247	54
12	0.2478	0.2453	0.9694	0.2530	3.952	1.3230	48
18	0.2496	0.2470	0.9690	0.2549	3.923	1.3212	42
24	0.2513	0.2487	0.9686	0.2568	3.895	1.3195	36
30	0.2531	0.2504	0.9681	0.2586	3.867	1.3177	30
36	0.2548	0.2521	0.9677	0.2605	3.839	1.3160	24
42	0.2566	0.2538	0.9673	0.2623	3.812	1.3142	18
48	0.2583	0.2554	0.9668	0.2642	3.785	1.3125	12
54	0.2601	0.2571	0.9664	0.2661	3.758	1.3107	06
15 00	0.2618	0.2588	0.9659	0.2679	3.732	1.3090	00 75
φ	x	cos φ	sin φ	cot φ	tan φ	x	φ

φ	x	sin φ	cos φ	tan φ	cot φ	x	φ
15° 00'	0.2618	0.2588	0.9659	0.2679	3.732	1.3090	00' 75°
06	0.2635	0.2605	0.9655	0.2698	3.706	1.3073	54
12	0.2653	0.2622	0.9650	0.2717	3.681	1.3055	48
18	0.2670	0.2639	0.9646	0.2736	3.655	1.3038	42
24	0.2688	0.2656	0.9641	0.2754	3.630	1.3020	36
30	0.2705	0.2672	0.9636	0.2773	3.606	1.3003	30
36	0.2723	0.2689	0.9632	0.2792	3.582	1.2985	24
42	0.2740	0.2706	0.9627	0.2811	3.558	1.2968	18
48	0.2758	0.2723	0.9622	0.2830	3.534	1.2950	12
54	0.2775	0.2740	0.9617	0.2849	3.511	1.2933	06
16 00	0.2793	0.2756	0.9613	0.2867	3.487	1.2915	00 74
06	0.2810	0.2773	0.9608	0.2886	3.465	1.2898	54
12	0.2827	0.2790	0.9603	0.2905	3.442	1.2881	48
18	0.2845	0.2807	0.9598	0.2924	3.420	1.2863	42
24	0.2862	0.2823	0.9593	0.2943	3.398	1.2846	36
30	0.2880	0.2840	0.9588	0.2962	3.376	1.2828	30
36	0.2897	0.2857	0.9583	0.2981	3.354	1.2811	24
42	0.2915	0.2874	0.9578	0.3000	3.333	1.2793	18
48	0.2932	0.2890	0.9573	0.3019	3.312	1.2776	12
54	0.2950	0.2907	0.9568	0.3038	3.291	1.2758	06
17 00	0.2967	0.2924	0.9563	0.3057	3.271	1.2741	00 73
06	0.2985	0.2940	0.9558	0.3076	3.251	1.2723	54
12	0.3002	0.2957	0.9553	0.3096	3.230	1.2706	48
18	0.3019	0.2974	0.9548	0.3115	3.211	1.2689	42
24	0.3037	0.2990	0.9542	0.3134	3.191	1.2671	36
30	0.3054	0.3007	0.9537	0.3153	3.172	1.2654	30
36	0.3072	0.3024	0.9532	0.3172	3.152	1.2636	24
42	0.3089	0.3040	0.9527	0.3191	3.133	1.2619	18
48	0.3107	0.3057	0.9521	0.3211	3.115	1.2601	12
54	0.3124	0.3074	0.9516	0.3230	3.096	1.2584	06
18 00	0.3142	0.3090	0.9511	0.3249	3.078	1.2566	00 72
06	0.3159	0.3107	0.9505	0.3269	3.060	1.2549	54
12	0.3176	0.3123	0.9500	0.3288	3.042	1.2531	48
18	0.3194	0.3140	0.9494	0.3307	3.024	1.2514	42
24	0.3211	0.3156	0.9489	0.3327	3.006	1.2497	36
30	0.3229	0.3173	0.9483	0.3346	2.989	1.2479	30
36	0.3246	0.3190	0.9478	0.3365	2.971	1.2462	24
42	0.3264	0.3206	0.9472	0.3385	2.954	1.2444	18
48	0.3281	0.3223	0.9466	0.3404	2.937	1.2427	12
54	0.3299	0.3239	0.9461	0.3424	2.921	1.2409	06
19 00	0.3316	0.3256	0.9455	0.3443	2.904	1.2392	00 71
06	0.3334	0.3272	0.9449	0.3463	2.888	1.2374	54
12	0.3351	0.3289	0.9444	0.3482	2.872	1.2357	48
18	0.3368	0.3305	0.9438	0.3502	2.856	1.2339	42
24	0.3386	0.3322	0.9432	0.3522	2.840	1.2322	36
30	0.3403	0.3338	0.9426	0.3541	2.824	1.2305	30
36	0.3421	0.3355	0.9421	0.3561	2.808	1.2287	24
42	0.3438	0.3371	0.9415	0.3581	2.793	1.2270	18
48	0.3456	0.3387	0.9409	0.3600	2.778	1.2252	12
54	0.3473	0.3404	0.9403	0.3620	2.762	1.2235	06
20 00	0.3491	0.3420	0.9397	0.3640	2.747	1.2217	00 70
φ	x	cos φ	sin φ	cot φ	tan φ	x	φ

φ	x	sin φ	cos φ	tan φ	cot φ	x	φ
20° 00	0.3491	0.3420	0.9397	0.3640	2.7475	1.2217	00 70°
06	0.3508	0.3437	0.9391	0.3659	2.7326	1.2200	54
12	0.3526	0.3453	0.9385	0.3679	2.7179	1.2182	48
18	0.3543	0.3469	0.9379	0.3699	2.7034	1.2165	42
24	0.3560	0.3486	0.9373	0.3719	2.6889	1.2147	36
30	0.3578	0.3502	0.9367	0.3739	2.6746	1.2130	30
36	0.3595	0.3518	0.9361	0.3759	2.6605	1.2113	24
42	0.3613	0.3535	0.9354	0.3779	2.6464	1.2095	18
48	0.3630	0.3551	0.9348	0.3799	2.6325	1.2078	12
54	0.3648	0.3567	0.9342	0.3819	2.6187	1.2060	06
21 00	0.3665	0.3584	0.9336	0.3839	2.6051	1.2043	00 69
06	0.3683	0.3600	0.9330	0.3859	2.5916	1.2025	54
12	0.3700	0.3616	0.9323	0.3879	2.5782	1.2008	48
18	0.3718	0.3633	0.9317	0.3899	2.5649	1.1990	42
24	0.3735	0.3649	0.9311	0.3919	2.5517	1.1973	36
30	0.3752	0.3665	0.9304	0.3939	2.5386	1.1956	30
36	0.3770	0.3681	0.9298	0.3959	2.5257	1.1938	24
42	0.3787	0.3697	0.9291	0.3979	2.5129	1.1921	18
48	0.3805	0.3714	0.9285	0.4000	2.5002	1.1903	12
54	0.3822	0.3730	0.9278	0.4020	2.4876	1.1886	06
22 00	0.3840	0.3746	0.9272	0.4040	2.4751	1.1868	00 68
06	0.3857	0.3762	0.9265	0.4061	2.4627	1.1851	54
12	0.3875	0.3778	0.9259	0.4081	2.4504	1.1833	48
18	0.3892	0.3795	0.9252	0.4101	2.4383	1.1816	42
24	0.3910	0.3811	0.9245	0.4122	2.4262	1.1798	36
30	0.3927	0.3827	0.9239	0.4142	2.4142	1.1781	30
36	0.3944	0.3843	0.9232	0.4163	2.4023	1.1764	24
42	0.3962	0.3859	0.9225	0.4183	2.3906	1.1746	18
48	0.3979	0.3875	0.9219	0.4204	2.3789	1.1729	12
54	0.3997	0.3891	0.9212	0.4224	2.3673	1.1711	06
23 00	0.4014	0.3907	0.9205	0.4245	2.3559	1.1694	00 67
06	0.4032	0.3923	0.9198	0.4265	2.3445	1.1676	54
12	0.4049	0.3939	0.9191	0.4286	2.3332	1.1659	48
18	0.4067	0.3955	0.9184	0.4307	2.3220	1.1641	42
24	0.4084	0.3971	0.9178	0.4327	2.3109	1.1624	36
30	0.4102	0.3987	0.9171	0.4348	2.2998	1.1606	30
36	0.4119	0.4003	0.9164	0.4369	2.2889	1.1589	24
42	0.4136	0.4019	0.9157	0.4390	2.2781	1.1572	18
48	0.4154	0.4035	0.9150	0.4411	2.2673	1.1554	12
54	0.4171	0.4051	0.9143	0.4431	2.2566	1.1537	06
24 00	0.4189	0.4067	0.9135	0.4452	2.2460	1.1519	00 66
06	0.4206	0.4083	0.9128	0.4473	2.2355	1.1502	54
12	0.4224	0.4099	0.9121	0.4494	2.2251	1.1484	48
18	0.4241	0.4115	0.9114	0.4515	2.2148	1.1467	42
24	0.4259	0.4131	0.9107	0.4536	2.2045	1.1449	36
30	0.4276	0.4147	0.9100	0.4557	2.1943	1.1432	30
36	0.4294	0.4163	0.9092	0.4578	2.1842	1.1414	24
42	0.4311	0.4179	0.9085	0.4599	2.1742	1.1397	18
48	0.4328	0.4195	0.9078	0.4621	2.1642	1.1380	12
54	0.4346	0.4210	0.9070	0.4642	2.1543	1.1362	06
25 00	0.4363	0.4226	0.9063	0.4663	2.1445	1.1345	00 65
φ	x	cos φ	sin φ	cot φ	tan φ	x	φ

φ	x	sin φ	cos φ	tan φ	cot φ	x	φ
25° 00'	0.4363	0.4226	0.9063	0.4663	2.1445	1.1345	00' 65°
06	0.4381	0.4242	0.9056	0.4684	2.1348	1.1327	54
12	0.4398	0.4258	0.9048	0.4706	2.1251	1.1310	48
18	0.4416	0.4274	0.9041	0.4727	2.1155	1.1292	42
24	0.4433	0.4289	0.9033	0.4748	2.1060	1.1275	36
30	0.4451	0.4305	0.9026	0.4770	2.0965	1.1257	30
36	0.4468	0.4321	0.9018	0.4791	2.0872	1.1240	24
42	0.4485	0.4337	0.9011	0.4813	2.0778	1.1222	18
48	0.4503	0.4352	0.9003	0.4834	2.0686	1.1205	12
54	0.4520	0.4368	0.8996	0.4856	2.0594	1.1188	06
26 00	0.4538	0.4384	0.8988	0.4877	2.0503	1.1170	00 64
06	0.4555	0.4399	0.8980	0.4899	2.0413	1.1153	54
12	0.4573	0.4415	0.8973	0.4921	2.0323	1.1135	48
18	0.4590	0.4431	0.8965	0.4942	2.0233	1.1118	42
24	0.4608	0.4446	0.8957	0.4964	2.0145	1.1100	36
30	0.4625	0.4462	0.8949	0.4986	2.0057	1.1083	30
36	0.4643	0.4478	0.8942	0.5008	1.9970	1.1065	24
42	0.4660	0.4493	0.8934	0.5029	1.9883	1.1048	18
48	0.4677	0.4509	0.8926	0.5051	1.9797	1.1030	12
54	0.4695	0.4524	0.8918	0.5073	1.9711	1.1013	06
27 00	0.4712	0.4540	0.8910	0.5095	1.9626	1.0996	00 63
06	0.4730	0.4555	0.8902	0.5117	1.9542	1.0978	54
12	0.4747	0.4571	0.8894	0.5139	1.9458	1.0961	48
18	0.4765	0.4586	0.8886	0.5161	1.9375	1.0943	42
24	0.4782	0.4602	0.8878	0.5184	1.9292	1.0926	36
30	0.4800	0.4617	0.8870	0.5206	1.9210	1.0908	30
36	0.4817	0.4633	0.8862	0.5228	1.9128	1.0891	24
42	0.4835	0.4648	0.8854	0.5250	1.9047	1.0873	18
48	0.4852	0.4664	0.8846	0.5272	1.8967	1.0856	12
54	0.4869	0.4679	0.8838	0.5295	1.8887	1.0838	06
28 00	0.4887	0.4695	0.8829	0.5317	1.8807	1.0821	00 62
06	0.4904	0.4710	0.8821	0.5340	1.8728	1.0804	54
12	0.4922	0.4726	0.8813	0.5362	1.8650	1.0786	48
18	0.4939	0.4741	0.8805	0.5384	1.8572	1.0769	42
24	0.4957	0.4756	0.8796	0.5407	1.8495	1.0751	36
30	0.4974	0.4772	0.8788	0.5430	1.8418	1.0734	30
36	0.4992	0.4787	0.8780	0.5452	1.8341	1.0716	24
42	0.5009	0.4802	0.8771	0.5475	1.8265	1.0699	18
48	0.5027	0.4818	0.8763	0.5498	1.8190	1.0681	12
54	0.5044	0.4833	0.8755	0.5520	1.8115	1.0664	06
29 00	0.5061	0.4848	0.8746	0.5543	1.8040	1.0647	00 61
06	0.5079	0.4863	0.8738	0.5566	1.7966	1.0629	54
12	0.5096	0.4879	0.8729	0.5589	1.7893	1.0612	48
18	0.5114	0.4894	0.8721	0.5612	1.7820	1.0594	42
24	0.5131	0.4909	0.8712	0.5635	1.7747	1.0577	36
30	0.5149	0.4924	0.8704	0.5658	1.7675	1.0559	30
36	0.5166	0.4939	0.8695	0.5681	1.7603	1.0542	24
42	0.5184	0.4955	0.8686	0.5704	1.7532	1.0524	18
48	0.5201	0.4970	0.8678	0.5727	1.7461	1.0507	12
54	0.5219	0.4985	0.8669	0.5750	1.7391	1.0489	06
30 00	0.5236	0.5000	0.8660	0.5774	1.7321	1.0472	00 60
φ	x	cos φ	sin φ	cot φ	tan φ	x	φ

φ	x	sin φ	cos φ	tan φ	cot φ	x	φ
30° 00'	0.5236	0.5000	0.8660	0.5774	1.7321	1.0472	00' 60°
06	0.5253	0.5015	0.8652	0.5797	1.7251	1.0455	54
12	0.5271	0.5030	0.8643	0.5820	1.7182	1.0437	48
18	0.5288	0.5045	0.8634	0.5844	1.7113	1.0420	42
24	0.5306	0.5060	0.8625	0.5867	1.7045	1.0402	36
30	0.5323	0.5075	0.8616	0.5890	1.6977	1.0385	30
36	0.5341	0.5090	0.8607	0.5914	1.6909	1.0367	24
42	0.5358	0.5105	0.8599	0.5938	1.6842	1.0350	18
48	0.5376	0.5120	0.8590	0.5961	1.6775	1.0332	12
54	0.5393	0.5135	0.8581	0.5985	1.6709	1.0315	06
31 00	0.5411	0.5150	0.8572	0.6009	1.6643	1.0297	00 59
06	0.5428	0.5165	0.8563	0.6032	1.6577	1.0280	54
12	0.5445	0.5180	0.8554	0.6056	1.6512	1.0263	48
18	0.5463	0.5195	0.8545	0.6080	1.6447	1.0245	42
24	0.5480	0.5210	0.8536	0.6104	1.6383	1.0228	36
30	0.5498	0.5225	0.8526	0.6128	1.6319	1.0210	30
36	0.5515	0.5240	0.8517	0.6152	1.6255	1.0193	24
42	0.5533	0.5255	0.8508	0.6176	1.6191	1.0175	18
48	0.5550	0.5270	0.8499	0.6200	1.6128	1.0158	12
54	0.5568	0.5284	0.8490	0.6224	1.6066	1.0140	06
32 00	0.5585	0.5299	0.8480	0.6249	1.6003	1.0123	00 58
06	0.5603	0.5314	0.8471	0.6273	1.5941	1.0105	54
12	0.5620	0.5329	0.8462	0.6297	1.5880	1.0088	48
18	0.5637	0.5344	0.8453	0.6322	1.5818	1.0071	42
24	0.5655	0.5358	0.8443	0.6346	1.5757	1.0053	36
30	0.5672	0.5373	0.8434	0.6371	1.5697	1.0036	30
36	0.5690	0.5388	0.8425	0.6395	1.5637	1.0018	24
42	0.5707	0.5402	0.8415	0.6420	1.5577	1.0001	18
48	0.5725	0.5417	0.8406	0.6445	1.5517	0.9983	12
54	0.5742	0.5432	0.8396	0.6469	1.5458	0.9966	06
33 00	0.5760	0.5446	0.8387	0.6494	1.5399	0.9948	00 57
06	0.5777	0.5461	0.8377	0.6519	1.5340	0.9931	54
12	0.5794	0.5476	0.8368	0.6544	1.5282	0.9913	48
18	0.5812	0.5490	0.8358	0.6569	1.5224	0.9896	42
24	0.5829	0.5505	0.8348	0.6594	1.5166	0.9879	36
30	0.5847	0.5519	0.8339	0.6619	1.5108	0.9861	30
36	0.5864	0.5534	0.8329	0.6644	1.5051	0.9844	24
42	0.5882	0.5548	0.8320	0.6669	1.4994	0.9826	18
48	0.5899	0.5563	0.8310	0.6694	1.4938	0.9809	12
54	0.5917	0.5577	0.8300	0.6720	1.4882	0.9791	06
34 00	0.5934	0.5592	0.8290	0.6745	1.4826	0.9774	00 56
06	0.5952	0.5606	0.8281	0.6771	1.4770	0.9756	54
12	0.5969	0.5621	0.8271	0.6796	1.4715	0.9739	48
18	0.5986	0.5635	0.8261	0.6822	1.4659	0.9721	42
24	0.6004	0.5650	0.8251	0.6847	1.4605	0.9704	36
30	0.6021	0.5664	0.8241	0.6873	1.4550	0.9687	30
36	0.6039	0.5678	0.8231	0.6899	1.4496	0.9669	24
42	0.6056	0.5693	0.8221	0.6924	1.4442	0.9652	18
48	0.6074	0.5707	0.8211	0.6950	1.4388	0.9634	12
54	0.6091	0.5721	0.8202	0.6976	1.4335	0.9617	06
35 00	0.6109	0.5736	0.8192	0.7002	1.4281	0.9599	00 55
φ	x	cos φ	sin φ	cot φ	tan φ	x	φ

φ	x	sin φ	cos φ	tan φ	cot φ	x	φ
35° 00′	0.6109	0.5736	0.8192	0.7002	1.4281	0.9599	00′ 55°
06	0.6126	0.5750	0.8181	0.7028	1.4229	0.9582	54
12	0.6144	0.5764	0.8171	0.7054	1.4176	0.9564	48
18	0.6161	0.5779	0.8161	0.7080	1.4124	0.9547	42
24	0.6178	0.5793	0.8151	0.7107	1.4071	0.9529	36
30	0.6196	0.5807	0.8141	0.7133	1.4019	0.9512	30
36	0.6213	0.5821	0.8131	0.7159	1.3968	0.9495	24
42	0.6231	0.5835	0.8121	0.7186	1.3916	0.9477	18
48	0.6248	0.5850	0.8111	0.7212	1.3865	0.9460	12
54	0.6266	0.5864	0.8100	0.7239	1.3814	0.9442	06
36 00	0.6283	0.5878	0.8090	0.7265	1.3764	0.9425	00 54
06	0.6301	0.5892	0.8080	0.7292	1.3713	0.9407	54
12	0.6318	0.5906	0.8070	0.7319	1.3663	0.9390	48
18	0.6336	0.5920	0.8059	0.7346	1.3613	0.9372	42
24	0.6353	0.5934	0.8049	0.7373	1.3564	0.9355	36
30	0.6370	0.5948	0.8039	0.7400	1.3514	0.9338	30
36	0.6388	0.5962	0.8028	0.7427	1.3465	0.9320	24
42	0.6405	0.5976	0.8018	0.7454	1.3416	0.9303	18
48	0.6423	0.5990	0.8007	0.7481	1.3367	0.9285	12
54	0.6440	0.6004	0.7997	0.7508	1.3319	0.9268	06
37 00	0.6458	0.6018	0.7986	0.7536	1.3270	0.9250	00 53
06	0.6475	0.6032	0.7976	0.7563	1.3222	0.9233	54
12	0.6493	0.6046	0.7965	0.7590	1.3175	0.9215	48
18	0.6510	0.6060	0.7955	0.7618	1.3127	0.9198	42
24	0.6528	0.6074	0.7944	0.7646	1.3079	0.9180	36
30	0.6545	0.6088	0.7934	0.7673	1.3032	0.9163	30
36	0.6562	0.6101	0.7923	0.7701	1.2985	0.9146	24
42	0.6580	0.6115	0.7912	0.7729	1.2938	0.9128	18
48	0.6597	0.6129	0.7902	0.7757	1.2892	0.9111	12
54	0.6615	0.6143	0.7891	0.7785	1.2846	0.9093	06
38 00	0.6632	0.6157	0.7880	0.7813	1.2799	0.9076	00 52
06	0.6650	0.6170	0.7869	0.7841	1.2753	0.9058	54
12	0.6667	0.6184	0.7859	0.7869	1.2708	0.9041	48
18	0.6685	0.6198	0.7848	0.7898	1.2662	0.9023	42
24	0.6702	0.6211	0.7837	0.7926	1.2617	0.9006	36
30	0.6720	0.6225	0.7826	0.7954	1.2572	0.8988	30
36	0.6737	0.6239	0.7815	0.7983	1.2527	0.8971	24
42	0.6754	0.6252	0.7804	0.8012	1.2482	0.8954	18
48	0.6772	0.6266	0.7793	0.8040	1.2437	0.8936	12
54	0.6789	0.6280	0.7782	0.8069	1.2393	0.8919	06
39 00	0.6807	0.6293	0.7771	0.8098	1.2349	0.8901	00 51
06	0.6824	0.6307	0.7760	0.8127	1.2305	0.8884	54
12	0.6842	0.6320	0.7749	0.8156	1.2261	0.8866	48
18	0.6859	0.6334	0.7738	0.8185	1.2218	0.8849	42
24	0.6877	0.6347	0.7727	0.8214	1.2174	0.8831	36
30	0.6894	0.6361	0.7716	0.8243	1.2131	0.8814	30
36	0.6912	0.6374	0.7705	0.8273	1.2088	0.8796	24
42	0.6929	0.6388	0.7694	0.8302	1.2045	0.8779	18
48	0.6946	0.6401	0.7683	0.8332	1.2002	0.8762	12
54	0.6964	0.6414	0.7672	0.8361	1.1960	0.8744	06
40 00	0.6981	0.6428	0.7660	0.8391	1.1918	0.8727	00 50
φ	x	cos φ	sin φ	cot φ	tan φ	x	φ

φ	x	sin φ	cos φ	tan φ	cot φ	x	φ
40° 00'	0.6981	0.6428	0.7660	0.8391	1.1918	0.8727	00' 50°
06	0.6999	0.6441	0.7649	0.8421	1.1875	0.8709	54
12	0.7016	0.6455	0.7638	0.8451	1.1833	0.8692	48
18	0.7034	0.6468	0.7627	0.8481	1.1792	0.8674	42
24	0.7051	0.6481	0.7615	0.8511	1.1750	0.8657	36
30	0.7069	0.6494	0.7604	0.8541	1.1708	0.8639	30
36	0.7086	0.6508	0.7593	0.8571	1.1667	0.8622	24
42	0.7103	0.6521	0.7581	0.8601	1.1626	0.8604	18
48	0.7121	0.6534	0.7570	0.8632	1.1585	0.8587	12
54	0.7138	0.6547	0.7559	0.8662	1.1544	0.8570	06
41 00	0.7156	0.6561	0.7547	0.8693	1.1504	0.8552	00 49
06	0.7173	0.6574	0.7536	0.8724	1.1463	0.8535	54
12	0.7191	0.6587	0.7524	0.8754	1.1423	0.8517	48
18	0.7208	0.6600	0.7513	0.8785	1.1383	0.8500	42
24	0.7226	0.6613	0.7501	0.8816	1.1343	0.8482	36
30	0.7243	0.6626	0.7490	0.8847	1.1303	0.8465	30
36	0.7261	0.6639	0.7478	0.8878	1.1263	0.8447	24
42	0.7278	0.6652	0.7466	0.8910	1.1224	0.8430	18
48	0.7295	0.6665	0.7455	0.8941	1.1184	0.8412	12
54	0.7313	0.6678	0.7443	0.8972	1.1145	0.8395	06
42 00	0.7330	0.6691	0.7431	0.9004	1.1106	0.8378	00 48
06	0.7348	0.6704	0.7420	0.9036	1.1067	0.8360	54
12	0.7365	0.6717	0.7408	0.9067	1.1028	0.8343	48
18	0.7383	0.6730	0.7396	0.9099	1.0990	0.8325	42
24	0.7400	0.6743	0.7385	0.9131	1.0951	0.8308	36
30	0.7418	0.6756	0.7373	0.9163	1.0913	0.8290	30
36	0.7435	0.6769	0.7361	0.9195	1.0875	0.8273	24
42	0.7453	0.6782	0.7349	0.9228	1.0837	0.8255	18
48	0.7470	0.6794	0.7337	0.9260	1.0799	0.8238	12
54	0.7487	0.6807	0.7325	0.9293	1.0761	0.8221	06
43 00	0.7505	0.6820	0.7314	0.9325	1.0724	0.8203	00 47
06	0.7522	0.6833	0.7302	0.9358	1.0686	0.8186	54
12	0.7540	0.6845	0.7290	0.9391	1.0649	0.8168	48
18	0.7557	0.6858	0.7278	0.9424	1.0612	0.8151	42
24	0.7575	0.6871	0.7266	0.9457	1.0575	0.8133	36
30	0.7592	0.6884	0.7254	0.9490	1.0538	0.8116	30
36	0.7610	0.6896	0.7242	0.9523	1.0501	0.8098	24
42	0.7627	0.6909	0.7230	0.9556	1.0464	0.8081	18
48	0.7645	0.6921	0.7218	0.9590	1.0428	0.8063	12
54	0.7662	0.6934	0.7206	0.9623	1.0392	0.8046	06
44 00	0.7679	0.6947	0.7193	0.9657	1.0355	0.8029	00 46
06	0.7697	0.6959	0.7181	0.9691	1.0319	0.8011	54
12	0.7714	0.6972	0.7169	0.9725	1.0283	0.7994	48
18	0.7732	0.6984	0.7157	0.9759	1.0247	0.7976	42
24	0.7749	0.6997	0.7145	0.9793	1.0212	0.7959	36
30	0.7767	0.7009	0.7133	0.9827	1.0176	0.7941	30
36	0.7784	0.7022	0.7120	0.9861	1.0141	0.7924	24
42	0.7802	0.7034	0.7108	0.9896	1.0105	0.7906	18
48	0.7819	0.7046	0.7096	0.9930	1.0070	0.7889	12
54	0.7837	0.7059	0.7083	0.9965	1.0035	0.7871	06
45 00	0.7854	0.7071	0.7071	1.0000	1.0000	0.7854	00 45
φ ° '	x	cos φ	sin φ	cot φ	tan φ	x	φ ' °

TABLE OF
PROPORTIONAL PARTS

	1	2	3	4	5	6	7	8	9	10	11	12	13	14	15
1	0·1	0·2	·0·3	0·4	0·5	0·6	0·7	0·8	0·9	1·0	1·1	1·2	1·3	1·4	1·5
2	0·2	0·4	0·6	0·8	1·0	1·2	1·4	1·6	1·8	2·0	2·2	2·4	2·6	2·8	3·0
3	0·3	0·6	0·9	1·2	1·5	1·8	2·1	2·4	2·7	3·0	3·3	3·6	3·9	4·2	4·5
4	0·4	0·8	1·2	1·6	2·0	2·4	2·8	3·2	3·6	4·0	4·4	4·8	5·2	5·6	6·0
5	0·5	1·0	1·5	2·0	2·5	3·0	3·5	4·0	4·5	5·0	5·5	6·0	6·5	7·0	7·5
6	0·6	1·2	1·8	2·4	3·0	3·6	4·2	4·8	5·4	6·0	6·6	7·2	7·8	8·4	9·0
7	0·7	1·4	2·1	2·8	3·5	4·2	4·9	5·6	6·3	7·0	7·7	8·4	9·1	9·8	10·5
8	0·8	1·6	2·4	3·2	4·0	4·8	5·6	6·4	7·2	8·0	8·8	9·6	10·4	11·2	12·0
9	0·9	1·8	2·7	3·6	4·5	5·4	6·3	7·2	8·1	9·0	9·9	10·8	11·7	12·6	13·5

	16	17	18	19	20	21	22	23	24	25	26	27	28	29	30
1	1·6	1·7	1·8	1·9	2·0	2·1	2·2	2·3	2·4	2·5	2·6	2·7	2·8	2·9	3·0
2	3;2	3·4	3·6	3·8	4·0	4·2	4·4	4·6	4·8	5·0	5·2	5·4	5·6	5·8	6·0
3	4·8	5·1	5·4	5·7	6·0	6·3	6·6	6·9	7·2	7·5	7·8	8·1	8·4	8·7	9·0
4	6·4	6·8	7·2	7·6	8·0	8·4	8·8	9·2	9·6	10·0	10·4	10·8	11·2	11·6	12·0
5	8·0	8·5	9·0	9·5	10·0	10·5	11·0	11·5	12·0	12·5	13·0	13·5	14·0	14·5	15·0
6	9·6	10·2	10·8	11·4	12·0	12·6	13·2	13·8	14·4	15·0	15·6	16·2	16·8	17·4	18·0
7	11·2	11·9	12·6	13·3	14·0	14·7	15·4	16·1	16·8	17·5	18·2	18·9	19·6	20·3	21·0
8	12·8	13·6	14·4	15·2	16·0	16·8	17·6	18·4	19·2	20·0	20·8	21·6	22·4	23·2	24·0
9	14·4	15·3	16·2	17·1	18·0	18·9	19·8	20·7	21·6	22·5	23·4	24·3	25·2	26·1	27·0

	31	32	33	34	35	36	37	38	39	40	41	42	43	44	45
1	3·1	3·2	3·3	3·4	3·5	3·6	3·7	3·8	3·9	4·0	4·1	4·2	4·3	4·4	4·5
2	6·2	6·4	6·6	6·8	7·0	7·2	7·4	7·6	7·8	8·0	8·2	8·4	8·6	8·8	9·0
3	9·3	9·6	9·9	10·2	10·5	10·8	11·1	11·4	11·7	12·0	12·3	12·6	12·9	13·2	13·5
4	12·4	12·8	13·2	13·6	14·0	14·4	14·8	15·2	15·6	16·0	16·4	16·8	17·2	17·6	18·0
5	15·5	16·0	16·5	17·0	17·5	18·0	18·5	19·0	19·5	20·0	20·5	21·0	21·5	22·0	22·5
6	18·6	19·2	19·8	20·4	21·0	21·6	22·2	22·8	23·4	24·0	24·6	25·2	25·8	26·4	27·0
7	21·7	22·4	23·1	23·8	24·5	25·2	25·9	26·6	27·3	28·0	28·7	29·4	30·1	30·8	31·5
8	24·8	25·6	26·4	27·2	28·0	28·8	29·6	30·4	31·2	32·0	32·8	33·6	34·4	35·2	36·0
9	27·9	28·8	29·7	30·6	31·5	32·4	33·3	34·2	35·1	36·0	36·9	37·8	38·7	39·6	40·5

	46	47	48	49	50	51	52	53	54	55	56	57	58	59	60
1	4·6	4·7	4·8	4·9	5·0	5·1	5·2	5·3	5·4	5·5	5·6	5·7	5·8	5·9	6·0
2	9·2	9·4	9·6	9·8	10·0	10·2	10·4	10·6	10·8	11·0	11·2	11·4	11·6	11·8	12·0
3	13·8	14·1	14·4	14·7	15·0	15·3	15·6	15·9	16·2	16·5	16·8	17·1	17·4	17·7	18·0
4	18·4	18·8	19·2	19·6	20·0	20·4	20·8	21·2	21·6	22·0	22·4	22·8	23·2	23·6	24·0
5	23·0	23·5	24·0	24·5	25·0	25·5	26·0	26·5	27·0	27·5	28·0	28·5	39·0	29·5	30·0
6	27·6	28·2	28·8	29·4	30·0	30·6	31·2	31·8	32·4	33·0	33·6	34·2	34·8	35·4	36·0
7	32·2	32·9	33·6	34·3	35·0	35·7	36·4	37·1	37·8	38·5	39·2	39·9	40·6	41·3	42·0
8	36·8	37·6	38·4	39·2	40·0	40·8	41·6	42·4	43·2	44·0	44·8	45·6	46·4	47·2	48·0
9	41·4	42·3	43·2	44·1	45·0	45·9	46·8	47·7	48·6	49·5	50·4	51·3	52·2	53·1	54·0

	61	62	63	64	65	66	67	68	69	70	71	72	73	74	75
1	6·1	6·2	6·3	6·4	6·5	6·6	6·7	6·8	6·9	7·0	7·1	7·2	7·3	7·4	7·5
2	12·2	12·4	12·6	12·8	13·0	13·2	13·4	13·6	13·8	14·0	14·2	14·4	14·6	14·8	15·0
3	18·3	18·6	18·9	19·2	19·5	19·8	20·1	20·4	20·7	21·0	21·3	21·6	21·9	22·2	22·5
4	24·4	24·8	25·2	25·6	26·0	26·4	26·8	27·2	27·6	28·0	28·4	28·8	29·2	29·6	30·0
5	30·5	31·0	31·5	32·0	32·5	33·0	33·5	34·0	34·5	35·0	35·5	36·0	36·5	37·0	37·5
6	36·6	37·2	37·8	38·4	39·0	39·6	40·2	40·8	41·4	42·0	42·6	43·2	43·8	44·4	45·0
7	42·7	43·4	44·1	44·8	45·5	46·2	46·9	47·6	48·3	49·0	49·7	50·4	51·1	51·8	52·5
8	48·8	49·6	50·4	51·2	52·0	52·8	53·6	54·4	55·2	56·0	56·8	57·6	58·4	59·2	60·0
9	54·9	55·8	56·7	57·6	58·5	59·4	60·3	61·2	62·1	63·0	63·9	64·8	65·7	66·6	67·5

	76	77	78	79	80	81	82	83	84	85	86	87	88
1	7·6	7·7	7·8	7·9	8·0	8·1	8·2	8·3	8·4	8·5	8·6	8·7	8·8
2	15·2	15·4	15·6	15·8	16·0	16·2	16·4	16·6	16·8	17·0	17·2	17·4	17·6
3	22·8	23·1	23·4	23:7	24·0	24·3	24·6	24·9	25·2	25·5	25·8	26·1	26·4
4	30·4	30·8	31·2	31·6	32·0	32·4	32·8	33·2	33·6	34·0	34·4	34·8	35·2
5	38·0	38·5	39·0	39·5	40·0	40·5	41·0	41·5	42·0	42·5	43·0	43·5	44·0
6	45·6	46·2	46·8	47·4	48·0	48·6	49·2	49·8	50·4	51·0	51·6	52·2	52·8
7	53·2	53·9	54·6	55·3	56·0	56·7	57·4	58·1	58·8	59·5	60·2	60·9	61·6
8	60·8	61·6	62·4	63·2	64·0	64·8	65·6	66·4	67·2	68·0	68·8	69·6	70·4
9	68·4	69·3	70·2	71·1	72·0	72·9	73·8	74·7	75·6	76·5	77·4	78·3	79·2

	89	90	91	92	93	94	95	96	97	98	99	100	101
1	8·9	9·0	9·1	9·2	9·3	9·4	9·5	9·6	9·7	9·8	9·9	10·0	10·1
2	17·8	18·0	18·2	18·4	18·6	18·8	19·0	19·2	19·4	19·6	19·8	20·0	20·2
3	26·7	27·0	27·3	27·6	27·9	28·2	28·5	28·8	29·1	29·4	29·7	30·0	30·3
4	35·6	36·0	36·4	36·8	37·2	37·6	38·0	38·4	38·8	39·2	39·6	40·0	40·4
5	44·5	45·0	45·5	46·0	46·5	47·0	47·5	48·0	48·5	49·0	49·5	50·0	50·5
6	53·4	54·0	54·6	55·2	55·8	56·4	57·0	57·6	58·2	58·8	59·4	60·0	60·6
7	62·3	63·0	63·7	64·4	65·1	65·8	66·5	67·2	67·9	68·6	69·3	70·0	70·7
8	71·2	72·0	72·8	73·6	74·4	75·2	76·0	76·8	77·6	78·4	79·2	80·0	80·8
9	80·1	81·0	81·9	82·8	83·7	84·6	85·5	86·4	87·3	88·2	89·1	90·0	90·9

	102	103	104	105	106	107	108	109	110	111	112	113	114
1	10·2	10·3	10·4	10·5	10·6	10·7	10·8	10·9	11·0	11·1	11·2	11·3	11·4
2	20·4	20·6	20·8	21·0	21·2	21·4	21·6	21·8	22·0	22·2	22·4	22·6	22·8
3	30·6	30·9	31·2	31·5	31·8	32·1	32·4	32·7	33·0	33·3	33·6	33·9	34·2
4	40·8	41·2	41·6	42·0	42·4	42·8	43·2	43·6	44·0	44·4	44·8	45·2	45·6
5	51·0	51·5	52·0	52·5	53·0	53·5	54·0	54·5	55·0	55·5	56·0	56·5	57·0
6	61·2	61·8	62·4	63·0	63·6	64·2	64·8	65·4	66·0	66·6	67·2	67·8	68·4
7	71·4	72·1	72·8	73·5	74·2	74·9	75·6	76·3	77·0	77·7	78·4	79·1	79·8
8	81·6	82·4	83·2	84·0	84·8	85·6	86·4	87·2	88·0	88·8	89·6	90·4	91·2
9	91·8	92·7	93·6	94·5	95·4	96·3	97·2	98·1	99·0	99·9	100·8	101·7	102·6

	115	116	117	118	119	120	121	122	123	124	125	126	127
1	11·5	11·6	11·7	11·8	11·9	12·0	12·1	12·2	12·3	12·4	12·5	12·6	12·7
2	23·0	23·2	23·4	23·6	23·8	24·0	24·2	24·4	24·6	24·8	25·0	25·2	25·4
3	34·5	34·8	35·1	35·4	35·7	36·0	36·3	36·6	36·9	37·2	37·5	37·8	38·1
4	46·0	46·4	46·8	47·2	47·6	48·0	48·4	48·8	49·2	49·6	50·0	50·4	50·8
5	57·5	58·0	58·5	59·0	59·5	60·0	60·5	61·0	61·5	62·0	62·5	63·0	63·5
6	69·0	69·6	70·2	70·8	71·4	72·0	72·6	73·2	73·8	74·4	75·0	75·6	76·2
7	80·5	81·2	81·9	82·6	83·3	84·0	84·7	85·4	86·1	86·8	87·5	88·2	88·9
8	92·0	92·8	93·6	94·4	95·2	96·0	96·8	97·6	98·4	99·2	100·0	100·8	101·6
9	103·5	104·4	105·3	106·2	107·1	108·0	108·9	109·8	110·7	111·6	112·5	113·4	114·3

	128	129	130	131	132	133	134	135	136	137	138	139	140
1	12·8	12·9	13·0	13·1	13·2	13·3	13·4	13·5	13·6	13·7	13·8	13·9	14·0
2	25·6	25·8	26·0	26·2	26·4	26·6	26·8	27·0	27·2	27·4	27·6	27·8	28·0
3	38·4	38·7	39·0	39·3	39·6	39·9	40·2	40·5	40·8	41·1	41·4	41·7	42·0
4	51·2	51·6	52·0	52·4	52·8	53·2	53·6	54·0	54·4	54·8	55·2	55·6	56·0
5	64·0	64·5	65·0	65·5	66·0	66·5	67·0	67·5	68·0	68·5	69·0	69·5	70·0
6	76·8	77·4	78·0	78·6	79·2	79·8	80·4	81·0	81·6	82·2	82·8	83·4	84·0
7	89·6	90·3	91·0	91·7	92·4	93·1	93·8	94·5	95·2	95·9	96·6	97·3	98·0
8	102·4	103·2	104·0	104·8	105·6	106·4	107·2	108·0	108·8	109·6	110·4	111·2	112·0
9	115·2	116·1	117·0	117·9	118·8	119·7	120·6	121·5	122·4	123·3	124·2	125·1	126·0

EXPLANATIONS OF USE OF TABLES

A. Method of linear interpolation

If, for the sake of greater accuracy in calculation, intermediary values must be found lying between the tabulated values, linear interpolation is usually used. The interval between two values given is divided into equal parts (usually 10), intermediary values of the function tabulated being obtained corresponding to the points of division (see Fig.).

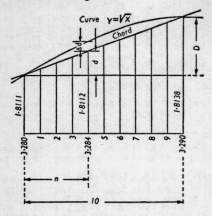

Geometrically, this means that the chord between the two known values is used as an approximation to the actual segment of the curve corresponding to the given function between these points. The ordinate corresponding to the required value of the function then extends up to the chord instead of to the curve. The error Δd is then markedly dependent on the form of the function and, for curves which depart considerably from linearity, can be so large as to render such interpolation impermissible. An idea of the error attending an interpolation procedure can best be obtained by plotting three or four points of the function concerned. For large deviations, the intermediary values can be more accurately obtained by graphical than by numerical interpolation. The error is further dependent on the distance apart

706

of the values tabulated. Accordingly it must be kept in mind that interpolation should not be used where there are large differences D (often at the beginnings of tables). But usually the error is so small that it is contained within the uncertainty occasioned by rounding off the last place.

Example:

Given $x = 3.284$, to find $\sqrt{x} = \sqrt{3.284}$. The root cannot be taken directly from Table I. If we had a Table in which the x-values were given at intervals of 0.001 instead of 0.01, we could extract the following values from it:

x	$\sqrt{x}$
$\left.\begin{array}{l} 3.280 \\ \\ 3.284 \end{array}\right\} n = 4$	$\left.\begin{array}{l} 1.8111 \\ \\ 1.8122 \end{array}\right\} d = 11$
$\left.\begin{array}{l} \\ \\ \\ 3.290 \end{array}\right\} 10$	$\left.\begin{array}{l} \\ \\ \\ 1.8138 \end{array}\right\}$

with $D = 27.$

In the problem we have

$x = 3.28,\ \sqrt{3.28} = 1.8111$;

$x = 3.29,\ \sqrt{3.29} = 1.8138$;

$x = 3.284,\ \sqrt{3.284}$ required;

$n = 4$ (more correctly, $3.284 - 3.280 = 0.004$);

$D = 27$ (more correctly, $1.8138 - 1.8111 = 0.0027$);

$$n:10 = d:D.$$

These values yield d and hence the required value $\sqrt{3.284}$. For the sake of simplicity we use only digits in the last two decimal places (in the example, 4, 10, 11, 27). Since $n:10 = d:D$, we have

$$d = \frac{D}{10}\, n.$$

Thus in the example

$$d = \frac{27}{10} \times 4 = \frac{108}{10} = 10 \cdot 8, \text{ or } 11 \text{ after rounding-off.}$$

$$
\begin{array}{r}
3 \cdot 284 \text{ is thus} \quad 1 \cdot 8111 \\
+ \quad 11 \\
\hline
1 \cdot 8122.
\end{array}
$$

This value coincides with the value which would have been obtained from a more refined tabulation.

An inverse procedure is necessary if we have to start out from the table-values, *i.e.* if we have to determine an argument corresponding to a given function-value.

Thus in our example, suppose the root-value, namely 1·8122, is given and the radicand (3·284) is to be found. In this case the equation $n : 10 = d : D$ must be solved for n:

$$n = \frac{d}{D/10}.$$

In the example

$$n = \frac{11}{27/10} = \frac{110}{27} \approx 4;$$

thus the radicand is

$$
\begin{array}{r}
3 \cdot 280 \\
+ \quad 4 \\
\hline
3 \cdot 284.
\end{array}
$$

To simplify the calculation we frequently use a table of proportional parts.

B. Table of Proportional Parts

From such a table (see p. 704) can be read off directly the value $\frac{D}{10} n = d$ corresponding to D, or the value $\frac{d}{D/10} = n$ corresponding to d. The table is so arranged that D is found in the horizontal border, n in the perpendicular border and d in the table itself. Thus in our example, for $D = 27$ and $n = 4$, $d = 10 \cdot 8 \approx 11$.

C. Hints for Individual Tables

Table 1, p. 601

This table may be used for more purposes than appear at first sight.

(a) *Powers of x.*

Proceeding from the x-column to x^2, x^3 and $\dfrac{1}{x}$ yields squares, cubes and reciprocals of x.

$$E.g. \quad x = 1 \cdot 28 \to x^2 = 1 \cdot 6384, \; x^3 = 2 \cdot 097, \; \frac{1}{x} = 0 \cdot 78125.$$

But we can also obtain squares and cubes by proceeding from the $\sqrt{x}$- and $\sqrt[3]{x}$-columns to the x-columns;

> *e.g.* $x = 1 \cdot 2207$ (found in the $\sqrt{x}$-column) gives $x^2 = 1 \cdot 49$ (found in the x-column); $x = 2 \cdot 0793$ (found in the column $\sqrt[3]{x}$-column) gives $x^3 = 8 \cdot 99$ (found in the x-column).

If we operate with the columns x^2, x^3, $\sqrt{x}$, $\sqrt[3]{x}$ we can obtain powers with fractional exponents, powers of roots or roots of powers.

> *E.g.* semi-cubical parabola $y = x^{3/2}$: for x (found in the x^2-column) we find $y = x^{3/2}$ in the x^3-column.

$$x = 1 \cdot 96 \to y = 2 \cdot 744.$$

The column for $\sqrt{10x}$ extends the range $[1 \cdot 00 – 10 \cdot 00]$ to $[10 \cdot 00 – 100 \cdot 0]$;

> *e.g.* $\sqrt{79 \cdot 9}$: $x = 7 \cdot 99 \to \sqrt{10 \times 7 \cdot 99} = \sqrt{79 \cdot 9} = 8 \cdot 939.$

(b) *Roots of x*

Square- and cube-roots are in general obtained by passing from the x-column to the columns for $\sqrt{x}$ and $\sqrt[3]{x}$;

> *e.g.* $x = 3 \cdot 41 \to \sqrt{x} = 1 \cdot 8466, \; \sqrt[3]{x} = 1 \cdot 5052.$

But the roots can also be obtained by passing from the x^2- and x^3-columns to the x-column.

> *E.g.* $x = 2 \cdot 1316$ (found in the x^2-column) $\rightarrow \sqrt{x} = 1 \cdot 46$ (found in the x-column);
>
> $x = 42 \cdot 144$ (found in the x^3-column) $\rightarrow \sqrt[3]{x} = 3 \cdot 48$ (found in the x-column).

In obtaining values corresponding to numbers outside the range given in the table, careful attention must be paid to rules for moving the decimal point (a preliminary estimate of the position of the decimal point is always advisable).

Examples:

1. If a value n is given which is 10 times as large as the available value in the x-column, we make the following modifications in arriving at

> n^2: multiplication of the value corresponding to x in the x^2-column by 100;
>
> n^3: multiplication of the value corresponding to x in the x^3-column by 1,000;
>
> $\sqrt{n}$: look for the value corresponding to x in the $10x$-column;
>
> $\sqrt[3]{n}$: look for the value n in the x^3-column corresponding to x^3 such that $\sqrt[3]{n}$ appears in the x-column;
>
> $\dfrac{1}{n}$: multiplication of the value corresponding to x in the column for $\dfrac{1}{x}$ by $0 \cdot 1$.

Numerical example: $n = 14 \cdot 5$; to find n^2, n^3, $\sqrt{n}$, $\sqrt[3]{n}$, $\dfrac{1}{n}$.

$$n^2: \quad x = 1 \cdot 45 \rightarrow x^2 = 2 \cdot 1025 \rightarrow n^2 = \underline{210 \cdot 25};$$

$$n^3: \quad x = 1 \cdot 45 \rightarrow x^3 = 3 \cdot 049 \rightarrow n^3 = \underline{3049};$$

$$\sqrt{n}: \quad x = 1 \cdot 45 \rightarrow \sqrt{10x} = \underline{3 \cdot 808} = \sqrt{n}.$$

Intermediary values can be found by interpolation provided D is not too large:

$$\sqrt[3]{n}: \quad x^3 = 14 \cdot 349 \rightarrow x = 2 \cdot 43 \quad D = 178 \quad n = \frac{151 \cdot 10}{178} \approx 8$$

$$x^3 = 14 \cdot 527 \rightarrow x = 2 \cdot 44 \quad d = 151$$

$$x^3 = 14 \cdot 5 \rightarrow x = 2 \cdot 438 = \sqrt[3]{n}.$$

$$\frac{1}{n}: \quad x = 1 \cdot 45 \rightarrow \frac{1}{x} = 0 \cdot 68966 \rightarrow \frac{1}{n} = 0 \cdot 068966.$$

2. If on the other hand we have a value n which is one-tenth of some value in the x-column, we obtain

n^2: by multiplication of the value corresponding to x in the x^2-column by $0 \cdot 01$;

n^3: by multiplication of the value corresponding to x in the x^3-column by $0 \cdot 001$;

$\dfrac{1}{n}$: by multiplication of the value corresponding to x in the $\dfrac{1}{x}$ column by 10;

$\sqrt{n}$: by multiplication of the value corresponding to x in the $10x$-column by $0 \cdot 1$;

$\sqrt[3]{n}$: by looking up $1000n$ in the x^3-column and then multiplying the associated value in the x-column by $0 \cdot 1$.

Numerical example: $n = 0 \cdot 343$; to find n^2, n^3, $\dfrac{1}{n}$, $\sqrt{n}$, $\sqrt[3]{n}$;

$$n^2: \quad x = 3 \cdot 43 \rightarrow x^2 = 11 \cdot 7649 \rightarrow n^2 = 0 \cdot 117,649;$$

$$n^3: \quad x = 3 \cdot 43 \rightarrow x^3 = 40 \cdot 354 \rightarrow n^3 = 0 \cdot 040,354;$$

$$\frac{1}{n}: \quad x = 3 \cdot 43 \rightarrow \frac{1}{x} = 0 \cdot 29155 \rightarrow \frac{1}{n} = 2 \cdot 9155;$$

$$\sqrt{n}: \quad x = 3 \cdot 43 \rightarrow \sqrt{10x} = 5 \cdot 857 \rightarrow \sqrt{n} = 0 \cdot 5857;$$

$$\sqrt[3]{n}: \quad x^3 = 343 \rightarrow x = 7 \rightarrow \sqrt[3]{n} = 0 \cdot 7.$$

Table 2, p. 621

The logarithms in this table are taken with respect to base 10, *i.e.* are Briggsian or common logarithms. The logarithms of a number occurs in two parts, the characteristic and the mantissa;

e.g. log 38 = 1·57978   1 = characteristic   57978 = mantissa.

With respect to base 10, the logarithms of numbers with the same digits (*e.g.*: 240; 24, 2·4; 0·24) are distinguished only by the characteristic—they each have the same mantissa (38021). Since the characteristic is easily determined, it is sufficient in Table 2 to give mantissas. These are given to 5 places. To save space, the first two figures are omitted from all but the first column. Where the second figure changes within a row, this is indicated by an asterisk (*). Thus from the number indicated onwards the initial 2 figures from the next row are to be used.

Determination of the characteristic

If a number is expressed as a power of ten, the exponent of the power is equal to the logarithm of the number;

$$\log 100 = 2\cdot000,00 \text{ since } 10^2 = 100,$$

$$\log 38 = 1\cdot579,78 \text{ since } 10^{1\cdot579,78} = 38.$$

The characteristic indicates how many times 10 or an integral (positive or negative) power of ten is contained in the number concerned. For this reason it is useful, in determining the characteristic, to split up the numbers occurring as follows:

Factorisation		Characteristic	Logarithm
3·15	= 3·15 . 10^0	0	0·49831
31·5	= 3·15 . 10^1	1	1·49831
315	= 3·15 . 10^2	2	2·49831
:	:		
etc.			
0·315	= 3·15 . 10^{-1}	−1	0·49831 − 1
0·0315	= 3·15 . 10^{-2}	−2	0·49831 − 2
0·00315	= 3·15 . 10^{-3}	−3	0·49831 − 3.

Negative characteristics are written either after the mantissa, or in front of the mantissa with a bar above to indicate the negative sign. *E.g.* log 0·0315 = 0·49831 − 2 = $\bar{2}$·49831.

Rules to note

1. (a) The characteristic of the logarithm of a number greater than 1 is 1 less than the number of digits to the left of the decimal point:

> *e.g.* log 1000 has characteristic 4 − 1 = 3;
>
> log 10 has characteristic 2 − 1 = 1.

(b) Conversely, a number always has one more digit to the left of its decimal point than the characteristic of its logarithm gives.

E.g. 3·55023 is the log of 3550; 1·49831 is the log of 31·5.

2. (a) The characteristic of the logarithm of a number less than 1 is negative and its absolute value is one greater than the number of zeros immediately following the decimal point.

> *E.g.* log 0·315, characteristic −1;
>
> log 0·00315, characteristic −3.

(b) Conversely, a number has one less zero immediately after its decimal point than the characteristic of its logarithm.

> *E.g.* $\bar{3}$·49831 is the log of 0·00315;
>
> 0·49831 − 1 is the log of 0·315.

Rules for calculating

To multiply numbers, their logarithms are added.

To divide numbers, their logarithms are subtracted.

To take the power of a number, its logarithm is multiplied by the exponent.

To take the root of a number, its logarithm is divided by the index of the root.

Conversion of common logarithms to natural logarithms (base $e = 2\cdot71828\ldots$):

$$\log x = \log e \times \ln x, \qquad \log x = 0\cdot43429 \times \ln x,$$
$$\ln x = 2\cdot3026 \times \log x.$$

Table 3, p. 641

This table has as argument the angle x measured in radians (arc-length of the unit circle). Corresponding values in degrees are given in the second column. sin x, cos x, tan x, cot x are the abbreviations for sine, cosine, tangent and cotangent, the trigonometric functions.

Table 4, p. 660

In the ln x column we have the natural logarithms of numbers appearing under x. Natural logarithms are based on the number $e = 2·71828...$ and are abbreviated as ln.

Powers of e are to be found in the e^x and e^{-x} columns.

Conversion of natural logarithms to common logarithms:

$$\log x = \log e \times \ln x \qquad \log x = 0·43429 \times \ln x$$

$$\log e = 0·43429$$

$$\ln x = \frac{\log x}{\log e} \qquad \qquad \ln x = 2·3026 \times \log x.$$

Table 5, p. 694

This table has as argument the angle ϕ measured in degrees. Corresponding arc-lengths of the unit circle (ϕ in radians) are given in the x-column and values of the four principal trigonometric functions in the remaining columns.

Since $\sin (90° - \phi) = \cos \phi$, $\tan (90° - \phi) = \cot \phi$ and conversely $\cos (90° - \phi) = \sin \phi$, $\cot (90° - \phi) = \tan \phi$, ϕ runs on the left side of the table (reading from top to bottom) from 0° to 45° and on the right side of the table (reading from bottom to top) from 45° to 90°. Similarly with x. For angles between 0° and 45° the designations at the head of the table are the relevant ones, for angles between 45° and 90° those in the lower border.

E.g.: $\sin 33° = 0·5446 = \cos 57°$,

$$\sin 78° = 0·9781 = \cos 12°.$$

Functions of angles greater than 90° can also be obtained directly, by observing the following rules:

$$\sin (90° \mp \phi) = \cos \phi \qquad \sin (180° \mp \phi) = \pm \sin \phi$$

$$\cos (90° \mp \phi) = \pm \sin \phi \qquad \cos (180° \mp \phi) = - \cos \phi$$

$$\tan (90° \mp \phi) = \pm \cot \phi \qquad \tan (180° \mp \phi) = \mp \tan \phi$$

$$\cot (90° \mp \phi) = \pm \tan \phi \qquad \cot (180° \mp \phi) = \mp \cot \phi$$

e.g. $\tan 131° = \tan (90° + 41°) = - \cot 41° = -1·1504$

$\cos 168° = \cos (180° - 12°) = - \cos 12° = -0·9781$

$\sin 253° = \sin (180° + 73°) = - \sin 73° = -0·9563$

$\cot 210° = \cot (180° + 30°) = + \cot 30° = +1·7321.$

The trigonometrical functions of angles between 720° and 360° are obtained by referring to values $\phi - 360°$ in the table, since the trigonometrical functions repeat themselves after 360°; and so on.

The radian-measure of angles greater than 90° can easily be obtained by taking $\frac{\pi}{2} \approx 1·5708$ for each 90° contained in the angle, reading off the residual angle from the table, and adding;

e.g. $\phi = 288° = 3 \times 90° + 18°,$

and so $x = 3 \times 1·5708 + 0·3142 = \underline{\underline{5·0266}}$